"A comprehensive anatomy of the exciting world of American homeschooling written with straightforward and sparkling clarity. The *Homeschooling Almanac 2000–2001* should save you at least three years of confusion and jitters as you negotiate your way into a realm of freedom and promise Paine and Jefferson understood but which modern families who undergo forced government schooling have been denied. And while these pages are practical enough to make you cry with relief, they capture all the vitality and promise of what has become a national movement for remaking families and reinvigorating society. Mary and Michael Leppert write with insight, intelligence, utility, and best of all, a generous spirit. Trust me, this one is a treasure. Quick, buy it before someone snatches the last copy!"

—John Taylor Gatto, former New York State and New York City Teacher of the Year; author of *Dumbing Us Down: The Hidden Curriculum of Compulsory Schooling*

———————

"A winner! The *Homeschooling Almanac* is mandatory reading for new home educators, as well as a must-have reference for experienced homeschooling families. With you-can-do-it enthusiasm, Michael and Mary Leppert describe a wide range of educational approaches. Especially helpful are the typical daily schedules, informative interviews with homeschoolers nationwide, and state-by-state resource lists."

—Cafi Cohen, author of *And What About College?*

———————

"Most homeschooling parents were themselves public-schooled, so it takes some time and research to find out the various methods of homeschooling, compare them, and choose what to do. Now Mary and Michael have done the work for you so that you can get right to work doing what really matters—helping your children get a superb education."

—Oliver Van DeMille, president, George Wythe College

In loving memory of Bernard J. Oakar, Sr. (alias Sydney Burns)
(August 2, 1932–July 13, 1999)
who taught us every single thing we know about Life,
one way or another.

In loving acknowledgment of Rose M. Leppert,
whose constant, nonjudgmental support and faith
has helped form the foundation of this book
and all of our work.

And to Lennon, without whom our eyes
would not have been opened.

Homeschooling
ALMANAC
2000–2001

Mary and Michael Leppert

Prima Publishing

PRIMA PUBLISHING and colophon are registered trademarks of Prima Communications, Inc.

All products mentioned in this book are trademarks of their respective companies. None of the manufacturers of such products have underwritten or in any way sponsored or endorsed this book. Neither the publisher nor the author have any financial interest in the products mentioned in this book. The coupons provided at the end of this book should be redeemed with the appropriate manufacturer. Neither the author nor the publisher can accept any responsibility with respect to any coupons. In addition, the author and publisher disclaim any warranties regarding the products, whether express or implied, and shall not be responsible for any loss, damage, injury, or liability arising from any product referred to herein.

Every effort has been made to make this book accurate as of the date of publication. Although the publisher and authors cannot be liable for any inaccuracies or omissions in this book, they are always grateful for corrections and suggestions for improvement. Contact the authors at hompaper@gte.net or at The Link, PMB 911, 587 N. Ventu Park Rd., Ste. F, Newbury Park, CA 91320.

This book is not intended to be legal advice.
Always consult a competent attorney concerning any legal issues.

Library of Congress Cataloging-in-Publication Data
Leppert, Mary.
Homeschooling almanac 2000–2001 / Mary Leppert & Michael Leppert.
    p.   cm.
   Includes index.
   ISBN 0-7615-2014-7
   1. Homeschooling—United States Handbooks, manuals, etc.   I. Leppert, Michael.
II. Title. III. Title: Homeschooling almanac, 2000.
LC40.L48 2000
371.04'2—dc21   96-9245
                                                      CIP

00 01 02 DD 10 9 8 7 6 5 4 3 2
Printed in the United States of America

How to Order
Single copies may be ordered from Prima Publishing, 3000 Lava Ridge Court, Roseville, CA 95661; telephone (800) 632-8676. Quantity discounts are also available. On your letterhead, include information concerning the intended use of the books and the number of books you wish to purchase.

Visit us online at www.primalifestyles.com

Contents

Foreword

by David Colfax

Twenty-five years ago, in the fall of 1974, when boys and girls across the country were heading off to begin another year of school, Micki and I and our three boys were building a house and establishing a homestead on a logged-over piece of land in the hills of California. It wasn't that we decided that the boys, at the ages of 9, 6, and 4, wouldn't go to school. It was only that what was happening in a dilapidated frame building six miles away and down in the valley that passed for the local elementary school was simply . . . irrelevant. We were doing *important stuff,* and confronting new challenges on a daily basis. It was *hard work* and *interesting,* and, perhaps if we had been more self-conscious about it, we might have even said it was *educational.* But it never occurred to us to call it *schooling.* When friends and relatives asked us why our kids weren't in school, we simply said that we didn't send them to school. Most of the time that was sufficient, but if pressed, we might reluctantly—and sometimes inadvertently and even provocatively—add that they were learning too much at home to waste time in school.

Nearly a decade later, though, we found that explanation wasn't good enough. In 1983, the media discovered that Grant, our oldest son, who had developed a nationally recognized herd of Alpine dairy goats, had been admitted to Harvard. The sound bite—on *Good Morning America, Today, Johnny Carson, Nightline, Donahue,* and dozens of local programs—was some version of "Goat Boy Goes to Harvard—And Never Spent a Day in School!" Repeatedly we found ourselves explaining how and why we had done what the media— and to our amusement and surprise, the general public—found both fascinating and disturbing. We soon learned that John Holt, whom we knew from the '60s only as an alternative education activist, had given up on schools in general and was advocating what we had been doing for the past decade—"teaching our own"; and Raymond Moore called to tell us that we, unknowingly, had been implementing some of the ideas he and his wife, Dorothy, had been promoting for years. What we had been doing, it appeared, was something called "home schooling."

We didn't care for the term, even when it was contracted by advocates into one word, "homeschooling"—a word that very soon found its way into ordinary dictionaries. To us, it connoted "doing school at home," and many of those who were hearing the word for the first time seemed to think that that was precisely what it meant. That's why the questions we were asked took the form they did: what about curriculum, how do you teach subjects you know nothing about, how do you know your kids are keeping up to grade level, what about testing? We tried calling ourselves "home educators," and just plain "educators," but that didn't help. Somehow—and someday some etymologist might be able to explain precisely how that came about—we were stuck with "homeschooling." Like it or not, we spoke prose and did . . . homeschooling.

And so we had to make the best of it. A quick look around told us there was not too much out there about homeschooling that was easily accessible to the general public. Worse, it seemed that Grant had become the poster boy for homeschooling because of the Harvard sound bite. Too often we found ourselves trying to explain—and echoing Mae West—that "Harvard had nothing to do with it." We merely wanted our boys to develop a love of and respect for learning, and school, at least for us, simply didn't figure into that process. It took us a couple more years, and the admission of Drew, and then Reed, into Harvard, and all the attendant publicity, before we sat down and wrote *Homeschooling for Excellence*, in which we tried to convey a sense of what we did and, in a very limited way, what materials we used. Still, we continued to get requests for information as to how, exactly, we did what we did, and what our educational philosophy and beliefs were. In order to put what we experienced as a family, learning together over many years and in the face of many challenges, into context, we wrote what some have called, with some accuracy, our "real" homeschooling book, *Hard Times in Paradise*.

How much easier it would have been back then to have been able to point people to something like the *Homeschooling Almanac*. Of course things have changed dramatically in the past quarter century. We're still stuck with the word "homeschooling," but homeschoolers who are admitted to tony colleges, who get Rhodes and Fulbright awards and wipe out the competition in national science, geography, and spelling contests, are barely noticed by a public that has come to recognize that kids who are educated at home are capable of such achievements. Most parents today know something about homeschooling, and many have a friend or relative who is a homeschooler. Today there are dozens of books, hundreds of homeschooling material vendors, support groups, and experts, accessible and more than willing to help homeschooling families at all levels shape their homeschooling lives. A couple of decades ago our task was to make the general public more aware of the world of possibilities that homeschooling presented. Today the challenge is to be more able to hear one's own voice, to ensure that one's own values and concerns prevail, and to make reasoned choices amidst the din and chaos of a wonderfully rich and diverse homeschooling movement.

Every Christmas, when our boys were growing up, one of them would receive a copy of the current *World Almanac*, and, over the year, its 900-plus pages presented more than enough to fill our "curriculum" needs. In its pages one could learn about the Gregorian and Julian calendars, who was who in the worlds of sports, music, and politics, temperature ranges in San Francisco and on Jupiter, and what was deemed worthy of noting in politics and culture in the preceding 12 months—or 6,000 years. It was not a volume to be read from cover to cover, but browsed through and used, to stimulate thought and debate. And so, too, I would suggest, is the *Homeschooling Almanac*. It contains more than its share of facts and information about where to get more information, materials, and ideas.

But it is more than an encyclopedia, a compendium of information and facts, or a how-to-do-it manual. The *Homeschooling Almanac* provides various perspectives on homeschooling and is refreshingly free of the top-down, "this is the *right* way to do it" tone that mars altogether too many books that offer homeschooling advice. You will find ideas here with which you may disagree and approaches to homeschooling that just don't fit your family or children's needs. You may disagree with some of the points of view expressed by those featured in its pages. And that is as it should be. Homeschooling is not of a single piece, a finished product. If anything at all can be said about it with near certainty, it is, in each family, *a work in progress*. And the *Homeschooling Almanac*, for all its attention to detail, takes cognizance of the immense and energizing variety and prospects of what is arguably the single most significant social movement in this country over the past 20 years. Inevitably, homeschooling in practice and as a movement will undergo changes of unknown magnitude and character over the next couple of decades. So in a sense, *The Homeschooling Almanac*, in this edition, is both a benchmark and a guide, and it should prove interesting, in some future time, to chart its evolution as both a record and shaper of what our children and their children will call homeschooling. But more than that, because we are teachers and learners above all, the *Homeschooling Almanac* is a tool, and as all experienced homeschoolers know, tools need to be used, and used hard if any good. The *Homeschooling Almanac* is a good tool. Use it. Hard.

Introduction

In our opinion the natural way for families to live is for parents to nurture, raise, and educate their young themselves. Parents know best what their children need to know to survive, as well as what will lead them to satisfying, happy lives. Before the 1850s and the advent of the public school system and compulsory attendance, parents accepted this responsibility, teaching their own children at home. The colonial Americans followed this lifestyle—all the founding fathers were homeschooled and then mentored to become tradesmen or professionals. In modern society, parents have largely abdicated this natural responsibility, leaving the educating and raising of their children to an impersonal system that operates as an immense business.

Today more and more parents, for various reasons, are going back to the pre-1850s status, returning to the job of educating and training their offspring for adulthood. As a result, schooling at home, popularly know as "homeschooling," is experiencing a resurgence. Over two million children were homeschooled in the United States in 1999, and that number is expected to reach four million by the year 2000. Of course, many forces are at work in our society to make homeschooling attractive to more families with each passing month, so even four million home-taught students could prove to be a conservative estimate. There has been a steady increase in homeschooling in the '90s, as more families become attracted to the natural parenting mentioned above and/or become disenchanted with disintegrating public school systems. This trend, which started primarily in large urban areas, is now reaching into the suburbs as well.

This book is intended for all parents—those who are considering it for their children, as well as those who are already homeschooling and want to expand and obtain more resources. It is also for parents who would never consider homeschooling but want more educational resources to supplement their child's education at home.

How We Got Our Start in Homeschooling

Our journey into the homeschooling world and away from institutional schooling began when our son, Lennon, was born in late 1987. At the time of his birth, we both had jobs we really enjoyed. Mary had just received a promotion and was looking forward to a long-term relationship with her company. Getting out of the "mainstream" living pattern was not part of our future plan.

Researching Parenting Issues

Like many couples who are expecting a baby, we began reading about parenthood. During this discovery process, we read the large amount of material detailing the inherent dangers of vaccines and determined that we would not be vaccinating our child. Many people told us that if we did not vaccinate our baby, he would not be allowed to attend school. (We subsequently discovered that this was not true.)

While researching this aspect of parenting, we discovered many books on homeschooling. One book on alternative education was written by A. S. Neill, the founder of Summerhill School in England. Another was by John Holt, the late author, teacher, and modern proponent of the "unschooling" method. The idea of teaching our own child struck a resonant chord within us both so we began our journey into the world of homeschooling!

Summerhill, John Holt, and Early American Education

Michael had read *Summerhill: A Radical Approach to Child Rearing* (New York: Hart Publishing Company, 1960) in the late '60s. Summerhill is the name of an experimental boarding school A. S. Neill founded and operated in England for many years. All Summerhill students had been expelled from other schools and were considered "problem children."

Neill had developed some theories about how best to teach children, based on his observations as a teacher in various English schools. His ideas about teaching are illustrated by two quotes from his book: "I hold that the aim of life is to find happiness, which means to find interest" (p. 24) and "Learning should come after play. And learning should not be deliberately seasoned with play to make it palatable" (p. 26). Neill's school had no mandatory class attendance, no grades, and a number of other revolutionary aspects to schooling children. Classes were offered, but the students were not forced to attend. If a child wanted to simply gaze at his navel all day, that was permitted.

Contrary to what you might expect, only two Summerhill students attended no classes at all. The rest of the children would become curious about something or other and eventually begin happily attending classes. Neill insisted that voluntary attendance was part of why Summerhill "worked." Neill had great success with his students and proved that children do not do their best work in the way that professional educators reasoned and assumed they do.

As we read books by John Holt, the well-known Boston school teacher, school reformer, and later staunch homeschool advocate, we noticed that Holt made some of the same observations that Neill had: Children are naturally curious, naturally want to learn, and the typical school does more *stifling* than *promoting* of this natural urge.

Coupled with that, we discovered that there was a huge Christian/ religious homeschooling movement. We attended several conferences and talks about homeschooling from this religious perspective. These people felt that it was their biblical duty and American right to educate their children at home and have each family with its unique belief system and environment be the main spiritual and social influence of the child. The two points of view—the religious and the Holt/Neill— helped us see that homeschooling was the way for us. We saw that we had broad choices in how our son was raised, spiritually and academically. As time passed, homeschooling grew as the centerpiece of the life we *really* wanted to live.

After all this research, we knew that Mary was not going back to work and that day care was not going to happen. Of course, life was considerably tougher without her substantial income. However, we believe that people, especially our son, matter more than money!

We *wanted* Lennon, *wanted* to be his mom and dad, and *wanted* to build a close-knit, loving family of three. We considered family our most important occupation; everything else was (and still is) secondary. We didn't consciously realize it then, but we were seeking the lifestyle Americans before us had—until World War II, anyway. The colonials, pioneers, and immigrants in the 1800s and 1900s followed a family-living path thousands—or millions—of years old (depending upon your belief system).

At that time, the religious movement probably represented the largest number of homeschoolers in the country. We did a lot of reading and research in that area as well. Michael is a Christian and Mary is not, though both of us were brought up Catholic and have basically the same family values—to raise our children (we thought we would have a large family) in a wholesome environment and teach them to be respectful of adults. We both envisioned a family in which our children would find it unnecessary and inappropriate to rebel against us and our values when they reached puberty. Michael's generation had rebelled in the '60s, a backlash against three assassinations and the Vietnam War—an aberration, a dysfunction rather than a healthy dynamic to be encouraged and repeated.

Our research revealed that for centuries, parents and children had gladly shared values. The founders of our country had not rebelled against their parents' values; on the contrary (according to Dr. Oliver DeMille's writings), their generation was homeschooled until college! Because they learned and were influenced at home, the values the founders brought to fruition had seeds in their parents! The same is true of the pioneer Americans and later immigrants, primarily those from Europe, who proudly learned to speak English and became Americans as quickly as possible but cherished their traditions, values, and cultures as well. They lovingly passed these spiritual heirlooms on to their children as a birthright. Much of our country's greatness came from the work ethic and attitude of gratitude nurtured and bolstered and passed on to succeeding generations. These people had a strong sense of what is right and what is wrong; of fairness and injustice; of productivity and dissipation; of what strengthened and what weakened one's family. Despite their different cultures and different native languages, all seemed to share basic views.

It took a few years for us to consciously realize that we, too, share basic family values that we want our son to learn. From then on, our personal family experience with homeschooling became integral to us and expanded to encompass our professional lives as well. Our involvement led to launching a national homeschooling newspaper, *The Link*, which has become our full-time vocation, along with sponsorship of an annual homeschooling conference.

Helpful Information

Starting twelve years ago, as we anticipated our son's arrival, we began to sift through much of the information available on homeschooling. We're familiar with the difficulty of finding accurate answers to many questions and with the satisfaction of uncovering helpful information to make the homeschooling task easier and more gratifying. Since launching *The Link*, we regularly encounter parents starting out as we did, with no homeschooling experience and little knowledge to help them begin and make the most of this unique opportunity to produce truly well educated, happy children. Here we share the results of our personal and professional quest for information so others can more easily reap the rewards of being part of a homeschooling family.

Despite its dramatic increase in recent years, homeschooling is still the exception rather than the norm. Few parents of today's school-age children experienced homeschooling themselves, and so, through habit or fear of the unknown, they often stay on familiar ground rather than strike out into new territory without a guide to follow or a map to consult. Some may simply not question whether to send their children to school, which seems the "natural" choice. Yet the system that has evolved over the years is far from natural, shifting the responsibility from parents to society. And as schools become increasingly ineffective in achieving even basic goals (and often are dangerous places for children!), more and more parents are thinking, "There must be another way. I could do a better job!" This book is intended to provide the guide and the map so parents can follow a smoother path to successfully educating their children. You'll find the roads are far more traveled than you think, and you'll meet many homeschoolers with whom you share values and from whom you can learn.

What You'll Get from This Book

Part 1 consists of eight chapters designed to provide the background and insight into what homeschooling is and how it works. Like most people considering, beginning, or already homeschooling, you probably have many questions.

Chapter 1, "More Home Than School," explores in depth why you should consider homeschooling. An interview with Day Farenga, who shares her experiences with both the homeschooling and school perspectives, caps this chapter. In chapter 2 you'll get advice on how to begin homeschooling, including the philosophy of David Colfax, well-known father of four homeschooled sons, three of whom graduated from Harvard and then earned degrees in medicine or law. Chapter 3 offers information on determining your child's learning style, culminating with a discussion with learning styles analysts Mariaemma Pelullo-Willis and Victoria Kindle Hodson.

Chapters 4, 5, and 6 present three basic methods—the parental approach, the unschooling method, and the eclectic method—that various homeschoolers follow. Each chapter includes an interview with a homeschooling parent who shares unique perspectives and experiences. Chapter 6 also discusses lesser-known methods of homeschooling, including the delayed academic approach and the Charlotte Mason method, among others.

Chapter 7 covers the goal of many homeschooling parents: college. You'll read how homeschoolers in general fare through the admissions process and in college academics, hear in detail from one homeschooler about her college experience, and view the transcript that helped her gain admission.

Finally, chapter 8 answers some of the most frequently asked questions about homeschooling from our own and veteran homeschoolers' experience. You'll also find more of these questions and answers scattered throughout the other seven chapters.

Products for Homeschoolers

Besides everyday family living and nature itself, which provide opportunities to educate your children, hundreds of companies and publishers offer assistance to homeschoolers in the form of virtually everything from boxed curriculums and books to art supplies and games. We highlight the best of these in part 2. We chose products to include based on our positive experience in using them for our own homeschooling curriculum, by testing them for review in *The Link*, or by testing them because they were recommended and used by friends and colleagues. There is usually more than one excellent product for any given subject. Your family is likely to use some and hear of many others, either from other parents or from those who offer consultation and advice to homeschoolers. We also bring to your attention some of the suppliers that commonly provide materials to schools but are often unfamiliar to individual families.

By scanning part 2, you'll get an idea of what is available to help homeschooling families with the education process. Should a particular item appeal to you, you'll find the product name, descriptions, and ordering information. Note: We provide this information for your convenience, not as an endorsement of a particular product or brand.

Resources

The proliferation of homeschooling has meant a surge of information on homeshooling in bookstores, in libraries, and on the Internet—far more than you could possibly read. Part 3 is designed to help you zero in on the truly helpful information. In addition to books, periodicals, and websites, special sections cover diverse religious or ethnic homeschooling groups and the various methods of homeschooling.

State-by-State Information

Whether you hail from Mississippi, Minnesota, or another of the fifty states, you'll find pertinent information on your state's regulations and brief descriptions of each state's political climate regarding homeschooling, along with contact information for statewide homeschooling groups and the state's department of education. In addition, part 4 lists local homeschooling organizations, groups, and conferences, along with general descriptions of locale, philosophy, activities, and the contact information that will enable you to access the specifics.

Who's Who and What's What

This section will familiarize readers with the movers and shakers behind homeschooling and with various terms used in the special world of homeschooling.

Valuable Coupons

Although it is possible to homeschool without spending an extra cent, most homeschoolers do purchase at least a few of the many available products. We provide a coupon section that will help you stretch often-scarce budgets. The coupons can be used when you purchase many of the items listed in part 2, "Products for Homeschoolers."

What This Book Is Not Meant to Do

This book is *not* meant to *tell* you how to homeschool "our" way. We love the diversity we encounter among homeschool families and feel this is a tremendous asset to our community and yours. We do not know your family; you do. We do not know your children; you do. The essence of teaching your own children is that *you* learn what they need and make your own decisions rather than passing the responsibility to someone else. You and your children decide how they will spend their time.

If you do not currently homeschool and it seems to be something you would like to try for your family, we offer as much help and encouragement as we can. No matter what you think your situation is, you can do it! If you do not feel comfortable teaching your own children, you can become more involved with what goes on at your children's school and with their overall education. Either way, you and your children will be much better off for your increased involvement and attention.

PART 1
The Nuts and Bolts of Homeschooling

CHAPTER 1

More Home Than School

Today's homeschooling is far more about "home" than "school." Few Americans today have the close-knit family life that so many Americans once had—before compulsory education pulled the children from their parents' responsibility, beginning in 1852 in Massachusetts. Children who attend school are raised by strangers more than by their parents. Family circles are more loose and ephemeral than ever before. In the past 150 years, schools have gained an increasing stranglehold on culture while families have lost more and more influence over their children. Is this a coincidence?

Many modern families consider eating a meal together unusual. And more often than not, they spend their "together" time watching television or a movie rather than looking at each other while discussing and listening to what other family members have to say. Compared to Americans of the early 1800s, modern families in general are strangers to each other.

Regaining Traditional Values

Homeschooling affords the families who value this traditional child-parent relationship a way to regain their own family culture and closeness. Teaching your own children academic subjects as well as your religious, spiritual, cultural, moral, and ethical beliefs is the heart and soul of homeschooling today. Watching a movie or television show is a passive function in which observers view a "third party" rather than relating to one another.

You Are Homeschooling Already

We are here to tell you this: You already know how to homeschool. You knew what your child needed and how he or she should progress before your child was six years old. Nothing has changed. If you are talking, seeing, hearing, or playing with your child, you are doing a simplified version of home "schooling."

Now, add to this interaction a planned activity, such as "playing" with simple addition/subtraction facts using sticks, blocks, or coins; "playing" with the phonetic sounds of English (as the precursor to learning to read); or "playing" with crayons or pencils to develop the early fine-motor skill necessary for much later handwriting. You are now home "schooling" your very young child in the "three R's," that foundation of academic knowledge early Americans learned at home, before mandatory schooling. All you need to do is develop a sense of connectedness with your own past and continue parenting.

Homeschooling is simply a matter of finding out what your "school-age" child (over age six) needs and then becoming resourceful. This information is readily obtainable in today's world, due to the growth of homeschooling, the widespread existence of good educational stores, and the phenomenon of the Internet. In most U.S. towns and cities, you can find a series of workbooks for math, reading, and other academic subjects in many large grocery and discount stores. We are not saying that this is the sum total of academics in homeschooling, but it *could* be that easy.

If you picked up this book, you either are interested in "bringing your children home" for any of a variety of reasons or have already done so. You are taking the first step to regaining traditional values in your life. Whether you are a single parent with one child or married with six or more children, or somewhere in between, homeschooling is the way to make your family circle closer, more authentic, and valuable to all of you. In this book, you'll find that "academic educa-

Homeschoolers Say . . .

I'm considering homeschooling my children who are under age 7. When should I begin?

Does your child know how to walk, feed himself, go to the toilet? Does he know numbers, colors, days of the week? If so, you have already begun!

---

tion" is a relatively small part of the entire picture. Often families come to homeschooling because of a negative experience at "school," only to find that homeschooling affords them not just a wonderful education, but closer relationships, less peer dependency, deeper spiritual or religious values, and a resurgence of their family uniqueness.

Homeschooling Is the Traditional Way of Educating

Homeschooling today is actually a return to the *truly* traditional method of children being instructed by their parents. In the 1700s and 1800s, members of our society were less diverse than we are today. Most held relatively similar Judeo-Christian religious beliefs and shared more or less the same value system. It was understood that one's children studied the Bible and learned their basic moral and ethical values at home, along with the elementary subjects necessary for further education. The expected and anticipated way of life was that *all elementary* aspects of life were taught by the parents. Children had to learn the three R's *before* they were accepted into school. Times have changed; we think maybe people have not.

Thirty-year veteran Manhattan junior high school teacher John Taylor Gatto states in *Dumbing Us Down* that it takes an average of 120 hours to teach a child to read. He goes on to say that the elongation of this process in America came about as a result of some teachers' organizations wishing to create job security. Instead of teachers exclusively continuing in their role of imparting *higher* forms of information, the imparting of the *basic* information became "complicated," requiring "specialists" and "experts" trained to do so over a long period of time. Slowly, over a many-year span, each bit of information became smaller and more repetitive.

If Homeschooling Is for Your Family, Then What?

Now that we have established that you are "qualified" to teach your own child the academic subjects at the elementary level—and

beyond—what next? You have to ascertain whether it is *right* for your family and yourself. Parents whose children are or have been in a school setting, whether public, private, or parochial, will have different considerations from those whose children have not yet attended school. Let us discuss the decision-making process for each one separately. An effective method frequently recommended for decision making in general is to list pros and cons of the possible change. Since the whole family is involved, it's important to consider the pluses and minuses for your child, yourself, your lifestyle, and your spouse.

If Your Child Is in School

We suggest that you begin thinking about how you and your child feel about his or her school experience. You are probably dissatisfied, or you would not be considering a change to homeschooling. First, track your dissatisfaction to its source(s) before you make any decision, homeschooling or otherwise. The simplest way to sort out your family's feelings and thoughts on this issue is to take a sheet of notebook paper, draw a line vertically down the center and write "Pros" as the left column heading and "Cons" on the right.

Your Child

Place the subheading "Child" on the next line and list, as honestly as you can, the positive and negative aspects of school from your child's standpoint. Don't omit anything. Include sports programs, music programs, anything that has importance to him and his development. Take into consideration who he is and what sort of person you would like to help him grow up to be (from a moral, ethical, and personality point of view). If you don't know how your child feels about school, *ask!* The process of homeschooling entails lots of talking and listening between parents and child. Just as with all other skills in life, "practice makes perfect" applies to communicating, too.

Yourself

Next, start a new page using the same format and headings, but make the subheading for yourself. List positive and negative elements of school from *your* viewpoint. If your child's school is rife with drug use, violence, lackadaisical teachers, less-than-acceptable performance on standardized tests, and so forth, the cons list will fill rapidly. If your child's school experience includes a highly skilled favorite teacher, large budget for materials and special programs, and so on, the pros list will contain these. Your good/bad lists may well be equal in length.

Your Lifestyle

Next, consider the pros and cons of school in terms of your lifestyle issues. What will life be like if you and your child are home together all day? Think carefully about this, especially if you have been working outside the home for a few years and are now contemplating becoming a stay-at-home parent. Some of the lifestyle changes that happen when you begin homeschooling may be very welcome; others may not be. Now is the time to think carefully about it. As above, list the positive and negative changes that you think will occur if you change your child's education situation from school to home.

Remember that teaching your child at home, one-on-one, takes only about two to three hours per day—not the six to eight she is used to in school. Dr. Oliver DeMille states that while researching public school classroom practices to prepare for the Mentorship course he teaches at George Wythe College, he found many studies showing that up to 80 percent of school time is nonacademic. You can teach children in grades 1 to 8 all they need in only about three hours per day, supplementing here and there for extra subjects you want to delve into, perhaps art history, drawing, or pottery. If you have an unusual work schedule, you can skip two weekdays and teach Saturday and Sunday, or teach extra hours for a few days and then reduce the time to two to three hours per day again. It is wonderful to discover how flexible and fun life can be when you're removed from the constraints of a rigid timetable!

After you've listed the positive and negative effects that discontinuing schooling will have on your lifestyle, do the same for your child's lifestyle. If you and your mate are both working full-time outside the home, one of you may have to alter your work schedule or even change jobs to homeschool. If you work days and your mate works second or third shift, homeschooling can easily be accommodated within this schedule. In many instances, the second income is used mostly to finance expenses relating to that extra job and the child's school attendance, and many expenses can be erased when one parent and the child remain at home.

Although it's more commonly the mother who stays home, fathers can teach as well as mothers! Also, a professional mom may make substantially more than the dad, or the father may simply welcome the opportunity to stay home with his child for a change. Dads often miss out on enjoyable aspects of child rearing because they are usually the breadwinners throughout the child's life. In the American colonial period, fathers taught their sons from about the age of 10 or 11 in the ways of the world and commerce as they taught them farming, smithing, or other family business—no matter what the boy eventually chose for an occupation. While modern-day fathers often think of teaching the children as "woman's work," that concept did not exist prior to the 1900s.

Your Spouse

If your mate is vitally involved in decisions of this type, have him or her create a separate list of pros and cons—without input from you. Then compare and discuss your separate lists. It's best that you "sleep" on your lists for a few days and talk again. If time is of the essence, however, you may have to make a tough decision quickly.

Let us assume that each of you filled about two pages with pros and cons from every point of view in your family. Take a good, long look at what is listed before you and answer these questions:

- Is homeschooling necessary in my life?
- Feasible?
- Desirable?
- For all concerned?
- You?
- Your child?

At this point, the *decision* has been made. By the time you distill the emotions and logistics down to these bare bones—two or three pages of black and white—you can see the writing on the wall. If your decision is to homeschool, what remains is implementing the necessary changes. If your decision is not to homeschool, then you will proceed to finding the best educational solution for you—private school, different public school, changes within the current school. Sometime in the future you may again consider whether to take the teaching reins and can re-read this book from a different slant.

If homeschooling seems right for you and your family, continue reading. You will find answers regarding legal curriculum and scheduling issues that will help you proceed.

Homeschoolers Say . . .

What if my spouse is against homeschooling?

When a husband (or wife) is against homeschooling, one approach is to make a deal with the spouse to try homeschooling for a certain amount of time—maybe one semester or one full school year. You can use this time to gather positive information about homeschoolers in general, such as their track record at getting into top colleges. Also, try taking your spouse with you to homeschooling activities such as park days, science fairs, and field trips. The resistive spouse usually sees such a positive change in the child's attitude that initial concerns fade away.

If Your Child Has Never Attended School

The situation is completely different for the child and parent who have not yet been involved in school. As we demonstrated above, you have actually begun homeschooling without realizing it. Games you play to keep your baby or toddler content are beginning home-schooling exercises. Counting games, shape-and-color games, and sound games followed by word games build the foundation to what homeschoolers do on a "larger" scale in "grades" 1 to 12. Families who have never been involved with school seldom think in grade (or age) terminology; they view each child as unique. For example, your child may be a "first-grade reader" but a "third-grade mathematician" and should be taught accordingly.

If your child has never attended school, you have by far the easier route to take in continuity and adjustment. If you have been at home all during this time, you probably know your child so well by the time he is five or six that your home-educating experience is likely to be a seamless transition. You won't have to quit a job, find another, or work from home. You'll have no need to adjust to a sun-time day to replace

Not long ago, I received a call from a woman who asked to ride with me to a homeschooling seminar. On the approximately 80-mile drive, all she talked about was how much against homeschooling her husband was. During the seminar she was very excited about what she learned but followed each expression of enthusiasm with "but my husband is *so* against it." Although I didn't see her again for about a year, this woman's plight remained vivid in my mind. I saw her at a local park day recently, and she happily related that her husband began asking his co-workers (police officers) what they knew about homeschooling and learned that many of them homeschooled their children. He decided there was nothing to worry about, and the matter was settled. Now he is a completely convinced homeschool dad! I find that this transformation happens 99 percent of the time.

some time-clock world. You won't have to deal with negative social "issues" often born of schooling, and your child won't need to take time off from academic work to adjust to the change.

If your child has been cared for by someone else while you were working, you can begin really getting to *know* her now. Observe her more closely than you had time to before. Interact with your young child and see how she moves from one interesting thing to another all day long. Unless someone stops this flow of curiosity, it will continue on its own. You can take the time to read to her now, play "math" games, and just be involved with her. Try to train yourself to remain interested for long periods of time. Prepare yourself mentally to enjoy your child's company, and both of you will benefit

One Family's Decision to Homeschool

The fact that families can return to a more traditional way of schooling, making home the center of learning, has been more than proven by the nearly two million families who are currently homeschooling.

Day Farenga and her family are one of the examples that homeschooling can and does work. The following interview sheds light on the dramatic differences between school education and home education.

Interview with Day Farenga

Day Farenga, who lives with her husband and children in the Boston area, is the homeschooling mother of three girls. She is the conference manager and coordinator for *Growing Without Schooling*'s annual homeschool conference. Her husband, Pat Farenga, is president of Holt Associates and publisher of *Growing Without Schooling* (GWS) magazine.

Recently, two of Day's three daughters, none of whom had ever attended school, entered school for different reasons. Here she shares her family's experiences with those who may be confronted with homeschooled children wanting to attend school.

MARY LEPPERT: *What are the ages of your daughters?*

DAY FARENGA: Twelve, nine, and six.

MARY: *Was it your oldest daughter who went to school?*

DAY: Yes, although the youngest one went this year for six weeks. I think there's a lot of pressure as you're heading into first grade. Everyone from the dentist to your friends is talking about school. She figured she was missing out on something. I was able to counter that with the other children, but this one—even though she has been home doing work with us for the past two years—really wanted to go. I finally decided I did not want to be teaching a reluctant learner. I wanted her to be interested.

MARY: *So what was that experience like?*

DAY: A lot of people who know us were surprised to see us at school the first day. But the teacher was wonderful. I had a feeling she might want to go to school, so I actually spoke to the kindergarten and first-grade teachers back in June and had really good interviews with them. I asked what their teaching styles were, what was important to them, and how they handled various subjects. Also, they let me choose the teacher I wanted Audrey to be with. That was one concession you know, "We'll do anything to get your child into school." Audrey *did* like it for the first couple of weeks. Having her backpack made her feel very important. She is a social kid, and by the tenth day she had a crowd around her all the time. She liked those aspects. Then we (GWS) had our big conference out of town in September, and I went to the site ahead of time and stayed a day after to wrap things up, so she was out of school a full week. She went back to school for a few days and then came down with lice. At first I thought it came from the camp (at the conference) but discovered it was rampant through the school. So she was out again for over a week.

Things with the school were becoming difficult. Audrey was becoming restless. She was seeing us going on homeschool field trips and doing all the neat things we do, and she was missing her sisters. She had some very hard times when she'd come home, expecting everybody to give her a big hug and tell her how much they missed her, but they'd been doing their home-thing and were ready to go off into the world—dance class or a friend's house. So it was like, "Oh hi, Audrey, see ya." She was also frustrated with the slowness of the class.

> I finally decided I did not want to be teaching a reluctant learner. I wanted her to be interested.

MARY: *Where did she fit in, academically?*

DAY: Well, she was certainly doing three-letter reading. Maybe one or two kids were ahead of Audrey, but some of her classmates didn't even know their ABC's. That's a teacher's nightmare, to teach a class with such a span. This teacher spent an awful lot of time on books and reading and writing.

MARY: *Were they printing?*

DAY: Printing, making little books, everybody contributing a little page to "What I Did over My Summer Vacation," reading a book aloud, taking a book home, doing worksheets, and all kinds of things. At Parents' Night, the teacher was talking about the reading, the writing, and the books, and needing parents' input. I looked around the room and saw two math things—one little box that was probably some kind of manipulative and a number line on the wall. I thought, "Where are pictures of animals and plants? Holidays?" or any of the things kids *can* do. They can learn so much in all different kinds of sciences—weather or natural sciences or animals or planets—without needing to read or write. You can do experiments and physically see all these things working, growing. There was none of it there.

MARY: *Did you talk to the teacher about it?*

DAY: Yes. She said, "Well, we do a unit in March. We read a book about a dog." It really hit me at that moment how exciting and diversified our home studies are, just by living our life! The Boston area museums have really picked up on the homeschooling market. Classes are offered at just about every museum around here. The natural history museum runs one four-week course after another for homeschool groups. They have huge stuffed animals you can draw and learn about, or you can study the cutting ants that carry leaves around, or just bugs. A lot of homeschoolers take advantage of it, even though there is a charge. The Audubon Society runs a huge habitat exhibit—a ten-week course, two and a half hours a week—for five- to eight-year-olds. They do all kinds of card games, build bird feeders, and go outside for a walk through nature, pointing out snakeskins and owl nests and things like that. There is so much kids this age can do that is not just learning to read!

> They can learn so much in all different kinds of sciences—weather or natural sciences or animals or planets—without needing to read or write.

MARY: *Did she want to leave school?*

DAY: She started wanting to leave the boredom of the school, but not her nice teacher or class friends. She started complaining about how everything was so slow and boring and she couldn't believe that the kids didn't know "this" and when were they ever going to do "that." Then on a Friday morning, she said, "I'm not going." I said, "Let's finish the week. Come on, let's go." She just refused, wouldn't get dressed. So I said, "Look, if this is really it, I have to go in and talk to these people." Around 2:00, I asked her again, "Do you want me to go in and make this official, or what?" She said, "I'm not going back!" I said, "Okay, but that means we are going to start your work here." She was fine about that. In fact, she insisted I buy her the next-level workbook. She took it everywhere and finished it in two and a half days—I guess to prove that she was going to be self-taught.

MARY: *The school let you go, just like that?*

DAY: They knew I had been homeschooling the older girls already and, in fact, felt I was quite successful. It was the first time I had gotten any support or encouragement from the school. The first-grade teacher said, "It seems like you're doing excellent work with the kids. Too many parents are not involved at all, but you are *very* involved, doing lots of different educational things. I understand that she feels like she is missing out." My experience with Lauren (my oldest) brought me to really understand the difference between the at-home system and the school system. It also made me feel better about saying, "The home system is pretty good and I'm not going to take people's criticism anymore."

MARY: *What was it like when Lauren went to school?*

DAY: It's a very long, upsetting story. She attended the sixth grade. She had a lot of pressure to go to be with friends, especially from the girl next door. They've known each other since they were five and there has always been a real feeling of the neighbor girl looking down her nose at us.

MARY: *Was it difficult for you to let Lauren go?*

DAY: Yes, very hard. It was a lot of personal torture. Since the second half of fifth grade, Lauren had been strongly voicing that she wanted to go to school. We decided it wouldn't make sense for her to start towards the end of a year, especially since fifth grade is the last year of elementary, then they all go to this magnet middle school.

In June Lauren and I went to an Introduction Day at the middle school to meet the rest of the kids. That way, she got to know her way around. If we *did* let her go in September, nobody would necessarily know that she had come from homeschooling but would think she came from another of the three schools coming together.

MARY: *So she ended up going to the middle school with her friend?*

DAY: Right. And every subject is a different class, so they were in a few classes together.

MARY: *Do you think that Lauren had an innocence compared to the other kids?*

DAY: Well, innocent in a good sense. She was innocent regarding prejudice—people being against someone because she is tall or pretty or came from this street or whatever. She also saw that adults could be uncaring. Some teachers really don't care about you and can be extremely mean and harmful to your self-esteem. She had chosen all her teachers and classes until then. And if she didn't like the teacher, we might try to change a few things by talking with the teacher, or somehow switch the teacher but keep the subject. She knew that "These teachers are wrong; this isn't the right way to be. There are other choices."

> It wasn't what you were learning in school, or how you were learning it; it was the final product that mattered.

For example, she knew from the first day which teachers were nice, which ones weren't, who was too quick with a particular kid or were immediately labeling certain students as troublemakers. She knew that was not necessary. She also had experience with not being graded, then she came home on the third or fourth day and said, "We're going to be getting a grade in Phys. Ed. What sense does that make?" She was blown away by that thought. Then there was Foreign Culture. She's very into different languages and has studied all kinds of foreign cultures. I actually let her go to Rome with her father on a speaking engagement this year because she has been so interested in studying this for so long. So, now Foreign Cultures is going to be pass or fail. She also was upset when she put in a very good effort, learned a lot about the subject, but turned an assignment in the next day because she was sick, and therefore got a D.

MARY: *What did that do to her desire to learn?*

DAY: Somewhere between two and three weeks in school, she started to catch on that it wasn't *what* you were learning, or *how* you were learning it; it was the final product that mattered.

MARY: *So what happened?*

DAY: Well, her grades were pretty bad at first—especially with social studies and history. (She *loves* history!) Well, she would be doing her homework for three or four hours, getting exhausted and getting mad about the homework. Her sisters were mad because she never had any time, and everything was "school, school, school." I said, "Let me work with you and see how you're going about it." I noticed she was reading the whole story or chapter for interest, as we do at home. I said, "Oh, Lauren, no; you don't read it! You read the paragraph around the word and that's how you answer it."

MARY: *She was absorbing the whole thing?*

DAY: She was interested! She wanted to know about it. But that type of learning was not rewarded. It took too long, and she couldn't get other work done.

MARY: *So the overall experience was a negative one for both you and her?*

DAY: Yes, negative for me all the way through because I was already aware of that sort of experience, but she had to live through it. I was picking up on the subtleties, and being in the *Growing Without Schooling* support network for so long made me very aware of the group management needs of the school. But I had to let her suffer because she really wanted to try this and do well at it. I did go on to teach her the tricks of the trade. "Okay, this is how you take a test. See how many questions there are and how much time you have, divide your time into each question, do the ones you know, skip the others, then come back to them. When in doubt, pick C." The second semester, she was on the honor roll!

MARY: *How was the whole "learning" experience in general?*

DAY: Quite often she had already studied it before she got there. She had been very interested in ancient Egypt, so we had done it for years. That's what they were doing for the middle semester. She did learn a few more things, but she was also kind of bored and very discouraged that she couldn't pick exactly what to study. They divided ancient Egypt into five different parts for a little history fair. If she could have chosen what she wanted to learn, she would have picked an area that she didn't know anything about yet. But instead, she was just told, "You're going to do the library part of it; bring in books and stuff people would use to do research on it." Talk about having done that *ad nauseam!*

MARY: *So there were no choices, really?*

DAY: There were no choices. And that's one of the things that finally broke her spirit. She was thinking about leaving school during Christmas vacation, then decided, "I want to try to see this through." She came home that day just delighted. "Everything's going to be great! We're going to do the science fair, pick our project, and do all this neat stuff." Of course, I'm thinking, "Uh-oh. I'll bet this and this are not going to hap-

> There were no choices in school. And that's one of the things that finally broke her spirit.

pen." But I said, "Okay, that sounds good. Let's see what happens." Well, to make a long, sad, and aggravating story short, she was not allowed to pick her subject. She chose one of two projects, and the teacher said, "No, you're smarter than that. This is what you're going to do . . . this is how you're going to do it." It involved interviewing boys and girls, and she's a very shy person. This was not something she was going to do well at.

MARY: *What does that have to do with science?*

DAY: Well, her project was to see if your heart rate changed when you listen to music. She had to interview five girls and five boys and say what her hypothesis was, how she was going to do the research, and create this whole bulletin board–type thing.

MARY: *Did she end up doing it?*

DAY: She did it slowly, painstakingly, with her mouth turned down. And it was such a shame, because she thought, "Hey, here's something I haven't done yet—a complete science project from beginning to end with a hypothesis and all." She and her friend were going to find out about Planet X, how they discovered it and all of that. Well, that just wasn't part of the teacher's plan. It was just amazing how much she had to step 'n' fetch it—being enthusiastic, being interested, having your own ideas is absolutely not an option. I think it's because teachers have so many kids, they're afraid they're going to lose control.

MARY: *So what happened with her relationship with her friend?*

DAY: Well, these girls who were best friends from five to eleven years old were not speaking to each other by the middle of October—all this nit-picking, "Who's talking to who? Who's in what group? Did you know she said this? Neh-neh-neh-neh-neh." Somewhere around January, they started being a little bit more friends, then another big, horrible thing happened in April. She was punched twice while trying to defend a friend.

MARY: *Was this type of dynamic something that happened when she went to school?*

DAY: This hurtful gossip was brand new to her. The whole point seemed to be to pass bad information to make the person feel excluded. Everything is, "Are you in the group or not?" And as it turns out, you're in the group this week, but next week you're not.

MARY: *And this is "socialization"?*

DAY: Exactly! She did finally make it through to the end of the year. I think she has a very strong character. She set this challenge before herself and was going to finish it. Also, "I'm dropping out; I'm staying in" was very unsettling. We finally said, "Just make a decision. Either you're in or you're out." She decided to stay in and it actually became less stressful because I said, "Okay, here's how you play the game. This is what you're agreeing to." She finished the year, did the best she could in every subject, then practically disappeared into her room for the first month of the summer.

> It's amazing how much she had to "step 'n' fetch it" in school.

MARY: *Was that uncharacteristic of her personality?*

DAY: Yes. I think she needed to find herself again. She did a lot of cleaning up her room, rearranging, writing, listening to music, staring out the window.

MARY: *Was your family peace disrupted by her going to school?*

DAY: Oh, yes! And it took a while to restore it. A lot of resentment built up in the middle child (Alison) because they had been such good friends. When Lauren was at school, she didn't have time for her sisters. She was talking about other people in school that Alison didn't know, and Lauren suddenly went from being 11 to 14.

MARY: *What were the kids like in comparison?*

DAY: A lot of attitude copping: "Let's go to the mall." "What clothes are you wearing?" "Did you see the show last night?" I'd hear, "I have to watch that TV show, Mom, because they're all going to be talking about it tomorrow." And, for the first time, boys.

MARY: *Did that go away when she came back? Did her innocence return?*

DAY: Well, once that's broken, that's it. We had to find a way not to make her feel like a dork, absolutely different from everybody, but not compromise our values either. A good example of that is when she came home one day totally psyched and said she was going to meet this boy at the playground, and could I drop her off. I was shocked, but had learned previously in my raising of the children to not give an answer right away. I'd just say, "Let me think about that. I'll give you an answer later today." For three or four hours, I kept going 'round and 'round on this, trying to figure it out. The solution I presented to her was, "You know, I feel really uncomfortable with just dropping you off. That's not like anything we've ever done. What I'd like to do is handle it the same way we've always handled meeting new friends and going new places. Our whole family is going to the playground. I'll sit there and read a book, and your sisters will play on the jungle gym, and you can talk to your friend. I *do* expect to be introduced. Then we're leaving at 5:00 to come home for dinner." She said, "Okay. That makes sense." I think she appreciated the protection, the reminder of her upbringing. It was a very good thing we made that decision because he didn't show up at the park. Then we thought it was a different park, but he wasn't there either. It was a wild-goose chase all over town in which they never saw each other.

MARY: *Did she ever come home and say, "Boy, you guys were right about school."*

DAY: Yes. She wrote me this wonderful letter, sometime during Christmas vacation, saying, "I went because I thought you were wrong, I needed to find out for myself. You were right. Now help get me out of here!"

MARY: *Are you glad you had the experience?*

DAY: Yes. Because now I don't have to be the bad guy. She saw the school for what it is. I think she felt an awful lot of support from me, though I was working very hard to hold my tongue.

CHAPTER 2
Beginning the Homeschooling Process

Once you have done whatever soul-searching, planning, and arranging you have to do to decide to homeschool, you are ready to contemplate a new future and tackle the basic elements involved in the process.

Say "Adios" to the "Hi/Good-bye" Life

If your family has been living the rat-race routine of school and work with its "hi/good-bye" level of communication, take some time off and relax! I strongly urge any parent who has just taken a child out of school to spend at least a week or two getting to know each other again before jumping into the academic routine. Throw out schedules and routines as much as possible for a while. (If you can't live "open-ended," expand your former schedule to make room for your new freedom!) Re-think your life and time values; find out your child's values. You have a clean slate and a piece of chalk, so to speak; if you make a "mistake," erase and write over it! Avoid starting the first week with "schooling." You might instead go to a good museum at 11:00 A.M. Monday, when it is quiet and virtually empty. Have lunch together out in a world that may be novel to your child. Show him what fun can be had in this newfound, free world of maturity. Let him see that important matters go on "out here." Go to the library or a large bookstore and let him browse as long as he wants. These experience may re-kindle curiosity in a subject not taught in school, and he may feel the spark of desire for learning! He may find a number of topics to explore that would never be possible in school.

In the ensuing days, take hikes or have picnics; do the things you could not do when you were working and he was in school. Get to know each other well. Enjoy being his parent and help him enjoy being your child. He will soon respond favorably to being treated in a more mature fashion than he was in the school world. If you talk to him with your faith and belief in him showing through, he *will* rise to your expectations. Give it time, lots of time—maybe even a year. Your day is now determined more by the rising and setting of the sun than by clocks and schedules. You aren't in the hamster-wheel anymore, so let it sink in . . . and enjoy it!

When Michael quit his day job to work full-time at home, it took us *over a year* to completely adjust to the fact that he was indeed free from someone else's time clock—not just between jobs or on a long vacation! His "commute" was from one end of the house to the other. His work uniform was no longer a suit and tie. Although we had always enjoyed each other's company, we had never been together seven days a week except briefly between jobs. We had to make new room for one another and restructure our time and space boundaries. It took some quarreling and discomfort, but now we love nearly every minute. You and your child will have to do the same sort of re-adjusting and re-thinking your former values and schedules. Your child will have the freedom and responsibility of living with his teacher(s); you will have the duty of knowing when to teach and when to be just mom or dad.

Define Your Homeschooling Philosophy

Let us assume that to homeschool in your state, you must simply notify the superintendent of your child's school that she is leaving and you will be homeschooling. Now, what do you do? You first need to determine what homeschooling philosophy you believe in *at this time*. Unlike what you may be used to from school experience, you need not make hard-and-fast decisions when you teach your own child. No career-track nail-biting, no college-prep or "general education" track decisions will shape the next few years. Nothing written in stone. You can decide today to be a strict curriculum devotee, following an absolute schoolwork schedule from 8:00 A.M. to noon Monday through Friday, only to find next month that you and your child hate this "school-brought-home" routine and want a freer approach. Then you may explore the techniques and theories written about and utilized by such educators and teachers as Charlotte Mason, Dr. Raymond and Dorothy

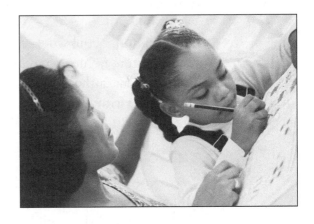

Moore, and John Holt. As you discover more about your child and yourself, you may interject more of your personalities into your homeschooling efforts. After all, this family you have built and maintained is your "world," and its road(s) to academic excellence are as uniquely individual as is your daily diet, wardrobe, and vacations. Above all, be yourselves!

Read This Book

To choose a philosophy that fits your family's personality and needs, you'll find it helpful to read the methods chapters in this book (chapters 4, 5, and 6). Let each one—parenting, unschooling, eclectic (and other approaches)—sink in, and try to gauge which one(s) might suit your family's personality. Then look in the Products and Resources sections, particularly for companies that offer catalogs you can pore over to learn about available resources. Order the complimentary copies of the homeschool publications offered in the Coupon section, and read them to discover which philosophy each favors. Each publication has a different slant, and each is enlightening in its own way. Even if you strongly disagree with a philosophy, that is part of your self-discovery.

Homeschooling is like a smorgasbord where you can pick and choose whatever sounds interesting—a math book, an English word game, a history workbook, a map puzzle, whatever strikes your fancy. You will find a *huge* amount of learning/teaching material, all of which is useful to some homeschooling family—maybe yours! Go to an educational bookstore or large all-purpose bookstore and browse for as long as you can. Ask a salesclerk for information about the educational books and materials. Most also have catalogs available containing many, many titles. Even 20 minutes spent looking here and there will prove invaluable.

Visit Your Public Library

Go to your local library and, once again, just browse through the general information sections, such as American history, world history, math, English, spelling, poetry, and art instruction. Check into whether the library has the Internet. I'll wager you will be surprised at what you have been overlooking at the library! I found an incredible little history book succinctly detailing all the signers of the Declaration of Independence with a color painting of each—a perfect way to learn about them, especially the less famous ones! Most libraries are excellent (and practically free!) resources for educational and supplemental materials that can help you determine your overall homeschooling philosophy.

Choosing a Philosophy
If Your Child Has Never Attended School

Even though you may have a leg up on your schooling counterparts, it is still very wise to really examine what is "out there" for homeschooling. Up until your child reached five or six, you may have had a fuzzy picture of what you wanted for him or her; perhaps a little counting, some word play, reading aloud was enough. Now that he or she is progressing to the "big" world, you may be putting his learning into clearer focus. Avail yourself of the excellent resources at your fingertips; they're invaluable in determining how to handle homeschooling.

Homeschoolers Say . . .

How long does homeschooling take each day?

This depends upon your approach or philosophy. Many people consider simply living and interacting with the family each day to be "education" enough.

Other families follow a rigid or semi-rigid daily academic schedule that can accomplish the basics in two to three hours. This doesn't mean the child covers the same amount as in six hours of school per day—homeschooling is far more intense and time-productive. Homeschooling can cover in one week (of two- or three-hour days) what can take two weeks or more in a traditional school setting. One-on-one teaching and the advantage of flowing, uninterrupted focus and attention on the part of the student make homeschooling very efficient. When you consider the field trips, park days, and other extracurricular activities available to homeschoolers, a great deal is going on.

Rethink Your Concept of Schooling

Homeschooling the child who has been in school may seem like an extended summer vacation; in some ways, it is. Much school time is spent on nonacademic activities, such as taking attendance and quieting disruptions. Now your child will be able to devote 100 percent of his study time on point. This means that in only two to three hours per day, he can cover far more than he would during an entire day in the classroom. Some families estimate that more learning takes place in a week of working at home two to three hours per day than can be accomplished in a month of school. Of course, this varies with each school, the family, and the specific experience. Our son will read for hours on end but may fight tooth and claw over five minutes of math presented in a "boring" fashion, such as memorizing times tables or repeating something he has done many times.

If we take a more relaxed, creative approach, giving him the same math facts in a slightly different setting—real measurements, sports statistics, or calculating the number of miles in a light-year—he enjoys the "work" and remembers what he learned! Keep in mind that you can't always make the work fun, but you can usually give it some real-life connection or purpose; if you cannot, maybe it isn't worth learning. No one, especially your child, needs his head crammed full of *useless* information. Be prepared to re-think your opinion of subjects you may have once thought of as acceptable.

Ask Your Child's Opinion

As you progress in this transition period, ask your child what she wants to *know* (not just what she wants to *learn*). What puzzles her? Does she know how your city operates its business day in and day out? Does he know and understand what you and your mate do or did for work? How your bank functions? What credit cards do? Such important real-life topics typically aren't covered in school. Combine academics and real-life knowledge. One characteristic of schooled children is the lack of initiative when it comes to *knowing* things. They often say, "We haven't learned that yet" or "They haven't taught us that." This demonstrates that the teacher, not the child, is responsible for knowing. Homeschooling families believe in raising a knowledgeable, self-teaching child who knows how and when to use the dictionary, atlas, phone book, and other reference books on his or her own.

One day, our son asked who owned the Walt Disney Company, so Michael explained about stockholders, publicly owned corporations, boards of directors and presidents, and that anyone, including Lennon, could purchase Disney stock. This widened his eyes for a few seconds and set the wheels turning! We haven't purchased Disney stock yet but probably will for a good lesson in the stock market.

Lennon also began helping with our bank deposits when he was nine and is involved in every aspect of our businesses. He knows much more than you would expect of an eleven-year-old. Whenever we give him responsibility and authority, he comes through with flying colors. We have been careful, though, to let him grow into these tasks by not giving him jobs we don't think he can handle. Other homeschooled children we've met have similar knowledge and abilities. We contend that your children will respond favorably if given opportunity to grow in this way. Kids are dying to know about and perform "adult" tasks, especially to elicit the praise of their parents and other important elders.

In college, classes you are allowed to choose (as opposed to those required) are called electives. In homeschooling, it helps to remain aware that electives keep the learning process interesting and alive. Children flourish in the autonomy of making such decisions, and you will be delighted how rewarding the learning experience can be.

The "Day After" Day One

Once you have given yourself and your child time to make the transition, you can go to work on the academic portion of home teaching. According to experiences reported through our newspaper, parents feel most comfortable using a prepackaged curriculum for the first year or six months. Thereafter, they often switch to a more customized approach, as discussed below. A prepackaged curriculum (see part 3) comes with virtually everything you need to begin work immediately—textbooks for each subject, workbooks, supplemental books, and any materials referred to in the year's plan (some even supply pencils and crayons!). Each package includes a detailed teacher's manual that tells you *exactly* what to do, and how and when to do it (no guesswork whatsoever!). Prepackaged curriculums are excellent for your introduction into homeschooling, but a word of clarification: The texts included are often written for classes of 30 or more students. As you gain insight into your child as a student and yourself as a teacher, you may lose your taste for such "school mentality." You will certainly become more skilled at selecting materials, thus producing a customized curriculum that meets your particular needs and goals.

Homeschoolers Say . . .

What exactly do homeschoolers do all day?

This depends on the family's educational philosophy. A family who "un-schools" may not adhere to a rigid schedule of academic work. Their days might be spent gardening, making a papier-mâché volcano as a science project, or doing other activities such as pottery, drawing, and music. Children in this type of environment are encouraged to follow their own interests, and all their interests are considered valid. We don't wish to give the impression that unschoolers are *always* working on something super-fantas-

Planning and Organizing

While enjoying your transitional week or two, get a spiral notebook at the drugstore or be fancy-schmancy and buy a Day Runner, Franklin, or other organizer to be utilized *exclusively* for your home-schooling (some specifically for homeschoolers made by homeschoolers are available, too). On scratch paper, begin roughly arranging your week, Monday through Friday (or whatever days you intend to do schoolwork).

If you use a packaged curriculum, you can still change the order of study the teacher's manual suggests. For example, you need not start with math on day one just because the manual recommends that. You may do certain subjects daily, based on your student's "weaknesses." You may do others, such as an art or craft project, or a "strong" subject, only once or twice a week. Because interests and needs change over time, be prepared to adapt your schedule at a moment's notice.

The flexibility of homeschooling is a strong feature. After working with you to improve a "weak" subject, your child will probably power ahead in that subject and you can modify his or her schedule

tic. Many spend days playing with Legos, reading a book, rearranging their rooms, or doing nothing at all.

On the other hand, a family using a boxed curriculum or teaching the trivium method (which suggests two hours daily of the parent reading aloud to the child) or another approach requiring regular, daily attention will have a more planned routine. When a parent is at home all day with the children, part of home educating is teaching each child grooming, cleanliness, and caring for one's surroundings. Therefore, housecleaning, yardwork, and picking up after one's self are included in the regimen.

to suit changing needs. Home teaching is like a gym for "brain" training, and you are the trainer. As you work a muscle group, it becomes stronger; then you shift your regimen to maintaining that first muscle group's strength while working another group to make it stronger. With faithful, *patient* effort, a person can evenly condition his entire body by changing the routine to fit the current situation. Like his muscles, your child's brain and personality constantly change as he or she *works* at the various subjects with you at home.

Water can wear a hole in a stone just by a constant, gentle drip, drip, drip. Be flexible and open to change when you see a "problem" develop with your original schedule. Be self-disciplined instead of obsessive. Raising a knowledgeable, well-adjusted young person involves growing *around* as well as through obstacles, as trees often do.

Once you have roughed out your ideal schedule, copy it in pencil in your organizer or notebook. The organizer will also help you keep attendance and daily progress records (good for peace of mind and beneficial if your state requires them). If your student is doing high school work, this type of planning and organizing will serve as the basis for your homemade transcripts when the time comes.

A typical homeschooling day is generally based on the schedule you and your child find most comfortable. If your child was in school by 8:30 or 9:00 each morning, you may not have considered what his work personality and habits are. Some students work best first thing in the morning; some need personal time to wake up; some prefer afternoons; others work great in the evening; and still others can work any time, any place, so it doesn't matter what time they begin and end their daily academic regimen. If your child is the type who must "work" before he plays, or else will accomplish nothing in a day, he should start right after breakfast. The order of the day's studies will be purely personal, too. Some students have to start with 20 to 30 minutes of their least-favorite subject, when attitudes are fresh. A different sort of personality might like to begin with an English assignment—or writing, reading a history lesson silently or aloud, or doing a geography lesson. The order of studies should depend on personal considerations, which you and your student can work out as you go. Below, we list a sample weekly schedule for those beginning the homeschooling process. In the unschooling chapter, you will find a sample weekly schedule for that approach.

Sample Weekly Schedule

Monday

9:00–9:40	*Math Lesson 1*
9:45–10:00	*Penmanship Exercise 1*
10:20–11:00	*Read Geography Lesson 1 and answer 5 of the 10 questions at the end.*
11:10–11:50	*Spelling Lesson 1*

Tuesday

9:00–9:40	*Math Lesson 2*
9:45–10:30	*American History Lesson 1*
10:35–10:55	*Reading Assignment 1*
11:05–11:20	*Penmanship Exercise 2*
11:25–12:00	*Poetry & Literature Lesson 1 (one each week for now)*

Wednesday

9:00–9:40	*Math Lesson 3*
9:45–10:00	*Penmanship Exercise 3*
10:05–10:45	*Read Geography Lesson 2; make a simple map*
10:50–11:30	*Spelling Lesson 2*
11:35–12:00	*Art History Lesson 1*

Thursday

9:00–9:40	*Math Lesson 4*
9:45–10:30	*American History Lesson 2*
10:35–11:00	*Reading Assignment 2*
11:05–11:30	*Grammar Lesson 2*
11:35–12:00	*Spanish (or French) Lesson 1*

Friday

9:00–9:40	*Math Lesson 5*
9:45–10:00	*Penmanship Exercise 5*
10:05–10:45	*Spelling Lesson 3*
10:50–11:20	*Music Appreciation*
11:25–12:00	*Spanish/French Lesson 2*

When Your Child Isn't Following the Schedule

You start right in Monday morning to follow the schedule, but your child is so happy to be home that she drills right through Math Lesson 1. When you come back at 9:40 to check on her and move on to the next subject, she is doing Lesson 4! What do you do? Celebrate and let her keep going! You can easily adjust your schedule to fit the other study topics or have her work into the afternoon. Now you have all day to stretch out!

Another *very* popular aspect of home teaching is that it's much more fluid than a classroom setting, in which teachers and sometimes the entire school must control the activities of large numbers of students. Often just as a child's mind is "warming up" to and becoming focused on a subject, the bell rings and he must tear himself away and

Homeschoolers Say . . .

What subjects should I teach?

In some states, you're required to teach a basic curriculum, which is just about universally accepted as "standard." It consists of reading, writing, math, English, American history, the history of your state, and possibly civics or health. In other states, parents are not *required* to teach this curriculum, but it is suggested. This core material can be amply covered in two to three hours per day. Over and above this, the parent and student are free

do something else for 50 minutes, only to be interrupted again 50 minutes later. Rigid scheduling does not allow the natural functioning of the human mind, which can concentrate for long periods of time and learn a great deal when interested and engaged in the subject. Your child's power drive through four math lessons indicates just what she can do when interested in and happy about her work.

On the other hand, your daughter may loathe penmanship and do *anything* to avoid writing even the simplest note or list. Because literacy involves being able to write as well as read (information in and information out), you may have to bear down the way a trainer or coach does. You may try any technique to inspire your student to practice penmanship (or any subject); you might even bribe him for good performance (not a dangerous precedent unless you have to bribe your child to do *any* scholastic work). Practice common sense and bribe/reward on a case-by-case basis.

Let's say your schedule is shaping up well. Monday everyone is happy and working along. So, Tuesday's schedule also includes math, which is to be a daily subject. Of course, if your student did four math lessons on Monday, she could skip math on Tuesday and work on a subject she needs to spend time on. Since your child is accusto add whatever they wish to their course of study—another wonderful thing about homeschooling! If you want to study astronomy, you can spend as much time as you wish—staying up late to view the sky through a telescope from a remote area, for instance. If you are interested in ancient history, you can delve into it at the museum and library for hours on end—especially at midday, when the crowds are small. If your student is a musician or artist, she or he can focus on music or art for hours. Homeschoolers have the opportunity to study a topic much more deeply than they would in a conventional school setting.

tomed to the teacher assigning work to be done independently, you will be able to do the same.

In the case of a hated subject, however, you may want to *sit down* and work with your student. The novelty may propel her to work harder—not out of fear that you'll correct her, but out of love. Nearly every child wants her parents to be involved with her work and views a parent *patiently* giving time as fun. By "patiently" I do not mean saintly; I simply mean squelching the desire to say anything negative or impatient, to verbally judge your child harshly. Your generosity of self can turn the tide toward a child's success in academic and nonacademic pursuits.

Have faith that your child will succeed, rather than the expectation that he will fail. Feeling in your gut that he will "screw it up" is, believe it or not, having faith—but faith in the negative rather than the positive, the "bad" rather than the "good." If you anticipate that he may not do the assignment correctly, hold your tongue. If you are frustrated at her slowness to catch on to what you think is crystal clear, treat her as you would your spouse's boss, whom you are compelled to treat with deference. Or pretend she is your minister's child or someone else you respect. Suddenly treating your child with respect and care is easy! So, if possible, occasionally sit and work together on the hated subject. You may enjoy working with your child so much that you work with him or her every session—as a partner rather than only an assigner of work.

As you progress through your daily schedule, you will see more and more how to adjust or re-vamp the regimen and will develop a longer-range view—weekly and monthly—for setting and accomplishing goals. Recognize that we all have good days and bad days, and that too narrow a view is bound to become distorted. Once you know how your child averages out over a month or six weeks, you will see his or her progress much more clearly and satisfactorily.

Following your plan over a few weeks will give you ample insight into how this home-educating process will work over the long haul. You may reach a point where you need absolutely no packaged curriculum but can confidently assemble your own, composed of favorite and supplemental books in each topic. Don't worry if this doesn't happen. Many families happily achieve academic excellence using a boxed curriculum throughout their homeschooling time, even in high school!

Now you are on your way! We now offer a step-by-step summary that provides some additional information you will need.

The Steps to Homeschooling

A primary goal of *The Homeschooling Almanac* is to answer four often-asked questions: "What do I do? How do I start? Is it legal? Where do I go?" If you are new to homeschooling, we suggest that you follow the following procedure.

Step One: Ask yourself why you are considering keeping your children at home. Answering this question will steer you in the "right" direction when you consider a method (see chapters 5, 6, and 7). Your answer will also guide you if and when you decide to choose a homeschooling support group for field trips and social and other activities.

Step Two: Find out how to homeschool legally in your state. In part 4, look up the state in which you intend to homeschool. You'll

Homeschoolers Say . . .

Is homeschooling legal?

Yes. In every state and province, homeschooling is legal. However, the level of state supervision and regulation varies widely, from very strict in some states to no regulation at all in many others. Check with your local parent-run homeschool organization (listed in part 4) about the legal responsibilities in your state *before* you contact any state agency.

find information you need to know about your locale—laws and procedures regarding homeschooling, as well as descriptions and contact information for resource centers, support groups, conferences, and other organizations. Homeschooling is currently legal in all states, and many states offer a variety of ways to teach your own children. Do the research and make a general decision about how you will go about it. This will be especially helpful if you want to remove your children from school and keep them home. Summaries of each state's homeschooling laws are provided. Be aware that these laws may represent the cutting edge of legislation (and one never knows how the political winds may change!). Inquire every few months to be sure you know your precise legal standing in your own locale. Note: Do not construe anything you read in this book as legal advice.

Step Three: Read the interviews in this book. Since there are a variety of ways to homeschool, we have chosen real homeschooling parents, each with a unique method of homeschooling, for our interviews. Our intention is that *Almanac* readers can glimpse lives of an "unschooling" family, a traditional school-at-home family, a large family, a small family, and others. We've used a conversational style to provide you with a real feel of what goes on in these homes. Such interviews with real people will show that *you can do this.* You'll see that parents who are experienced in homeschooling also have doubts, but they carry on—successfully. Also, do some interviewing on your own. Get to know other parents; spend time with other families to see what their day is like. Once again, don't expect to re-create school at home—six hours of one-on-one teaching is *very* intense and not necessary.

Step Four: Roughly define your own family's educational goals. Keep in mind that you are an individual and your family is an individual family. A great strength of homeschooling is that *you* can customize everything to fit your family and your children's personalities, tastes, and interests. And, like that of a ship on the ocean, your course can change. Re-examine and adjust as time goes by and your family changes. You know pretty quickly whether you want your child to have a "classical" education (studying great literature, logic, and rhetoric); a "traditional" education (based on reading, 'riting, and 'rithmetic); or one based on your child's interests. As you grow into homeschooling, you naturally extend your ability and grow more!

Early on, as we met many people with many different homeschooling styles, we made the mistake of not defining our family point of view. We were tempted to change our concept of homeschooling each time we encountered a new, viable family outlook, which caused a lot of inner turmoil. We experimented with different methods and thought and re-thought until we found out enough about our family to formulate our unique and usable "Leppert method." A word of advice: When defining your family educational outlook, avoid re-creating the school day. Relax, be flexible, and be easy on yourself and your family. Our emphasis on this extends to "home-living," not just "home-schooling."

Once you define your initial educational outlook and goals, then choose which books, materials, or tools (if any) you wish to use, and plan how your children will spend their time. Notice as you read chapters 5, 6, and 7 on methods that you can take any of many, many paths to achieve your family goals—from "conservative" (more school-like) to liberal (less school-like). You can complete curriculums-in-a-box, design your own curriculum from a huge variety of available printed materials, or teach without buying anything at all. Your community library is a treasure trove of books, videos, tapes, and other materials that can aid you in your work. Or you can create nearly all the "curriculum" work from scratch—write your own math papers and read to your child. Your imagination is the primary "limiting" factor.

    Step Five: Contact a local support group and meet people face-to-face who are homeschooling. In the beginning stages, surround yourself with those of like mind. For example, if you are homeschooling for religious reasons, find other homeschoolers of the same background. After you become more experienced and comfortable, branch out and meet other homeschoolers.

One Family's Homeschooling Way

The popularity of homeschooling received a huge push in 1983 when the homeschooling success of David and Micki Colfax was first publicized. Their dramatic story of sending three of their four homeschooled sons from California's remote Mendocino County to Harvard and then on to medical and law school caught the nation's attention. Here, David shares his experience and thoughts on homeschooling, carefully including the advice that each family must determine its own philosophy and then create and continually revise the methods that fit their unique circumstances.

Interview with David Colfax

For those of you who don't know of them, David and Micki Colfax are real pioneers of homeschooling. In the early 1980s they bought property in northern California with virtually nothing on it and took their four boys there to live. Homeschooling evolved from this experience. The Colfaxes became famous after three of their completely homeschooled children went to Harvard and then on to Yale and Michigan law schools and Harvard Medical School. The fourth son is an international chef. All four children turned out happy and successful. David and Micki frequently speak at homeschooling conferences, have produced tapes, and have authored two books about their experiences with homeschooling: *Hard Times in Paradise* and *Homeschooling for Excellence*. Early in the homeschooling years, I (Mary) read *Hard Times in Paradise* and kept the Colfaxes' experience in a neat little corner of my psyche for times when people would criticize me or warn me against homeschooling.

Q
A

MARY LEPPERT: *What did you and your wife do on a daily basis as you and your children lived the homeschooling experience?*

DAVID COLFAX: We did as little as possible and as much as possible. I think most people are uncomfortable with that kind of answer; it sounds like we are trying to be evasive, but that is really at the heart of it. That is one of the things we try to convey to parents in our very short conversations with them. If you come into homeschooling with a ideology of education that is fully fleshed out, I think you are going to have some very serious problems at some point in your educational endeavors.

> ## We did as little as possible and as much as possible.

MARY: *So when you say you did as little and as much as possible, describe the "much."*

DAVID: Well the "much" was to provide the kids with a sense that there is a world of possibilities out there. In life, you will be dealing with people who have theories, ideas, and concepts—views that make sense in certain contexts; some that make no sense in certain contexts; and some stuff that makes no sense at all. Basically, what we tried to do is give them a sense of the fact that the world is filled with theories, filled with things to do, and that you can create and carve out any of millions of lives within your own life.

MARY: *So are you saying that you tried to expose them to as many different ideas and theories as possible?*

DAVID: Well, it's not so much trying to expose them as a process of discussing and debunking, if you will. Nowadays the academics would call it "deconstructing reality." Basically, we were being very radical in terms of looking at the systems of thought. Micki and I are very, very unsympathetic toward the grandiose theories—history, art, religion, interpersonal relations, and so forth. The old phrase that there are more things in heaven and earth than are dreamed in your philosophy is kind of a bellwether. The point was to go into these different realms and feel free to pick up any book and get what is good out of it. It also means don't pick up anything with the idea that it has certain value because it is a book or because somebody said this or that, or that they, by publishing this or publicizing that, give it any authority. The ultimate authority resides in you and what you know and what sense you are able to make of it.

> ## Don't buy into anyone's system! Create your own system. Be yourself.

So, in some sense, we anticipated educationally a lot of what is now being taught at the university level. It's not surprising because we have come through the same generation and the same kinds of events. We operated under what is called deconstructionism; that is, you have to look at things in the context in which they happen, you have to be highly critical, to make meaning out of what is perhaps meaningless, and so on. That's not the sort of thing you can get across to people when they say, "What should I be teaching my 12-year-old?" It's rather an orientation, and we present that to people, more in the context of, "Relax! It's a serious business, but you don't have to be *deadly* serious about it. The kids will do all right as long as you are showing them that you are concerned and providing them with opportunities."

That's what it evolves into, but, as you probably well know, we are very reluctant to recommend one system or another, even to recommend what we did, on the grounds that you know your kids better than we do, and we don't know you as well as you know your kids. So don't come to us asking for clarification, guidance, or expertise. We can say, "We thought this book was great, but be prepared to say, 'I didn't get anything out of it.'" Be prepared to say, "This might work for the Colfaxes, but it sure doesn't work for me." We're saying, "Good! You're not afraid. You're not buying into our system." Don't buy into anyone's system! Create your own system. Be yourself.

MARY: *Did you have a plan?*

DAVID: We were constantly revising, from our perspective at least. It's almost as if we reinvented the curriculum every day. Let's say you pick up the paper and read about someone who just died, and one of the boys says, "He was pretty interesting." But another says, "That guy was a real bum! Why is the newspaper celebrating someone who did more harm than good?" So we have the makings of what becomes a history lesson, or a lesson on the way the media distorts rules, or a lesson in newspaper economics, or an opportunity to talk about ideology. You can take off on somebody's obituary that you happened upon and talk about it in a dozen different categories. On the other hand, one of the boys may walk away from the whole thing and find a dead bird outside that becomes his concern for the day.

Now if you have a curriculum and say, "Put the dead bird down and forget about what we were talking about; you have to get onto your 'real' studies," you are saying to them that experiences and concerns are not as valuable as having a structured environment. I know that having a structured environment makes most people much more comfortable, safer than being essentially out there in the open.

MARY: *If one of the kids wanted to talk about a dead bird the rest of the day, or find out why the wings were a certain way, what would happen?*

DAVID: It would depend on how old they were. We would say, "What books do we have on birds back there?" And one might say, "Well, there is nothing in them; let's not bother." That would be the end of it. We would not say, "Oh, here's a great learning opportunity." That's what we call the overbearing or the didactic homeschooling parent, where the child can't have an experience without having it turn into an "educational experience."

> It's almost as if we reinvented the curriculum every day.

Just because they found a bird that died in the backyard that morning did not have to mean they were going to sacrifice building a telescope or finishing a novel. By having certain freedoms and allowing priorities to evolve in a child's mind naturally, you're not saying, "What you are doing right now is not as important as what may come up immediately."

What you are saying is, "We are letting you make these choices. Here is a wonderful opportunity—a woodpecker just died in the backyard. Let's dissect the thing and take the feathers and start making Indian baskets with them." If you do that, you are saying, in effect: "If this bird had not died and we had not found it, you would have been doing something less important, less significant." That demeans the ongoing process. There is real tension between being open to new experiences and still taking seriously what you are doing. I think we lose sight of that fact because we regard ourselves as teachers; maintaining the equilibrium is difficult.

MARY: *So do you think each kid has a path within the environment that he will follow if you leave him alone?*

DAVID: It's not "leaving alone." This is where you get people saying, "Did you let them just grow up, like Topsy?" The answer is "No." What we did was interact with them. It doesn't mean they had total access to us at all times, that we just sat there and said, "Do you have a question?" We did things with them, and disagreed with them, and they knew they could disagree with us. We wouldn't say, "You don't know what you are talking about." We didn't just tell them to shut up and go read, but we might suggest, "Maybe you need to read more and talk less." We had that kind of dynamic. The lack of dynamism concerns me about some of what is going on in the homeschooling movement. I think there is a tendency to rigidify and to buy into theories and methods and styles. Micki and I believe that you are engaged in a constant dynamism in the learning process. There is a tendency also to say, "Well, then you just lived your life." Well, yes . . . and no.

MARY: *You had to have structure to do what you were doing on the farm, right?*

DAVID: Right. As I was saying, we were living our lives; but at the same time, we were also bringing up children, we were educating them, we were in the process of preparing children for the time when they would no longer be with us. That has to be made clear to anybody trying to figure out what we were doing. We didn't just come here and raise some chickens and some ducks and say, "Well, if you learn something that's great, and if you don't, that's okay too." A very big part of our experience was that we had a clear sense of our responsibilities to our kids to make sure they learned how to be critical, to interact, to raise tough questions. You have to do these things in order not to accept conventional notions.

In one regard, I think that is why our kids are in very conventional professions, but at the same time are unconventional within those professions. I think the reason is that we said, "Hey, listen, this is the real world out there. You want to talk about what it is like to be a sociology professor? I'll talk about it. But let's also talk about what it is like to be a sociology professor in a context in which you don't accomplish very much, or in a context in which the university makes sure that the sociology professors don't teach sociology. Big difference."

MARY: *So you tell them the truth.*

DAVID: A big part of it is truth telling; the other side is that they develop a kind of critical edge, a critical view. We felt that our job was simply to present a view when it was called for. "What is good about this? What is bad about this? Is this truth, or is this somebody's ideology? Is somebody's value system being presented as if it were some timeless verity?" So, our boys have very little tolerance as adults for grand theorists. They tend to be (I don't think they would put it in these terms, but I would) pragmatists. Micki's signaling that I'm getting too abstract. But this is abstract. I think it's involved in everybody's way of looking at life. People are told that they have to categorize, to compartmentalize, to arrange information in hierarchies.

> We had a clear sense of our responsibilities to our kids to make sure they learned how to be critical, to interact, to raise tough questions.

MARY: *The same thing is done with subjects. Is that whole thing a marketing illusion?*

DAVID: Yes, absolutely. The marketing of education has had a very strong historical basis for 150 years. There is no reason we have to be thrown into this but, on the other hand, the whole culture is organized in this fashion today. The whole large of our society is compartmentalizing, categorizing, hierarchializing.

MARY: *Do people live real lives within that realm?*

DAVID: Again, that is why we have the commercialization of modern life. If you buy your entertainment or purchase it in blocks, you spend most of your time doing work so you can buy whatever products are out there. We are reluctant to get out too far—some reviewers of our second book, *Hard Times in Paradise*, said we came across as self-righteous and arrogant. Well gee, if we did, I'm sorry, but the fact is we did what we were doing. And we told how we did it and why we did it.

It wasn't all homeschooling, but we were trying to get more control over the way we lived and not be subject to larger blandishments of the society. It's very compelling. We didn't have television—not because we dislike television as such, but rather because of the insidious aspects of how television came to be and what kept it going and what mind-set the kids fall into. We would become uncritical because there is no reason to become critical of TV if you are a kid— unless you have a frame of reference, and most kids do not have that frame of reference. We have to be careful (I have to be careful) about becoming way too abstract. It's not something we talked about on a daily, weekly, or even monthly basis, or sat down and worked out a philosophy; but basically, our philosophy is one of going against the grain.

For example, we're in contact with a group of homeschooling parents who are getting harassed by the county building department. They're telling these parents who meet once a week in a house, "You cannot have your kids in your house because that does not meet the school standards." From my perspective it's a wonderful opportunity for the parents, the kids, and everybody involved to talk about the nature of government and civil rights, about constitution and politics. But in this case, some of the parents are conservative and have good jobs as professionals; they don't want to talk about the abuse of authority.

They just want a quiet life, and challenging even illegitimate authority is not their style. But when you take that kind of perspective, what kind of response can you make to abusive authority? Our kids would have grabbed hold of it and said, "Let's see where we go with this." I'm not saying these folks are unresponsive; they are just not approaching education as being potentially a very subversive activity. True education is truly subversive. It subverts a system that functions as a whole set of untested assumptions and ideas. If you are not prepared to examine each and every aspect in the course of your day-to-day activities in life, you are not making full use of your faculties, as it were.

MARY: *So where do the three R's fit into this?*

DAVID: It would go something like this: The guy across the road, who is a hippie, believes that he read a book once and didn't like it. He thinks that sitting under a redwood tree gives more knowledge and information than anything else does. So, you are seven or eight years old and told to sit under a redwood tree and see if you have the same feeling. If you do, fine. But when you want to do something, discover that you want to know more about Indians, I guarantee that redwood tree is not going to give you that information. It may make you feel the way they felt, but that is not the kind of information you are seeking. Perhaps your friend across the road does not really care about history. Now that you are asking about history, you are talking about literacy. You have to learn to read. We're not going to be your research assistants. We live in a literate society, and if you are not literate, you are going to have more problems than you can imagine. Reading is a simple process, if you don't allow it to be turned into something frightening or overwhelming. The same with math. You don't need to know much math (most people know very little math). You have to add, subtract, divide, and multiply, and that's it. You learn your multiplication tables to the 10s.

> We live in a literate society, and if you are not literate, you are going to have more problems than you can imagine.

MARY: *So you didn't make your kids do math?*

DAVID: I don't know what you mean by "make." I think we made it clear, "If you're not interested in this, fine. But at some point you are going to come up against it. When you do, you can either cram and be ready for it or simply say, 'I never bothered to learn that.' But you had better have a good explanation; otherwise you sound like a fool." By the time you're nine years old, you'll want to do things that might require a degree of literacy. It's not learning to read or do math that's important; it's what you can *do*. Math and reading are nothing more than tools, means to an end. So as you say, "I'd really like to explore this in more detail" or "I'd like to talk to somebody other than the people in the neighborhood," you have access to everything that's out there in the larger culture.

MARY: *Would you advise people who are living the "modern" life to get rid of TV, video games, and such and have a richer environment?*

DAVID: No, I wouldn't. I don't know that hearing that would do anybody any good. Most people are not going to be able to go back and live lightly on the earth and at the same time raise a family and live in a society where you need money to function. You may be willing to trade off certain things, but we don't need people advising us how we *should* live. We need people who say, "I'm going to take a look at what our priorities are."

MARY: *As a friend of mine said last week, "They want the cure, but they don't want to take the medicine."*

DAVID: That's a good way of putting it. I've had fathers come up to me and Micki at conferences—I can't tell you how many times—and say, "I want our kids to grow up and become successful professionals like your kids, but I think it's important for my nine-year-old son to do math on a regular basis; otherwise he's not going to have the skills and abilities to get to where your kids are." In that situation, I could either go into a long speech about "Well, there are many ways to this end . . ." (at that point, his eyes will probably glaze over) or I can tell him, "I think you're just plain wrong," and alienate him, which I wouldn't do.

Basically, I'm looking at someone who has a certain mind-set, who's not open to alternatives, who's not used to thinking the way I do. Someone I would call a very conventional guy with very conventional ideas about how you suc-ceed. I'm not going to tell him, "Many, many parents have the same aspirations for their kids that you have. The only question is how to achieve them and, quite frankly, I don't know that what you're saying is any different from what thousands of parents out there who are doing very conventional things are say-ing as well." The idea that you can do homeschooling and do the means and ends connection in the way the schools do is entirely possible. But it doesn't guarantee you anything. If you go that particular route, chances are your kids will do better than they would in school because you're putting more energy into them. But this is not what we would call real education. You're merely serv-ing as a substitute teacher-parent. If you really question some of your values about where you're going and why you're doing what you're doing, you might not like what you discover.

MARY: *Why do you think your kids became doctors and lawyers? Is it just a coincidence?*

DAVID: We raised our kids with the value of being involved in a profession that allows a person to try to make it a better world, which is something we highly value. Whether or not we had been homeschooling the kids, those values would have been there. So they carried forward values that were predominant in our family. At the same time, they are very much at the margin of their professions. Defending death row inmates in Alabama makes most lawyers shudder. That's what Drew is doing. He could be making big money if he were simply to cross to the other side of the street. But this is something he feels very, very deeply about. He feels that if *he* doesn't do it, who is going to do it? He's tough enough and young enough to do it for a few years.

So we have Grant, a physician working with AIDS patients and Reed working for the NAACP on housing cases; Garth is working with developmentally disabled kids. I can hear somebody saying, "Yeah, but they're not making any money." If your standard is making a lot of money, having a big house in the suburbs, and collecting a regular paycheck that allows you all kinds of freedom, then you just won't understand. I guess two of the kids own cars; the other two don't. They're barely able to pay their debts for law and medical school, but they're doing work that most people—especially their peers—believe needs to be done. Grant comes home and starts talking about cases he deals with, and it's pretty difficult to keep from wincing when he starts talking about homeless people that need medical care. It's not like being in a comfortable office doing the same kind of work with "nice" people, which he *could* do (and I don't want to demean anybody who is doing that). The point is that this takes a particular style of looking at the world—basically a subversive value.

> We raised our kids with the value of being involved in a profession that allows a person to try to make it a better world.

MARY: *When did your kids start reading, writing, and math? Or should people just relax and trust their kids to learn?*

DAVID: Relax *and* let the kids know what you think is important, what your values are. We're not saying, "Just go into free fall" and things will be fine. Don't be afraid to let the kids know what you think is important, but at the same time, try to create the conditions where the kids can say, "I don't agree with you on that." Instead of saying, "I hate math," I'd rather hear a kid say,

"What good is this?" or "Why do I have to learn it?" Then you are in a position of having to answer them honestly, and you may find yourself confronting your own values. Why is it important that kids learn geometry? Why do we waste time on teaching kids geometry? Mathematicians tell me all kinds of reasons; it was important to them because they are mathematicians!

Relax and let the kids know what you think is important, what your values are.

So you have to put it into some sort of social context, put it into a context of saying, "Well, you're right, but keep in mind that if you want to go into some scientific studies, you're going to need some math to do *some* things. And geometry is one of the steps in the process." Now, of course, mathematicians may come roaring out with, "This guy has no sense of what math is really all about." But I don't see warping your child's view of learning or frightening the child (or yourself or anybody else) because somebody says, "I really don't feel like doing math." Parents have to be able to say, "I think it's important," and the kids have to be in a position to say, "Why?" Maybe the most important thing we can hope for in kids is their ability to say, "Why?" when presented with ideas or new experiences or a new set of demands.

MARY: *I've heard you say that you told your kids, "If you want to play the college game, this is what you have to do."*

DAVID: Right. But you do that when they understand that they *do* want to play the college game. Fifteen or 16. You don't tell a 6-year-old, "This will help you get into college." What could be more intimidating or off the wall to a kid than to make this a standard, that everything you do is done in order to be able to do something else! It should not be the peak of one's life experiences. But again, it's matter of being very pragmatic and open. At each step in growing up, kids should be allowed to say, "Why am I doing this?" and parents should be secure enough to say, "Now that you ask, I don't have a good answer." And go on to something else.

MARY: *Did reading, writing, and math come differently with each child?*

DAVID: Yes—at very different times and in different ways. For Reed, it was a matter of imitation. This stuff called "math" was something his older brothers were doing and talking about, and kids will do what other kids do. To show that he was just as tough and grown up as they were, he would do math. By the time he was their age, he was far ahead of where they had been back then. On the other hand, Garth did not feel the need to be competitive. He learned math, but never vis-à-vis his brothers, because he wasn't as close in age and wasn't sitting alongside them every day, seeing what the big guys were doing.

MARY: *At approximately what age did they start doing reading, writing, math?*

DAVID: Much of it emerged from practical experience. They were out there building a house and helping do the sub-flooring. We'd tell them, "Put the nails every 6 inches around the perimeter of the piece of plywood; space them every 12 inches as you go across." They quickly learned what they needed and what we wanted. They'd see the marks on the tape measure and say, "What do these mean?" "What's 2½ inches?" "What's ¼ inch?" So on and so forth. Then you want to add fractions, then decimals, so you get into those kinds of things. Most families aren't nailing down sub-flooring, but they are doing things that are every bit as important. Education means drawing out, and that means being able to utilize experiences of all kinds.

CHAPTER 3
What Type of Learner Is Your Child?

Finding out what type of "learner" your child is can mean treading on foreign ground for most parents. "Learning styles" is still a relatively new, largely uncharted territory for everyone but specialists in this field. "Learning styles" is a philosophy that recognizes that we all perceive and process information in unique ways. Discovering your own or your child's learning styles is time- and energy-consuming—but worthwhile.

The majority of schools and teaching institutions are just starting to consider "learning styles" a meaningful way to analyze how children learn, and few have a clue how to use the information. Given the limitations of mass-schooling, school systems that choose to analyze and sort children by their learning styles may find it a logistic impossibility to accommodate all learners. Or perhaps it could be done along the lines of the magnet school method. For instance, all students whose intelligence is predominantly linguistic could attend one school, those with primarily musical intelligence another, and so forth. Still, given the highly individual nature of learning styles, it's unlikely that institutions like public schools will ever use this valuable tool.

Fortunately for the family who chooses to homeschool, there is no logistic problem. You can read the excellent material available on learning styles, possibly visit a counselor who specializes in advising families about learning styles (such as our interviewees at the conclusion of this chapter), and then implement your own personalized teaching plan for your child based on your findings.

Learning styles analysis can also be used in the home to understand the relationships between family members. By understanding ourselves and our family, we can build a healthy family of individuals with a strong, unique self-image. They, in turn, can go into the world and work with other people with different personalities and learning styles and, in general, be tolerant, understanding, and happy.

How We Discovered Our Child's Learning Style

Before we knew anything about learning styles, we realized that certain ways of learning would make it possible for our son to *really* learn—have the knowledge at his fingertips "forever," the authority to discuss it, and the ability to use it when necessary and repeat it when desired. If his particular learning way was not followed, the "learning" would be like writing in water—gone immediately after he went through the motions.

For example, the math book we used introduced skip-counting (1, 3, 5 . . .) by each number from 1 to 9 as preparatory practice to learning multiplication. The author said that multiplying these simple numbers is the same as fast addition, and skip-counting teaches that. So we began and quickly realized that incorporating skip-counting into a game would facilitate the learning. So we began playing catch with a bean bag, saying "our" number aloud as we threw the bag back and forth. We could practice all nine sets of numbers every day without breaking a sweat—speeding up, slowing down, throwing behind our backs, between our legs, fooling around with the game within the game. He would often beg to do them again and again!

Later, we tried having him sit and do multiplication worksheets of larger numbers. It was like dragging a heavy stone through the desert—nothing could have been less fun or more unproductive! We wanted him to practice the material and to prove that he knew it (as every program advised), and when you begin multiplying two-digit numbers by two-digit numbers, skip-counting cannot be used.

After struggling with the worksheet method, we finally took to using a lecture approach (which we still use, by the way). Michael would stand at a dry-erase board where Lennon (lounging on his bed, possibly holding one of his cats) could easily see him write, for instance, a two-digit number times a three-digit one. Then Michael would say, "Okay, now walk me through this problem." Lennon would tell him what to do at each step, instructing Michael exactly what to do before he'd write *anything* down. This activity has an immediate cause-and-effect dynamic, to which Lennon responds very well. He must tell Michael to "put down the 0 and carry the 1" before *anything* is written down; therefore, Lennon *must* know what to do. This method allows him to use his knowledge in a functional way in a comfortable atmosphere, and we can also teach him new concepts and skills at the board just as effectively. We receive tremendous satisfaction from actually teaching him and seeing him learn from us!

We use this dry-erase/lecture method for English grammar and vocabulary, too. At any given time we have spent over an hour telling him about the history of the English language, the wars and fortunes of it, or explaining why pronunciation and spelling are not standardized. He has listened raptly without being distracted until he has a question. We've heard him repeat this information to someone else days later, showing that it "stuck" with him. This gives us both such satisfaction that we look for-

ward to working the next day, and often, when we have to stop after twenty minutes, he will groan and moan, "Do we *really* have to stop so soon?" He never groaned about not doing a worksheet!

Since Lennon hates to sit and write problems out, the lecture method is about the only way that works for us. Were he in school all day, the teacher would definitely be telling us he had "problems."

Here is another anecdote illustrating that you can realize great profits by catering to your child's learning style. While Michael was still working his day job, Mary was doing most of the homeschooling. At the time, we were using a boxed curriculum and following the teacher's manual fastidiously. Then Mary started *The Link*, our homeschool newspaper and soon, due to lack of time, started homeschooling in a different manner. For example, while she was doing the bulk mailings, she would open the spelling book and ask then-seven-year-old Lennon a word. If he spelled it correctly, she "let" him do two laps around the inside of the house. He would run laughing through the den/kitchen/living room twice, thinking it was great fun! He would work on spelling for hours if Mary continued the game. We had previously used the workbook approach, which he went along with because he took pride in being a good speller, but his enthusiasm multiplied with the running/spelling method.

For all children, there is at least one "right" way (the most productive one) and a few "wrong" ways (those that are unproductive and merely drudgery). Finding out your child's learning style can be easiest when you know what he or she likes (within learning) and dislikes. Dislikes are often simply a matter of a different learning styles.

The Seven Human Intelligences

Howard Gardner, a psychologist at Harvard University, studied and developed his analytical outlook based on organizing human intelligence not as one element, but by the following seven categories of intelligence. Gardner submits that everyone is a mixture of all seven, in varying degrees. By looking through this "lens" of Gardner's, we can see one or two predominant intelligences standing out in each person we know, including ourselves. The other intelligences are apparent in decreasing dominance and strength the further we analyze. Let us list the seven and discuss each a bit.

Bodily-Kinesthetic Intelligence

People with this form of intelligence just can't sit still. They wiggle constantly, make noises with their mouths, fingers, feet, hands, by

Homeschoolers Say . . .

I am intimidated by the incredible news stories about what home-schoolers do. What if my child doesn't measure up?

There is nothing to measure up to. We consider each child unique, and no two can be intelligently compared, except for considerations of taste. Contests like spelling bees and geography bees are not barometers of intelligence. A brilliant person may "freeze" in front of a crowd and be unable to demonstrate his intelligence, but give him a quiet room with a computer or notebook and pen, and he might illuminate pages and pages with his thoughts. Try not to fall into the trap of comparing. *Everyone* is good at certain things and not so good at other things. If you can let your child manifest the best "self" he or she can be, and you love and respect *that* person, both of you will have an enjoyable experience, no matter what.

either constantly tapping or by squeaking and squawking. They can't wait to be outside playing, running, climbing trees—you name it. As adults, they fidget, probably doodle while on the phone. If a bodily-kinesthetic person has athletic skill as well, she or he will probably be very good at sports, dancing, and other such activities.

This type of person often has intuitive feelings about academic material. Such a one may know an answer to a problem, but not how to arrive at it. They "feel" it. They learn through their bodies, so to speak, doing best in atmospheres of action, touching, physical contact, working with their hands. One boy with a great deal of this type of intelligence memorized the capitals of the 50 states over a period of about five days while rollerblading on the family's patio and repeating them after his father. To do this work sitting down would have been more than he could endure, plus might have required ten days of struggle rather than five days of fun.

A child with this type of intelligence will not get along well in a typical school setting. Most schools teach children in a way that is more conducive to the logical-mathematical intelligence.

Interpersonal Intelligence

People with this form of intelligence have a strong personality and are sensitive to others and what is going on around them in general. They make great social types. Successful society hosts and hostesses who throw parties in large commercial cities would have strong interpersonal intelligence, knowing exactly who to invite to these important networking events as well as who to seat together and who to separate.

Great salespeople have this type of intelligence as well. They can ferret out a person's need and successfully connect it with their product. Of course, they can also manipulate people in their negative manifestations. These people also tend to have "street smarts," which help one navigate in the world. Interpersonally intelligent people can also be excellent politicians, both in getting elected and in putting empathy for others into practical use on a large scale. Children with this type of intelligence may enjoy playing group games and activities, and they tend to be very outgoing, often serving as the peacemakers in disputes. As adults, they can also use their interpersonal skills as counselors and mediators.

Intrapersonal Intelligence

Those whose intrapersonal intelligence is their primary intelligence have strong personalities also, but they manifest it in a more personal way than do those with the interpersonal variety. The intrapersonal type can happily work alone. They possess a deep awareness of themselves and have a highly developed inner world, which they do not characteristically enjoy exposing or sharing with others. If a person of this type is also skilled in music or another art, she or he can become very accomplished in the art form, although performing may not be appealing due to shyness.

Children with this predominant form of intelligence can be bookish and quietly knowledgeable, but they do not necessarily fare well in school. They are often autodidacts—people who teach themselves—

and may become self-educated once they get beyond the high school or college academic imposition of grades and such. They possess an inner discipline and will to learn *real* things, not achieve synthetic grades. They also manifest themselves as independent and express strong opinions and feelings in heated discussions.

Linguistic Intelligence

Those with linguistic intelligence predominating are likely to be born poets and writers, loving to play with words just for the fun of it. Lewis Carroll probably possessed this form of intelligence, as do many famous song lyricists and poets. If they are less predisposed to writing, they may make excellent verbal storytellers and good yarn-spinners. Possibly Homer, who made up and recited epic poems, was of the linguistic group.

People with linguistic intelligence tend to love to read books and other forms of print and are naturally good spellers, possessing a strong memory for words in all of their forms, both as children and adults. They also may enjoy playing Scrabble and doing crossword puzzles or anagrams and other types of word puzzles and games. They are probably skilled at learning more than one language as well, noting the universal similarities among all the spoken/written forms of communication. Such people learn best by seeing, speaking, or hearing words, so reading print, listening to lectures, and taking notes are comfortable, successful ways for them to take in information. Telling others about this information often helps them to reinforce the learning process.

Logical-Mathematical Intelligence

People who possess logical-mathematical intelligence think logically and easily see patterns. For instance, great chess players are successful because they reportedly "see" the patterns of moves—both theirs and their opponent's. Logical-math people are also very good at transferring abstract concepts to reality and are often able to communicate these concepts to others. They may also enjoy solving life's puzzles through the sciences and can be very good inventors, having the skill to visualize—and conceptually alter—an invention before they even make a prototype. A person such as this may enjoy Mensa puzzles and games or a card game such as Set, in which players must compete against each other to find the most combinations of similarities or differences in designs and shapes drawn on a deck of special cards. This requires lightning-fast visual analysis and the ability to process information in a certain way. These people normally do well in school, which was designed for their type of intelligence. The old-fashioned IQ tests measured this form of intelligence more than any other.

Musical Intelligence

People with musical intelligence often hum or sing to themselves. They have a great aptitude for music in general, being able to remember melodies after only three or four hearings, and they possess excellent pitch and usually a good sense of rhythm in varying degrees. Often, when a piece of music is playing, they cannot help but move some part of their bodies in time with it. These children and adults have a keen awareness of sounds other than music as well, such as the wind blowing, insects buzzing and chirping, and traffic noise. They can often learn by hearing information set to music or by writing their own music to it.

Not surprisingly, many of them are very talented musicians and often exhibit this ability early in life. Some who are not particularly gifted with playing or composing ability make *sure* critics, keenly interested in music and understanding it. Those having this type of intelligence often concentrate better with music playing in the background. To teach one with musical intelligence, you might use tapes that contain the information set to music, for instance. Or use music as a mood-enhancing tool to decrease stress and increase relaxation and concentration. A particular piano concerto by Mozart has actually been shown to exert a scientifically measurable change in the brains of listeners—a very interesting phenomenon! It increases concentration in some and just gives others a sense of clarity. Hopefully, in-depth study in this area of brain research will continue, and a musical catalog of "brain" tunes can be developed!

Spatial Intelligence

Having this form of intelligence imparts the ability to think and see in pictures and images. This would be a form of intelligence of a painter or sculptor who can "see" in his or her mind's eye and bring forth in detail what others might miss. Those with this form of intelligence love to make charts and maps, so get your student involved by having him or her make simple maps of your house, your neighborhood, and your city. Let him work in geography as much as he likes.

Analyzing the learning styles and personalities is really no more than carefully examining the dynamics and fibers of every individual. Imagine putting 30 different people in one room and then wondering why they don't do things the same way, see things the same way, agree on everything, and desire the same things. Yet this is exactly what is expected in mass-schooling today.

Homeschooling the "ADHD" or the "Gifted" Child

Since you have read this far, chances are you recognize your own child in the above descriptions. But what the identification of learning styles provides is a way out of the "system" way of thinking—out of categorizing, labeling, grading, and consequently disabling children.

Once you have decided to homeschool your children, labeling is no longer necessary. If your child has been labeled "gifted" or "ADHD," perhaps you can view him or her in a different light now that he or she is at home.

Here are examples of two children classified by the school system with these popular but misleading labels.

Peter, a Kinesthetic Learner

Peter is 11 years old and cannot sit still. Given a choice, he'd rather be out riding his bike, playing ball, or in-line skating than doing anything else. A very creative boy with a vivid imagination, Peter can dictate stories at will and punctuate them with his own sound effects. At times, he has shown his parents how to repair things around the house. For example, once the washing machine quit working, and his father pulled the front panel off, exposing the motor. Peter was able to see that the belt was ¼-inch off track. Another instance showing

Peter's mechanical inclination occurred when his parents bought a camcorder. Peter had never operated or even held one before, yet within 30 minutes, he was filming like a pro. He was also able to advise and instruct his parents on how to operate the camera and recharge the battery, explain the more detailed features of the camera, and even transfer and edit videotape. His father often thought that he would become an engineer or an architect because of his natural ability to solve problems.

Peter's school life is a different story. He has problems sitting still and has a propensity toward audio learning, so the logical-mathematical way in which material is presented leaves him high and dry—and confused and frustrated.

When his teacher announced that he had scored at the bottom of the class in tests and subsequently placed him in a different room for the "learning disabled," he felt insecure, like any 11-year-old boy would. He became prone to certain personality problems. His parents attended several meetings, and there was talk that Peter had ADHD (Attention Deficit Hyperactivity Disorder), along with hyperactivity. He was faced with living down the label of "slow learner" and a childhood of Ritalin. Peter would have faced a rough road in a conventional school. Luckily, his parents decided to homeschool him.

Six months after removing Peter from school, his family reported in all sincerity that they felt homeschooling saved Peter from possibly turning to crime one day. This might sound dramatic, but the labeling put him on such a downward path that he felt he wasn't smart and was unable to do the right things. Based on other stories we've read and heard, his family's fears were not overstated but were all too true.

Ann Marie, a "Gifted" Child

Ann Marie was labeled "gifted" when she was ten because she could read at a college level. This was a *relative* label, though, because her class of 25 students contained three children who were musically intelligent, seven who were kinesthetically intelligent, and approximately ten who had a high degree of spatial intelligence. None of them fared well with the linguistic, logical-mathematical material that was used as the yardstick for judging ability and intelligence. Ann Marie went all through her school years in the "gifted" program feeling the need to live up to her labeling. She felt impelled to be perfect and to produce so she would not disappoint her parents, teachers, or school peers. This caused Ann Marie a great deal of internal turmoil, and by the age of 16, she had developed anorexia. Through her therapy for this disorder, it was revealed that what Ann Marie really dreamed of was getting married, having a large family, living out in the country, and having a simple life. Ann Marie felt she could never attain her dream without letting down the many people who expected her to live up to their high image of her as "gifted."

Homeschooling the "Gifted" Child

When we asked author and professional learning styles analyst Mariaemma Pelullo-Willis what it means to be "gifted," she replied, "All children are gifted! In our culture, we define areas in which we think children should be smart and then call them 'gifted' when they show the 'right' kind of intelligence and 'learning disabled' when they don't." We were not surprised by her remark. We've asked many friends and acquaintances whose kids are labeled "gifted" in the public school system exactly what this label means and how their kids are treated differently. Many related stories of magnet schools, special field trips, and special activities.

One mother related that the magnet school her son attends has children do two in-depth (four months each) unit-type studies about particular subjects, such as the judicial system. I (Mary) followed what this child did during the four months; as her mother and I are friends, I was able to inquire along the way just exactly what the child covered. I found that these "gifted" children were not doing anything differently than we were doing in our diverse homeschool group. At the time in this group we had two 12-year-old boys, one who could not read at all and one who could read at his "age" level. We had two children who were talented in the arts, drama, and painting. One was nine and not writing yet. We also had a variety of other children just out of mass-school who, if studied, would be considered ordinary. I found it very curious that we, with our diverse

Homeschoolers Say . . .

My child is in the "gifted" program. Do you recommend homeschooling for us?

A very good friend of ours whose child is in the public school "gifted" program told us that the program covered three special topics extensively each school year. They were currently working on the judicial system, which included activities such as taking a field trip to a courthouse while trials were in progress and talking with a judge. What they are doing is not much differ-

group of children, were doing the same things that these kids were doing in the magnet schools in the special "gifted" program.

I was bothered most thinking about all the children not in the "gifted" program, who did not go to the courthouse or do other "gifted" activities. In our homeschool group, all children participate and all are "gifted" in one area or another. Homeschooling fosters "giftedness" by its very nature and can bring out the best in your "gifted" child and yourself as well.

Valuable Analysis for the Family

Not only can recognizing different learning styles make you a better homeschooler, it can also make your family unit stronger. In our family, we have found great value in realizing that Michael is gifted with intrapersonal intelligence and Mary is blessed with interpersonal intelligence. When we are working together on a project such as this book, Michael thrives in an environment with the door closed, locked away from all external stimuli. On the other hand, Mary feels strangled with the door closed, as if all her creativity goes out the window and she's being cut off from her personal strength. In the past, such differences could cause a huge eruption between us.

ent from what we do any given week or month. It was much like a unit-study approach. (See chapter 6 for more information on unit study.) If your child is in the gifted program, you can satisfy him or her by being an active home-schooler—going on field trips, studying topics in depth, challenging him or her, entering science fairs, participating in geography bees. Much is available for homeschoolers and all children. Tour a plastics factory; see how bagels are made; go to a potato chip factory; visit an auto manufacturing plant, the post office, police station, or fire station; do a weekend cartooning workshop. The list is limited only by your imagination!

Now, more fully understanding the basic qualities a person with a particular intelligence possesses makes it easier to work together and to be married, in general. The same thing goes for our relationship with our son. We can now look at each other with deeper understanding of how each of our personalities functions. Life is smoother, and we are all a great deal happier. In the past, these differences in intelligences caused us to think that perhaps one of us was being stubborn or always wanted to have his or her own way, or perhaps one of us was not all that smart. Now we know we just have different styles.

Skills and Work

Think about your skills in childhood and their relationship to your adult means of earning a living. If your child loves to dissect things and study biology and then grows up to be a doctor, there is apparent continuity. If your child is a gifted musician and grows up to earn a substantial living as a musician, the perception is one of continuity. So imagine how unimportant algebra might seem to a gifted musician—or chemistry or any of a number of academic subjects

Homeschoolers Say . . .

My child has been labeled learning disabled. Would homeschooling be good for him?

Yes. We receive many calls from parents who say their children have been labeled ADHD since first or second grade. By the time these children get to grade 5 or 6, they're labeled troublemakers. Mothers who have taken these 11- and 12-year-old children out of school often find, after two or three months, that the child's personality completely changes, and he or she becomes an absolute delight to be around.

---

that are given a great deal of weight in our current view of what children should learn. Much of the hand-wringing and soul-searching parents do results from this underlying "job search" way of thinking. We submit that parents should analyze what they consider important for their children based on a number of factors, including the child's learning styles—not just on a blind acceptance of the academic curriculum conceived in another time under another philosophy of what is important.

When Parents Discover the Concept of Learning Styles

Very often at *The Link*, we get phone calls from distressed parents of schoolboys, 10–11 years old, saying that their children have been diagnosed with ADD or ADHD. This is one of the situations that brings many people to homeschooling. I have always found it curious that many of these parents who begin homeschooling call in a few months to say that there has been a drastic change for the better in

Parents whose children have been labeled as having severe learning disabilities worry that they'll have no idea how to teach them. We usually recommend that these parents visit a learning styles consultant. More often than not, these children simply have a different learning style.

We recently interviewed Dr. Rene Fuller, creator of the reading program Ball-Stick-Bird. When we asked what she thought about the widespread diagnoses of ADHD and ADD in public schools, she said that these labels are, unfortunately, groundless. Had such terms existed when she was in grade school, she would have been labeled hyperactive because she is a fidgety person.

their children's attitude, behavior, and lives in general. What usually happens is that when these children, who have been labeled "behavioral problems" and/or "troublemakers," are at home all day instead of in a school setting, they are allowed to blossom and grow in a more organic way. As a result they become attuned to their own personal learning style and they become happy, well-adjusted children.

The attitude of the public school system is that these children must be put on Ritalin or some other personality-controlling drug and should learn how to sit and do as they are told. One reason for this is that the public school system gets more ADA (average daily attendance) money for a child who is considered to have special needs. Many times the parents get no help from the public system; instead, their kids are placed on a sidetrack of negativity that involves drugs and sometimes psychiatric intervention. We believe that in 90 percent of these cases, the child is simply not in a learning setting that is suited to how he functions and thrives best. This is what brings the family to homeschooling, as a last resort.

About three years ago, I (Mary) attended a workshop called "Learning Styles or Learning Disabilities" at a homeschooling conference. It was presented by Mariaemma Pelullo-Willis, co-owner, with Victoria Kindle Hodson, of Reflective Educational Perspectives. I only attended Mariaemma's workshop because the one I wished to attend was full. My son does not have learning disabilities, and I was not that interested in the topic. After about 20 minutes, I was teary-eyed because all of my school life I had felt different because I could not sit still and always wished to be someplace else. (My husband says this was "good taste.") Also, I learned better by listening to information rather than reading it. I discovered that day that my learning modality was auditory; I had never thought about it much before.

In the workshop, Mariaemma described different learning styles that I was completely unfamiliar with—not just auditory, visual, tactile-kinesthetic. From the point of view of Reflective Educational Perspectives, these are learning modalities, and modalities represent only one-fifth of the entire learning personality. Most homeschoolers I know define learning styles as purely auditory (one who learns best by hearing); tactile-kinesthetic (one who learns best by feeling/moving); or visual (one who learns best by seeing, including reading). These modalities are only one of the five aspects Mariaemma and Victoria analyze to provide a person with a full learning profile.

The other aspects include such things as Environment. Do you learn best with noise in the background? Maybe you require a completely quiet room. Or maybe you need something in between the two. Couple environmental requirements of your personality with the modality that you use to process information, and you have two-fifths of your entire profile. The other three aspects of learning style are talents (word, music, math/logic, mechanical reasoning, and so on), interests (favorite subjects, pastimes, jobs, and so on), and disposition (performing, producing, inventing, and so on).

Mariaemma's workshop changed my entire self-image. I took *A Self-Portrait* Learning Style Profile and found it to be dead accurate in describing me. All the things I used to consider inadequacies, I was eventually able to see as strengths. They are not "bad" or "weak"; they are simply my way, which is different from the way schools teach people.

Is Learning Styles a Homeschooling Method?

Mariaemma and I have become friends over the years, and when I was telling her about this book, we discussed where we should list Reflective Educational Perspectives, the Learning Styles company that offers *A Self-Portrait*. Mariaemma said, "Under the methods section, of course." I myself had never thought of defining and using learning styles as a method, but I saw her point.

If you imagine all the methods of homeschooling to be in a room, lined up like a display, Mariaemma and Victoria's Learning Style Profiles approach to learning is the doorway. You cannot fully and effectively teach your child five or six different subjects until you know how she or he learns best. One method of homeschooling might work for only one "subject" in your total program, so you will benefit highly from a thorough analysis of your child's profile. The Learning Style method of homeschooling will help you choose the curriculum and materials, for each subject, that are right for your child.

Interview with Mariaemma Pelullo-Willis and Victoria Kindle Hodson

Mariaemma Pelullo-Willis and Victoria Kindle Hodson, partners in the consulting company Reflective Educational Perspectives, frequently offer workshops on learning styles for homeschooling groups. Their methods have proven of particular value to homeschooling parents who wish to determine and apply the most effective methods for teaching each individual child.

Mariaemma and Victoria are very quiet, gentle people, sensitive and patient. I know that the following interview will help all of us in our parenting, including those whose children have been labeled with learning "disabilities."

Q
A

MARY LEPPERT: *What does your company, Reflective Educational Perspectives, do?*

MARIAEMMA PELULLO-WILLIS: Our company works with children and their families to evaluate all aspects of the child's learning style to learn the child's strengths and how he or she learns best.

VICTORIA KINDLE HODSON: With the information we gather, we make specific environmental and curricula suggestions for that child's learning needs. We want to rekindle the natural curiosity in our children that makes them eager, self-directed learners. We do this by using our *A Self-Portrait* profiles, which have been designed to assess learning needs for various age groups: preschool, elementary school, junior high school, and high school–adult.

MARY: *Can you elaborate on the different learning styles?*

MARIAEMMA: There is confusion about what these are. Most people think "learning style" means auditory, visual, tactile-kinesthetic; but there is so much more to it than that. We look at five aspects of learning style.

VICTORIA: We've come up with a mnemonic to remember them: TIMED. "T" is for talents, "I" is for interests, "M" is for modalities, "E" is for environment, and "D" is for dispositions. Saying that a person is auditory, visual, or tactile-kinesthetic is only telling us about the modality aspect.

MARY: *How do you do an assessment?*

VICTORIA: Each person taking the profile answers simple questions (an unusual feature is that children answer the questions themselves), which tell us what the person's talents, interests, modalities, environmental needs, and disposition are. The scores of the five aspects of learning style are then summarized to create the child's learning portrait.

MARY: *Earlier you spoke of environmental needs; what are they?*

MARIAEMMA: For instance, do kids need bright light or dim light? Do they need a very cool temperature or warmer?

VICTORIA: Quiet and noise would be another aspect of environment. Do they need to have other people in the room or be alone? Sitting at a desk or lying down to study is another consideration.

MARIAEMMA: In other words, there are several areas to consider when determining a person's learning style. For example, let's say in the talent section you selected "Taking care of animals" and "Being good with other people" and "math/logic" kinds of activities. Then we look at your Interests and see that you are really interested in playing the piano, and in hiking and skateboarding. Next we look at modality and find you are more of a visual learner who does best with videos, movies, and CD-ROMs (moving visuals). That is, if you watch a video about something you are studying, you are more apt to learn it.

> We want to rekindle the natural curiosity in our children that makes them eager, self-directed learners.

VICTORIA: Then we would assess environment and might find that you do best with a radio on in the room with your pet sitting next to you. And, you prefer sitting on the floor with all your papers spread out around you. We don't *have to* be sitting at a desk all by ourselves to learn! Another important aspect of environment is determining your best study time. Is morning better for "hard" subjects that require more focus, or afternoon? These natural cycles are more important to successful learning than people realize.

MARY: *Tell me more about the five aspects of Learning Style and how they relate to homeschooling.*

VICTORIA: Disposition, the fifth aspect, has five categories of its own: performing, producing, inventing, relating/inspiring, and thinking/creating.

MARIAEMMA: A Learning Styles model of education is a method for homeschooling. A person's whole philosophy of education is different when it comes out of this model. You continually look at your child in terms of all the components of his or her unique learning style. You constantly want to set things up so your child can learn as well as possible. In addition, you're able to teach your child about his or her learning style so she or he can be a competent, self-directed learner in any situation.

VICTORIA: When you have a Learning Styles approach to homeschooling, you are sure your materials are appropriate for your child, so you don't spend a lot of time and money on materials that don't work.

MARY: *Can someone have a Visual Modality preference for learning some things and a Kinesthetic Modality for learning other things?*

MARIAEMMA: That's possible, too. To see a model of the body or to watch a CD-ROM with pictures that show the inside of a cell rather than read about human biology in a book makes all the difference to some learners. For math that same person might need to use his whole body to "get it," a kinesthetic approach. For example, I often use a number mat like a hopscotch board with numbers. The kids walk to the number 2 square, and you say, "What happens if you get five more pencils?" and the child walks the squares until he gets to number 7. For subtraction, he walks backwards. This way kids get a feeling inside their bodies of what it means to add and subtract.

> Natural cycles are more important to successful learning than people realize.

VICTORIA: Or some people might memorize multiplication tables while jumping on a mini-trampoline or while clapping their hands rhythmically. Bouncing a ball can also help a child to memorize math facts.

MARY: *Can you elaborate a little on ADD and ADHD?*

VICTORIA: Well, ADD stands for Attention Deficit Disorder, but it's not the child who has the deficit—it's a deficit in the way he's being taught! Schools are saying, "You must fit the environment we have, so you must change." What happens to children who urgently need to move about, or who get headaches from fluorescent lights, or who have difficulty remembering auditory instructions when they are made powerless to say or do anything about it? What happens when a child receives the message over and over again that his or her needs are not important?

MARIAEMMA: Every student I have worked with who had been diagnosed with learning disabilities and who was either on or had been recommended to go on

Ritalin showed no symptoms of learning disabilities within a few months after he or she (1) began homeschooling, (2) took the Learning Styles Profile, and (3) followed the recommendations for the appropriate curriculum and materials. In addition, they start to shine in all ways—even improve in their problem areas or weak areas. I've had kids who couldn't read at all, and a couple of years later are avid readers despite being told this could never happen.

MARY: *How would you sum up the benefits of the Learning Styles method?*

MARIAEMMA: Being willing to work with a child's learning style is one of the most important ways to show respect for that child.

VICTORIA: And you will be rewarded with an eager, self-directed learner who will experience success in school and in life.

For more information about A Self-Portrait *Learning Styles consultation, please see Resources, page 504. Also see coupon.)*

CHAPTER 4
The Parental Approach

While writing this book, we met people from all different walks of homeschooling. We discovered—as we'd expected—that few parents rigidly follow any particular approach in and of itself. Most do, however, want their children to learn certain things, such as the three R's and other academic subjects based on the nature of their children and family as a whole. Some parents, when asked which approach they use, said, "I guess we just teach them what we think that they need to know."

Our family handles homeschooling in much the same way. As our son's parents, we surround him with an environment we think is wholesome and suitable. We create the setting and choose from a variety of styles and philosophies. One hundred years ago, when parents raised their kids with little outside influence, this approach would have needed no explanation or name.

We have realized that we homeschool Lennon with what we call the parental approach. As his parents, we believe in the traditional idea of the three R's, the flexibility of the unschooling approach (see chapter 5), and the creativity of the eclectic approach (see chapter 6). The following scenario provides an example of our lifestyle. One evening we were working in our little office, the extra room in our house. While we were all there, Lennon converted a vacant desk into a science lab, pulled out some Wild Goose kits he'd used three years ago, and made slime—all the while joining in on our conversations about this book. While writing the trivium section (chapter 6, page 140, and Resources, page 511), we were looking up terms and reading the dictionary definitions aloud for all to hear and discuss. It became a mini-prelim course in the trivium for us all. If one were to analyze that scenario in terms of "educational" style, it could be considered *unschooling* because it was driven by Lennon's own interest (he pulled out five old science kits from the back of a closet at 10:30 P.M.); *classical* because of the nature of the discussion; *eclectic* because while we were discussing rhetoric, he was filling a balloon with air using a bicycle pump, both of which were attached to PVC pipe he had assembled. *Charlotte Mason* would have loved it because we were living in a "rich" educational environment.

In the months of working on the book, these situations have arisen many times. It is how we live our life. It was midnight, and if Mary got into one frame of mind (the traditional school-at-home approach because she is not fully "de-institutionalized"), she could have felt anxiety about it being midnight and our not following a structured science curriculum with the Wild Goose kits. If she looked at one aspect of Charlotte Mason, Mary would be wondering, "Are we forming good habits by allowing our son to stay up until midnight?" Then it hit us, when we were discussing the old definition of rhetoric compared to its modern definition (which assumes only "political rhetoric") that this is a tremendous environment for Lennon! He is like a colonial farmboy, learning many "trades" while working with his parents.

Our society has lost the flexibility that once allowed families to let their children work alongside them—on farms, in family-owned shops, restaurants, and delicatessens. Our quest to "get educated" and "give our children what we did not have" has cost us our ability to be real, true, organic people who pass who we are *on* to the next generation.

That night writing, we were just being who we are, and *our life* is how we homeschool our son. We write for a living, put out our newspaper, have a conference once a year—and Lennon is intimately involved in it all. When we cooked for people and held various other newspaper jobs, he was right alongside us. Whatever you do for a liv-

Homeschoolers Say . . .

Am I really a good influence for my child all day long?

This is an ironic question, but one we hear from parents all the same. We think it reflects a truly humble self-image, which is admirable but for its blind spot. What makes you think you are any less a good influence than a teacher who is doing his or her job? Or a group of children your child's age? Any way you look at it, for better or for worse, your child's destiny is to be *your* child, which includes your being his or her main influence. Just as your child has your genetic makeup, she or he should have your cultural and so-cietal makeup as well.

Homeschooling is also a wonderful reason for spending time to better yourself. The better you are as a person, the better parent you'll be. So if you're not the best influence for your child, become so!

ing, wherever you live, you too can be your child's parent and guide his or her life. Have an educational plan, raise the child up "politically correct" or not, in a religion or not, exposed to or sheltered from a wide array of ideas. This right is a gift of being a parent—and its greatest fun. Be yourself, relax, be patient, and experiment—take the parental approach!

Mass-school has permeated not only the world of children, but the adult world as well. Once you break away from it, you will be amazed at how free and easy successful learning/living can be. Our country, which was founded by courageous pioneers who became entrepreneurs and leaders, is now dominated by people who are influenced by mass-marketing and mass-schooling schemes that drastically change lives for the worse.

This manifests itself in many different ways. Among them are children fighting—even killing—over brand-name tennis shoes and other apparel and children being violent to the point of murder, stating the strong influence over them of movies, song lyrics, and pop singers. Couple this with parents whose primary goal is climbing the corporate ladder, attaining a new car, boat, larger TV, more credit—bigger, better, richer, cooler—and you have the recipe for social disaster. All members of the family leave each day on separate tracks for six hours or more and are influenced by marketing from different angles. These people grow further apart each day, hardly ever coming together in more than superficial ways; and when they do, they are virtual strangers. Compare this with the family life 100 years ago, when everyone in the family worked day and night together for a common goal—the well-being of the family.

Homeschooling is taking our past and futures back from Madison Avenue and Washington, all in one fell swoop. A beautiful gift of being human is the opportunity to raise our own children and extend ourselves. No matter how much money you make or what you do for a living, get to know your children and realize that *you are good enough* for them to get to know you. Accept the job of raising, shaping, and influencing your own children!

To Follow the Parental Approach, Know Yourself

First of all, to follow the parental approach you must have a firm conviction that your values are right for your family and appropriate to form the bedrock upon which all else is built. You must believe that even your "tastes" are valid. We don't mean that every detail about your philosophy needs to be fully developed, iron-clad, and wrapped up in a neat little package you can recite at will. (If we all waited to reach that level of self-knowledge, *nothing* would get done!) But if you know at least 50 percent about what kind of person you would like your child to grow up to be, and *how to help him do it*, the parental approach is your way! We all want a child who is a blessing—to be around, to work for, to work with, to be married to, to have as a caregiver one day, to have as a fellow citizen and neighbor. If you can define what a "blessing" would be, the parental approach is your way. If you can't clearly define that ideal, don't try the parental approach. Instead, first evaluate, judge, and think a great deal more.

Know Your Religious Beliefs

If you are a believer—whatever your religion, God-based or otherwise—know your beliefs. If you are not a believer in a religion, know that, too. If your belief includes attending a worship service of some sort, whether in a building, in a meadow, at night, in the morning, on Saturday, on Sunday, at the Solstice, or whenever-you-feel-like-it, *do it!* If taking this action is not important, *don't do it!* Know that being the main influence in your child's life is your proper role, guiding your child in the values and ways that you follow.

Know Your Cultural Heritage

You are the preserver of your unique family culture. You and your spouse, each from a different family culture, create a unique environment when you come together. Even if you were raised half a block apart, are of the same religion, ethnicity, age, and financial strata, you are still *not* the same people; your families were not the same family. When you marry and children enter your lives, they are a by-product—biologically and otherwise—of your unique mix; they carry on this cultural uniqueness themselves.

Your job is to *know* your personal culture, and to teach these ways to your offspring, both in word and in deed. Make decisions about all of these important issues. Know your ways, let your children know that you know your ways, and let them know your ways, too. Obviously, children will make their own decisions about life values when they are old enough, and if you do the moral, ethical, and intellectual work now, you can probably predict their decisions. Until that self-determining time, you must take this responsibility upon yourself and teach them the way.

Be Your Child's Guide and Mentor

Next, you must believe that you are the right person to be your child's guide, mentor, and authority figure. If you are uncomfortable

Homeschoolers Say . . .

What if I don't feel qualified to teach my child myself?

This is a frequent concern. Virtually every instructional book available—for math, English, history, writing—is self-explanatory because homeschooling is a do-it-yourself field. Many book/learning material companies are owned by homeschooling families; others want to court the vast, growing market in home education. These companies provide detailed instructions for the successful use of their products. Any parent with average reading comprehension skills can successfully teach his or her own children.

with these important functions, or if you're waffling back and forth over nearly every issue, I recommend you stick with a curriculum-in-a-box format with a conservative approach. If you are unsure that you're qualified for this leadership role, you can probably find someone you think *is* qualified. For example, you may trust a writer of a homeschooling curriculum, so let that person lead in that area. There is nothing wrong with admitting that you need someone else to tell you what to do; we all need guidance in various endeavors. The mistake is not seeking guidance when you're unable to guide yourself. If you're unable to say, "I don't know" or "I need help," your family will suffer.

Determine Your Schedule

We advise beginning homeschoolers to spend four hours per day with their child, say from 9:00 A.M. to 1:00 P.M. We, for example, decided that our son needs to learn certain things to function properly in life. These include cursive writing (despite what anyone says about computers and typing replacing handwriting!), reading (both aloud and silently), and music (instruction in at least one musical in-

As a sidelight, most teachers at conventional schools don't choose their own curriculum but are assigned a curriculum selected by the school board or administrator. Teachers present textbook material to 30 or 40 children in a classroom each day, moving them through the school year on time. Home-schooling your own children is very different: The parent and student have much more time together, teaching is one-on-one, you can use your time more effectively, and you can always ask someone else if you find you don't know something.

strument and voice training). If Lennon possessed a tin ear rather than being musically inclined, we would not insist on this intense level of musical training. We would focus instead on another strength—perhaps artistic or mechanical—and provide appropriate private instruction to develop that area.

We also value spelling, basic math, world history and American history, critical thinking (to be expanded to logic later on), English grammar, and a foreign language (most likely Spanish, perhaps Latin). We teach these subjects often and intersperse them with "real" work on the newspaper, conference, or household chores. Of course, we have taught him our moral and ethical code, but not in a rigid time frame. Rather, we've talked with him daily over the years (and still do) about the right and wrong ways to be, to think, to live. He knows right from wrong by the Judeo-Christian code and knows that others live by different codes of behavior, or by even lack of such.

We spend a certain number of hours per week instructing Lennon, knowing that we will do less during conference time but make up for it the rest of the year. We arrange our curriculum format in an organizer and then follow it as closely as we can for a day at a time, hopefully a week at a time. If we do exactly what we plan two weeks in a row (which happens about twice a year), we feel like Super Homeschoolers!

How Will I Know Which Curriculum to Choose?

This is a tough question for us to answer with our parental approach background. This is because you may consider one or two of the subjects we value and teach Lennon a complete waste of time. Or you may value something highly that we don't teach at all. The parental approach is completely individualized. But remember that we started with a boxed curriculum, heavily supplemented with storybooks and workbooks on various topics, until we grew into this experience. Our growth into homeschooling included talking to many, many other homeschooling families, reading countless magazines and catalogs, attending conferences and curriculum fairs, and shopping in educational and regular bookstores for things that caught our eyes. Some great-looking materials were dismal failures once we tried teaching with them—some dumbed down, others were not what Lennon responds to.

If I had it to do over, I wouldn't change a thing. The boxed curriculum gave us a great outline and high-quality, well-written materials to learn with as teachers and pupil. After the second year, we began customizing our core work materials. By now, we have a clear picture of what subjects to teach Lennon, what will come in the near future, and what will come after that. We can safely say that we see what his learning career looks like up to high school and somewhat into high school. Math considerations will be determined by whether or not Lennon decides to "play the game" of college entrance (as David Colfax puts it).

Determining the Direction of Your Curriculum

Our family has compiled a curriculum we're very comfortable and satisfied with, chosen from among the many fine materials available to homeschoolers. Before using some of these materials, we tested them a little bit, doing a lesson here or there or the introductory lessons to see if we liked the entire program. The ones we use now are "it" for our purposes. Remember, however, that these are personal

Homeschoolers Say . . .

Are all subjects taught in school really necessary?

No. In some school districts the curriculum is determined by the school administration based on a well-thought-out philosophy of what children need to learn to be well-rounded; in other districts, the decision is based on what books are available at a discount; in others, still other forces are at work. But even well-thought-out and well-meaning educational philosophies can be "wrong" for your family or your child. That is why getting to know yourselves and making decisions based on this knowledge is important.

choices—as much so as favorite styles of clothing, food, entertainment, and friends. The materials that make up your child's curriculum will become a part of your family for the years you use them. A poor fit can lead to negative, unproductive experiences common in mass-school. As an example, we list below the materials we use.

Math

We use the Saxon math series (see page 293), created by the late John Saxon. Until this year, we'd been using a boxed-curriculum math book, which had obviously been written for a class of 30 children. Because some examples and illustrations of certain points did not satisfy us, it wasn't exactly what we wanted. We looked at the Saxon textbooks and talked to various homeschooling friends who pointed out the strengths of the series. We recently reached the point where we felt it necessary to skip ahead a few lessons to keep our son challenged. Lennon is chomping at the bit to do "interesting" multiplication and division work, so we moved to more challenging lessons dealing with three-digit by three-digit multiplication and simple division, soon to be followed by more difficult division.

We don't follow the exact Saxon guidelines but use this math book as an overall "scope and sequence" guide. In other words, it helps us figure out what to cover and in what order. Addition first? Subtraction? When do we move on to the next skill? Even though we use the book as an overall guide, we still customize the course in true parental approach fashion—we are our son's parents and know what he likes and needs, and

what causes him to actually *learn* the material. Doing it lecture style on a wipe-off board in a relaxed setting is *our* style—teacher *and* pupil.

We don't believe everything in the book is necessary. If Lennon decides he wants to be a space engineer and work for NASA, he may have to go back and bone up on a few things—which we are completely confident he will do with ease. This is another of homeschooling's most pleasurable and satisfying aspects—you can keep you child challenged! Rather than waiting for perhaps 25 children in class to catch up, mom or dad simply has a "skull" session with the eager pupil and moves ahead in the book or program to a section that once again interests and challenges. Remember that many homeschoolers begin taking college classes around the age of 14 or 15. This would not be possible if they were unable to move ahead when they master something quickly, such as an entire math curriculum.

In schools, most subjects are taught not when the child is ready but when the *system* is ready. Schools group children by age, not because children of that age are magically capable of learning a particular subject but because that is best for the system and makes crowd management easier.

Saxon math is designed to allow flexibility if you want it, within a rigid framework, if you want *that*.

Writing (Creative)

Around our home, writing has been more difficult than other subjects. Our son does not usually enjoy the physical act of sitting down and writing even a sentence by hand. We have tried a few approaches and are very pleased with Writing Strands (see page 237). Even if we only do a lesson per month, the program provides continuity through an appealing logical order and is geared toward building a good written communicator.

Dave Marks, the creator of Writing Strands, is a homeschool dad and writing teacher who developed an excellent set of 10 books for homeschoolers to use through high school (and beyond). They help the student learn to think in an orderly fashion and then put the results on paper. He also wrote *Communication and Interpersonal Relationships*, which is designed to teach "how to say what you mean to say." We use it from time to time to supplement our work in developing thinking skills.

We also use a book from the early twentieth century, by Emma Serl, reproduced by Lost Classics Books Company (see page 189). It is a comprehensive book of daily language arts lessons, covering short writing assignments, short poetry memorization, vocabulary drills, and more, in the way that our grandparents learned.

Thinking Skills

As parents, we agree that the ability to actually reason (rather than merely form opinions) and to discern is the most important intellectual quality. To help Lennon master this skill, we used books 1 and 2 from *Building Thinking Skills* (see page 427) part of the Critical Thinking Books and Software collection. We are all very pleased with them. Lennon will do the problems for hours. When we ultimately begin the study of logic, we're sure these Critical Thinking books and our instruction will be an excellent foundation.

Reading

We taught Lennon to read many years ago using Hooked on Phonics. Although the music background was pretty boring, he did learn to read and enjoyed other aspects of the program.

If we were teaching reading today, we would use Blumenfeld's Alpha Phonics (see page 213), which we have examined closely. This excellent program does not have a lot of frills, yet it is not "dumbed down." An interesting videotape explains the essentials, and a number of well-designed, attractive components—cards, books, audiotapes—provide the lessons. All are packaged in "relaxed" colors, rather than the blaring, overstimulating fluorescent colors found in most mass-school-appeal packaging.

For silent reading and reading aloud, we use a number of different volumes, including the G. A. Henty books available from Lost Classics Books Company (see page 384) and also from Preston Speed Publishers (see page 233). These moral stories written in the 1800s develop good examples of moral character and offer a glimpse into early America. They also include a glossary, which enables users to expand their storehouse of words. We also favor many other titles from the Lost Classics collection, such as *The Minute Boys of Lexington*.

Geography

The Atlasphere is one of the greatest learning aids for geography we have ever seen! This standard-size globe includes a mini-computer inside the base, which is wired to the globe (see page 402). You plug a cartridge containing a set of geography "games" into a slot in the side of the base. The globe then "talks," asking questions about location, population, and so on. of various countries, cities, and continents, which you answer by touching a connected stylus pen to the globe's surface at the appropriate location. You can play the games with up to eight people. We have a great time competing with each other, or with the timer on the globe. Lennon learned more in a week of daily playing with the Atlasphere than in months of studying books and maps. When he reviewed the maps, he could grasp more information, as his interest had been piqued.

These descriptions of our favorite materials are intended to spark your imagination and help you to find your own favorites.

Interview with Kellie G.

Kellie has a no-nonsense approach to homeschooling that we felt readers of the *Almanac* would benefit from hearing. One of the most sensible and level-headed people we know, Kellie has a simple and secure approach to life and homeschooling.

Kellie was born and raised in the Los Angeles suburb where she now lives with her husband and two sons, ages 11 and 10. She does what we call the parental approach with her two boys, whom she has homeschooled their entire lives.

MARY LEPPERT: *When did you decide to homeschool your boys?*

KELLIE G.: I would say it was when my oldest was three or four years old.

MARY: *How did you first hear about homeschooling?*

KELLIE: I first heard about homeschooling when I was playing with my children at a park and met a lady there. Our children were playing together, and during the course of our conversation, she mentioned homeschooling. At first I thought she was crazy; it was an extremely foreign idea at the time. I recall thinking that homeschooling was a primitive concept that would greatly change what I envisioned for my future—going back to work as soon as my kids set foot through the door of kindergarten. That plan slowly changed. The lady in the park also mentioned the book *Summerhill* by A. S. Neill, which got me started on an expedition to the library. Once my interest was piqued, I started thinking about their future, my future, and their education. I looked into all sorts of education—the Waldorf School, A. S. Neill and Summerhill, John Holt, Christian home education, and Montessori.

MARY: *What did your husband think?*

KELLIE: He was completely "with" me. We took the journey together, which was fortunate. He was always interested and supportive and immediately loved the idea of us spending more time together and our family staying more of a cohesive unit.

MARY: *How do you define yourself as a homeschooler—eclectic, unschooler, school-at-home?*

KELLIE: All of the above. It's hard to put a title on what you do. I consider myself semi-structured, in that we do use some textbooks and library books. We do specifically designate a time of day for organized learning, but I don't buy a packaged curriculum or have anyone overseeing or telling us what to do.

> We had to trickle down to the homeschooling style that felt most comfortable to ourselves and our family as a whole.

MARY: *Did you ever buy a packaged curriculum?*

KELLIE: I believe I started with the Weaver curriculum, a unit-study approach that is less structured than others. I only used that for one year, then switched to Sonlight, which is in itself an eclectic gathering of materials from different sources.

MARY: *How did you move from reading A. S. Neill and John Holt to feeling that you needed to do school-at-home.*

KELLIE: Through reading about the different learning styles and methods, we had to trickle down to what felt most comfortable to ourselves and our family as a whole. Coming from the experience of being publicly schooled with an average, middle-class American upbringing, we felt more comfortable with a little more structure than what we anticipated in either John Holt's method or in *Summerhill.*

MARY: *Did you ever try that method?*

KELLIE: I believe we did more when the boys were young. I have gone back to it sometimes, when I'm feeling jaded with what we're doing, trying to give the children more free time and just to see what their interests would be and how we could be led by that. I find our home is not as peaceful when we loosen up. The children sometimes have a problem filling their time. I don't see them being interest-led in a particular way, so they seem agitated because they are bored. I don't doubt that less structure works for other people or that, if we had the determination to wait out that period of boredom, it might work for us. But we are all conditioned to a certain level of activity, and some structure feels more comfortable at this point.

MARY: *Could you tell me what your structure is like?*

KELLIE: Our day is only semi-structured in that we don't wake anybody up to get started. We have a list of chores that the boys need to accomplish before 9:00 A.M. They take their showers, make their beds, clean their rooms, unload the dishwasher. It feels good to have the house in order before we make another mess.

MARY: *Do your sons wake up naturally before 9:00 A.M.?*

KELLIE: Absolutely. My older son wakes up around 6:30 or 7:00, the younger one as late as 8:00 sometimes, but he still gets his stuff done before 9:00. Then, at 9:00, or even 9:15, we generally meet in the living room, where we first spend time together, reading something from the Bible or spiritually related material to start our day. We usually take turns reading the Bible, and I generally read aloud to them if I'm reading from a book.

MARY: *How did your children learn to read?*

KELLIE: Watching them learn to read was one of my favorite parts of homeschooling. I taught the first child to read but would give the credit mainly to the book *Teaching Your Child to Read in 100 Easy Lessons.* Fortunately, both of them were very easy to teach. It was just a forward progression over a period of time. With the first-born, it took some normal time without any hindrances. With my second child, who is 13 months younger, I didn't do any organized teaching. I have to mention that we read aloud as a family very, very frequently—especially when the boys were younger.

> Watching my children learn to read was one of my favorite parts of homeschooling.

MARY: *So getting back to your "day," what is your school time like?*

KELLIE: There is a pretty fair pattern to it from 9:00 to noon. Math is usually the first academic subject. I teach a number of different ways; my methods are changing as they grow older. Last year, I was with them every day, went over the lesson with them every day, and sat with them while they did it. This year, they're moving into maturity, natural growth, and I use more variety. One day I'll sit through the whole thing; the next day they'll do it completely on their own.

MARY: *What do you do after math?*

KELLIE: The order changes. I give them a list they can do in whatever order they like as long as they accomplish what's on the list. It would normally include something from Writing Strands. We also use Usborne Books' grammar puzzles and capitalization and apostrophe exercises. And we're using *Simply Grammar* by Charlotte Mason, too. We would do all these maybe one day a week or every other week for variety. Basically, everyday activities include math, writing, and reading—to themselves and listening to me read some novel aloud. Other things, such as science and Spanish, are usually done on alternating days. For science, we're using *Switched on Schoolhouse*, a CD-ROM program by Alpha Omega. It's text and pictures on the computer with a test at the end of each lesson. They also do projects and write essays in conjunction with that. It's all provided right there on the computer screen. We do some but not all of the extras. For Spanish we're using *Learn to Speak Spanish*, made by the Learning Company.

MARY: *Are the kids doing cursive writing? That seems to be an issue with many people.*

KELLIE: I don't really have an issue with it, but it's not terribly important to me and they don't like it. So I just ask them to do their assignments in cursive once in a while to make sure they remember how. They prefer printing and I find that most men print in their adult life. My father and husband both print, for example. When the boys are adults, they probably will use a computer keyboard or print, so I'm not going to make a huge issue out of it.

MARY: *What do you do after noon, when the academics are finished?*

KELLIE: The boys are free to do whatever they want to do. Basically they play with Legos or play outside with other homeschool friends and neighborhood friends later in the afternoon. Their extracurricular activities include taking piano lessons, swimming and baseball for the older son, and gymnastics for the younger son.

MARY: *Do you think the dynamics in your home are more difficult because you are homeschooling and together all the time?*

KELLIE: I think the dynamics are far *better because* we spend more time together. We definitely have flare-ups because we spend so much time together, but I think working through those times, getting along with each other, and spending time alone when we don't want to be with each other makes us better people, able to handle situations more competently. I feel the dynamics would definitely be worse if we weren't homeschooling.

> I think the dynamics are far better because we spend more time together.

MARY: *Do you feel everyone should homeschool?*

KELLIE: I feel every family would be better off if they homeschooled and spent their lives more as a family unit. When I decided to homeschool, part of my philosophy was that the family unit was God's creation and His intention was for families to live together, work together, have extended families together, and die together—not to the exclusion of everybody else in the world, but as part of the design for whole people and happy lives. What and how children are educated is secondary to being with their natural family—learning how to work together, take care of a home, make an income, and do whatever a family needs to do to survive.

MARY: *Looking back at your homeschooling experience to this point, do you see things you would do differently?*

KELLIE: I am pretty happy with the choices I've made. My only regrets have to do with who I am and what I can give them and not give them. For example, I would have been happy if they had had more artistic experiences in their childhood, if their mother were a natural sculptor, painter, or somebody who had some other gifts, because I would like them to have the most wonderful experience possible. I would be happier if I could provide everything for them, be this amazing Superperson who has all the gifts available to mankind to give them. My only regret is that they weren't exposed to everything and that some things didn't come naturally to me to share with them. But realizing that that's not who I am and it is their destiny to be my children, I'm happy with how it's gone.

MARY: *How important is a homeschool group in your life?*

KELLIE: A group is not terribly important to me. Initially, I found a lot of encouragement with a group by going to meetings and hearing what homeschoolers were and could be doing and how busy I could be doing those things with them. That was valuable primarily for the personal validation. But as I became more comfortable and found a few close friends for my children and for myself, we find our support through them. An organized group with meetings, supervision, field trips has little importance to me now.

MARY: *How do you picture the kids' future?*

KELLIE: I don't think too much about that, though I am open to anything for them, open to the idea of them going to college. I picture that they might dabble in community college when they reach the age of 15 or 16, let's say, and we'll see what happens then. I imagine them spending a lot of time with their father at work and probably having part-time jobs there. We'll just see what their interests are then and where they are led to go.

MARY: *Is it difficult for you to think about sending them off to college before the age of 18?*

KELLIE: I would consider them more adults by then. I certainly have strong feelings about what is valuable and not valuable in a college experience. I am not a parent who would say that it is important for them to go to college, or to a good college. But if, at their adult ages of 17 or 18, they would like to go to college, we would support them in that and we would encourage them to live at home, stay at home, and go to a college nearby. I would not, however, feel they were outside the realm of problems. I believe college-age children are still too young to handle some of the temptations, and that being far away from home is definitely a bad idea, even near home is risky. But I believe they are formed enough to start to handle it, with the accountability of their family still nearby.

MARY: *Do you have any advice to give new homeschoolers?*

KELLIE: Take it one day at a time. Ride through the low points and the feelings of insecurity, and appreciate the fact that you are definitely doing something special by providing a haven and loving environment for your children. That is an incredible gift.

CHAPTER 5
The Unschooling Method

In the late 1960s, Boston educator John Holt came up with some ideas about learning that startled many of his colleagues and formed the basis of the unschooling movement in homeschooling. After formulating his basic theories that children are naturally curious and will lead themselves in exploring and finding out about the world around them, Holt worked to bring about school reform, attempting to implement his ideas in the classroom setting to which he was accustomed.

After a time he gave up on reforming school, realizing that "school" was part of the problem, and began to exhort parents to teach their own children and to "un" school. By this he meant, "Don't do what schools do—stifle natural learning impulses, force intellectual activity to be subject to a rigid timetable, and so on." This approach was the topic of numerous books by Holt, wherein he discussed his findings on how children take in information and what things stop them from doing so. (See page 505 for selected Holt titles.) At the same time that Holt was working in Boston, Dr. Raymond Moore and his wife, Dorothy, were in Washington state developing theories similar to Holt's, in a slightly different format referred to as Delayed Academics. (For a further discussion of their work, see page 137.)

Today, many parents have interpreted "unschooling" as meaning "Don't do anything academic unless your child initiates the interest." Despite first impressions, this is not a complete negation of academics. If the child *wants* to study chemistry, you can still teach him or her as an unschooler . . . maybe by doing chemistry all day and foregoing anything not required for the study of chemistry. Printing may be necessary to copy formulas or take notes, so the child will eagerly learn to print well as a furtherance of his or her chemistry exploration. This would be classic unschooling: "Forget what the school agenda is; teach chemistry."

You could be an unschooling parent of a child who loves to go through a curriculum and would sit and do it for six hours a day—if it was his or her *idea to do so*. The whole point is for the parent to follow the child's lead.

In this chapter, we will attempt to shed some light on the trail of thought and action that led from what we consider the birth of this "movement" to its present-day issues.

Some Historical Background on Unschooling

The initial idea of unschooling can be traced to Jean-Jacques Rousseau (1712–1778), a French writer and philosopher, father of the French Revolution, and an influence in the American Revolution. Rousseau created and developed a creed that valued feeling above thought. He can be considered the father of unschooling. Rousseau never intended his ideas on children's upbringing and education to be applied broadly to society; they were purely his *personal* views. In spite of this, his ideas were later appropriated by European educators in the eighteenth and nineteenth centuries, who then applied them to society at large.

Despite the fact that he was not a teacher beyond his early employment as tutor to two young children, Rousseau wrote a didactic novel, *Emile* (1762), which presents Rousseau's theory that education is not the imparting of knowledge but a drawing out of what is already in a child. In *Emile*, Rousseau describes his views of how children of means should be taught, offering advice to the children's professional tutors in these matters. Rousseau states, for instance, the idea that before age 12, the "ideal" child should be taught nothing at all, and certainly nothing "bookish." Instead, he should be encour-

Homeschoolers Say . . .

What if I love homeschooling and the kids hate it, and they want to go back to school?

This question always reminds me of a comment that John Holt, an educator and subsequent developer of the modern unschooling philosophy, used in answering similar queries: "If your child wanted to jump off a cliff, would you let him?"

aged by the tutor to follow his instincts about what he wants to study. Age 12 is also when the child should be allowed to read his first book.

Rousseau believed that the tutor should introduce into the day's conversation topics he wants the child to know about, creating an opportunity to teach without seeming to do so. There is a connection from Rousseau to the modern-day unschooling and John Holt's observations, analyses, thoughts, and writings on the subject of child-led learning.

Some people who practice unschooling agree with this approach of subtly controlling the environment and also of letting the child lead the parent with his or her interests.

Others believe that children are born curious and that their intellectual drives must come from within.

To many "unschooling" parents, the self-motivated child—one who is constantly exploring and discovering relevant information hands-on, not just in books—is the ideal they are striving to preserve. The information the child learns becomes integrated into his or her personality—possibly for life. To unschoolers, gardening is just as important as math; building a soapbox racer is equal in importance to reading; and watching baby kittens being born is on a par with (if not superior to) knowing the definitions of nouns and verbs.

All too many parents recall being vitally curious about life until school "educated" out their zest for taking in information, and they began avoiding anything that resembled "learning." The last thing these people intend to impose on their children is "education" or "school," so they "un-school." To them that means no schedule, no externally imposed curriculum, no hoops to jump through or bars to jump over. Just be alive each day and, if you find a thread, follow it to see where it leads.

If Unschooling Interests Me, What Should I Do?

First, read the following two interviews with Barb Lundgren and Kathleen Jacobs. Both of these women are unschooling moms, but each one has a different interpretation of what unschooling means and how to "practice" it. Barb provides stimulus to her children but believes their prime motivation must come from within themselves. She does not believe she should tell them what to do. Kathleen, on the other hand, believes in intentionally offering certain stimuli— making suggestions about possible projects, steering her children into certain interests to "test the waters"—and then she observes how her offspring react to the stimulus before determining how to proceed.

After you have read the two interviews and digested some of the information, check our Resources section, page 505, for books of interest. (Most can be found at your local library.) Also, obtain the free copies of *Growing Without Schooling* magazine and *Homefires, Journal of Homeschooling* by sending in the coupons you will find in the Coupon section.

Creating an Unschooling Environment

Note that the families we interviewed, and most families that follow the unschooling approach, do not allow television, video games, or other activities prevalent in today's society to creep into their children's lives. Most children, when given a choice between overstimulating activities such as TV or video games and more wholesome

Homeschoolers Say . . .

What if my child just wants to watch TV all day?

If your child wanted to eat sugar three meals a day, you would know that's not healthful. The same is true about watching television all day. If you remove TV from your home, you'll be going a long way toward ending your problem. No matter how "addicted" to television someone is, other activities soon replace it, and the controversy is resolved.

---

pastimes, will generally choose the more stimulating. To really see how your child's interests flow, create an environment conducive to worthwhile, natural interests and experiences by surrounding him or her with natural things, not synthetics.

Have lots of great books around and read those books together as a family. When we gave up our TV four years ago, at first it seemed too quiet and depressing after the sun went down. Then we began reading at night, going through about one great book each week. Soon we looked forward to our evening readings. Be sure you pick books the whole family enjoys. Sometimes we each read our own books silently, and Lennon is usually the last to turn the lights out.

You can take just about any topic that you or your child is interested in and create an environment conducive to natural learning. If you really want your kids to be interested in a variety of topics, then show interest in them yourself! Listen to all forms of music. Try learning a new instrument. Take a cooking class or two and bring home interesting and different recipes with different spices for the family to try. I guarantee your children will come to the kitchen to see what's going on.

Another activity that helps foster interest in your child is playing games. Some great games on the market include Scrabble, Uno, chess, and Set, to name a few. These games teach spelling, math, and critical thinking. Many other games cover a variety of topics.

One way that our family created an interest for Lennon was by establishing an art wall in our home. Our wall features a Monet, a Diego Rivera, and some van Goghs. A wonderful company called Art Extension Press (see page 341) sells prints and a 75-page workbook very inexpensively. So many prints come in the Extension Press set that it would take you over a year to complete a study of them at two per week. We frame them, and then we discuss the artist and his times. The workbook can also be used for an art class by those who school-at-home. For the unschooling approach, you might simply hang the art on the wall and be amazed at your child's interest in it. Many nights during dinner, we talk about our prints. One night Lennon turned a painting upside down, and we all saw it differently from that point on. This led to a fascinating discussion about conceptualization. (Note: Those following the unschooling approach would simply drop the discussion if the child wasn't interested in the art.)

But When Will They Learn the Three R's?

If you want to live the unschooling approach, an important element is *trust!* Trust your child to go in the direction in which he or she is meant to go, and the child's natural flow will occur. If the child is not learning long division by 13 or 14, let it go and realize that the child might learn long division in due time. David Colfax, popular author and conference speaker, has mentioned at our conferences that when his children wanted to "play the game" of getting into college, they learned their math quickly. Many teachers have reported to our newspaper, *The Link*, that junior high school math is simply a review of what most kids do not learn very well in the elementary years. This is one reason why unschoolers have a practice of not pushing math in general and especially complicated "higher" forms of math (trigonometry, algebra, calculus) onto their children, unless the child decides to enter a field of study which requires it— engineering for instance—or wishes to enter a university and needs the math for entrance requirements. Unschoolers feel that much of the creativity and curiosity of youth is wasted on academic work.

One mother tells me her 11-year-old son does math division in his head and can multiply very quickly. When I asked how her son learned these skills so well, she stated that she never made him drill, never showed him how to multiply or divide, and never even forced him to learn the math facts for the numbers under 10. The child simply has a love for money, earns money any way he can, and has savings of over $500. He saves his pennies for various expensive toys, pets, and hobbies. The family does not have a large income, so the child has to earn everything he has. This boy's math situation is a perfect example of "unschooling"!

Another mother of three boys claims that her middle son displays a natural gift for numbers. When multiplication or quick addition is necessary during family games, she has been amazed how quickly he figures out the answers, especially considering that he has had no formal math training whatsoever. His older and younger brothers do not have the same ability. This illustrates what unschooling parents believe—that children who have a love for something will pursue it on their own. Learning does not have to be drilled into them.

Writing is another concern for many parents. This is a favorite topic of Richard Prystowsky, the inspirational homeschooling conference speaker, writer, and teacher. He and his wife homeschool their three boys. I (Mary) will never forget the first time I heard him speak, to a roomful of 40 women. He asked how many had boys between the ages of 7 and 12, and every single person in the room raised her hand. Then he asked how many had boys who liked to write; not one raised her hand! Prystowsky stated that boys between these ages are not ready to "do" writing. They are too interested in building Legos, playing basketball, and so on to care about writing. To the unschooling parent, this is the natural flow; and if necessary or desired, the act of writing with grammatical form and proper syntax will be emulated from the world that the child lives in.

Homeschoolers Say . . .

What if my child just wants to read all day?

Most in-school reading is controlled by teachers who assign chapter-by-chapter segments of fiction or textbooks. When children are free to read, they become excited about a book and often want to read it straight through. Let them! Rather than interrupting our son's reading to practice multiplication tables, for instance, we prefer waiting until he is tired of reading or finishes the book. However, we do make a point of having plenty of high-quality reading material available at home.

Many unschooling parents have their children dictate stories that the parent types into a word processor. Creating a story is a completely separate act from the mechanical one of writing. The rote part of learning grammar and syntax is also mechanical, as is the skill of cursive writing (which many unschooling parents feel is unnecessary). The unschooler is confident that in due time their children will learn all these things separately and put them together when and if it becomes necessary.

The academic world and educational community are especially concerned about reading. In one way or another, that means all of us. As parents we want our children to learn to read and improve related skills such as spelling, grammar, punctuation, and writing. If you are beginning an "unschooling" journey with a child who has been in school for a number of years, chances are he or she already knows how to read. Even if the child doesn't read, unschooling parents are seldom concerned. In the 1850s, most children did not learn to read until they were 10 or 11 years old; the average age for entry into college was 16. Modern society is in a "Head Start" mode, putting kids on the "fast track." Is this working?

John Taylor Gatto states that he learned to read by sitting on his mother's lap and following along as she read to him. All of a sudden, he discovered that he could do it himself! Unschooling parents often say they never taught their children how to read; the child simply started to read to them! I recall reading about a homeschooling family with five children. The 12-year-old boy was not reading. One day the boy couldn't be found for the entire day. When the mother finally found him and asked where he'd been, she learned he had spent the whole day hiding away with a book that he didn't want to put down until he finished reading it!

"Trust" is the key word here. Trust that you have made the right decision to try unschooling. Trust that as a parent, you've created an environment conducive to your child's developing into all he or she can be! Most important, the unschooling parent must trust that the child is independent and strong. Many unschooling parents believe that they are raising their children to walk their own paths, and each child's destiny will unfold.

The following two interviews with unschooling mothers will enable you to get a feel for what an unschooling family does each day. Barb Lundgren homeschools her three children in central Texas, and Kathleen Jacobs unschools her three boys in Southern California. Note that these parents run their households in much the same way any parent does, giving the children chores and responsibilities. However, in the area of learning, they have an interest-led existence.

Interview with Barb Lundgren

Barb, a veteran homeschool mother, has a fearless attitude about parenting—or at least she doesn't show any fear. Her confidence and strength come through when you talk to her and seem to pass to others through osmosis.

Married and the mother of three, Barb is a leader in the homeschooling community of the state of Texas and creates the annual

Mindful Conference, which focuses on deeper issues than the actual "school" of homeschooling. A radical unschooler, Barb homeschools her children with almost total freedom. Her first influences in homeschooling were John Holt and *Growing Without Schooling* magazine.

MARY LEPPERT: *What are the ages of your children?*

BARB LUNDGREN: They are 16, 14, and 10.

MARY: *What made you decide to homeschool?*

BARB: Having a home birth. I planned a home birth while enmeshed in mainstream culture, which is where I was, with a full-time university contract in St. Louis, Missouri. Midwifery is illegal in Missouri, so I had to hire a doctor. As much as I tried to educate myself about home birthing and what could happen, I had a long labor (a pretty scary process), but once it was over, I was profoundly struck with the natural power of it all. Moments after that—like a lightning bolt—I was forced, almost in an organic way, to say, "If they were wrong about birth, what else are they wrong about?" "They" being all the naysaying friends and professionals I'd consulted during my pregnancy, all of whom were saying I was crazy, careless, or both for attempting to home birth.

MARY: *Were you the sort of person who always listened to your intuition?*

BARB: No. I had to train myself. Possibly when I was a teenager I was more in touch with myself. However, I lived in a world that did not support intuition—a typical world of church officials, teachers, and parents who want you to check all the right boxes, their boxes. The boxes they think are important have titles like "Take this course," "Get this degree," "Mind your manners," and "Do as you're told."

MARY: *What was school like for you?*

BARB: I was brought up in public school just outside of Chicago, Illinois. I never remember liking anything about school. At times I really dreaded it. My mother tells me I would cry before I had to go to school in first grade. I was extremely shy, all the way through high school. I'm not anymore.

MARY: *So you decided you would homeschool?*

BARB: It wasn't that I decided I was going to homeschool. What I realized was that they were wrong about the birthing process and could be wrong about other things. So as I went along, I got grief about not vaccinating; lots of grief about extended, on-demand nursing; lots of grief about our family bed—all the while being fully enraptured in all of this thinking. To have my first baby latched onto me for eight hours straight was not hard work; it was the natural order of things. I simply saw it as something he needed; it never occurred to me that something was wrong with it.

> I did not start out as an unschooler.

Of course, it all segued into homeschooling because what I found in the birth process was that I had the ability to listen to my child. Because he was born at home, that connection between him and me was there, never broken. I was able to listen to what he needed from the first millisecond he was born and help him get it. Of course, I mean much more than listening to his voice. I mean watching his facial expressions, his gestures, his body posturing, and connecting with my intuition—the metaphysical forces that exist between mother and child.

MARY: *You are definitely an "unschooler"! What is your everyday life like?*

BARB: Well, I did not start out as an unschooler. Because my first son was an early and articulate talker, I assumed he would read and become a good student early and easily. We had a very active lifestyle—lots of traveling and visiting friends, visiting museums, zoos, plays, concerts. We also went to the library once or twice a week. We had the typical active life of any homeschool family. I thought that when he was six years old, we would sit down and start doing schoolwork, which back then was still pretty much my idea of education.

When I tried to introduce formal structure in his learning, he laughed at me. As I think back on it now, I'm sure I was a little offended because I thought this was the way it was going to work. I bought this "stuff" for learning letters and practicing writing and doing workbooks, and we would do it. He looked at it like, "This looks like garbage. Why on earth would I want to sit and do this?"

So we did not struggle with it very long. The turning point for me was when I had to say, "What are we going to do, then?" I can't force him to do this just because I'm the mother.

MARY: *What did you do then? Dive deeper into John Holt?*

BARB: Yes, I started to piece together complex questions—What is education? What is parenting? What makes a good parent, a bad parent? What is happiness? How do our kids get it? What are the components of good character? What creates a good quality of life? Through that much more complicated process of thinking and doing lots of reading of all kinds, and talking to people and observing them, I really began to feel comfortable with not the dogma of unschooling, but simply taking the cues from my child. In today's vernacular, "unschooling" is the best word for that.

> I began to feel comfortable with not the dogma of unschooling, but simply taking the cues from my child.

MARY: *Do you listen to your children 100 percent of the time?*

BARB: What I *try* to do is listen to them 100 percent of the time, but that doesn't mean I always do what they say. The listening process opens up the whole complex array of questions, such as: How do you create a stimulating atmosphere or environment that causes all those who live in that environment to want to "learn" (a silly word). What and how do we create an environment, a home, a community that stimulates our children to feel happy and productive? What is responsibility—something we teach, something we take away, or something they learn on their own?

MARY: *Have you found the answers to those questions?*

BARB: I don't think I'll feel like I have conclusive answers until my kids are in their 30s, and maybe not even then. In fact, I'm not sure "answers" are the goal. But I've been experimenting enough that, yes, my two teens are extremely responsible, and more responsibility may come developmentally, with age. I see them taking on responsible roles in the world both within and outside our home through self-initiated interests. For example, I see their follow-through in both projects and work. I see them asking responsible questions about their peers, treating others with fairness and diplomacy. I see them succeeding and being rewarded in "real world" opportunities, through jobs, volunteer opportunities, and friendship.

MARY: *So, you never force responsibility, never say: "You must do this at a certain time."*

BARB: If they were on the verge of killing each other (and I really mean "killing" each other), then I would jump in. I make it a policy not to get involved in any disputes between my children unless they physically ask me to.

MARY: *You once mentioned that for a period your kids were sleeping until 1:00 in the afternoon and staying up almost all night.*

BARB: Well, I didn't tell them they couldn't. I did say, "You know, I am really bummed by this schedule of yours. It just does not work for me to have you guys sleeping until 1:00 in the summer. If we want to do anything before it gets too hot, we need to be out of here by 9:00 in the morning!"

MARY: *Did they agree to what you wanted?*

BARB: Yes. And that's closer to consensus, rather than dictatorial. They still had a choice and chose to give up the late-night experiment in deference to my unhappiness and my desire to spend time with them.

MARY: *So you're never dictatorial with the kids? You let them do—within reason—educationally and around the house whatever they want?*

BARB: Definitely educationally (and everything is educational, right?). Clearly, I've learned to live with some chaos, commotion, and untidiness. I can let it drive me crazy or teach myself to adapt to the needs of my children. I've found almost no need to parent like a dictator. Instead, I've found that the more opportunities I give myself to challenge the traditional beliefs about children, the easier it is for all of us to live together.

MARY: *Getting back to the basics, how would you feel if your 15-year-old son couldn't read at all? Or if your kids never showed interest in the alphabet or learning?*

BARB: I would be extremely nervous; but I was extremely nervous when they weren't reading at age 6, 7, or 8 (all three of my kids began reading at 9).

I would say that having no interest in learning would be impossible in a home where the parents have written or printed material around. If you put a kid in a closet with a video game for his whole life, he'll probably never show an interest in reading. But if the child's parents read, write letters, receive letters, communicate with the written word, the child will want to emulate his or her role models.

MARY: *So you don't think a child should be forced to learn how to read—or that it's even possible to force it?*

BARB: Every situation is different. If I were helping someone figure out why their child wasn't reading, I would need to pick apart a lot of different variables—developmental stages, learning environment, genetics, attitudes of the child and others around him, other interests, and so forth. I think it's really important for a parent, for example, to keep the TV off. If my kids knew I was watching soap operas while they're outside playing, it wouldn't make sense for me to say, "I don't want you watching TV because it isn't good for your brain." I would give up the television. My activities such as the reading and writing are examples, too. But on the other hand, I had to give up the idea that my kids would be like me.

> The more opportunities I give myself to challenge the traditional beliefs about children, the easier it is for all of us to live together.

MARY: *Were you hoping they would be?*

BARB: I used to hope, even to believe, that they would adopt the same interests I have—gardening, cooking, art, learning music, and enjoying lots of things that are natural interests to me. I just assumed that, because I was *doing* them, they would also do them; that did not happen. They develop interests of their own.

MARY: *What is the typical day like at your house?*

BARB: It's different every day; we don't really have routines. I've found that the classes they take tend to be pretty short-lived because most are geared toward being extracurricular classes for public-school kids. They're treated like little subordinates. The things that work long-term for us are completely self-directed. My daughter is interested in reading, for instance. She reads all the time.

MARY: *What about writing? Do you make your kids write?*

BARB: My kids have actually come to me and said things like, "I want to learn how to do cursive writing; will you make me do this until I learn it?" They knew it wasn't going to be much fun but they did want to learn and asked me to be the driving force behind their doing it. I did that for a time, until it became obvious I was the only one doing the work. When my son was in fifth grade, he really wanted to buy a curriculum. I couldn't talk him out of it, so we shopped around, picked one out, and bought it for around $300.

Even though it was a nice selection of books, we could tell right away that it might not work. For example, all of the novels were ones he'd already read. He didn't want to do the science book because, he said, "These experiments are really stupid." When I asked, "What's stupid about them?" he said, "Well, they're so simple." I said, "How about picking an experiment out for the assignment and if you can predict the results and why it happened, then you don't have to do the experiment." So he would tell me, "Okay, this is what's going to happen and this is why it happened," just from living in the world and experimenting on his own terms.

MARY: *Did you do the rest of the curriculum?*

BARB: No. It wanted him to do something like make a quilt. Now, he is just not the sort of person who would ever make a quilt. And some of the stuff seemed really boring—very textbooky. He still very much wanted to do it, though, I think to show himself he *could* do it. But I found I was doing most of the work trying to get him to do it.

> Having no interest in learning would be impossible in a home where the parents have written or printed material around.

At that point, someone called me right out of the blue and said, "I hear you have this fifth-grade curriculum you don't want; I'll pay you full price for it." I told my son, "Guess what, we can sell this curriculum and haven't lost anything!" He said, "No, I really want to do this." So I said, "The way it's been going so far, you're not very interested. If you decide to keep the curriculum, that's fine. I'm willing to pay for it. But, if you don't follow through, you have to pay me for it." We agreed that every week he didn't keep up with the curriculum, he would pay me $8, which was a lot of money for a 10-year-old. He wound up paying me for every penny of it from allowance, working, whatever. He paid me every week on his own accord.

MARY: *What did he ever say about it?*

BARB: When the whole year was finally over, summertime had come, and we were talking about the future, he said, "You know, it probably makes more sense to do what I'm really interested in, instead of trying to force myself to do things that aren't very interesting."

MARY: *Why did he want to do a curriculum? Was it structure he wanted?*

BARB: I don't think it was structure he wanted. His best friends were public-schooled and . . . I'm sure you've run into this with some kids who come to your house and wind up so envious that your son is homeschooled, that they go home and ask their parents, "Can we homeschool?" Then the parents come up with all these weird reasons about why they can't homeschool. His best friend's parents were saying, "Well, when Quinn does go to school, if he ever goes, he is going to have to start out as a kindergartner." That would always put their kids off wanting to be homeschooled. Even though he and the boy are still really good friends, this friend made my son feel insecure about how he fits in. He felt like, "Is he smarter than I am? Could I really do the work if I had to?"

MARY: *Why do you think most parents don't homeschool?*

BARB: As popular as homeschooling is becoming, it will never appeal to Western civilization on a grand scale. Our culture has become inordinately focused on work to buy stuff, pay bills—even though they all complain about it. Work outside the home has become far more important to many families than unpaid work at home. Many parents, too, simply don't enjoy the company of their children, which is certainly a requirement for homeschooling with any success. I believe that a major determinant to good health is psychological well-being, which is one reason I unschool. As I was dealing with the "happiness" issue—

what makes a happy person, what's a good quality of life, what kind of environment do we need, what kind of messages do we need to hear—everything pointed toward a child-led lifestyle. Everything pointed to, We're born with wisdom, we're here to express it and get our needs met.

MARY: *Is your husband in favor of unschooling and homeschooling?*

BARB: Yes, he is. He wasn't in the beginning and has never been one to read much about it, but I did the thinking, read the books, and told him about it. He has always been supportive of my ideas. He's very comfortable having me "do the homework" and recommend some action. Once in a while he gets nervous: One of our kids isn't reading, what if our teen doesn't do well on the SAT, that sort of thing.

> The degree of natural compatibility, the ability to cooperate and share that homeschooled children show, is remarkable.

MARY: *What about academic excellence? Do you want your kids to be able to be excellent spellers or do math really well or be great writers?*

BARB: I would love for all those things to be true, but I try consciously to separate the fantasies I have for my children from the fantasies they have for themselves. I think it's a parent's responsibility to present information, have intelligent conversations, and help the child see how the world works without too much bias. While I believe in expressing my opinions and beliefs, I also teach my children that they have an obligation to think things through on their own and come to their conclusions.

MARY: *How important is a homeschool (support) group in your life?*

BARB: It's not very important to me now because my kids are older. Early on, however, the homeschool support was integral to my succeeding. I very much needed to hear others' experience, bounce my ideas off other homeschoolers, make like-minded friends. To tell you the truth, I am not sure I could have been successful at homeschooling without a support group. I have found that home-schooled kids are quite different from "normal" kids. All ages and abilities can play and work together without prejudice. The degree of natural compatibility, the ability to cooperate and share that homeschooled children show, is remarkable. There are no words in our language to describe such children.

They are different away from you than they are at home, and it's through their interactions with other people that you really step back and say, "Wow, these are really different kids." If I had to describe them, I guess "extraordinary" is the most useful nutshell sort of word. Extremely mature, responsible. Passionate, sensitive, careful, respectful. I would never use academic descriptions for my kids like "straight-A student," "good academically," or "college-bound." When I think about those phrases, I realize that I could describe almost no adults in that way. Before we end this interview, I want to tell you that my oldest son has enrolled in high school.

MARY: *How did that come about?*

BARB: He just really wanted to go. I enrolled him in a little Jesuit school his first year, when he was 12. The classes were small, they didn't issue grades, and they were willing to enroll him despite his lack of prior formal instruction.

MARY: *Was he able to keep up with everything?*

BARB: No. But he had no problem with some subjects because he liked them so much. For example, he really came to love classic literature that year. He still loves it, but the public school where he is now doesn't offer anything in classic lit. He made a lot of friends that first year, and even the older kids liked him because he was so different. I would say in terms of his academic work, even though they didn't issue grades, he probably succeeded with the equivalent of a C average—did enough and understood enough and kept up enough. But it was definitely a struggle because, until that point, there was no way I could find to manipulate his environment to get him interested in things like spelling, grammar, writing.

MARY: *So what happened when he went to public school?*

BARB: He learned the ropes. He was interested in sports and computers and science, subjects that the Jesuit school wasn't offering. He went to the public school for his freshman year and did pretty well—A's, B's, and C's—and figured out how the system works. This year, as a sophomore, he finds it quite easy to earn straight A's in algebra, chemistry, Spanish, anything he has taken. He gets all his homework done in school within the time they give him.

MARY: *Do you think he'll continue until he graduates?*

BARB: I'm not sure. He was just asking me the other day if he could read the *Encyclopaedia Britannica* and have that be his curriculum. And he is also talking about going to college. I have become comfortable with not needing to predict my children's futures. The best I can do for them comes one day at a time.

Interview with Kathleen Jacobs

Kathleen Jacobs seems to have some sort of secret in raising children. Her three boys are the most well behaved, kind, sweet-spirited children we have ever known. They seem to have a fresh interest in things that any parent would want to foster in their children. Kathleen has an unobtrusive way about her, along with an inquisitive quality that expresses security.

MARY LEPPERT: *How old are your three boys?*

KATHLEEN JACOBS: They are 7, 9, and 11.

MARY: *Did they ever experience going to school?*

KATHLEEN: My oldest went to public school kindergarten. He was bored there because he was starting to read by that age, and they were making him sit down and color alphabet pages. Until the Christmas holiday, I would drive him to school and he would say, "Turn around; I don't want to go." That lasted until Christmas, then after Christmas break, he just sort of resigned himself to "this is life" and got used to it. That made me realize how most kids just get used to school because they're so adaptable.

MARY: *So you felt sad because you saw him being bored and he was so intelligent?*

KATHLEEN: It was more than that. It was dealing with the teacher and the whole school mentality; seeing that school offered nothing of value that couldn't be duplicated at home or in the community; that I could eliminate so many things that I felt were negative. I especially disliked how competitive the school environment was. They turned everything into a contest and my oldest was always "winning," which I felt was as bad as always "losing." In fact, I believe he acquired a distaste for math because he wasn't at the top of the class in performance, so he ended the year with an "I hate math" attitude. Another example was "Student of the Month," when the teacher picked a student to be honored for some positive trait (honesty, cooperation, helpfulness, and so on). On the surface, that might seem fine, but during any given year, only 9 of the 30 get to be Student of the Month, so most are "losers." When I pointed this out to the teacher, she said that the ones who don't get picked the first year will get picked in later years (never mind that some kids won't be Student of the Month for three or four years!). To me, this was pure manipulation to get the kids to cooperate.

> Most kids just get used to school because they're so adaptable.

MARY: *Did you think school would be that negative before you sent your son?*

KATHLEEN: I went into the whole experience thinking, "Well, maybe it's not as bad as I remember." I think the reality was worse. I needed that last little push to try homeschooling.

MARY: *So how did you first hear about homeschooling?*

KATHLEEN: I remember a cousin's wife talking about homeschooling when the kids were really little, but the idea didn't appeal to me. When my kids were young, I looked towards the school years as a kind of mother's respite. But as they got older, I realized school would take them away when they started to be really fun.

MARY: *So did you research homeschooling?*

KATHLEEN: Yes. I went back to my cousin's wife and asked her questions about homeschooling. She mailed me years of back issues of *Growing Without Schooling*, so I got to read all those without spending a penny. I loved them. Then I began reading John Holt's books. I was shocked and delighted about the concept of "unschooling." What appealed to me from the very beginning was rejecting the school model. You don't have to say, "Okay, kids. I'm not a mother now; I'm your teacher now." That's the image most people have of homeschooling. Unschooling sounded a lot like what I did with the kids before they were school age, and it made sense to just continue with the same approach to living and learning.

MARY: *So what exactly does the term "unschooling" mean to you?*

KATHLEEN: Unschooling means not separating school from the rest of life; following the kids' interests and realizing that's the best type of learning; trying to lead them to learning in fun and interesting ways, but being willing to drop it if the kids reject what is on *your* agenda. It also means surrounding them with interesting materials and seeing what appeals to them and what doesn't; being available to answer their questions. Unschooling is not buying into the term "grade level" but instead watching and enjoying them "moving forward" academically, socially, and emotionally in a more natural way.

MARY: *So what is a typical day like for you guys?*

KATHLEEN: There's no typical day. There's a typical week that's based on outside activities. Our oldest usually has a private archery lesson once a week. The two younger kids take gymnastics one night a week. They attend classes through the local parks and recreation department. We participate in field trips with local support groups, and plan play times with friends. I schedule in grocery shopping and errands when we are out. At home, our structure would include daily family read-aloud sessions before bedtime, any ongoing projects, lots of play inside and out, and documentaries or nature shows on public television two to three times a week. My youngest enjoys cartoons and is allowed to watch for an hour in the mornings when we are home. (I believe limited television watching is critical to a positive learning

> Unschooling is not buying into the term "grade level" but instead watching and enjoying them "moving forward" in a more natural way.

environment at home.) The kids are responsible for certain things around the house as well.

MARY: *Do you have a schedule as to when everyone gets up?*

KATHLEEN: They just get up whenever they get up, and it's usually within an hour to half an hour of each other. That usually starts by 7:00 A.M.

MARY: *When they get up, for example on a day when you don't have a class at the park, is there a flow to your day? Or is it mostly parenting/mom-type stuff.*

KATHLEEN: Parenting/mom-type stuff.

MARY: *Are days at home focused on anything like math or science or any other school-type subject?*

KATHLEEN: Not planned in any conscious way, but it might turn out that way. For example, I might be working in the yard and see an interesting insect and we will try to identify it. Or the kids might be fishing in the pond and pull out a water beetle that we try to identify and look at under a magnifying lens. The boys might plan things themselves. On a "free day," my oldest might decide he wants to work in his math book, update his stamp collection, or walk around the neighborhood looking for mushrooms to bring home and identify. My younger two spend most of their free time in pretend play. I have noticed that they often re-create in play what we are reading about during our family reading time. And we'll discuss certain things, like my oldest and I decided together how quickly he wanted to get through his math book.

MARY: *Did he just say he wanted to learn math?*

KATHLEEN: No, he has always struggled with math until this year, which I be-lieve was a mental block. Each year we have tried different approaches to math, either together or he tries something independently. Last year, I asked him to try the *Key To . . .* workbooks. He enjoyed the first one in each subject, but then the material would get too hard and he didn't want to do it. I asked him to work in the books once a week and he agreed to that. How much time he worked at each session was up to him. This year, I asked him to try Saxon math. We read the beginning of the book together and decided how many lessons to do each week to complete the book by the end of the year. Since then, he has been on his own and enjoying it (enjoying the fact that he "gets it," I think). I have not had to remind him to do it, and he is more than halfway through the book now.

MARY: *How did you know he struggled in math?*

KATHLEEN: Well, we'd be playing a game and you could see him really struggling to add numbers. With my middle child, I've never had him work on math at all because it's all very natural to him. He finds mental math easy to do and he doesn't try to avoid it when a math problem comes up.

MARY: *When you see them struggling, do you say, "I think you need to work on this or that," or do you say, "You have to do it"?*

KATHLEEN: It's definitely not a command type of situation; it's more like, "I'm concerned that you're frustrated with trying to add stuff together when we're playing games. A lot of math is just repetitive and easy stuff, and once you get to a certain point it's really easy." He agreed with that and decided how much time he was willing to spend in a week. Then it's up to him to set up his own schedule.

MARY: *What would you have done if he had said, "I don't want to learn how to do math"?*

KATHLEEN: I'd have let it go, which is basically what I've done. This is the first year he's had any success with math. Before this, he'd never spend more than maybe an hour a week doing it. The year before that, he'd always end up in tears when I tried to teach him

> I kept trying different approaches until something clicked, but I think what clicked was age and maturity.

math concepts. He'd get so frustrated when he didn't understand that we'd just drop it for a while and try again later.

MARY: *When you started out, did you think, "When he's ready then he'll do it"?*

KATHLEEN: I would just keep trying different approaches until something clicked, but I think what clicked was age and maturity. I don't regret anything I did because it was sort of dabbling and experimenting, and I didn't make a big deal about it. We would just drop it. The other kids do math all the time, just naturally—in the grocery store, doing mental math, money, such as figuring out their weekly allowance, what they can and can't buy.

MARY: *Are you worried about long division problems?*

KATHLEEN: No, I don't think that's any big deal since you can learn that at any time. I also don't think it makes a lot of sense to kids because when do you use that? Long division is a pretty abstract concept.

MARY: *Does your older son do the math program willingly because he set that goal for himself?*

KATHLEEN: Exactly. We had an argument the other day about his priorities. I asked him why he remembered to work in his Saxon math book but always forgot to practice his archery. I asked him, "Why is it that I have to remind you to do archery, and I have never once had to remind you to get that math book out? It makes me wonder if you don't really like archery." And he said, "No, I love it." But for some reason he needs me to remind him about archery. But with the math, I've seen him doing it on the weekend. He'll be walking through the house thinking, "I need to do a math lesson." It's too bizarre. I'm not sure he has developed a love for it, but I think he's relieved that he understands it.

> I don't think long division is any big deal.

MARY: *So is he a self-governing kid?*

KATHLEEN: Not really. I have to remind him to do chores and things.

MARY: *What about writing? Would you make your kids write if they didn't want to do it?*

KATHLEEN: Well, my middle child had the same experience with writing that the older one had with math. He was really frustrated doing any sort of writing because he didn't like the way it looked. I discussed it with him last year, and now he's been working in a cursive handwriting book for the second year. I try to reinforce the message that some things get easier with practice and become less frustrating. After he used the book for a while, his handwriting improved noticeably. I can't say for sure whether it was the book or that he's just a bit older now. But whatever it was, I didn't force him. If he'd said he hated the book and didn't want to do it, we would have dropped it. I have to remind him sometimes, but he does it.

MARY: *What types of chores are the kids required to do as part of a daily routine?*

KATHLEEN: Cleaning up after themselves, brooming outside, folding and putting away laundry, watering the vegetable garden, washing the car, stuff like that.

MARY: *Do they initiate anything else that would be considered academic?*

KATHLEEN: Well, my older two spend lots of time reading and often are so engrossed that they go back to a really good book as often as possible. My oldest likes to read a book straight through; my middle child likes short reading sessions often throughout the day.

MARY: *So you are kind of like an overall, quiet guide for them, sort of subtle in the background?*

KATHLEEN: Yes, I'm always suggesting stuff. For example, I suggested my middle child start writing a journal about the hamster he bought—when he bought it, what kinds of things the hamster learned (you're supposed to be able to teach them stuff). He wasn't interested in doing that. He was very adamant, and I don't think any real learning would take place if I required him to write a journal.

MARY: *What do you think about learning that requires the everyday discipline of practice, such as writing or playing piano?*

KATHLEEN: I handle those things in the way I already described, as a way of handling weaknesses. Beyond that, if there is genuine opposition, I believe the learner is in the best position to know the best time to learn something. In the meantime, I will try to get to the bottom of the reason by trying different approaches, or having materials available that might spark an interest. To take writing as an example, I think they first have to see a reason to write, know that it serves a purpose. They must reach a certain maturity level before they can see that. For example, my oldest was required to keep a record book of his 4-H activities. He did a large amount of writing, which was hard work. He worked on editing and rewriting because he had an audience, people who were interested in what he had to say and gave him feedback. Since then he has done very little writing, but I am confident that the next time he needs to or wants to, he will.

MARY: *Would you ever force your kids to learn certain things?*

KATHLEEN: No. If they're adamant about not learning something, there must be some reason. Another way to look at this is that there are only so many hours in a day, and we are always picking and choosing how to spend that time. I limit what I believe are time-wasting and mind-numbing activities, mainly television.

> My goal is to create an interesting, varied, and appropriate environment for them, and an important element in that environment is trusting their choices.

Even if they are daydreaming, or playing, how can I be sure that's not what they should be doing? I feel much more useful when they ask me for help. My goal is to create an interesting, varied, and appropriate environment for them to live and learn in, and an important element in that environment is trusting their choices.

It might be appropriate here to make a distinction between educational freedom and parental permissiveness. We feel that part of our job is instilling a set of values in the boys. These are parental issues, not educational ones. But my values influence my decisions when choosing materials and creating an appropriate environment. That's why I limit television, and why I would never own a Nintendo. So an important first step is deciding what your long-range goals are for your kids and then to focus on that instead of worrying that they haven't memorized their multiplication tables. Many, many things are more important than that.

MARY: *What do you think is the hardest thing about homeschooling?*

KATHLEEN: Probably the hardest part is trusting my instincts instead of what the neighbor's kids are doing, and having to live in the society we live in, where it seems so many people have gone astray. I also feel bad that my husband has to work so much, subsidizing the rest of us, while we are together having lots of fun.

For resources for unschoolers, see page 505.

CHAPTER 6

Eclectic Approach and Other Methods

The previous two chapters introduced the opposite ends of the homeschooling spectrum: the parental (parent-centered) and unschooling (child-centered) approaches. In fact, most homeschoolers fit somewhere between the extremes, perhaps leaning toward either a parent-centered or a child-centered philosophy. As our examples and interviews illustrate, homeschoolers often gravitate toward whatever methods work best for their family. Those who don't adhere to a particular philosophy or style but select what appears to be the best in various methods are often considered "eclectic." The term comes from the Greek word "eklektos," which originally meant chosen. During the time of Alexander the Great, his "chosen" inner circle of generals and advisors was of such a mix of backgrounds—Mongolian, Arab, Persian, Athenian, Macedonian, African, and so forth—that "eclectic" came to mean any widely varied mix.

What Is the Eclectic Approach?

The eclectic approach is more a way of doing the other methods than a strict approach in itself. Yours could probably be a strict school-at-home family yet still be eclectic (although you might find it difficult to feel "right" and validated). An eclectic family might have a plan for what the child *should* learn and master over, say, a year's period of time, just as a family using the parental approach would, but is flexible about how to accomplish this end. For example, if the eclectic parent believes a child must cover certain topics in history, and the child is not a sit-down-read-a-book type, the parent might read aloud about the American colonial era, take the child to a Civil War re-enactment as a project, and obtain a video that portrayed that historical period. On the other hand, the unschooling parent who follows a child's interests may be led to anything from closely inspecting a snail on a nature walk to using a boxed math curriculum—again, the learning methods could be termed eclectic.

Eclectic homeschoolers take their educational information from widely varied materials. Eclectic homeschooling families often follow a "patchwork" curriculum, and their teaching schedules may be more innovative and flexible than are those of families who follow either a strict parental or unschooling approach. There is very little an eclectic homeschooling family would *not* utilize in its learning life. Imagine using a series of travel brochures and maps to teach geography! Or better yet, imagine using actual travel to various locales as the background for a series of geography lessons. An eclectic family believes in teaching academics, but rather than using only books, they like to put a twist on the process, making learning much more interesting.

Here's another example of an eclectic approach: Suppose you went into a favorite used bookstore and found an interesting, old second-grade reading book for $1. You brought it home and had your third-grader read it, and you both realized she didn't know more than one-fourth of the vocabulary in the book. If you were already homeschooling your child, you might immediately decide to include the "new" book in your daily work, as both a reading text and as a vocabulary builder.

If an eclectic homeschool family purchased a curriculum-in-a-box, before long they would replace, supplement, or fine-tune some element to suit their exact needs. Perhaps they buy a math book here, borrow a history book there, order a grammar book that caught their fancy at a curriculum fair, and dust off a handwriting book they found in grandmother's attic—you get the picture. Eclectic families are not haphazard, however. They use grandmother's penmanship book because it is the right tool for the right job. The operative word for an eclectic family is "confidence." If you don't have confidence in your ability to assemble a curriculum from diverse materials and sources, eclecticism will not work for you. In fact, always second-guessing whether you are using the "right" book or program would drive you crazy.

But unless you have already plotted a course you're happy with, the eclectic approach is by far the most interesting way of home-schooling, if you can muster the confidence to do it. It combines the conservatism of teaching academic subjects with the freedom of taking advantage of anything and everything as a learning resource. So many wonderful resources are available to homeschoolers that you need not restrict yourself to any one choice. Whether you are Christian, Muslim, Mormon, Jewish, or none of the preceding, you can use Christian materials in varied styles from ultra-conservative to liberal, non-Christian materials, and non-homeschool-specific materials, as well as books, videos, and other resources made specifically for home-schoolers. Those who use the eclectic approach may use materials from *all* the above resource types, if it suits their family's fancy. If you don't mind references to evolution, old-earth theories, and such, then you could use any of the science videos and books, for instance.

Eclectic homeschoolers are always asking other families what they use and how they like it because they're continually shopping for good products that suit their family's tastes and goals, for either the present or the future. By contrast, a strictly religious home-schooler might purchase only products suitable for a Christian or even her specific denomination of Christianity because of certain doctrinal differences of opinion. Orthodox Jewish homeschoolers have similar considerations, as do Muslim homeschoolers.

Eclectic homeschoolers are much more aggressive and inquisitive about materials, programs, books, even theories of imparting information to their children than non-eclectics. Eclectics are always searching. A fundamentalist Christian family is not likely to use a product not approved specifically for fundamentalist Christians—sometimes even for their particular denomination! An eclectic trusts his or her own judgment about a product. What better way to shop than through vicarious test-drives by friends and fellow support-group

Homeschoolers Say . . .

How do I put together my own curriculum?

The best way to create your own curriculum is to decide what your educational philosophy and goals are. This is not easy when you are just beginning. I advise new homeschoolers to relax in the first year. Don't bring school home! In our house, music and reading are very important; they are who we are, so naturally we go in that direction. Neither of us is very interested or good in math or the careers that good math skills would bring. Decide what is important to your family and find materials that help you reach your goals in that direction.

members? Although the eclectic approach would seem the most "labor-intensive" way to choose materials, it is typically an outgrowth of the family itself, a blend of homeschooling methods that is a definite expression of the family character.

There are curriculum guides for the eclectic family, which help cut down on having to make *every* choice all the time. Of course, catalogs and online resources are scoured and worn out quickly, because this homeschooling style is a total environment, a constant commitment, a never-ending but happy search for elusive pieces of the knowledge puzzle. If you have three partial sets of dishes and unmatching silverware and like it that way because it is more interesting, you are probably an eclectic! Now just add homeschooling to the mix, and the adventure begins!

Using the Eclectic Approach

If you are a person who requires an externally imposed structure or authority (such as someone else's curriculum choices and lesson plans), the eclectic approach is not for you. This method of home-

Go to homeschooling conferences and curriculum fairs and see what is out there. Many curricula are produced by homeschooling parents who started out just like you.

After you decide what you want to do, then decide when and how you will do it. This will be different for each family. In our family, we put books on our mantle in June that we decide we will read before the next June. We also decide what skill our son will learn—fractions or division, for instance—during the coming year. For example, if we decide to study word roots over the next year, we'll purchase materials at our conference or another one.

schooling requires an individual touch and the ability and desire to customize one's curriculum, as well as the confidence to exercise freedom and independent judgment and creativity. Some eclectic families do use a boxed curriculum but usually chafe at something and just *have* to replace that element or book with one of their own choosing. For instance, the history book included in the boxed set may not be as good as another one they know of, so they switch those books. Or an eclectic mom finds an excellent workbook at a bookstore—just what her daughter needs as a spelling supplement—so she buys it to add to the curriculum.

You could use the eclectic approach with a child who is fresh from school if you have been giving these learning styles a great deal of thought. Let's say you had a feeling you wanted to homeschool, but you let your child remain in school another year before making the final decision. During this year you've been reading and thinking about the various approaches to homeschooling, weighing each one in relation to you and your child, and you now feel confident that you can assemble a curriculum from many different sources. You have found a reading book you love, a spelling book that is just right,

Homeschoolers Say . . .

If my child is currently in public school, how do I get him or her out?

The procedure varies with each state or province and with each school district to some degree. In some districts, all you have to do is notify them, usually in writing, that you are removing your child from the school and will be teaching him or her at home. Since all states and provinces provide for homeschooling as a legal option, the state's regulation and overseeing of your homeschooling activity will be similar to that of a private school.

and a math book you can both work with. You could take your child out of school and begin teaching her with the eclectic method right away. Or you might first purchase these books and materials and look them over at odd moments.

Many families who homeschool with an eclectic approach also consider activities such as private music lessons, classes with other homeschoolers, science classes outside of home, hiking, docent training, going to various museums, and visiting convalescent homes to be part of their studies.

Making the Transition from School

If your child has been in school, we again recommend taking about a week or two off just to be together to relax and get used to having control of your lives before you settle into a routine. Near the end of this week off, make a list of strengths and weaknesses, as discussed below.

Identifying Strengths, Weaknesses, and the In-Betweens

The following information and outline is placed here because eclectic homeschoolers have a definite idea of the things they want their children to know, and they tend to build their own systems for

You may have to keep and submit attendance records; possibly turn in a broadly described lesson plan (including only the areas of study you intend to teach, not details such as what books you will use); and submit your child to taking a standardized test every other year or in specified years sprinkled throughout the elementary and high school career. Some states have testing; many do not. Some have attendance record requirements; many do not. (See part 4 for details on how to contact each parent-run homeschool organization in your state. Talk with them before you do anything.)

homeschooling *almost* from the ground up. Eclectics don't reinvent the wheel, but they build their own car.

Ascertain your child's academic strengths, weaknesses, and in-betweens by listing them on paper. Divide the paper into three sections, placing "Strengths" as the left-side heading, "In-Betweens" as the middle heading, and "Weaknesses" as the right-side heading. Now, using the school curriculum your daughter has just left as your basic guide, carefully and honestly categorize each subject by these headings. Enlist your child's opinion, too, as she has insight into her academic makeup.

Once you feel you have categorized all the subjects she was studying in school, discuss any other supplemental subjects either of you feel are appropriate additions to the list. There are bound to be subjects of interest that the school didn't offer. By looking at your combined lists of school and other subjects, you have your curriculum before you. The weak subjects will receive priority right now, while strengths and "in-between" ones might receive less attention. We recommend that weak subjects be taught every day for a period of weeks or months, and they should have top priority on the daily time schedule to bring them to at least the "in-between" level.

If math is weak, teach it early in the day, when your student's mind is freshest. If she is enthusiastic about it, spend more time doing math than you might have planned. If you spend an hour or more, one-on-one, working on math (if that's your child's weakness), it will not be a weak area for long! The strengths simply have to be maintained and can be further developed at a slower pace. This plan can be an effective course of study for at least the first few months. You will want to review and revise your program whenever you feel the need.

Setting Your Schedule

Hopefully, you have been stockpiling the books and materials you want to use for homeschooling. Now look each over and, based on your subject lists, compile a daily schedule. Make some rough drafts before settling on a "typical" day that will work for you. Maybe each day of the first teaching week should be a "dry run" that will give you the opportunity to test your plan and book choices for kinks and bugs. As you proceed through this experimental week, take notes and have your child do the same so you can fine-tune your curriculum. Once you have completed this week, look over your plan and notes and make any necessary adjustments, which may include shopping for alternative materials.

During the second week, you can teach your child with the specialized plan you devised for improving her weaknesses and maintaining her strengths, using the curriculum and materials you have chosen. Below is a sample schedule that will give you a general idea of what might be covered in a week. Note that it lacks rigid times because an eclectic parent might spend hours reading aloud to her child or playing Scrabble as a spelling lesson.

Sample Schedule

Monday

MATH	*Make a trip to the grocery store, with the child totaling the bill and budgeting with a calculator.*
PENMANSHIP	*Copy poems from a favorite poem book.*
GEOGRAPHY	*Plan a trip to Washington, D.C., using travel brochures and maps.*

SPELLING — *Play Scrabble.*

OUTSIDE CLASS — *Child might have a series of classes outside of home, such as music, art, or dance.*

Tuesday

MATH — *Spend 20 minutes or so calculating how far it is to Alpha Centauri, a star system 4½ light-years from earth.*

AMERICAN HISTORY — *Read the selection "The Men Who Built the Railroad Across America" from American Adventures, Pt 1 by Morrie Greenberg (see page 395), and then watch the Kaw Valley video about the same topic and discuss it.*

READING — *Student reads aloud 20 minutes to mom from "With Lee in Virginia" by G. A. Henty (see page 384).*

GRAMMAR — *Mom and student spend 20 minutes working from grammar workbook Explode the Code.*

POETRY AND LITERATURE — *Mom reads Uncle Tom's Cabin aloud 20 or 30 minutes. Or the child could begin memorizing a favorite poem, possibly the same one she copied for penmanship on Monday.*

Wednesday

MATH — *Mom writes out and explains the times tables from 1 to 5.*

PENMANSHIP — *Child writes a letter to grandma.*

GEOGRAPHY — *The family plays Take Off, a popular geography game.*

SPELLING — *Mom and student spend 20 minutes looking at the book English from the Roots Up (page 193) about words with Latin and Greek roots.*

OUTSIDE CLASS — *Ballet.*

Thursday

MATH — *Student skipped math to watch kittens being born for two hours in the morning. Later helped Mom balance the checkbook.*

AMERICAN HISTORY — *Began reading a novel by Oliver Optic (Lost Classics Books).*

READING — *This is covered by the American history assignment above.*

GRAMMAR — *The student could work in the grammar workbook for 20 minutes, or mom and the student could discuss how different the language is in the Oliver Optic book compared to how we speak today.*

SPANISH — *If the student is studying the language at home, one of the many excellent self-teaching methods can be utilized; otherwise, an outside teacher can do the instructing.*

Friday

This could be a day off or a free day when the student chooses what she wants to do.

Homeschoolers Say . . .

What if we have too much time on our hands?

Before our family started *The Link,* Mary felt many days that we had too much time on our hands. Sometimes she and Lennon were so bored that they'd follow the volunteer police (usually senior citizens looking for crime) around the neighborhood just for fun! It brought up discussion topics such as "Are these citizens in their middle to late seventies capable of doing this job?" Some swerved and weaved when they drove; others were excellent drivers. This led to more questions: "What is discrimination about? Should we let someone have or not have a job just because of age?" Another time-filling (and money-saving) activity was visiting thrift stores. Once we found a pottery wheel for $10.

Idle time can become a Petri dish for new experiences for parents and children alike—a delight!

This outline gives you an overview of how you can arrange your daily schedule. You can see from this schedule that real-life activities are combined with academic skill development to produce an interesting and rewarding curriculum that prepares the child for adulthood.

Another aspect of eclectic homeschooling is that the subjects are often tied together one way or another. For instance, because Alpha Centauri is the nearest object to earth besides our own solar system components, calculating its distance segues right into a study or discussion of astronomy now or later. Dad might come home from work and take his daughter outside to find Alpha Centauri with the telescope. Or they may go to a planetarium on the weekend and find Alpha Centauri on the dome depiction of the sky. This creative, imaginative use of a single item to aid in learning both math and astronomy is characteristic of the eclectic approach. Teaching your child useful information that also has an academic value, such as balancing a checkbook, budgeting your grocery shopping, and so on, is another important aspect of the eclectic approach.

The following interviews with two homeschooling mothers from very different backgrounds illustrate how creative and flexible the eclectic method can be.

Interview with Diane Keith

Diane Keith is vital, funny, and warm. For those who aren't familiar with her, Diane is the editor and publisher of *Homefires Journal of Homeschooling*. This eclectic collection of homeschool academia and information is the type of periodical one keeps for years as a reference. Diane seems to have passed her own dynamism to her children, and I think the following visit will enable *Almanac* readers to experience some of her energy.

Diane Flynn Keith is married and homeschools her two sons, 11 and 13, in northern California. Except for brief encounters with school, she has homeschooled her children using the eclectic approach.

<big>Q
A</big> MARY LEPPERT: *How would you describe your homeschool approach?*

DIANE KEITH: I would call what we do eclectic. To me, eclectic means taking a little bit of academic learning mixed in with a whole lot of experiential learning. For us, it offers the best of both worlds.

MARY: *So do you have a plan with your eclectic approach?*

DIANE: Three mornings a week we have a large chunk of time, about three or four hours, when we don't have to run to classes or do anything else. So those mornings I usually ask them to sit down and maybe have them read some history or I will read it to them if they prefer. Sometimes I ask them to write down their impressions, in a paragraph or so that explains what they have just read.

Then they'll read it back to me so I know they understood the material and be-cause they need the practice in writing.

MARY: *If one of your boys said, "I want to write about in-line skating," would you let him?*

DIANE: Well, I think that is really following the child's lead, which is impor-tant. If you can accomplish the task by following the child's interest, I would al-ways say that's better than any textbook could ever be. I definitely think that anything interest-initiated or child-led is more on the unschooling bend.

MARY: *So with eclectic, you have a goal in mind that you're going to accomplish using a variety of sources?*

DIANE: Yes, and my goal is to give my kids as many skills as possible so they can jump through all the hoops they encounter in life; and if they want to go to college, they are going to be prepared. If they want to start their own business and fly air-planes or something, that's okay too. It's absolutely okay to utilize parental authority and responsibility to make sure your children are well prepared for the world. And I think some coercion is always okay. I remember when my kids were real little and occasion-ally didn't want to do math, they would say, "I'll do it if you pay me." I would give them 10 cents a page because they were learning about money. I don't see anything wrong with that approach—everything in moderation.

> It's absolutely okay to utilize parental authority to make sure your children are well prepared.

MARY: *So you decided you needed more structure than unschooling?*

DIANE: The problem with labeling is that I don't know any homeschoolers who don't guide or facilitate their children's learning in some way. I think un-schooling is a very difficult concept to define. I've seen many articles in many publications, and even online conversations, where people struggle to define what unschooling is, and nobody seems to agree. I believe that unschooling is following the child's interests. It doesn't mean you're not going to give them op-portunity; in fact, they won't allow you *not* to.

MARY: *Tell me what you do every day.*

DIANE: Three days a week we "do school." We have Saxon math, history, and writing that we do on a very regular, consistent basis. My younger child is a real visual learner who prefers reading the text himself and doing the practice questions. The older child is an auditory learner who learns better if he hears it. So I will actually sit down and read it with him. So we have two different things going on there, and they're working out of different textbooks.

> I have my children's good will.

MARY: *Do they complete the lesson each day?*

DIANE: Three days a week they're required to do one or two lessons. I will tell you this: I am very flexible when I use Saxon; I think it's insane for them to answer all 30 practice or drill questions at the end of every chapter. They already know how to add, subtract, multiply, and divide; so if the current chapter is about percentage, fractions, or something like that, I ask them to answer those questions at the end of the chapter. Once every 10 or 15 lessons, I ask them to do all 30 questions to see if they can do it. It's sort of a game, and they're very willing. I have my children's good will. A lot of respect has developed between us. This especially happens when you homeschool a long time with your kids.

MARY: *Do they see the value in learning math?*

DIANE: Yes, any time we are talking about money, for instance—probably because they're from a family of entrepreneurs. They're numismatists; they collect coins, and their grandfather talks about stocks and investing money.

MARY: *What brought you to homeschooling?*

DIANE: My oldest son went to preschool, kindergarten, and first grade. He went to a Montessori preschool program that he enjoyed very much. At the time I had never considered anything else; I just assumed my children would go to school. Quite frankly, I was on a fast track. I wanted "the best" and "the most" for my children. When my older son was born, he was one of those kids who never, ever slept, so I started reading the newspapers to him. He loved

"Dear Abby" because I could put a lot of expression in my voice and change characters. I realized he needed more, so I found a book called *How to Teach Your Baby to Read* from the Institutes for the Achievement of Human Potential, Glen Doman's organization. I decided to attend their Professional Mother Seminar.

The theory of the Institutes is that all children are geniuses; all of us are born with the potential of a Leonardo da Vinci. I believe that. Because I took the seminar, we joined their Evan Thomas off-campus program. Now, the Institutes believes in a parent's ability to educate his or her children, to give the children all the wonderful information they would need from the world. I started using that program with both my sons, and I can't describe to you how much they loved it. They would beg, "Can we please sit down and see the bits of information, please, please, please?"

MARY: *What are the "bits of information"?*

DIANE: Well, they're like flash cards—beautiful pictures by famous artists, like all of the Impressionists, on big cards—and you put the card in front of the child's face and tell him 30 seconds of information about it. "This is a painting by Monet. Do you see the watercolor that he used? The name of the painting is *The Seine at Bennecourt.* Then you move on to the next one, fast. The kids go, "Oh, that's cool."

My younger son started at birth on that program; my older son was about 2. I did that for a couple of years, and now they recognize a lot of famous paintings. I still interacted that way with my children—even while my older son had preschool experience—because it was so successful.

He was in preschool, getting ready for kindergarten in the fall, when I went to the classrooms and watched what was happening, I knew this was not the experience I wanted for my son.

MARY: *Did you know about homeschooling at that point?*

DIANE: Of course, through the Evan Thomas Institute, I learned that it was a possibility. I did not know anybody who was doing it. I was still searching.

MARY: *What about in your life?*

DIANE: I went to various colleges over a period of six years and couldn't decide on a major. Finally, I went to nursing school, then dropped out three months before graduation. I just decided I didn't want to do it. I wanted to be an at-home mom. That was all-important. I was 33 years old when I had my first child. We were having children because my husband and I *wanted* children; we wanted to raise them, spend time with them. We were not going to turn them over to someone else to raise; that was very clear. But I still had a "school" mind and didn't understand that I had other options, that I wouldn't have to turn my children over to the "system." This is when I decided to homeschool, because my younger son was miserable and bored.

So around that April, my husband said, "Why don't you homeschool him?" and I went, "Whoa! There's a totally new concept." I had heard of it once or twice, but I didn't know anybody who did it. But that's when the investigation started. I got every back issue of *Growing Without Schooling*, found *Home Education Magazine*, then attempted to find people in my own area. That was only seven years ago. It was a clandestine activity because of the homeschooling laws here. People were afraid that if they were outside with their kids, they'd get picked up for truancy.

I'm a very honest person and it just struck me that I'd live my life as usual and let everybody know I was homeschooling. Within a year I had made contacts with other people who felt like I did, and we started a newsletter and shared and networked information. That's how *Homefires* started.

MARY: *What do you do for writing?*

DIANE: You mean, an actual handwriting course? I use the Italics course from Portland State University. We did a page a day of writing so my older son would have legible handwriting. I used it with my younger son as well.

For the actual writing, about a year ago, I hired a tutor to work with them on writing development—stories and everything, informatory or expository writing. She would give them a topic like "Should the Drinking Age Be Lowered to 18?" or "Should Kids Be Able to Drive at 15?" and they had to present both sides of the argument in the course of writing. She helped them structure their thoughts, organize and present the facts through sentences and paragraphs, and then go back and edit the work. This worked out well for us.

MARY: *What do the kids do on the other two days?*

DIANE: The other two days they have private lessons—science, music (one takes drums; the other takes guitar). For the science classes, a group of homeschooling parents hired an engineer. He comes in and teaches about laser technology, blows things up, and does wonderful chemical experiments they would never do in school because of the liability. Also, they're taking programmed athletics fitness classes during the day. And at the same center, they are now offering a music mentoring program. The boys jam with professional musicians one night a week in a state-of-the-art recording studio. They recorded a CD and are having a good time. In reading and performing arts they do the *Boomerang* tapes, which is an audio magazine for kids.

> There's some textbook learning, there's some classroom learning, and then they'll spend the rest of the time investigating what they want.

Do you understand how that balance thing goes? There's some textbook learning, there's some classroom learning, and then they'll spend the rest of the time investigating what they want. They learned to fly airplanes over the summer and really want to pursue that this year. When you live in the San Francisco Bay Area, the resources are phenomenal.

MARY: *Can you say what your educational philosophy is in a sentence or two?*

DIANE: I believe that learning should be a joyful experience. I believe that we learn from everything in life, that you learn as long as you are awake and breathing. What I'm trying to accomplish is to raise children who are eventually autonomous, to raise an independent individual who loves learning and knows how to research and get the information he needs to get where he wants to go.

MARY: *Do you think homeschooling is for everyone?*

DIANE: In a perfect world, yes. This is not a perfect world. There are too many variables to make a blanket statement that homeschooling will work for everyone. Homeschooling is a profoundly joyful educational alternative, one that I wish *every* family would consider. Ultimately, I trust parents to make the right educational choices for their own children, based on their personal educational philosophy and on their child's learning styles and needs. I believe parents *are* the experts who should determine the best learning environment for their own children. It is a matter that should be reassessed from time to time based on changing needs and interests. But the option to homeschool should always be available and, even in an imperfect world, it should be acknowledged, accepted, and respected as a viable process.

Interview with Lisa K.

Lisa, who lives in Michigan, has a semi-large family that is very diverse. Lisa's interesting mix of qualities fits the definition of eclectic. She began raising her children with an unschooling approach and segued into an eclectic style as the children got older. Lisa is educated, sophisticated, and dedicated to motherhood in a wholesome way. She is very experienced in homeschooling.

Q A

MARY LEPPERT: *How old are your children?*

LISA K.: They're 17, 15, 13, and 9.

MARY: *And what made you decide to homeschool?*

LISA: In the beginning, we thought we would stay at home as a family just for the first few years, but it worked out well, so we kept on doing it.

MARY: *Are you homeschooling for religious reasons?*

LISA: That's a part of the total reason. It's very holistic for us, a whole integrated learning approach that's hard to separate out and say, "This is why."

MARY: *How did you first hear about homeschooling?*

LISA: Well, my husband had heard about homeschooling when he was in college. He had taken a couple of courses and ran across a book by Goodman. I believe it's called *Compulsory Miseducation at the Community of Scholars*. So he was familiar with the idea on a theoretical level. Then we had our first child and were having a wonderful time being a family. I had just read *The Magical Child*, by Joseph Pierce, about the natural, holistic, spiritual (as well as physical and cognitive) development of children and how our society has interfered with or not supported that development. We were starting to talk about those things, then we became pregnant with our second child and decided to have a home birth.

Our daughter, who was then 21 months, was present at the birth when our son was born. I never "went away and came back with a new baby." So now there were the four of us, and we were starting to think about what was going to happen next. We thought we'd send them to school when they were nine, because that would give them a chance to really learn who they were in the context of a loving family

As time went on, every year I had a new reason why we were homeschooling. "Well, this year we're homeschooling because my oldest really needs that sense of leadership that she gets in being in a one-on-one situation," or "She needs a little more time; she's too far ahead academically," or "She's too little; she's a tiny person." So, since it was working well, we decided to just keep going.

MARY: *When did you decide to keep doing this without making up a new reason every year?*

LISA: I guess as they got to be about 10 and 12. By then I was not asking questions like "Should we look into school?" They had a sense of community in the synagogue and we liked that better because they were in a *real* community, rather than an artificial community of people all within a year of their own age.

MARY: *What do you do as far as "school" goes?*

LISA: We have had lessons for piano, voice, and guitar. Music is also a discipline that builds on what you've learned before. You need to work on it every day to develop the facility. And so here we are "unschoolers," but every day we're doing math, music, and housework (which is a very important curriculum item in my house). I think people who homeschool often begin because they are into a Rousseau-type atmosphere and attitude of letting the child lead. Then at some point, we think, "We're going to take control of our education, and we're going to do school at home and be better than the school."

You kind of start out at one end or the other, and most of us drift closer to the center. If you say, "I'm an unschooler," it pushes you in the direction of diving into whatever your passion is. In our house, theater is a passion. For example, we are doing full-length Shakespeare productions with other homeschoolers, private schoolers, and local school kids. We're setting them in different eras, and all of a sudden we're "learning" history and the Elizabethan worldview and how that compares to our age of discovery. We're looking at languages, at poetry, and at costuming, which leads us into the art of the period. Do you see what I'm saying? Everything flows together.

MARY: *In education in general, labeling certain "subjects" is almost the same as labeling your homeschooling style.*

LISA: Exactly. It's like pulling a thread in a piece of clothing. If you keep pulling, the whole thing will come apart.

MARY: *Is the high school program you mentioned through a public school?*

LISA: It is Clonlara Home-Based Education program, located in Ann Arbor. I want my kids to have a diploma, to have transcripts because they all want to go to college.

> You kind of start out at one end or the other of the homeschooling spectrum, and most of us drift closer to the center.

MARY: *Have you ever vacillated in your approach to homeschooling?*

LISA: I think that we always evolve in our approach to homeschooling. Like I said about people moving toward the middle, it would change from week to week for us. Now, my oldest two are teaching assistants for a Hebrew program in our town. My daughter drives there, so Tuesday mornings and Thursday mornings we do world history or science projects. We just finished doing a biology lab with dissection with some other homeschoolers on Thursday.

MARY: *Is homeschooling a full-time job for you?*

LISA: It's like two or three full-time jobs! Being a mom is a full-time job. It always has a piece of your mind—whether you're home with your children, or your children are going to school and you're going to work, they're always occupying part of your time and energy. And as far as being an educator, that's a full-time job, too.

MARY: *Lisa, do you think homeschooling is a way to a better society?*

LISA: I think it is one answer. A central issue for me is that I see our society as having a machine approach to living. We all fit into our paradigm and make things work; and it's better to be faster, more efficient, do more. That is organization without being organic, not seeing the whole picture of life. It is living in a very linear rather than broad and holistic structure.

I think the family should be the model for being human.

I think most of society doesn't examine the relatedness of the whole, where you fit in. If you're seeing a career track, you think of a career track (or even the mommy track). Or you think, "Have I found my niche?" or "Have I found what the next step on the ladder is?" All those are very linear images, thinking about success as a specific kind of goal. Society is not as human as I would like it to be. Part of being human is being whole and able to relate to other people.

MARY: *When you say that "society is not as human," do you mean it's more machine-like? Or heartless?*

LISA: I think it is machine-like in the sense that it isn't thinking or feeling, which also implies heartlessness. But a machine is not heartless in a way that a human would be heartless. We need a different model, and I think the family should be the model for being human. Technology changes; people don't. People still want to belong, to feel connected. I think that homeschooling is one way—not the only way, but an important way. It's been a very good way for *our* family. We've had our bad days when I'm tearing out my hair and thinking, "I'm letting everybody down." But taking the long view, and looking at the whole picture, my children are doing very well academically. All of them are people I would be delighted to call my friends if I met them in another context, if they weren't my own flesh and blood. They have heart, compassion, kindness. They want to do the right thing. You cannot pick up those qualities in a textbook. The best prep school is not going to give you that edge. Those qualities come from investing time in other human beings. And that happens for us through having a family-centered lifestyle.

MARY: *Do you think these qualities can come from the lifestyle of homeschooling?*

LISA: Homeschooling gives us opportunity to spend time together as a family so we can put things in perspective. It has been a wonderful experience for us; it is who we are!

For resources for eclectic schoolers, see page 508.

Other Homeschooling Methods

The eclectic style draws upon the unlimited resources available to people who are interested in knowing more. Everywhere you go, there is something potentially worth knowing. In the homeschooling realm, the eclectic style not only combines the parental and unschooling approaches, but draws from the other methods to teach, several of which are explained below. Each approach has a number of adherents who follow the method successfully.

Many parents are intimidated by the prospect of being teachers. They feel they don't know how to do it or where to begin. You will notice that many products and resources come with teacher's manuals that can be helpful (see Products and Resources). That is why homeschooling parents are able to say (without smugness or judgment) that teaching your own children does not require special ability or intelligence, just the desire to do so and the ability to read and then impart the information. Most parents soon realize that they can teach their own children up to at least the high school level. There is no end to the help available to those who seek it.

Delayed Academic Approach

The inventors of this method are Dr. Raymond Moore and his wife, Dorothy. They partially homeschooled their two children and are pioneers in the homeschooling movement and responsible for many homeschooling laws in California. They began in the homeschooling movement at the same time John Holt did and were friends of his.

Raymond Moore is known worldwide for establishing highly successful work-study programs in colleges and universities. Dorothy is a child specialist and reading and curriculum authority. Their methods have been used by thousands of families, schools, and homeschools around the world that want to develop high achievement, social ability, and character in their students and children.

The delayed academic approach involves following the Moore formula (as quoted from a Moore Foundation manual): "1. Study every day, from a few minutes to hours. 2. Manual work, at least as much as study. 3. Home and/or community service, an hour or so per day. Focus on kids' interests and needs; be an example in consistency, curiosity and patience. Live with them! Worry less about tests. With the Moore formula, if you are loving and can read, write, count and speak clearly, you are a master teacher."

The Moore Foundation has conducted thousands of studies and paired them with studies from Stanford University and the University of Colorado Medical School. They concluded after observing children's senses, brain, cognition, and so on that no evidence shows that children are ready or need formal study or homeschool before the ages of 8 to 10. Therefore, the Moores advocate reading, singing, and playing with your children from birth. They suggest that children will learn to read in their own time, if someone reads to them often. Some children are not actually ready until the age of 14! Dr. Moore claims that the older readers often become the best readers of all. They also experience less damaged vision, more adult-like reasoning, more mature brain structure, and less blocking of creative interests.

This is not an unschooling program; it is placing service and work interests before "book-ish" academics.

For resources for the delayed academic method, see page 509.

The Charlotte Mason Approach

Nourish a child daily with loving, right and noble ideas . . . which may bear fruit in his life.

—Charlotte Mason

Charlotte Mason was born in England in 1842, did most of her work from Ambleside, and died in 1923. Her basic philosophy was that, most importantly, children should love to learn. According to popular lecturer, author, and Charlotte Mason expert Catherine Levison, "The most important thing is that they have a love of learning." Catherine advocates in her book that parents should not get burned out but should enjoy learning along with their children.

The basic philosophy includes "regular school" plus the humanities. Originally the humanities meant things people make—music, art, and crafts. Charlotte also believed this should include the study of folk art and the humanities of common people, as well as the "art" produced by trained practitioners.

A typical day using the Charlotte Mason approach would include one hour of structured academic time. Charlotte believed the parents should schedule as little as an hour per day in the morning to do serious academics, and then the parents and child should go out into nature and sketch. The children should have plenty of free time to pursue their own interests.

Charlotte grew up in the Victorian era, when children were not allowed to ask questions. Nor were they taken to museums to see fine art; they generally were not considered at all. This brought out her belief that children's input should be valued. Her educational philosophy grew out of this. She believed that education is an atmosphere, a way of life, a discipline.

Another basic tenet of the Mason philosophy is that parents should frequently read aloud to their children and then have the children paraphrase what they have learned. This is referred to as the narration process. Practitioners of Mason's philosophy spend a lot of time in nature, often sketching what they find, which fosters respect for nature and develops their observational skills.

Charlotte's view on literature is another important aspect. She believed children should spend their time with whole books and "living" books, meaning that the people in them are real-life characters to whom a child can make a connection. This is different from the textbook method, in which you read about a historical event but the people are not brought to life. Mason believed in the importance of exposing children to poetry, enforcing good habits, keeping nature diaries, and including dictation and spelling in their academic time. This would be an old-fashioned education at its most enjoyable.

For resources for the Charlotte Mason method, see page 510.

The Trivium Approach

The Latin word "trivium" means three roads. The trivium method focuses on a three-subject curriculum of grammar, logic, and rhetoric, which represented the lower division of the seven liberal arts taught in medieval universities. The method, which is very effective today, defines grammar, logic, and rhetoric differently than our modern definitions do. Allow us to explain further.

- *Grammar:* This means the *fundamental rules* of any science, art, or subject of study. In the trivium, it means obtaining basic information, facts, and knowledge (mechanics) when the student is in his or her elementary stage, up to approximately 12 years old.

- *Logic:* The literal meaning is the study of *reasoning and reliable inferences.* In modern English, we call this critical thinking, in which the student learns to look for truth in information, for instance, to discern untruth or manipulated fact, and to recognize how these manipulations take place.

- *Rhetoric:* One definition of this term is the study of the effective use of language. In the trivium context, this is *the act of combining and integrating the mechanics and the thinking skills into one's self, and then being able to communicate the synthesized fact to others.* Presumably, once the student has mastered this process, she or he may be able to extend the knowledge base of a topic beyond mere synthesis. A modern scientist, for instance, may integrate the mechanical knowledge and critical analysis of his field of endeavor and then follow a new path of discovery beyond.

The trivium approach has had a resurgence across the United States in private schools wishing to teach in the classical manner. Therefore, there are now many textbooks designed for classroom use. The Bluedorn family from Moline, Illinois, is one of the only connections today for homeschoolers wanting to use the trivium approach. The Bluedorns, who homeschool their five children, went through every logic, Latin, and Greek book they could and chose to offer those that are homeschool-friendly, useful for self-teaching. (See page 511 for the Bluedorns' catalog order information.) The Bluedorns also publish *Teaching the Trivium Magazine.*

For resources for the trivium approach, see page 511.

The Principle Approach

"There is a revival bubbling up in America—a healing in our land. It is a revival of America's Christian history and a desire to learn those

Biblical principles, which identify America as a Christian nation with a Christian form of government." This quote is from an article written by Rosalie Slater about the principle approach. Those who adhere to this approach believe our country was founded upon Christian principles and wish to bring back Christian leadership to our government and country.

The approach is based on the following seven Biblical principles:

1. God-given individuality
2. Christian self-government
3. Character (Biblical New Testament)
4. Conscience
5. A Christian form of government
6. Local self-government
7. A restoration of unity in government (Christian unity)

Proponents of this approach, which is very political in nature, believe that Christian leadership must be restored to our country and the world. The academics are taught from a biblical point of view with the quality of a classical education. Those outside the Christian realm could not follow the principle approach.

For resources for the principle approach, see page 511.

Unit Study Approach

Early in our homeschooling, we lived in the South and attended a small homeschooling conference at a church. The many workshops offered included one presented by a company called KONOS, a popular Christian unit study homeschool program. The workshop included a demonstration using the human ear as the topic of study. The presenter made a mock-up of an ear by strategically draping a table with a cloth and showed us how we could duplicate the inner ear for our children with basic materials found around the house.

Unit study involves taking a particular topic—such as ancient Rome—and studying it for a month or longer. During your study of Rome, you can incorporate different academics—by using Roman games, coin values, numerals, literature, history, and even Latin—to gain insight into the Roman world. You can also cook and eat Roman food; go to a museum to see Roman artwork; read history about Julius Caesar or the great orator Cicero; or read the poetry of Virgil (you get the picture!). Another unique aspect of unit study is that you can do it from an unschooling approach, by allowing your child to choose what to study. If you unit-study astronomy and your child is more interested in the planets than the constellations, you can concentrate on that aspect. Unit study is very flexible, yet effective.

If you prefer the parental approach and wanted to utilize unit study, you could create your own unit about the Romantic period (1820–1900) in European history. You could design your own time-line of Europe, showing the great achievements in art, music, and thought and study the cultural atmosphere, the attitudes of government, and the people around the Continent during that time. You could study Renoir's paintings and artistic methods for a few days and perhaps read a book about his life. Or you might listen to Beethoven's music and read biographical material about him. Or read the writings of Goethe and study the changes in the empires going on all around these great artists. While reading of them and their lives, you would learn about their food, which could lead to cooking a number of fine authentic meals from this period of excellent cuisine. Imagine a Beethovian meal of sausages, coffee, and Viennese pastry!

If you wish to use the unit study approach, you can purchase a curriculum from companies listed under "Unit Study" in the Resources section or assemble your own from library materials, used books, and anything that helps you get the "feel" for the unit you are doing.

For resources for the unit study approach, see page 512.

CHAPTER 7
The College Question

In the day-to-day operation of our newspaper, the second most frequently asked question about homeschooling (after "socialization") is "What about college?" The burning concern behind this query is parents' fear that major colleges and universities may reject the homeschooled child. This might have been the case 25 years ago, but not today. We read and hear about numerous examples and have personally met many people with college-entrance success stories. Some families find a system that works to their advantage; others mold themselves to fit the admissions process; and some fly right over it. Let us explain these three approaches to gaining entrance into college, starting with the third.

Fly over the Admissions Process

One completely legitimate way to enter a four-year college or university is to have your child take junior college courses as a high school student. Once she or he has acquired the proper number of units, it may be possible to transfer right into a four-year school as a junior. The junior college will not ask for high school transcripts because your child is technically a high school student, not seeking full entry into the junior college. This approach works quite well for many families since junior college systems in most states allow (and encourage) high school students to take courses without being formally enrolled as full-time college students. When a student transfers to a four-year

Homeschoolers Say . . .

Will my child have transcripts if I homeschool?

Yes. You can obtain an academic record of your child's schooling career in two ways. The first way is to keep records yourself and then create a transcript format document for such use (see Janelle Orsi's transcript on page 159). The other way is to enroll in an independent study program (ISP), either public or private, that maintains records and generates transcripts for you. (An independent study program is called something different in nearly every state.)

school as a junior, all required paperwork comes from the junior college; therefore, the fact that a student has been homeschooled, particularly during high school, usually does not come up.

Mold Yourself to the Admissions Process

A second path to institutions of higher learning is to keep your own transcripts, have your child take "the tests" (SAT, ACT, and/or CEB, depending on which universities she or he wants to apply to), and perform the standard application process required of all prospective college entrants. Many homeschoolers score very well in college entrance exams, and that fact alone can guarantee them a place at some schools. Other schools will also require transcripts, usually written in "educationalese." Usually it does not matter whether or not your high school work is from an accredited school.

Accreditation

Parents often worry about the high school accreditation issue. If this is a concern and you want your child to attend an accredited high school, simply enroll in one of the many nationally accredited correspondence institutions, such as The American School, Homestudy

International, or Keystone National High School. (See Resources for further information.)

When the Admissions Process Fits You

We interviewed Dr. Stephen Van Luchene for our newspaper, *The Link*. He is a faculty member and former dean of admissions at St. John's College, a highly respected private college in Santa Fe, New Mexico. Dr. Van Luchene provided us with this description of their admissions procedure: "An applicant, homeschooled or not, must demonstrate enough math and foreign language ability to undertake our program. The application itself consists of several essays the applicant must complete, describing his or her personal background, and she or he must make a case for him/herself as to ability to undertake our program . . . What we *do* want to see is that the person has done enough preliminary work to undertake our program. Personally, I think homeschooling is a great way to prepare for St. John's" (*The Link*, Vol. 2, Issue 2).

Dr. Van Luchene stated that the college also requires of all applicants—homeschooled or not—a written recommendation from an objective third party about the applicant's ability. St. John's doesn't look that closely at one's test scores, unless there is little else to examine. This unique college, which focuses on a cooperative rather than a competitive atmosphere, has a flexible attitude because they wish to attract students who are capable of completing their program, not those who put on a good "dog-and-pony show." St. John's intense but interesting classical curriculum includes teaching all students Greek and using the tutor method (as does Oxford University) to study logic, rhetoric, and so forth to aid in perfecting the thought process.

In other words, St. John's is not easy to enter or remain in. Yet homeschooled applicants fare as well as any, as they tend to have long-standing, *serious* attitudes about study and learning. Similar private, high-standard institutions report the same results—homeschoolers are accepted on an equal basis with their school-educated counterparts (who characteristically represent the upper 10 to 15

Homeschoolers Say . . .

Will my child be able to get into college?

Yes. You should keep good records, develop your own transcripts, and have your child take the college entrance exams—SAT, ACT, and CEB. You can obtain information about these tests from your statewide homeschool organization. (See state-by-state information in part 4.)

Characteristically, every major college and university accepts homeschooled students; some even seek out college-bound homeschoolers because they are typically serious about learning and do not attend college to

percent of their graduating classes), assuming their SAT scores are high and personal interviews are favorable.

In the past two years, all universities and colleges have come to accept homeschoolers, including those of the Ivy League, the Big 10, and Pac 10 and smaller state-run and private schools. Homeschooling is no longer an issue; individual ability is. Three excellent books will provide you with all the university/college information you need. *And What About College?* by Cafi Cohen and *From Homeschool to College and Work* by Alison McKee are discussed below. The third book is *Homeschooling for Excellence* by David and Micki Colfax. (Ordering information is contained in the Resources section.)

All colleges and universities have similar admissions attitudes in that they are looking for well-trained minds to educate further and recognize that homeschoolers' minds are as well trained as any.

Financial Aid

Dr. Van Luchene also mentioned that admissions and financial aid are two distinct functions at St. John's. Financial aid is based exclusively on need, so the homeschooled student, once admitted to St. John's, is on equal footing with other students regarding grants and scholarships.

party. A university in the South recently rejected a homeschooled applicant on the grounds that he hadn't attended an accredited high school (despite the fact that his homeschooling transcripts and high SAT score would be enough for Harvard!). The applicant took the school to court and won admission.

Check into the colleges to which your child wishes to apply to obtain their specific requirements. Many private colleges in the United States rely on an applicant interview as well as written recommendations to determine the student's ability to shoulder the school's workload. Homeschoolers are welcome at these institutions—provided they can show their mettle—and they do well in college.

Financial aid ground rules are nationally standardized, so they hold true for all institutions. Note: Be aware that the financial aid field is a prime one for illegitimate companies seeking to separate you from your money by "finding" you scholarship money for a "fee." A very good website (www.finaid.org), run by Mark Kantrowitz, will provide you with detailed information and links to other sites regarding legitimate scholarships and how to go about getting them. Or check with your local library for a book with the same information.

Other Considerations

Another burning question is, "How will our mostly homeschooled children fare when thrown into the college experience?" Since homeschooling fosters a collective family closeness and unity, some parents choose to have their children attend colleges close to home or even offer a homeschooled college experience through correspondence programs.

As for those who attend college far from home, we interviewed Janelle Orsi, who was homeschooled from fourth grade on, attended junior college, and is now a senior in a four-year college in Southern

California. A copy of the transcript Janelle used to gain admission to four colleges can be found on page 159.

Interview with Janelle Orsi

Janelle Orsi, who has worked for us in many capacities, is one of the most mature and composed individuals we have ever met. Janelle was 16 when she worked on ad creation for our newspaper, and she did the layout for the program of our first *Link* homeschool conference. She also worked at the conference, never losing her composure, even when facing hundreds of people who had various questions and needs. Her flexibility under pressure and adaptability to the high demands of the jobs were impressive, especially for a teenage girl.

Janelle Orsi is 19 years old, lives in southern Ohio, and is a student at Pomona College, near Los Angeles. Besides Pomona, she was accepted at Reed College and Wesleyan University and was on the waiting list at Amherst College.

Q
A

MARY LEPPERT: *Why did your mom begin homeschooling?*

JANELLE ORSI: We moved from North Carolina to California when I was 10, and the public school options just looked kind of bad. She wasn't really thinking of homeschooling as the answer to all educational problems but just didn't want to send us to school.

MARY: *Were you homeschooled in a particular type of way?*

JANELLE: It evolved. In the beginning it was more like regular school. We actually had this room called the schoolroom. Not quite with the flag, but it was close to repeating school. My mom wouldn't stand up in front and lecture at the board, but we had a daily schedule. We would start at 8:00 A.M. and sit at the desks and do this and then this. At first we had to do certain things *every single day*, then it slowly dissipated after a few years to the point where mom didn't pay much attention to anything we did. I think that if my sister and I weren't studying, then she would have been concerned. But she knew we were both pretty motivated and doing work, so she didn't have to say, "Okay, it's 8:00. Start doing your math."

MARY: *Do you think going to school up to the fourth grade gave you the tools to carry out your self-motivation?*

JANELLE: No, I think the opposite, because in school I was never doing it for any particular reason. "Why do math?" "Because all fourth-graders have to do math; that's the way life is." I had no motivation coming from myself at all. It was all about getting good grades and going home at 3:00 to forget about school. When I started homeschooling, I'd think, "Why are we doing this? We're not getting grades or report cards. What's the point?" It all seemed so pointless because there were no gold stars and all that. Well, I eventually figured out, maybe one or two years into homeschooling, that I was doing all this crazy learning stuff for myself. I was about 12 and got really into geology, and that was the major breakthrough for me. I started studying it like crazy and started to realize that I study because it's fun and worthwhile! But I've always wanted to be successful educationally.

> I eventually figured out, maybe one or two years into homeschooling, that I was doing all this crazy learning stuff for myself.

MARY: *Where do you think you got that idea of "successful educationally"?*

JANELLE: I don't know if this is an American ideal, but in our family at least, everybody has gone to college—my parents, my extended family. I think most of us are socialized by the ideal that people grow up, graduate from high school, then aspire to go to college. That's what is considered successful in this society and I got that into my brain, so I kept doing math even though sometimes I didn't want to or wasn't sure why I was doing it. Eventually I did start liking it and would do Saxon math for four hours a day and crazy things like that. That was in my "nerd" stage. I kind of finished all the books up to calculus when I was 14, then I stopped.

MARY: *What was your day like after that "school" phase?*

JANELLE: I would go through these weird motivation phases. Sometimes I'd wake up at 6:00 in the morning and do twelve lessons in math by noon and things like that. And other times it would be like, "I think I'll sleep in and stay up late and study." I was never on a fixed schedule, it was more what I felt like.

MARY: *Do you belong to a homeschooling group?*

JANELLE: Yes, my mom founded a group of about sixty families. There were just a few at first. After a couple of years it got really big and I was doing all kinds of stuff with them—drama, ice-skating, and other stuff. It was a big part of my life from the ages of 12 to 18, until I moved out of California. There were many young kids, and also a number of active teenagers—six or seven, I guess. I was particularly active because I did the newsletter and conducted the orchestra.

MARY: *You mean you were the conductor or the organizer of the orchestra?*

JANELLE: I was the organizer of it. I arranged the music and all. But I played in it—guitar, violin, piano, and flute. We didn't really have a conductor. I guess it wasn't really an orchestra, either, because it was just a lot of random instruments. But we played classical music, so . . . we called it an orchestra just to make ourselves feel good.

MARY: *When did you learn all those instruments?*

JANELLE: I'd been learning piano for a really long time, since before we were homeschooled. And then when I was 12 or 13, our homeschooling group had group guitar lessons and I really got into it, so I kept going. Then I got into playing violin and played in a community orchestra for four years. I took up flute because it was easy and because we had one. We also needed a flute player in our orchestra. I was just a little music maniac.

MARY: *It sounds like you went from being really into geology and math to music, or were you interested in all these things at the same time?*

JANELLE: I tend to go through phases of being interested in one thing for a long time. I went through a geology phase, then dropped that and went through an architecture phase. I once went through a painting phase where I did watercolor painting for an entire month. This is the beauty of being homeschooled.

MARY: *Now that you are in college, are you able to learn a lot of different things at once?*

JANELLE: That has been the main problem I've had with college. Lately I've been reading all these books about philosophy, yet this past semester I wasn't taking any philosophy courses so had no reason or time to be studying it. So, college is kind of keeping me from following this philosophy phase. I have other obligations and other classes, so that has been my biggest frustration with college. There's always a paper due the next day.

Another problem is that the fast pace and high pressure of college frequently do not allow students to slow down and enjoy what they're learning. One late night I was trying to finish a hundred pages of reading for an astronomy class for the next day, and it suddenly hit me that the reading was fascinating, yet I was not interested at all. I was just trying to memorize the information as fast as possible, and not actually enjoying it like I would if I were reading it on my own time. I realized that college was turning me into an apathetic, high-powered learning machine. One of the merits of homeschooling is that it allows people to slow down enough to take in what they are learning, to care about it, and to enjoy it by relating it to the greater spectrum of knowledge, thereby making learning relevant. That reading for my astronomy class was relevant only to the next day's class. Learning should never be that way.

> One of the merits of homeschooling is that it allows people to slow down enough to take in what they are learning, to care about it.

MARY: *What were the classes you were taking all at once?*

JANELLE: I was taking . . . I've forgotten them already . . . Advanced Spanish, Archaeoastronomy & World Cosmology, Semantics, and Colonial Latin American History. Another class Pomona has for first-year students is Critical Inquiry, which is a seminar class in which a very specific topic is studied in great depth. We're required to do a lot of writing and speaking. My class was about the history, politics, and economics of Los Angeles. That was really cool.

MARY: *Are most of the classes really interesting to you?*

JANELLE: I love my classes, but sometimes I'd be reading for them and wishing I could be studying philosophy or something that interested me more. However, I would not stop reading because I knew that I have to get good grades to get into grad school. In homeschooling I never really had to prove myself to anybody and now I'm proving myself constantly so I can get into grad school to get a Ph.D. and then teach.

MARY: *What do you want to teach?*

JANELLE: I'm not sure. My major at Pomona is a self-designed thing I'm calling Comparative Cultures and Ideologies. It's a lot like anthropology, but less about economics and politics and more about religion, mythology, and how various cultures form their worldviews. I'm taking a lot of art history classes and philosophy and religious studies. I have a general interest in culture, religion, and art. I want to teach something along those lines, maybe anthropology or art history.

MARY: *So what are you most interested in now? Anthropology or geology?*

JANELLE: Geology I dropped when I was about 14. That phase is long gone. And I wouldn't say anthropology just because I'm in such a philosophical mode right now. I keep thinking, "Maybe I should major in philosophy. No, I shouldn't do that." But I am interested in the humanities in general—art history, politics, and religion—and how all the topics relate because I don't like to isolate the topics too much. So I'm interested in anthropology, but also art history, politics, and religion, and how all of these topics are related.

MARY: *Are you a happier person when you follow your own drives rather than going after "success"?*

JANELLE: Definitely. When I was homeschooling, when I was doing it all for myself, I was much more motivated, much more passionate about everything I did. I didn't consider studying grueling work that I had to do because it was due the next day. It was pure enjoyment, so I was really motivated. I put a lot of pressure on myself, too, because I wanted to be really well educated. I wasn't just learning aimlessly and wandering around. I had some general educational goals that had nothing to do with getting into college. Now I have this extra weight on my shoulders that I *have* to get into a good grad school. That has replaced some other motivations I had.

MARY: *Did it replace your natural desire to learn and just enjoy things?*

JANELLE: Yes. As much as I try, I keep telling myself, "Janelle, you're doing this for yourself; you shouldn't write this paper just because it's for the grade." But if I do it all just for myself, I'll flunk out of college and never get into grad school.

MARY: *And would you consider yourself a loser if you did that?*

JANELLE: I don't think so. Well, one night I was writing an essay for my archaeoastronomy class that was due the next day. It got really elaborate and I was getting so excited about it, but I also had another essay due the next day, and a midterm. I decided I wasn't going to study for the midterm or write the other essay; I was just going to work on this astronomy essay because I wanted to do well on it. So I spent all night writing it and was really happy when I turned the essay in. But later it occurred to me that I just got

> When I was homeschooling, when I was doing it all for myself, I was much more motivated, much more passionate about everything I did.

an F on the one paper I didn't turn in and I did just okay on the midterm because I hadn't studied. I decided to do the "homeschooling thing" by following my interest but then was mad at myself because I had to make up for the work I didn't do.

MARY: *Will that affect your grade point average?*

JANELLE: Yes. I got straight A's my first semester, but that's just because I would drop things I was interested in and study something I didn't want to study.

MARY: *If you study subjects and write papers for "non-homeschooling" reasons over the next few years, do you think it will change you as a person?*

JANELLE: This is kind of a quandary of mine. I keep telling myself, "I'm not going to change. I'm still going to love learning just for the sake of it. I'm not going to be poisoned by the higher educational world." My goal is to spend the rest of my life in higher education—to get my Ph.D. and to teach because I think I would really love teaching.

MARY: *But you don't love the system?*

JANELLE: That's the problem I've been trying to work out. On one hand, I really love the college environment—being around so many people that learn, lectures and events and musical performances. Pomona is such a learning world. I've fallen in love with that aspect. It would be so nice to be at a university or college and be in this environment.

MARY: *So if you could find a forum for learning somewhere else in life, would you be as attracted to an institutional setting?*

JANELLE: I'm going to get Bill Gates to give me a billion dollars so I can create a private museum/university that people go to for the sole purpose of learning; it will not be for grades or diplomas. It would be my learning Utopia, what I wish all universities were like. But in the society we live in now, people have to prove themselves in order to succeed. Fixing that is just overthrowing the entire system of the world.

MARY: *How would you feel if you were a Ph.D. at a prestigious university, forced to teach things a certain way and follow a curriculum that stopped students from going further with their natural curiosity?*

JANELLE: This is a really hard one. If I didn't have enough freedom to design a curriculum, I'd probably try to get out of it. Maybe I'm being too optimistic. Maybe I won't find a position that will give me that much freedom. That's why I want to start my own with that billion dollars from Bill Gates.

MARY: *Why do you want to teach?*

JANELLE: I just love learning and love watching other people learn. It's so great to see someone else take the same interest that I took in something. I love sharing what I've learned with others. I hope I find people in academia who learn just for the sake of learning.

MARY: *Tell me about your study of Spanish.*

JANELLE: I started two and a half years ago at community college because of the language requirement. I wasn't really interested in learning Spanish at that point, but now I am minoring in Spanish because I love it so much. I'm going to Spain in the spring, to the University of Salamanca.

MARY: *So you went to community college before you attended Pomona?*

JANELLE: I went to community college for four years, starting when I was 14. To get in I just had to show them my high school transcript. There were no entrance exams, just placement exams. In California, it isn't hard to get in, though it varies from school to school. My high school transcript came from my own R-4 (that's the way families declare themselves a private school in California). I just typed it up on my computer, like, "Hmm, yes, I studied geology."

MARY: *When you took the proficiency test, was it pretty easy?*

JANELLE: Yes. Actually, I think it has gotten harder since I took it, but then it was no big deal. When I first enrolled in community college, I was a concurrently enrolled high school student, because my diploma did not become valid until I turned 16. When I turned 16, I enrolled in community college as a high school student and went there for four years.

MARY: *Then you used those credits to transfer to the four-year college?*

JANELLE: Yes. When I first applied, I had no intent of transferring those credits. I viewed all my community college work as high school work and did not plan to apply it toward a bachelor's degree. But then Pomona College informed me that they would not take a freshman with so many credits, so I'm suddenly a junior in college.

MARY: *What did they say about your being a homeschooler?*

JANELLE: They looked at my high school record, which was mainly a five-page overview of everything I learned during my high school years, what books I'd used, and how I'd gone about studying these subjects. I wrote that up in essay format but listed all the subjects and described them in detail. They paid a lot of attention to that. And they also looked at my SAT scores. So they looked at both the college and the homeschool work. [See Janelle's Academic Summary, reproduced in its entirety, at the conclusion of this interview.]

MARY: *Did you take the SAT before or after your four years at community college?*

JANELLE: I took it during. They didn't require SAT scores for community college.

MARY: *How did you do on the SAT?*

JANELLE: I got 1450, and 1600 is the top so I was very happy with it. I studied a lot, too.

MARY: *When you are in school every day, where do you think you fit?*

JANELLE: Pomona is a very good school, so the students there are generally well educated and well prepared. However, at times I've sensed that I'm ahead, mainly because I studied nontypical subject areas during my "high school" years—sociology or anthropology, for instance. I've also read independently in subjects such as literary theory and cultural studies that many students do not explore until they reach college. I've watched some freshmen struggle to apply more complex and abstract ideas to their studies, while I had the opportunity to study and use these ideas earlier. Almost all traditionally educated students followed a similar path of study: Four years of high school math, one year of biology, one year of chemistry, and so on. My education was completely different, and I had more opportunity to dabble in the subjects that high schools don't teach; this has worked to my advantage now that I'm in college.

> I've sensed that I'm ahead, mainly because I studied nontypical subject areas during my "high school" years—sociology or anthropology, for instance.

MARY: *Are the majority of kids in the dorm basically like you? Or do they do things differently from your lifestyle as a homeschooler?*

JANELLE: They do things differently. I don't know if it's as much homeschooling as personal preference. Some of these students have just gone crazy at college, done the drug thing and alcohol and parties. I've stayed out of that—a lot of people have. Socially, I wouldn't say there's a big difference. I worried that it would be kind of strange to be suddenly thrown in with people my own age. It was never like that before. There were so many adults in community college, and I was constantly around people of different ages playing in the orchestra and being in homeschool groups. But then I got there and felt really at home—not more so than in a multi-age environment, but it wasn't as strange as I thought it would be.

Academic Summary for

Janelle Elizabeth Orsi
SSN: [inserted here]
DOB: [inserted here]
Address: [inserted here]
Phone: [inserted] E-mail: [inserted]

Since I have been nontraditionally educated, it is necessary to describe my coursework in more detail than is usually required of an applicant. I ask your patience with the length of this résumé. Below is a brief sketch of how I pursued academic study in each discipline as well as descriptions of my extracurricular activities:

Independent Study in Homeschool

Mathematics: Textbooks: *Algebra 1/2, Algebra 1, Algebra 2,* and *Advanced Mathematics* by John Saxon, covering high school algebra, geometry, trigonometry, and pre-calculus. Calculus will be studied during the second half of my senior year.

English: Coached by my mother, who is a professional writer, I've practiced writing reports and essays. I've studied basic concepts of grammar and English from various textbooks and written for publications, including *The Coastside HomeScholar* (of which I was editor for three years), *Homefires* (an education magazine for which I wrote a bimonthly astronomy column for two years), *Circa* (a history publication), and *California Homeschool News.* I've just completed a second-semester college-level course called Composition, Literature, and Critical Thinking, in which I learned various critical approaches to poetry, short stories, novels, and drama. I've read widely, sampling of the classics and modern fiction, with a particular enjoyment of science fiction.

Linguistics: Learning languages has become a hobby of mine; I study languages partially out of a desire to travel and learn about other cultures, but also out of an interest in anthropological linguistics. I have studied the following languages:

Latin: Two years of Latin. Primary text: *Artes Latinae,* books 1 and 2, by Waldo Sweet.

Spanish: I've studied Spanish independently as well as taken three semesters at Skyline College. In the past eight months, I have taken up the study of Spanish and Latin American Literature, sampling authors such as Garcilaso de la Vega, Gabriel García Márquez, Miguel de Unamuno, Carlos Fuentes, Rigoberta Menchú, and others.

Other Languages: I completed a summer course in conversational Japanese and continue to study the language independently. I have also been studying the Yucatec and Quiché dialects of the modern Maya of Guatemala and Mexico.

Continues . . .

. . . Continued

American History and Social Studies: A college-level book, *The Pursuit of Liberty,* served as my main text, as well as numerous other sources. I did an extra study of the Civil War, which included a family trip to Gettysburg, PA, and Washington, DC. I also took an American Politics course at Skyline College.

World History: Out of a sincere interest in world history, I've read numerous historical treatises, travel accounts, historical novels, and books about anthropology and social science, from which I've gained my knowledge of world history. I've taken two semesters of Western Civilization at Skyline College. I've been studying current international issues, such as the Israeli/Palestinian conflict and issues in Cambodia, Guatemala, and Chiapas, Mexico.

I've been particularly interested in pre-Columbian Meso-American history and have read many books about it. During the summer of '96, I traveled to Belize and spent two weeks on a post-classic Mayan excavation with a group from Earthwatch. I am currently studying Asian art, history, and ideas.

Economics: Textbooks: *Our Economy: How It Works,* by Elmer Clawson (high school–level economics textbook); *Whatever Happened to Penny Candy?* by Richard Maybury; *The Stock Market Explained for Young Investors,* by Clayton Fisher; *Understanding Today's Economics,* by Robert Crane. I also followed the stock market via the Internet and set up my own technology stock index, which I recorded daily with a spreadsheet software program.

Geography: Primary text: *The Real World,* by Bruce Marshall, and additional related reading.

Computers: I have acquired competency in the following: MS-Word (word processing), PageMaker (publishing), Photoshop (graphics), Excel (spreadsheets), Access (databases), MIDI (digital music), HTML (web programming).

Photography: I set up a darkroom at home with the help of my dad and learned how to develop black-and-white film. From there I progressed into astrophotography and did occasional experimentation with black-and-white infrared and color infrared film. I've also done digital photography with the aid of a digital camera plus color scanner, which I use in computer graphic design.

Art History and Appreciation: I studied from a high school–level book on Western painting and read from various other sources, such as *More Than You See: A Guide to Art* by Fredrick Horowitz. This past fall semester, I audited an Asian art class at Skyline College and I'm working on writing a comparative study of Asian garden design. I also took a class in pre-Columbian art of the Americas at Skyline College.

Architecture: Because architecture is an interest of mine, I've read extensively, studying from more than 35 books on both engineering and style. I learned some basics of drafting and designed experimental houses, using the computer software Floorplan Plus as an aid in design.

Astronomy: For several years this was my passion. I read numerous books about astronomy and planetary science and kept up with astronomical journals and research for three years. I authored a bimonthly astronomy column for *Homefires* magazine for two years (600 subscribers) and was very active in online astronomy clubs.

I spent many nights stargazing with my 3.5-inch telescope and made several trips to the Chabot College and Foothill College observatories. I did much experimentation in astrophotography with my telescope and developed many of my photos at home.

Chemistry: I audited a semester of college-level general chemistry at Skyline College and studied independently, ultimately earning 720 on the Chemistry SAT II.

Biology: I took a semester of college-level biology at Cañada College (including lab) and read independently on biotechnology, including its applications in nanotechnology.

Geology: Starting at age 12, I collected rocks, minerals, and fossils, eventually amassing a collection of 300+ identified specimens. I studied mineralogy, plate tectonics, and volcanology and learned to recognize geological features of the San Mateo County coast. I taught a class about mineralogy to a group of homeschooled children ages 7–10.

Environmental Science: Primary textbooks: *Endangered Environments*, by Anna Maria Caldara, *Living in the Environment: Principles, Connections, and Solutions*, by Tyler Miller (Wadsworth, Inc, college textbook).

Psychology: Primary textbook: *Introduction to Psychology*, Kalat (Brooks/Cole college textbook). I also took an introductory course through College of San Mateo.

Physical Education: Hiking, mountain biking, and ice-skating.

Extracurricular Activities

Drama: In the past few years I've acted in four plays produced by Coastside Home-Scholars, including *Kangaroo Court, Red Riding Hood Goes '90s, A Christmas Carol,* and *Who Killed Aunt Edna?*, a comedy/mystery that I co-wrote and co-directed. *Who Killed Aunt Edna?* featured nine actors, ages 12–17, and was performed in three locations in the San Francisco Bay Area for other homeschooling groups.

Music: I consider myself a serious student of music. Since age 14, I have been playing violin in the Coastside Community Orchestra, which has 60 members and does two or three concerts per year. I have also played in string and other small ensembles, including a string quartet. A couple of years ago I organized a small orchestra of 13

Continues . . .

. . . Continued

homeschooled kids, which performed four times for homeschooled audiences. I directed and arranged the music for this orchestra.

For four years I have been taking guitar lessons and have studied various forms, including classical, Spanish, Brazilian, Cuban, and Hawaiian. I've been playing piano for nine years but have been self-taught for the past six. I have also been self-taught on Western classical flute and Andean pan-pipes.

I've studied music theory with my guitar teacher and done some composition. Ethnomusicology has been an interest of mine, and I took a world music course at Skyline College. I've read about and listened to music of South America, India, Indonesia, Japan, Africa, Mexico, and Polynesia.

Painting and Drawing: I became interested in painting two years ago, particularly watercolors. I also experimented with pastel and acrylic and took a drawing class at Skyline College. I've produced much of the graphic art that has been used in *The Coastside Homescholar* newsletter. My drawings have also been published in *California Homeschool News* and *Notes*, the newsletter for the Coastside Community Orchestra.

Writing, Publishing, and Editing

The Coastside HomeScholars Newsletter: For almost three years I was the editor of the newsletter for a homeschooling group that consists of approximately 60 families located just south of San Francisco. The newsletter featured news, stories, poetry, drawings, essays, reports, and reviews by homeschooling kids and parents. The newsletter ranged in size each month from 8 to 16 pages.

Coastside Community Orchestra Newsletter: For six months I published *Notes*, the monthly newsletter for the Coastside Community Orchestra, which consisted of news and articles written by various orchestra members. The newsletter was usually six to eight pages long. I also designed many of the posters and flyers advertising our concerts and activities.

Column for *Homefires* Magazine: For two years I wrote a bimonthly astronomy column for *Homefires* magazine, which reaches over 600 California homeschool families. I wrote about astronomical events, research and exploration, astrophotography, telescope buying, and astronomy books and talked about black holes, galaxies, planets, and other astronomical objects.

California Homeschool Network Homepage: Two years ago I created the web page for the California Homeschool Network (http://www.comenius.org/chn). The page, which has been taken over by my sister, is considered one of the best resources on homeschooling and recently received favorable mention in *Family PC*, a national magazine.

Mayan Archaeological Dig: During August of 1996, I spent two weeks on a post-classic Mayan excavation near Orange Walk Town, Belize. Prior to the dig, I read many books about Meso-American civilization and did research at the Stanford University library into the particular area that I would be studying in Belize. I also designed and continue to manage the official website for the project (http://www.comenius.org/laguna_de_on).

Volunteer Work and Community Service: For the past six years I have done volunteer work of various sorts for the Half Moon Bay Friends of the Library, helping to set up and work the book sales and helping with membership recruitment. I've created websites for various organizations, including California Homeschool Network (http://www.comenius.org/chn), Laguna de On Archaeological Project (http://www.comenius.org/laguna_de_on), and Coastside Working Women, a photographic essay on women in their various work situations (http://www.canopyweb.com/ww). I designed flyers and other forms of desktop publishing for the Coastside Community Orchestra, Coastside HomeScholars, and others. I've also done odd jobs (database development and concert go-fer) for the San Francisco-based Omni Foundation for the Performing Arts. During the fall 1997 semester, I helped in fundraising activities for Skyline College Environmental Club.

Employment: Since June, I have been working for Stanly Insurance Brokerage in San Francisco, doing market research, advertisement design, and accounting and designing a database to manage client information. I will continue working on advertisement for this company while I'm living in Ohio. I've also worked for a national homeschooling newspaper called *The Link*, doing advertisement design and page layouts. Over the past few years I have been hired to do various computer jobs, including database work, MIDI and digital music–related jobs, desktop publishing, web-page design, and computer graphics. Additionally, Bay Area breeders of champion Abyssinian show cats employed me for three years to assist with the care of their cats.

CHAPTER 8

Frequently Asked Questions About Homeschooling

As homeschooling parents and disseminators of information about homeschooling, we are constantly asked questions by parents considering homeschooling their children, or by the just plain curious. Here we offer our responses to some of the questions that come up most frequently. You'll find more questions and answers in the sidebars of the previous seven chapters.

Q *What about socialization?*

A Because this is the *most* frequently asked question, we have placed it first. Parents need to consider that in the average school day of 6 hours, the child spends approximately 1½ hours "socializing"—two 15-minute recesses and 1 hour at lunch. The rest of the time the child usually sits at his desk, separated from the other children by the invisible wall of "good behavior." Plus, as the school atmosphere becomes increasingly restricted and dangerous, the socialization that occurs is not particularly "social."

Homeschooling parents, on the other hand, often find their children have too much socialization—weekly park days, skate days, and field trips. Besides planned events, children who live in urban or suburban areas come in contact with people all day long. Most neighborhoods, which is where a child's playmates usually come from (and always have), include children of varying ages, whether homeschooled or conventionally schooled (that is, attending public or private school). Families in rural areas have to take steps to ensure that their children—whether homeschooled or not—come in contact with others on a regular basis. The fact is, children taught at home have more time to socialize freely without being told what to play, when to play, and where to play. If organic, pure socialization is to take place, it is in the homeschool setting.

Q *What about critical or skeptical family members?*

A Usually, a skeptical family member is concerned about academic and socialization issues. (People who don't live with your children may not see the positive spiritual and psychological changes they go through once they are no longer in an age- or peer-dependent environment.) Try inviting the skeptic to park days or field trips to let them see what your daily life is like.

This brings to mind Michael's mother, who was very skeptical when she first heard our plans to homeschool. Before our son reached the age of six, she didn't believe we wouldn't send him to school. When school enrollment time came and went, and we didn't change our plan, she was worried and decided to pay for our first-grade boxed curriculum. She also came out to Los Angeles from Chicago and accompanied us on our routine the first week of her visit.

We remember the week distinctly: Monday, a field trip to the J. Paul Getty Art Museum; Tuesday, homeschool gymnastics class (with about 15 families); Wednesday, Yamaha Music School (with 10 other children who weren't homeschoolers); Thursday, park day (with 20 to 40 other homeschooled children, playing for approximately four hours); Friday, chorus at the Yamaha School (with 25 non-homeschooled children). Our son was occupied with trips to the library, doing his curriculum in the early mornings, and listening to Michael read to all of us in the evenings. She quickly realized that not only was her grandson not socially deprived, but he had a culturally and academically rich life, filled with music, chorus, gymnastics—training he would not receive in a school setting. After her visit, we heard from relatives that Michael's mother spoke with much pride about what a great life Lennon had!

Q *What if all my child's friends are schooled and she feels "different"?*

A Had you asked us this question five years ago, we would have answered differently. We probably would have said to do little things like buy a lunch pail and pencil and paper pads at the beginning of each school year and try to incorporate more "school-type" things into your lives. We would not have said

> Our son has taught us that we should be proud to be homeschoolers.

with the pride we now have, how fortunate and privileged he is to be homeschooled! We were squeamish in the early years and sometimes felt that we had to hide. Over these years, our son has taught us that we should be proud to be homeschoolers, that we should feel different because we are. We view his sense of pride in being homeschooled as righteous and healthy. In today's society, there is constant talk about building self-esteem in children. If you knew that homeschooling your child would give her a tremendous sense of self-esteem—far beyond what she would gain in a school—would you do it? Foster the difference and be proud of it!

Q *How much does homeschooling cost?*

A Homeschooling can cost from $0 to $2,500 per year. Starting at $0, a family can create their entire curriculum with materials available at the local library. The advent of the Internet also makes it possible to homeschool for only the cost of your online service. (Online schools, however, *do* charge a fee.) Once again, cost depends on your philosophy. If you use a boxed curriculum, you can purchase an excellent one for as little as $300 per year, with an optional correspondence-teacher review service available for approximately another $200 to $500. Or you can spend as much as $2,500 per year in the boxed-curriculum category. This cost, in most cases, would include an advisory teaching service, networking, private "networked" park days available only to those enrolled in the school, field trips, resource libraries, and many other extracurricular services, which amount to a private-school-at-home. Resourceful families purchase materials at bookstores, garage sales, curriculum fairs, homeschool conferences—virtually anywhere.

Q *What if my child goes back to school? Will the school accept him?*

A Children who are U.S. citizens cannot be denied public education unless they have been legally expelled or some other extenuating circumstance exists. Therefore, the question really should be: "What is the easiest way to get my child back into school after he or she has been homeschooled?" The answer depends on which state you live in. If you declare yourself a private school, then keeping good records of daily activities and the subjects studied is crucial should you eventually decide to enroll your child in school. If you enroll in an independent study program (ISP), either private or through a public school, you will have no problems transferring back into the system. (In some states, an ISP is called a "church school.") Call your state's parent-run state organization (see part 4) for in-depth information.

> Some teenagers seem relieved to be taken out of a peer-dependent environment.

Q *What if my child does not want to leave his school friends?*

A This can be a tough situation. That question comes up often when we talk with parents who choose to homeschool because of the negative peer pressure involved in school. We have seen repeatedly that most children, when removed from a negative situation, feel a sense of relief, as if the parents rescued them from something they were attracted to but were uncomfortable with. After-school hours and weekends allow plenty of time for children to continue seeing school friends who are a positive influence. Homeschooling doesn't mean you are going to another planet! You will still live in your house, in your neighborhood, with the same phone number; and your child's friends will know that.

Q *How will I know if a homeschool group is right for me?*

A Fitting into a homeschool group is much like the dynamics between any human beings. You may know two completely opposite people who get along great. Or you may know of people with similar personalities and interests who don't care for each other's company. You'll have to visit a homeschooling group to find out if you feel comfortable. For instance, I have met born-again Christian mothers who attend secular groups that feel just right. I have also met mothers who are not religious yet attend Christian groups because they like the structure and the organization such groups tend to have. Try many different groups, and then stick with the one that feels best for you, or join more than one!

Q *My teenager wants to be homeschooled, but my husband and I both work. Is this a good idea?*

A This depends on your teenager and your relationship with him or her. Some teenagers seem relieved to be taken out of a peer-dependent environment and are pleased to do schoolwork while mom and dad are away in order to keep this latitude. Other teenagers fare better working a part-time job during the day and doing their academic work in the evening and on weekends. Teenagers are at a perfect age to benefit from an apprentice situation or mentoring relationship. We know of one teenager who works 25 hours a week in a pet store and plans on becoming a veterinarian. Another works part time at a newspaper office, typesetting and learning about newspapers.

Q *What will the neighbors think?*

A Your child is the best example of the fruits of homeschooling. However, we admit that even we have sometimes felt uneasy when our son plays basketball in front of our house at 10:00 on a Monday morning, when all of the other kids have gone to school. What will the very active 85-year-old man across the street think?—that we are neglecting our son? But after the voice of fear whispers in my ear, my "brave self" quickly remembers my true opinion: Homeschoolers no longer need to be afraid of recrimination from those with incorrect and preconceived notions. We can express our pride in being home-schoolers and confidence in the certainty of our decision.

Q *Should I let my children play outside while regular school is in session?*

A Since homeschooling is legal in every state and province, there's no reason to fear having your child playing on your block. If your child wants to play at the park and is under adult supervision, most communities will not bother him or her. Get to know your community's attitude toward homeschoolers and, if it is unfavorable, work to change it. Some California communities have "curfew laws" that are being successfully challenged in the courts when they are not enforced with good faith and common sense by police departments or truancy-control agencies. Be open and honest about home-schooling, and help local officials be aware of homeschooling and its benefits to your community.

> Your child is the best example of the fruits of homeschooling.

Q *Should I follow the regular school year?*

A This depends first on your state laws and second on your lifestyle. Following the school year is a necessity when your state requires teaching parents to keep and submit very accurate attendance records. A more flexible schedule is realistic in states that do not require this. Children whose parents are writers or actors or engaged in seasonal occupations may follow an academic calendar that co-incides with the parents' work schedules rather than the school-year calendar. Further, many parents who use a scheduled curriculum enjoy the simplicity of the school year: You teach 180 days per year and that's that. Of course, since homeschooling is much more aca-demically active than conventional schooling, your student will cover more than one grade in 180 days, which is fine. Many home-schoolers attend college at 15 or 16!

Q *Is it harder to teach high school than the elementary grades?*

A Most people who homeschool high schoolers don't find teaching them a problem. Usually, study habits are already set up; the child is accustomed to completing a certain amount of "work." Also, students who have been in school usually enjoy finishing their schoolwork early, leaving enough time to work a part-time job, become an apprentice, practice a sport, or take college classes.

Parents of teenagers who have never been in school might have to be more involved in finding out how to teach algebra, chemistry, or other "difficult" subjects. Many families in both categories solve this problem by pooling resources and hiring a tutor to instruct a small group (often 5 to 10 children) in a particular subject once or twice a week. Usually, this type of arrangement is conducive to a positive learning experience: The children know why they are there and want to be there, so it works out well for all. With homeschooling becoming more popular each year, "help" is available to any family who wants it.

Q *What if I can't stand to be with my kids all day?*

A People don't ask this question often, but when they do, we are always shocked and saddened. We believe parents who cannot stand to be with their children don't really know them. And if they don't like their children, they are probably seeing a child who isn't "real" but is a creation of marketing, school peer pressure, fear, low self-esteem, and alienation. When your child is home with you, person-to-person, these external forces can—and do—fall away over time.

Children are people in formation (still under "construction") and should be protected from what many adults today call "real" life—which translates into exposure to social horrors (news coverage of mass deaths, heinous crime descriptions, desensitization to violence) and personal "stylistic" degradation, such as pierced body parts, tattoos, and moshing (slam dancing), that would have made a sailor blush 50 years ago. Our American society has duped itself into thinking that children are short adults with adult sensibilities—mature enough to make intelligent decisions about all they do and believe. A few minutes of close observation of an 11-year-old or even a 15-year-old discloses that this "short adult" assumption is faulty.

Children are capable of making some decisions, but they have to be guided and steered in many others. We all learn progressively how to navigate life—to make choices, determine what we believe and who we are. To become skilled at such decision making takes years. John Taylor Gatto, in his book *Dumbing Us Down*, comments that today's public school children never get the time alone required to build a personality but instead are constantly moved along the conveyor belt or bombarded with media stimuli. Homeschooling provides such private time. So it is no surprise that once your child has an opportunity to return to his or her appropriate age and stop being a reflection of the external forces, you are likely to find a pretty likeable person.

Q *Am I abandoning the system by homeschooling?*

A This depends on what you think your duty is to "the system." We are believers in the old adage "Charity begins at home." Our allegiance and support are more with our *son* than to a mass system developed by special interests in the mid-1850s to educate the children of the very poor (public school). When Mary attended her first homeschooling meeting, someone stood up and said, "Aren't we abandoning society by leaving the public system and homeschooling our children?" A mother in the audience explained that at first she had felt that, by not sending her five children to school, she was withholding her contribution to society. But she couldn't justify sending these fine people into a system that advocated so many things she was against. She remedied this by volunteering two days per month at a local elementary school—a wonderful answer for

> Most people who homeschool high schoolers don't find teaching them a problem.

anyone who feels the need to help the system. (And don't forget—you still pay taxes that fund the system!)

Q *Are there African Americans who homeschool?*

A Yes. Many African-American families are turning to homeschooling to ensure excellence in the education their children receive. An African-American homeschooling mom giving a workshop at a conference a few years ago was asked why so few African-American families homeschool. She stated that since the group fought so long and hard to be included in the full public school system, they were not in a hurry to leave it. The African-American homeschooling community is growing quickly as they, along with people of other ethnicities, choose homeschooling as a means of retaining their culture.

Q *Should I get involved with the independent study program (ISP) with a public school?*

A People who begin homeschooling often feel they need the warm hand of a certified teacher on their shoulder, guiding them along until they get the hang of doing it themselves. That is exactly what the public ISP appears to do. In most states, ISPs use the same curriculum that children at the local public school would use. If you choose such a program, you are assigned an ISP counselor, a certified teacher for the public school system who usually keeps track of between 100 and 300 families like yours. You are given the curriculum to follow and must report to the counselor weekly, bimonthly, or monthly. Most families find, after two or three months, that they *love* the freedom of homeschooling and want to be their own drivers.

Q *I've never been a bookish person and did not like school. How can I possibly teach my children?*

A We repeatedly hear that homeschooling has afforded many parents the opportunity to educate or re-educate themselves in certain subjects. For example, Mary wasn't interested in early history or word roots and grammar because of the negative feeling she carried over from school. But upon reading about these to our son, she found herself becoming more interested as time went on. She also never considered herself artistic (in school she couldn't sketch an apple even if she wanted to!). When our son was about seven, we obtained the Usborne How to Draw art series, which gives you the exact layout of different objects. Mary was so amazed at how well her rockets, spaceships, and buildings came out that she has actually considered taking drawing classes! Use homeschooling as an opportunity to learn new things and add dimension to your life!

Q *Homeschoolers seem to occupy the far left or the religious right, whereas I am somewhere in the middle. Where or how do I fit into all of this?*

A You are right on point. Possibly your perception of the political orientation of homeschoolers is left over from an earlier era. In the '70s (and even earlier), most homeschoolers were of a religious persuasion or were leftist radicals who wanted to "drop out" of society. Since the late '80s, however, homeschooling has become increasingly mainstream, attracting more and more professional or upper-income parents (along with lower- and middle-income families) opting to teach their own children at home—especially as they approach high school age.

Q *We live on two incomes now. How could we ever survive on one income?*

A The best answer is to be creative! It also helps to realize that when one parent chooses to leave a job, they also leave behind hidden expenses: dry-cleaning bills, lunches out, even something as financially trivial as the cost of a tube of mascara! In addition, having one person stay at home allows families to have more at-home meals, maybe even bread and pizza dough made from scratch, which can be quite economical.

One thing Mary did for many years before we started *The Link* was to cook for families who were too busy to cook for themselves and could afford to have home-cooked meals delivered. Our son was right with her from the time he was three, helping her cook, pack, and deliver the food. Parents can do many, many things besides cooking for extra money and have their children help them. All can be tied into "education."

Many people who need to supplement a single income become small-time entrepreneurs. These small businesses often grow into the family's main source of income, sometimes making them more financially sound than ever. I believe this happens because, first, we drop the desire to look "outside" for educational sustenance, and second, as a natural progression, we stop looking outside for other things as well. Subsequently, this flows into the rest of our lives, making us more like the American colonials and pioneers—self-sustaining, independent families.

Q *Don't teachers know something about "teaching" that we as parents should know to teach our own?*

A No. As mentioned above, a school teacher's job is to present the curriculum chosen by the school administration to 25 or 40 children in a classroom setting, moving them through the school year on time. A homeschooling parent's job is very different. You will be working with your child in a setting you choose and recognize to be what is right for him or her. You can adjust your focus at any time to meet the changing needs of your student and your family. You can work more during one part of the year, less

> Use homeschooling as an opportunity to learn new things and add dimension to your life!

during another (provided your state doesn't require school-year-strict attendance records). You can spend more time on a "weak" academic topic and less time on a "strong" one. The list of reasons we are most qualified to teach our own is long and different for each family.

Q *If I have three children I want to homeschool, do I have to teach three levels of math, science, and English each day?*

A Probably not. One great thing about having two or more children in a homeschooling setting is that the younger ones want to keep up with the older ones. There is less total work when children are fairly close rather than far apart in age. Some families report that their children set up a natural, healthy competition among themselves. In the case of English, the younger child may have to catch up to be on a par with the older but will do that on his or her own. A few subjects may require individual, separate teaching; but that is probably the exception rather than the rule.

Q *When will my child ever use calculus, trigonometry, algebra, or geometry?*

A For two years we've been trying to find a mathematician to write a column for *The Link*. Parents often ask us whether we think the higher math subjects are valuable. Do my children really need algebra, other than to get into college? The mathematicians we asked to write a column have declined, saying they can't offer a valuable use except for students meeting college entrance requirements or pursuing degrees in math-heavy subjects such as architecture, engineering, or computer programming. It's not necessary for families homeschooling children in the early teen years to stress out about the higher math subjects.

Q *I enjoyed school activities like the prom and the science fair. Aren't we denying our children these things if we homeschool them?*

A Homeschoolers tend to be very innovative. Most homeschool groups have science fairs and social activities, and some even have graduations for their students. The beauty of something so grassroots is that you can

make it anything you want it to be. Parents whose children are in the public school system often comment that they like a particular activity—a dance or what-have-you—but they don't like the music being played. In homeschooling, we can create these activities for our children in an environment that is in harmony with our beliefs and values. I don't want to mislead anyone that you can have these things for your children without putting in work and effort. It takes all families in a group to contribute to the grand scheme. If you are not the doer type, you can always join an ISP, and most of the planning and prep could be done for you. Such groups usually cost $160 to $800 per year and will advise you of the services they provide when you sign up. Be sure to ask, however; don't assume.

Q *Are we losing a sense of community when we remove our children from school?*

A No. You are building a true sense of community when you decide to homeschool *if* you also choose to meet with other homeschooling families and participate in the field trips, park days or play days, and any special programs they do. Through programs like Goals 2000, the government is trying to make public schools into synthetic "village centers," so to speak. We think individual parents and families doing it themselves is better. If you are used to having community activity planning done for you, you may have an adjustment to make. It is not difficult, however; most homeschoolers have phones, many are on the Internet, and most have cars. You can communicate with them as easily as with someone in the PTA, Boy Scouts, or other community organization. It all comes down to this: *You* make the community—not homeschooling.

Q *What about homeschooling an only child?*

A As parents of an only child, we can answer, "Yes, it can be done very successfully." We won't say it is easy; in fact, we believe it's harder to homeschool an only child. (Most of our homeschooling friends have two to eight children.) Much depends on the type of child as well. If the child is incredibly social, it takes extra effort to plan a social life in which the child feels he or she interacts enough with other children. At least one parent must be the social type to plan a social life for the homeschooled child. Most homeschooling functions are not "drop-off" activities. If you are the parent caring for the child, you might find yourself spending hours on end with other homeschooling parents (mostly mothers). If you are not comfortable with this much socializing, it could be a problem for you.

From the academic standpoint, homeschooling an only child can be loads of fun. It is much easier to jump into the car and take off to the desert to see the wildflowers with one than with five or six children. One is also cheaper; you may be able to afford lessons that a large family might not be able to afford.

Another advantage to homeschooling one child is the closeness that develops between the parents and the child. For us, spending day in and day out with our son gives us hours to talk and get to know each other well. Mary has taken him along on many jobs to which she would not be able to take two or three children. She's even attended college classes with him right alongside her.

Q *Will my child have a high school diploma?*

A Depending on your state's laws, probably yes—if you choose to obtain one. But check first. Generally speaking, your child can acquire a GED diploma through your state, or you, as the principal of your own certified, private school (if you establish one), can create your own high school diploma. You may also use a nationally recognized, certified correspondence school to obtain a diploma. Check with the parent-run organization in your state (listed in part 4) to find out firsthand your state's requirements and guidelines.

Q *How will I know if my child is "where he should be" in various subjects?*

A Our son is a member of a choir comprising some homeschooled kids and (a majority of) school kids. This year he came home asking, "What grade am I in?" He said that's the first thing the school kids in choir ask. Well, the last boxed curriculum we did was fourth grade; that was three years ago and he is now 11. After fourth grade we created our curriculum using our own parental approach. We worried that his self-image would be damaged because he felt that he was not "where he should be." He seemed bothered by this because he kept saying that maybe we should "do grades." We wanted him to realize that we were living a different life than most families in the chorus.

Mary began thinking about "grades" and, to sort out our concerns about them, took out an old textbook from her first college

English class. It was the type with short stories that measures comprehension at the end of each selection. She had Lennon read a story and answer the questions. He read the story aloud with perfect pronunciation and answered all the questions in the back of the book, 100 percent correct. We told him the next time anyone asked what grade he is in to tell them, "In reading and comprehension, I am in college."

Lennon has perfect penmanship (seventh grade?) and he does math at a fifth-grade level.

Our point is that homeschooling affords the student the opportunity to soar ahead in favored topics of study while spending more time on less-popular academic areas. Keep in mind, grades are used in school settings mainly to keep some children at one place and move others along. We are talking about a for-profit business—BIG business at that! The system is not a benevolent grandfather who has your child's best interest at heart.

Homeschooling can lead to the greatest metamorphosis of your life!

Q *Should I use a prepackaged curriculum?*

A If you are new to homeschooling and don't know where to begin, then a prepackaged curriculum could be ideal for you and your homeschooled child or children. Prepackaged curriculums give beginning homeschooling parents a direction. Our advice is to try one and feel free to tailor it after your child's own needs.

Q *Why should I homeschool?*

A There are two primary reasons to homeschool—one is social and the other, academic. In discussing both of them, it all depends on your point of view and what you are satisfied with.

Socially speaking, if you live in a small community where . . .

- the parents have autonomy in how the schools are run;

- the children are *not* exposed to inappropriate information and behavior—be it sexual, criminal, antisocial, disrespectful, or other; and

- the family is the main influence in each child's life, inculcating their beliefs, standards, and philosophy in him or her and determining what sort of children the child socializes with . . .

then you would not need homeschooling for social reasons as far as we can see.

Academically speaking, the quality of public school learning varies widely from state to state. In California, which has one of the highest costs per pupil in the country, the school performance has been among the worst—consistently in the bottom three or four states. Homeschooling could not possibly do *worse*, could it? On the other hand, if your local school system does the following . . .

- provides parents with autonomy and produces academic results the parents approve of, and

- teaches a curriculum parents believe will mold their children's minds to obtain work and make them well-rounded enough to enjoy life and its many advantages . . .

then your situation would not require homeschooling. I have not heard of such a community—have you?

Q *Is there a "downside" to homeschooling?*

A Hardships such as living on one income, learning how to be together day in and day out, and having to re-learn or learn certain academic subjects at first may seem like negatives, but if you give yourself the opportunity to discover that these negatives can be positives, homeschooling can lead to the greatest metamorphosis of your life! We are so happy and satisfied with our decision to homeschool that there has not been a downside that we consider worthy of mention. What at first seemed like adversity has grown into a new, freer, and much larger life than we dreamed of.

PART 2
Products for Homeschoolers

Over the past four years of publishing a nationwide homeschool newspaper, we've had a unique opportunity to hear about, review, and use many excellent homeschooling products. We review products as a regular feature of our newspaper, and we are always discussing with parents, publishers, and manufacturers how to make products more effective, efficient, and even fun! From the thousands of homeschooling products on the market today, we've selected what we think are the best for you, no matter what your method of homeschooling, your level of experience, or whether you're religious or nonreligious.

Many of the products are from companies not well known to most homeschoolers. For instance, Sax Arts & Crafts, Carolina Biological, and Learning Services are well known to teachers and institutions that purchase their products in large quantities but are largely unknown to the private family. Our goal is to expose our readers to these companies and bring the same educational atmosphere, items, prices, and opportunities to the home-educated child as his school counterpart.

We've included certain information about each product for you. For instance, we list age ranges. Keep in mind that the age ranges you'll see are approximations only; every child is unique. Also, we have used a ✝ symbol to help you easily spot products and resources best suited for Christian homeschoolers.

Next, many of the products are CD-ROM programs. These products are compatible with certain types of computers. CD-ROMs are designated by WIN (Windows), MAC (Macintosh), hybrid (Windows 95 or Macintosh), or tribrid (Windows 3.1, Windows 95, or Macintosh). Last, please note that the books we list are available through commercial bookstores unless otherwise noted.

Finally, be sure to look through the two-color Coupons section at the back, which offers discounts for specific products and company-wide offerings. Note that neither we nor the publisher have any financial interest in listing products or offering coupons.

Language Skills

English Books, Programs, and Reference Materials

Vocabulary Companion (Ages 7 to 13)

This CD-ROM will revolutionize the way you teach vocabulary! Instantly create complete instructional packets covering phonics, word analysis, and vocabulary development. With over 200 language arts objectives and a database of over 12,000 words, you can easily create worksheets to use right at home. MAC CD-ROM: VISIO150-MC3S or WIN CD-ROM: VISIO150-W31S, $59.95. Available from Learning Services, P.O. Box 10636, Eugene, OR 97440-2636; Western Region: 800/877-9378; Eastern Region: 800/877-3278. (See coupon.)

Compton's Interactive Reference Bundle (Ages 7 to 18)

Two comprehensive resources on CD-ROM—*Compton's Interactive Encyclopedia Deluxe '99 Edition* and *Compton's 3D World Atlas Deluxe '98 Edition*. This 26-volume encyclopedia includes a thesaurus, dictionary, and interactive timelines. Electronic notebook and highlighter help students track findings. The *World Atlas* covers geography, geology, climate, environmental issues, economies, and cultures, with 3D globes, narrated video documentaries, and detailed articles (Each program sold separately elsewhere in this book.) WIN CD-ROM only: LSPK1340-MPC, $62.95. Available from Learning Services, P.O. Box 10636, Eugene, OR 97440-2636; Western Region: 800/877-9378; Eastern Region: 800/877-3278. (See coupon.)

Noah Webster's 1828 Dictionary   (Ages 6 to 18) †

This CD-ROM will make a great addition to your reference library. It defines 70,000 words. Noah Webster was one of our country's founding fathers, a lawyer, teacher, and finally, compiler of the first *American Dictionary of the English Language*, published in two volumes in 1828. Webster held to high Christian standards, refusing to admit vulgarities or slang into his dictionary. WIN CD-ROM, $29.95. Available through Christian Technologies, Inc. (CTI), P.O. Box 2201, Independence, MO 64055; 800/366-8320; 816/478-8320; www.christiantech.com. (See coupon.)

DK Encyclopedia of Space and the Universe (Ages 7 to 13)

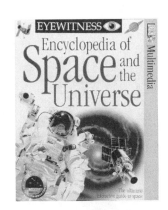

This CD-ROM includes the birth and death of stars, the Big Bang theory, black holes, Planet X, and much more! MAC CD-ROM: DORLOO8O-MCCDS or WIN CD-ROM: DORLOO8O-MPCS, $54.95 each. Available from Learning Services, P.O. Box 10636, Eugene, OR 97440-2636; Western Region: 800/ 877-9378; Eastern Region: 800/877-3278. (See coupon.)

DK Children's Encyclopedia   (Ages 7 to 13)

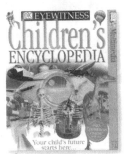

This is a must-have CD-ROM reference tool for any home. MAC CD-ROM: DORLO12O-MCCDS or WIN CD-ROM: DORLO12O-MPCS, $49.95 each. Available from Learning Services, P.O. Box 10636, Eugene, OR 97440-2636; Western Region: 800/877-9378; Eastern Region: 800/877-3278. (See coupon.)

Carmen Sandiego Word Detective   (Ages 9 to 13)

In this CD-ROM program, the power of speech is at stake. Speaking, reading, and writing as we know them will cease unless players can stop Carmen's plans to steal language and wreak havoc. Your child will encounter activities covering grammar, spelling, and vocabulary. Hybrid CD-ROM: BRODO1OO-CDB, $27.95. Available from Learning Services, P.O. Box 10636, Eugene, OR 97440-2636; Western Region: 800/877-9378; Eastern Region: 800/877-3278. (See coupon.)

DK My First Incredible Amazing Dictionary 2.0 (Ages 3 to 9)

A talking dictionary on CD-ROM! What could capture and hold your young child's attention better? Covers recognition and spelling of 1,000 words. Helps expand your child's vocabulary and teaches alphabetical order—handy for later dictionary use! Hybrid CD-ROM: Item # 8392, $24.95. Available from DK Family Learning, 11124 N.E. Halsey, Suite 460, Portland, OR 97220; 888/225-3535. (See coupon.)

DK American Heritage Children's Dictionary (Ages 7 to 14)

This CD-ROM has 45,000 entries with clear definitions. It contains games to improve spelling, writing, and vocabulary. WIN CD-ROM: Item #819, $24.95; MAC CD-ROM: Item #861, $24.95. Available from DK Family Learning, 11124 N.E. Halsey, Suite 460, Portland, OR 97220; 888/225-3535. (See coupon.)

The DK Picture Encyclopedia (Primary Reference Tool) (Ages 6 and up)

This 160-page large hardcover book will enthrall your child with facts, maps, and the famous DK illustrations and photographs. Over 1,500 topics about nature, science, history, geography, sports, and art. Item #036, $16.95. Available from DK Family Learning, 11124 N.E. Halsey, Suite 460, Portland, OR 97220; 888/225-3535. (See coupon.)

DK My First Encyclopedia (Ages 4 to 8)

This picture information book (80 pages, hardcover) answers questions most first-grade children ask. It encourages your child to read alone, too. The index features cross-referencing. Item #061, $16.95. Available from DK Family Learning, 11124 N.E. Halsey, Suite 460, Portland, OR 97220; 888/225-3535. (See coupon.)

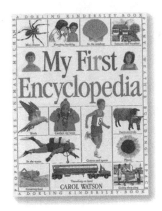

DK Millennium Family Encyclopedia (Ages 8 and up)

This 5-volume, 1,036-page hardcover set provides in-depth reference coverage of 6,500 topics in the famous DK "Eyewitness" style. Crammed with the top-quality characteristic DK artwork, photos, charts, and more. Item #537, $149.95. Available from DK Family Learning, 11124 N.E. Halsey, Suite 460, Portland, OR 97220; 888/225-3535. (See coupon.)

DK Concise Encyclopedia (Ages 10 and up)

This handy little book (512-page paperback) is an illustrated guide to the world. Bright, clear illustrations and photographs make it a pleasure to use. $9.95. Available from DK Family Learning, 11124 N.E. Halsey, Suite 460, Portland, OR 97220; 888/225-3535. (See coupon.)

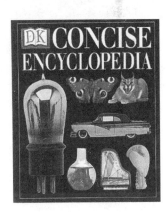

DK Dictionary & Thesaurus   (Ages 11 and up)

This 512-page paperback volume provides definitions and synonyms for thousands of words at your fingertips. Its compact size is perfect for a briefcase, desk drawer, or desktop. $9.95. Available from DK Family Learning, 11124 N.E. Halsey, Suite 460, Portland, OR 97220; 888/225-3535. (See coupon.)

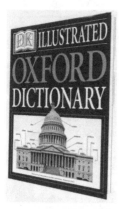

DK Illustrated Oxford Dictionary   (Ages 11 and up)

This 1,008-page book, the best of family reference books, is a combination of DK's visual mastery and the Oxford University Press's intellectual mastery. Well known for its ability to de-complicate the most complicated entries, it is useable by virtually everyone. $50. Available from DK Family Learning, 11124 N.E. Halsey, Suite 460, Portland, OR 97220; 888/225-3535. (See coupon.)

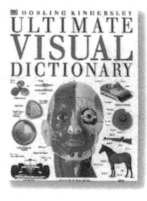

DK Ultimate Visual Dictionary   (Ages 11 and up)

This 640-page hardcover book is an extensive and unique reference work, filled with thousands of entries, clearly labeled. $39.95. Available from DK Family Learning, 11124 N.E. Halsey, Suite 460, Portland, OR 97220; 888/225-3535. (See coupon.)

English

Primary Language Lessons   (Ages 7 to 9)

This 148-page hardcover by Emma Serl is a drill book, but much more interesting. Serl was an experienced teacher of the early twentieth century. She recognized the two most salient points for teaching English: Capture your student's interest and drill, drill, drill! Each lesson is slightly different from the one before and after, providing a refreshing approach to each day's English work. $14.95. Available from Lost Classics Book Co., P.O. Box 1756, Ft. Collins, CO 80522; 888/611-BOOK (2665); www.lostclassics-books.com. (See coupon.)

Intermediate Language Lessons   (Ages 9 to 12)

This 344-page hardcover by Emma Serl is the second volume of the author's English-language series. Designed to ease the task of teaching English in grades 4, 5, and 6, this volume includes the work of outstanding authors (including Alcott, Longfellow, and Shakespeare), literature and poetry studies, letter writing, creating an outline, grammar, word usage, composition, memorization, oral presentation, debating, and dictation. $21.95. Available from Lost Classics Book Co., P.O. Box 1756, Ft. Collins, CO 80522; 888/611-BOOK (2665); www.lostclassicsbooks.com. (See coupon.)

DK Children's Illustrated Dictionary   (Ages 8 and up)

This 256-page hardcover is an excellent reference and resource book for children as they develop their reading skills. Clear definitions for 5,000 words, illustrated as only DK does—with full-color photos and drawings. $19.95. Available from DK Family Learning, 11124 N.E. Halsey, Suite 460, Portland, OR 97220; 888/225-3535. (See coupon.)

DK Children's Illustrated Encyclopedia   (Ages 8 and up)

This 644-page hardcover book is a tremendous one-volume encyclopedia, packed with over 450 main entries and 1,500 subentries covering all of the facts children want to know. $39.95. Available from DK Family Learning, 11124 N.E. Halsey, Suite 460, Portland, OR 97220; 888/225-3535. (See coupon.)

Student Reference Library   (Ages 9 to 18)

Your student can increase his or her report writing effectiveness by using this CD-ROM program's easily accessible information. It is filled with great photographs, sound clips, and video presentations. It has a suggested report format and can be used with nearly any word-processing program. MAC CD-ROM: MIND0690-MCCDS or WIN CD-ROM: MIND0690-MPCS, $69.95. Available from Learning Services, P.O. Box 10636, Eugene, OR 97440-2636; Western Region: 800/877-9378; Eastern Region: 800/877-3278. (See coupon.)

Grolier 1999 Multimedia Encyclopedia   (Ages 9 to 18)

This powerful CD-ROM program contains over 58,000 articles, 22,000 Internet links, thousands of images, 1,200 maps, and 15 hours of sound. Includes interactive timelines, guided tours, an atlas, and much more. MAC CD-ROM: GROL0075-MCCDS or WIN CD-ROM: GROL0075-MPCS, $69.95. Available from Learning Services, P.O. Box 10636, Eugene, OR 97440-2636; Western Region: 800/877-9378; Eastern Region: 800/877-3278. (See coupon.)

Middle School Learning Resource Library
(Ages 9 to 13)

This comprehensive set of six CD-ROMs is for the achievement-oriented student. It contains self-help tutorials and/or references for the following topics: book report, typing tutor, *Webster's Concise Encyclopedia*, grammar, pre-algebra, and fractions. WIN CD-ROM: SOFS0040-MPC, $29.95. Available from Learning Services, P.O. Box 10636, Eugene, OR 97440-2636; Western Region: 800/877-9378; Eastern Region: 800/877-3278. (See coupon.)

High School Learning Resource Library
(Ages 14 to 18)

This is a set of six CD-ROMs that provide in-depth self-help tutorials for the self-motivated high school student. It includes the following: vocabulary, term paper, *Webster's Concise Encyclopedia*, algebra, geometry, and high school grammar. WIN CD-ROM: SOSF0035-MPC, $29.95. Available from Learning Services, P.O. Box 10636, Eugene, OR 97440-2636; Western Region: 800/877-9378; Eastern Region: 800/877-3278. (See coupon.)

Compton's Interactive Encyclopedia '99 Edition
(Ages 7 to 18)

Your student can access all the reference information she or he needs in seconds in this easy-to-use CD-ROM format. It includes a thesaurus, dictionary, current U.S. and world maps, 16,000 vivid photos, 20 hours of sound clips, and Ask the Librarian, which suggests additional online resources. (See "bundle" in this section, also.) WIN 95 CD-ROM: CMPT0015-MPC, $32.95. Also available is the 1998 Edition for MAC: CMPT0010-MCCD, $54.95. Available from Learning Services, P.O. Box 10636, Eugene, OR 97440-2636; Western Region: 800/877-9378; Eastern Region: 800/877-3278. (See coupon.)

The Ultimate Children's Encyclopedia (Ages 8 to 11)

This CD-ROM program is a complete reference library for children. It contains thousands of articles for children's reading levels along with child-friendly features to make it easy to research and write using its information. Includes the Kingfisher series of children's books, an illustrated dictionary, illustrated thesaurus, a *Book of Words and Great Lives*, and an atlas and historical timeline. WIN CD-ROM: SKSW0175-MPC, $39.95. Available from Learning Services, P.O. Box 10636, Eugene, OR 97440-2636; Western Region: 800/877-9378; Eastern Region: 800/877-3278. (See coupon.)

ABC World Reference: Wide World of Animals (Ages 11 and up)

Using this CD-ROM program, your student can explore over 700 species of animals using text, photos, sound clips, and full-screen videos. Watch animals in their native habitats, learn about endangered species, and view documentaries on animal-related stories. MAC CD-ROM: ELEC9020-MCCD or WIN CD-ROM: ELEC9020-MPC, $24.95. Available from Learning Services, P.O. Box 10636, Eugene, OR 97440-2636; Western Region: 800/877-9378; Eastern Region: 800/877-3278. (See coupon.)

Good Grammar Matters!   (Ages 8 to adult)

Each of the lessons in this four-hour audiocassette course begins with a simple, nontechnical explanation and examples of incorrect usage. This is an easy way to learn or review good English grammar. Parts I and II each contain four one-hour audiocassettes and a 24-page booklet. Part I, #S04050, $39.50; Part II, #S04060, $39.50. Available from Audio-Forum, 96 Broad St., Ste. C70, Guilford, CT 06437; 203/453-9794; e-mail: info@audioforum.com; www.audioforum.com. (See coupon.)

English from the Roots Up (Ages 7 to 16)

This interesting and easy to use non-workbook approach by Lundquist can expand your child's vocabulary and spelling skills. It gives you 100 Greek and Latin root words that you can teach to students from elementary through high school. You don't need to have a background in Latin or Greek to teach these words. $19.95. Available from Excellence in Education, 2640 S. Myrtle Ave., Unit A-7, Monrovia, CA 91016; 626/821-0025; Fax: 626/357-4443; www.excellenceineducation.com. (See coupon.)

Latin and Greek Root Word Cards (Ages 7 to 16)

Students of *English from the Roots Up* can use this set of 100 easy-to-use and color-coded flashcards to complement the text. This is an ideal travel companion. $15. Available from Excellence in Education, 2640 S. Myrtle Ave., Unit A-7, Monrovia, CA 91016; 626/821-0025; Fax: 626/357-4443; www.excellenceineducation.com. (See coupon.)

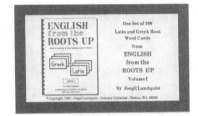

Rummy Roots, More Rummy Roots (Ages 7 to 12)

These card games were created to increase English vocabulary in a fun and stress-free way by helping users become more familiar with Greek and Latin roots. There are four different card games in one deck. The Pre-Roots is played like "Go Fish." The highest level of play utilizes a "Rummy"-style game combining up to three roots into one word. $10.95. Available from Excellence in Education, 2640 S. Myrtle Ave., Unit A-7, Monrovia, CA 91016; 626/821-0025; Fax: 626/357-4443; www.excellenceineducation.com. (See coupon.)

English

Vocabulary from Classical Roots   (Ages 12 to 18)

This five-book series by Norma Fifer and Nancy Flowers teaches junior and senior high students words derived from important Greek and Latin roots. Drawings, illustrative sentences, and challenging exercises help students master the vocabulary they need to read works of literature and prepare for the new SAT tests. It features literary, historical, and geographical references, and writing is integrated with vocabulary study. Workbooks A–E: $8.95 each; Teacher's Guide & Answer Key for A–E, $6.95 each. Available from Excellence in Education, 2640 S. Myrtle Ave., Unit A-7, Monrovia, CA 91016; 626/821-0025; Fax: 626/357-4443; www.excellenceineducation.com. (See coupon.)

Wordly Wise   (Ages 10 to 13)

These highly acclaimed vocabulary enrichment workbooks by Kenneth Hodkinson will be a definite asset to your child's quest in mastering the English language. The workbooks were created with four objectives in mind: 1. Learn new words. 2. Show how words are formed and used. 3. Discover where many of our words come from. 4. Make learning interesting and enjoyable. Books A, B, and C, $5 each; Answer Key, $2.25 for each level; Books 1–6, $7.50 each; Answer Key $5 each level. Available from Excellence in Education, 2640 S. Myrtle Ave., Unit A-7, Monrovia, CA 91016; 626/821-0025; Fax: 626/357-4443; www.excellenceineducation.com. (See coupon.)

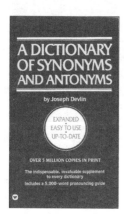

Webster's Dictionary of Synonyms and Antonyms (Ages 9 to 13)

Clear descriptions explain the subtle variations in meaning and connotation to help you select the appropriate word. Over 4,000 entries are arranged alphabetically and organized in a collection of articles. Following each list of words in an article is a concise statement that defines the element of meaning the words have in common and sample phrases that illustrate the correct usage. $7.95. Available from Excellence in Education, 2640 S. Myrtle Ave., Unit A-7, Monrovia, CA 91016; 626/821-0025; Fax: 626/357-4443; www.excellenceineducation.com. (See coupon.)

Webster's New Young American Dictionary   (Ages 7 to 10)

This dictionary is written especially for young students. It is more advanced than the simple picture dictionaries meant for children who are not in school yet. The definitions are in plain language, yet the dictionary has many features of larger dictionaries designed for adults. Contains the meanings and uses of more than 32,000 words. $9.95. Available from Excellence in Education, 2640 S. Myrtle Ave., Unit A-7, Monrovia, CA 91016; 626/821-0025; Fax: 626/357-4443; www.excellenceineducation.com. (See coupon.)

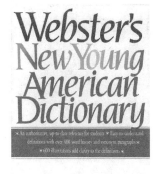

Created in Cooperation with the Editors of
MERRIAM-WEBSTER

Webster's Concise Reference Library
(Ages 10 to adult)

This dictionary is a reference to those words that form the very core of the English vocabulary. This dictionary is one of the smallest of the family of dictionaries published by Merriam-Webster. It is intended to serve as a quick reference, especially for questions of spelling, pronunciation, and hyphenation of the most common words in everyday use. $9.95. Available from Excellence in Education, 2640 S. Myrtle Ave., Unit A-7, Monrovia, CA 91016; 626/821-0025; Fax: 626/357-4443; www.excellenceineducation.com. (See coupon.)

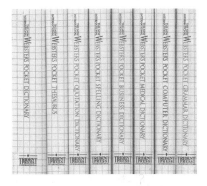

Scholastic Children's Dictionary   (Ages 9 to 13)

This dictionary is your guidebook to the English language. You can refer to it to find out what a word means, check its spelling or pronunciation, or figure out how to use it in a sentence. Special features make this an excellent choice for your children. Large print and the use of nice color illustrations make this a fine publication. $16.95. Available from Excellence in Education, 2640 S. Myrtle Ave., Unit A-7, Monrovia, CA 91016; 626/821-0025; Fax: 626/357-4443; www.excellenceineducation.com. (See coupon.)

Classic Curriculum Series for Writing and Grammar (Ages 7 to 10)

EIE proudly offers this complete line of workbooks for grades 1 to 4, skillfully written by Dr. Rudy Moore. This series precedes *Harvey's Revised English Grammar*. Please specify grade level 1 through 4 and quarter 1 through 4. Books are $8.99 each. Available from Excellence in Education, 2640 S. Myrtle Ave., Unit A-7, Monrovia, CA 91016; 626/821-0025; Fax: 626/357-4443; www.excellenceineducation.com. (See coupon.)

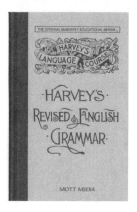

Harvey's Revised English Grammars   (Ages 10 and up)

Two English grammar volumes written by educator Thomas W. Harvey have had answer keys added. *Elementary Grammar and Composition*, designed for ages 10 to 12, will guide the student from simple words and sentences to complex sentences. Punctuation and the eight parts of speech are covered as well. *English Grammar*, designed for ages 13 to 14 as well as high school, includes orthography, etymology, syntax, and prosody. *Elementary Grammar* $11.95, answer key, $3.95. *English Grammar* $16.95, answer key, $5.95. Available from Excellence in Education, 2640 S. Myrtle Ave., Unit A-7, Monrovia, CA 91016; 626/821-0025; Fax: 626/357-4443; www.excellenceineducation.com. (See coupon.)

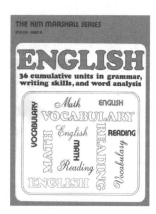

The Kim Marshall Series: *English*   (Ages 10 to 13)

These books contain a total of 36 cumulative units in grammar, writing skills, and word analysis in four general categories. Each unit introduces one skill, with four pages to teach the new material and the fifth page a test. The unit ends with a review page of short practice questions. English Part A (grades 4 to 6), $9.95; Teacher's Guide, $5.95; English Part B (grades 6 to 8), $9.95; Teacher's Guide, $6.95. Available from Excellence in Education, 2640 S. Myrtle Ave., Unit A-7, Monrovia, CA 91016; 626/821-0025; Fax: 626/357-4443; www.excellenceineducation.com. (See coupon.)

Learning English with the Bible   (Ages 7 to 12) ✝

These four attractive volumes (163-page text; 47-page answer guide; 50-page diagramming text; and 50-page pronunciation and capitalization text—all in softcover) use passages from the entire Bible for examples and exercises. They are the perfect teaching tools for the Christian family wanting everything they do to be Bible-based. The three English books constitute a set for $17.99 plus shipping. *The Punctuation Guide* is $7.99 plus shipping. Order from AMG Publishers, 6815 Shallowford Road, Chattanooga, TN 37421; 800/251-7206; e-mail: amgpublish@aol.com. Ask for their catalog. (See coupon.)

Language Arts

This section includes phonics, spelling, vocabulary skills, grammar and syntax, developing reading ability, and study guides.

Progeny Press Study Guides   (Ages 8 to 18) ✝

Progeny Press produces study guides for literature, which are written with a Christian perspective in mind. Each averages 50 pages and provides vocabulary lessons, biblical application, content questions, literary terms, and much more. The guide is designed to spend two months on a book or just do a cursory study of it. $13.95 per guide. Books from $3.99 to $6.99. Available from Progeny Press, 200 Spring St., Eau Claire, WI 54703-3225; 715/833-5261; Fax: 715/836-0105; e-mail: progeny@mgprogeny.com; www.mgprogeny.com/progeny. (See coupon.)

Calvert Study Guides for *Little House on the Prairie* Books   (Ages 8 to 11)

These detailed lesson guidebooks use recipes, music, puzzles, writing activities, and more. They are very interactive. $70 each. Available from Calvert School, 105 Tuscany Rd, Baltimore, MD 21210; 888/487-4652; www.calvertschool.org.

Language Arts

DK My First Reading Adventure: I Want to Read! (Ages 3 to 5)

This CD-ROM program helps your young child to begin developing important reading skills and enthusiasm for reading using phonics, letter sounds, spelling patterns, and sentence construction. Hybrid CD-ROM Item # 8482, $19.95. Available from DK Family Learning, 11124 N.E. Halsey, Suite 460, Portland, OR 97220; 888/225-3535. (See coupon.)

DK My First Reading Adventure: Now I'm Reading! (Ages 5 to 8)

This CD-ROM continues the skill development begun on the earlier CD-ROM in this series. This one promotes grammatical awareness and punctuation skill. Hybrid CD-ROM Item # 8512, $19.95. Available from DK Family Learning, 11124 N.E. Halsey, Suite 460, Portland, OR 97220; 888/225-3535. (See coupon.)

DK I Love Spelling! (Ages 7 to 11)

This CD-ROM is a fun way to learn and practice spelling. It teaches irregular spellings and recognition of word families (one of the keys to spelling mastery). It also broadens vocabulary and improves reading and writing ability. Hybrid CD-ROM Item #8682, $29.95. Available from DK Family Learning, 11124 N.E. Halsey, Suite 460, Portland, OR 97220; 888/225-3535. (See coupon.)

DK First Steps to Reading, Starter Sets 1 & 2 (Ages 4 to 6)

Start your neophyte reader with these two fun sets from DK. Each set consists of five books—four illustrated storybooks and one for sharing with an adult (Parents' Notes); gold star stickers display your child's progress. Set 1 (introduces 30 words): Item # 406, $14.95; Set 2 (includes 50 words): Item #407, $14.95. Available from DK Family Learning, 11124 N.E. Halsey, Suite 460, Portland, OR 97220; 888/225-3535. (See coupon.)

Super Solvers Midnight Rescue!   (Ages 9 to 11)

This CD-ROM helps your child develop his or her reading comprehension while participating in an adventure. Requires reading for the main idea, recalling key facts, and drawing inferences. Hybrid CD-ROM: LEARO1OO-CDBS, $46.95. Available from Learning Services, P.O. Box 10636, Eugene, OR 97440-2636; Western Region: (800) 877-9378; Eastern Region: 800/877-3278. (See coupon.)

Super Solvers Spellbound!   (Ages 8 to 12)

This CD-ROM program will provide your child with a fun and challenging atmosphere for practicing and improving basic spelling abilities. Includes visual and auditory word recognition, word recall, concentration, keyboard familiarity, and problem solving. Hybrid CD-ROM: LEAR0015-CDB, $27.95. Available from Learning Services, P.O. Box 10636, Eugene, OR 97440-2636; Western Region: 800/877-9378; Eastern Region: 800/877-3278. (See coupon.)

Spelling Rules   (Ages 9 to 14)

This CD-ROM program is designed to help your child improve his or her spelling accuracy, master plurals, capitalization rules, and other skills. Tribrid CD-ROM: WEEK0730-CDB, $41.95. Available from Learning Services, P.O. Box 10636, Eugene, OR 97440-2636; Western Region: 800/877-9378; Eastern Region: 800/877-3278. (See coupon.)

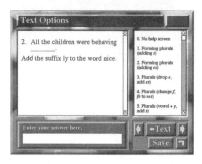

Vocabulary Development (Ages 9 to 14)

Illustrated in this CD-ROM program are synonyms, antonyms, prefixes, suffixes, homophones, multiple meanings, and context clues. This aids your student in developing the ability to figure out unfamiliar words. Tribrid CD-ROM: WEEK0060-CDB, $41.95. Available from Learning Services, P.O. Box 10636, Eugene, OR 97440-2636; Western Region: 800/877-9378; Eastern Region: 800/877-3278. (See coupon.)

Reading Comprehension Series (Ages 9 to 14)

This CD-ROM series consists of eight separate volumes packed with multilevel stories. They will keep your child's attention while helping him or her develop reading comprehension skills. Titles include Famous People, Science, Geography, History, Sports, and American Wildlife. $41.95 each. Available from Learning Services, P.O. Box 10636, Eugene, OR 97440-2636; Western Region: 800/877-9378; Eastern Region: 800/877-3278. (See coupon.)

Punctuation Rules (Ages 9 to 14)

The material in this CD-ROM program ranges from the categories of sentences to forming possessives. It offers your child the opportunity to learn and strengthen use of periods, commas, apostrophes, question marks, colons, hyphens, exclamation points, and more. The add-on question feature makes it very flexible. Tribrid CD-ROM: WEEK0040-CDB, $41.95. Available from Learning Services, P.O. Box 10636, Eugene, OR 97440-2636; Western Region: 800/877-9378; Eastern Region: 800/877-3278. (See coupon.)

Children's Literature Companions   (Ages 8 to 12)

With this set of five CD-ROMs, you can guide your child through the process of writing about books he or she reads for the program. Each volume covers several titles and includes an easy-to-use word processing program, on-screen activities, and illustrations to add to reports. Hybrid CD-ROMs: Volume 1 (includes *Charlotte's Web*) SVE-0225-CDBS; Volume 2 (includes *Stone Fox*) SVE-0230-CDBS; Volume 3 (includes *Sounder*) SVE-0235-CDBS; Volume 4 (includes *James and the Giant Peach*) SVE-0240-CDBS; Volume 5 (includes *The Cricket in Times Square*) SVE-0245-CDBS. $44.95 each. Complete set (five CD-ROMs): SVE-0250-CDBS, $209.95 Available from Learning Services, P.O. Box 10636, Eugene, OR 97440-2636; Western Region: 800/877-9378; Eastern Region: 800/877-3278. (See coupon.)

How to Read and Understand Poetry
(Ages 12 to 18)

Help your child learn to understand and appreciate poetry by using this excellent CD-ROM program. Contains extensive readings from many of the world's greatest poets, including visual presentations to help explain techniques while children learn about the content and form of a poem and how to interpret it. Hybrid CD-ROM: CLEA0445-CDB, $49.95. Available from Learning Services, P.O. Box 10636, Eugene, OR 97440-2636; Western Region: 800/877-9378; Eastern Region: 800/877-3278. (See coupon.)

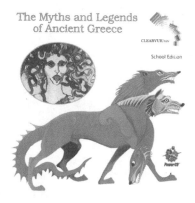

Myths and Legends of Ancient Greece
(Ages 12 to 14)

With this CD-ROM program your student can gain familiarity with ten of the famous stories of the ancient Greeks. Also included are book notes about the themes and characters from European literature. Hybrid CD-ROM: CLEA-0430-CDB, $74.95. Available from Learning Services, P.O. Box 10636, Eugene, OR 97440-2636; Western Region: 800/877-9378; Eastern Region: 800/877-3278. (See coupon.)

Language Arts

Language Arts

The History of English Literature   (Ages 13 to 18)

With this CD-ROM program, your student can study and learn about approximately 1,400 years of English Literature. Part 1 covers early literature—Chaucer, the Elizabethans, and the Renaissance. Part 2 deals with the poetry, themes, and ideals of Blake, Wordsworth, Keats, Byron, and others. Hybrid CD-ROMs: Part 1, CLEA0200-CDB, $74.95; Part 2: CLEA0205-CDB, $74.95; package of both CD-ROMs, CLEA-0206, $134.95. Available from Learning Services, P.O. Box 10636, Eugene, OR 97440-2636; Western Region: 800/877-9378; Eastern Region: 800/877-3278. (See coupon.)

Literature Classics Companions: Shakespeare
(Ages 13 to 18)

This disk is intended to help supplement your literature curriculum—or use it to study Shakespeare more in depth. The following plays are analyzed in detail: *A Midsummer Night's Dream, Julius Caesar, Othello, Romeo & Juliet, Hamlet,* and *Macbeth.* Hybrid CD-ROM: CLEA0750-CDB, $74.95. Available from Learning Services, P.O. Box 10636, Eugene, OR 97440-2636; Western Region: 800/877-9378; Eastern Region: 800/877-3278. (See coupon.)

The History of American Literature   (Ages 13 to 18)

In this CD-ROM program you will find study notes containing information on the plots, themes, and characters from 15 selected works. Part 1 covers the literature from the Colonial period to the Civil War. Part 2 deals with the period from Mark Twain to the present. Hybrid CD-ROMs: Part 1, CLEA-0400-CDB, $74.95; Part 2, CLEA0401-CDB, $74.95; package of both CD-ROMs, CLEA0402-CDB, $134.95. Available from Learning Services, P.O. Box 10636, Eugene, OR 97440-2636; Western Region: 800/877-9378; Eastern Region: 800/877-3278. (See coupon.)

Shakespeare's Theater   (Ages 13 to 18)

This CD-ROM package takes your child on a guided tour of the Globe Theatre and gives information about the emergence of the London theatre during the reign of Queen Elizabeth. Gain insight into the tastes and manners of the Bard's audience; learn about how the actual productions were created. Hybrid CD-ROM: CLEA0385-CDB, $49.95. Available from Learning Services, P.O. Box 10636, Eugene, OR 97440-2636; Western Region: 800/877-9378; Eastern Region: 800/877-3278. (See coupon.)

The Time, Life, and Works of Shakespeare (Ages 13 to 18)

This CD-ROM allows you to see into Shakespeare's life and achievements in light of the social and intellectual developments of his time. Included is a 35-minute survey of 1,000 years of English pronunciation, a 19-minute program of excerpts from 22 of his sonnets, and study notes relating to the plots, themes, and characters from 14 of his plays. Hybrid CD-ROM: CLEA0210-CDB, $49.95. Available from Learning Services, P.O. Box 10636, Eugene, OR 97440-2636; Western Region: 800/877-9378; Eastern Region: 800/877-3278. (See coupon.)

Women in Literature   (Ages 13 to 18)

This CD-ROM program informs your child about the portrayal of women in literature from the times of the Bible and Greece to the recent past. Hybrid CD-ROM: CLEA0235-CDB, $49.95. Available from Learning Services, P.O. Box 10636, Eugene, OR 97440-2636; Western Region: 800/877-9378; Eastern Region: 800/877-3278. (See coupon.)

Language Arts

Literature Classics Companions: American Literature (Ages 13 to 18)

If report-writing skill is important to your agenda, this CD-ROM will be of help. Your student will choose a title and the program will guide him or her through analysis, themes, characterizations, and many other topics. Study titles include *The Crucible, Little Women, The Red Badge of Courage,* and more. Hybrid CD-ROM: CLEA0740-CDB, $49.95. Available from Learning Services, P.O. Box 10636, Eugene, OR 97440-2636; Western Region: 800/877-9378; Eastern Region: 800/877-3278. (See coupon.)

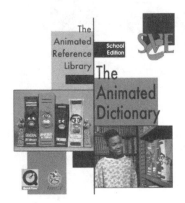

The Animated Dictionary   (Ages 10 to 14)

This disk teaches your child alphabetizing, explains the use of guide words, and tells how to read the pronunciation key. It also includes an overview of the thesaurus and other specialized dictionaries. Hybrid CD-ROM: CLEA895-CDBS, $74.95. Available from Learning Services, P.O. Box 10636, Eugene, OR 97440-2636; Western Region: 800/877-9378; Eastern Region: 800/877-3278. (See coupon.)

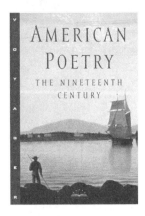

American Poetry: The Nineteenth Century   (Ages 11 and up)

The timeframe of this CD-ROM program is from Phillip Freneau to Stephen Crane. It includes large selections from Dickinson, Longfellow, and Poe, as well as other poets who are not as famous. Hybrid CD-ROM: VOYA0325-CDB, $27.95. Available from Learning Services, P.O. Box 10636, Eugene, OR 97440-2636; Western Region: 800/877-9378; Eastern Region: 800/877-3278 (See coupon.)

Secret Writer's Society   (Ages 8 to 10)

This CD-ROM program can teach your child the fundamentals of effective writing. It guides the student through the steps of planning, drafting, revising, editing, and presenting. The skills covered in the first six lessons are then applied in 20 creative writing missions. Features a direct feedback function so that your child can learn more quickly and easily. Hybrid CD-ROM: PANA0090-CDB, $24.95. Available from Learning Services, P.O. Box 10636, Eugene, OR 97440-2636; Western Region: 800/877-9378; Eastern Region: 800/877-3278. (See coupon.)

Scholastic's Diary Maker   (Ages 11 to 14)

This new CD-ROM program contains example diaries from Anne Frank (Amsterdam Jewish girl in WWII), Zlata Filipovic (girl caught between the warring factions in Sarajevo), and Latory Hunter (an immigrant teenager in New York City). Enable your student to create his or her own journal of daily thoughts, feelings, and experiences. Hybrid CD-ROM: SCH09005-CDB, $27.95. Available from Learning Services, P.O. Box 10636, Eugene, OR 97440-2636; Western Region: 800/877-9378; Eastern Region: 800/877-3278. (See coupon.)

An Odyssey of Discovery: Skills of Writers
(Ages 10 and up)

This disk provides practice in vocabulary development, word usage, sentence structure, punctuation, capitalization, spelling, and poetic form and style through three 3-D activities. Hybrid CD-ROM: PIER0275-CDB, $29.95. Available from Learning Services, P.O. Box 10636, Eugene, OR 97440-2636; Western Region: 800/877-9378; Eastern Region: 800/877-3278. (See coupon.)

Language Arts

An Odyssey of Discovery: Writing for Readers (Ages 10 and up)

In this CD-ROM program, four activities help your student brainstorm ideas; develop plots, characters, and settings; and then write and edit dialogue. Included are interviews with writers who talk about their writing habits. Hybrid CD-ROM: PIER0280, $29.95. Available from Learning Services, P.O. Box 10636, Eugene, OR 97440-2636; Western Region: 800/877-9378; Eastern Region: 800/877-3278. (See coupon.)

Beginning Reading at Home   (Ages 3 to 6)

This is a home-produced, take-apart kit that teaches reading the old-fashioned way. The set contains ten take-apart kits—sound cards, touch cards, word cards, nine storybooks, a test, and a guide book. In its simplicity, it gets the job done. $36. Request a brochure from Individualized Education, P.O. Box 5136, Fresno, CA 93755; 209/299-4639; e-mail: bette1234@aol.com.

Language Patterns & Usage Series   (Ages 7 to 12)

This series of 72-page workbooks is a multi-use resource that begins with learning to print capital letters. It progresses to writing invitations and RSVPs, as well as short but complete sentences about daily life. Sturdy workbooks, $6.95 each. Level A (G-1) #1064-4; Level B (G-2) #1065-2; Level C (G-3) #1066-0; Level D (G-4) #1067-9; Level E (G-5) #1068-7; Level F (G-6) #1069-5. Teacher's Guide, $3. Available from Continental Press, 520 E. Bainbridge St., Elizabethtown, PA 17022; 800/233-0759. (See coupon.)

Chall-Popp Phonics Series   (Ages 7 to 11)

This is a series of workbooks ranging from very simple for the beginning reader to the more advanced user of 4th to 5th grade. The attractive, four-color books cover the English topic at hand, and provide interesting insight into living information as well. Full-color workbooks, $7.75 each. Level A (K) #0137-8; Level B (G-1) #0138-6; Level C (G-2) #0387-7; Level D (G-3) #0388-5. Teacher's Editions, $12.95 each level. Level A (K) #1249-3; Level B (G-1) 1250-7; Level C (G-2) 1251-5; Level D (G-3) 1252-3. Available from Continental Press, 520 E. Bainbridge St., Elizabethtown, PA 17022; 800/233-0759. (See coupon.)

Reading for Comprehension Series   (Ages 9 to 12)

These workbooks take your student through the process of reading a short passage then answering pertinent questions to build the ability to determine what is important and to retain it. They are attractive, spot-color books of approximately 56 pages each. An audio cassette is available to accompany each workbook. $6.75 to $12.95. Available from Continental Press, 520 E. Bainbridge St., Elizabethtown, PA 17022; 800/233-0759. (See coupon.)

Phonics Pathways (All ages)

This complete 256-page reading manual is an effective program for beginning and remedial readers of all ages. Sounds and spelling patterns are slowly and systematically built into syllables, words, phrases, and sentences. The author adds one word at a time, making it very user-friendly. Its multisensory method makes it usable for a dyslexic or a learning disabled student. Includes a comprehensive guide of spelling rules. $29.95. Available from Dorbooks, P.O. Box 2588, Livermore, CA 94551; 925/449-6983.

Analytical Reading Program   (Ages 8 to 10)

This multilevel workbook series (3 vols per year) takes an analytical approach to developing the student's ability to see the main idea and secondary ideas in a reading sample and then analyze the order in which they occur. Questions are included at the end of each sample. Order by cover color: Building Basic Reading Skills (blue cover), Main Idea & Details (green cover), Inference & Sequence (red cover). Workbooks, $6.95 each; Teacher's Guide, $2.75. Continental Press, 520 E. Bainbridge St., Elizabethtown, PA 17022; 800/233-0759. (See coupon.)

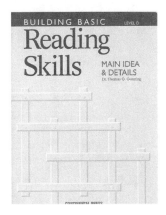

Phonics and Word Analysis Series   (Ages 9 to 11)

These attractive, high-quality workbooks (approximately 72 pages per volume) include crossword puzzles, paragraphs, and word comparisons to enable the user to progress in his or her phonics and overall English ability. $6.95 each. Level A (G-1) #1070-9; Level B (G-2) #1071-7; Level C (G-3) #1072-5; Level D (G-4) #1073-3; Level E (G-5) #1074-1; Level F (G-6) #1075-X. Teacher's Guide, $3 Continental Press, 520 E. Bainbridge St., Elizabethtown, PA 17022; 800/233-0759. (See coupon.)

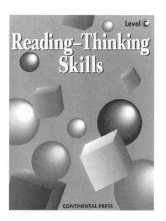

Reading-Thinking Skills Series   (Ages 10 to 12)

This group of workbooks includes Substituting Synonyms, Understanding Multiple Meanings, Organizing Ideas, and Time Sequence to more advanced levels of Vocabulary and Organization. Attractive and well made, it is a perfect tool to teach your child English and help him or her work independently. $6.95 each. Level A (G-1), 1058-X; Level B (G-2) 1059-8; Level C (G-3), 1060-1; Level D (G-4), 1061-X; Level E (G-5), 1062-8; Level F (G-6), 1063-6. Teacher's Guide, $3.25. Continental Press, 520 E. Bainbridge St., Elizabethtown, PA 17022; 800/233-0759. (See coupon.)

How to Teach Your Child to Read and Spell Successfully (Ages 4 to adult)

This 131-page softcover book is by Sheldon R. Rappaport, Ph.D., who has many years' experience in the field of teaching reading to children with severe learning disorders and helping them to overcome their disability. He discusses some case histories that will prove helpful to parents. He also suggests word-games and lists words that often present particular difficulty to children with various reading difficulties. $21.50. Available from Effective Educational Systems, Inc., 164 Ridgecrest Rd., Heber Springs, AR 72543; 501/362-0860; 800/308-8181. (See coupon.)

Writing Through the Year: Building Confident Writers One Month at a Time (Ages 8 to 12)

Written by Sandy Woolley, this book is arranged as a teacher's guide. The Sentence of the Day features lower and upper grade work, which is very handy in families of more than one child. The other monthly sections include dictionary work, journal topics, poetry, and vocabulary development. The book also features an almanac section of dates and their significance, which supplements history work as well. Item # DL119, $15.95. Available from Dandy Lion Publications, 3563 Sueldo, Ste. L, San Luis Obispo, CA 93401; 800/776-8032. Free catalog.

Junior Literature Companion (Ages 7 to 10)

This 64-page illustrated glossy softcover book by Dianne Draze is a junior writing companion; it has excellent exercises for the beginning writer. Many novel fill-ins and short assignments (such as writing a note to a friend) do not tax the concentration of a little one, but allow for practice in organizing thoughts and actually putting them on paper. Item #DL 67, $9.95. Available from Dandy Lion Publications, 3563 Sueldo, Ste. L, San Luis Obispo, CA 93401; 800/776-8032; Fax: 805/544-2823. Free catalog.

Beginning Writing Lab (Ages 9 to 10)

This 64-page illustrated, glossy softcover by Nancy Atlee is designed to be used one hour a week as a writing lab, allowing your student to develop his or her writing skills and also enjoy the process of writing. Weekly lessons develop fluency, clarity, revision, style, and more. Complete instructions and reproducible sheets make it a real value. Item #DL 121, $9.95. Available from Dandy Lion Publications, 3563 Sueldo, Ste. L, San Luis Obispo, CA 93401; 800/776-8032; Fax: 805/544-2823. Free catalog.

Writing Lab   (Ages 10 to 13)

This 112-page, glossy softcover by Nancy Atlee is the intermediate book for developing writing skills. Like the *Beginning Writing Lab* (p. 209), it is designed to be used one hour per week, which allows your student to develop writing skills but still enjoy the process. Lessons include instructions and examples. Item #DL 69, $13.95. Available from Dandy Lion Publications, 3563 Sueldo, Ste. L, San Luis Obispo, CA 93401; 800/776-8032; Fax: 805/544-2823.

Advanced Writing Skills   (Ages 11 to 14)

This 80-page, glossy softcover text by Nancy Atlee will be your companion when your older student is ready to hone his or her writing skill to actually communicate personal experiences, feelings, and opinions. Included are samples, advice on techniques, and assignments. Item #DL 99, $10.95. Available from Dandy Lion Publications, 3563 Sueldo, Ste. L, San Luis Obispo, CA 93401; 800/776-8032; Fax: 805/544-2823.

Discover Intensive Phonics for Yourself   (Ages 7 to 13)

This attractive, packaged reading course was developed by Charlotte Lockhart, a teacher with many years' experience. The course includes a large, 307-page, 3-ring binder with over 75 lessons teaching your child to read with intensive phonics; an audiocassette; and two packs of 8½" × 11" card stock with drill cards and letters and words printed on the standard three-line "printing" guide paper. $185. Available from Lockhart Reading Systems, 1420 Lockhart Dr., Ste 211, Kennesaw, GA 30144; 800/501-6767; www.lockhart-reading.com.

Play N' Talk—The Phonics Multimedia Solution   (Ages 7 to 11)

This program comes in many forms from 18 phonic readers with two activity books to audiocassettes and CD-ROMs. It contains two distinctive parts: (1) a 144-page Instructor's Manual and (2) four textbooks. With only two daily 10-minute lessons, your child can learn to read and spell as a simple process. $45 to $395. Available from Play N' Talk International, 7105 Manzanita St., Carlsbad, CA 92009; 800/472-7525.

The Institute for Excellence in Writing   (All Ages)

This company provides a highly acclaimed two-day seminar where they come to you and your homeschool group. You will leave this program with concrete tools to teach note-making and summarizing of notes, library research, report writing, and their special topic-clincher paragraph formatting. Also covered are creative writing, formal essays, critiques, and varied stylish and grammatical constructions. It is also available on video correspondence. $12 to $130. P.O. Box 96, Fort Valley, VA 22652; 800/856-5815.

English Vocabulary Quick Reference Guide   (Ages 12 and up)

This 182-page hardcover helps build a vocabulary of over 10,000 high school and college-level words. For each Greek or Latin word root, you will find a complete list of dozens of words that contain that root. Each one has a complete etymology, definition, and pronunciation. Common words are marked in red and key words in blue. This is very helpful when studying for the SAT. Available from Lexadyne Publications, Inc., P.O. Box 4498, Leesburg, VA 20177; 888/559-4700; www.quickreference.com.

Spelling Workout   (Ages 7 to 14)

This is a complete phonics-based spelling workbook series by Modern Curriculum Press. These workbooks (which have perforated pages so you can remove them) consist of eight levels ending with eighth grade. Levels A–H (grades 1 to 8), $7.50 each; Teacher's Editions, $7.50. Available from Excellence in Education, 2640 S. Myrtle Ave., Unit A-7, Monrovia, CA 91016; 626/821-0025; Fax: 626/357-4443; www.excellenceineducation.com. (See coupon.)

Spellbound (Ages 10 and up)

This workbook by Educators Publishing Service is probably one of the most complete books on learning the rules of spelling. The student is encouraged to use words, not just memorize. Even though it was designed with older students in mind, this nongraded workbook is ideal for anyone with a basic third-grade level of reading and writing skills. $8.95. Available from Excellence in Education, 2640 S. Myrtle Ave., Unit A-7, Monrovia, CA 91016; 626/821-0025; Fax: 626/357-4443; www.excellence-ineducation.com. (See coupon.)

Spellwell (Ages 8 to 11)

This new eight-book spelling series makes possible an organized, effective spelling program in just 30 minutes a week. Each book is suitable for half a school year. The first 10 to 12 words in each lesson are grade-level words that follow a certain pattern. In addition, words from the student's lessons or readings can be added. Series includes Book A & AA, 2nd grade; B & BB, 3rd grade; C & CC, 4th grade; D & DD, 5th grade. Each book is $7.50; Teacher's Guide, $1.95. Available from Excellence in Education, 2640 S. Myrtle Ave., Unit A-7, Monrovia, CA 91016; 626/821-0025; Fax: 626/357-4443; www.excellenceineducation.com. (See coupon.)

Ball-Stick-Bird (Ages 6 and up)

Ball-Stick-Bird is a scientific method of teaching reading that seeks to clarify the alphabet mystery by showing how each letter can be composed using just three basic forms: circle, line, and angle. It is taught through four sense modalities instead of two—visual, auditory, tactile, and kinesthetic. This program seeks to use the student's greatest potential by compensating for deficits in one area by using strengths in another. Set 1 (books 1–5 and Instructor Manual), $92.45; Set 2 (books 6–10 and Instructor Manual), $92.45; Sets 1 and 2 purchased together, $175.95. Available through Ball-Stick-Bird Publications, P.O. Box 13, Colebrook, CT 06021; 860/738-8871. (See coupon.)

The McGuffey Reader   (Ages 7 and up)

Here is the legendary high-water mark in American reading developmental programs in this reproduction edition. Primer (almost 1st grade), RB 8029, $4.25. First Reader (beginning 1st grade), RB 8030, $4.25. Second Reader (almost 4th grade), RB 8031, $5. Third Reader (beginning 6th grade), RB 8032, $5.75. Fourth Reader (almost 8th grade), RB 8033, $6.50. Fifth Reader (middle of 8th grade), RB 8034, $7.50. Sixth Reader (into college), RB 8035, $8.50. Entire boxed set, RS 8028, $39.95. First Reader Workbook: RB, 8036, $15.95; Second Reader Workbook: RB 8027, $12.95. Available from Alpha Omega Publications, 300 N. McKemy Ave., Chandler, AZ 85226-2618; 800/622-3070; www.home-schooling.com.

Come, Read with Me   (Ages 4 and up)

This videocassette program is designed for children who know their alphabet and have the desire to learn to read. Parents can play games, sing songs, and explore with their children to develop important skills and concepts. Included in the kit are 40 lessons on eight tapes, a comprehensive guide, activity book, and extensive supplies such as crayons, erasers, glue, pencil, and scissors. $175. Available from Calvert School, 105 Tuscany Rd., Baltimore, MD 21210; 888/487-4652; www.calvertschool.org.

Alpha Phonics   (Ages 5 and up)

This popular program comes with audiotapes, an introduction videotape, workbook, instruction manual, lesson tapes, flash cards, first readers, a flip book, and a writing tablet. Developed by teacher, lecturer, and author Dr. Samuel Blumenfeld of Boston, Alpha Phonics focuses on the 26 letters and 44 sounds of the English alphabet, letter by letter, sound by sound. $239.95. Available from Literacy Unlimited, 2575 Knox Dr., Rockford, IL 61114; 888/922-3000. (See coupon.)

The Phonics Game   (Ages 7 and up)

This is a popular reading improvement product consisting of many books, tapes, card decks, and other learning aids. $179. Available from Excellence in Education, 2640 S. Myrtle Ave., Unit A-7, Monrovia, CA 91016; 626/821-0025; Fax: 626/357-4443; www.excellenceineducation.com. (See coupon.)

Learning Wrap-Ups Early Reading Sets (Preschool age)

Alphabet and Phonics are the early reading skills development version of this innovative system of learning and practicing. Every Wrap-Up set consists of various notched and labeled plastic boards. A piece of precut yarn (supplied) is wrapped up around the board following the proper pattern to produce the correct answer to the problem. Alphabet LWU 112 and Phonics LWU 115; $7.95 each. Available from Learning Wrap-Ups, 2122 East 6550 South, Ogden, UT 84405; 800/992-4966. (See coupon.)

Bring Phonics to Life (Preschool age)

This book and its accompanying cassettes, are products of the Learning Wrap-Ups company. The book contains stories your child will love. There are 85 reproducible pages that your children can color while you read the stories to them. The cassettes are the narrated stories. Book only: LWU 901, $9.95; book with cassettes: LWU 911, $19.95. Available from Learning Wrap-Ups, 2122 East 6550 South, Ogden, UT 84405; 800/992-4966. (See coupon.)

Leap into Phonics   (Ages 4 to 7)

This CD-ROM program contains 26 activities to help your pre-reader master eight beginning phonics skills. Techniques include nursery rhymes, rhyming words, sounds/syllables in words, beginning/middle/ending sounds, and more. Also offers a printable progress report. Hybrid CD-ROM: BRIG0005-CDB, $29.95. Available from Learning Services, P.O. Box 10636, Eugene, OR 97440-2636; Western Region: 800/877-9378; Eastern Region: 800/877-3278. (See coupon.)

Reader Rabbit's Interactive Reading Journey (Ages 5 to 7)

An exciting CD-ROM journey through 20 Letter Lands, your student stops at Skill Houses along the way, developing the skills that will aid her in reading 40 stories. Hybrid CD-ROM: LEAR0135-CDB, $34.95. Available from Learning Services, P.O. Box 10636, Eugene, OR 97440-2636; Western Region: 800/877-9378; Eastern Region: 800/877-3278. (See coupon.)

Reader Rabbit's Reading 1   (Ages 7 to 9)

This CD-ROM program contains four games to develop pattern and letter recognition, beginning spelling, and vocabulary. There are over 200 three-letter words and more than 70 pictures to provide comprehensive coverage of early reading material. Hybrid CD-ROM: LEAROO71-CDB, $24.95. Available from Learning Services, P.O. Box 10636, Eugene, OR 97440-2636; Western Region: 800/877-9378; Eastern Region: 800/877-3278. (See coupon.)

Reader Rabbit's Toddler   (Ages 2 to 4)

This is one of four CD-ROMs that, while not exclusively a reading program, does expose your littlest student to various skills, some of which are necessary for his or her future reading. The program demonstrates color and shape recognition, counting, and the alphabet. Attractive playland scenes, characters, and music keep your toddler's attention. Hybrid CD-ROM: LEAR0415-CDB, $17.95. Available from Learning Services, P.O. Box 10636, Eugene, OR 97440-2636; Western Region: 800/877-9378; Eastern Region: 800/877-3278. (See coupon.)

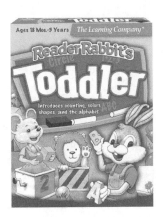

Reader Rabbit's Preschool   (Ages 3 to 4)

This CD-ROM program, although not geared exclusively to reading mastery, includes letter mastery, numbers, and patterns, and boosts memory skills through games, music, songs, and movement activities. Hybrid CD-ROM: LEAR0420-CDB, $17.95. Available from Learning Services, P.O. Box 10636, Eugene, OR 97440-2636; Western Region: 800/877-9378; Eastern Region: 800/877-3278. (See coupon.)

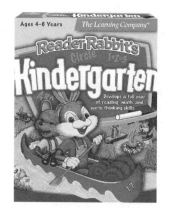

Reader Rabbit's Kindergarten   (Ages 4 to 6)

This third CD-ROM in the series includes reading development along with math, time concepts, and early thinking skills. Hybrid CD-ROM: LEARN0425-CDB, $17.95. Available from Learning Services, P.O. Box 10636, Eugene, OR 97440-2636; Western Region: 800/877-9378; Eastern Region: 800/877-3278. (See coupon.)

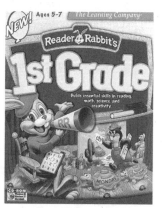

Reader Rabbit's 1st Grade   (Ages 5 to 7)

This fourth CD-ROM rounds out the set of programs that teach a variety of skills, reading included, for the young child. This 1st grade disk works on building skills in reading, math, science, and creativity. Hybrid CD-ROM: LEAR0505-CDB, $17.95. Also available is Reader Rabbit's 2nd Grade. Hybrid CD-ROM: LEARO51O-CDB, $17.95. Available from Learning Services, P.O. Box 10636, Eugene, OR 97440-2636; Western Region: 800/877-9378; Eastern Region: 800/877-3278. (See coupon.)

Reader Rabbit's Early Learning Bundle   (Ages 5 to 8)

This is a great set of three CD-ROMs. RR's Reading 2 develops recognition of over 1,000 words. RR's 2nd grade covers a full year of essential skills for this age: reading, writing, math, science, and thinking. It includes over 20 exploratory and arcade-style activities. RR's Math helps develop real-world math skills through an action-packed adventure game. Item #LSPK1345-CDB, $59.95. Available from Learning Services, P.O. Box 10636, Eugene, OR 97440-2636; Western Region: 800/877-9378; Eastern Region: 800/877-3278. (See coupon.)

Language Arts

Franklin's Reading World   (Ages 5 to 8)

This CD-ROM program is a reading-skills builder including hundreds of animations. It offers 320 words and 250 sentences to build, four songs, and 10 six-page coloring books you can print out. MAC CD-ROM: SANCOO4O-MCCDS or WIN CD-ROM: SANCOO4O-MPCS, $37.95. Available from Learning Services, P.O. Box 10636, Eugene, OR 97440-2636; Western Region: 800/877-9378; Eastern Region: 800/877-3278. (See coupon.)

Reading Comprehension Series/Famous People (Ages 9 to 14)

This CD-ROM includes eight individual volumes. Each one will capture the interest of your student while increasing reading comprehension skills. Bilingual English/Spanish. Tribrid CD-ROM: WEEKO7O9-CDB, $41.95. Available from Learning Services, P.O. Box 10636, Eugene, OR 97440-2636; Western Region: 800/877-9378; Eastern Region: 800/877-3278. (See coupon.)

Reading Comprehension Series/Sports (Ages 9 to 14)

This CD-ROM offers eight individual volumes of stories about sports. Bilingual English/Spanish. Tribrid CD-ROM: WEEKO712-CDB, $41.95. Available from Learning Services, P.O. Box 10636, Eugene, OR 97440-2636; Western Region: 800/877-9378; Eastern Region: 800/877-3278. (See coupon.)

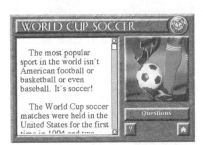

Reading Comprehension Series/History (Ages 9 to 14)

This CD-ROM is designed to increase your student's reading comprehension by offering multi-level stories about historical events and people. Bilingual English/Spanish. Tribrid CD-ROM: WEEKO715-CDB, $41.95. Available from Learning Services, P.O. Box 10636, Eugene, OR 97440-2636; Western Region: 800/877-9378; Eastern Region: 800/877-3278. (See coupon.)

Reading Comprehension Series/Punctuation Rules (Ages 9 to 14)

This CD-ROM program covers material from types of sentences to forming possessives. It helps your student gain strength in using periods, commas, apostrophes, question marks, colons, quotation marks, and more. In bilingual English/Spanish, the program also includes a teacher's section. Tribrid CD-ROM: WEEKOO4O-CDB, $41.95. Available from Learning Services, P.O. Box 10636, Eugene, OR 97440-2636; Western Region: 800/877-9378; Eastern Region: 800/877-3278. (See coupon.)

Reading Comprehension Series/Vocabulary Development   (Ages 9 to 14)

Synonyms, antonyms, prefixes, suffixes, homophones, multiple meanings, and more are covered on this CD-ROM. Also aids your student to more accurately define known words. Bilingual English/Spanish. Tribrid CD-ROM: WEEKOO6O-CDBS, $41.95. Available from Learning Services, P.O. Box 10636, Eugene, OR 97440-2636; Western Region: 800/877-9378; Eastern Region: 800/877-3278. (See coupon.)

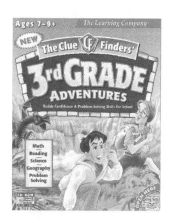

The ClueFinders' 3rd Grade Adventures   (Age 9)

Your 3rd-grade student will enjoy the more than 20 activities on this CD-ROM, which covers important areas such as math, reading, language arts, geography, science, and logic in four different levels of difficulty. Hybrid CD-ROM, LEARO44O-CDB, $17.95. Also available: The ClueFinders' 4th Grade Adventures, Hybrid CD-ROM: LEARO53O-CDB, $17.95. Available from Learning Services, P.O. Box 10636, Eugene, OR 97440-2636; Western Region: 800/877-9378; Eastern Region: 800/877-3278. (See coupon.)

Read, Write & Type! (Pre-reading)   (Ages 3 to 5)

This colorful approach to early language learning on CD-ROM allows your student to learn phonics and typing skills by working with a talking keyboard. She or he will then use the learned information to make words, sentences, and stories. Program consists of many activities and games and 40 ability levels to ensure your student's continued interest. LEAR0145-CDBS, $54.95. Available from Learning Services, P.O. Box 10636, Eugene, OR 97440-2636; Western Region: 800/877-9378; Eastern Region: 800/877-3278. (See coupon.)

Reading Search: In Search of Lost Folktales (Ages 8 to 12)

Your student can improve his or her reading comprehension with this CD-ROM. Players use a variety of reading and cognitive skills to find clues, gather artifacts, and perform other functions in the "game" setting. Includes over 80 activities and more than 60 stories. Hybrid CD-ROM: GREATOO55-CDBS, $49.95. Available from Learning Services, P.O. Box 10636, Eugene, OR 97440-2636; Western Region: 800/877-9378; Eastern Region: 800/877-3278. (See coupon.)

Punctuation: Building Better Language Skills (Ages 8 to 11)

On this CD-ROM, your child will be challenged to locate and correct punctuation errors. You can select specific rules to practice, or you can include all 12 basic rules presented in the program. A more in-depth learning experience can occur when you ask your student to identify which rule applies to the error. Hybrid CD-ROM: MICGO1OO-CDB, $24.95. Available from Learning Services, P.O. Box 10636, Eugene, OR 97440-2636; Western Region: 800/877-9378; Eastern Region: 800/877-3278. (See coupon.)

Reading for Critical Thinking   (Ages 11 to 18)

Sharpen your student's critical thinking skills by making inferences, summarizing, reasoning, and drawing conclusions. Topics include history, culture, and science. This three-level program also includes a game of reasoning and logic. Hybrid CD-ROM: Level A (grades 5 to 7), GAMCO515-CDB, $48.95. Level B (grades 7 to 9), GAMCO517-CDB, $48.95. Level C (grades 9 to 12), GAMCO520-CDB, $48.95. All three levels in one, GAMCO521-CDBS, $132.95. Available from Learning Services, P.O. Box 10636, Eugene, OR 97440-2636; Western Region: 800/877-9378; Eastern Region: 800/877-3278. (See coupon.)

Reading Concepts   (Ages 10 to 13)

This CD-ROM gives you an optional diagnostic test to help you to place your child at his or her "appropriate" reading level. Your student will then answer a series of questions in vocabulary, sequence, main idea, fact or opinion, factual recall, inference, and drawing conclusions. Incorrect answers receive helpful feedback. Correct answers lead to a challenging activity. Hybrid CD-ROM: GAMCO640-CDBS, $55.95. Available from Learning Services, P.O. Box 10636, Eugene, OR 97440-2636; Western Region: 800/877-9378; Eastern Region: 800/877-3278. (See coupon.)

Phonics Mastery   (Ages 3 to 9)

This three-level CD-ROM series will aid achievement of mastery of over 100 phonemes. There are four parts: pretests, instructions, practice/evaluation, and mastery games. Hybrid CD-ROM: Level A (PreK to 1), GAMCO975-CDBS, $48.95. Level B (grades 1 to 2), GAMCO980-CDBS, $48.95. Level C (grades 2 to 3), GAMCO985-CDBS, $48.95. All three levels in one, GAMCO990-CDBS, $132.95. Available from Learning Services, P.O. Box 10636, Eugene, OR 97440-2636; Western Region: 800/877-9378; Eastern Region: 800/877-3278. (See coupon.)

Undersea Reading for Meaning   (Ages 9 to 12)

Your student can dive to recover artifacts from a sunken ship by correctly answering questions in reading comprehension in this two-level CD-ROM program. The skills include drawing conclusions, determining cause and effect, and making inferences. The disk includes 135 paragraphs and a glossary the student can access. Hybrid CD-ROM: Level A (grades 3 to 4), GAMCO710-CDBS, $48.95. Level B (grades 5 to 6), GAMCO715-CDBS, $48.95. Both levels in one, GAMCOO9-CDBS, $88.95. Available from Learning Services, P.O. Box 10636, Eugene, OR 97440-2636; Western Region: 800/877-9378; Eastern Region: 800/877-3278. (See coupon.)

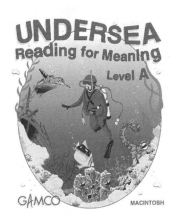

Essential Language Series   (Ages 9 to 14)

In this multipart CD-ROM series (three different skills, two levels each), your student will identify grammar, punctuation, and parts of speech usage errors. The material is presented in a standardized test format to help prepare him or her for test-taking. The program also includes a tutorial, practice with help, and other features. Hybrid CD-ROM: *Essential Grammar:* Level A (grades 3 to 6), GAMCO330-CDBS, $41.95; Level B (grades 6 to 8), GAMCO331-CDBS, $41.95. *Essential Punctuation:* Level A (grades 3 to 5), GAMCO250-CDBS, $41.95; Level B (grades 6 to 8), GAMCO251-CDBS, $41.95. *Parts of Speech:* Level A (grades 3 to 6), GAMCO370-CDBS, $41.95; Level B (grades 6 to 8), GAMCO371-CDBS, $41.95. All A titles, GAMCO327-CDBS, $111.95; all B titles, GAMCO9328-CEBS, $111.95. Available from Learning Services, P.O. Box 10636, Eugene, OR 97440-2636; Western Region: 800/877-9378; Eastern Region: 800/877-3278. (See coupon.)

Phonics Patterns   (Ages 5 to 10)

This book by Edward Fry is a wonderful addition to your tools for teaching phonics. It combines the centuries-old tradition of "phonograms" and the newer concepts of "onset," the initial consonant(s) sound at the beginning of a syllable, and "rhyme," the vowel plus final consonant. Breaking syllables into onset and rhyme aids spelling. $5.95. Available from Excellence in Education, 2640 S. Myrtle Ave., Unit A-7, Monrovia, CA 91016; 626/821-0025; Fax: 626/357-4443; www.excellenceineducation.com. (See coupon.)

How To Teach Reading for Teachers, Parents, Tutors (All Ages)

This book was originally written for Peace Corp volunteers by Professor Edward Fry as a tool to teach reading skills to non-readers. The current six-step program puts more emphasis on the use of better literature for story content, on writing, and on a longer list of phonic words, high frequency words, and reading materials. $14.95. Available from Excellence in Education, 2640 S. Myrtle Ave., Unit A-7, Monrovia, CA 91016; 626/821-0025; Fax: 626/357-4443; www.excellenceineducation.com. (See coupon.)

Fun with Phonograms   (Ages 5 to 12)

Enjoy this delightful Spalding-compatible program by Cindy Franklin. There are four levels, with each kit containing 25 separate activities, plus several pages of teaching aids. Fun with Phonograms (K to 1) covers 26 single-letter Phonograms. Fun with Phonograms 1 includes multi-letter phonograms. Fun with Phonograms 2 introduces more multi-letter combinations. Fun with Handwriting features pictures illustrating multi-letter phonograms. Per package, $8; all four for $28. Available from Excellence in Education, 2640 S. Myrtle Ave., Unit A-7, Monrovia, CA 91016; 626/821-0025; Fax: 626/357-4443; www.excellenceineducation.com. (See coupon.)

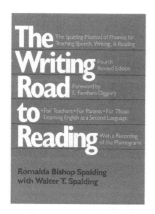

Writing Road to Reading   (Ages 5 to adult)

This comprehensive phonics program, including writing and spelling through college level, works well with primary phonics primers. $17.95. Available from Excellence in Education, 2640 S. Myrtle Ave., Unit A-7, Monrovia, CA 91016; 626/821-0025; Fax: 626/357-4443; www.excellenceineducation.com. (See coupon.)

Teaching Reading at Home   (Ages 5 to 10)

This easy-to-follow, step-by-step guide by Wanda Sanseri is user friendly—the best and most comprehensive phonics program we have seen. Guide, $19.95; Phonogram Cards, $12.95; Chart Masters, $3.95. Available from Excellence in Education, 2640 S. Myrtle Ave., Unit A-7, Monrovia, CA 91016; 626/821-0025; Fax: 626/357-4443; www.excellenceineducation.com. (See coupon.)

The New England Primer of 1777   (Ages 8 to 12) ✝

Features that made *The New England Primer* the most popular reader during the colonial period include the use of the alphabet to teach letter sounds and the use of Christian material. With some careful editing to meet current grammar and spelling rules, this book by Gary and Wanda Sanseri maintains its original flavor and intent. $14.95. Available from Excellence in Education, 2640 S. Myrtle Ave., Unit A-7, Monrovia, CA 91016; 626/821-0025; Fax: 626/357-4443; www.excellenceineducation.com. (See coupon.)

Explode the Code   (Ages 7 to 10)

This program by Nancy Hall with Rena Price helps children learn to read by teaching them to use the sounds of letters. A carefully sequenced variety of exercises provides experience recognizing and combining sounds in order to read words, phrases, sentences, and stories, as well as to build vocabulary. Teachers Key (covers all books), $2.50. Book 1 (consonant pretest, short vowels), $6.95. Book 2 (initial consonant blends, final consonant blends), $6.95. Book 3: (one-syllable words ending in a long vowel), $6.95. Book 4: (compound words, common endings, syllable division, dipthong syllables, three syllable words), $6.95. Available from Excellence in Education, 2640 S. Myrtle Ave., Unit A-7, Monrovia, CA 91016; 626/821-0025; Fax: 626/357-4443; www.excellenceineducation.com. (See coupon.)

Saxon Phonics   (Ages 6 to 9)

This program teaches the sounds of English to the child, then progresses to teach each letter—one per week—using the tried and true Saxon approach of daily review of previously covered material and one new piece of information each day. After three letters are learned, blends using them are learned, and so on. Prices range from $55 to $130, depending upon what is ordered. Available from Eagle's Nest Educational Supplies, 6024 Vivian Road, Modesto, CA 95358-8643; 209/556-9551.

Literature

Andre   (Ages 7 and up)

The true story of a harbor seal that charmed the world, this word-for-word audiocassette of the children's book will capture young imaginations. $14.95. Available from Audio Bookshelf, 174 Prescott Hill Road, Northport, ME 04849; 800/234-1713; www.agate.net/~audbkshf. (See coupon.)

Wild Fox   (Ages 5 and up)

Cherie Mason, a naturalist and environmentalist, tells her story of what transpired between an injured wild fox and her own heart in this touching audiocassette for all ages. Mason also shares the many things she learned about foxes while learning how to better understand her new friend. Cassette: 5-98, $10.95; Available from Audio Bookshelf, 174 Prescott Hill Road, Northport, ME 04849; 800/234-1713; e-mail: audbkshf@agate.net. (See coupon.)

Talking Walls/The Stories Continue
(Ages 6 and up)

This 90-minute audiocassette explores the question, Do walls talk? If they did, what would they tell us? Each wall has a story to tell and here author Margy Burns Knight reads the stories of 28 walls from Australia to Zimbabwe with accompanying music. Cassette: 2-98, $15.95; Teacher's Guide: TG2-98B, $9.95. Available from Audio Bookshelf, 174 Prescott Hill Road, Northport, ME 04849; 800/234-1713; e-mail: audbkshf@agate.net. (See coupon.)

Poems & Folktales   (Ages preschool and up)

In this audiocassette, award-winning author, artist, and performer Ashley Bryan will leave you breathless with his poems and animated retelling of four African folktales. Cassette, 6-94, $14.94; *Sing to the Sun* (only poems), Available from Audio Bookshelf, 174 Prescott Hill Road, Northport, ME 04849; 800/234-1713; e-mail: audbkshf@agate.net. (See coupon.)

Island Boy/Miss Rumphius
(Ages preschool and up)

This 32-minute audiocassette is read by Tracy Lord, with original music by Bruce Boege. *Miss Rumphius*—one of the best-selling children's books in the country—is paired with *Island Boy*, a story of the circle of life (and author Barbara Cooney's own favorite). Cassette, 4-96, $12.95; Available from Audio Bookshelf, 174 Prescott Hill Road, Northport, ME 04849; 800/234-1713; e-mail: audbkshf@agate.net. (See coupon.)

Time of Wonder   (Ages 3 and up)

This 21-minute cassette of Robert McCloskey's timeless classic of a child's summer on a coastal Maine island makes listeners of all ages dream of summer's magic. Cassette, 7-95, $11.95. Available from Audio Bookshelf, 174 Prescott Hill Road, Northport, ME 04849; 800/234-1713; e-mail: audbkshf@agate.net. (See coupon.)

Eleanor and Hattie and the Wild Waves
(Ages preschool and up)

This 46-minute cassette contains the unabridged book with original music by Paul Sullivan. Barbara Cooney records her work for the first time ever in this award-winning duo: *Eleanor,* the touching story of Eleanor Roosevelt's sad and lonely beginning in life, and a second story of childhood, *Hattie and the Wild Waves,* based on the life of Cooney's mother. Cassette, 6-97, $13.95. Available from Audio Bookshelf, 174 Prescott Hill Road, Northport, ME 04849; 800/234-1713; e-mail: audbkshf@agate.net. (See coupon.)

Newberry: The Life and Times of a Maine Clam (Ages 5 and up)

Unabridged, the story on this 1½-hour cassette is read by David Skigen. Newberry is a curious clam. He also wears a warm purple muffler, prescribed for his sore neck. From starfish to sandpipers, barnacles to crickets, Newberry and his friends on the shore are hilariously brought to life by zoologist Vincent Dethier. Cassette, 4-95, $14.95. Available from Audio Bookshelf, 174 Prescott Hill Road, Northport, ME 04849; 800/234-1713; e-mail: audbkshf@agate.net. (See coupon.)

Lost! On a Mountain in Maine   (Ages 5 and up)

Unabridged, this 2-hour story on two audiocassettes is read by Amon Purinton with original music by Brent Thompson. Alone, starving, and without shelter, yet determined to survive, Donn Fendler's true story of his ordeal as told to Hoseph B. Egan, is a timeless adventure for listeners of all ages. Cassette, 5-93, $17.95. Available from Audio Bookshelf, 174 Prescott Hill Road, Northport, ME 04849; 800/234-1713; e-mail: audbkshf@agate.net. (See coupon.)

Soup   (Ages 7 and up)

Unabridged, this 1½-hour story by Robert Newton Peck on cassette is read by Amon Purinton. What on earth will best friends Rob and Soup get into next? More mischief, you can bet on it! Cassette, 3-95, $14.95. Available from Audio Bookshelf, 174 Prescott Hill Road, Northport, ME 04849; 800/234-1713; e-mail: audbkshf@agate.net. (See coupon.)

Rachel Carson: Voice for the Earth   (Ages 10 and up)

These two cassettes (2 hours) present an unabridged version by Ginger Wadsworth, read by Melissa Hughes. Here is the behind-the-scenes story of Rachel Carson and the writing of her profound book *Silent Spring*. Cassette, 3-96, $17.95. Available from Audio Bookshelf, 174 Prescott Hill Road, Northport, ME 04849; 800/234-1713; e-mail: audbkshf@agate.net. (See coupon.)

Tuck Everlasting   (Ages 8 and up)

Two audiocassettes (3 hours) present this unabridged modern classic from Natalie Babbitt read by Melissa Hughes. Cassette, 2-95, $21.95. Available from Audio Bookshelf, 174 Prescott Hill Road, Northport, ME 04849; 800/234-1713; e-mail: audbkshf@agate.net. (See coupon.)

Toby Tyler   (Ages 7 and up)

An unabridged version by James Otis Kaler is presented on four audiocassettes (4½ hours) read by Amon Purinton. "Couldn't you give more'n six peanuts for a cent?" And so begins a small boy's adventure with the circus, and a much-loved children's classic first published in 1879. Cassette, 3-97, $21.95. Available from Audio Bookshelf, 174 Prescott Hill Road, Northport, ME 04849; 800/234-1713; e-mail: audbkshf@agate.net. (See coupon.)

My Brother Sam Is Dead   (Ages 10 and up)

This unabridged book (4½ hours on four cassettes) by James Lincoln Collier and Christopher Collier is read by John C. Brown. The Revolutionary War—a war with no clear-cut loyalties—divided families, friends, and towns. A story rich in historical detail and action as told from the viewpoint of young Tim Meeker. Cassette, 2-96, $24.95. Available from Audio Bookshelf, 174 Prescott Hill Road, Northport, ME 04849; 800/234-1713; e-mail: audbkshf@agate.net. (See coupon.)

American Fairy Tales from Rip Van Winkle to the Rootabaga Stories   (Ages 10 and up)

Compiled by Neil Phillip, preface by Alison Lurie, this 5-hour version (four audiocassettes) is unabridged, read by Taylor Mali. American fairy tales? You bet! And this stellar collection is as entertaining as it gets—12 tales that capture the zest of the American spirit as it emerged over the last 200 years. Cassette, 1-98, $26.95. Available from Audio Bookshelf, 174 Prescott Hill Road, Northport, ME 04849; 800/234-1713; e-mail: audbkshf@agate.net. (See coupon.)

Literature

The Man Who Was Poe (Ages 10 and up)

This unabridged book (5½ hours on four audiocassettes) is read by David Case. Award-winning author Avi spins an intriguing tale where young Edmund finds himself alone on the murky streets of Providence, Rhode Island, in 1848 until he hooks up with a temperamental writer, Edgar Allan Poe. Then it seems that things are never what they appear to be at first . . . or are they? Cassette, 6-95, $24.95. Available from Audio Bookshelf, 174 Prescott Hill Road, Northport, ME 04849; 800/234-1713; e-mail: audbkshf@agate.net. (See coupon.)

Whirligig (Ages 13 and up)

On this audiocassette hear Newbury Medal–winner Paul Fleischman's profoundly moving story of connected-ness—to one's self, to others, and to nature. Sixteen-year-old Brent Bishop commits a drastic act without thought of how far-reaching the results could be. Weaving four other voices in and out of Brent's story, Fleischman reveals to what extent his actions can impact the lives of strangers—even years later. This is a story of a young soul's journey of self-discovery—a story ultimately of hope and promise. Cassette, 1-99, $24.95. Available from Audio Bookshelf, 174 Prescott Hill Road, Northport, ME 04849; 800/234-1713; e-mail: audbkshf@agate.net. (See coupon.)

American Student's Package (Ages 8 to 18) ✝

This package incorporates *Noah Webster's 1828 Dictionary, Webster's 1833 Bible, The King James Version, Strong's Greek & Hebrew Definitions, Nave's Topical Index,* and *American Quotations* by William J. Federer into one volume. Federer's *Quotations* is a compilation of nearly 4,000 passages, phrases, and quotes influencing early and modern American history, listed by sources in literature, speeches, letters, and other categories. $49.95. Available through Christian Technologies, Inc., P.O. Box 2201, Independence, MO 64055; 800/366-8320; 816/478-8320; www.christiantech.com. (See coupon.)

Reading Strands   (Ages 9 to 15)

This is a program designed to teach the parent and student to comprehend and interpret fiction by learning to extract meaning on his or her own level. Therefore, it is designed so that any homeschooling parent—experienced or not—can guide his or her child through this development. The publisher provides several techniques (such as action, allegory, dialogue, domain, and evaluation) and advises how to use them. $22.95. National Writing Institute, 810 Damon Ct., Houston, TX 77006-1329; 800/688-5375 or 713/529-9396.

Hope and Have   (Ages 8 to 12) ✝

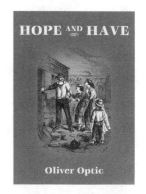

This 272-page softcover fiction book, by the late nineteenth-century storyteller Oliver Optic, tells the story of a young orphan girl in upstate New York who undergoes a 360-degree transformation. The first part of the book recounts how Fanny comes to have faith in God, and her subsequent change of heart produces new adventures of all sorts. Includes a build-your-vocabulary glossary. $14.95. Available from Lost Classics Book Co., P.O. Box 1756, Ft. Collins, CO 80522; 888/611-BOOK (2665); www.lostclassics-books.com. (See coupon.)

DK Oliver Twist   (Ages 10 and up)

This 64-page hardcover is a retelling of the English classic by Charles Dickens of an orphan boy in London, his friends, adventures, and triumph over poverty. Sidebars on each page provide depth for today's child in understanding the complete story of the original novel. $14.95. Available from DK Family Learning, 11124 N.E. Halsey, Ste. 460, Portland, OR 97220; 888/225-3535. (See coupon.)

Inside Stories—Study Guides for Children's Literature   (Ages 9 to 14)

This attractive five-volume series of study guides in glossy softcover (94 to 101 pages each) will aid the parent who is home teaching by offering a path to follow using some of your child's favorite books. Books 1 to 3 cover 10 titles each. Books 4 and 5 cover 11 titles each. $12.95 each. Available from Dandy Lion Publications, 3563 Sueldo, Ste. L, San Luis Obispo, CA 93401; 800/776-8032; Fax: 805/544-2823.

Zane Grey and Cameron Judd   (Ages 9 to 13)

Two 90-minute cassettes tell stories and ballads from the heartland in the rich tradition of America's storytellers. John Chandler presents prose, poetry, and ballads of the Wild West. Observations on Blue Moons, Smilin' Coyotes, and Campfire Logic. $9.95 each. Contact for brochure, Newport Publishers,100 N. Lake Ave., Ste. 203, Pasadena, CA 91101-1883; 800/579-5532; 626/796-0404. (See coupon.)

Family Classics/Children's Classics Series
(Ages 6 to 12 and adult)

This timeless radio theater collection is complete with multi-voice narrations, sound effects, and original music. Gather your family together to listen to these great classics from our rich heritage in Western Civilization literature—Dickens, Conan Doyle, Mark Twain, Washington Irving, and many more. Each audiocassette is 60 minutes long. Each library—Family Classics or Children's Classics—contains 40 cassettes.$49.95 each library. Contact for brochure, Newport Publishers, 100 N. Lake Ave., Ste. 203, Pasadena, CA 91101-1883; 800/579-5532; 626/796-0404. (See coupon.)

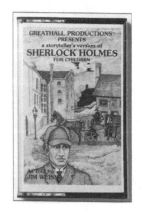

Greathall Productions Presents Jim Weiss Master Storyteller
(Ages 5 to adult)

On audiocassette or CD-ROM, Jim Weiss is America's premiere storyteller. He has appeared at the White House twice and received every major award—his work is superb! It stands up to repeated listening, always retaining its freshness and inspiring value. Included in his over 20 titles are stories from Sherlock Holmes, Shakespeare, the Old Testament, the *Arabian Nights*, and numerous other classic sources. Audiocassettes $9.95 each plus $2.50 S&H. CD-ROMs $14.95 each plus $2.50 S&H. 10% discount for two or more units; 20% discount for entire set. Write for a free catalogue. Greathall Productions, Inc., P.O. Box 5061, Charlottesville, VA 22905-5061; 800/477-6234; Fax: 804/296-4490. (See coupon.)

An Interview with J. R. R. Tolkien   (Ages 12 to adult)

On this cassette Oxford Don and creator of the wondrous trilogy *Lord of the Rings* Tolkien gave this interview to the BBC in 1964, at which time he discussed his imaginary world and the languages he created for it, as well as his views on other topics. Side two features an interview with Basil Bunting, friend of Ezra Pound and a poet himself. #ECN 117, $12.95. Available from Audio-Forum, 96 Broad St., Ste. C70, Guilford, CT 06437; 203/453-9794; e-mail: info@audioforum.com; www.audioforum.com. (See coupon.)

Anthony Burgess on Writing and the English Language   (Ages 13 to adult)

This cassette was recorded in 1980 with Burgess, author of *A Clockwork Orange, 2001—A Space Odyssey*, and many other titles. This conversation is highly entertaining with valuable insights into the development of English. Side two contains The Use and Abuse of English, a panel discussion of lexicographers, a linguist, writers, and a broadcaster. Item #ECN162, $12.95. Available from Audio-Forum, 96 Broad St., Ste. C70, Guilford, CT 06437; 203/453-9794; e-mail: info@audioforum.com; www.audioforum.com. (See coupon.)

Hamlet (BBC Production)   (Ages 12 to adult)

A British cast including Ronald Pickup, Angela Pleasance, and Martin Jarvis bring this Shakespeare classic to your ears via four audiocassettes. Item #SCN 085, $24.95. Available from Audio-Forum, 96 Broad St., Ste. C70, Guilford, CT 06437; 203/453-9794; e-mail: info@audioforum.com; www.audioforum.com. (See coupon.)

The Rime of the Ancient Mariner (BBC Production)   (Ages 12 to adult)

Douglas Leach reads this incomparable English classic composition by Samuel Taylor Coleridge in its entirety on one audiocassette. #ECN 179, $12.95. Available from Audio-Forum, 96 Broad St., Ste. C70, Guilford, CT 06437; 203/453-9794; e-mail: info@audioforum.com; www.audioforum.com. (See coupon.)

William Blake—The Book of Thel and Ralph Richardson Reads Blake
(Ages 12 to adult)

If you are a fan of William Blake, you will love this single audiocassette. *The Book of Thel* is read by Cecil Day-Lewis, late British poet-laureate. On side two, Ralph Richardson reads 21 of Blake's poems, including "The Lamb," "The Tiger," "Infant Joys," and more. #ECN213, $12.95. Available from Audio-Forum, 96 Broad St., Ste. C70, Guilford, CT 06437; 203/453-9794; e-mail: info@audioforum.com; www.audioforum.com. (See coupon.)

Literature

The Aeneid by Virgil   (Ages 12 to adult)

This recording in English (on six audiocassettes plus glossary booklet) was released in 1983 and today is acknowledged as a masterpiece. Read by Christopher Ravenscroft, this great Roman epic poem is a classic to be heard and re-heard by today's audiences. It was a tremendous success in the time of its creation during the reign of Emperor Augustus, the poet's friend and patron. Item #S11281, $39.95. Available from Audio-Forum, 96 Broad St., Ste. C70, Guilford, CT 06437; 203/453-9794; e-mail: info@audioforum.com; www.audioforum.com.

Insights into Biblical Greek Vocabulary   (Ages 12 to adult) ✝

This 60-minute audiocassette is a powerful resource for the serious Bible student who wishes to pursue the depth of the Greek of the New Testament, which far surpasses English in its shades of meaning and variety of available words. #CGK100, $12.95. Available from Audio-Forum, 96 Broad St., Ste. C70, Guilford, CT 06437; 203/453-9794; e-mail: info@audioforum.com; www.audioforum.com. (See coupon.)

Learning History Through Literature   (Ages 10 to 15)

G. A. Henty was a prolific, nineteenth-century storyteller—called "The Prince of Storytellers" in his time. His books are available from Preston Speed Publication, RR4, Box 705, Millhall, PA 17751; 570/726-7844.

By Right of Conquest: Or with Cortez in Mexico   (Ages 10 to 15)

This book has 375 acid-free pages, ten illustrations, two maps, and a special foreword. G. A. Henty has interwoven the adventures of an English youth, Roger Hawkshaw, the sole survivor of the good ship *Swan*, which had sailed from a Devon port to challenge the mercantile supremacy of the Spaniards in the New World. Hardcover, $20; softcover, $11. Available from Preston Speed Publication, RR4, Box 705, Millhall, PA 17751; 570/726-7844.

By Pike & Dyke—A Tale of the Rise of the Dutch Republic   (Ages 10 to 15)

This book has 366 acid-free pages, 12 illustrations by Maynard Brown, and four maps, including one foldout map. In this story G. A. Henty traces the adventures and brave deeds of an English boy in the household of the ablest man of his age—William the Silent. Hardcover, $19. Available from Preston Speed Publication, RR4, Box 705, Millhall, PA 17751; 570/726-7844.

Under Drake's Flag: A Tale of The Spanish Main   (Ages 10 to 15)

This hardcover book by G. A. Henty has 298 acid-free pages and 12 illustrations. It is the story of the days when England and Spain struggled for supremacy of the sea. The heroes sail as lads with Drake in the Pacific expedition and in his great voyage of circumnavigation. $18. Available from Preston Speed Publication, RR4, Box 705, Millhall, PA 17751; 570/726-7844.

St. Bartholomew's Eve: A Tale of the Huguenot Wars   (Ages 10 to 15)

This 376-page book by G. A. Henty includes a special foreword detailing history of Huguenot Cross, 12 illustrations by H. J. Draper, and a foldout map of France. The hero, Philip Fletcher, is a right true English lad, but he has a French connection on his mother's side. This kinship induces him to cross the Channel in order to take a share in the Huguenot wars. Hardcover, $20; softcover, $11. Available from Preston Speed Publication, RR4, Box 705, Millhall, PA 17751; 570/726-7844.

The Cat of Bubastes: A Tale of Ancient Egypt   (Ages 10 to 15)

This 339-page book set in 1250 B.C. has a special foreword and eight illustrations by J. R. Weguelin. G. A. Henty drew on the pictured records of Egyptian life and history to produce a story that will give young readers an unsurpassed insight into the customs of one of the greatest of ancient peoples. Hardcover, $18; softcover, $11. Available from Preston Speed Publication, RR4, Box 705, Millhall, PA 17751; 570/726-7844.

The Young Carthaginian: A Story of the Times of Hannibal   (Ages 10 to 15)

Those reading the history of the Punic Wars in the historic setting of 220 B.C. seldom have a keen appreciation of the merits of the contest. To let them know more about this momentous struggle for the empire of the world, G. A. Henty wrote this story in graphic style, giving a brilliant description of a most interesting period of history. This tale is of exciting adventure. Hardcover, $18. Available from Preston Speed Publication, RR4, Box 705, Millhall, PA 17751; 570/726-7844.

Beric the Briton: A Story of the Roman Invasion   (Ages 10 to 15)

This 398-page book by G. A. Henty, with 12 illustrations, has a historic setting: A.D. 61. This story deals with the invasion of Britain by the Roman legionaries. Beric, who is a boy-chief of a British tribe, takes a prominent part in the insurrection. Ultimately Beric is defeated, trained in a school of gladiators, organizes a band of outlaws, and at length returns to Britain. Hardcover, $20. Available from Preston Speed Publication, RR4, Box 705, Millhall, PA 17751; 570/726-7844.

For the Temple: A Tale of the Fall of Jerusalem (Ages 10 to 15)

This hardcover book has 335 pages, 11 illustrations by Solomon J. Solomon, and a map/plan of the siege of Jerusalem. G. A. Henty weaves into the record of Josephus a lad who passes from the vineyard to the service of Josephus. Hardcover, $17; softcover, $11. Available from Preston Speed Publication, RR4, Box 705, Millhall, PA 17751; 570/726-7844.

The Dragon & The Raven: Or the Days of King Alfred (Ages 10 to 15)

This 238-page book set in A.D. 870 includes nine illustrations by C. J. Staniland. In this story, G. A. Henty gives an account of the fierce struggle between Saxon and Dane for supremacy in England and presents a vivid picture of the misery and ruin to which the country was reduced by the ravages of the sea-wolves. Hardcover, $16; softcover, $11. Available from Preston Speed Publication, RR4, Box 705, Millhall, PA 17751; 570/726-7844.

Winning His Spurs: A Tale of the Crusades (Ages 10 to 15)

In 324 acid-free pages with numerous illustrations and a special foreword by Byron Snapp, G. A. Henty weaves a story of the life and times of King Richard the Lion-hearted that is yet to be equaled. Set in A.D. 1190, this book tells the heroic story of Cuthbert de Lance, who is of Norman blood on his father's side and Saxon by his mother. Hardcover, $18. Available from Preston Speed Publication, RR4, Box 705, Millhall, PA 17751; 570/726-7844.

In Freedom's Cause: A Story of Wallace and Bruce (Ages 10 to 15)

In 351 pages with12 illustrations by Gordon Browne, G. A. Henty relates the stirring tale of the Scottish War of Independence in A.D. 1314. The extraordinary valor and personal prowess of Wallace and Bruce rival the deeds of the mythical heroes of chivalry. The research of modern historians has shown, however, that Wallace was a living, breathing man—and a valiant champion. Hardcover, $18. Available from Preston Speed Publication, RR4, Box 705, Millhall, PA 17751; 570/726-7844.

Wulf the Saxon: A Story of the Norman Conquest (Ages 10 to 15)

This book by G. A. Henty includes 361 pages, 12 illustrations, and a special foreword by Douglas Jones. The hero is a young thane who wins the favor of Earl Harold and becomes one of his retinue. Hardcover, $18; softcover, $11. Available from Preston Speed Publication, RR4, Box 705, Millhall, PA 17751; 570/726-7844.

A Knight of the White Cross: A Story of the Siege of Rhodes **(Ages 10 to 15)**
This book, which includes 12 illustrations and a special foreword by Dr. R. J. Rushdoony, is set when England was embroiled in the War of the Roses. This much-neglected area of history is brought to life by the masterful storytelling hand of G. A. Henty. Hardcover, $18. Available from Preston Speed Publication, RR4, Box 705, Millhall, PA 17751; 570/726-7844.

Creative and Technical Writing

Ultimate Writing & Creativity Center **(Ages 8 to 11)**
This CD-ROM features Penny, the interactive help character, who speaks to users and coaches them through the five stages of the writing process: prewriting, drafting, revising, editing, and presenting. There are seven levels plus a Writing Exposition course and a Creating Fiction course. The publisher recommends that you not begin at any "age" but rather at the appropriate writing level for each child. Hybrid CD-ROM: LEAR0220-CDB, $54.95. Available from Learning Services, P.O. Box 10636, Eugene, OR 97440-2636; Western Region: 800/877-9378; Eastern Region: 800/877-3278. (See coupon.)

The Amazing Writing Machine **(Ages 8 to 11)**
This CD-ROM is a creative writing, illustration, and idea-generating system that will invite your student to begin writing with any of the five projects offered: story, journal, essay, poem, and letter. Each provides the child special tools to help with that writing form. For example, the outlining feature helps the user organize his or her thoughts when writing essays. Hybrid CD-ROM: BROD1010-CDBS, $46.95. Available from Learning Services, P.O. Box 10636, Eugene, OR 97440-2636; Western Region: 800/877-9378; Eastern Region: 800/877-3278. (See coupon.)

Storybook Weaver Deluxe   (Ages 7 to 12)

This CD-ROM is one of the most popular programs on the market today. It can encourage your child to bring ideas to life in his or her own multimedia story. Excellent visuals, inspiring music, and wonderful sound effects draw the student into the creative writing process. Write in English and Spanish and perform many other sophisticated activities with added scanning or other software. Tribrid CD-ROM: MECCO850-CDBS, $46.95. Available from Learning Services, P.O. Box 10636, Eugene, OR 97440-2636; Western Region: 800/877-9378; Eastern Region: 800/877-3278. (See coupon.)

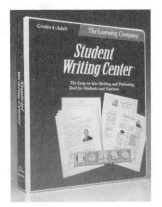

Student Writing Center   (Ages 11 to 18)

This CD-ROM offers your child five different document types: report, newsletter, journal, letter, and sign. Provides easy page layout, over 30 specially designed letterheads and sign borders, and over 150 clip-art pictures. MAC CD-ROM: LEAROO90-MC3L5 or WIN CD-ROM: LEARNOO90-PC3S, $54.95 each. Available from Learning Services, P.O. Box 10636, Eugene, OR 97440-2636; Western Region: 800/877-9378; Eastern Region: 800/877-3278. (See coupon.)

Student Writing & Research Center   (Ages 11 to 18)

This CD-ROM combines two great programs into one: Student Writing Center and *Compton's Concise Encyclopedia*. This is a full-featured word processor designed just for students. Contains more than 8,000 full-color and b&w pictures, over 75 full-motion videos, over 15 hours of sound! Atlas, illustrated timelines, dictionary, and thesaurus are included. WIN CD-ROM: LEARO160-MPC, $54.95. Available from Learning Services, P.O. Box 10636, Eugene, OR 97440-2636; Western Region: 800/877-9378; Eastern Region: 800/877-3278. (See coupon.)

mPower 2.8   (Ages 13 to adult)

This authoring CD-ROM combines many multimedia tools in one. Great for all sorts of multimedia presentations, the product combines video, sound, photographs, and charts with one of 64 different backgrounds to make the project look stunning. MAC CD-ROM: MINDOOO5-MCCD or WIN CD-ROM: MINDOOO5-MPC, $74.95 each. Available from Learning Services, P.O. Box 10636, Eugene, OR 97440-2636; Western Region: 800/877-9378; Eastern Region: 800/877-3278. (See coupon.)

Ultimate Writing & Creativity Center   (Ages 8 to 11)

This CD-ROM provides young writers with exciting hi-tech tools to use in writing, illustrating, and presenting their ideas clearly and imaginatively. It features an easy-to-use word processor, too. Hybrid CD-ROM: LEARO22O-CDB, $29.95. Available from Learning Services, P.O. Box 10636, Eugene, OR 97440-2636; Western Region: 800/877-9378; Eastern Region: 800/877-3278. (See coupon.)

The Negro Writer in America   (Ages 13 to 18)

In this 46-minute audiocassette of a 1961 Pacifica radio broadcast, two giants of American writing, James Baldwin and Langston Hughes, participate in a panel discussion addressing the situation of the Negro writer in America. Also on the panel are Lorraine Hansberry, Alfred Kazin, and Emile Capouya. Item #C23062, $12.95. Available from Audio-Forum, 96 Broad St., Ste. C70, Guilford, CT 06437; 203/453-9794; e-mail: info@audioforum.com; www.audioforum.com. (See coupon.)

Writing Strands   (Ages 7 to adult)

This multipart program is designed to teach children how to write and organize their thoughts. The publisher calls it a "complete program to writing and composition, assuring continuity and control." Each level can be purchased separately The publisher also has a program for the learning disabled. Request the "Scope & Sequence" to help you determine which level to begin with. $18.95 to $20.95. Available from National Writing Institute, 810 Damon Ct., Houston, TX 77006-1329; 800/688-5375 or 713/529-9396.

Creative and Technical Writing

Penmanship

SmartWrite Software   (Ages 5 and up)

This CD-ROM program teaches your child to develop printing penmanship and other skills—spelling, phonics, and numbers. A child or parent simply inserts the disk, types a letter, prints it out, and a work page is produced that the child can then trace over. WIN 3.1, 486 processor, $39.95. Available from IdeaMaker, Inc., 80 S. Redwood Road, Ste. 212, North Salt Lake, UT 84054; 888/WRITE-ABD or 801/936-7779; www.startwrite.com. (See coupon.)

Legible Handwriting and *Write Now*   (Ages 5 to 12)

Legible Handwriting uses the italic handwriting method and includes an instruction manual and each letter introduced with worksheets. There is also an adult book, *Write Now,* available for those who want to change their penmanship to the Getty/Dubay style. *Legible Handwriting,* $5.75. *Write Now,* $12.95. Continuing Education Press, Portland State University, Dept. P, P.O. Box 1394, Portland, OR 97207; 800/547-8887, ext. 4891.

Christian Liberty Press Handwriting Series   (Ages 8 to 12) ✝

This is a five-part program written in the traditional Palmer style. Biblical references are found throughout the series. The first two books fully develop the basic principles of cursive handwriting. Each workbook is approximately 75 pages and comes with a detailed Instruction Guide. Books 4 and 5 have additional material featuring the topic of home education. Book 1: In the Beginning; Book 2: Writing with Diligence; Book 3: Writing with Prayer; Book 4: Writing with Grace; Book 5: Writing with Power. $5.50 each. Available from The Eagle's Nest, 6024 Vivian Road, Modesto, CA 95358-8643; 209/556-9551.

D'Nealian Handwriting   (Ages 8 to 12)

This program is similar to italic handwriting, in that those using it experience a very simple transition from manuscript to cursive handwriting. Workbook activities range from copying (to learn letter formation at the early stages), to creative writing exercises in the grades 4 to 6 book. More than a handwriting series, students are exposed to classifying, alphabetizing, alliteration, and a host of other writing skills. $6.95 each. Available from The Eagle's Nest, 6024 Vivian Road, Modesto, CA 95358-8643; 209/556-9551.

D'Nealian Handwriting Readiness for Preschoolers (Ages 4 to 6)
In Book 1, while adults recite directions, children trace with their fingers or crayon. In Book 2, children learn lowercase manuscript letters. Consumable books, $6.95 each. Available from The Eagle's Nest, 6024 Vivian Road, Modesto, CA 95358-8643; 209/556-9551.

D'Nealian Home/School Activities Manuscript Practice (Ages 5 to 9)
Directions are provided for forming each lower and uppercase letter, plus numbers, with special space for practice. Activities use letters in words and sentences. Consumable practice books, $6.95. Cursive Practice book, $6.95. Available from The Eagle's Nest, 6024 Vivian Road, Modesto, CA 95358-8643; 209/556-9551.

D'Nealian Handwriting Accessories
Washable foam rubber mat contains upper and lowercase manuscript alphabet and five practice lines. The practice slate is an 11-inch square chalkboard with cut-out handle, imprinted with upper and lowercase alphabets and practice lines on both sides. Mat $3.95, manuscript or cursive practice slate, $7.95. Available from The Eagle's Nest, 6024 Vivian Road, Modesto, CA 95358-8643; 209/556-9551.

Italic Handwriting Series (Ages 6 to 12)
This package removes the frustration of learning two different types of writing—manuscript and cursive. Using this series, your child learns only one simple way of writing the alphabet that is both manuscript and cursive. Books A–G (K to 6), $5.75 each. Available from The Eagle's Nest, 6024 Vivian Road, Modesto, CA 95358-8643; 209/556-9551.

Spencerian Penmanship (Ages 8 to 14)
These little books (six volumes) can help restore the lost art of good penmanship. Developed in the 1860s, they teach children how to write neatly and clearly. Each of five copybooks has sheets with guidelines and examples. A theory book is also available for the instructor. Grades 2 to 8, $15.99. Available from The Eagle's Nest, 6024 Vivian Road, Modesto, CA 95358-8643; 209/556-9551.

Traditional Manuscript & Traditional Cursive (Ages 7 to 12)
Instructional Fair's humorous illustrations and activities keep students' attention as they learn basic handwriting. $4.95 for either volume. Available from The Eagle's Nest, 6024 Vivian Road, Modesto, CA 95358-8643; 209/556-9551.

Foreign Language

Power-glide Foreign Language Courses
(Ages 6 to adult)

This foreign language program includes six 90-minute tapes and a student workbook. It combines fun and easy-to-use effective methods into one comprehensive language-learning program, even for parents who know nothing about the chosen language. There is an array of additional products available—tests, CD-ROMs, complete kits, teacher's guides, comprehension tapes, and much more. Languages available are German, Spanish, Japanese, Russian, French, and Latin. Spanish comes with a CD-ROM (Win only). $12.95 to $159.95. Available through Power-glide Language Courses, 988 Cedar Ave., Provo, UT 84604; 800/596-0910; www.power-glide.com. (See coupon.)

Learning Wrap-Ups Spanish Intro Kit   (Ages 7 to 11)

This kit, which covers 480 words and phrases, includes four sets of Wrap-Ups, two audiocassettes to indicate proper pronunciation, and a 16-page teacher's guide. Every Wrap-Up set consists of various notched and labeled plastic boards. A piece of precut yarn (supplied) is wrapped up around the board following the proper pattern to produce the correct answer to the problem. Alphabet Set or Phonics Set, $7.95 each. Available through Learning Wrap-Ups, 2122 East 6550 South, Ogden, UT 84405; 800/992-4966. (See coupon.)

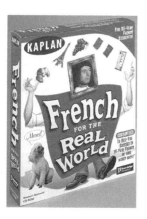

French for the Real World   (Ages 11 and up)

This CD-ROM presents first-year French for real-world settings, taught through arcade-type games and other video activities. The program includes an onscreen French-English dictionary with grammar and usage tips, and also teaches about the culture of France. Hybrid CD-ROM: DAVIO61O-CDBS, $59.95. Available from Learning Services, P.O. Box 10636, Eugene, OR 97440-2636; Western Region: 800/877-9378; Eastern Region: 800/877-3278. (See coupon.)

Spanish for the Real World   (Ages 11 and up)

This CD-ROM program offers great learning of real-world Spanish in an entertaining and fun setting. Also includes onscreen Spanish-English dictionary, tips on grammar and usage, and information about the culture of Mexico. Hybrid CD-ROM: DAVIO605-CDBS, $59.95. Available from Learning Services, P.O. Box 10636, Eugene, OR 97440-2636; Western Region: 800/877-9378; Eastern Region: 800/877-3278. (See coupon.)

Smart Start Language   (Ages 13 and up)

In Spanish, French, or German, this CD-ROM starts your student speaking a new language right away. An interactive trainer teaches correct pronunciation of key words. Your student and you can compete in game-style formats, using the mouse. As you progress through the many levels, you master words, phrases, and conversations! WIN CD-ROM: French, KADVO370-CDBS, $94.95; German, KADVO375O-CDBS, $94.95; Spanish, KADVO380-CDBS, $94.95. Available from Learning Services, P.O. Box 10636, Eugene, OR 97440-2636; Western Region: 800/877-9378; Eastern Region: 800/877-3278. (See coupon.)

Brighter Paths' Interactive English   (Ages 7 and up)

If you have a special-needs student or want to teach English as a second language, this CD-ROM program will be the ideal instruction aid. It provides practice in understanding spoken phrases and vocabulary. It has a record and playback feature so that your student can speak into the microphone and have the computer play it back to hear and adjust to the correct pronunciation. Hybrid CD-ROM: BRPAO020-CDB, $49.95. Available from Learning Services, P.O. Box 10636, Eugene, OR 97440-2636; Western Region: 800/877-9378; Eastern Region: 800/877-3278. (See coupon.)

Foreign Language

Language for Everyone   (Ages 7 and up)

This CD-ROM program allows you to practice conversing in French, German, or Spanish with native speakers in various everyday situations. It contains extensive video and audio, a printed phrase book, online dictionary, and grammar guidebook. WIN CD-ROM: Spanish, LEARO515-MPC; French, LEARO520-MPC; German, LEARO535-MPC. $27.95 each. Available from Learning Services, P.O. Box 10636, Eugene, OR 97440-2636; Western Region: 800/877-9378; Eastern Region: 800/877-3278. (See coupon.)

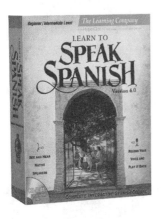

Learn to Speak . . . Spanish, English, German, French (Ages 13 to 18)

Here is an interactive, self-paced language CD-ROM program to aid your student in becoming proficient in these foreign languages. Includes everyday vocabulary, pronunciation, thorough grammar, reading, and writing. Hybrid CD-ROM: Spanish, LEARO213-CDB; French, LEARO217-CDB; German, LEARO215-CDB; English, LEARO205-CDB, Hablemos Ingles, LEARO210-CDB. $74.95 each. Available from Learning Services, P.O. Box 10636, Eugene, OR 97440-2636; Western Region: 800/877-9378; Eastern Region: 800/877-3278. (See coupon.)

The Language Solution   (Ages 6 to adult)

Learn English or Spanish naturally on CD-ROM. This user-friendly, self-paced, natural approach to language learning includes no grammar, no translation, no boring drills. It comes in either beginner or intermediate level; both include a microphone and dictionary. Level 1 and 2 combined on WIN CD-ROM, English (INTIO012-CDB) or Spanish (INTIO013-CDB), $139.95. Level 1 or 2 separately: English (INTIO005) or Spanish (INTIO010-CDB); $97.95 each. Available from Learning Services, P.O. Box 10636, Eugene, OR 97440-2636; Western Region: 800/877-9378; Eastern Region: 800/877-3278. (See coupon.)

History and Culture of Mexico   (Ages 13 to 18)

This multimedia CD-ROM program provides a full look at Mexico past and present. It includes video action and many illustrations. Requires 13-inch monitor. Hybrid CD-ROM: QUEO009-CDB, $125. Available from Learning Services, P.O. Box 10636, Eugene, OR 97440-2636; Western Region: 800/877-9378; Eastern Region: 800/877-3278. (See coupon.)

Spanish Reading Comprehension
(Ages 13 and up)

This unique non-multimedia CD-ROM (no sound or graphics) offers a student who is learning Spanish 144 lessons of high-interest reading selections on a variety of subjects. The student reads a passage in Spanish, then answers several questions, testing both comprehension and vocabulary. Hybrid CD-ROM: QUEU4525-CDB, $95. Available from Learning Services, P.O. Box 10636, Eugene, OR 97440-2636; Western Region: 800/877-9378; Eastern Region: 800/877-3278. (See coupon.)

Spanish Grammar   (Ages 13 to 18)

This CD-ROM provides a complete tutorial and review of all elements of Spanish grammar. It includes the most frequently used idioms and over 150 exercises that test one's mastery of Spanish grammar and syntax. Covers all of the elements of grammar. Hybrid CD-ROM: QUEU4530-CDB, $95. Available from Learning Services, P.O. Box 10636, Eugene, OR 97440-2636; Western Region: 800/877-9378; Eastern Region: 800/877-3278. (See coupon.)

Let's Visit Mexico   (Ages 12 to 18)

This CD-ROM shows Mexico City, Acapulco, Teotihuacan, and six other major cities of this fabulous country to the south. Two separate narrations are included: The English provides cultural and historical background; the beginning-level Spanish uses a carefully controlled vocabulary including an easily accessible translation. Hybrid CD-ROM: QUEUO2220-CDB, $59.95. Available from Learning Services, P.O. Box 10636, Eugene, OR 97440-2636; Western Region: 800/877-9378; Eastern Region: 800/877-3278. (See coupon.)

French Grammar (Ages 12 to 18)

This non-multimedia CD-ROM (no sound, no graphics) offers 150 exercises to test your student's knowledge of French grammar and syntax. It is a complete tutorial program. Hybrid CD-ROM: QUEU4520-CDB, $95. Available from Learning Services, P.O. Box 10636, Eugene, OR 97440-2636; Western Region: 800/877-9378; Eastern Region: 800/877-3278. (See coupon.)

History & Culture of France (Ages 13 to 18)

Add to your language study of French by visits to France via your computer's CD-ROM drive. This disk will provide you with an in-depth look at the history, geography, and culture of France. The narration is accessible in both French and English. A teacher's guide is included. MAC CD-ROM: QUEU0012-MCCD or WIN CD-ROM: QUEU0012-MPC, $95 each. Available from Learning Services, P.O. Box 10636, Eugene, OR 97440-2636; Western Region: 800/877-9378; Eastern Region: 800/877-3278. (See coupon.)

DK Spanish-English Pocket Dictionary (Ages 9 and up)

This handy size dictionary fits in a backpack or briefcase. Also available in a French-English version, it uses standard format for cross-referencing words in both languages. Spanish-English, $9.95; French-English, $9.95. Both are available from DK Family Learning, 11124 N.E. Halsey, Suite 460, Portland, OR 97220; 888/225-3535. (See coupon.)

150 First Spanish Phrases (Ages 7 to 12)

This 48-page DK paperback provides your student with a significant number of beginning phrases to learn, as well as great illustrations. Item #107 $9.95. Available from DK Family Learning, 11124 N.E. Halsey, Suite 460, Portland, OR 97220; 888/225-3535. (See coupon.)

Hey, Andrew, Teach Me Some Greek! (Ages 8 to 13) ✝

This five-level series of workbooks by Karen Mohs accompanies the reader of the same level and is designed to give the student practice work in everything from writing and naming each letter of the Greek alphabet to translating complete pages of the New Testament. Instructions on when to use flashcards, as well as an answer key and quizzes/exams, are all available. $3 to $18.95. Call or check website for specific prices. Available from Greek 'n' Stuff, P.O. Box 882, Moline, IL 61266-0882; 309/796-2707; e-mail: Workbooks@greeknstuff.com; www.greeknstuff.com. (See coupon.)

Latin's Not So Tough (Ages 8 to 16)

This is a three-level workbook format method of teaching elementary and older students. The Latin alphabet and blends of letter sounds are covered in Workbook 1. Workbook 2 allows you to put your newfound alphabetic knowledge to work learning 50 Latin words. Workbook 3 then offers translating simple Latin sentences. An answer key for each level can be purchased as well as flashcards sets and quizzes/exams. $7 to $18.95. Call or check website for specific prices. Available from Greek 'n' Stuff, P.O. Box 882, Moline, IL 61266-0882; 309/796-2707; e-mail: Workbooks@greeknstuff.com; www.greeknstuff.com. (See coupon.)

Arabic You Need (Lebanese) (Ages 10 to adult)

This program (two audiocassettes and a 176-page text) is a brief self-study course in the Lebanese dialect. One of the easiest to learn, this dialect is spoken primarily in Lebanon, Syria, Jordan, and the Gulf area. There are 25 lesson units, each divided into five parts. For example, Part 1 is Conversational Situations and Part 2, Listen, Read & Say. Each unit includes a glossary with a grammatical classification. Item #SAR300, $49.50. Available from Audio-Forum, 96 Broad St., Ste. C70, Guilford, CT 06437; 203/453-9794; e-mail: info@audioforum.com; www.audioforum.com. (See coupon.)

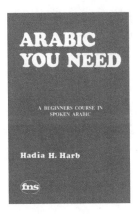

Foreign Language

Speak Mandarin (Ages 10 to adult)

This program of seven audiocassettes, a 238-page text, and a 165-page workbook teaches Mandarin, the official language of China. The user is not required to learn Chinese characters; rather, the focus is on new sounds, words, and language patterns, just as Chinese children (and others) learn: speak first, write later. The course consists of 20 lessons with vocabulary, sentence patterns, notes, and a translation. Item #AFM201, $185. Available from Audio-Forum, 96 Broad St., Ste. C70, Guilford, CT 06437; 203/453-9794; e-mail: info@audioforum.com; www.audioforum.com. (See coupon.)

Speaking Chinese in China (Ages 13 to adult)

This is a second-year conversational course teaching current Chinese via six audiocassettes and a 314-page text. Item #AFM320, $155. Available from Audio-Forum, 96 Broad St., Ste. C70, Guilford, CT 06437; 203/453-9794; e-mail: info@audioforum.com; www.audioforum.com. (See coupon.)

China & the Forbidden City (Ages 8 to adult)

This 60-minute videocassette is an insider's film into the culture, people, and some of the greatest treasures of man. Item #V72404, $34.95. Available from Audio-Forum, 96 Broad St., Ste. C70, Guilford, CT 06437; 203/453-9794; e-mail: info@audioforum.com; www.audioforum.com. (See coupon.)

Tai Chi Ch'uan   (Ages 12 to adult)

This 90-minute videocassette (in English) teaches about Tai Chi, which has been referred to as Chinese Yoga. This ancient fitness regimen, practiced all over the world, is great for stress reduction, muscle toning, and increasing flexibility. Item #V72668, $24.50 Available from Audio-Forum, 96 Broad St., Ste. C70, Guilford, CT 06437; 203/453-9794; e-mail: info@audioforum.com; www.audioforum.com. (See coupon.)

Basic French (and German, Greek, Italian, Japanese, and Spanish)   (Ages 13 to adult)

This was among the first language programs developed for the State Department. Each lesson concludes with a "culture capsule" in English, providing you with insights into the foreign life and language usage. Packages range from $155 to $245. Available from Audio-Forum, 96 Broad St., Ste. C70, Guilford, CT 06437; 203/453-9794; e-mail: info@audioforum.com; www.audioforum.com. (See coupon.)

French Business Culture Course on Video   (Ages 18 to adult)

This 70-minute videocassette and 64-page workbook provide an innovative way to understand the differences between French and American business cultures. The video presents a meeting between a French bank and an American computer software company, conducted in French. An English-subtitled version is given at the end of the program. After the meeting, two English-speaking commentators analyze the cultural differences and use instant replays to illustrate. Book and video, item #SV7120, book & video, $195. Workbook only, item #BO7120, $19.95. Available from Audio-Forum, 96 Broad St., Ste. C70, Guilford, CT 06437; 203/453-9794; e-mail: info@audioforum.com; www.audioforum.com. (See coupon.)

Foreign Language

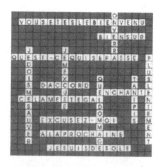

Cultural Crosswords   (Ages 13 to adult)

This unique audiocassette/48-page book/crossword puzzles combination provides a fresh approach to studying French language and culture for intermediate/advanced levels. Item #SFR310, $19.95. Available from Audio-Forum, 96 Broad St., Ste. C70, Guilford, CT 06437; 203/453-9794; e-mail: info@audioforum.com; www.audioforum.com. (See coupon.)

French or Spanish Scrabble   (Ages 13 to adult)

This version of the world's most popular word game is designed for French (with rules in French only!). Spanish Scrabble is the same game in a different language. Rules are in Spanish and English. French, Item #AF8981, $39.95. Spanish, Item #AF8980, $29.95. Available from Audio-Forum, 96 Broad St., Ste. C70, Guilford, CT 06437; 203/453-9794; e-mail: info@audioforum.com; www.audioforum.com. (See coupon.)

French or Spanish Monopoly   (Ages 13 to adult)

The world's most popular board game allows you to buy/sell/rent properties with French names. Rules are in French only; play money is in U.S. dollars. Spanish Monopoly is the same game in Spanish without English translations. French, item #AF8991, $39.95. Spanish, item #AF8990, $24.95. Available from Audio-Forum, 96 Broad St., Ste. C70, Guilford, CT 06437; 203/453-9794; e-mail: info@audioforum.com; www.audioforum.com. (See coupon.)

French/English or German/English Translator
(Ages 12 to adult)

This great invention for the French student is a handheld calculator-type language translator with 80,000 words for dining, business, and more. French Translator, Item #AF8878, $99.95; German/English Translator, Item #ACCG301, $99.95. Available from Audio-Forum, 96 Broad St., Ste. C70, Guilford, CT 06437; 203/453-9794; e-mail: info@audioforum.com; www.audioforum.com. (See coupon.)

The Pronunciation and Reading of Ancient Greek:
A Practical Guide   (Ages 12 to adult)

This novel product, which combines audiocassettes and booklets, was produced under the editorship of a professor of classical languages at the City College of New York to provide the restored pronunciation of Greek. There are eight packages available, including selections of Homer, Plato, Euripides, and many others. Ask for a list of titles; $34.95 to $199. Available from Audio-Forum, 96 Broad St., Ste. C70, Guilford, CT 06437; 203/453-9794; e-mail: info@audioforum.com; www.audioforum.com. (See coupon.)

The Pronunciation and Reading of Classical Latin:
A Practical Guide   (Ages 12 to adult)

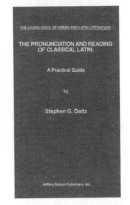

These are recordings of Latin literature with pronunciation based upon newest linguistic evidence, so you can hear as the ancients did. Included are selections from Catallus, Horace, Cicero, and Virgil. $34.95 to $39.95. Available from Audio-Forum, 96 Broad St., Ste. C70, Guilford, CT 06437; 203/453-9794; e-mail: info@audioforum.com; www.audioforum.com. (See coupon.)

Jen Nia Mondo   (Ages 13 to adult)

This 45-minute audiocassette and 72-page book course designed to teach Esperanto consists of 12 lessons of dialogs, vocabulary, grammar, and exercises. Each of Esperanto's 28 alpha letters has only one sound, its grammar has only 16 basic rules with no exceptions or irregularities, and each word is pronounced as spelled. Item #AFES10, $22.95. Available from Audio-Forum, 96 Broad St., Ste. C70, Guilford, CT 06437; 203/453-9794; e-mail: info@audioforum.com; www.audioforum.com. (See coupon.)

Foreign Language

Storybridges to French (or German, or Spanish) for Children (Ages 4 to 12)

Familiar stories such as Little Red Riding Hood are told in words and phrases in a foreign language on these audiocassettes. The child listener participates with the storyteller and his child assistants on the tape. Each set includes three audiocassettes (53 minutes each). French, Item #SFR125; German, Item #SGE125; Spanish, Item #SSP125, $29.95 per set. Item #BSP125 Spanish 48-page illustrated activity workbook, $8.95. Available from Audio-Forum, 96 Broad St., Ste. C70, Guilford, CT 06437; (203) 453-9794; e-mail: info@audioforum.com; www.audioforum.com. (See coupon.)

Sing, Dance, Laugh, and Eat Quiche (Ages 4 to 12)

This features a one-hour audiocassette and 35-page book of traditional and original French songs that provide a fun introduction to French vocabulary. Explanations between songs are in English so your child can follow along. The full-color illustrated book includes "actions" and "suggestions" in English plus a good and easy recipe for quiche. Item #SRF275 (one audiocassette, 35-page book), $21.95. Available from Audio-Forum, 96 Broad St., Ste. C70, Guilford, CT 06437; 203/453-9794; e-mail: info@audioforum.com; www.audioforum.com. (See coupon.)

Sing, Dance, Laugh, and Learn German (Ages 4 to 12)

Catchy songs introduce your child listener to German; this 30-minute audiocassette and 18-page book help children learn the alphabet and count. Item #SGE375, $17.95. Available from Audio-Forum, 96 Broad St., Ste. C70, Guilford, CT 06437; 203/453-9794; e-mail: info@audioforum.com; www.audioforum.com. (See coupon.)

Foreign Language

"Teach Me" and "Teach Me More" Italian for Children (Ages 4 to 12)

Popular children's songs such as "Mary Had a Little Lamb" are translated into Italian, making it easy for children to repeat and remember Italian words and phrases. A 15-page read-along coloring book with song translations is included with this 25-minute audiocassette. "Teach Me More" is a 45-minute audiocassette and 20-page follow-along coloring book. "Teach Me," Item #SIT200; "Teach Me More," Item #SIT205, $19.95 each. Available from Audio-Forum, 96 Broad St., Ste. C70, Guilford, CT 06437; 203/453-9794; e-mail: info@audioforum.com; www.audioforum.com. (See coupon.)

Spanish Songs for Children   (Ages 4 to 12)

This audiocassette contains 12 songs, many of which are hundreds of years old, as well as a Spanish lyric sheet. Item #SSP120, $14.95. Available from Audio-Forum, 96 Broad St., Ste. C70, Guilford, CT 06437; 203/453-9794; e-mail: info@audioforum.com; www.audioforum.com. (See coupon.)

Biblical Hebrew Flashcards   (Ages 8 to adult) ✝

Each vocabulary word is used a minimum of 200 times and many are used over 500 times in the Bible. Set of 333 cards, Item #SFLHE1, $27.95. Available from Audio-Forum, 96 Broad St., Ste. C70, Guilford, CT 06437; 203/453-9794; e-mail: info@audioforum.com; www.audioforum.com. (See coupon.)

Foreign Language

Learning Irish   (Ages 11 to adult)

This is a beginning level course of 36 lessons (in the form of four one-hour audiocassettes and a 336-page book), featuring the Irish spoken in County Galway. Textual spelling is that of standard Irish. English translations of text, key vocabulary, and exercise instructions are provided for each lesson. Item #AFIR10, $89.95. Available from Audio-Forum, 96 Broad St., Ste. C70, Guilford, CT 06437; 203/453-9794; e-mail: info@audioforum.com; www.audioforum.com. (See coupon.)

Calliope Books   (Ages 6 to adult)

This company provides high-quality foreign-language materials for all ages and abilities in over 30 languages. They will help you plan a curriculum and choose the right books and will answer all of your questions. You will receive very personalized service. Write or call for catalog ($1): Calliope Books, Rt. 3, Box 3395, Saylorsburg, PA 18353; 610/381-2587.

The Learnables   (Ages 7 to adult)

This has been a homeschooling foreign language favorite for over 20 years. The lessons of this full-immersion program use native speakers and are easy to use. Students are not confused by mixing English with foreign words, nor does the program require translation from English or rote memorization of words or phrases. It prepares students for college study. $50 to $109. Available from International Linguistics Corporation, 3505 East Red Bridge, Kansas City, MO 64137; 800/237-1830; www.learnables.com.

"Periodic Tables" of Languages or Money   (Ages 10 to 16)

Full-color 24" × 36" posters are a great way to learn a representative phrase or word from 40 countries and view the country's corresponding flag. The money poster displays the official and slang terms for 40 different currencies of the world. Languages, Item #AF9960; Money, Item #AF9961, $16.50 each. Available from Audio-Forum, 96 Broad St., Ste. C70, Guilford, CT 06437; 203/453-9794; e-mail: info@audioforum.com; www.audioforum.com. (See coupon.)

Math, Science, and Technology

Computer Products: Games, Books, Word Processing

Pablo   (Ages 13 to adult)

This state-of-the-art computer drawing tablet uses a pressure-sensitive pen. You will be amazed at your child's drawings, tracings, and animations created with Pablo's superior technology. Your child will be designing web pages and original artwork that would never be possible with an ordinary mouse. MAC CD-ROM: KIDB0020-MCCDS, $118.95; WIN CD-ROM: KIDB0020-MPCS, $98.95. Available from Learning Services, P.O. Box 10636, Eugene, OR 97440-2636; Western Region: 800/877-9378; Eastern Region: 800/877-3278. (See coupon.)

Trail Mix Social Studies CD Bundle   (Ages 10 to 18)

Three great programs—Oregon Trail, 3rd Ed., Amazon Trail II, and MayaQuest Trail! In Oregon Trail students learn about and experience the famous path to the Northwest. In Amazon Trail children are immersed in the ecology, history, and geography of the rainforest. MayaQuest explores the Yucatan Peninsula in an attempt to discover why the Maya civilization collapsed over 1,000 years ago, for no apparent reason. Tribrid CD-ROM: LSPK1350-CDBS, $136.95. Also available individually—MayaQuest Trail, Tribrid CD-ROM: MEDD0505-CDBS, $46.95; Africa Trail, Hybrid CD-ROM: MECCO500-CDBS; Yukon Trail, Hybrid CD-ROM: MECC0900-CDB, $46.95. Available from Learning Services, P.O. Box 10636, Eugene, OR 97440-2636; Western Region: 800/877-9378; Eastern Region: 800/877-3278. (See coupon.)

Computer Products

King Arthur Through the Ages (Ages 10 and up)

This beautifully illustrated CD-ROM program by Calvert School comes with a booklet consisting of seven different sections. There are beautiful maps of Britain in an overlay style, a written history of Arthurian England, a real-sound pronunciation guide, and a multi-level game concerning the actual history of Arthur or his legend. This WIN CD-ROM is also part of Calvert's 5th grade curriculum. Item #1KA, $40. Available from Calvert School, 104 Tuscany Road, Baltimore, MD 21210.

Adobe PageMaker 6.5 (Ages 13 to adult)

One of the best professional publishing software programs ever. Allows you to perform many functions of composition, word processing, text editing, and more. Used alone or in combination with other Adobe products, this program is all the publishing software you'll need for projects. MAC CD-ROM: ALDU0035-MCCD or WIN 95/WIN CD-ROM: ALDU0035-MPC, $189.95. Available from Learning Services, P.O. Box 10636, Eugene, OR 97440-2636; Western Region: 800/877-9378; Eastern Region: 800/877-3278. (See coupon.)

Adobe PageMill 3.0 (Ages 15 to adult)

This software makes building your Web pages a simple drag-and-drop operation! Just type in text or import it directly from standard office applications. What you see is truly what you get. Create image maps or linked hotspots. Includes audio, video, animated GIFs, PDF files, and more! PageMill 3.0 for WIN 95: ADOBO107-MPC, $48.95; PageMill 2.0 for MAC: ADOBO107-MCCD, $48.95. Available from Learning Services, P.O. Box 10636, Eugene, OR 97440-2636; Western Region: 800/877-9378; Eastern Region: 800/877-3278. (See coupon.)

Adobe Illustrator 8.0   (Ages 15 to adult)

The industry-standard illustration software makes your creativity stand out in sophisticated artwork for print and the Web. Integration with Adobe's professional graphics programs, including Photoshop 5.0, PageMaker, Premiere 5.0, and ImageReady software provides an efficient workflow. MAC CD-ROM: ADOBOO70-MCCD or WIN CD-ROM: ADOBOO70-MPC, $142.95. Available from Learning Services, P.O. Box 10636, Eugene, OR 97440-2636; Western Region: 800/877-9378; Eastern Region: 800/877-3278. (See coupon.)

Adobe Photoshop 5.0   (Ages 13 to adult)

Provides the power to create compelling images and the precision to prepare them for the printed page, the Web, and virtually any other medium. Superimpose images, graphics, and text on multiple layers. Create original artwork with a complete set of adjustable brushes and pens. Retouch and refine scanned photos with darkroom-style tools. Correct color on adjustment layers that preserve your original. Add special effects with more than 95 filters. MAC CD-ROM: ADPBPP50-MCCD or WIN CD-ROM: ADOBOO5O-MPC, $269.95. Available from Learning Services, P.O. Box 10636, Eugene, OR 97440-2636; Western Region: 800/877-9378; Eastern Region: 800/877-3278. (See coupon.)

Adobe PhotoDeluxe   (Ages 13 to adult)

Use this great software to make the most of your photos! The entire family can have fun using photos to create cards, calendars, T-shirts, and much more. It has never been easier to improve contrast and color, remove red-eye, apply cool special effects, drop photos into included templates, and share your creations in print or on the Web. MAC CD-ROM: ADOB1025-MCCD or WIN CD-ROM: ADOB1025-MPC, $48.95. Available from Learning Services, P.O. Box 10636, Eugene, OR 97440-2636; Western Region: 800/877-9378; Eastern Region: 800/877-3278. (See coupon.)

Adobe Premiere 5.0 (Ages 15 to adult)

Designed for video professionals, this software offers an elegant interface with superb editing control for producing high-quality movies for video, multimedia, or the Web. Use the professional controls in the monitor window to mark source clips and play back your edited program. Add up to 99 video and 99 audio tracks. Then target, hide, display, and edit the content with ease. MAC CD-ROM: ADOBOO55-MCCD or WIN CD-ROM: ADOBOO55-MPC, $269.95. Available from Learning Services, P.O. Box 10636, Eugene, OR 97440-2636; Western Region: 800/877-9378; Eastern Region: 800/877-3278. (See coupon.)

Adobe Acrobat 4.0 (Ages 15 to adult)

This software is the fastest way to publish any document on your cooperative Intranet, the Web, or CD-ROM. It gives you everything you need to create and distribute electronic documents that can be searched, hypertext linked, and even animated with QuickTime movies. You can view and browse pdf files. Many more features you will appreciate! MAC CD-ROM: ADOB1035-MCCD or WIN CD-ROM: ADOB1035-MPC, $48.95. Available from Learning Services, P.O. Box 10636, Eugene, OR 97440-2636; Western Region: 800/877-9378; Eastern Region: 800/877-3278. (See coupon.)

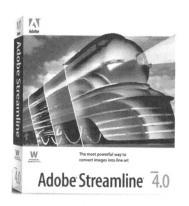

Adobe Streamline 4.0 (Ages 15 to adult)

This software product converts images into editable line art. You can quickly and easily convert scanned b&w or color images into PostScript language line art. You'll save hours over time-consuming manual tracing, and you can take advantage of many flexible and powerful controls that autotrace tools in drawing programs don't provide. MAC CD-ROM: ADOB1000-MC3 or WIN CD-ROM: ADOB1000-W31, $98.95. Available from Learning Services, P.O. Box 10636, Eugene, OR 97440-2636; Western Region: 800/877-9378; Eastern Region: 800/877-3278. (See coupon.)

Adobe ImageReady 1.0   (Ages 15 to adult)

This is the Web professional's powerhouse with everything you need to prepare images and graphics for the Web faster. Real-time image compression lets you instantly compare optimized images with the original and view file sizes and download times. MAC CD-ROM: ADOB1050-MCCD or WIN CD-ROM: ADOB1050-MPC, $127.95. Available from Learning Services, P.O. Box 10636, Eugene, OR 97440-2636; Western Region: 800/877-9378; Eastern Region: 800/877-3278. (See coupon.)

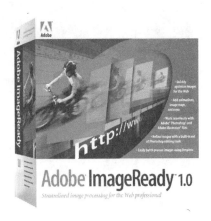

Adobe After Effects 4.0   (Ages 15 to adult)

Produce professional-quality film and video composites with sophisticated animation and special effects using this great software. Adobe is the leader in desktop composition and 2-D animation. MAC CD-ROM: ADBO1030-MCCD or WIN CD-ROM ADOB1030-MPC, $259. Available from Learning Services, P.O. Box 10636, Eugene, OR 97440-2636; Western Region: 800/877-9378; Eastern Region: 800/877-3278. (See coupon.)

Adobe Dimensions 3.0   (Ages 15 to adult)

This is an easy to use but powerful 3-D rendering tool that creates high-quality 3-D artwork in vector and raster formats. MAC CD-ROM: ADOBOO75-MCCD or WIN CD-ROM: ADOBOO75-MPC, $89.95. Available from Learning Services, P.O. Box 10636, Eugene, OR 97440-2636; Western Region: 800/877-9378; Eastern Region: 800/877-3278. (See coupon.)

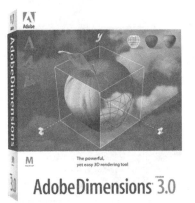

Computer Products

Claris Home Page 3.0   (Ages 13 to adult)

With this software anyone can create and manage great-looking Web pages. Easy-to-use assistants walk you through the entire process in minutes, handling all of the complex HTML work behind the scenes. Hybrid CD-ROM: CLA-ROO15-CDB, $59.95. Available from Learning Services, P.O. Box 10636, Eugene, OR 97440-2636; Western Region: 800/877-9378; Eastern Region: 800/877-3278. (See coupon.)

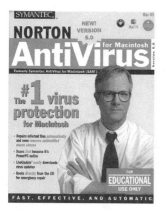

Norton AntiVirus 5.0 (Family use)

Now you can get the world's No. 1 antivirus protection for your computer. This software also allows a new way to recover data that has been damaged "beyond repair" by a particular virus. MAC CD-ROM: SYMA070-MCCD, $41.95; WIN CD-ROM: SYMA0070-MPC, $31.95. Available from Learning Services, P.O. Box 10636, Eugene, OR 97440-2636; Western Region: 800/877-9378; Eastern Region: 800/877-3278. (See coupon.)

Microsoft Office 98 (Family Use)

The office suite from the leader! Includes Word, Excel, Power-Point, and Mail in one great integrated package. WIN 95 CD-ROM: MICROO59-W95 or WIN CD-ROM: MICROO56-PC3, $155.95. Available from Learning Services, P.O. Box 10636, Eugene, OR 97440-2636; Western Region: 800/877-9378; Eastern Region: 800/877-3278. (See coupon.)

Print Shop PressWriter (Ages 9 to 18)

This software program gives your student all the tools he or she needs to practice essential information organization, writing, and publishing skills by creating "real world" writing projects. Choose from reports, letters, resumes, newsletters, journals, brochures, booklets, and flyers. You can easily edit and format your work with the excellent features included. MAC CD-ROM: BROD1405-MCCDS or WIN CD-ROM: BROD1405-MPCS, $59.95. Available from Learning Services, P.O. Box 10636, Eugene, OR 97440-2636; Western Region: 800/877-9378; Eastern Region: 800/877-3278. (See coupon.)

Inspiration (K to 12 Education Edition) (Ages 5 to 17)

This is a powerful visual learning software tool that inspires your student to organize his or her thinking. Remember using the web method for creative writing? This program includes concept webs, maps, and other graphic organizers. Useful for English, science, history, or any subject that relies on organizing. Hybrid CD-ROM: INSP0005-CDB, $65.95. Available from Learning Services, P.O. Box 10636, Eugene, OR 97440-2636; Western Region: 800/877-9378; Eastern Region: 800/877-3278. (See coupon.)

Digital Chisel 2.1.4 (Ages 9 and up)

This is a multimedia authoring tool that allows the user to create an animated alphabet book, a multimedia lesson in advanced science, and singing birthday cards! You can even convert your projects to HTML and make Web pages! MAC CD-ROM: PIERO150-MCCDS, $48.95. Available from Learning Services, P.O. Box 10636, Eugene, or 97440-2636; Western Region: 800/877-9378; Eastern Region: 800/877-3278. (See coupon.)

DK My First Incredible, Amazing Dictionary (Ages 4 to 9)

This DK Interactive Learning CD-ROM dictionary allows a child to learn potentially more than 1,000 words and their meanings at his or her own pace through the use of spoken words, pictures, sound effects, and animation. MAC CD-ROM: DORLOOO5-MCCDS or WIN CD-ROM: DORLOOO5-MPCS, $45.95. Available from Learning Services, P.O. Box 10636, Eugene, OR 97440-2636; Western Region: 800/877-9378; Eastern Region: 800/877-3278. (See coupon.)

A to ZAP!   (Ages 4 to 7)

This software program is crammed with 26 different activities. It can teach your student letters, numbers, and words in a fun setting. MAC CD-ROM: SUNBOO1O-MCCD or WIN CD-ROM: SUNBOO1OMPC, $59.95. Available from Learning Services, P.O. Box 10636, Eugene, OR 97440-2636; Western Region: 800/877-9378; Eastern Region: 800/877-3278. (See coupon.)

The World of Totty Pig: You Are Much Too Small   (Ages 4 and up)

On this CD-ROM Totty Pig is told she is much too small to do all of the things grown-up pigs do, so she sets out to teach them a lesson. Makes learning to read fun with its many features such as learning puzzles, games, and much more. MAC CD-ROM: ORANO48O-MCCD or WIN CD-ROM: ORANO480-MPC, $19.95. Available from Learning Services, P.O. Box 10636, Eugene, OR 97440-2636; Western Region: 800/877-9378; Eastern Region: 800/877-3278. (See coupon.)

Multisensory Kindergarten   (Ages 4 to 8)

This CD-ROM helps your little student develop skills in number ordering, sequencing, alphabet and keyboard identification, colors and shapes, drawing and coloring, and the concept of the days of the week. MAC CD-ROM: ORANO42O-MCCD, $49.95. Available from Learning Services, P.O. Box 10636, Eugene, OR 97440-2636; Western Region: 800/877-9378; Eastern Region: 800/877-3278. (See coupon.)

Highlights Hidden Pictures Workshop   (Ages 4 to 10)

Highlights is America's best-selling children's magazine and is now available on CD-ROM. This disk offers three skill levels, and at least one is sure to enthrall your child for hours of fun and learning value. Hybrid CD-ROM: PALLOO35-CDB, $29.95. Available from Learning Services, P.O. Box 10636, Eugene, OR 97440-2636; Western Region: 800/877-9378; Eastern Region: 800/877-3278. (See coupon.)

The Life Skills CD-ROM   (Ages 13 to 18)

This CD-ROM collection includes Life Skills English, How to Do Research, Dictionary Skills, Survival Math, Business Math, You and the Law, Needing Reading, You and Your Money, Reading Comprehension for Employment, and more. Hybrid CD-ROM: QUEUO615-CDB, $195.95. Available from Learning Services, P.O. Box 10636, Eugene, OR 97440-2636; Western Region: 800/877-9378; Eastern Region: 800/877-3278. (See coupon.)

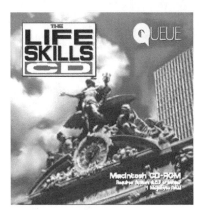

Computer Products

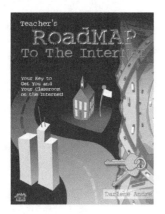

Teacher's Roadmap to the InterNET   (Ages 15 to adult)

This book/CD-ROM guides you onto the Internet so you can use the resources and information for study purposes. There is a wealth of information and services available through the Internet, and the 100-page book will help you track them down. Hybrid CD-ROM: FOREOOO5-CDB, $27.95. Available from Learning Services, P.O. Box 10636, Eugene, OR 97440-2636; Western Region: 800/877-9378; Eastern Region: 800/877-3278. (See coupon.)

Cyber Patrol   (Ages 5 to 18)

This CD-ROM program puts you in control of Net access. It is easy to use and allows you to restrict use to certain times of the day, limit the total amount of time spent online, or block access completely. Another feature (for Windows only) is that it prevents your child from revealing personal information online. Hybrid CD-ROM: MCRSOOO5-CDB, $34.95. Available from Learning Services, P.O. Box 10636, Eugene, OR 97440-2636; Western Region: 800/877-9378; Eastern Region: 800/877-3278. (See coupon.)

The Internet Schoolhouse (Adults)

This CD-ROM will help you to integrate the Internet and multimedia into your curriculum. It is a resource you will want to use again and again. Hybrid CD-ROM: VISIO175XX, $23.95. Available from Learning Services, P.O. Box 10636, Eugene, OR 97440-2636; Western Region: 800/877-9378; Eastern Region: 800/877-3278. (See coupon.)

FoolProof Internet (Family Use)

This CD-ROM program extends your protection and control over Internet access. Offers you intelligent content filtering, browser security, and much more. Hybrid CD-ROM: SMSTO105-CDB, $69. Available from Learning Services, P.O. Box 10636, Eugene, OR 97440-2636; Western Region: 800/877-9378; Eastern Region: 800/877-3278. (See coupon.)

Field Trap Internet Coach   (Ages 7 to 11)

A class trip teaches students about their ancestry on this CD-ROM. Gives information on more than 50 nationalities living in the United States. Hybrid CD-ROM: APTEOO4O-CDB, $35.95. Available from Learning Services, P.O. Box 10636, Eugene, OR 97440-2636; Western Region: 800/877-9378; Eastern Region: 800/877-3278. (See coupon.)

Mission to Planet X   (Ages 10 and up)

This CD-ROM is filled with space travel information. Your student can use his or her Internet knowledge to solve mysteries and learn all the features of the Internet. Hybrid CD-ROM: APTEOO1O-CDB, $35.95. Available from Learning Services, P.O. Box 10636, Eugene, OR 97440-2636; Western Region: 800/877-9378; Eastern Region: 800/877-3278. (See coupon.)

Search for the Black Rhino   (Ages 10 and up)

This CD-ROM is packed with information about scientific Web pages your student can use for Internet research. It also challenges users to put their skills to work. Hybrid CD-ROM: APTEOO3O-CDB, $35.95. Available from Learning Services, P.O. Box 10636, Eugene, OR 97440-2636; Western Region: 800/877-9378; Eastern Region: 800/877-3278. (See coupon.)

Computer Products

for Elementary Students

Internet ABCs for Elementary Students and Internet Skills for School Success   (Ages 6 to 18)

Despite the fact that these two books seem to have a "school" outlook, you should know of them. They contain information for quickly teaching you and your student to use the Internet's vast educational resources. A "Teacher's Guide to the Net" is also included. *ABCs for K-6:* FORFOOO5XX; *Skills for School Success:* FORFOO10XX; $9.95 each. Available from Learning Services, P.O. Box 10636, Eugene, OR 97440-2636; Western Region: 800/877-9378; Eastern Region: 800/877-3278. (See coupon.)

Crystal Composition—Language Arts on the Internet (Ages 12 to 14)

This CD-ROM program helps your student to write better by using some of the resources available on the Web. Internet experience is not necessary. Hybrid CD-ROM: BONUOO25-CDBS, $32.95. Available from Learning Services, P.O. Box 10636, Eugene, OR 97440-2636; Western Region: 800/877-9378; Eastern Region: 800/877-3278. (See coupon.)

Mavis Beacon Teaches Typing 9.0   (Ages 9 and up)

Your child can use the world's best-selling typing program to master typing skills. Many flexible features make this CD-ROM customizable to your student's strengths, weaknesses, and skills level. MAC CD-ROM: (v.2.0) SWTOO2O-MC3 or WIN CD-ROM: (v.3.0) SWTOO2O-PC3, $17.95. Available from Learning Services, P.O. Box 10636, Eugene, OR 97440-2636; Western Region: 800/877-9378; Eastern Region: 800/877-3278. (See coupon.)

All the Right Type   (Ages 10 and up)

With this CD-ROM you can create your own drills, lessons, tests, and timings for your child's use. Adapt the program to his or her needs. Blank screen can be employed, which allows your student to type from hardcopy while the program continues to mark and record. MAC CD-ROM: DIDAOO3O-MCCDS or WIN CD-ROM: DIDAOO3O-MPCS, $49.95. Available from Learning Services, P.O. Box 10636, Eugene, OR 97440-2636; Western Region: 800/877-9378; Eastern Region: 800/877-3278. (See coupon.)

Stickybear Typing   (Ages 7 and up)

Your young typist can sharpen his or her skills and improve keyboarding mastery with the program's three multilevel activities. The user can self-test for timing and accuracy while the program tracks progress and keeps records. The program contains 30 levels of difficulty. Tribrid CD-ROM: WEEKOO31-CDB, $41.95. Available from Learning Services, P.O. Box 10636, Eugene, OR 97440-2636; Western Region: 800/877-9378; Eastern Region: 800/877-3278. (See coupon.)

Roller Typing   (Ages 8 and up)

Your student can learn and practice his or her typing skills through five unique animated in-line skating events. Contains 20 levels of letters, numbers, and punctuation symbols. Hybrid CD-ROM: EDVEOO1O-CDBS, $33.95. Available from Learning Services, P.O. Box 10636, Eugene, OR 97440-2636; Western Region: 800/877-9378; Eastern Region: 800/877-3278. (See coupon.)

Computer Products

Speedskin   (Ages 4 to 18)

This is not a software program but an opaque orange sheet you place over the keys, covering the letters, and eliminating keyboard peeking. One size fits all keyboards, including most laptops. SPEEDOO5XX, $10.95. Available from Learning Services, P.O. Box 10636, Eugene, OR 97440-2636; Western Region: 800/877-9378; Eastern Region: 800/877-3278. (See coupon.)

LittleFingers   (Ages 8 to 12)

This is the world's first computer keyboard designed specifically for children's smaller hands. This makes touch-typing easier and more accurate for them. Built-in wrist-rest assures comfort and safety. Specially designed to allow a standard adult-sized keyboard to be connected at the same time, allowing parent and student to work side-by-side. MAC and PC compatible. DADEOOO5XX, $79.95. Available from Learning Services, P.O. Box 10636, Eugene, OR 97440-2636; Western Region: 800/877-9378; Eastern Region: 800/877-3278. (See coupon.)

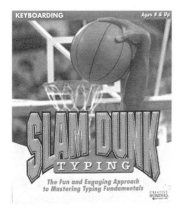

Slam Dunk Typing   (Ages 9 and up)

This program combines the thrill of a basketball game with exercises that develop typing speed and accuracy. Onscreen hands show correct positioning and typing method. There is even a coach who monitors your student's progress, offering tips and advice for improving his or her skills. Sound effects heighten the basketball analogy! Hybrid CD-ROM: CRE-WOO5O-CDB, $19.95. Available from Learning Services, P.O. Box 10636, Eugene, OR 97440-2636; Western Region: 800/877-9378; Eastern Region: 800/877-3278. (See coupon.)

JumpStart Typing   (Ages 8 and up)

A high-tech decathlon is the setting for learning to type with this CD-ROM program. The typist helps a coach and his Dream Team to success in the games while learning correct typing skills, hand placement, and posture. Hybrid CD-ROM: KADV9010-CDBS, $44.95. Available from Learning Services, P.O. Box 10636, Eugene, OR 97440-2636; Western Region: 800/877-9378; Eastern Region: 800/877-3278. (See coupon.)

Math

(For math games, please see Board Games, p. 457)

Great Ideas of Mathematics Posters (Family Use)

These 24" × 34" posters are available separately: Prime Numbers Poster (EB-91-6562); Pythagorean Theorem Poster (EB-91-6561); History of Pi Poster (EB-91-6564); Infinity Poster (EB-91-6563), $10.95 each. Set of four and Teacher's Guide EB-91-6860, $36.95. Available from Carolina Biological Supply Co., 2700 York Rd., Burlington, NC 27215; 800/334-5551; www.carolina.com.

Strength in Numbers: Discovering the Joy and Power of Mathematics in Everyday Life   (Ages 15 and up)

This 1996 book by Sherman K. Stein is a 272-page hardcover. Enjoy this survey of mathematics that takes the reader from Abel to zero over zero. EB-91-3966, $24.95. Available from Carolina Biological Supply Co., 2700 York Rd., Burlington, NC 27215; 800/334-5551; www.carolina.com.

Discovering the Joy and Power of Mathematics in Everyday Life

SHERMAN K. STEIN

Math

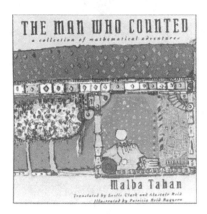

The Man Who Counted: A Collection of Mathematical Adventures (Ages 12 and up)

This 244-page softcover by Malba Tahan tells the story of a noted Brazilian mathematician who was seeking a way to bring the mysteries and delights of mathematics to a wider audience. Beremiz Samir summons extraordinary mathematical powers to settle disputes, give wise counsel, overcome dangerous enemies, and win fame, fortune, and rich rewards. EB-91-3995, $14.95. Available from Carolina Biological Supply Co., 2700 York Rd., Burlington, NC 27215; 800/334-5551; www.carolina.com.

Mathematical Scandals (Ages 12 to adult)

This 149-page softcover by Theoni Pappas was written in 1997. A series of stories points out the rivalries and deceptions that took place in the history of mathematics. This contradicts the average layman's view that mathematicians are detached from such things. EB-91-4713, $10.95. Available from Carolina Biological Supply Co., 2700 York Rd., Burlington, NC 27215; 800/334-5551; www.carolina.com.

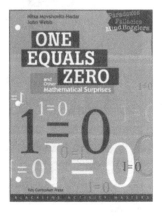

One Equals Zero: and Other Mathmatical Surprises (Ages 13 to 18)

This 192-page softcover by Nitsa Movshovitz-Hadar and John Webb presents activities that will perplex, pique curiosity, and stimulate your child's intellect. Many of them are applicable to lessons in algebra, geometry, trigonometry, statistics, and calculus. Detailed teacher's notes accompany each activity with thorough explanations of the paradoxes and/or problems presented. BC-91-3974, $13.95. Available from Carolina Biological Supply Co., 2700 York Rd., Burlington, NC 27215; 800/334-5551; www.carolina.com.

Math

Harper Collins Dictionary of Mathematics   (Ages 12 and up)

This 657-page softcover by E. J. Borowski and J. M. Borwein was written in 1991. More than 4,000 entries provide definitions, explanations, and examples from pure and applied mathematics. It includes over 400 illustrations, biographies of mathematicians, and explanations of paradoxes. A must-have for the math scholar in your home. EB-91-3925, $18.95. Available from Carolina Biological Supply Co., 2700 York Rd., Burlington, NC 27215; 800/334-5551; www.carolina.com.

Mathematical Investigations   (Ages 14 to 18)

The softcover books in this three-book series can be purchased separately, or more economically as a set. Book 1: topics include geometry, patterns, operations research, and genetics (1989, 200-page softcover); Book 2: problems involve networks, sports math, rates, using maps, and discovering rules (1992, 230 pages); Book 3: basic ideas about money, finance and loans, probability, scaling, and linear programming (1993, 208 pages). Book 1: EB-91-4240; Book 2: EB-91-4241; Book 3: EB-91-4242, $19.95 each. Set of all three: EB-91-4243, $56.85. Available from Carolina Biological Supply Co., 2700 York Rd., Burlington, NC 27215; 800/334-5551; www.carolina.com.

101 Mathematical Projects   (Ages 12 and up)

This 168-page softcover by Brian Bolt and David Hobbs was written in 1989. These projects were chosen to connect art, science, and the real world with mathematics. Classified into 13 broad categories, the projects range from room design to sports performance to the math of planning and raising a garden. A wide variety of interests are covered, and references are provided for each activity. EB-91-4215, $20.95. Available from Carolina Biological Supply Co., 2700 York Rd., Burlington, NC 27215; 800/334-5551; www.carolina.com.

Math

A Blueprint for Geometry (Ages 12 to 18)

This 96-page reproducible real-world geometry book by Brad Fulton and Bill Lombard provides scale measurement and spatial problem solving. Your student will read floor plans and design houses from the ground up. $16.95. Architectural Education Resource Center (AERC) 131 Hillside Road, Franklin, MA 02038; 508/528-4517; e-mail: aerc@norfolk-county.com; www.norfolk-county.com/aerc. (See coupon.)

Family Math Series (Ages 4 to 14)

This popular series of math books (3 volumes) by Grace Davila Coates and Jean Kerr Stenmark was developed through UC Berkeley. The books are written in a form that suits families learning together and in real-life settings (1) *Family Math for Young Children*, ages 4 to 8, 196 pages, $18.95; (2) *Family Math—The Middle School Years*, ages 10 to 14, 280 pages, $18.95; (3) *Family Math*, ages 5 to 14, 304 pages, $18.95. (Add $5 shipping per book or $7 for three.) Make checks payable to *Regents of the University of California* (California residents add appropriate sales tax) and send to: UC Berkeley, EQUALS Publications, Lawrence Hall of Science #5200, Berkeley, CA 94720-5200; 800/897-5036; 510/643-5757. Contact for credit card purchases or a complete catalog.

Basic Math Learning Wrap-Ups (Ages 8 and up)

Every Wrap-Up set consists of ten various notched and labeled plastic boards. A piece of precut yarn (supplied) is wrapped up around the board following the proper pattern to produce the correct answer to the problem. On the back of each board is etched the correct path the wound string should follow (the solution). Addition (LWU 101), Subtraction (LWU 102), Multiplication (LWU 103), Division (LWU 104), and Fractions (LWU 105); $7.95 each. Learning Wrap-Ups, 2122 East 6550 South, Ogden, UT 84405; 800/992-4966. (See coupon.)

The Happy Homeschool Money Kit (Ages 8 to 12)

With this kit your child will make coins, study the history of money, play Presto Chango, and do much more. $135. The Happy Homeschool, 60 Walker Ln., Lake Placid, FL 33852; Fax: 941/699-5808; www.happyhomeschool.com; for a free catalog, call, 877/540-1918.

Pre-Algebra Learning Wrap-Ups   (Ages 12 to 16)

This is the algebra version of the innovative plastic-board-and-yarn practice tools. Your child will be able to practice these concepts with the same self-correcting system as was described in the basic math version (p. 270) by wrapping the precut length of yarn around the plastic board in the appropriate pattern. The kit contains +/−,÷/× Integers, Solve for the Unknown, Algebraic Expressions, Mental Math, Prime Factors, Squares, and Formulas. LWU 821 $34.95. Learning Wrap-Ups, 2122 East 6550 South, Ogden, UT 84405; 800/992-4966. (See coupon.)

Math for Humans: Teaching Math Through 7 Intelligences (Parent Use)

This 240-page softcover by Mark Wahl was published in 1997. Learn about the theory of multiple intelligences and apply its principles to your teaching. Your lesson planning will benefit. EB-91-4106, $29.95. Available from Carolina Biological Supply Co., 2700 York Rd., Burlington, NC 27215; 800/334-5551; www.carolina.com.

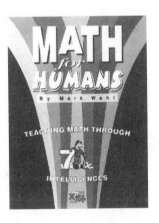

A History of Mathematics   (Ages 13 to 18)

This 715-page softcover second edition by Carl B. Boyer and Uta C. Merzbach was published in 1991. Read about the progress of mathematics including coverage of twentieth-century developments in computers and probability. Includes a time-line of mathematical and general historical events. EB-91-4740, $32.95. Available from Carolina Biological Supply Co., 2700 York Rd., Burlington, NC 27215; 800/334-5551; www.carolina.com.

Math

She Does Math!   (Ages 12 to 18)

Marla Parker edited this 1995 softcover collection of autobiographies of 38 women who worked in the fields of math. Each subject talks about what math she studied in high school and college, why she chose math as her field of endeavor, and how she obtained her job. EB-91-3935, $16.95. Carolina Biological Supply Co., 2700 York Rd., Burlington, NC 27215; 800/334-5551; www.carolina.com.

Men of Mathematics   (Ages 13 and up)

This 1965, 591-page softcover by E. T. Bell is a classic biographical work dealing with great mathematicians from Pythagoras to Einstein. EB-91-3934, $17.95. Available from Carolina Biological Supply Co., 2700 York Rd., Burlington, NC 27215; 800/334-5551; www.carolina.com.

Fantasia Mathematica   (Ages 13 and up)

This collection of essays (1997, 325-page softcover) by many famous authors first appeared in 1958 and was originally edited by Clifton Fadiman. It includes works by Aldous Huxley, H. G. Wells, Plato, Arthur C. Clarke, and others. EB-91-3967 $19.95. Available from Carolina Biological Supply Co., 2700 York Rd., Burlington, NC 27215; 800/334-5551; www.carolina.com.

Math

The Mathematical Magpie (Ages 13 and up)

This 300-page softcover is a 1997 version of a book originally edited by Clifton Fadiman and first published in 1962. The companion volume to *Fantasia Mathematica*, this book includes works by Arthur C. Clarke, Isaac Asimov, Mark Twain, and Lewis Carroll. Also includes poems, limericks, and other items. EB-91-3969, $19.95. Available from Carolina Biological Supply Co., 2700 York Rd., Burlington, NC 27215; 800/334-5551; www.carolina.com.

Multicultural Science and Math Connections (Ages 12 to 14)

This 1995, 193-page softcover volume by Beatrice Lumpkin and Dorothy Strong provides exploration of math discoveries of 13 different cultures and features 22 units of work using simple materials, readings, and project ideas. It connects science, math, history, art, and music. EB-91-5565, $24.95. Available from Carolina Biological Supply Co., 2700 York Rd., Burlington, NC 27215; 800/334-5551; www.carolina.com.

When Are We Ever Gonna Have to Use This? (Family Use)

This poster by Hal Saunders (Dale Seymour Publications, revised 1990) offers a summary of Saunders' interviews with people in 100 different occupations about the kinds of math they use. This 22" × 34" poster covers 71 math topics. EB-91-6580, $7.95. Available from Carolina Biological Supply Co., 2700 York Rd., Burlington, NC 27215; 800/334-5551; www.carolina.com.

When Are We Ever Gonna Have to Use This? (Ages 8 to 14)

This softcover book by Hal Saunders (Dale Seymour Publications, 1988, 3rd ed.) has 133 pages. This volume contains over 430 word problems using 60 different math topics correlated to occupations, math content, and three levels of difficulty. EB-91-4150, $10.95. Available from Carolina Biological Supply Co., 2700 York Rd., Burlington, NC 27215; 800/334-5551; www.carolina.com.

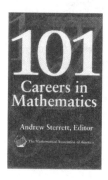

101 Careers in Mathematics (Ages 14 and up)

Edited by Andrew Sterrett, this 260-page softcover book contains a series of essays that describe various careers in which math or a preparation of it are utilized. Some require math on a daily basis; others simply require math-type problem solving. EB-91-3928, $22.95. Available from Carolina Biological Supply Co., 2700 York Rd., Burlington, NC 27215; 800/334-5551; www.carolina.com.

In the Wind (Ages 15 and up)

Learn about airplane navigation by forecast information and applying vectors to find an airplane's ground track in this 128-page softcover written in 1997 by Christine Johnson. It includes discussions of ratios, proportions, rates, patterns, and functions, angle and distance measurement, scale drawing, headings, orientation, maps, testing, and weather. EB-91-5559, $19.95. Available from Carolina Biological Supply Co., 2700 York Rd., Burlington, NC 27215; 800/334-5551; www.carolina.com.

Math Wizardry for Kids (Ages 11 and up)

This 325-page softcover written in 1995 by Martha Kenda and Phyllis Williams is a collection of over 200 math puzzles and activities. Full of tips for finding math outside a classroom setting. EB-91-4217, $13.95. Available from Carolina Biological Supply Co., 2700 York Rd., Burlington, NC 27215; 800/334-5551; www.carolina.com.

Yesterday's Sports, Today's Math   (Ages 10 to 14)

This 94-page softcover by Don Fraser was published by Dale Seymour Publications in 1997. Real data from the sports world can help your student build number sense and motivate them to use statistics in answering sports-related questions. If your child is a sports fan, this is likely to be a "hit" with him or her! EB-91-7867, $13.95. Available from Carolina Biological Supply Co., 2700 York Rd., Burlington, NC 27215; 800/334-5551; www.carolina.com.

Math for Real Kids   (Ages 12 to 14)

This sourcebook by David B. Spangler (1997, 136-page softcover) of math problems, applications, and activities provides 70 situations encountered in everyday life. Estimate change in a restaurant, figure out how many times a bike wheel turns, score a bowling game, and work with sports statistics. This book covers whole numbers, decimals, fractions, statistics, probability, measurement, geometry, and pre-algebra. EB-91-4510, $12.95. Available from Carolina Biological Supply Co., 2700 York Rd., Burlington, NC 27215; 800/334-5551; www.carolina.com.

Applying Algebra   (Ages 14 and up)

This 1994, 90-page softcover by John L. P. McCabe illustrates practical applications of algebra to everyday situations. Topics covered include formulas, ratios, proportion, percent, and equations. A discussion of the topic is followed by its application to real-life problems. Answers are included. EB-91-8971, $6.95. Available from Carolina Biological Supply Co., 2700 York Rd., Burlington, NC 27215; 800/334-5551; www.carolina.com.

Math

Hands-On Algebra! **(Ages 13 and up)**

This 622-page softcover book (1998) by Frances M. Thompson has 159 games and activities to make algebra more meaningful for kids of all ability levels. It consists of five sections: Real Numbers, Linear Forms, Linear Applications and Graphing, Quadratic Concepts, and Special Applications. Each activity includes complete teacher directions, and many also include reproducible worksheets. EB-91-8996, $28.95. Available from Carolina Biological Supply Co., 2700 York Rd., Burlington, NC 27215; 800/334-5551; www.carolina.com.

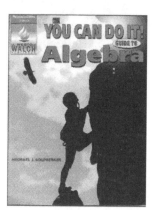

You Can Do It! Guide to Algebra **(Ages 13 and up)**

This volume (1996, 142-page softcover) by Michael J. Goldberger supplies clear explanations and advice for the first-year algebra student. There are understandable explanations, step-by-step directions, pointers, examples, and 62 topics covered with problems for each. Answers are included. EB-91-8956, $22.95. Available from Carolina Biological Supply Co., 2700 York Rd., Burlington, NC 27215; 800/334-5551; www.carolina.com.

Algebra Practice Exercises **(Ages 13 and up)**

This is a collection of worksheets by Thomas E. Campbell covering 50 topics, including vocabulary, order of operations, factoring, solving simple equations, simultaneous equations, and word problems. Complete answers are included. EB-91-8957, $19.95. Available from Carolina Biological Supply Co., 2700 York Rd., Burlington, NC 27215; 800/334-5551; www.carolina.com.

Math

80 Activities to Make Basic Algebra Easier
(Ages 13 and up)

This handy sourcebook (1983, 173-page softcover) by Robert S. Graflund is designed for the beginning algebra student. It contains reproducible puzzles, problems, and practice to reinforce basic skills in such areas as polynomials, factoring, equations, and graphing. Answers are included. EB-91-8962, $22.95. Available from Carolina Biological Supply Co., 2700 York Rd., Burlington, NC 27215; 800/334-5551; www.carolina.com.

A Blueprint for Geometry   (Ages 12 to 14)

Bill Lombard and Brad S. Fulton published this 62-page softcover in 1995. Offer your student the chance to exercise some creativity in geometry with this activity book. Helps develop skill in measurement and proportion; statistics, spatial visualization, and drawing; and perimeter, area, and volume in the context of apartment and house design. EB-91-9429, $16.95. Available from Carolina Biological Supply Co., 2700 York Rd., Burlington, NC 27215; 800/334-5551; www.carolina.com.

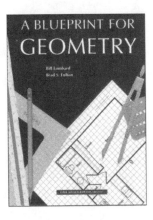

Trigonometry the Easy Way   (Ages 16 and up)

The essentials of trig are simply and clearly presented through an adventure story by Douglas Downing in this 307-page softcover (1990). EB-91-4605, $11.95. Available from Carolina Biological Supply Co., 2700 York Rd., Burlington, NC 27215; 800/334-5551; www.carolina.com.

Calculus Explorations (Ages 16 and up)

This 144-page softcover book (1997) by Paul Foerster encourages your student to learn by exploring on his or her own. Excellent supplements to textbooks, these activities are designed for use with a graphing calculator. The activities are indexed according to calculus functions and solutions to the problems are provided. EB-91-9633, $19.95. Available from Carolina Biological Supply Co., 2700 York Rd., Burlington, NC 27215; 800/334-5551; www.carolina.com.

The Candy-Coated World of Calculus (Age 15 and up)

Take the fear out of calculus with these approximately one-hour video reviews. Part 1 reviews functions and graphing, presents limits, asymptotes, continuity, the derivative, differentiation, the power rule, and second and higher derivatives. Part 2 presents applications of the derivative, including local maxima and minima, tangent lines, velocity and acceleration, antiderivatives, rules of integration, the definite integral, Riemann sums, and the Fundamental Theorem of Calculus. Part 1 (EB-91-5993), $19.95; Part 2 (EG-91-5994), $19.95. Available from Carolina Biological Supply Co., 2700 York Rd., Burlington, NC 27215; 800/334-5551; www.carolina.com.

Sunbuddy Math Playhouse (Ages 5 to 9)

Your youngster will enjoy learning about counting and numbers in this CD-ROM program. Basic addition and subtraction are reinforced; memory skills and problem-solving are improved. MAC CD-ROM: SUNBOO3O-MCCD or WIN CD-ROM: SUNBOO3O-MPC, $59.95. Available from Learning Services, P.O. Box 10636, Eugene, OR 97440-2636; Western Region: 800/877-9378; Eastern Region: 800/877-3278. (See coupon.)

Math

Numbers Undercover   (Ages 5 to 9)

This CD-ROM program asks the student to solve the mystery of the missing numbers. In doing so, she or he practices four math skills: telling time, measuring and estimating, counting, and working with money. MAC CD-ROM: SUNB9P35-MCCD or WIN CD-ROM: SUNB9O35-MPC, $59.95. Available from Learning Services, P.O. Box 10636, Eugene, OR 97440-2636; Western Region: 800/877-9378; Eastern Region: 800/877-3278. (See coupon.)

Moneywise Kids   (Ages 8 and up)

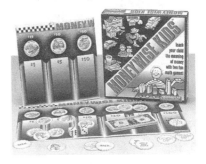

This kit offers your student the opportunity to learn about money in a real-life atmosphere. She or he will practice making change while earning a $100 bill, then work to budget the earnings on the necessities of life. Allows for practice with addition, subtraction, multiplication, and place values. B8-96-2459, $15. Available from Carolina Biological Supply Co., 2700 York Rd., Burlington, NC 27215; 800/334-5551; www.carolina.com.

DK My First Math Adventure—Counting & Sorting   (Ages 3 to 7)

This CD-ROM program helps your young child develop early math skills and two onscreen characters are always available to help. Item #8632, $19.95. Available from DK Family Learning, 11124 N.E. Halsey, Suite 460, Portland, OR 97220; 888/225-3535. (See coupon.)

DK My First Math Adventure—Adding and Subtracting   (Ages 5 to 8)

This CD-ROM will help your child master addition and subtraction with onscreen help available. Hybrid CD-ROM: Item #8642, $19.95. Available from DK Family Learning, 11124 N.E. Halsey, Suite 460, Portland, OR 97220; 888/225-3535. (See coupon.)

Math

DK I Love Math!   (Ages 7 to 11)

This CD-ROM covers addition, subtraction, multiplication, division, geometry, fractions, decimals, measures, percentages, data, tables, and ratios. A fun way to learn. Hybrid CD-ROM, Item #8662, $29.95. Available from DK Family Learning, 11124 N.E. Halsey, Suite 460, Portland, OR 97220; 888/225-3535. (See coupon.)

DK Times Tables!   (Ages 7 to 11)

This 32-page book and 40-minute audiocassette combine to provide your child with instruction in multiplication made easy. The times tables are set to music, and puzzles and games are also featured to make the task fun and productive. Item #370, $15.95. Available from DK Family Learning, 11124 N.E. Halsey, Suite 460, Portland, OR 97220; 888/225-3535. (See coupon.)

DK My First Math Book   (Ages 6 to 9)

This well-illustrated book (48 pages, hardcover) makes everyday objects into tools for learning basic math. Interactive games, puzzles, and exercises help children explore time, multiplication, division, fractions, geometry, graphs, and more. (Also available in Spanish.) Item #069, $14.95. Available from DK Family Learning, 11124 N.E. Halsey, Suite 460, Portland, OR 97220; 888/225-3535. (See coupon.)

The Quarter Mile Math Games   (Ages 5 to 14)

This six-section CD-ROM program allows your child to compete with himself or herself while acquiring all of the basic math skills. Sections include The Quarter Mile (Ages 5 to 15), a sampling of the other sections; Whole Numbers (ages 5 to 12); Fractions (ages 10 to 13); Decimals & Percents (ages 10 to 13); Integers & Equations (ages 11 to 15); and Estimation & Math Tricks (ages 9 to 15). Hybrid CD-ROM: (MAC, WIN & Apple II), $34.95 each. Value Set, (all six) $129.95 Available from Learning Services, P.O. Box 10636, Eugene, OR 97440-2636; Western Region: 800/877-9378; Eastern Region: 800/877-3278. (See coupon.)

Math

Math for the Real World   (Ages 9 to 14)

This CD-ROM program helps your student acquire math skills by using real-life situations. The setting is a U.S. travel tour, and your child is a member of the band of travelers who must use logic, critical thinking, time management, and other math areas. Hybrid CD-ROM: DAVI00030-CDBS, $59.95. Available from Learning Services, P.O. Box 10636, Eugene, OR 97440-2636; Western Region: 800/877-9378; Eastern Region: 800/877-3278. (See coupon.)

The Lost Mind of Dr. Brain   (Ages 11 and up)

With this CD-ROM program by Sierra, your student can develop higher level thinking skills and problem solving by using the thousands of puzzles in ten different game areas. The program incorporates the *Theory of Multiple Intelligences* of Dr. Howard Gardner, with each game challenging several of the seven intelligences. Hybrid CD-ROM: SIER0235-CDBS $59.95. Available from Learning Services, P.O. Box 10636, Eugene, OR 97440-2636; Western Region: 800/877-9378; Eastern Region: 800/877-3278. (See coupon.)

Math Workshop Deluxe   (Ages 6 to 12)

Your student will have the opportunity to learn, practice, and improve important math skills using puzzles, music, and animated characters on this CD-ROM. Eight activities include computation, estimation, fractions, logical reasoning, spatial visualization, and fractions. Hybrid CD-ROM: BROD1016-CDB $27.95. Available from Learning Services, P.O. Box 10636, Eugene, OR 97440-2636; Western Region: 800/877-9378; Eastern Region: 800/877-3278. (See coupon.)

Math

Carmen Sandiego Math Detective　(Ages 9 to 13)

Carmen Sandiego is at it again on this CD-ROM, shrinking world treasures faster than your student can count them. Your child will embark on 12 exciting missions involving multiplication, division, and conversion of fractions to decimals in order to save Mt. Everest, the Great Wall of China, and other sites. Hybrid CD-ROM: BROD1425-CDB, $27.95. Available from Learning Services, P.O. Box 10636, Eugene, OR 97440-2636; Western Region: 800/877-9378; Eastern Region: 800/877-3278. (See coupon.)

Carmen Sandiego Curriculum Library　(Ages 11 to 14)

This CD-ROM collection of the newest Carmen Sandiego titles is for upper elementary and middle school–aged students in history, language arts, and math. It includes the complete editions of *Where in Time Is Carmen Sandiego? Carmen Sandiego Word Detective*, and *Carmen Sandiego Math Detective*. Hybrid CD-ROM: BROD2030-CDBS, $109.95. Available from Learning Services, P.O. Box 10636, Eugene, OR 97440-2636; Western Region: 800/877-9378; Eastern Region: 800/877-3278. (See coupon.)

Astro Algebra　(Ages 13 to 15)

This CD-ROM teaches the concepts and problem-solving skills your student will need to master basic algebra and develop math confidence. As captain of the spaceship *Algebra Centauri*, your student can assist aliens from around the galaxy by completing over ten missions using algebra and pre-algebra concepts. Hybrid CD-ROM: EDMK0405, $29.95. Available from Learning Services, P.O. Box 10636, Eugene, OR 97440-2636; Western Region: 800/877-9378; Eastern Region: 800/877-3278. (See coupon.)

Math

Mighty Math Cosmic Geometry   (Ages 13 to 16)

This CD-ROM is a conceptual learning journey through the wonderful world of geometry. It covers shapes, solids, constructions, transformations, 2-D and 3-D coordinates, length, perimeter, area, and volume. Your student will assemble robots, work through a 3-D maze, and much more! Hybrid CD-ROM: EDMK0400-CDB, $29.95. Available from Learning Services, P.O. Box 10636, Eugene, OR 97440-2636; Western Region: 800/877-9378; Eastern Region: 800/877-3278. (See coupon.)

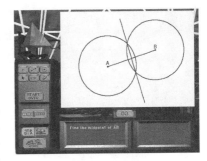

Treasure MathStorm!   (Ages 5 to 9)

Your child can develop his or her critical thinking skills to solve real-life math problems on this CD-ROM. New photo-realistic graphics help lead your child through seven progressively difficult activities. Hybrid CD-ROM: LEAR0055-CDB, $17.95. Available from Learning Services, P.O. Box 10636, Eugene, OR 97440-2636; Western Region: 800/877-9378; Eastern Region: 800/877-3278. (See coupon.)

Odyssey of Discovery: Exploring Numbers
(Ages 10 and up)

This CD-ROM program consists of five different activities giving students practice in order of operations, prime number identification, comparing and ordering integers, real numbers classification, square roots, bases, and exponents. Hybrid CD-ROM: PIER1055-CDB, $29.95. Available from Learning Services, P.O. Box 10636, Eugene, OR 97440-2636; Western Region: 800/877-9378; Eastern Region: 800/877-3278. (See coupon.)

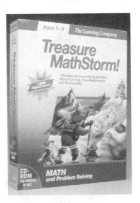

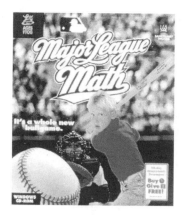

Major League Math (Ages 10 to 14)

This CD-ROM program is packed with real statistics, and your child will field over 4,000 math questions covering such topics as measurements, percentages, and basic computation. Your baseball fan can team up with his or her favorite professional club to play against another person or the computer. Includes math workshops and 28,000 potential questions. Hybrid CD-ROM: SANC00085-CDBS, $37.95. Available from Learning Services, P.O. Box 10636, Eugene, OR 97440-2636; Western Region: 800/877-9378; Eastern Region: 800/877-3278. (See coupon.)

Crash Course Basic Accounting (Ages 13 and up)

This CD-ROM offers study aid for one taking a first-year accounting course or seeking a quick review of basic accounting principles. MAC or WIN CD-ROM: HIGT0025-MPCS, $39.95. Available from Learning Services, P.O. Box 10636, Eugene, OR 97440-2636; Western Region: 800/877-9378; Eastern Region: 800/877-3278. (See coupon.)

Crash Course Algebra 1 (Ages 13 and up)

This animated CD-ROM program introduces the user to the concepts of symbols and equations, then moves quickly to graphing and quadratic equations. It is the equivalent of two semesters of algebra. WIN CD-ROM: HIGT0005-MPCS, $39.95. Available from Learning Services, P.O. Box 10636, Eugene, OR 97440-2636; Western Region: 800/877-9378; Eastern Region: 800/877-3278. (See coupon.)

Crash Course Personal Finance   (Ages 14 and up)

This CD-ROM provides information and instruction about personal investing, taxes, budgeting, financing options—everything important to gaining financial security. WIN CD-ROM: $39.95. Available from Learning Services, P.O. Box 10636, Eugene, OR 97440-2636; Western Region: 800/877-9378; Eastern Region: 800/877-3278. (See coupon.)

Crash Course Precalculus   (Ages 14 and up)

This course on CD-ROM offers an introductory mode into calculus by covering the math concepts needed before going on—a combination of algebra, analytic geometry, and trigonometry. WIN CD-ROM: HIGT0010-MPC, $39.95. Available from Learning Services, P.O. Box 10636, Eugene, OR 97440-2636; Western Region: 800/877-9378; Eastern Region: 800/877-3278. (See coupon.)

Crash Course Easy Statistics   (Ages 14 and up)

With this CD-ROM program, your student can learn the basics of statistics by dealing with practical, everyday situations. The principles are explained visually in easy-to-understand lessons. Hybrid CD-ROM: HIGT0015-MPC, $39.95. Available from Learning Services, P.O. Box 10636, Eugene, OR 97440-2636; Western Region: 800/877-9378; Eastern Region: 800/877-3278. (See coupon.)

Math

Crash Course Integral Calculus   (Ages 14 and up)

This CD-ROM program leads the student into the world of integration. It offers beneficial preparation in physics, chemistry, and other sciences. WIN CD-ROM: HIGT0030-MPC, $39.95. Available from Learning Services, P.O. Box 10636, Eugene, OR 97440-2636; Western Region: 800/877-9378; Eastern Region: 800/877-3278. (See coupon.)

Crash Course Differential Calculus   (Ages 14 and up)

This CD-ROM program teaches limits, simple functions, rate of change, derivatives, and much more. WIN CD-ROM: HIGT0045-MPC, $39.95. Available from Learning Services, P.O. Box 10636, Eugene, OR 97440-2636; Western Region: 800/877-9378; Eastern Region: 800/877-3278. (See coupon.)

Wild West Math   (Ages 10 to 12)

In this CD-ROM program, your student can join up with a host of animated Old West characters singin' and ridin' through great math activities. See how long she or he can stay on a bucking bronco by answering math questions correctly. Hybrid CD-ROM: MICG0015-CDB, $49.95. Available from Learning Services, P.O. Box 10636, Eugene, OR 97440-2636; Western Region: 800/877-9378; Eastern Region: 800/877-3278. (See coupon.)

Math

10 Secrets to Addition/Subtraction Fact Mastery and 10 Days to Multiplication Mastery (Ages 8 to 13)

These softcover books by Marion Stuart (160 and 124 pages respectively) offer ten lesson plans each with support material, as well as charts to enable your student to visualize and understand number families, games, worksheets, and answer pages. It is an ideal supplement to your regular math book to provide some extra practice, where needed. LWU-715 $9.95. Available from Learning Wrap-Ups, 2122 East 6550 South, Ogden, UT 84405; 800/992-4966. (See coupon.)

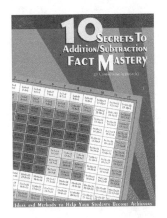

Activities for Learning—A Complete Program for K to 5 (Ages 5 to 11)

This unique math program consists of a wooden abacus and study materials. A volume of worksheets provides a visual depiction of what the abacus bead arrangement should be and the corresponding Arabic numerals. Includes two Plexiglas triangle templates, a T-square, a booklet instructing how to study geometry with these tools, and a number of other booklets and card decks. Items can be purchased separately as well. $120 plus shipping. Available from Activities for Learning, 21161 York Road, Hutchinson, MN 55350-6705; 320/587-9146; e-mail: joancott@hutchtel.net.

Mathematics: Skills, Concepts, Problem Solving Series (Ages 7 to 14)

These seven fine workbooks cover math from simple to advanced with exercises in multiplication, fractions, geometry, and so on. This series is attractive with spot color throughout and illustrations on each page. Available from Continental Press, 520 East Bainbridge St., Elizabethtown, PA 17022; 800/233-0759; www.continentalpress.com. (See coupon.)

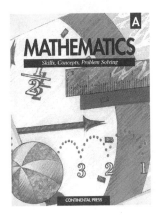

Math

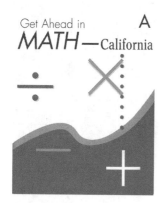

Get Ahead in Math—California (Ages 7 to 14)

This series of seven attractive workbooks is a high-quality set that can be used as a daily supplement for drilling in each math skill, from simple to geometry. Illustrated, each volume is over 75 pages. Available from Continental Press, 520 East Bainbridge St., Elizabethtown, PA 17022; 800/233-0759; www.continental-press.com. (See coupon.)

No Problem! Taking the Problem Out of Mathematical Problem Solving (Ages 10 to 12)

This 96-page illustrated, glossy, softcover book contains eight problem-solving techniques that will enable young math workers to become experts. Reproducible. DL 45, $11.95. Available from Dandy Lion Publications, 3563 Sueldo, Ste. L, San Luis Obispo, CA 93401; 800/776-8032; Fax: 805/544-2823.

Mathematics (Ages 5 to 12)

From problem-solving strategies and critical thinking to estimation and mental math, this newly revised program by Modern Curriculum Press presents a developmental sequence that introduces and extends skills taught in basal math programs. Develop high-level process skills for more problem solving using an effective four-step teaching strategy: see, plan, do, check. Alternate chapter tests to provide more testing opportunities. Levels K, A, B, C, D, E, F, $9.95 each. Teachers Edition Levels, $24 each. Available from Excellence in Education, 2640 S. Myrtle Ave., Unit A-7, Monrovia, CA 91016; 626/821-0025; Fax: 626/357-4443; www.excellenceineducation.com. (See coupon.)

The Kim Marshall Series   (Ages 10 to 14)

The 35 cumulative units in these two books cover basic computation skills, Roman numerals, English and metric measurements, graphing, fractions, and basic geometry. Theory and generalizations are minimized; practice and application are stressed. Each one-week unit covers a specific skill. Math Part A, (ages 10 to 12), $9.95; Teachers Manual, $6.95. Math Part B, (ages 13 to 14), $9.95; Teachers Manual, $6.95. Available from Excellence in Education, 2640 S. Myrtle Ave., Unit A-7, Monrovia, CA 91016; 626/821-0025; Fax: 626/357-4443; www.excellenceineducation.com. (See coupon.)

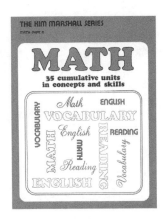

Ray's New Arithmetic Series   (Ages 7 to 18)

This classic series skillfully directs the student through the three growth stages in arithmetic: manipulative, mental image, and abstract. Done primarily through word problems, the student is taught arithmetic in an orderly fashion, starting with simple rules and principles working toward more complex applications. *Primary Arithmetic* (ages 7 to 8), $7.99. *Intellectual Arithmetic* (ages 9 to 10), $9.99. *Practical Arithmetic* (ages 11 to 12), $16.99. *Key to Ray's Arithmetic: Primary, Intellectual and Practical*, $12.99. *Higher Arithmetic* (ages 13 to 14 and high school), $20.99. *Key to Ray's Higher Arithmetic*, $12.99. *Parent-Teacher Guide for Ray's Arithmetic* by Ruth Beechick. $10.99. The full set (contains all the above books), $99.99. Available from Excellence in Education, 2640 S. Myrtle Ave., Unit A-7, Monrovia, CA 91016; 626/821-0025; Fax: 626/357-4443; www.excellenceineducation.com. (See coupon.)

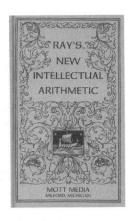

Classic Curriculum Workbooks, Ray's New Arithmetic Series (Ages 7 to 10)

These workbooks are for use with the corresponding Ray's Arithmetic series. A large $8^{1}/_{2}$" × 11" format allows the student to see the pages more clearly. Each workbook (quarter) is $8.99: Series 1, quarter 1 (none); quarters 2–4 use Ray's *Primary Arithmetic*. Series 2, quarters 1–4 use *Ray's Primary Arithmetic*. Series 3, quarters 1–4 use *Ray's Intellectual Arithmetic*. Series 4, quarters 1–4 use *Ray's Practical Arithmetic*. Available from Excellence in Education, 2640 S. Myrtle Ave., Unit A-7, Monrovia, CA 91016; 626/821-0025; Fax: 626/357-4443; www.excellenceineducation.com. (See coupon.)

The Wonder Number Game   (Ages 7 to adult)

This game applies over 100 mathematical concepts. The introduction of odd and even numbers, prime and composite numbers, multiples, addition, subtraction, multiplication, division, formulae for finding the areas of geometric forms, and reading comprehension when used with mystery numbers are but a few. The basic game consists of no less than ten individual games. $34.95. Available from Excellence in Education, 2640 S. Myrtle Ave., Unit A-7, Monrovia, CA 91016; 626/821-0025; Fax: 626/357-4443; www.excellenceineducation.com. (See coupon.)

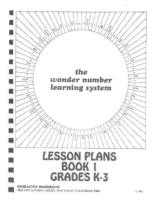

Curriculum Guides for the Wonder Number Game (Ages 5 to 14)

Utilize these curriculum guides to expand on the educational value of the game. Using both the game and curriculum guides will greatly enhance your child's "mastering" level of the number system and math. Ages 5 to 9, Ages 9 to 12, Ages 12 to 14, $14.95 each. Available from Excellence in Education, 2640 S. Myrtle Ave., Unit A-7, Monrovia, CA 91016; 626/821-0025; Fax: 626/357-4443; www.excellenceineducation.com. (See coupon.)

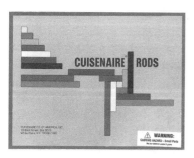

Cuisenaire Rods   (Ages 5 to 18)

Cuisenaire Rods spark children's interest in math concepts. Introductory Set contains a single set of 74 rods, a colorfully illustrated wall poster, a booklet, and teacher guide. Basic Set contains 155 rods in a self-sorting tray. It can be used to extend other rod sets or as a stand-alone set for three to five students working together. Introductory Set, $17.50. Basic Set (Ages 5 to 12), $10.25. Available from Excellence in Education, 2640 S. Myrtle Ave., Unit A-7, Monrovia, CA 91016; 626/821-0025; Fax: 626/357-4443; www.excellenceineducation.com. (See coupon.)

Math

Mathematics Made Meaningful   (Ages 4 to 14)

Designed for one to three children, this kit introduces addition, subtraction, multiplication, and division with Cuisenaire Rods. Includes 155 rods, 50 topic cards, and 80-page teacher guide. $29.95. Available from Excellence in Education, 2640 S. Myrtle Ave., Unit A-7, Monrovia, CA 91016; 626/821-0025; Fax: 626/357-4443; www.excellenceineducation.com. (See coupon.)

Starter Set   (Ages 5 to 12)

Perfect for four students to share, this set includes 155 rods in a self-sorting tray, the *Idea Book for Cuisenaire Rods at the Primary Level*, and Cuisenaire's *Learning with Cuisenaire Rods* teacher guide. $34.50. Available from Excellence in Education, 2640 S. Myrtle Ave., Unit A-7, Monrovia, CA 91016; 626/821-0025; Fax: 626/357-4443; www.excellenceineducation.com. (See coupon.)

Rod Tracks   (Ages 5 to 12)

Build rod trains and match them to numbers. Tracks are 50 cm or 100 cm long and the width of a Cuisenaire Rod. 50 cm Rod Track, $3.50; 100 cm Rod Track, $5.95. Available from Excellence in Education, 2640 S. Myrtle Ave., Unit A-7, Monrovia, CA 91016; 626/821-0025; Fax: 626/357-4443; www.excellenceineducation.com. (See coupon.)

Math

Cuisenaire Publications (Ages 4 to 15)

A wide variety of publications help you teach with Cuisenaire Rods, including: *Idea Book for Cuisenaire Rods at the Primary Level* (ages 4 to 8), $17.95; *Using Cuisenaire Rods—A Photo/Text Guide for Teachers* (ages 5 to 14), $18.95; *Everything Is Coming Up Fractions with Cuisenaire Rods* (ages 9 to 12) $9.50; *From Here to There with Cuisenaire Rods Area, Perimeter and Volume* (ages 10 to 12), $9.50; *Hidden Rods/Hidden Numbers* (ages 7 to 14), $7.50; *Multiplication and Division Rod Patterns and Graph Paper* (ages 10 to 14), $9.50; *Spatial Problem Solving with Cuisenaire Rods* (ages 10 to 15), $9.50. Available from Excellence in Education, 2640 S. Myrtle Ave., Unit A-7, Monrovia, CA 91016; 626/821-0025; Fax: 626/357-4443; www.excellenceineducation.com. (See coupon.)

Miquon Math (Ages 7 to 10)

Students use hands-on experience building models for concepts as preparation for the written equation. $5.95. Available from Eagle's Nest Educational Supplies, 1411 Standiford Ave, Ste. A, Modesto, CA 95350; 209/529-7720; Fax: 209/529-7115.

Audio Learning Tapes (Ages 8 to 12)

Contains a long-playing musical cassette by Cathy Troxel with lively sing-along tunes to reinforce math skills. The music in these tapes is refreshing and pleasant to hear. The child is encouraged to repeat the songs, with blanks left in them requiring a correct response. This is a good addition to your car tape library. "Addition," "Subtraction," and "Multiplication," $9.95 each. Available from Excellence in Education, 2640 S. Myrtle Ave., Unit A-7, Monrovia, CA 91016; 626/821-0025; Fax: 626/357-4443; www.excellenceineducation.com. (See coupon.)

Math

Math for Every Kid (Ages 13 to 18)

This great "hands on" approach to math utilizes easy activities, exciting ideas, projects, and things to do to make math come alive. Covers measurement, fractions, graphs, geometry figures, problem solving, and more. $11.95. Available from Excellence in Education, 2640 S. Myrtle Ave., Unit A-7, Monrovia, CA 91016; 626/821-0025; Fax: 626/357-4443; www.excellenceineducation.com. (See coupon.)

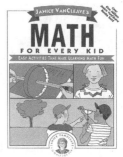

Cuisenaire Fraction Strips Set (Ages 5 to 14)

Excellent for teaching fractions, equivalence, addition, and subtraction, this 51-piece set is made of heavy plastic in for instance, halves, thirds, fourths, fifths, sixths, eighths, tenths, twelfths, and one whole. $7.95. Available from Excellence in Education, 2640 S. Myrtle Ave., Unit A-7, Monrovia, CA 91016; 626/821-0025; Fax: 626/357-4443; www.excellenceineducation.com. (See coupon.)

Saxon Math (Ages 5 to 18)

This program is the most popular homeschooling math program! Slowly introduce concepts to the student with continual repetition of what has been learned the days and weeks before. The program can be completed by working 20 to 30 minutes per day. There is a revised edition especially for homeschoolers that includes an answer key, solution manuals, and a student text. $33 to $90. Available from Eagle's Nest Educational Supplies, 1411 Standiford Ave, Ste. A, Modesto, CA 95350; 209/529-7720; Fax: 209/529-7115.

The Mathematics of Buying (Ages 13 and up)

An interactive workbook designed for the math of everyday living. This is the real thing. $19.95. Available from Meridian Creative Group, 5178 Station Road, Erie, PA 16510; 800/695-9427; www.meridianch.com. (See coupon.)

Leap Frog Math   (Ages 5 to 12)

This series of seven interactive CD-ROMs will not allow children to move to the next level until they have mastered the level below. Students can keep track of their progress and view an explanatory video of certain mathematical principles. This excellent series is the next-best thing to having an actual instructor in front of your child. $95. Available from Meridian Creative Group, 5178 Station Road, Erie, PA 16510; 800/695-9427; www.meridianch.com. (See coupon.)

Larson's TI-73 Mastery Module   (Ages 12 to 15)

This middle-school math tutorial is a software application which when downloaded, allows students to utilize cutting-edge graphing calculators to practice computational skill building. Covers three years of study in one program. This is a one-of-a-kind product $34.95. Available from Meridian Creative Group, 5178 Station Road, Erie, PA 16510; 800/695-9427; www.meridianch.com. (See coupon.)

Science and Biology

DK Encyclopedia of Nature 2.0   (Ages 8 to adult)

This CD-ROM covers more than 250 species of plants and animals. Hybrid CD-ROM: DORLOO3O-DBS, $54.95. Available from Learning Services, P.O. Box 10636, Eugene, OR 97440-2636; Western Region: 800/877-9378; Eastern Region: 800/877-3278. (See coupon.)

Take a Ride on the Magic School Bus Series (Ages 7 to 10)

Six different CD-ROM explorations of habitats. Sold separately. (1) Age of Dinosaurs, WIN CD-ROM: MICRO338-MPC, $33.95; (2) Rainforest, WIN CD-ROM: MICRO339-MPC, $33.95; (3) Human Body, Hybrid CD-ROM: MICR0330-CDB $33.95; (4) Inside the Earth, WIN CD-ROM: MICRO337-MPC, $22.95; (5) Ocean, MAC CD-ROM: MICRO336-MCCD or WIN CD-ROM: MICRO336-MPC, $22.95; (6) Solar System, WIN CD-ROM: MICRO335-MBC, $22.95. Available from Learning Services, P.O. Box 10636, Eugene, OR 97440-2636; Western Region: 800/877-9378; Eastern Region: 800/877-3278. (See coupon.)

Science Investigator (Ages 12 to 14)

With this CD-ROM, your student will affect the future! Through fun interactive activities on websites, she or he can explore physical science or chemistry or learn about elements and their symbols, static electricity, atoms, forces, waves, light, motion, Newton's laws, and more! Hybrid CD-ROM: BONUOO3O-CDBS, $32.95. Available from Learning Services, P.O. Box 10636, Eugene, OR 97440-2636; Western Region: 800/877-9378; Eastern Region: 800/877-3278. (See coupon.)

Amazing Animals CD-ROM Activity Pack (Ages 4 to 9)

This is one of a series of DK Interactive Learning CD-ROM packages based upon the *Amazing Animals* TV series. This package introduces your child to the world of animals through 20 activities on animal appearance, behavior, and habitat. Hybrid CD-ROM: DORLO13O-CDBS, $45.95. Available from Learning Services, P.O. Box 10636, Eugene, OR 97440-2636; Western Region: 800/877-9378; Eastern Region: 800/877-3278. (See coupon.)

Can O' Worms Composting Bin   (Family use)

This odorless, user-friendly system allows recycling and garden enrichment through the process of composting. Plastic, recycled, stackable trays create an ideal situation for studying many science-related topics in a controlled environment. Standing on five sturdy legs, each unit (29" × 20") also features a tap drain for the collection of natural liquid fertilizer. Under normal indoor use, the bin is designed to last many years. Bin with worms, AA-14-1590 $134.95; Bin with 75–100 red worms, AA-14-1592 $143.95. Available from the Carolina Biological Supply Co., 2700 York Rd., Burlington, NC 27215; 800/334-5551; website; www.carolina.com.

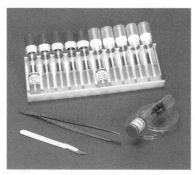

Plant Tissue Culture Kit: African Violet Micropropagation   (Ages 10 to adult)

Using a stage-two African violet, the student can initiate multiplication and rooting stages. Instructions included. Contents: African violet, Stage 2 culture; 5 tubes African violet Multiplication Medium; 5 tubes African violet Pre-transplant Medium, forceps, scalpel; 2 Petri dishes; tissue culture rack. AA-19-1113, $32.25. Available from the Carolina Biological Supply Co., 2700 York Rd., Burlington, NC 27215; 800/334-5551; www.carolina.com.

Floating Bog Plant Kit   (Ages 10 to adult)

For use indoors or out. Float the container with bog plant in a well-lit 10-gallon (or larger) aquarium or in a pond. Includes miniature cattail or similar bog plant, 8" × 5" floating bog container anchor kit, potting mix, waterworn pebbles, and instructions. AA-16-2410, $38.50. Available from the Carolina Biological Supply Co., 2700 York Rd., Burlington, NC 27215 800/334-5551; www.carolina.com.

Floating Bog Container   (Ages 10 to adult)

This container adds a focal point to any pond or room aquarium. Arrange a bog plant in the container with wet potting mix and set the assembly afloat. Suitable for mosses, rushes, sedges, and many other bog-loving plants (including carnivorous plants). Constructed of durable, nontoxic, UV-resistant material that is reusable year after year. Includes anchoring kit. Available in three sizes; dimensions listed are internal. AA-16-2482 (8" × 5"), $16. AA-16-2484 (10" × 7"), $20. AA-16-2486 (13" × 10"), $22. Available from the Carolina Biological Supply Co., 2700 York Rd., Burlington, NC 27215; 800/334-5551; www.carolina.com.

Cascading Creek System (Kit)   (Ages 10 to adult)

Basic kit converts a 10-gallon or larger tank into a fully functional viquarium (with waterfall) where fish, amphibians, and reptiles can live together. Includes textured base, pump, and bio-bag for water filtration. Tank, hood, gravel, plants, and animals not included. Deluxe kit also contains cascading creek system plus 10-gallon tank, with hood, gravel, net, tropical plants, 3 fish, 3 snails, 2 newts. Living materials will be shipped 2–3 weeks after kit arrives. Basic kit AA-16-1959, $59.95. Deluxe kit AA-16-1960, $135.95. Available from the Carolina Biological Supply Co., 2700 York Rd., Burlington, NC 27215; 800/334-5551; www.carolina.com.

Small Basic River Tank Ecosystems
(Ages 10 to adult)

Study the flora and fauna typical at a river's edge! The 10- and 20-gallon models are not covered, allowing plant growth through the top of the tank. A pair of stands holds the light above the tank. Smaller systems are not suitable for keeping terrestrial animals, as the animals will escape. Kits include tank with plant pockets, fluorescent strip light, pump, submersible heater, filter cartridge, and owner's guide. B8-16-1561, 10 gallon (20" × 10" × 12.5") $164.50. B8-16-1563, 20 gallon (24" × 12" × 16") $298. Available from the Carolina Biological Supply Co., 2700 York Rd., Burlington, NC 27215; 800/334-5551; www.carolina.com.

Plant Assortment Set   (Ages 10 to adult)

A great assortment of plants suitable for the 10-gallon River Tank Ecosystem (p. 297). Also suitable for a 10-gallon terrarium. Set includes moss, *Conocephalum*, mini glacier ivy, a parlor palm, *Lycopodium*, a Venus flytrap, fern, and moneywort. B8-15-1106, $42.50. Available from the Carolina Biological Supply Co., 2700 York Rd., Burlington, NC 27215; 800/334-5551; www.carolina.com.

Terraset Kits   (Ages 10 to adult)

These units convert a standard 10- or 20-gallon aquarium or any 12-inch-wide aquarium into a beautiful habitat. The kits offer a waterfall and plant area in the aquarium as well as built-in biological filtration. The Complete Kits include Terraset form, tank, gravel, power-head water pump, filter cartridge, lift tube and diffuser, cover, and light. Complete Small Terraset Kit (with 10-gallon tank, top, light), B8-16-1949, $139.95. (Small set without tank, top, light, B8-16-1951, $79.95); Complete Medium Terraset Kit (with 20-gallon tank, top, light), B8-16-1952, $194.95; (Medium set without tank, top, light, B8-16-1954, $99.95). Available from the Carolina Biological Supply Co., 2700 York Rd., Burlington, NC 27215; 800/334-5551; www.carolina.com.

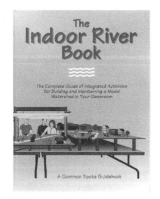

The Indoor River Book   (Ages 10 to 12)

This is a step-by-step teacher's guidebook to building and maintaining a "classroom river" by Jim Higgins and Martin Kimple. Homeschool families can make a low-cost, tabletop, indoor aquatic habitat. Includes dozens of photos, illustrations, and hands-on curricular activities in the life sciences, math, social studies, and the arts. B8-95-9710, $14.95. Available from the Carolina Biological Supply Co., 2700 York Rd., Burlington, NC 27215; 800/334-5551; www.carolina.com.

Lobster Lab Kit   (Ages 8 and up)

You receive nine baby lobsters. After the lobsters grow too large for your home, send them to the release program! Each kit includes a lobster condominium, water pump, return tube, bio-media rocks, activated carbon, filter pad, water-conditioning bacteria, three-month supply of lobster food, and a storybook. (Small crayfish may be substituted if lobsters are not available.) Dimensions are approximately 12" × 16". B8-L588, $119.95. Food—nutritionally balanced sinking pellets, 250 g bag, B8-L595, $4.99. Available from the Carolina Biological Supply Co., 2700 York Rd., Burlington, NC 27215; 800/334-5551; www.carolina.com.

How Living Things Are Classified   (Ages 10 to 14)

This 18-minute video introduces the basic principles of biological classification and describes the limiting characteristics for each of the five kingdoms. Includes teacher's guide with questions. B8-49-0950-V, $79.95. Available from the Carolina Biological Supply Co., 2700 York Rd., Burlington, NC 27215; 800/334-5551; www.carolina.com.

Animals in the Classroom   (Ages 7 to 14)

This book details the housing, handling, and feeding of 29 animals, ranging from worms and insects to birds and mammals. For each animal, author David C. Kramer gives natural history information and suggests observation activities. Includes information on where to obtain animals and what to do with them once your projects are completed. B8-45-1597, $29.95. Available from the Carolina Biological Supply Co., 2700 York Rd., Burlington, NC 27215; 800/334-5551; www.carolina.com.

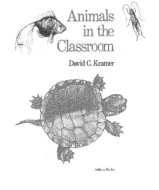

Animals in the Classroom

David C. Kramer

Aqua Scope   (Ages 10 to 18)

This completely waterproof 25" × 6" system is designed so children can study pond life at close quarters. Just place one end in the water and view undisturbed underwater life. B8-95-1401, $32.95. Available from the Carolina Biological Supply Co., 2700 York Rd., Burlington, NC 27215; 800/334-5551; www.carolina.com.

Complete Classroom Pond System   (Ages 13 to adult)

These above-ground pools can be assembled indoors or out for a whole year of learning. The 36-gallon pond measures 33" in diameter × 13" depth. The system includes a 20-milliliter liner, 60-gallon/hour water pump, tubing, and water bell fountain attachment. Easy to assemble and take down. The system also comes with a generous selection of aquatic plants and snails shipped about 3 weeks after the pond. B8-16-23981, $165. Available from the Carolina Biological Supply Co., 2700 York Rd., Burlington, NC 27215; 800/334-5551; www.carolina.com.

Ghost Shrimp Habitat Set   (Ages 13 to adult)

Designed for maintaining ghost shrimp in the home, this kit includes 12 shrimp, 1½ gallon plastic aquarium, gravel, water plant, food, air pump, air stone, and instructions. B8-L591, $24.95. Available from the Carolina Biological Supply Co., 2700 York Rd., Burlington, NC 27215; 800/334-5551; www.carolina.com.

Living Fossil Life Cycle Kit (Triops)   (Ages 5 to 12)

Study the life cycle of the tadpole shrimp, *Triops longi-caudatus,* a branchiopod that resembles an extinct trilobite. Kit includes a vial of dry soil containing Triops eggs (Daphnia and fairy shrimp eggs are also present). The eggs hatch within 24 to 36 hours after water is added and adults will be present in 2 to 3 weeks. Kit also includes plastic container, food, and instructions. B8-L520, $8.79. Available from the Carolina Biological Supply Co., 2700 York Rd., Burlington, NC 27215; 800/334-5551; www.carolina.com.

Raise a Sea Monkey Kit   (Ages 5 to 12)

Actually grow brine shrimp to adult stage with this unique kit. Includes small "Micro-Vue" aquarium, eggs, water purifier, growth food, feeding spoon, and instructions. To refurbish the kit, order Brine Shrimp combo, 3 bags per set. Kit: B8-L608A, $8.79. Brine Shrimp Combo: B8-L609E, $4.65. Available from the Carolina Biological Supply Co., 2700 York Rd., Burlington, NC 27215; 800/334-5551; www.carolina.com.

Raise a Snail Kit   (Ages 5 to 12)

Your student can raise snails from eggs. Includes mature pond snails, water conditioner, 1½ gallon plastic aquarium, food, and complete instructions. Species vary with availability. B8-L489F, $14.95. Available from the Carolina Biological Supply Co., 2700 York Rd., Burlington, NC 27215; 800/334-5551; www.carolina.com.

Minipond Ecosystem   (Ages 5 to 12)

An outdoor habitat for microorganisms, this maintenance-free habitat simulates a pond, yet can be brought indoors for study of microscopic algae and protists. Activities include discovering pond traffic and observing the organisms' feeding habits. Kit requires the use of a microscope and includes a minipond container, pond substrate, protozoan mixture, algae mixture, pH test strips, nutrient solution, and instructions. B8-13-1207, $18.50. Carolina Student Microscope (30x), B8-60-2376, $22. Available from the Carolina Biological Supply Co., 2700 York Rd., Burlington, NC 27215; 800/334-5551; www.carolina.com.

Plastic Aqua-teriums   (Ages 8 to adult)

Ideal for holding small animals such as insects as well as fish, amphibians, reptiles, and plants. Optional hood light with bulb provides light and heat. Mini (7" × 4" × 5½"), B8-67-4337, $3.30. Small (9" × 6" × 6¾"), B8-67-4337A, $5.35. Medium (12" × 7½" × 8"), B8-67-4337B, $9.75. Large (15" × 8½" × 9¾"), B8-67-4337C, $15.25. Hood with light, B8-67-4338, $6.95. Available from the Carolina Biological Supply Co., 2700 York Rd., Burlington, NC 27215; 800/334-5551; www.carolina.com.

Carolina Living Wonders Habitats   (Ages 10 to 18)

This habitat is an ideal way for your child to maintain his or her own pet at home. Each kit contains at least two animals of one kind, plastic terrarium with escape-proof lid, colored gravel, plastic plant, water dish, food, and complete instructions. Choose your own animal. Land Hermit Crab, B8-16-3558, $19.98; Painted Lady Butterfly, B8-16-3560, $19.98; Dwarf Aquarium Frog, B8-16-3562, $19.98; Fantail Goldfish, B8-16-3563, $19.98; American Chameleon, B8-16-3564, $19.98. Available from the Carolina Biological Supply Co., 2700 York Rd., Burlington, NC 27215; 800/334-5551; www.carolina.com.

Science and Biology

Sea Shell Assortment   (Ages 8 to adult)

About 150 shells of all sizes. B8-95-1662, $9.50. Available from the Carolina Biological Supply Co., 2700 York Rd., Burlington, NC 27215; 800/334-5551; www.carolina.com.

In the Company of Whales   (Ages 12 and up)

Eighteen months in the making, beautifully filmed in 15 locations around the world, this spectacular 90-minute video reveals phenomenal whale encounters never before captured on film. Includes their natural history, ecology, near extinction from whaling and interactions with man, and prospects for their future. B8-49-2977-V, $19.95. Available from the Carolina Biological Supply Co., 2700 York Rd., Burlington, NC 27215; 800/334-5551; www.carolina.com.

The Ocean Book   (Ages 5 to 12)

This activity book by with foreword by Isaac Asimov on the oceans and the living things that inhabit them is filled with experiments, investigations, puzzles, games, and all sorts of fun things to do and learn. The activities are designed to learn by doing. B8-95-1010, $12.95. Available from the Carolina Biological Supply Co., 2700 York Rd., Burlington, NC 27215; 800/334-5551; www.carolina.com.

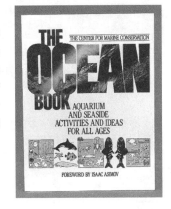

Monterey Bay Aquarium (Ages 4 to 18)

Plunge via this 30-minute video into the world's tallest aquarium exhibit where schools of fish weave among swaying kelp fronds. Discover how biologists feed a giant octopus, rear an orphaned sea otter pup, and care for thousands of creatures on exhibit. Then join scientists for the first-ever expedition into Monterey Bay's 2,000-foot deep canyon. B8-49-1116-V, $24.95. Available from the Carolina Biological Supply Co., 2700 York Rd., Burlington, NC 27215; 800/334-5551; www.carolina.com.

Life Cycle Wooden Sequencing Puzzles (Ages 5 to 8)

Each puzzle piece illustrates a separate stage in the logical progress of the life cycle. Six interlocking pieces per puzzle. Measures 18" × 6". Frog, B8-95-2375, $14.25; Duck, B8-95-2375, $14.25; Butterfly, B8-95-2377, $14.25. Available from the Carolina Biological Supply Co., 2700 York Rd., Burlington, NC 27215; 800/334-5551; www.carolina.com.

Raise-a-Frog Kit (Ages 5 and up)

This kit includes everything you need to raise a small frog from a tadpole. Students will be fascinated to observe the growth of the legs and disappearance of the tail as tadpole becomes frog. Kit includes two healthy tadpoles, small plastic aquarium, food, colored gravel, and instructions. B8-L1542, $10.50. Available from the Carolina Biological Supply Co., 2700 York Rd., Burlington, NC 27215; 800/334-5551; www.carolina.com.

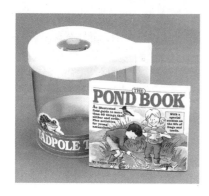

The Pond Book and Tadpole Tank Set (Ages 8 to 11)

The Pond Book is a full-color field guide to frogs, toads, turtles, and water bugs; over 40 species are covered. The shatterproof, see-through Tadpole Tank is topped by a combination lid/strainer with special magnifying glass in the center for observing the tiniest creatures. B8-95-1718, $14.95. Available from the Carolina Biological Supply Co., 2700 York Rd., Burlington, NC 27215; 800/334-5551; www.carolina.com.

Chameleon Condos — Critters & Critical Thinking (Ages 10 to 15)

This 56-page book by Craig Berg of activity-based life science shows you how to build and use condos: Low-cost, small-critter habitats that students make from 2-liter recycled plastic soda bottles. Condos will provide your home with highly visible habitats for anoles, crickets, and ants. The author demonstrates via flowcharts, examples, and student blackline masters, how to use condos and children's questions in order to initiate a creative problem-solving model. B8-45-5040, $9.95. Available from the Carolina Biological Supply Co., 2700 York Rd., Burlington, NC 27215; 800/334-5551; www.carolina.com.

Live American Chameleons (anoles)   (Ages 10 to 15)

Your children will light up when this little lizard changes color right before their eyes! The American chameleon is hardy and lively as well as being affordable, very easy to care for, long-lived, and docile. Recommended foods include mealworms, crickets, and wingless fruit flies. Anoles come with instructions. B8-L1656, $13.95 for 3. Available from the Carolina Biological Supply Co., 2700 York Rd., Burlington, NC 27215; 800/334-5551; www.carolina.com.

Painted Lady Butterfly Larvae   (Ages 8 and up)

One or two larvae are shipped in a rearing chamber with food, along with instructions. Ideal for individual student use. B8-L911, $13.59 per set of 3. Available from the Carolina Biological Supply Co., 2700 York Rd., Burlington, NC 27215; 800/334-5551; www.carolina.com.

Science and Biology

Raise-a-Butterfly Kit   (Ages 8 and up)

Everything you need to raise your own painted lady butterflies. Includes five larvae, caterpillar food, 1½ gallon plastic cage, water and food vial, climbing mat, and instructions. B8-L913, $19.98. Available from the Carolina Biological Supply Co., 2700 York Rd., Burlington, NC 27215; 800/334-5551; www.carolina.com.

Carolina Butterfly Sanctuary

Give your butterflies room to stretch their wings in this spacious and attractive habitat. The 36" × 12" habitat is preassembled and is designed to hang from a hook on the ceiling or wall. Feeder and detailed instructions are included. B8-L920H, $12.99. Available from the Carolina Biological Supply Co., 2700 York Rd., Burlington, NC 27215; 800/334-5551; www.carolina.com.

Swallowtail Butterfly Pupae   (Ages 8 and up)

Add excitement and depth to your science projects with living swallowtail pupae. You can store the pupae for over three months in the refrigerator; they take about two weeks to develop at room temperature. The adult butterflies can be used to start or add to an insect collection. Wingspans range from 3 to 5½ inches. Available October through May. Spicebush Swallowtail Pupa, B8-L919A, $3.70; Tiger Swallowtail Pupa, B8-L919B, $3.70. Available from the Carolina Biological Supply Co., 2700 York Rd., Burlington, NC 27215; 800/334-5551; www.carolina.com.

Butterfly Habitat Set   (Ages 8 to 15)

Ideal for maintaining two or three adult butterflies. Includes container with escape-proof lid, climbing mat, watering vial and wick, and instructions. Order butterflies separately (see previous entry). B8-L919H, $9.95. Available from the Carolina Biological Supply Co., 2700 York Rd., Burlington, NC 27215; 800/334-5551; www.carolina.com.

Science and Biology

Caterpillar Puppet   (Ages 8 to 12)

18 inches long. B8-95-2159, $26. Available from the Carolina Biological Supply Co., 2700 York Rd., Burlington, NC 27215; 800/334-5551; www.carolina.com.

Jewels of the Rain Forest Butterfly Collection (Ages 5 and up)

This fun and easy-to-assemble kit contains 13 replica butterflies. These are convincingly detailed reproductions of actual specimens from a world-famous collection. When assembled, these high-quality paper reproductions are pin-mounted and secured to a rigid foam base and framed in a handsome display box. B8-27-2742, $19.95. Available from the Carolina Biological Supply Co., 2700 York Rd., Burlington, NC 27215; 800/334-5551; www.carolina.com.

Butterfly Feeder   (Ages 5 and up)

The only feeder that presents nectar for butterflies to feed naturally. Designed and tested by biologists. A combination of wicks and tubes mimic actual flower blossoms. Small spikes also hold fresh fruit pieces. Easy to assemble, clean, and fill. Holds 6 ounces and comes with enough mix for making one quart of nectar. B8-L950, $14.95. Available from the Carolina Biological Supply Co., 2700 York Rd., Burlington, NC 27215; 800/334-5551; www.carolina.com.

The Curiosity Club: Kids' Nature Activity Book (Ages 10 and up)

Why do we need trees? Where do animals make their homes? How does a feather work? Allene Roberts' 184-page book uses illustrations, games, puzzles, and hands-on activities to answer these and other questions and to involve children in dialog about the world around them. B8-96-0724, $14.95. Available from the Carolina Biological Supply Co., 2700 York Rd., Burlington, NC 27215; 800/334-5551; www.carolina.com.

The Very Hungry Caterpillar Game   (Ages 5 to 7)

Students set off on a journey with The Very Hungry Caterpillar. Along the way they learn about shapes and colors as they create a new butterfly every time they play. Designed for 1 to 4 players; no reading skills are required. B8-95-1532 $18.95. Available from the Carolina Biological Supply Co., 2700 York Rd., Burlington, NC 27215; 800/334-5551; www.carolina.com.

Land Hermit Crabs   (Ages 5 and up)

Unlike most crabs, hermits are gentle and timid and can be trained to eat food from your hand. Hermit crabs use empty snail shells to protect their soft abdomens, and students find it fascinating to observe them changing shells. Study activities can include observation of hermit crab social interactions, shell preferences, and response to different colors or flavors in food. Care instructions are included. B8-L600, $11.55 for 3. Available from the Carolina Biological Supply Co., 2700 York Rd., Burlington, NC 27215; 800/334-5551; www.carolina.com.

Science and Biology

Hermit Crab Terrarium Kit   (Ages 5 and up)

Designed for maintaining a group of land hermit crabs at home. Includes six land hermit crabs with extra shells, 10-gallon all-glass tank, incandescent hood with bulbs, tree branch for climbing, water bowl, coarse sand, food, and instructions. Hermit crabs will be shipped about 2 weeks after terrarium and supplies are shipped. B8-L598, $82.45. Available from the Carolina Biological Supply Co., 2700 York Rd., Burlington, NC 27215; 800/334-5551; www.carolina.com.

Create-a-Cage   (Ages 10 to 15)

Create a beautiful and natural living environment for amphibians, reptiles, and other small animals. This collapsible cage, which uses kid-safe Plexiglas wall panels, assembles in minutes. Comes with a dam accessory to separate soil from water, plastic molded lid with built-in screen top to accommodate lighting, and space underneath for optional under-the-tank heater. Plants, animals, and decorations are not included. Cage is 16" × 16" × 19" (20-gallon). B8-67-4100, $69.95. Available from the Carolina Biological Supply Co., 2700 York Rd., Burlington, NC 27215; 800/334-5551; www.carolina.com.

Praying Mantis Egg Cases   (Ages 8 and up)

An egg cluster of the Chinese praying mantis produces 25 to 50 young mantises in 3 to 6 weeks at room temperature. Children can perform experiments and make observations of growth and molting, interactions among baby mantises, and predatory behavior. Egg cases can be stored in the refrigerator until ready for use. Available from September to June. B8-L738, $11.70. Available from the Carolina Biological Supply Co., 2700 York Rd., Burlington, NC 27215; 800/334-5551; www.carolina.com.

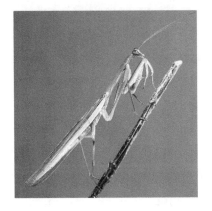

The Praying Mantis Nursery Kit   (Ages 8 and up)

Students can raise their own praying mantises. Everything needed for a group of 30 children, including Chinese praying mantis egg case; fruit fly culture kit with wingless fruit flies (for feeding baby mantises); 30 clear plastic mantis nursery vials with foam plugs; and 30 cotton swabs (to provide water.) Directions for building a terrarium for larger mantises are included. B8-L739, $39.95. Available from the Carolina Biological Supply Co., 2700 York Rd., Burlington, NC 27215; 800/334-5551; www.carolina.com.

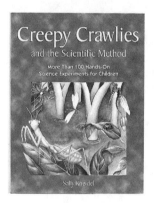

Creepy Crawlies and the Scientific Method   (Ages 7 to 12)

From beetles to bugs, ant lions to slime molds, praying mantises to earthworms, this book by Sally Kneidel shows parents how to use a full spectrum of insects and other crawling creatures to teach children the five steps of the scientific method. These experiments will encourage students to understand science through observation of small animals in their natural surroundings. B8-95-6520, $16.95. Available from the Carolina Biological Supply Co., 2700 York Rd., Burlington, NC 27215; 800/334-5551; www.carolina.com.

Lyrical Life Science: Science They'll Remember (Ages 10 to 12)

Each volume comes with cassette, teacher's guide, and reproducible student workbook. The lyrics of each tune are content-rich and loaded with scientific terms and concepts. Vol. 1 has 96 pages and 11 songs, including "Scientific Method," "Invertebrates," "Cold-blooded Vertebrates," "Birds," "Vascular Plants," "Algae," "Fungi," "Protozoa," "Viruses," "Bacteria." Vol. 2 has 112 pages and 16 songs in a systematic study of mammalian orders, ecology, and biomes. Vol. 1, B8-95-2284, $25.50; Vol. 2, B8-95-2285, $25.50. Available from the Carolina Biological Supply Co., 2700 York Rd., Burlington, NC 27215; 800/334-5551; www.carolina.com.

Exploring the Secrets of the Meadow-Thicket   (Ages 5 to 9)

Throughout the seasons, children are guided on a journey filled with stories, activities, and adventures in this 265-page book by Joanne Dennee, Julia Hand, and Carolyn Peduzzi. The meadow-thicket comes alive with all the buzz, beauty, and song of the summer and fall. Winter's hush is explored with hands-on activities and in the spring the awakening landscape is celebrated. B8-95-2245, $18.95. Available from the Carolina Biological Supply Co., 2700 York Rd., Burlington, NC 27215; 800/334-5551; www.carolina.com.

Life in a Rotting Log Kit   (Ages 5 to 12)

This kit includes a generous-size decaying piece of wood, leaf mold, and an assortment of at least five different kinds of harmless creatures (at least 15 total) that can be found in or under a rotting log. Each kit comes with a 1½–gallon terrarium. Keep your rotting log moist and watch it change over time. Complete instructions and age-appropriate activities are included. B8-L718, $24.95. Available from the Carolina Biological Supply Co., 2700 York Rd., Burlington, NC 27215; 800/334-5551; www.carolina.com.

Giant Ant Farm   (Ages 5 and up)

The scientifically designed, escape-proof ant farm comes with a year's supply of food, special tunneling sand, illustrated manual, and a certificate good for a generous supply of ants. The Refill includes sand and a year's supply of food. Customers in Arizona, Hawaii, and Tennessee must apply for a USDA permit to receive ants (we will supply necessary information and forms). Ants cannot be shipped into Canada. Ant Farm, B8-L1052, $26.65; Refill, B8-L1052A, $4.99; replacement unit (ants only), B8-L1054B, $9.75. Available from the Carolina Biological Supply Co., 2700 York Rd., Burlington, NC 27215; 800/334-5551; www.carolina.com.

Planet Ant Kit   (Ages 5 to 11)

Packed full of safe experiments, guided observations, and entomology facts, Planet Ant introduces kids to the social structure of an ant colony, the habits and skills of ants, and lots of weird ant trivia. The kit includes a 48-page full-color book, a 4" × 6" ant farm, and a coupon for ants. B8-95-1753, $14.95. Available from the Carolina Biological Supply Co., 2700 York Rd., Burlington, NC 27215; 800/334-5551; www.carolina.com.

Dirt Makers: The World of Earthworms (Ages 5 to 9)

Students collect food to feed worms and learn how recycling leftover food makes soil. They also learn to maintain the worm habitat. Each kit comes with redworms, a 1½–gallon terrarium with lid, soil, worm closet (for keeping worms in the dark), rocks, and a fork for stirring food in the soil. Complete with teacher information on habitat and feeding. B8-95-1630, $18.95. *The Wonderful World of Wigglers* (155-page book), B8-95-1675 $17.25. Available from the Carolina Biological Supply Co., 2700 York Rd., Burlington, NC 27215; 800/334-5551; www.carolina.com.

Worm Composting   (Ages 10 to 14)

The book *Worms Eat Our Garbage* by Mary Aggelhef, Mary Frances Fenton, and Barbara Less Harris is a group activity for a better environment. This comprehensive, integrated curriculum guide contains activities with earthworms and recycling garbage. *Worms Eat My Garbage* is a manual for setting up and maintaining a system for processing organic waste by means of redworms. *Worms Eat Our Garbage*, B8-95-1681, $26.50; *Worms Eat My Garbage*, B8-95-1682, $11.95. Available from the Carolina Biological Supply Co., 2700 York Rd., Burlington, NC 27215; 800/334-5551; www.carolina.com.

Bugwise   (Ages 7 to 12)

An eye-opening look at the world of insects and spiders, this book by Pamela M. Hickman has 30 exciting experiments to make children "bug-wise." Fun activities can be done individually or in groups. Illustrations are realistically detailed. B8-95-1704, $9.95. Available from the Carolina Biological Supply Co., 2700 York Rd., Burlington, NC 27215; 800/334-5551; www.carolina.com.

Pet Bugs: A Kid's Guide to Catching & Keeping Touchable Insects   (Ages 5 and up)

No bug-lover's library should be without this book by Sally Kneidel. Information about each insect includes what it looks like, where to find it, how to catch, keep, and feed it, and what its behavior is like. Details are given on insects that we see every day. Complete with information on how to catch insects and create a habitat. B8-95-1708, $10.95. Available from the Carolina Biological Supply Co., 2700 York Rd., Burlington, NC 27215; 800/334-5551; www.carolina.com.

Build Your Own Bugs and Stamp Kit   (All ages)

Budding entomologists will find the answers to all their bug questions in this 32-page, full-color paperback book by Dennis Schatz featuring colorful and educational drawings. Includes an ink pad and 29 different stamps of parts of insects so children can create their own bugs or follow the directions in the book. B8-95-1710, $14.95. Available from the Carolina Biological Supply Co., 2700 York Rd., Burlington, NC 27215; 800/334-5551; www.carolina.com.

Bug Play   (Ages 5 to 9)

Twenty-six sections offer activities using basic classroom materials and include recording the different songs of crickets and observing the life cycle of beetles. Poems and black-line masters reinforce the unique features of 17 insects. An accompanying music cassette of creative, lively songs extends and reinforces activities. B8-95-6505, $29.95. Available from the Carolina Biological Supply Co., 2700 York Rd., Burlington, NC 27215; 800/334-5551; www.carolina.com.

Magnifying Bug Viewer   (Ages 5 and up)

This 3-inch diameter viewer features a sizing grid and air holes. It can also be used for examining coins, stamps, flowers, and other small items. B8-67-4274, $6.95. Available from the Carolina Biological Supply Co., 2700 York Rd., Burlington, NC 27215; 800/334-5551; www.carolina.com.

The Bug House   (Ages 5 and up)

This safe container for keeping and observing insects measures 5" high × 3" in diameter. B8-67-4276, $6.50. Available from the Carolina Biological Supply Co., 2700 York Rd., Burlington, NC 27215; 800/334-5551; www.carolina.com.

Ant Homes Under the Ground   (Ages 5 to 7)

This kit features activities that delve into many aspects of the ubiquitous and fascinating social insects. Children learn about body structures, jobs, and homes by observing ants in nature and in an ant farm. Item #NB-95-1754, $16. Available from the Carolina Biological Supply Co., 2700 York Rd., Burlington, NC 27215; 800/334-5551; www.carolina.com.

Do Bees Sneeze? And other questions kids ask about insects   (Ages 5 to 12)

Discover many fascinating facts in this entertaining and informative book, which was prompted by an entomologist's classroom visits and correspondence with young people from across the United States. Item #NB-95-1706, $17.95. Available from the Carolina Biological Supply Co., 2700 York Rd., Burlington, NC 27215; 800/334-5551; www.carolina.com.

Don't Bug Me   (Ages 7 and up)

This charming game of backyard gardening pits farmer against farmer as they attempt to grow eight prize specimens. But don't let your guard down! When you least expect it, hungry veggie-eating bugs can spoil the fun. Little gardeners will delight in planting the packet of real vegetable seeds, included with every game. B8-95-2210, $18. Available from the Carolina Biological Supply Co., 2700 York Rd., Burlington, NC 27215; 800/334-5551; www.carolina.com.

Flying Insect Net   (Ages 5 to 12)

Make your field trip a sure-fire success with this custom-made net. Our Pacific aerial net is especially designed for catching butterflies and other flying insects. Net has 15-inch hoop, 3-inch handle, and medium mesh. B8-65-1380, $16.10. Available from the Carolina Biological Supply Co., 2700 York Rd., Burlington, NC 27215; 800/334-5551; www.carolina.com.

Alpha Animals Game   (Ages 8 to 11)

With this A-to-Z classification game, young students move their animal playing pieces through the letters of the alphabet, naming animals as they go. The older students name animals in important classification groups: mammals, birds, fish, reptiles, and many more. The game comes with a list of 700 animals for double-checking answers. B8-95-2526, $25.95. Available from the Carolina Biological Supply Co., 2700 York Rd., Burlington, NC 27215; 800/334-5551; www.carolina.com.

Alpha Animals Junior   (Ages 5 to 8)

Students roar like lions and growl like bears as they explore the world of animals. This A-to-Z alphabet game will teach young students about the animal world while having lots of fun. B8-95-2527, $19.95. Available from the Carolina Biological Supply Co., 2700 York Rd., Burlington, NC 27215; 800/334-5551; www.carolina.com.

Fun with Your Cat   (Ages 10 to 12)

Games, activities, and experiments for a group of 25 to journey into the world of cats. Students explore the different ways pet cats learn and perceive the world through their senses. This fun kit introduces children to the world of the large cat through activities with their own pets. B8-95-1460A, $76. Available from the Carolina Biological Supply Co., 2700 York Rd., Burlington, NC 27215; 800/334-5551; www.carolina.com.

Fun with Your Dog Kit   (Ages 9 to 12)

A class of 25 can conduct experiments to find out how their pets process information with their remarkable senses. Discover why dogs love cookies and how to make a healthy dog snack. Do dogs see blue skies overhead? With special glasses they make, students take a look at a dog's view of the world. B8-95-1462A, $76. Available from the Carolina Biological Supply Co., 2700 York Rd., Burlington, NC 27215; 800/334-5551; www.carolina.com.

Who's At Home In the Animal Habitat?
(Ages 8 to 12)

Players race from start to finish to find out who's at home in eight different animal habitats. Students discover the amazing wonders of the animal kingdom and learn how animals adapt to their diverse habitats. This board game with 320 questions at two levels of difficulty comes with an instruction booklet and recommended reading list. B8-95-1140, $24.95. Available from the Carolina Biological Supply Co., 2700 York Rd., Burlington, NC 27215; 800/334-5551; www.carolina.com.

Exploring the World of Animals: Linking Fiction to Nonfiction (Ages 5 to 11)

Focusing on animals, a subject of intense fascination for young students, this book by Phyllis J. Perry contains four sections: animals as pets, on the farm, in the woods, and in the wild. Activities link language arts to science, math, social studies, and the arts. B8-95-2003, $24.50. Available from the Carolina Biological Supply Co., 2700 York Rd., Burlington, NC 27215; 800/334-5551; www.carolina.com.

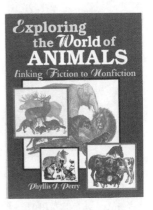

The Visible Horse (Ages 9 and up)

This is a scaled-down model of a thoroughbred, measuring over 14 inches long and 12 inches high. Highly detailed parts represent the skeleton and vital organs. A fully illustrated guide and complete instructions for assembly are included (paint not included). B8-95-1750, $21.95. Available from the Carolina Biological Supply Co., 2700 York Rd., Burlington, NC 27215; 800/334-5551; www.carolina.com.

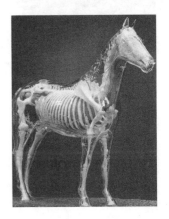

Life Sequences Cards Set   (Ages 5 to 8)

Capture your student's imagination and arouse curiosity with these 5¾" × 8¼" cards. Forty beautifully detailed photographs in five life stories of five different life forms help students learn about concepts of change, time, growth, and development. Set includes teacher's notes. B8-95-2020, $30. Available from the Carolina Biological Supply Co., 2700 York Rd., Burlington, NC 27215; 800/334-5551; www.carolina.com.

City Kids and City Critters!   (Ages 8 to 12)

City children need to know about wildlife preservation as much as their country cousins. This field guide/activity book by Carole Huelbig and Janet Roberts gives you creative alternatives to specimen collection, photography, drawing, observation, constructing models, and building mini-habitats to help students develop science skills as they learn about creatures living in urban environments. B8-95-2007, $15.95. Available from the Carolina Biological Supply Co., 2700 York Rd., Burlington, NC 27215; 800/334-5551; www.carolina.com.

Animal Families Game   (Ages 5 to 8)

This card game for 2 to 4 players (which can be played as five different games) makes readers and nonreaders alike experts on animal families. Students learn about 13 animal families. B8-95-2380, $8. Available from the Carolina Biological Supply Co., 2700 York Rd., Burlington, NC 27215; 800/334-5551; www.carolina.com.

Who's Endangered on Noah's Ark?   (Ages 5 to 14)

Your child can learn about endangered species with this fine, sensitive volume. Examines ten animals within the framework of children's literature. Activities are provided for literature, art, and writing. B8-95-2001, $23.95. Available from the Carolina Biological Supply Co., 2700 York Rd., Burlington, NC 27215; 800/334-5551; www.carolina.com.

Endangered! (Ages 10 to 12)

Four books that focus on the "at-risk" animals and environments around the world, why they are endangered and what is being done. Full-color illustrations with detailed text. *Endangered Birds*, B8-95-1550; *Endangered Environments*, B8-95-1551; *Endangered Mammals*, B8-95-1552; *Endangered Sea Life*, B8-95-1553: $18.50 each; Set (one of each), B8-95-1554, $65.25. Available from the Carolina Biological Supply Co., 2700 York Rd., Burlington, NC 27215; 800/334-5551; www.carolina.com.

Rubber Stamp Sets (Ages 5 to 15)

Enhance science projects with rubber stamps. Each set includes stamps and washable inkpad. Number of stamps in each set shown in parentheses. Farm Animals (10), B8-95-1779, $8; African Animals (6), B8-95-1780, $8; Rain Forest (7), B8-95-1781, $8; Butterflies (10), B8-95-1782, $8; Life on a Coral Reef (33), B8-95-1783, $19.95; Bone Zone (30), B8-95-1784, $14.95. Available from the Carolina Biological Supply Co., 2700 York Rd., Burlington, NC 27215; 800/334-5551; www.carolina.com.

Rubber Stamps Sets (Ages 5 to 15)

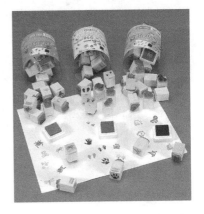

18 individual ¾-inch square stamps, plus 2 small inkpads. Animal Tracks, B8-95-2232, $14.95; Bugs, B8-95-2233, $14.95; Natures Creatures, B8-95-2234, $14.95; Sea Life, B8-95-2235, $14.95. Available from the Carolina Biological Supply Co., 2700 York Rd., Burlington, NC 27215; 800/334-5551; www.carolina.com.

Insect Lotto Game   (Ages 5 and up)

Authenticated and licensed by the Smithsonian Institution, it makes learning about the insects fun. B8-95-2349, $11.95. Available from the Carolina Biological Supply Co., 2700 York Rd., Burlington, NC 27215; 800/334-5551; www.carolina.com.

National Geographic's Really Wild Animals (Ages 5 to 10)

These lively music videos will keep your child's interest. Meet some of the most amazing animals on Earth. Approx. 45 minutes each. Amazing North America, B8-49-2985; Totally Tropical Rain Forest, B8-49-2986; Adventures in Asia, B8-49-2987; Swinging Safari, B8-49-2988; Wonders Down Under, B8-49-2989; Deep Sea Dive, B8-49-2990; Polar Prowl, B8-49-2991; Dinosaurs and Other Creature Features, B8-49-2992; Monkey Business and Other Family Matters, B8-49-2993, $14.95 each. Available from the Carolina Biological Supply Co., 2700 York Rd., Burlington, NC 27215; 800/334-5551; www.carolina.com.

DK Nature Bundle   (Ages 8 to adult)

Learn about the web of life with this CD-ROM/video package, which includes: Eyewitness Encyclopedia of Nature 2.0 CD-ROM; Eyewitness Insect Video, and Eyewitness Reptile Video. Hybrid CD-ROM: LSPK1135-CDB, $49.95. Available from Learning Services, P.O. Box 10636, Eugene, OR 97440-2636; Western Region: 800/877-9378; Eastern Region: 800/877-3278. (See coupon.)

DK Encyclopedia of Science 2.0   (Ages 13 to 18)

This CD-ROM covers chemistry, math, physics, and the life sciences in full-motion video. Hybrid CD-ROM: DOR-LOO15-CDBS, $54.95. Available from Learning Services, P.O. Box 10636, Eugene, OR 97440-2636; Western Region: 800/877-9378; Eastern Region: 800/877-3278. (See coupon.)

DK Science Bundle   (Ages 10 to 18)

Learn broadly about the field of science with this detailed CD-ROM/video/book package. It includes Eyewitness Encyclopedia of Science 2.0 CD-ROM; Eyewitness Volcano Video; and *Dictionary of Science*. Hybrid CD-ROM: LSPK1165-CDB, $65.95. Available from Learning Services, P.O. Box 10636, Eugene, OR 97440-2636; Western Region: 800/877-9378; Eastern Region: 800/877-3278. (See coupon.)

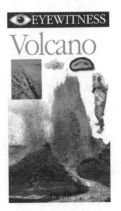

DK The Way Things Work Bundle   (Ages 8 to 13)

Discover the scientific principles behind inventions and meet the great inventors in this CD-ROM/book set! It includes The Way Things Work 2.0 CD-ROM; The Way Things Work: Pinball Science CD-ROM; *Think Tank Book*. WIN CD-ROM: LSPK1200-CDB, $79.95. Available from Learning Services, P.O. Box 10636, Eugene, OR 97440-2636; Western Region: 800/877-9378; Eastern Region: 800/877-3278. (See coupon.)

Animal Tracks Kit   (Ages 7 to 12)

Your student will learn about domestic animals by studying their footprints. Each kit includes footprint molds of six barnyard animals. Children make their own cases and use them to identify the appropriate animals. B8-95-2015, $39.95. To make tracks, Model Magic modeling compound by Crayola (plain color, 4 ounces): BC-96-440, $3.60. Available from Carolina Biological Supply Co., 2700 York Rd., Burlington, NC 27215 800/334-5551; www.carolina.com.

Bird Wise   (Ages 7 to 12)

If you have a bird lover in your home, this book is a great companion. It includes 40 hands-on exercises to help your child learn about birds and have fun, too. Activities explore the shapes of beaks and feet, camouflage, the structure of feathers, and much more. Plans for building birdhouses and feeders are also included. B8-95-2006, $10.50. Available from Carolina Biological Supply Co., 2700 York Rd., Burlington, NC 27215 800/334-5551; www.carolina.com.

Bird Feeder Kit   (Ages 8 to 15)

This do-it-yourself kit is great for the novice bird enthusiast. Recycled plastic soda bottles serve as the birdseed holder. The kit includes screw-on plastic base, funnel for easy filling, hanger for mounting, and instructions. B8-65-1796, $2.55. Available from Carolina Biological Supply Co., 2700 York Rd., Burlington, NC 27215 800/334-5551; www.carolina.com.

Science and Biology

Top Hatch Incubator for Chicks
(Ages 5 and up with adult supervision)

The built-in fan keeps heat evenly distributed. Heat source is a 60-watt bulb with a candelabra base. The unit is designed so the light is also an egg candler. Eggs can be manually turned without removing the clear top. The egg-holding unit is dishwasher safe. Egg capacities: 48 chicken eggs, 140 quail eggs, 64 pheasant eggs, 32 turkey eggs, or 16 goose eggs. Diameter, 18 inches; weight, 9½ pounds. Incubator, B8-70-1195, 110-V, $123.58. Automatic turner, B8-70-1196, 110-V, $36.20. Available from Carolina Biological Supply Co., 2700 York Rd., Burlington, NC 27215 800/334-5551; www.carolina.com.

Picture Window Egg Incubator (Ages 5 and up)

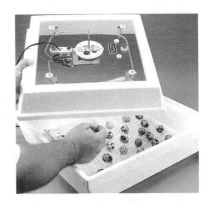

Your child will be able to view incubation and hatching through the 14" × 14" clear plastic window on top. Incubator (18" × 18" × 7½") holds up to 70 chicken eggs. B8-70-1194, $61.28. Available from Carolina Biological Supply Co., 2700 York Rd., Burlington, NC 27215; 800/334-5551; www.carolina.com.

Fertile Chicken Eggs (Ages 5 and up)

These eggs, suitable for incubation, will hatch in 21 days (fertility varies with the season—highest is February to June). *Perishable; we must receive your order at least 2 weeks in advance of the use date. Shipped on Tuesdays only.* Unit of 12 eggs, B8-13-9290, $18.54. Available from Carolina Biological Supply Co., 2700 York Rd., Burlington, NC 27215 800/334-5551; www.carolina.com.

Fertile Quail Eggs   (Ages 5 and up)

Coturnix quail eggs hatch in 17 days; the birds mature in 6 weeks. *Perishable; we must receive your order at least 2 weeks in advance of the use date.* Eggs come 12 per unit; minimum order is 2 units. B8-13-9330, $19.95 per unit. Available from Carolina Biological Supply Co., 2700 York Rd., Burlington, NC 27215; 800/334-5551; www.carolina.com.

The Bat Book and See-Through Model Set (All ages)

This set combines the fun of creating a snap-together bat model with a 48-page book full of valuable information, such as how bats use echolocation to navigate and find food. Your child can learn anatomy while assembling the model. B8-95-1756, $14.95. Available from Carolina Biological Supply Co., 2700 York Rd., Burlington, NC 27215 800/334-5551; www.carolina.com.

The Wisconsin Fast Plants Teaching System, Special Get-Acquainted Mini-Trial Kit   (Ages 11 and up)

This one-quad unit contains everything you need: seeds, soil, fertilizer, wicks, miniature watering system, pollination supplies, stakes, labels, plus complete *Growing Instructions* manual. Proper lighting is essential for success. The minimum light requirement is a 24-hour cool-white fluorescent light, placed within several inches of the growing tips. B8-15-8690, $6.75 per kit. Available from Carolina Biological Supply Co., 2700 York Rd., Burlington, NC 27215; 800/334-5551; www.carolina.com.

Solar Circle Plant Light   (Ages 10 to adult)

This compact fluorescent light is excellent for all plant-growing needs. The lighted growing space accommodates up to 64 plants in quads, 48 plants in pots, or any other plants up to 27 inches tall. The light requires only 16 square inches of table space, stands 31 inches tall, and uses a special 30-watt compact fluorescent ring bulb (included) for the necessary high light intensity. B8-15-8995, $99.95. (Replacement bulb: B-15-8996, $14.50). Available from Carolina Biological Supply Co., 2700 York Rd., Burlington, NC 27215; 800/334-5551; www.carolina.com.

Science Adventure Kits   (Ages 7 to 14)

Each of these five kits is basically self-contained (except batteries). Each deals with a particular topic of science—Astronomy, Discovering Birds, Microscopic Explorations, Magnetism, and the Wonders of Light. The program is laid out in approximately 12 to 14 lessons, two lessons per week to complete one subject kit. The pages are suitable for copying. $24.95 to $29.95; triple set of Astronomy/Birds/Magnetism, $59.95. Home Science Adventures, 17650 1st Ave. S, PMB186, Seattle, WA 98148; 800/694-7225; www.homeschoolscience.com. (See coupon.)

DK Space/Weather Bundle   (Ages 8 to 15)

This great CD-ROM/video/book set brings you the challenges of outer space and its explorers. It includes Eyewitness Encyclopedia of Space & Universe CD-ROM; Eyewitness Weather Video; *Eyewitness Visual Dictionary Universe Book*. MAC CD-ROM: LSPK1170 or WIN CD-ROM: LSPK1170-MPC, $57.95. Available from Learning Services, P.O. Box 10636, Eugene, OR 97440-2636; Western Region: 800/877-9378; Eastern Region: 800/877-3278. (See coupon.)

DK Guide to Space   (Ages 8 and up)

Strap into your favorite reading chair and blast off to the solar system and beyond in this beautiful 64-page hardcover by Peter Bond. The book includes the latest NASA and Hubble telescope photos, over 300 color photographs total. LC: 9842054, $19.95. Available from DK Family Learning, 11124 N.E. Halsey, Suite 460, Portland, OR 97220; 888/225-3535. (See coupon.)

Stars & Stories Astronomy Program   (Ages 11 to 18)

Lawrence Bangs developed this great astronomy CD-ROM as a part of a larger curriculum he is working on. Stars & Stories contains 13 different sections, including: Constellations, Myths, Distance, Trigonometry, Surf the Stars, a suggested list of websites, and Internet access. The graphics in Stars & Stories are beautiful and make it all the more fun to use. $89.95. Wildridge Software, Wildridge Farm Road, Box 61, Newark, VT 05871; 888/244-4379.

Solar System Chart Set   (Ages 10 to 12)

Each chart has up to six reproducible worksheets on the back. The charts are printed on 22½" × 28½" heavy stock for long use. Set of six: B8-95-7110, $13.95. Available from Carolina Biological Supply Co., 2700 York Rd., Burlington, NC 27215; 800/334-5551; www.carolina.com.

Star Projection Theater   (Ages 8 to 14)

This is a battery-operated sound and light show suitable for indoor and outdoor use. It consists of a 5-inch transparent globe, a horizon ring, halogen projection lamp, plastic base, user's guide, and a 56-minute audiocassette. Requires 2 AA alkaline batteries, not included. B8-61-2064, $47.90. Available from Carolina Biological Supply Co., 2700 York Rd., Burlington, NC 27215 800/334-5551; www.carolina.com.

Be Your Own Astronomy Expert   (Ages 8 to 12)

This book contains dozens of entertaining projects and colorful photographs which help unravel the mysteries of the galaxy for students. Learn about the sun, moon, and how they interact with the earth. B8-95-7122, $14.95. Available from Carolina Biological Supply Co., 2700 York Rd., Burlington, NC 27215; 800/334-5551; www.carolina.com.

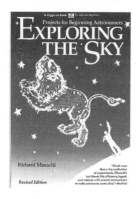

Exploring the Sky: Projects for Beginning Astronomers (Ages 10 to 14)

This book by Richard Moeschl is a guide for teaching people to help their students explore the nighttime sky through history, mythology, and science. B8-95-7130, $17.95. Available from Carolina Biological Supply Co., 2700 York Rd., Burlington, NC 27215; 800/334-5551; website; www.carolina.com.

Repogle Moon Globe   (Ages 8 to 12)

This 12-inch globe, which is the official NASA model, comes with a molded base and 11-page handbook. It has a 3-D look with the seas and craters standing out in great detail. The landing site of the first Apollo mission is shown. B8-61-2060, $39.95. Available from Carolina Biological Supply Co., 2700 York Rd., Burlington, NC 27215; 800/334-5551; www.carolina.com.

Solar System Planetary Science Kit   (Ages 9 to 12)

Assemble, paint, and then display this scale model of the solar system, including nine planets, principal moons, and a 12" × 36" sun poster. The accompanying 64-page book offers instructions, planetary information, and more than 20 experiments. B8-95-7115, $39.95. Available from Carolina Biological Supply Co., 2700 York Rd., Burlington, NC 27215; 800/334-5551; www.carolina.com.

Where in Space Is Carmen Sandiego?
(Ages 9 to 12)

In this space version of the popular global geography board game, players race through the solar system, visiting the planets and answering questions about them. Complete instructions and introductory solar system map. B8-95-7166, $22.95. Available from Carolina Biological Supply Co., 2700 York Rd., Burlington, NC 27215; 800/334-5551; www.carolina.com.

Natural Science Chart Set   (Ages 9 to 12)

This is a set of six charts, 22½" × 28½", each with a teacher lesson plan, activity sheets you can copy, and answer keys. B8-95-9030, $46. Available from Carolina Biological Supply Co., 2700 York Rd., Burlington, NC 27215; 800/334-5551; www.carolina.com.

Rock & Mineral Hunt   (Ages 8 to 12)

Teach geology with real rocks and minerals! This kit contains over 25 specimens, cleaning brushes, 3-lens magnifier, identification labels, specimen bags, teacher's guide, and 160-page *Golden Guide to Rocks and Minerals*. B8-95-9042, $23.95. Available from Carolina Biological Supply Co., 2700 York Rd., Burlington, NC 27215; 800/334-5551; www.carolina.com.

DK Rocks, Fossils & Gems   (Ages 8 and up)

Part of the DK Eyewitness Anthologies, this 128-page hardcover book is packed with the famous DK illustrations and readable text, bringing geology to life for your child. Item #777, $19.95. Available from DK Family Learning, 11124 N.E. Halsey, Suite 460, Portland, OR 97220; 888/225-3535. (See coupon.)

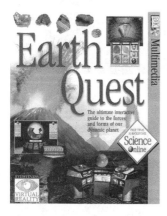

DK Geology Bundle   (Ages 8 to 15)

Study the geologic features that make up our dynamic planet in this exciting CD-ROM/video set! It includes EarthQuest CD-ROM, Eyewitness Rocks and Minerals Video; Eyewitness Volcano Video. Hybrid CD-ROM: LSPK1145-CDB, $54.95. Available from Learning Services, P.O. Box 10636, Eugene, OR 97440-2636; Western Region: 800/877-9378; Eastern Region: 800/877-3278. (See coupon.)

Rock Tumbler Kit   (Ages 10 and up)

Turn rough rocks into polished gemstones with this kit. Includes an electric tumbling machine with heavy-duty motor, rough semiprecious stones to polish (amethyst, jasper, agate), grits, polish, and instruction manual. B8-95-9300, $35.95. Refill: B8-95-9302, $12.95. Available from Carolina Biological Supply Co., 2700 York Rd., Burlington, NC 27215; 800/334-5551; www.carolina.com.

Ring-of-Fire   (Age 10 and up)

If you have a budding geologist in your household, Igneous Rock Kits, Sedimentary Rock Kits, and/or Metamorphic Rock Kits will be appreciated. The rock samples come with a small hand microscope for close inspection. A booklet in each kit contains blank pages for the student's journal notes, and has detailed descriptions of the subject rocks and their properties for identification and understanding how they were formed and why they differ. Each kit is $19.95 plus $4.50 shipping. Order from Ring-of-Fire, P.O. Box 489, Scio, OR 97374; 888/785-5439; Fax: 503/394-3100; e-mail: myrnam@teleport.com. (See coupon.)

Geode Studies   (Ages 8 to 15)

If you have never cracked open a geode, you don't know what you are missing. These are great additions to your student's rock collection. The machine-cut geodes make beautiful paperweights or coffee-table decorations. Deluxe Geode Kit includes three large (approximately 2-inch diameter) and 16 medium (approximately 1-inch diameter) crack-open geodes and one large, machine-cut and polished geode (approximately 1 lb./4-inch diameter). 51-110-4751, $48. Available from Delta Education, P.O. Box 3000, Nashua, NH 03061-3000; 800/442-5444; www.delta-ed.com.

Tub of Geodes   (Ages 8 to 15)

200 1-inch-diameter crack-open geodes in a recyclable plastic tub. 51-180-8982, $74.98. Available from Delta Education, P.O. Box 3000, Nashua, NH 03061-3000; 800/442-5444; www.delta-ed.com.

Geode Accessories   (Ages 8 to 15)

Rock Pick Hammer, 51-080-1800, $15; Adult Safety Goggles, 5N-190-0092, $4.78; Child Safety Goggles, 5N-190-0030, $5.50. Available from Delta Education, P.O. Box 3000, Nashua, NH 03061-3000; 800/442-5444; www.delta-ed.com.

Volcanoes Earth Science Kit   (Ages 9 to 12)

Here is a kit you can paint while you read the 32-page science book covering facts, legends, activities, and more. Includes paint, brushes, and instructions. B8-95-9100, $14.95. Available from Carolina Biological Supply Co., 2700 York Rd., Burlington, NC 27215; 800/334-5551; www.carolina.com.

Stream Table Kit   (Ages 10 to 15)

Want to study stream erosion of soil? This portable table unit is perfect! Includes plastic tray, drain trough, tray support, and siphon tube. Teacher's guide, too. B8-GEO-9888, $49.95. Available from Carolina Biological Supply Co., 2700 York Rd., Burlington, NC 27215; 800/334-5551; www.carolina.com.

The Sedimentator   (Ages 10 to 12)

Here is a simple device that demonstrates the process of sedimenting as in river erosion. Two sediment tubes plus teacher manual and student information with activities are included. B8-95-9025, $17.95. Available from Carolina Biological Supply Co., 2700 York Rd., Burlington, NC 27215; 800/334-5551; www.carolina.com.

Fossil Hunt   (Ages 8 to 12)

This kit provides the opportunity for your student to "dig" into clean volcanic gravel for 20 fossil specimens, including a 550-million-year-old trilobite and a genuine dinosaur fossil! Teaches how to discover, observe, identify, and exhibit fossils. Includes cleaning brushes, 3-lens magnifier, I.D. labels, specimen bags, 160-page *Golden Guide to Fossils*, 480 full-color illustrations. B8-95-9405, $23.95. Available from Carolina Biological Supply Co., 2700 York Rd., Burlington, NC 27215; 800/334-5551; www.carolina.com.

Mold Making Kit   (Ages 10 and up)

If your student already has a fossil collection, she or he can make replicas or use the two fossils included in the kit. Comes with the booklet *Mold Making*, which provides instructions and photographs, as well as small unfinished Ammonite cast, small unfinished Crinoid cast, latex rubber casting and backup medium (gypsum cement), clay, paint brushes, wooden sculpturing tool, and gauze. B8-GEO5200, $35.50. Latex rubber refill: B8-GEO5102, $11; Gypsum cement, 4-lb. bag: B8-GEO5202, $11.80. Available from Carolina Biological Supply Co., 2700 York Rd., Burlington, NC 27215; 800/334-5551; www.carolina.com.

Fossilworks Interactive Casting Kits (Ages 10 and up)

Two kits (four-mold or six-mold) both of rubber, offer your student the opportunity to make fossil replicas. Both kits include gypsum cement, lesson plans, complete instructions, and watercolors. The four-mold kit includes an ammonite, crinoid, trilobite, and a cave bear tooth. B8-GEO5210, $31.15. The six-mold kit has an additional shark tooth and dinosaur claw. B8-GEO5412, $41.55. Available from Carolina Biological Supply Co., 2700 York Rd., Burlington, NC 27215; 800/334-5551; www.carolina.com.

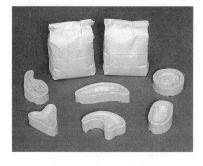

Science and Biology

Bones and the Secrets They Tell (Ages 9 to 12)

By assembling a 176-piece, 3-D life-size puzzle of a Neanderthal skull, your student will learn about the work of paleontologists, forensic scientists, anthropologists, and others who study bones for a living. The puzzle comes with a 16-page booklet with instructions. B8-95-9408, $17.50. Available from Carolina Biological Supply Co., 2700 York Rd., Burlington, NC 27215; 800/334-5551; www.carolina.com.

DK Books' Dinosaur Bundle (Ages to 8 to 13)

Delve into the fascinating world of these incredible beasts in this CD-ROM/video package. Includes Dinosaur Hunter CD-ROM; Eyewitness Dinosaur Video; *Eyewitness Visual Dictionary: Dinosaurs*. MAC CD-ROM: LSPK1140-MCCD or WIN CD-ROM: LSKP1140-MPC, $59.95. Available from Learning Services, P.O. Box 10636, Eugene, OR 97440-2636; Western Region: 800/877-9378; Eastern Region: 800/877-3278. (See coupon.)

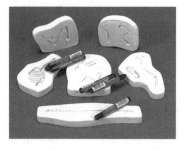

Dinosaur Traces Kits (Ages 9 to 12)

Using these three kits, students "rub" six different plastic molds representing parts of one dinosaur skeleton and assemble them into a version of the dinosaur. Each kit includes information about the dinosaurs, instructions on how to use the molds, suggested exercises, further reading list, six molds, six crayons, and skeletal key for exact positioning of the rubbings. Velociraptor, B8-GEO-6040; Triceratops, B8-GEO6042; Tyrannosaurus, BI-GEO6044; $39 each. Available from Carolina Biological Supply Co., 2700 York Rd., Burlington, NC 27215; 800/334-5551; www.carolina.com.

The Weather Book (Ages 5 to 14)

An easy-to-understand, scientifically accurate weather guide by *USA Today*. Makes a great addition to your weather station. B8-95-9840, $19.95. Available from Carolina Biological Supply Co., 2700 York Rd., Burlington, NC 27215; 800/334-5551; www.carolina.com.

Science and Biology

Weather Whys   (Ages 5 to 9)

Help your younger child understand more about the weather and how it affects us with this book by Mike Artell. Filled with facts, riddles, things to do, and even a tear-out weather wheel with weather terms and definitions. B8-95-9842, $12.95. Available from Carolina Biological Supply Co., 2700 York Rd., Burlington, NC 27215; 800/334-5551; www.carolina.com.

Weather Watch Rain Gauge   (Ages 5 and up)

This gadget is a little self-contained weather station, suitable for mounting on a pole or a fence or other stationary object. The gauge measures rainfall, wind speed and direction, and temperature. B8-95-9848, $6.95. Available from Carolina Biological Supply Co., 2700 York Rd., Burlington, NC 27215; 800/334-5551; www.carolina.com.

Cloud Chart & Flash Card Set   (Ages 5 to 12)

Want to get lost in the clouds? This set is a great way to do it. Students can study the three basic families of clouds with both the cards and the poster. A guide is also included with more than 101 sky-centered activities. B8-95-9868, $16.95. Available from Carolina Biological Supply Co., 2700 York Rd., Burlington, NC 27215; 800/334-5551; www.carolina.com.

Storms and Weather Forecasting Kit   (Ages 10 to 12)

With this kit, your student can build his or her own weather station and learn how to predict storms. The kit includes a 16-page instruction book, chart to record daily weather, map, sticker, cloud charts, and lots more. B8-95-9836, $17.50. Available from Carolina Biological Supply Co., 2700 York Rd., Burlington, NC 27215; 800/334-5551; www.carolina.com.

Humidity Test Strips

These inexpensive strips come in handy as an addition to your student's weather study program. The strips' color varies with the humidity, from blue (low) to pink (high). Package of 100 strips, B8-89-5571, $1.67. Available from Carolina Biological Supply Co., 2700 York Rd., Burlington, NC 27215; 800/334-5551; www.carolina.com.

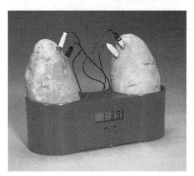

Two Potato Clock   (Ages 8 to 13)

Remember this classic science experiment? Making an "electrical" device, in this case a digital clock, run on the acid content of two certain objects—potatoes or lemons, for instance. Your student can discover which materials provide the longest-running amount of energy. B8-96-2270, $15.95. Available from Carolina Biological Supply Co., 2700 York Rd., Burlington, NC 27215; 800/334-5551; www.carolina.com.

Color-Coded Spring Scales   (Ages 9 and up)

These clear plastic, tubular spring scales have two calibrations, newtons (N) to measure force and grams (g) for weighing mass. Available in six values from 250 g (2.5 N), B8-96-2092; up to 5,000 g (50 N), B8-96-2096; $6.15 each. Available from Carolina Biological Supply Co., 2700 York Rd., Burlington, NC 27215; 800/334-5551l; www.carolina.com.

Pyrex Graduated Glass Beakers (Family use)

Low-cost beaker with spout and uniform wall thickness. 250 ml, B8-72-1223, $2.10; 600 ml, B8-72-1225, $3.20. Available from Carolina Biological Supply Co., 2700 York Rd., Burlington, NC 27215; 800/334-5551; www.carolina.com.

Pyrex Erlenmeyer Flasks   (Family Use)

Flasks (see picture at top of page) come in three sizes: 125 ml, B8-72-6670, $2.35; 250 ml, B8-72-6672, $2.55; 500 ml, B8-72-6676, $3.35. Available from Carolina Biological Supply Co., 2700 York Rd., Burlington, NC 27215; 800/334-5551; www.carolina.com.

Graduated Cylinder Set   (Family Use)

Six clear, easy-reading plastic graduate vessels (see picture at top of page). They are short and have a wide base to help prevent spills. B8-96-1968, $43 per set. Available from Carolina Biological Supply Co., 2700 York Rd., Burlington, NC 27215; 800/334-5551; www.carolina.com.

Microscale Vacuum Apparatus Kit   (Ages 11 to adult)

This kit allows you to perform all sorts of vacuum-necessary experiments and learn about air pressure and how it affects various objects under differing conditions. High school and college-level experimenters can study many of the laws of air pressure. The kit includes a 3½" bell jar, base plate, vacuum pump syringe, suction cup, balloons, pipettes, and instructions. Item #VAC-10, $34.95. Available from Education Innovations, Inc., 151 River Rd., Cos Cob, CT 06807-2514; Fax: 203/629-2739; 206/629-6049 or (for orders) 888/912-7474.

Science Accessories (Family use)

Alcohol lamp with metal cap: 2 oz., B8-70-6600, $6.05; wood splints: 500 per bundle, B8-70-6860, $3.10; plastic dropping pipettes: 6 inches long, B8-73-6898, $6.85 per 100; plastic medicine dropper: 3½ inches, B8-73-6907, $2.60 per 12. Available from Carolina Biological Supply Co., 2700 York Rd., Burlington, NC 27215; 800/334-5551; www.carolina.com.

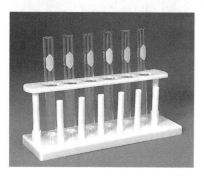

Test Tube Rack (Family use)

This handy addition to your in-home lab equipment has six 25 mm–diameter holes for upright test tubes and six vertical pins for drying inverted tubes after cleaning. Rack is 9½" × 3" × 3⅝". B8-73-1876, $5.45. Available from Carolina Biological Supply Co., 2700 York Rd., Burlington, NC 27215; 800/334-5551; www.carolina.com.

Pyrex Test Tubes (with rim) (Family use)

Each pack contains 72 (20 mm by 150 mm) tubes. B8-73-1-19, $45.50 per pack. Available from Carolina Biological Supply Co., 2700 York Rd., Burlington, NC 27215; 800/334-5551; www.carolina.com.

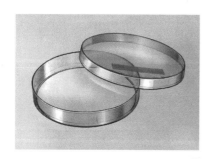

Petri Dishes (plastic) (Family use)

These are sterile, disposable round dishes for lab use. B8-74-1346 (60 × 15 mm), $5.10 per 20; B8-74-1350 (100 × 15 mm), $4.45 per 20. Available from Carolina Biological Supply Co., 2700 York Rd., Burlington, NC 27215; 800/334-5551; www.carolina.com.

Science and Biology

Lab Apron for the Beginning Scientist   (Ages 5 to 12)

Heavy, translucent 24" × 36" plastic aprons with cotton trim at waist and neck to protect your budding Pasteur/Curie's clothing while experimenting in your home lab. One size fits all. Pack of 6 aprons, B8-95-3101, $23.95; pack of 12 aprons, B8-95-3102, $42.95. Available from Carolina Biological Supply Co., 2700 York Rd., Burlington, NC 27215; 800/334-5551; www.carolina.com.

Outside Celsius/Fahrenheit Thermometer (Family use)

This outdoor thermometer has a plastic molded frame, with aluminum mounting bracket for permanent installation. B8-95-9872, $4.25. Available from Carolina Biological Supply Co., 2700 York Rd., Burlington, NC 27215; 800/334-5551; www.carolina.com.

101 Great Science Experiments   (Ages 7 to 11)

This 120-page hardcover by Neil Ardley, from the beautiful DK collection, will keep your student enthralled! Item # 500, $16.95. Available from DK Family Learning, 11124 N.E. Halsey, Suite 460, Portland, OR 97220; 888/225-3535. (See coupon.)

101 Great Nature Experiments   (Ages 7 to 11)

This great 96-page DK book by David Burnie offers your child many, many hours of science fun. Item # 501, $16.95. Available from DK Family Learning, 11124 N.E. Halsey, Suite 460, Portland, OR 97220; 888/225-3535. (See coupon.)

Protozoa Review/Book Set   (Ages 10 to 15)

Designed for a group of 30 students, this set consists of four individually labeled cultures (Amoeba, Euglena, Paramecium, and Volvox), the book *How to Know the Protozoa*, and a pad of 30 Bioreview sheets for each protozoan. Comes with culturing instructions, AA-13-1090, $53.55. Available from the Carolina Biological Supply Co., 2700 York Rd., Burlington, NC 27215 800/334-5551; www.carolina.com.

Fly The Space Shuttle Plus 3-D Model   (Ages 8 and up)

A 32-page hardcover action book and model from DK's collection. With this great set, your student can read the book and play with the 3-D model of the shuttle, providing a real-feel connection between the two. Item # 304, $16.95. Available from DK Family Learning, 11124 N.E. Halsey, Suite 460, Portland, OR 97220; 888/225-3535. (See coupon.)

Inside Guides   (Ages 7 to 11)

These superbly written, beautifully illustrated 48-page hardcovers by DK Books cover a broad range of scientific explorations. *Amazing Bugs*, Item #289. *Animal Homes*, Item #288. *Animal Reproduction*, Item #296. *Forest*, Item #300. *Human Body*, Item #293. *Incredible Earth*, Item #290. *Incredible Plants*, Item #292. *Microlife*, Item #295. *Ocean*, Item #294. *Poisonous Animals*, Item #297. *Robot*, Item #301. *Superstructures*, Item #291. $12.95 each. Available from DK Family Learning, 11124 N.E. Halsey, Suite 460, Portland, OR 97220; 888/225-3535. (See coupon.)

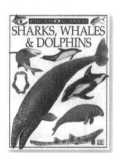

Sharks, Whales & Dolphins   (Ages 8 and up)

This deep-sea DK Eyewitness Anthology (128-page hardcover) takes your child on a illustrated tour of the largest and most intelligent denizens of the watery blue. Item #776, $19.95. Available from DK Family Learning, 11124 N.E. Halsey, Suite 460, Portland, OR 97220; 888/225-3535. (See coupon.)

Museum of Science-by-Mail   (Ages 8 to 13)

This is a nonprofit program of the Museum of Science, Boston. Students register at the end of summer and receive a packet of three projects to work on throughout the year. They are also "assigned" a science pen pal, a practicing scientist in the particular field. The student can then correspond with the scientist one-on-one. Cost is $54 per school year, with two different science activity packets. Please request the registration information by writing: Science-by-Mail, Museum of Science, Science Park, Boston, MA 02114; 800/729-3300.

Science and Biology

Wild Goose Science Kits   (Ages 5 to 14)

This company produces three different lines of great science experimentation kits, suitable for various ages. Megalabs are six different complete kits covering a specific field of scientific experimentation. Slime Chemistry (ages 5 to 12); Out to Launch (ages 8 to 12); Volcanoes, Dinosaurs & Fossils (ages 5 to 12); Crash & Burn Chemistry (ages 10 to 12); Kitchen Table Chemistry (ages 9 to 12); and Ooh Aah Chemistry (ages 9 to 12); $29.99 each. Goose Eggs are smaller experimentation kits, $5 each. Newton's Kits is a series of eight kits for ages 10 to 14, each containing a scientific detective game

that the student must solve, $17.99. Available from Wild Goose Science, 888/621-1040; e-mail: wgoose9150@aol.com; www.wildgoosescience.com.

Protozoans   (Ages 6 to12)

Do you know where your protozoans are? Find out the answer using the Carolina Student Microscope (30x). Set includes at least four protozoans of our choice, plastic deep-well slides, and the microscope. B8-13-1140, $15.25. Available from the Carolina Biological Supply Co., 2700 York Rd., Burlington, NC 27215; 800/334-5551; www.carolina.com.

Basic Microorganisms Set   (Ages 10 to 15)

This set includes a selection of living microorganisms representing algae, protozoa, bacteria, and fungi—16 organisms total—in appropriate containers, plus three booklets: *Carolina Protozoa and Invertebrates Manual, Techniques for Studying Bacteria and Fungi,* and *Culturing Algae.* Contains these organisms: Amoeba proteus, Euglena, Paramecium multimicronucleatum, Chalamydomonas, Oedogonium cardicaum (male), Oscillatoria, Volvox aureus, Spirogyra, Bacillus subtillis, Micrococcus luteus, Rhodospirillum rubrum, Coprinus cinereus, Pencillium notatum, Rhizopus stolonifer, Saccharomyces cerevisiae, and Saprolegnia. AA-13-0900, $112. Available from the Carolina Biological Supply Co., 2700 York Rd., Burlington, NC 27215 800/334-5551; www.carolina.com.

Science and Biology

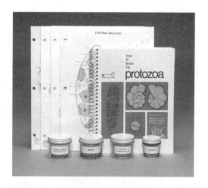

Protozoa Review Sets   (Ages 10 to 15)

Each set contains one culture and a pad of 30 anatomy Bioreview Sheets (with instructions)—enough review material for 30 students. It is perfect for a homeschool support group, which offers a biology class or supplemental study. Amoeba, AA-13-1070, $8.93; Euglena, AA-13-1072, $8.93; Paramecium, AA-13-1074, $8.93; Volvox, AA-13-1076, $8.93; Amoeba, Paramecium, and Euglena combined, AA-13-1085, $25.45 (includes instructions for culturing each form). Available from the Carolina Biological Supply Co., 2700 York Rd., Burlington, NC 27215 800/334-5551; www.carolina.com.

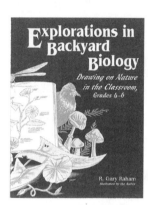

Explorations in Backyard Biology: Drawing on Nature in the Classroom   (Ages 10 to 12)

Young students discover life science adventures in this book by R. Gary Raham. Using drawing and writing skills, the author offers activities in four areas of natural history: size, scale, and the world of the very small; predator-prey relationships among animals; animal communication; and the ecology of living communities, including their human members. The activities can be integrated with other curricula. B8-95-6560, $25. Available from the Carolina Biological Supply Co., 2700 York Rd., Burlington, NC 27215; 800/334-5551; www.carolina.com.

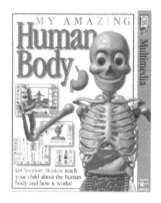

DK Books' My Amazing Human Body Bundle (Ages 8 to 15)

Explore the most wondrous invention of all—the human body in this CD-ROM/book/video set! includes My Amazing Human Body 2.0; *The Amazing Pop-Up, Pull-Out Body in a Book*, and Eyewitness Human Machine Video. Hybrid CD-ROM: LSPK1130-CDB, $49.95. Available from Learning Services, P.O. Box 10636, Eugene, OR 97440-2636; Western Region: 800/877-9378; Eastern Region: 800/877-3278. (See coupon.)

Liberal Arts

Art Instruction

Art History   (All ages)

This is a flexible art history program that can be purchased in any one of three levels—Primary (ages 7 to 10), Intermediate (ages 10 to 12), Upper (ages 13 to 15)—each featuring 30 glossy prints of paintings in junior prints (4.25" × 5") or large prints (8½" × 11"). *Learning More About Pictures* (100 pages) is comprised of an outline essay of the development of painting in Europe and America followed by explanatory paragraphs relating to each of the prints included in the package. $2.50 to $130. Available from Art Extension Press, P.O. Box 389, Westport, CT 06881; 203/256-9920. (See coupon.)

Draw Today   (Ages 10 and up)

A great, complete beginning charcoal drawing course in a box, created by Steven Golden. Included are a 75-minute instructional video and complete start-up amounts of materials—charcoal, erasers, paper, and rulers. Steven guides the neophyte artist in the "forgiving" medium of charcoal, using the grid overlay approach. The program progresses from hand copying very simple black and white drawings to complex drawings with many shades of gray. Draw Today Master Set, $59.95; Draw & Paint Set, $79.95; Da Vinci Perspective Grid $19.95. Available from Steven Golden & Associates, 217 Ferry St., Easton, PA 18042; 800/552-3729.

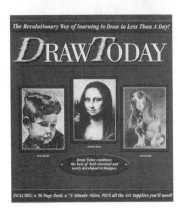

Calvert's Discovering Art Program   (Ages 9 to 14)

This is one of those programs that is really worth the money. It is 32 lessons on six 1-hour videocassettes. Included is a comprehensive parent/teacher guide and a fully packed art kit. This art program begins with a lesson about contour lines and covers such topics as African shapes, pattern, texture, light, and value. $200. Available from Calvert School, 107 Tuscany Road, Baltimore, MD 21210; 410/243-6030; www.calvertschool.org.

Lives of the Artists — Masterpieces, Messes (and What the Neighbors Thought) (Ages 10 and up)

This book by Kathleen Krull is produced on two 2-hour audiocassettes. This unabridged collection of miniature biographies of the great artists and how the people in their lives saw them is read by John C. Brown/Melissa Hughes. Cassette, item #7-96, $15.95. Available from Audio Bookshelf, 174 Prescott Hill Road, Northport, ME 04849; 800/234-1713; audbkshf@agate.net. (See coupon.)

Architecture in Education   (Ages 5 to 18)

This 224-page book by Jan Ham is full of imaginative activities and is a perfect beginning place for teaching design, materials, structures, homes, and cities. Can also be used to tie into other topics such as math and science. $25. Available from Architectural Education Resource Center (AERC), 131 Hillside Road, Franklin, MA 02038; 508/528-4517; e-mail: aerc@norfolk-county.com; www.norfolk-county.com./aerc. (See coupon.)

Designing Playgrounds   (Ages 9 to 14)

This 64-page reproducible book by Jan Ham includes ten activities that cover topics such as why children play and includes to-scale plans and models. $12.95. Available from Architectural Education Resource Center (AERC), 131 Hillside Road, Franklin, MA 02038; 508/528-4517; e-mail: aerc@norfolk-county.com; www.norfolk-county.com./aerc. (See coupon.)

Art Instruction

Why Design? (Ages 12 to 18)

This 224-page book by Jan Ham is an excellent guide to the design process. Includes landscapes, buildings, and products. $19.95. Available from Architectural Education Resource Center (AERC), 131 Hillside Road, Franklin, MA 02038; 508/528-4517; e-mail: aerc@norfolk-county.com; www.norfolk-county.com./aerc. (See coupon.)

I Know That Building! Discovering Architecture with Activities and Games (Ages 5 to 14)

Here is a great 88-page book by Jane D'Alelio filled with 30 games, puzzles, building cutout models, and more! Have fun trying to identify famous, distinctive buildings and skylines when you see magazine photos or video clips—especially from great cities such as New York, Chicago, Nashville, Cleveland, Cincinnati, Columbus, San Francisco, Oklahoma City, and Los Angeles. $14.95. Available from Architectural Education Resource Center (AERC), 131 Hillside Road, Franklin, MA 02038; 508/528-4517; e-mail: aerc@norfolk-county.com; www.norfolk-county.com/aerc. (See coupon.)

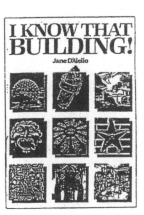

Frank Lloyd Wright for Kids (Ages 10 to 14)

This 136-page biography of the genius by Kathleen Thorne-Thompsen includes 21 activities based on his houses. From his never-built, mile-high skyscraper in Chicago to his beautiful cantilevered homes and buildings, the legendary Frank Lloyd Wright is the best-known American architect to all of us non-architects. $14.95. Available from Architectural Education Resource Center (AERC), 131 Hillside Road, Franklin, MA 02038; 508/528-4517; e-mail: aerc@norfolk-county.com; www.norfolk-county.com/aerc. (See coupon.)

The Art of Construction: Projects and Principles for Beginning Engineers and Architects   (Ages 10 to 18)

In this 60-page text by Mario Salvadori, your student will use common materials to test principles. If you want to instruct your child in structure, this is the book to start with. $12.95. Available from Architectural Education Resource Center (AERC), 131 Hillside Road, Franklin, MA 02038; 508/528-4517; e-mail: aerc@norfolk-county.com; www.norfolk-county.com/aerc. (See coupon.)

Structures   (Ages 10 to 14)

This 64-page book by Bernie Zubrowski is a four- to six-week investigation of force, tension, compression, equilibrium, and stress. Your student will build and test straw and paper clip structures. $11.50. Available from Architectural Education Resource Center (AERC), 131 Hillside Road, Franklin, MA 02038; 508/528-4517; e-mail: aerc@norfolk-county.com; www.norfolk-county.com/aerc. (See coupon.)

Box City   (Ages 5 to 18)

This 160-page reproducible book by Ginny Graves gets your child involved in city planning and community building. $30. Available from Architectural Education Resource Center (AERC), 131 Hillside Road, Franklin, MA 02038; 508/528-4517; e-mail: aerc@norfolk-county.com; www.norfolk-county.com/aerc. (See coupon.)

Building Toothpick Bridges   **(Ages 10 to 14)**

This 32-page reproducible book by Jeanne Pollard helps you and your child to have experience with real-world math and science. Your student orders materials, keeps a budget, designs, and tests bridges. $9.95. Available from Architectural Education Resource Center (AERC), 131 Hillside Road, Franklin, MA 02038; 508/528-4517; e-mail: aerc@norfolk-county.com; www.norfolk-county.com./aerc. (See coupon.)

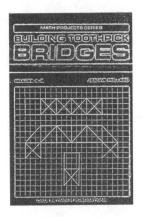

SimCity Card Game   **(Ages 9 to 18)**

This game is great to use with more than one student because it enables the participants to debate various city issues such as land use. Players earn "sim" points as the city grows. Great way to teach the concepts of city planning. $15. Available from Architectural Education Resource Center (AERC), 131 Hillside Road, Franklin, MA 02038; 508/528-4517; e-mail: aerc@norfolk-county.com; www.norfolk-county.com./aerc. (See coupon.)

3-D Home Kit   **(Ages 12 to 18)**

This complete cardboard modeling kit includes plans, walls, windows, furniture, people, and a booklet of design and math. $24.95. Available from Architectural Education Resource Center (AERC), 131 Hillside Road, Franklin, MA 02038; 508/528-4517; e-mail: aerc@norfolk-county.com; www.norfolk-county.com./aerc. (See coupon.)

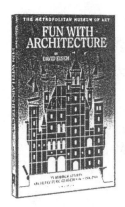

Fun with Architecture Stamp Set (Ages 9 to 18)

A great product from New York's Metropolitan Museum of Art, this set helps your child create historic, modern, and fantasy buildings. $22.50. Available from Architectural Education Resource Center (AERC), 131 Hillside Road, Franklin, MA 02038; 508/528-4517; e-mail: aerc@norfolk-county.com; www.norfolk-county.com./aerc. (See coupon.)

Block Building for Children (Ages 5 to 14)

If you have a set of blocks and this 166-page book by Lester Walker you can take advantage of its 18 projects from skyscrapers to castles. Teach your child about planning and spatial problem-solving while having fun! $22.95. Available from Architectural Education Resource Center (AERC), 131 Hillside Road, Franklin, MA 02038; 508/528-4517; e-mail: aerc@norfolk-county.com; www.norfolk-county.com./aerc. (See coupon.)

Architects Make Zigzags (Ages 5 to 13)

This is an alphabet book by Roxie Munro that introduces architectural vocabulary and concepts. $9.95. Available from Architectural Education Resource Center (AERC), 131 Hillside Road, Franklin, MA 02038; 508/528-4517; e-mail: aerc@norfolk-county.com; www.norfolk-county.com./aerc. (See coupon.)

The Visual Dictionary of Buildings (Ages 5 to 18)

This is a clearly portrayed 64-page reference book edited by Fiona Courtenay-Thompson, Roger Tritton, and Nicola Liddiard covering building solutions from ancient to modern day. $14.95. Available from Architectural Education Resource Center (AERC), 131 Hillside Road, Franklin, MA 02038; 508/528-4517; e-mail: aerc@norfolk-county.com; www.norfolk-county.com./aerc. (See coupon.)

N.C. Wyeth's Pilgrims (Ages 9 to 12)

Wyeth painted pictures of Pilgrims to dispel the ideas of their dourness. The book includes photos of Wyeth paintings with text by Sam Souci. Hardcover, $14.95; paperback, $5.95. Available from Beautiful Feet Books, 139 Main St., Sandwich, MA 02563; 800/889-1978; 508/833-8626. www.bfbooks.com. Call for catalog.

Drawing for the Terrified! (Ages 12 to adult)

This complete course for beginners comes in a 128-page hardcover by Richard Box with 168 color and b&w illustrations. Overcome fear and draw with complete confidence! Exercises for drawing in monochrome, tonal values, color, and shading, along with relaxation techniques, methods for enhancing perception, and creative ways to tap into your emotions. Item #570-1446, $24.95. Available from Sax Arts & Crafts, P.O. Box 510710, New Berlin, WI 53151-0710; 414/784-6880; 800/558-6696; e-mail: infor@saxarts.com; www.saxarts.com. (See coupon.)

Drawing on the Right Side of the Brain
(Ages 13 to adult)

This 207-page illustrated softcover presents Betty Edwards' revolutionary "Right Brain" approach to drawing! See things not as objects but as a series of lines and shapes. Sharpen your powers of perception and express individuality through your own drawing style. Access the part of your mind that works in a style conducive to creative, intuitive thought. Item #570-0497, $15.95. Available from Sax Arts & Crafts, P.O. Box 510710, New Berlin, WI 53151-0710; 414/784-6880; 800/558-6696; e-mail: infor@saxarts.com; www.saxarts.com. (See coupon.)

Pastel for the Serious Beginner   (Ages 13 to adult)

Beginning with materials and methods, this 144-page softcover by Larry Blovits includes helpful, step-by-step demonstrations and 150 full-color illustrations. Learn how to use the delicate pastel medium to create light-filled landscapes, sophisticated still-lifes, and pleasing portraits. Find out how to blend pastels into radiant gradations, bring contrasts of light and shadow, build basic shapes into 3-D forms, and handle perspective to create the feeling of depth and space. Item #570-1479, $19.95. Available from Sax Arts & Crafts, P.O. Box 510710, New Berlin, WI 53151-0710; 414/784-6880; 800/558-6696; e-mail: infor@saxarts.com; www.saxarts.com. (See coupon.)

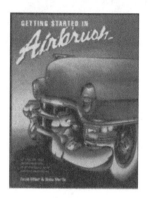

Getting Started in Airbrush   (Ages 13 to adult)

This 120-page softcover by Miller and Martin includes dozens of full-color airbrush illustrations. It also presents 22 step-by-step demonstrations of all the basic airbrush techniques used to create a wide variety of effects, whether you are doing illustration or air-brushing a T-shirt. The book covers lettering, highlighting, metallic effects, textures, edge basics, masking, gradation basics, and includes advice on equipment to get started. Item #570-2204, $23.95. Available from Sax Arts & Crafts, P.O. Box 510710, New Berlin, WI 53151-0710; 414/784-6880; 800/558-6696; e-mail: infor@saxarts.com; www.saxarts.com. (See coupon.)

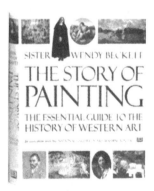

The Story of Painting   (Ages 13 to adult)

This 400-page hardcover by Sister Wendy Beckett focuses entirely on painting, promotes greater understanding and renewed appreciation of fine art through the ages. Over 450 masterpieces chronicle the developments and movements in painting from ancient art through Medieval, Gothic, Renaissance, Impressionism, and other eras to Modernism. Includes timelines for an instant review of the important artists of each era. Item #570-2436, $39.95. Available from Sax Arts & Crafts, P.O. Box 510710, New Berlin, WI 53151-0710; 414/784-6880; 800/558-6696; e-mail: infor@saxarts.com; www.saxarts.com. (See coupon.)

Using Liquid Frisket   (Ages 13 to adult)

This 48-page book by Griffith includes b&w illustrations and a full-color gallery of examples. Learn what frisket is, what different types are available, and how to work with various paper surfaces. The book takes you step-by-step through the frisket process—planning your painting and demonstrating watercolor, airbrush, and decorative techniques. Includes practice exercises to help you perfect basic techniques. Item #570-2576, $10.95. Available from Sax Arts & Crafts, P.O. Box 510710, New Berlin, WI 53151-0710; 414/784-6880; 800/558-6696; e-mail: infor@saxarts.com; www.saxarts.com. (See coupon.)

The Encyclopedia of Watercolor Techniques (Ages 13 to adult)

This 192-page hardcover by Harrison presents numerous full-color illustrations that depict exciting creative techniques for watercolor, gouache, ink, and acrylic. Learn the basics of masking, wax resist, variegated wash, sponging, dry brushing, glazing, and more. Practical applications of widely differing styles by professional artists. Item #570-2717, $24.95. Available from Sax Arts & Crafts, P.O. Box 510710, New Berlin, WI 53151-0710; 414/784-6880; 800/558-6696; e-mail: infor@saxarts.com; www.saxarts.com. (See coupon.)

Color Theory Made Easy   (Ages 13 to adult)

This 112-page softcover includes hundreds of color illustrations. Ames suggests that the true primary colors are not red, blue, and yellow, but cyan, magenta, and yellow. These "new" primaries form the foundation for a fresh approach to mixing color. Step-by-step watercolor procedures show students how to paint portraits, reflective light, shadows, landscape, and more. Item #570-2774, $19.95. Available from Sax Arts & Crafts, P.O. Box 510710, New Berlin, WI 53151-0710; 414/784-6880; 800/558-6696; e-mail: infor@saxarts.com; www.saxarts.com. (See coupon.)

Authentic American Indian Beadwork and How to Do It   (Ages 13 to adult)

This 48-page softcover by Pamela Stanley-Miller presents 50 charts and 21 full-size patterns for beadwork. Item #570-3103, $4.95. Available from Sax Arts & Crafts, P.O. Box 510710, New Berlin, WI 53151-0710; 414/784-6880; 800/558-6696; e-mail: infor@saxarts.com; www.saxarts.com. (See coupon.)

Color Woodblock Printmaking   (Ages 13 to adult)

This 88-page text by Kanada includes 54 full-color illustrations. Behind the famous major artists were scores of anonymous craftsmen who carved woodblocks, made paper, and performed other tasks. This book spotlights these specialized techniques and discusses the many steps involved in the creation of a color woodblock print. Item #570-6221, $19.95. Available from Sax Arts & Crafts, P.O. Box 510710, New Berlin, WI 53151-0710; 414/784-6880; 800/558-6696; e-mail: infor@saxarts.com; www.saxarts.com. (See coupon.)

Learning to Weave   (Ages 13 to adult)

This hardcover by Chandler has 232 pages, color photos, and b&w illustrations throughout. In it, the mysteries of four-harness weaving are made easy! All you need to know to weave with confidence—step-by-step warping, weaving technique, project planning, reading and writing drafts, common weave structures, as well as lots of handy hints. The book is for beginners and seasoned weavers alike. Item #570-9027, $21.95. Available from Sax Arts & Crafts, P.O. Box 510710, New Berlin, WI 53151-0710; 414/784-6880; 800/558-6696; e-mail: infor@saxarts.com; www.saxarts.com. (See coupon.)

Sculpture as Experience (Ages 11 to adult)

This 192-page softcover by Peck presents 116 b&w illustrations. Interesting projects for all skill levels! Experience the wide range of methods and materials used to create contemporary sculpture by trying many uncomplicated projects that do not require major equipment. A broad variety of methods demonstrate usage of clay, wire, plaster, wax, and more. Also explains mounting and finishing. Item #571-3259, $17.95. Available from Sax Arts & Crafts, P.O. Box 510710, New Berlin, WI 53151-0710; 414/784-6880; 800/558-6696; e-mail: infor@saxarts.com; www.saxarts.com. (See coupon.)

Start Sculpting (Ages 13 to adult)

The 20 projects in this 144-page hardcover by Plowman provide experience in five ways of making a sculpture: carving, modeling, construction, casting, and assemblage. Create original sculptures using readily available materials, such as scrap wood, empty cans, clay, and modeling wax. The guide includes clear, step-by-step instructions and color photos. Item #571-3458, $17.98. Available from Sax Arts & Crafts, P.O. Box 510710, New Berlin, WI 53151-0710; 414/784-6880; 800/558-6696; e-mail: infor@saxarts.com; www.saxarts.com. (See coupon.)

The Book of Candlemaking (Ages 13 to adult)

Make molded, double-molded, dipped, rolled, and floating candles with this step-by-step 128-page hardcover guide by Larkin. Learn how to melt wax and add hardeners, dyes, and scents. Decorate candles using techniques such as decoupaging, embossing, and leafing or creatively add paint, beads, foil, glitter, and other materials. Item #571-3987, $24.95. Available from Sax Arts & Crafts, P.O. Box 510710, New Berlin, WI 53151-0710; 414/784-6880; 800/558-6696; e-mail: infor@saxarts.com; www.saxarts.com. (See coupon.)

The Great Origami Book (All ages)

Enjoy the beautiful and inexpensive art of paperfolding through this 80-page illustrated softcover by Ayture-Scheele! Full-color diagramed patterns present unique ideas for both the novice and experienced student of origami. Eight basic forms provide the foundation for 40 different figures, which can be used as novelties, decorations, or toys. Simple, rewarding projects for all ages. Item #571-7194, $12.95. Available from Sax Arts & Crafts, P.O. Box 510710, New Berlin, WI 53151-0710; 414/784-6880; 800/558-6696; e-mail: infor@saxarts.com; www.saxarts.com. (See coupon.)

Origami American Style (All ages)

This 32-page softcover by Zulat Asture-Scheele with b&w illustrations is the first book of its kind; clear, concise directions and diagrams follow an easier logic than most traditional Japanese books. Finally—origami designs developed by an American folder for Americans to fold! Beginners as well as expert folders will love these everyday-to-unusual designs. Item #571-7467, $5.95. Available from Sax Arts & Crafts, P.O. Box 510710, New Berlin, WI 53151-0710; 414/784-6880; 800/558-6696; e-mail: infor@saxarts.com; www.saxarts.com. (See coupon.)

Getting to Know the World's Great Artists Series (Ages 5 to 9)

Expose children to the fine works of famous master artists at an early age. Clever full-color illustrations and often humorous text by Venezia teach and entertain at the same time, while providing a light, yet realistic overview of each of 17 artist's life and style of painting. Large print with grade 2 reading level. Each softcover book has 32 pages and full-color reproductions. $6.95 to $146.95. Contact for catalog. Available from Sax Arts & Crafts, P.O. Box 510710, New Berlin, WI 53151-0710; 414/784-6880; 800/558-6696; e-mail: infor@saxarts.com; www.saxarts.com. (See coupon.)

Children and Painting   (All ages)

This 160-page hardcover by Topal presents 250 full-color illustrations. This fresh look at art instruction emphasizes a step-by-step strategy of teaching basic concepts and techniques, fine-tuning aesthetic awareness, and slowly introducing new creative challenges. Includes 40 activities that coordinate with the elementary curriculum and are appropriate for any beginning painter. Item #572-1402, $24.95. Available from Sax Arts & Crafts, P.O. Box 510710, New Berlin, WI 53151-0710; 414/784-6880; 800/558-6696; e-mail: infor@saxarts.com; www.saxarts.com. (See coupon.)

Discovering Great Artists: Hands-On Art for Children in the Styles of the Great Masters   (Ages 5 to 15)

This 141-page softcover by Kohl and Solga includes more than 200 b&w illustrations, as well as 110 fascinating art activities. Activities are designed to help children experience the styles and techniques of the great masters from the Renaissance to the present, while brief biographies acquaint children with each artist. Fully illustrated, child-tested activities feature painting, drawing, sculpture, photography, and more. Item #572-2343, $14.95. Available from Sax Arts & Crafts, P.O. Box 510710, New Berlin, WI 53151-0710; 414/784-6880; 800/558-6696; e-mail: infor@saxarts.com; www.saxarts.com. (See coupon.)

Child Art Therapy: Understanding and Helping Children Grow Through Art   (Ages 7 to 12)

This 320-page softcover with b&w illustrations by Rubin is a superior reference for all special needs teachers and anyone who nurtures the creative process in children. The book includes updated information on progress in child art therapy, as well as photos of children's original artwork and suggestions for children with special needs. Item #572-7998, $48.95. Available from Sax Arts & Crafts, P.O. Box 510710, New Berlin, WI 53151-0710; 414/784-6880; 800/558-6696; e-mail: infor@saxarts.com; www.saxarts.com. (See coupon.)

Geology Crafts for Kids: 50 Nifty Projects to Explore the Marvels of Planet Earth   (Ages 10 to 14)

This cross-curricular book (144 pages, hardcover) by Anderson, Diehn, and Krautwurst combines earth science and art with exciting activities, information, and experiments. Children will learn about a broad spectrum of geologic phenomena—including continental drift, minerals, volcanoes, earthquakes, rocks, crystals, erosion, fossils, and much more. Item #572-8027, $14.95. Available from Sax Arts & Crafts, P.O. Box 510710, New Berlin, WI 53151-0710; 414/784-6880; 800/558-6696; e-mail: infor@saxarts.com; www.saxarts.com. (See coupon.)

The Metropolitan Museum of Art Activity Book (Ages 9 to 12)

This 88-page softcover by Brown with b&w and color illustrations enables you to bring some of the things that most fascinate children about a trip to the art museum right into your home! Children construct ancient objects, models, puppets, mosaics, games, and puzzles inspired by treasures in the museum's collection. Item #72-7532, $12.95. Available from Sax Arts & Crafts, P.O. Box 510710, New Berlin, WI 53151-0710;   414/784-6880;   800/558-6696;   e-mail: infor@saxarts.com; www.saxarts.com. (See coupon.)

Career Opportunities in Art, Rev. Ed.   (Ages 13 to adult)

This 191-page softcover by Haubenstock and Joselit is an up-to-date, comprehensive source of opportunities for an exciting career in art. Contains indispensable and realistic information on over 80 job titles in art education, graphic arts, journalism, museums, galleries, and other art-related businesses. Details on requirements, in-depth descriptions, advancement prospects, salaries, and other topics are included. Helpful appendix lists schools, scholarships, internships, and more. Item #572-8241, $18.95. Sax Arts & Crafts, P.O. Box 510710, New Berlin, WI 53151-0710; 414/784-6880; 800/558-6696; e-mail: infor@saxarts.com; www.saxarts.com. (See coupon.)

Art Journal Topics **(Ages 10 to 14)**

This bookmark-sized tablet holds 200 incredibly creative topics to stimulate young minds to express themselves in drawing and writing. Imaginative topics include "Design or describe an original postage stamp that commemo-

rates an important event in history" or "What color is a yawn?" or "If you could meet any artist, whom would you choose and why?" Topics can be adapted for all age levels. Item #572-8696, $4.95. Available from Sax Arts & Crafts, P.O. Box 510710, New Berlin, WI 53151-0710; 414/784-6880; 800/558-6696; e-mail: infor@saxarts.com; www.saxarts.com. (See coupon.)

The Encyclopedia of Cartooning Techniques
(Ages 13 to adult)

This 176-page hardcover by Whitaker includes many b&w and color illustrations that inspire students to create cartoons with powerful visual impact! Jam-packed volume shows the importance of choosing the right art materials, acquiring technical skills, and developing a personal style. Artwork and step-by-step demonstrations help students learn to translate colorful ideas into cartoon form. Importance is placed on learning to depict figures, body language, movement, foreshortening, caricature, and

more. Item #573-7077, $24.95. Available from Sax Arts & Crafts, P.O. Box 510710, New Berlin, WI 53151-0710; 414/784-6880; 800/558-6696; e-mail: infor@saxarts.com; www.saxarts.com. (See coupon.)

Masters of Illusion **(Ages 13 to adult)**

This unique 30-minute video uses new technology to look at old masters in new ways. It examines artistic and scientific discoveries of the Renaissance, focuses on the discovery of perspective and the development of visual tools that create the magic of illusion; and shows how extraordinary special effects of today's movies are based on principles established more than 500 years ago by Renaissance masters! Item #586-1646, $29.95. Available from Sax Arts & Crafts, P.O. Box 510710, New Berlin, WI 53151-0710; 414/784-6880; 800/558-6696; e-mail: infor@saxarts.com; www.saxarts.com. (See coupon.)

Degas   (Ages 13 to adult)

This 68-minute video features many paintings, drawings, and prints that represent Degas's favorite settings: the ballet class, racecourse, and railway. Item # 586-1729, $39.95. Available from Sax Arts & Crafts, P.O. Box 510710, New Berlin, WI 53151-0710; 414/784-6880; 800/558-6696; e-mail: infor@saxarts.com; www.saxarts.com. (See coupon.)

Paul Cezanne   (Ages 13 to adult)

This 58-minute video traces Cezanne's career to his final recognition as the father of modern painting. Cezanne focused on the use of a single image—the Mont St. Victoire in Provence—to define form, color, and light. Item #586-1737, $39.95. Available from Sax Arts & Crafts, P.O. Box 510710, New Berlin, WI 53151-0710; 414/784-6880; 800/558-6696; e-mail: infor@saxarts.com; www.saxarts.com. (See coupon.)

In a Brilliant Light: van Gogh in Arles   (Ages 13 to adult)

This 58-minute video portrait of van Gogh's last days in the south of France focuses on the artist's work rather than on his life and dispels many of the myths surrounding this legendary painter. Item #586-1745, $29.95. Available from Sax Arts & Crafts, P.O. Box 510710, New Berlin, WI 53151-0710; 414/784-6880; 800/558-6696; e-mail: infor@saxarts.com; www.saxarts.com. (See coupon.)

Seurat   (Ages 15 to adult)

This 74-minute video of Seurat's revolutionary pointillist technique of applying paint in small dots (coupled with his masterful draftsmanship) is highlighted by conversations with modern artists Henry Moore and Bridget Riley. Contains some nudity. Item #586-1752, $39.95. Available from Sax Arts & Crafts, P.O. Box 510710, New Berlin, WI 53151-0710; 414/784-6880; 800/558-6696; e-mail: infor@saxarts.com; www.saxarts.com. (See coupon.)

With Open Eyes   (Ages 5 to 18)

With this CD-ROM children and adults can take a personalized tour of over 200 works of art from The Art Institute of Chicago's enormous collection. Beautiful full-screen pictures with audio clips make it possible for you to get a close-up view of an Egyptian mummy, Japanese kimono, or Picasso portrait. Includes other study features as well. Hybrid CD-ROM: VOYA8115-CDB, $27.95. Available from Learning Services, P.O. Box 10636, Eugene, OR 97440-2636; Western Region: 800/877-9378; Eastern Region: 800/877-3278. (See coupon.)

The Louvre Museum   (Ages 9 to 14)

This is a CD-ROM tour of a great art museum of the world. Approximately 150 art treasures are shown—each next to a person to provide a concept of scale. Includes other study features, too. Hybrid CD-ROM: VOYA1000-CDB, $27.95. Available from Learning Services, P.O. Box 10636, Eugene, OR 97440-2636; Western Region: 800/877-9378; Eastern Region: 800/877-3278. (See coupon.)

Art Instruction

van Gogh: Starry Night   (Ages 13 to 18)

This CD-ROM explores Vincent's beautiful picture of the swirling night, known to art lovers all over the world. After the famous Griffith Observatory in Los Angeles established the fact that the painting represented the predawn sky of June 19, 1889, Professor Albert Boime determined there was much more to this classic painting than meets the eye. Hybrid CD-ROM: VOYA8210-CDB, $29.95. Available from Learning Services, P.O. Box 10636, Eugene, OR 97440-2636; Western Region: 800/877-9378; Eastern Region: 800/877-3278. (See coupon.)

3-Part Watercolor Program   (Ages 13 to adult)

This VHS video with Cecile Johnson, A.W.S., contains three parts, for a total of 41 minutes and includes six watercolors of various scenes and seasons, enabling the student to see equipment and techniques in use. *Watercolor Equipment & Basic Principles*, Part 1: 14 minutes, 83 frames. *Watercolor Composition & Techniques*, Part 2: 15 minutes, 88 frames. *Watercolor Demonstration*, Part 3: 12 minutes, 87 frames. Complete three-part program, VHS videos/frame format, and teacher's guide: Item #586-2529, $49.95. Available from Sax Arts & Crafts, P.O. Box 510710, New Berlin, WI 53151-0710; 414/784-6880; 800/558-6696; e-mail: infor@saxarts.com; www.saxarts.com. (See coupon.)

Norman Rockwell: An American Portrait   (Ages 13 to adult)

This 60-minute VHS video features the art of Rockwell, as well as commentary and remembrances from friends, art historians, and the artist himself. In his portraits of everyday life, Rockwell chronicled regular people while capturing essential truths about human strengths and weaknesses, success and failure. Item #586-2784, $19.98. Available from Sax Arts & Crafts, P.O. Box 510710, New Berlin, WI 53151-0710; 414/784-6880; 800/558-6696; e-mail: infor@saxarts.com; www.saxarts.com. (See coupon.)

How to Draw Blitz Cartoons   (Ages 10 and up)

Professional cartoonist Bruce Blitz introduces you to the fun and wacky world of cartooning in this 60-minute VHS video. Discover how easy it is to create your own characters and situations with Bruce's expert guidance. See how a few simple lines can convey a range of emotions—from hilarity to anger. This is a great introductory course. Item #586-6447, $17.95. Available from Sax Arts & Crafts, P.O. Box 510710, New Berlin, WI 53151-0710; 414/784-6880; 800/558-6696; e-mail: infor@saxarts.com; www.saxarts.com. (See coupon.)

How To Draw Cartoon Animals   (Ages 10 and up)

This lively 35-minute VHS video will have you sketching expressive dogs, cats, birds, monkeys, and even outrageously popular dinosaurs! Turn simple shapes into zany cartoon animals following the Blitz method of cartooning. Item #586-6439, $17.95. Available from Sax Arts & Crafts, P.O. Box 510710, New Berlin, WI 53151-0710; 414/784-6880; 800/558-6696; e-mail: infor@saxarts.com; www.saxarts.com. (See coupon.)

How To Draw Cartoon Doodle Tricks   (Ages 10 and up)

See a cartoon develop right before your eyes as this fun and easy-to-follow 35-minute VHS video shows you how to turn numbers, letters, and words into Blitz cartoon drawings. Item #586-6470, $17.95. Available from Sax Arts & Crafts, P.O. Box 510710, New Berlin, WI 53151-0710; 414/784-6880; 800/558-6696; e-mail: infor@saxarts.com; www.saxarts.com. (See coupon.)

Learn Basic Blitz Drawing   (Ages 10 and up)

You'll be able to draw anything from this step-by-step, 60-minute VHS video using the four basic forms: the cube, cylinder, cone, and ball. Item #586-6488, $17.95. Available from Sax Arts & Crafts, P.O. Box 510710, New Berlin, WI 53151-0710; 414/784-6880; 800/558-6696; e-mail: infor@saxarts.com; www.saxarts.com. (See coupon.)

Draw Your Own Blitz Comic Strips   (Ages 10 and up)

Create comic characters in your own cartoon world with this unique 60-minute VHS video. Includes tips on writing gags and even shows how to market your comic strips. Item #586-6595, $17.95. Available from Sax Arts & Crafts, P.O. Box 510710, New Berlin, WI 53151-0710; 414/784-6880; 800/558-6696; e-mail: infor@saxarts.com; www.saxarts.com. (See coupon.)

Blitz Video Library Set   (Ages 10 and up)

A total collection of five Bruce Blitz instructional VHS videos in one set (4 hours, 10 minutes) presents a complete course on cartooning and drawing. The video includes the following titles: How to Draw Cartoons, How to Draw Cartoon Doodle, How to Draw Cartoon Animals, Learn Basic Drawing, and Draw Your Own Comic Strips. Item #586-6959, $49.99. Available from Sax Arts & Crafts, P.O. Box 510710, New Berlin, WI 53151-0710; 414/784-6880; 800/558-6696; e-mail: infor@saxarts.com; www.saxarts.com. (See coupon.)

The Young Masters Home Study Art Program   (Ages 4 to adult)

This full art curriculum includes three modes of instruction: teacher manual, video demonstration, and home correspondence. The program offers instruction from beginner to professional level. It is very easy to follow; everything is broken down into the smallest steps possible. $190 plus $10 shipping. Available from Gordon School of Art, P.O. Box 28208, Green Bay, WI 54324; 800/210-1220; www.newmasters.com. (See coupon.)

How Great Thou Art   (Ages 3 to Adult) ✝

This is a complete, Godly art curriculum designed to for students working in an independent environment. Teaches the fundamentals of drawing, color theory, painting, and more. Teacher's Manuals for each level are easy to understand and use. Prices range from $14.95 to $42.95. Available from How Great Thou Art, P.O. Box 48, McFarlan, NC 28102; 800/982-DRAW; www.howgreatthouart.com.

Visual Manna   (Ages 4 to 18) ✝

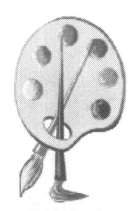

This Christian company specializes in producing many unique art instruction programs, especially from a Biblical perspective. A project newsletter is included with all orders. *Teaching English Through Art*, $17.95; *Teaching Science Through Art*, $10.95; *Teaching History Through Art*, $14.95; *Teaching American History Through Art*, $14.95; *Teaching Renaissance History Through Art*, $14.95. Art kit with supplies and the *ABC's of Art*, $39.95; *Bible Arts & Crafts*, $9.95. Available from Visual Manna, P.O. Box 553, Salem, MO 65560; Orders: 888/275-7309; www.rollanet.org/~arthis. Free catalog. (See coupon.)

Homeschooling Today   (Family use) ✝

This bimonthly Christian homeschool magazine is an excellent resource for homeschoolers in general. The "Understanding the Arts" column featured in each issue has a full-color, full-page reproduction of a famous painting along with a mini-study guide discussion of the work, its history, and more. Annual subscription is $19.99 prepaid. Available from Homeschooling Today, 6011 Rodman St., Suite 301, Hollywood, FL 33023; 954-962-1930; www.homeschooltoday.com. (See coupon.)

You Can Draw   (Ages 12 and up)

On this CD-ROM seven elements of drawing are covered including gesture, shape, line, and value. There are timed sketching exercises, puzzle exercises, and shading exercises carried out on a regular sketchpad (not included). Biographical outlines of two famous painters per element are included. MAC CD-ROM or WIN CD-ROM, $49.95. Available from Cognitive Technologies Corporation (CTC), 5009 Cloister Dr., Rockville, MD 20852; 301/581-9652; Fax: 301/581-9653.

History

DK My First Amazing History Explorer   (Ages 4 to 9)

This DK Interactive Learning CD-ROM serves as a valuable introduction to history. Your child can visit the Roman Empire, the Great Plains of the Sioux, and the high mountain home of the Incas. Hybrid CD-ROM: DORLO21O-CDBS, $45.95. Available from Learning Services, P.O. Box 10636, Eugene, OR 97440-2636; Western Region: 800/877-9378; Eastern Region: 800/877-3278. (See coupon.)

Bull Run   (Ages 10 and up)

This two-hour, two-audiocassette version of Paul Fleischman's book is unabridged. Multiple narrators represent sixteen voices—not the heroes eulogized in history books, but the voices of the common soldiers, their leaders, their families, and their comrades. North/South, White/Black, adult/child—this disparate and compelling choir of voices weaves an intimate tapestry of the first battle of the Civil War. Cassette, item #2-99, $17.95 Available from Audio Bookshelf, 174 Prescott Hill Road, Northport, ME 04849; 800/234-1713; e-mail: audbkshf@agate.net. (See coupon.)

Early American History: A Literature Approach
(Ages 5 to 9) ✝

This teacher's study guide by Rea C. Berg suggests books and materials to study and/or offers material within its covers. The suggested books are the products of a diverse group of authors. This guide is designed for a one-year course teaching American history, from pre-English colonies through the Civil War. The daily lesson plans incorporate biblical principles, poetry, geography, and other disciplines. $12.95. Available from Beautiful Feet Books, 139 Main St., Sandwich, MA 02563; 800/889-1978; 508/833-8626; www.bfbooks.com. Call for catalog.

Early American History: A Literature Approach
(Ages 10 to 12) ✝

This intermediate edition of the study guide on p. 362, also by Rea C. Berg, carries on with the same pattern of utilizing (mostly) external literary sources to study American history, going into greater depth and detail for older students. It adds the skills of journal-keeping and map-making, includes student tests, and explains the use of an Early American Timeline. There is also an extended supplemental reading list for Grades 7 to 8. $13.95. Available from Beautiful Feet Books, 139 Main St., Sandwich, MA 02563; 800/889-1978; 508/833-8626; www.bfbooks.com. Call for catalog.

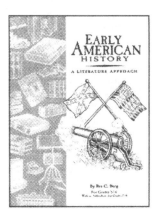

Lives of the Presidents — Fame, Shame (and What the Neighbors Thought)
(Ages 10 and up)

This three-hour, two-audiocassette unabridged version of Kathleen Krull's book is read by John C. Brown. From George Washington to Bill Clinton, Kathleen Krull goes beyond politics and photo ops, revealing the complex and very real lives of the 41 American Presidents to date. Always respectful, but entertaining. Cassette, item #3-98, $17.50. Available from Audio Bookshelf, 174 Prescott Hill Road, Northport, ME 04849; 800/234-1713; e-mail: audbkshf@agate.net. (See coupon.)

U.S. and World History: A Literature Approach
(Ages 16 to 18) ✝

This literature-based study guide by Rea C. Berg covers the events and people of the period from the Civil War to Vietnam. Literary sources include: *Uncle Tom's Cabin*, *The Red Badge of Courage*, *Around the World in 80 Days*, *House of Sixty Fathers*, and many more. The volume also includes biographies of Robert E. Lee, Josef Stalin, Theodore Roosevelt, and other important people of this time period. $13.95. Available from Beautiful Feet Books, 139 Main St., Sandwich, MA 02563; 800/889-1978; 508/833-8626; www.bfbooks.com. Call for catalog.

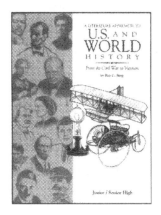

Medieval Reformation and Renaissance History (Ages 13 to 18) †

This study guide by Rea C. Berg covers the Magna Carta in England, 1215, to the Elizabethan era of England in the early 1600s. The great master writers and poets of our "modern" English are represented as well as adventurers of faith. The junior and senior high school courses are separate two-year plans. A Medieval Timeline is also employed to illustrate the high points of European civilization. $12.95. Available from Beautiful Feet Books, 139 Main St., Sandwich, MA 02563; 800/889-1978; 508/833-8626; www.bfbooks.com. Call for catalog.

Ancient History: A Literature Approach   (Ages 13 to 18) †

This study guide by Rea C. Berg takes in the Sumerians, Egyptians, Greeks, and Romans and their respective civilizations. It is designed for the mature student. Biblical history, geography, mythology, and vocabulary are included and there are tests with answer keys provided. $12.95. Available from Beautiful Feet Books, 139 Main St., Sandwich, MA 02563; 800/889-1978; 508/833-8626; www.bfbooks.com. Call for catalog.

History of California: A Literature Approach (Ages 10 to 12) †

This read-aloud program by Rea C. Berg charts the history of California from the Native Americans and early Spanish explorers and missionaries through the Gold Rush of the 1850s and completion of the Transcontinental Railroad in 1869. The volume includes the California Timeline, Biblical principles, and poetry, and touches upon geography and map-making. $12.95. Available from Beautiful Feet Books, 139 Main St., Sandwich, MA 02563; 800/889-1978; 508/833-8626; website:www.bfbooks.com. Call for catalog.

History of Science: A Literature Approach
(Ages 9 to 13) ✝

This read-aloud program by Rea C. Berg takes you and your student into the world of science. It begins with Archimedes and includes Galileo, Newton, and Einstein, with hands-on experiments to prove each one's theories. This is a wonderful way to introduce your student to the worlds of biology, chemistry, and physics. $10.95. Available from Beautiful Feet Books, 139 Main St., Sandwich, MA 02563; 800/889-1978; 508/833-8626; www.bfbooks.com. Call for catalog.

History of the Horse: A Literature Approach
(Ages 9 to 13) ✝

This study guide on a novel topic begins in the 1700s with the Godolphin Arabian and continues through the early 1900s, covering Lippizzaner stallions, the wild mustangs of the American west, Chincoteague ponies, and other breeds. The course, by Hilary Berg, utilizes such great books as *Black Stallion* and *Black Beauty*. $10.95. Available from Beautiful Feet Books, 139 Main St., Sandwich, MA 02563; 800/889-1978; 508/833-8626; website:www.bfbooks.com. Call for catalog.

Early American History Jumbo Pack (Ages 5 to 9) ✝

This history-curriculum-in-a-box contains 19 different books by various authors, four "Your Story Hour" audiocassettes, a student composition notebook, and the *American History Study Guide* by Rea C. Berg. Books include *Leif the Lucky, Columbus, Pocahontas, Benjamin Franklin, George Washington, Abraham Lincoln,* and *Buffalo Bill*—all written by Ingri and Edgar Parin D'Aulaire and originally published in the 1950s; *Squanto, Friend of the Pilgrims* by Clyde Bulla; *Stories of the Pilgrims* by Margaret Pumphrey; *Meet Abe Lincoln* by Barbara Cary; *The Courage of Sarah Noble* by Alice Dalgliesh; and *Boys and Girls of Colonial Days* by Carolyn Bailey. $189.95. Available from Beautiful Feet Books, 139 Main St., Sandwich, MA 02563; 800/889-1978; 508/833-8626; www.bfbooks.com. Call for catalog.

Early American History Jumbo Pack (Ages 11 to 12) ✝

This history-curriculum-in-a-box contains 16 books written by various authors, four "Your Story Hour" audiocassettes, an intermediate composition notebook, and an *American History Timeline* and *American History Study Guide*, both written by Rea C. Berg. Titles include: *Sacajawea, Guide to Lewis and Clark*; *America's Providential History* by Steven McDowell and Mark Beliles; *Leif the Lucky, Columbus, Pocahontas*, and *Benjamin Franklin*, all by Ingri and Edgar D'Aulaire; and *Abe Lincoln Grows Up* by Carl Sandburg. $174.95. Available from Beautiful Feet Books, 139 Main St., Sandwich, MA 02563; 800/889-1978; 508/833-8626; www.bfbooks.com. Call for catalog.

Medieval History Jumbo Pack (Ages 13 to 15) ✝

This boxed history curriculum includes 14 books by assorted authors, and the *Medieval Timeline* and *Medieval History Study Guide*, both by Rea C. Berg. Among the volumes are: *Magna Carta* by Charles Daugherty; *The World of Columbus and Sons* by Genevieve Foster; *The Story of Liberty* by Charles Coffin; *Otto of the Silver Hand* by Howard Pyle; *Fine Print, A Story About Johann Gutenberg* by Joann Burch; and *The Canterbury Tales* by Geoffrey Chaucer. $149.95. This pack can be upgraded to the Senior High School pack for $109.95. Available from Beautiful Feet Books, 139 Main St., Sandwich, MA 02563; 800/889-1978; 508/833-8626; www.bfbooks.com. Call for catalog.

Medieval History Jumbo Pack (Ages 16 to 18) ✝

Twelve books by assorted authors are included in this boxed history curriculum along with the *Medieval History Study Guide* by Rea C. Berg. Among the volumes are: *Westward Ho!* by Charles Kingsley; *Scottish Chiefs* by Jane Porter; *Ivanhoe* by Sir Walter Scott; *King John* and *Henry VIII* by William Shakespeare; *Men of Iron* by Howard Pile; *Joan of Arc* by Mark Twain; and *Martin Luther* by Sally Stepanek. $169.95. (The other volumes are also contained in the Junior High School Pack; to avoid needless duplication of materials, the publisher offers families an upgrade from the Junior High Pack for $109.95.) Available from Beautiful Feet Books, 139 Main St., Sandwich, MA 02563; 800/889-1978; 508/833-8626; www.bfbooks.com. Call for catalog.

Ancient History Jumbo Pack (Ages 13 to 18) ✝

This great package contains 14 books plus the *Ancient History Study Guide* by Rea C. Berg. The volumes include: *City* by David Macaulay; *Pyramid* by David Macaulay; *The D'Aulaires' Book of Greek Myths* by Ingri and Edgar D'Aulaire; *Tales of Ancient Egypt* by Roger Lancelyn Green; *Quo Vadis?* by Henryk Sienkiewicz; *Caesar's Gallic Wars* by Olivia Coolidge; *The Children's Homer* by Padraic Colum; and *The Bronze Bow* by Elizabeth Speare. $164.95. Available from Beautiful Feet Books, 139 Main St., Sandwich, MA 02563; 800/889-1978; 508/833-8626; website:www.bfbooks.com. Call for catalog.

Ancient History Literature Pack (Ages 13 to 18) ✝

This package contains 7 of the 14 books found in Ancient History Jumbo Pack. $64.95. Available from Beautiful Feet Books, 139 Main St., Sandwich, MA 02563; 800/889-1978; 508/833-8626; www.bfbooks.com. Call for catalog.

California History Jumbo Pack (Ages 10 to 12) ✝

This is a complete course study in California history in one package! Besides the *California Study Guide* and the *California Timeline* both by Rea C. Berg, this set includes 12 other books. Among the titles are: *Island of the Blue Dolphins* by Scott O'Dell; *Junipero Serra, Brave Adventurer* by F. White; *Our Golden California* by Juanita Houston; and *The Making of American California: A Providential Approach* by Dorothy Dimmick. Also included are three "Your Story Hour" audiocassettes. $146.95. Available from Beautiful Feet Books, 139 Main St., Sandwich, MA 02563; 800/889-1978; 508/833-8626; www.bfbooks.com. Call for catalog.

California Literature Pack (Ages 10 to 12) ✝

This package includes nine of the books in the Jumbo Pack for a lesser price. $52.95. Available from Beautiful Feet Books, 139 Main St., Sandwich, MA 02563; 800/889-1978; 508/833-8626; www.bfbooks.com. Call for catalog.

History of Science Pack   (Ages 9 to 13) ✝

This package of books by Rea C. Berg follows the read-aloud approach to study science. Besides the *History of Science Study Guide* and Scientists Card Game are 11 titles, including *Science Around the House* by Robert Gardner; *Explorabook* by Joan Cassidy; *The Picture History of Great Inventors*; *The Way Things Work* by David Macaulay; *Galileo and the Universe* by Steve Parker; *Archimedes and the Door of Science* by Joanne Bendick; *The Story of Thomas Edison* by Margaret Cousins; and *Marie Curie's Search for Radium* by Beverly Birch. $134.95. Available from Beautiful Feet Books, 139 Main St., Sandwich, MA 02563; 800/889-1978; 508/833-8626; www.bfbooks.com. Call for catalog.

U.S. & World History for Senior High Pack, Part I (Ages 16 to 18) ✝

This self-contained history curriculum by Rea C. Berg includes many great titles. Besides the *U.S. & World History Study Guide*, the pack includes such books as *Uncle Tom's Cabin* by Harriet Beecher Stowe; *Rifles for Watie* by Harold Keith; *The Red Badge of Courage* by Stephen Crane; *Virginia's General* by Albert Marrin; *Reconstruction: Binding the Wounds*, edited by Cheryl Edwards; and *Up from Slavery* by Booker T. Washington. $124.95 Available from Beautiful Feet Books, 139 Main St., Sandwich, MA 02563; 800/889-1978; 508/833-8626; www.bfbooks.com. Call for catalog.

Augustus Caesar's World   (Ages 10 and up) ✝

Augustus' world ranged from 44 B.C. to A.D.14, but the scope of this 334-page book by Genevieve Foster includes events beginning in 3000 B.C. and culminating in the birth of Jesus of Nazareth. In story form, it covers the major events of Egyptian, Greek, and Roman history, and includes timelines, charts, maps, and illustrations. $14.95. Available from Beautiful Feet Books, 139 Main St., Sandwich, MA 02563; 800/889-1978; 508/833-8626; www.bfbooks.com. Call for catalog.

Ancient Rome How It Affects You Today (Ages 10 and up) ✝

Used together with *Augustus Caesar's World* (p. 368) this paperback by Richard J. Maybury makes for a challenging study of how history, no matter how old, affects us today. It sheds new light on the Roman Emperor's world by making it more relevant to our own. $8.95. Available from Beautiful Feet Books, 139 Main St., Sandwich, MA 02563; 800/889-1978; 508/833-8626. www.bfbooks.com Call for catalog.

City (Ages 10 and up) ✝

This paperback book by David Macaulay sets forth in detail all of the elements of building a Roman city, from planning to construction. VHS companion was partially shot in Italy. It shows construction methods of the Romans and everyday life as well. Book, $7.95; video, $21.95. Available from Beautiful Feet Books, 139 Main St., Sandwich, MA 02563; 800/889-1978; 508/833-8626; www.bfbooks.com. Call for catalog.

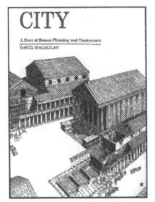

D'Aulaire's Book of Greek Myths (Grades 4 and up) ✝

This book by Ingri and Edgar D'Aulaire has been a favorite of many readers for many years. It is a perfect introduction to the mythical beliefs of the Greeks and Romans. Hardcover: $24.95; paperback: $16.95. Available from Beautiful Feet Books, 139 Main St., Sandwich, MA 02563; 800/889-1978; 508/833-8626; www.bfbooks.com. Call for catalog.

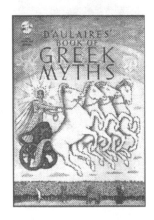

Pyramid   (Ages 10 and up) ✝

This paperback book by David Macaulay is another glimpse at ancient building techniques—the Great Pyramid at Giza. The video is partially shot on location in Egypt. It shows planning and construction of this wonder of the ancient world. Paperback, $7.95; video, $21.95. Available from Beautiful Feet Books, 139 Main St., Sandwich, MA 02563; 800/889-1978; 508/833-8626; www.bfbooks.com. Call for catalog.

Castle   (Ages 10 and up) ✝

This great book by David Macaulay shows the how and why of castle building in Medieval Europe. Detailed drawings accompany text. The video uses both live-action and animation to show the building of a thirteenth-century castle in Wales. Paperback, $7.95; video, $21.95. Available from Beautiful Feet Books, 139 Main St., Sandwich, MA 02563; 800/889-1978; 508/833-8626; www.bfbooks.com. Call for catalog.

Cathedral   (Ages 10 and up) ✝

This book by David Macaulay details the centuries-long building of a Medieval European cathedral. Detailed drawings and text explain this great achievement of Man. The video shows footage of eight different, spectacular cathedrals in France. Paperback, $7.95; video, $21.95. Available from Beautiful Feet Books, 139 Main St., Sandwich, MA 02563; 800/889-1978; 508/833-8626; www.bfbooks.com. Call for catalog.

Bard of Avon: The Story of William Shakespeare
(Ages 8 to 12) ✝

This book by Diane Stanley and Peter Vennema is one of the few children's books available about the great dramatist's life, and can be enjoyed by the entire family. Richly illustrated as well, *Bard of Avon* provides a complete view of the man and his life. Hardcover, $15. Available from Beautiful Feet Books, 139 Main St., Sandwich, MA 02563; 800/889-1978; 508/833-8626; www.bfbooks.com. Call for catalog.

Famous Men of the Renaissance and Reformation   (Ages 10 and up) ✝

This great volume by Robert Shearer will aid your study of this important period of Western Civilization. Some men you know and some you don't. Paperback, $15.95. Available from Beautiful Feet Books, 139 Main St., Sandwich, MA 02563; 800/889-1978; 508/833-8626; www.bfbooks.com. Call for catalog.

Fine Print: A Story about Johann Gutenberg
(Ages 10 and up) ✝

This is Joann Burch's biography of the man who brought movable type printing and, consequently, mass-availability of books to people everywhere. The hardships and challenges he faced to make this dream a reality are recounted here. Paperback, $5.95. Available from Beautiful Feet Books, 139 Main St., Sandwich, MA 02563; 800/889-1978; 508/833-8626; www.bfbooks.com. Call for catalog.

Joan of Arc   (Ages 13 and up) ✝

Few people know that the great American author Mark Twain spent over 10 years studying the life of this courageous young woman who overcame many obstacles to save France. This book is the result. Paperback, $17.95. Available from Beautiful Feet Books, 139 Main St., Sandwich, MA 02563; 800/889-1978; 508/833-8626; www.bfbooks.com. Call for catalog.

The Magna Carta   (Ages 10 and up) ✝

As author James Daughtery relates, June 15, 1215, marks a turning point in Anglo-American history. This is the date that King John bowed to the pressure of the Englishmen who wanted to expand the freedom of citizens and diminish some of the power of the crown in Britain. It was the beginning of the end of the absolute power of the monarchy in England that culminated (for Americans) in the Revolutionary War over 500 years later! Paperback, $8.95. Available from Beautiful Feet Books, 139 Main St., Sandwich, MA 02563; 800/889-1978; 508/833-8626; www.bfbooks.com. Call for catalog.

The Story of Liberty   (Ages 10 to 12) ✝

This book by Charles Coffin was first published in 1879. It begins by relating the story of the Magna Carta all the way up to the early colonization of North America. Paperback, $14.95. Available from Beautiful Feet Books, 139 Main St., Sandwich, MA 02563; 800/889-1978; 508/833-8626; www.bfbooks.com. Call for catalog.

The Trumpeter of Krakow   (Ages 10 to 12)

This book by Erik P. Kelly details the world of fifteenth-century Poland and an adventure, as narrated by the 15-year-old boy who is the main character. Hardcover, $15.95; paperback, $4.50 Available from Beautiful Feet Books, 139 Main St., Sandwich, MA 02563; 800/889-1978; 508/833-8626; www.bfbooks.com. Call for catalog.

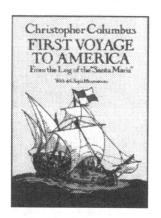

First Voyage to America   (Ages 5 to 9) ✝

This book by Bartholomew Las Casas provides insight into the day-to-day life of this important voyage. Includes firsthand accounts taken from Captain Columbus' logbook, as well as pen and ink drawings. Paperback, $6.95. Available from Beautiful Feet Books, 139 Main St., Sandwich, MA 02563; 800/889-1978; 508/833-8626; www.bfbooks.com. Call for catalog.

Faith Unfurled: The Pilgrims' Quest for Freedom (Ages 10 to 12) ✝

This book by Sheila Foley is an unusual collection of journal entries and poetry. Paperback, $6.95. Available from Beautiful Feet Books, 139 Main St., Sandwich, MA 02563; 800/889-1978; 508/833-8626; www.bfbooks.com. Call for catalog.

Pocahontas (Ages 10 and up) ✝

The famous team of Ingri and Edgar d'Aulaire brings the true story of the Indian woman and the struggling colonists to life in their unique style. Paperback, $11.95. Available from Beautiful Feet Books, 139 Main St., Sandwich, MA 02563; 800/889-1978; 508/833-8626; www.bfbooks.com. Call for catalog.

Amos Fortune, Free Man (Ages 10 to 12) ✝

This powerful book by Elizabeth Yates is written to read aloud to the entire family. It presents the true story of a young African who was kidnapped and sold into slavery in Boston. Hardcover, $15.99; paperback, $4.99. Available from Beautiful Feet Books, 139 Main St., Sandwich, MA 02563; 800/889-1978; 508/833-8626; www.bfbooks.com. Call for catalog.

Boys and Girls of Colonial Days (Ages 5 to 9) ✝

This reader was written by Carolyn Bailey to provide today's child with a better understanding of how the events and people of colonial America affected the youngsters alive at that time. Paperback, $5.95. Available from Beautiful Feet Books, 139 Main St., Sandwich, MA 02563; 800/889-1978; 508/833-8626; www.bfbooks.com. Call for catalog.

America's Paul Revere (Ages 5 to 9)

This life story of a great American patriot, written by Ester Forbes, is heavily illustrated. Paperback, $7.95. Available from Beautiful Feet Books, 139 Main St., Sandwich, MA 02563; 800/889-1978; 508/833-8626; www.bfbooks.com. Call for catalog.

The Great Little Madison (Ages 10 and up)

The life story of the father of the Constitution, written by Jean Fritz. Hardcover, $15.95. Available from Beautiful Feet Books, 139 Main St., Sandwich, MA 02563; 800/889-1978; 508/833-8626; www.bfbooks.com. Call for catalog.

DK Eyewitness History of the World (Ages 8 to adult)

This CD-ROM covers the period from early humans to the events of the 1990s with clarity and precision. World 1.0 MAC CD-ROM: DORLO19O-MCCD or World 2.0 WIN CD-ROM: DORLO19L-MPCS, $54.95. Available from DK Family Learning, 11124 N.E. Halsey, Suite 460, Portland, OR 97220; 888/225-3535. (See coupon.)

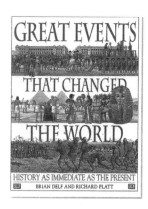

DK Great Events That Changed the World (Ages 8 and up)

This 32-page hardcover DK book brings history alive in your child's hands with its top-quality illustrations and well-written text. Item #515, $15.95. Available from DK Family Learning, 11124 N.E. Halsey, Suite 460, Portland, OR 97220; 888/225-3535. (See coupon.)

DK The Atlas of Ancient Worlds (Ages 9 and up)

Arranged by civilization, this beautifully illustrated 64-page DK hardcover provides children with insight into the origins of many ideas and objects we take for granted, such as writing, crafts, sailing, and more. Covers the period from the Sumerians in 3500 B.C. to the New World Incas of A.D.1500. Item # 526, $19.95. Available from DK Family Learning, 11124 N.E. Halsey, Suite 460, Portland, OR 97220; 888/225-3535. (See coupon.)

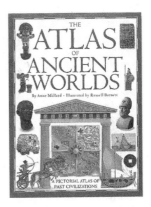

DK How Children Lived from Ancient Egypt to the 20th Century (Ages 6 and up)

This DK 48-page beginning history book allows your student to compare his or her own life with the lives of 16 children living in the past. This hardcover book is illustrated in the famous DK style. Item # 279, $14.95. Available from DK Family Learning, 11124 N.E. Halsey, Suite 460, Portland, OR 97220; 888/225-3535. (See coupon.)

DK Visual Timelines from DK Books (Ages 8 and up)

Inventions (64-page hardcover) gives your child the view of inventions on a timeline from stone tools to superconductors. *20th Century* (48-page hardcover) offers a timeline from atomic bombs to virtual reality. *Inventions*, Item #524; *20th Century*, Item #534, $14.95 each. Available from DK Family Learning, 11124 N.E. Halsey, Suite 460, Portland, OR 97220; 888/225-3535. (See coupon.)

DK Eyewitness Anthologies (Ages 8 and up)

These beautifully illustrated 128-page volumes will take your child on a journey into many past events. Each of the four anthologies makes use of maps, color photos, artwork, and well-written text to bring the period alive. *Knights & Castles*, Item #769; *American Peoples*, Item #771; *Ancient Egyptians*, Item #772; *Ancient Civilizations*, Item #768, $19.95 each. Available from DK Family Learning, 11124 N.E. Halsey, Suite 460, Portland, OR 97220; 888/225-3535. (See coupon.)

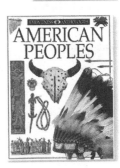

DK Kings & Queens of England & Scotland (Ages 11 and up)

This 96-page paperback DK book by Plantagenet Somerset Fry, replete with over 100 full-color illustrations, provides a reign-by-reign history of England and Scotland. Included are the family trees that linked one dynasty to the next, as well as key events in each monarch's reign, offering insight into the larger picture against which these kings and queens "strutted upon Life's stage." $12.95. Available from DK Family Learning, 11124 N.E. Halsey, Suite 460, Portland, OR 97220; 888/225-3535. (See coupon.)

DK Aztecs: The Fall of an Empire (Ages 10 and up)

In this richly illustrated 48-page hardcover your student can read and see the drama of the Spanish conquest of the lofty land of the Aztecs. $14.95. Available from DK Family Learning, 11124 N.E. Halsey, Suite 460, Portland, OR 97220; 888/225-3535. (See coupon.)

DK Moon Landing: The Race for the Moon
(Ages 10 and up)

To commemorate the 30th anniversary of Man's walk upon the moon, DK Books is offering a glowing 48-page hardcover, filled with illustrations and photographs of this momentous feat. $14.95. Available from DK Family Learning, 11124 N.E. Halsey, Suite 460, Portland, OR 97220; 888/225-3535. (See coupon.)

History

DK Trojan Horse (Ages 10 and up)

This 48-page book by David Clemens presents the story of how the Greeks gained victory at Troy by ingenuity and craft—with a little help from the Trojans. Factual side panels enlighten the story for your child, increasing his or her reading pleasure. Hardcover, $12.95; paperback, $3.95. Available from DK Family Learning, 11124 N.E. Halsey, Suite 460, Portland, OR 97220; 888/225-3535. (See coupon.)

DK My First Amazing History Explorer (Ages 5 to 10)

With this CD-ROM program from DK Books, your child will track down a Time Fugitive to recover a stolen map. In doing so, she or he will learn about eight different historical periods from Ancient Egypt to a 1920s city. Provides an insight into how life has changed over this vast time. Includes 14 historical destinations, four games with historical themes, an interactive journal, notes for parents, and more! Hybrid CD-ROM: $29.95. Available from DK Family Learning, 11124 N.E. Halsey, Suite 460, Portland, OR 97220; 888/225-3535. (See coupon.)

DK Eyewitness History of the World 2.0 (Ages 10 and up)

This CD-ROM program, updated to cover 1997, offers you the clarity and quality of DK books with early man up to nearly present day as the topic. This disk includes a comprehensive U.S. history section, a *Who's Who* with over 200 new biographies, 35 new maps, a brain-teasing game, and a Quiz Master feature. WIN CD-ROM: $29.95. Available from DK Family Learning, 11124 N.E. Halsey, Suite 460, Portland, OR 97220; 888/225-3535. (See coupon.)

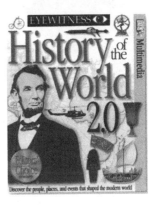

Chronicle of the 20th Century   (Ages 12 and up)

This CD-ROM program contains entries for each day from January 1, 1900, through July 1996. The selections are presented in text, film, photos, and audio, presenting a comprehensive view of the century of our birth. Includes biographies and timelines. MAC CD-ROM or WIN CD-ROM: $29.95 each. Available from DK Family Learning, 11124 N.E. Halsey, Suite 460, Portland, OR 97220; 888/225-3535. (See coupon.)

Castle Explorer   (Ages 10 and up)

With this CD-ROM, your child will learn about medieval life while carrying out the King's secret mission. Contains DK Books' quality and vividness. $29.95. Available from DK Family Learning, 11124 N.E. Halsey, Suite 460, Portland, OR 97220; 888/225-3535. (See coupon.)

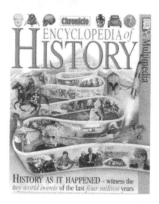

Chronicle Encyclopedia of History   (Ages 12 and up)

This CD-ROM program, produced with the high quality for which DK books are famous, lets your child witness key events occurring over a 4 million-year period. $29.95. Available from DK Family Learning, 11124 N.E. Halsey, Suite 460, Portland, OR 97220; 888/225-3535. (See coupon.)

Smithsonian Timelines of the Ancient World
(Ages 11 and up)

This 256-page hardcover edited by Chris Scarre is separated into five global study regions and four categories, covering the period from the origins of life to A.D.1500. Such a reference book will prove invaluable to any study of ancient history. $49.95. Available from DK Family Learning, 11124 N.E. Halsey, Suite 460, Portland, OR 97220; 888/225-3535. (See coupon.)

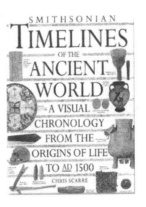

DK A Young Person's Guide to Philosophy   (Ages 11 and up)

This 64-page hardcover by Jeremy Wheate is well written and illustrated. The book takes your child through the history of the great philosophers and their ideas. $16.95. Available from DK Family Learning, 11124 N.E. Halsey, Suite 460, Portland, OR 97220; 888/225-3535. (See coupon.)

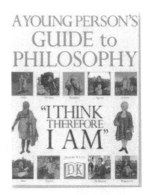

DK Cross-Sections Castle   (Ages 9 and up)

This 32-page DK book by Richard Platt comes in hardcover. Ever wonder exactly what a medieval castle looked like inside? You can be sure your child does. Here's the answer—a sliced castle, suitable for viewing in all details! Dazzling photographs and illustrations in the original, unique DK style display everything imaginable about this centerpiece of the medieval town and much about its inhabitants, too. $16.95. Available from DK Family Learning, 11124 N.E. Halsey, Suite 460, Portland, OR 97220; 888/225-3535. (See coupon.)

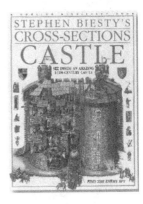

History

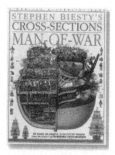

DK Cross-Sections Man-of-War   (Ages 9 and up)

This 32-page hardcover by Stephen Biesty unlocks another mystery—what does a tall sailing ship look like inside? Where did the crew eat, sleep, live? This fascinating DK book takes you into the world below-deck by offering you a sliced ship, with views from all sides! $16.95. Available from DK Family Learning, 11124 N.E. Halsey, Suite 460, Portland, OR 97220; 888/225-3535. (See coupon.)

DK A Street Through Time   (Ages 10 and up)

This 32-page hardcover by Dr. Anne Millard is an imaginative volume that covers 12,000 years of life and living in the form of a pictorial story with labels. Highly detailed, the book is illustrated as only DK does. $16.95. Available from DK Family Learning, 11124 N.E. Halsey, Suite 460, Portland, OR 97220; 888/225-3535. (See coupon.)

DK In the Beginning...A Nearly Complete History of Almost Everything   (Ages 10 and up)

This 72-page hardcover by Richard Platt is stuffed with interesting illustrations and photographs, with corresponding factual text. The book provides hours of quiet reading and learning. $19.95. Available from DK Family Learning, 11124 N.E. Halsey, Suite 460, Portland, OR 97220; 888/225-3535. (See coupon.)

DK Tutankhamun—A DK Discovery Guide   (Ages 10 and up)

King Tut comes to your home via this sparkling 48-page hardcover with four gatefolds by David Murdoch. Anyone familiar with DK Books knows of their reputation for providing the most beautifully illustrated and clearly written books available. This is no exception. $14.95. Available from DK Family Learning, 11124 N.E. Halsey, Suite 460, Portland, OR 97220; 888/225-3535. (See coupon.)

DK Pompeii: The Day a City Was Buried   (Ages 10 and up)

Read about this tragic but fascinating phenomenon in this DK gem of illustration and text (48 pages with four gatefolds, hardcover by Christopher Rice and Melanie Rice). In a matter of a few hours, the Roman city of Pompeii was buried by the eruption of Mt. Vesuvius. The story of the people's lives has been told by scientists excavating the ruins. $14.95. Available from DK Family Learning, 11124 N.E. Halsey, Suite 460, Portland, OR 97220; 888/225-3535. (See coupon.)

DK Castle at War   (Ages 10 and up)

Witness the preparations and actions of a medieval castle in warfare through this 48-page hardcover with four gatefolds by Andrew Langley and Peter Dennis. Exciting illustrations and detailed text bring this period of history to stunning life! $14.95. Available from DK Family Learning, 11124 N.E. Halsey, Suite 460, Portland, OR 97220; 888/225-3535. (See coupon.)

DK Polar Exploration   (Ages 10 and up)

Read this book by Martyn Bramwell, Marjorie Crosby-Fairall, and Ann Winterbotham (48 pages plus with four gatefolds, hardcover) in summer—it details the travails, tragedies, and triumphs of the ice-cap explorers in richly illustrated and clear, easy-to-read text. $14.95. Available from DK Family Learning, 11124 N.E. Halsey, Suite 460, Portland, OR 97220; 888/225-3535. (See coupon.)

DK Transportation   (Ages 9 and up)

See the fascinating story of the progression in people-moving through the centuries come alive in the sparkling illustrations and bright text of this 48-page hardcover book by Anthony Wilson! $16.95. Available from DK Family Learning, 11124 N.E. Halsey, Suite 460, Portland, OR 97220; 888/225-3535. (See coupon.)

History

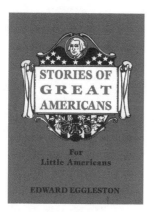

Stories of Great Americans for Little Americans (Ages 6 to 8)

In this 163-page hardcover, Edward Eggleston teaches American history in the best way possible for children: with 52 imaginative stories about great Americans. Stories about war heroes, statesmen, explorers, inventors, writers, artists, scientists, and just plain ordinary people who made a difference. The lives of these men and women wonderfully illustrate the virtues children need to learn. $14.95. Available from Lost Classics Book Co., P.O. Box 1756, Ft. Collins, CO 80522; 888/611-BOOK (2665); www.lostclassicsbooks.com. (See coupon.)

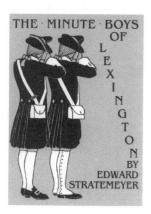

The Minute Boys of Lexington (Ages 8 to 12)

This 304-page softcover by Edward Stratemeyer is the first book in the author's series for young people about the American Revolution. Written in the late nineteenth century, it is the kind of adventure story missing from the ranks of today's children's books. The book includes a Build-Your-Vocabulary glossary. $14.95. Available from Lost Classics Book Co., P.O. Box 1756, Ft. Collins, CO 80522; 888/611-BOOK (2665); www.lostclassics-books.com. (See coupon.)

A First Book in American History (Ages 9 to 12)

In this 240-page hardcover history text, Edward Eggleston illustrates the development of the United States by using the stories of the real Americans who made it all happen. This is a teacher-friendly textbook complete with study questions after each chapter, definitions of pertinent words, maps, illustrations, and an index for easy cross-reference. $19.95. Available from Lost Classics Book Co., P.O. Box 1756, Ft. Collins, CO 80522; 888/611-BOOK (2665); www.lostclassicsbooks.com. (See coupon.)

The Minute Boys of Bunker Hill   (Ages 8 to 12)

This 316-page softcover by Edward Stratemeyer tells an exciting historical tale, which chronicles the events of the American Revolution through the experiences of a young patriot. Your child will learn the importance of such virtues as love of liberty, bravery, courage, fierce determination, and loyalty. The text includes a Build-Your-Vocabulary glossary. $14.95. Available from Lost Classics Book Co., P.O. Box 1756, Ft. Collins, CO 80522; 888/611-BOOK (2665); www.lostclassicsbooks.com. (See coupon.)

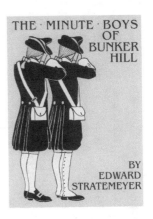

A History of the United States and Its People (Ages 12 to adult)

You won't find political correctness or revisionism in this 433-page hardcover volume by Edward Eggleston—just solid American history. This book includes study questions (some by topic), liberal use of maps, suggestions for diagrams, reviews, and other exercises. The book includes over 400 illustrations and maps as well as a comprehensive index. $24.95. Available from Lost Classics Book Co., P.O. Box 1756, Ft. Collins, CO 80522; 888/611-BOOK (2665); www.lostclassicsbooks.com. (See coupon.)

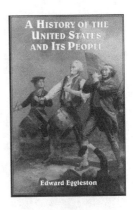

Mary of Plymouth   (Ages 8 to 12) †

This 178-page hardcover by James Otis tells the story of the Pilgrims' first ten years in the New World through the eyes of a young girl. Includes a Build-Your-Vocabulary glossary. $14.95. Available from Lost Classics Book Co., P.O. Box 1756, Ft. Collins, CO 80522; 888/611-BOOK (2665); www.lostclassicsbooks.com. (See coupon.)

History

History

With Lee in Virginia (Ages 10 to adult)

Readers are rediscovering G. A. Henty, the prolific author of nineteenth-century adventures. The story in this 415-page softcover opens just before the Civil War. Vincent joins General Lee in Virginia and the story weaves Vincent's adventures with the real-life characters and events of the war, teaching history while celebrating the virtues of family loyalty, honor, bravery, and determination in the face of adversity. The book includes a Build-Your-Vocabulary glossary. $16.95. Available from Lost Classics Book Co., P.O. Box 1756, Ft. Collins, CO 80522; 888/611-BOOK (2665); www.lostclassicsbooks.com. (See coupon.)

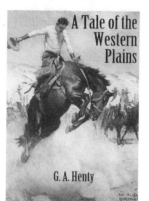

A Tale of the Western Plains (Ages 10 to adult)

Great nineteenth-century author G. A. Henty spins a tale of a world in this 444-page softcover where courage, daring, and virtue are all part of what made America great. Book includes a Build-Your-Vocabulary glossary. $16.95. Available from Lost Classics Book Co., P.O. Box 1756, Ft. Collins, CO 80522; 888/611-BOOK (2665); www.lostclassicsbooks.com. (See coupon.)

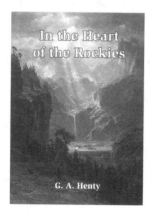

In the Heart of the Rockies (Ages 10 to adult)

This 388-page historical fiction softcover by G. A. Henty, set in the Rocky Mountains, describes gold mining, running the Colorado River rapids, and surviving a mountain winter with ingenuity, resourcefulness, and perseverance. It describes the challenges of the American West, a portion of our history that made our nation great. This book includes a Build-Your-Vocabulary glossary. $16.95. Available from Lost Classics Book Co., P.O. Box 1756, Ft. Collins, CO 80522; 888/611-BOOK (2665); www.lostclassicsbooks.com. (See coupon.)

The Life of Kit Carson   (Ages 10 to adult)

This 364-page softcover biography by Edward Ellis is an excellent supplement for teaching American history and geography, as well as virtue. Ellis' research includes original sources along with material exclusively commissioned for this book. The book includes a Build-Your-Vocabulary glossary. $14.95. Available from Lost Classics Book Co., P.O. Box 1756, Ft. Collins, CO 80522; 888/611-BOOK (2665); www.lostclassicsbooks.com. (See coupon.)

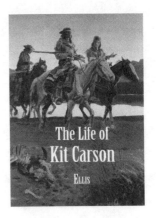

Taken by the Enemy   (Ages 10 to adult)

Oliver Optic was a prolific storyteller of the late nineteenth century. Among his best creations is the historical fiction *Blue and the Gray* Series; this 351-page softcover volume is the first volume in that series. As such, it introduces characters and events that will figure in the future volumes, providing children with a personal and historical picture of the Civil War. The book includes a Build-Your-Vocabulary glossary. $14.95. Available from Lost Classics Book Co., P.O. Box 1756, Ft. Collins, CO 80522; 888/611-BOOK (2665); www.lostclassicsbooks.com. (See coupon.)

DK See and Explore Library: Wonders of the World (Ages 10 to adul)

Here is an excellent DK See & Explore Library Edition supplement to the study of history—the wonders of the world—ancient as well as modern. This 64-page paperback provides beautifully illustrated examples of how Man's wondrous creations have changed over the centuries. $7.95. Available from DK Family Learning, 11124 N.E. Halsey, Suite 460, Portland, OR 97220; 888/225-3535. (See coupon.)

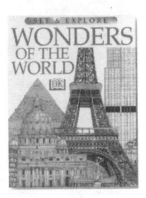

History

The DK History of the World   (Ages 10 to adult)

Written by Plantagenet Somerset Fry, this richly illustrated 384-page hardcover volume provides an informative and interesting view of world history. $39.95. Available from DK Family Learning, 11124 N.E. Halsey, Suite 460, Portland, OR 97220; 888/225-3535. (See coupon.)

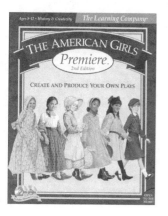

The American Girls Premiere   (Ages 8 to 12)

This great CD-ROM program replicates significant periods in American history, drawing your child into creative role-play with historically accurate characters. A different character stars in each of five eras: Colonial, Pioneer, Civil War, Victorian, and WW II. Your student can develop stories using 55 additional characters, 60 realistic sets, and scores of music and sound effects. Program includes tutorials, online help, and more! Hybrid CD-ROM: LEARO410-CDB, $19.95. Available from Learning Services, P.O. Box 10636, Eugene, OR 97440-2636; Western Region: 800/877-9378; Eastern Region: 800/877-3278. (See coupon.)

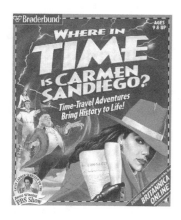

Where in Time Is Carmen Sandiego?   (Ages 9 to adult)

Your student will embark upon a voyage to the New World with Columbus, learn Shoshoni sign language, and help Beethoven reassemble his music in this CD-ROM program. History comes to life as players explore times from Ancient Egypt to the present-day USA. Hybrid CD-ROM: BRODO123-CDB, $27.95. Available from Learning Services, P.O. Box 10636, Eugene, OR 97440-2636; Western Region: 800/877-9378; Eastern Region: 800/877-3278. (See coupon.)

Elementary U.S. History (Ages 10 to 14)

These four CD-ROMs trace our history from the sixteenth-century European explorations to the settlement of the Wild West. Hybrid CD-ROMs: *Exploring & Colonizing*—Mexico, Canada, and the U.S. Atlantic Coast, CLEA0560-CDBS; *Becoming a Nation*—Examines the colonists' efforts to gain independence, CLEA0565-CDBS; *Expanding Our Nation*—settlers to move West, CLEA0570-CDBS; *Staying One Nation*—African slaves and the Civil War, $69.95 each. 4-Disk set, CLEA0555-CDBS, $264.95. Available from Learning Services, P.O. Box 10636, Eugene, OR 97440-2636; Western Region: 800/877-9378; Eastern Region: 800/877-3278. (See coupon.)

U.S. Government: The First 200 Years
(Ages 12 to 18)

This is a program of two CD-ROMs. Part 1 reveals the issues that led to the creation of the Constitution, the development of political parties, Federalism, the Civil War, and more. Part 2 explores Reconstruction, Johnson's impeachment, the ICC, increasing government influence on everyday life, special interests, presidential power, and more. Hybrid CD-ROMs: Part 1, CLEA0250-DB; Part 2, CLEA0255-CDB, $59.95 each. Both disks, CLEA0260-CDB, $109.95 Available from Learning Services, P.O. Box 10636, Eugene, OR 97440-2636; Western Region: 800/877-9378; Eastern Region: 800/877-3278. (See coupon.)

The American Pioneering Experience
(Ages 11 to 16)

These five hybrid CD-ROMs explore the taming of the Western frontier. Through the use of journals, maps, and print, a picture is painted of the daily life of the pioneers. *Daniel Boone and the First American Pioneer*, CLEA0920-CDBS; *Ohio Boatmen and the Pioneering Families*, CLEA0925-CDBS; *Mountain Men and Gold Seekers*, CLEA0930-CDBS; *Old Texas*, CLEA0935-CDBS; *Covered Wagons and Westward Expansion*, CLEA0940-CDBS, $89.95 each. Entire set, CLEAR9045-CDBS, $424.95. Available from Learning Services, P.O. Box 10636, Eugene, OR 97440-2636; Western Region: 800/877-9378; Eastern Region: 800/877-3278. (See coupon.)

Everyday Life in Ancient Egypt (Ages 10 to 14)

Your student will have the opportunity to learn about the lives of the Egyptians—their battles, traditions, beliefs, burial practices, and much more—with this CD-ROM program. Hybrid CD-ROM: CLEA015-CDBS, $69.95. Available from Learning Services, P.O. Box 10636, Eugene, OR 97440-2636; Western Region: 800/877-9378; Eastern Region: 800/877-3278. (See coupon.)

The Greek and Roman World (Ages 11 to 18)

This CD-ROM program covers the achievements in art, literature, politics, and philosophy of four important peoples of these ancient lands: the Aegean Greeks, the Mediterranean Greeks, the Italian Romans, and the Imperial Romans. Your student will learn how each of their cultures differed from one another and how important they are to us today. Hybrid CD-ROM: CLEA0510-CDBS, $69.95. Available from Learning Services, P.O. Box 10636, Eugene, OR 97440-2636; Western Region: 800/877-9378; Eastern Region: 800/877-3278. (See coupon.)

Columbus and the Age of Discovery (Ages 10 to 14)

Using this CD-ROM program, your student can trace global exploration from before Columbus to the Space Age and realize the importance these explorers had in our lives. Hybrid CD-ROM: CLEA0520-CDBS, $74.95. Available from Learning Services, P.O. Box 10636, Eugene, OR 97440-2636; Western Region: 800/877-9378; Eastern Region: 800/877-3278. (See coupon.)

The Civil War: Two Views   (Ages 12 to 18)

This CD-ROM program affords the student with the view of both sides of the war, allowing him or her to evaluate personally the many issues that gave rise to the conflict. Hybrid CD-ROM: CLEA0115-CDBS, $74.95. Available from Learning Services, P.O. Box 10636, Eugene, OR 97440-2636; Western Region: 800/877-9378; Eastern Region: 800/877-3278. (See coupon.)

The Great Depression   (Ages 12 to 18)

With this CD-ROM program, your student will be able to analyze the conditions that led to the long years of economic hopelessness and paralysis and learn its impact upon the ordinary citizen. Hybrid CD-ROM: CLEA0105-CDBS, $74.95. Available from Learning Services, P.O. Box 10636, Eugene, OR 97440-2636; Western Region: 800/877-9378; Eastern Region: 800/877-3278. (See coupon.)

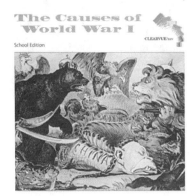

The Causes of World War I   (Ages 12 to 18)

The social, political, and economic factors leading to "the war to end all wars" are discussed on this CD-ROM. Hybrid CD-ROM: CLEA0110-CDBS, $74.95. Available from Learning Services, P.O. Box 10636, Eugene, OR 97440-2636; Western Region: 800/877-9378; Eastern Region: 800/877-3278. (See coupon.)

Hisotry

History

The Causes of World War II   (Ages 12 to 18)

The birth and growth of new totalitarian reigns, which ultimately led to another global conflict, are explored on this CD-ROM. Hybrid CD-ROM: CLEA0130-CDBS, $74.95. Available from Learning Services, P.O. Box 10636, Eugene, OR 97440-2636; Western Region: 800/877-9378; Eastern Region: 800/877-3278. (See coupon.)

Religions of the World   (Ages 12 to 18)

On this CD-ROM, four of the world's major religions are explored to promote understanding and respect of differing religious views. Hybrid CD-ROM: CLEA0420-CDBS, $74.95. Available from Learning Services, P.O. Box 10636, Eugene, OR 97440-2636; Western Region: 800/877-9378; Eastern Region: 800/877-3278. (See coupon.)

Leading Black Americans   (Ages 10 to 15)

This CD-ROM program examines over 200 years of contributions made by African-Americans in education, arts, government, science, business, and industry. Hybrid CD-ROM: CLEA0412-CDB, $99.95. Available from Learning Services, P.O. Box 10636, Eugene, OR 97440-2636; Western Region: 800/877-9378; Eastern Region: 800/877-3278. (See coupon.)

SkyTrip America   (Ages 10 to 18)

On this CD-ROM, your student can pick any state or region of the country, click the mouse, and take off on a time-travel adventure through U.S. history. Along the way she or he will learn about important people, events, and places in our history. MAC CD-ROM: DICH0060-MCCD or WIN CD-ROM: DICH0060-MPC, $27.95 each. Available from Learning Services, P.O. Box 10636, Eugene, OR 97440-2636; Western Region: 800/877-9378; Eastern Region: 800/877-3278. (See coupon.)

Founding of America   (Ages 10 to 15)

With this CD-ROM program, your student can role-play one of four Americans: a colonist in the Massachusetts Bay Colony, a Virginia tobacco farmer in 1670, a patriot during the Revolutionary War, or a naval captain during the War of 1812. Each character is confronted with realities of the times upon which his decisions are based. Hybrid CD-ROM: ENTR0135-CDB, $29.95. Available from Learning Services, P.O. Box 10636, Eugene, OR 97440-2636; Western Region: 800/877-9378; Eastern Region: 800/877-3278. (See coupon.)

Ancient Civilizations   (Ages 10 to 15)

On this CD-ROM your child can role-play a Phoenician merchant in 200 B.C. She or he can watch the rise of the Roman Empire, the decline of ancient Egypt, or visit the Pyramids and the Parthenon. Your student will also have to make decisions about business, career-plan for the eldest son, and other issues. Hybrid CD-ROM: ENTR0120-CDB, $29.95. Available from Learning Services, P.O. Box 10636, Eugene, OR 97440-2636; Western Region: 800/877-9378; Eastern Region: 800/877-3278. (See coupon.)

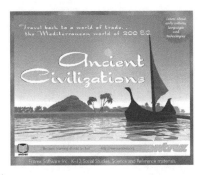

History

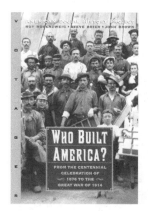

Who Built America? (Ages 14 to 18)

This CD-ROM program is based upon a two-volume history of the U.S. from 1876–1914. It tells the story of ordinary men and women who built this country and offers a new way to experience history through video, sound, and graphics. MAC CD-ROM: VOYA0255-MCCD or WIN CD-ROM: VOYA0255-MPC, $34.95 each. Available from Learning Services, P.O. Box 10636, Eugene, OR 97440-2636; Western Region: 800/877-9378; Eastern Region: 800/877-3278. (See coupon.)

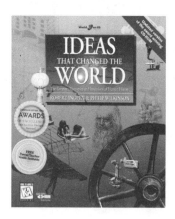

Ideas that Changed the World (Ages 14 and up)

This CD-ROM program presents ideas that have influenced the human race from early tools right up to the computer. Your inquiring student will love this disk. Hybrid CD-ROM: ICE10010-CDB, $24.95. Available from Learning Services, P.O. Box 10636, Eugene, OR 97440-2636; Western Region: 800/877-9378; Eastern Region: 800/877-3278. (See coupon.)

Jean Fritz Series of Book-Based CD-ROMs (Ages 9 to 14)

These three CD-ROMs are based on books by Jean Fritz. *Where Do You Think You're Going, Christopher Columbus?* (Ages 9 to 13) is a story about the man who refused to give up his dream of an all-water route to India. *What's the Big Idea, Ben Franklin?* (Ages 10 to 14) examines the man who helped forge our republic. *Shh! We're Writing the Constitution* (Ages 9 to 13) introduces your student to the delegates of the Philadelphia convention. Hybrid CD-ROMs: Columbus, SCHOOO75-CDBS; Franklin, SCHOOO80-CDBS; Constitution, SCHOOO85-CDBS; $55.95 each. Available from Learning Services, P.O. Box 10636, Eugene, OR 97440-2636; Western Region: 800/877-9378; Eastern Region: 800/877-3278. (See coupon.)

Origins of the Constitution   (Ages 12 to 16)

Through use of this CD-ROM program, your student can gain awareness of how our country was constructed, and how the differing personalities, beliefs, and philosophies of the Founders created the unique reality of America. Includes the Federalist Papers, Articles of Confederation, the Constitution, the Declaration of Independence, and the Bill of Rights. MAC CD-ROM: QUEU0250-MCCD or WIN CD-ROM: QUEU0250-MPC, $65.95 each. Available from Learning Services, P.O. Box 10636, Eugene, OR 97440-2636; Western Region: 800/877-9378; Eastern Region: 800/877-3278. (See coupon.)

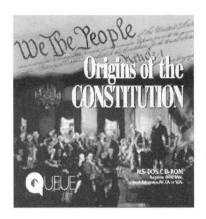

Illinois: The Prairie State   (Ages 11 to 13) †

This package includes a 110-page book, 80-page softcover teacher's guide, and reproducible 80-page test booklet. This Christian-oriented history and geography study of Illinois is rich with history and commerce. The "Inland Empire" has been occupied by many advanced native American tribes and later explored and settled by the French. Textbook, $17.95; Teacher's Guide, $20.95; Test Booklet, $13.95. Available from: ETC Publications, 700 E. Vereda del Sur, Palm Springs, CA 92262; 800/382-7869; 760/325-5352; Fax: 760/325-8841.

Our Golden California   (Ages 11 to 14) †

This package includes a 364-page textbook, 104-page teacher's guidebook, and 30-page student test booklet. This well-written Christian-oriented book by Juanita C. Houston chronicles the history and geography of the Golden State, from its initial colonization by the Spanish missionaries and soldiers to its present-day status as the most populous state and a leader in many areas. Includes an excellent Native American Tribal map. Textbook, $17.95; Teacher's Guide, $20.95; Test Booklet, $13.95. Available from ETC Publications, 700 E. Vereda del Sur, Palm Springs, CA 92262; 800/382-7869; 760/325-5352; Fax: 760/325-8841.

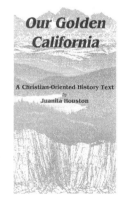

Exploring the Lost Maya   (Ages 10 and up)

This CD-ROM program explores the Mayan culture, which flourished in Central America between the years 150 B.C. and A.D. 1500. It shows 35 different archeological sites in four countries, and discusses the history, evolution, culture, and disappearance of these people. Includes over 600 photographs, a timeline, interactive map sites, original music and narration, a glyph index, and a travel sections. Hybrid CD-ROM: QUEU0625, $49.95. Available from Learning Services, P.O. Box 10636, Eugene, OR 97440-2636; Western Region: 800/877-9378; Eastern Region: 800/877-3278. (See coupon.)

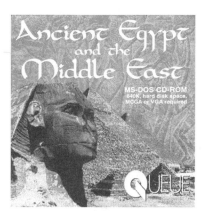

Ancient Egypt and the Middle East
(Ages 12 to 18)

This CD-ROM program focuses on the daily lives of the people of Egypt and neighboring ancient Middle Eastern civilizations. Includes a question section that tests your student's comprehension and reinforces the material. MAC CD-ROM: QUEU0290-MCCD or WIN CD-ROM: QUEU0290-MCCD, $145 each. Available from Learning Services, P.O. Box 10636, Eugene, OR 97440-2636; Western Region: 800/877-9378; Eastern Region: 800/877-3278. (See coupon.)

Total Titanic: A Night to Remember   (Ages 12 to adult)

This CD-ROM program is adapted from Walter Lord's book about the sinking of the giant ship and its last hours with great care and detail. Hybrid CD-ROM: ORAN0520-CDB, $20.95. Available from Learning Services, P.O. Box 10636, Eugene, OR 97440-2636; Western Region: 800/877-9378; Eastern Region: 800/877-3278. (See coupon.)

American Adventures: True Stories from America's Past (Ages 7 to 13)

This set consists of three 96-page illustrated softcover volumes by Morrie Greenberg. Part 1 covers 1770–1870; Part 2, 1870 to present; Part 3, American Heroes, 1735–1900. Many great men and women chronicled such as Dr. Walter Reed, Clara Barton, and inventor Cyrus McCormick. Mr. Greenberg uses his skill as a storyteller to bring to light a number of true but often unusual stories. After each story, there is a study section with questions and exercises. $9.95 each part. Available from Brooke-Richards Press, 818/893-8126.

The Illustrated Living History Series (Ages 10 to 16)

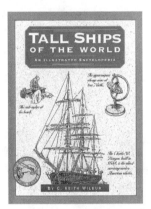

Nine softcover books, each between 94 and 123 pages, offer a close look at how various groups lived their everyday lives in the America of the sixteenth to nineteenth centuries. Careful research results in authentic detail, and all are thoroughly illustrated. Titles: *Tall Ships of the World; Early Explorers of North America; Homebuilding and Woodworking in Colonial America; Pirates & Patriots of the Revolution; Revolutionary Medicine, 1700–1800; The Revolutionary Soldier, 1775–1783.* $14.95 each. *Indian Handcrafts; The New England Indians; Woodland Indians* (all over 95 pages); $16.95 each. Available from Globe Pequot Press, P.O. Box 833, Old Saybrook, CT 06475. www.globe-pequot.com. Write for a free catalog. (See coupon.)

Our Beautiful America: A Christian-Oriented U.S. History Text (Ages 10 to 14) ✝

This book was written by Juanita C. Houston for Christian homeschoolers looking for an up-to-date American history text with strong moral values. Textbook (hardcover), $23.95; teacher's guide, $21.95; student workbook, $17.95; reproducible student test booklet, $19.95. Order from ETC Publications, 700 E. Vereda del Sur, Palm Springs, CA 92262; 800/382-7869; 760/325-5352; Fax: 760/325-8841.

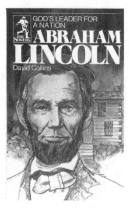

Assorted Titles—Pioneers and the Westward Movement (Ages 9 to 12)

Little House Cookbook, $6.95; *Little House Books*, $29.95; *Story of Laura Ingalls Wilder*, $3.50; *Children of the Wild West*, $6.95.

EASY BIOGRAPHIES BY TROLL: *Abe Lincoln, Davey Crockett, James Beckworth, Daniel Boone, Narcissa Whitman, Johnny Appleseed*, $3.50 each.

SOWER BIOGRAPHY SERIES: *Johnny Appleseed, Abraham Lincoln*, $7.99 each.

CHILDHOOD OF FAMOUS AMERICANS: *Daniel Boone, Buffalo Bill, Davey Crockett, Annie Oakley, Sacagawea*, $4.95 each.

TURNING POINT IN AMERICAN HISTORY SERIES: *Lewis and Clark Expedition, The Transcontinental Railroad, The Battle of Little Bighorn*, $7.95 each.

COLORING BOOKS: *Lewis and Clark*, $2.95; *Pioneers, Plains Indians, Southeast Indians, Southwest Indians, Northeast Indians, Northwest Indians*, $1.99 each.

Available from Excellence in Education, 2640 S. Myrtle Ave., Unit A-7, Monrovia, CA 91016; 626/821-0025; Fax: 626/357-4443; www.excellenceineducation.com. (See coupon.)

Assorted Titles—The American Revolution to the Civil War (Ages 9 to 12)

America's Paul Revere, $6.95. *Paul Revere's Ride* by Longfellow; *Boston Massacre* (Intrepid); *Benjamin Franklin* (Childhood of Famous Americans); *Federalist Papers*, $4.95 each. Also available are: *Autobiography of Benjamin Franklin*, $4.99; *Anti-Federalist Papers and Constitution Debates*, $6.99; *The Light and the Glory*, $9.95; *The Light and the Glory for Children*, $9.95; *From Sea to Shining Sea*, $9.95; *From Sea to Shining Sea for Children*, $9.95.

TROLL BIOGRAPHIES: *Andrew Jackson, John Adams, George Washington, Patrick Henry, Young Thomas Jefferson, Young Benjamin Franklin, Young Abigail Adams, John Paul Jones, Paul Revere, Noah Webster, James Monroe*, and *Lafayette*. $3.50 each.

MORE TROLL: *Yo Millard Fillmore*, $6.95; *Yo Sacramento*, $6.95.

SOWER SERIES BIOGRAPHIES: *Francis Scott Key, George Washington, Daniel Webster, Abigail Adams*, and *Stonewall Jackson*, $7.99 each. Available from Excellence in Education, 2640 S. Myrtle Ave., Unit A-7, Monrovia, CA 91016; 626/821-0025; Fax: 626/357-4443; www.excellenceineducation.com. (See coupon.)

Civil War and On—Assorted Titles   (Ages 9 to 12)

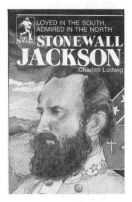

If You Lived at the Time of The Civil War, $4.95; *Up from Slavery* by Booker T. Washington (Dover), $2; *Gettysburg* (Landmark), $4.99; *Go Free or Die—Harriet Tubman*, $5.95; *Walking the Road to Freedom—Sojourner Truth*, $5.95;

TROLL SERIES BIOGRAPHIES: *Teddy Roosevelt, Harriet Tubman, Robert E. Lee*, $3.50 each.

SOWER SERIES BIOGRAPHIES: *George Washington Carver, Robert E. Lee, Abraham Lincoln*, $7.99 each.

EARLY CHILDHOOD OF FAMOUS AMERICANS: *Clara Barton, Robert E. Lee, Abe Lincoln*; $4.95 each.

THE HISTORY OF THE CIVIL WAR SERIES: *John C. Calhoun and the Roots of War; Harriet Tubman and the Underground Railroad; Robert E. Lee and the Rise of the South; Abraham Lincoln: To Preserve the Union; David Farragut and the Great Naval Blockade; John Ericson and the Inventions of War; Stonewall Jackson: Lee's Greatest Lieutenant; Ulysses S. Grant and the Strategy of Victory; Clara Barton: Healing the Wounds; Andrew Johnson: Rebuilding the Nation*, $7.95 each. *Go Free or Die: Tubman; Walking to the Road of Freedom; Pocketful of Goobers—George Washington Carver*, $5.95 each. Available from Excellence in Education, 2640 S. Myrtle Ave., Unit A-7, Monrovia, CA 91016; 626/821-0025; Fax: 626/357-4443; www.excellenceineducation.com. (See coupon.)

Family Tapestry   (Ages 11 to 14)

Here is a wonderful way to supplement your child's study of history—his or her own! This book by Barbara Maley Yamamoto helps children explore their own family histories—immigration, heredity, and more—to find their own unique part in the fabric of life. Item #122, $9.95. Available from Dandy Lion Publications, 3563 Sueldo, Ste. L, San Luis Obispo, CA 93401; 800/776-8032; Fax: 805/544-2823.

California History—Assorted Titles   (Ages 9 to 12)

Junipero Serra, $3.99; *Feliciana's California Miracle*, $8.75; *Vallejo and the Four Flags*, $8.75; *California Gold Rush*, $4.99; *Island of the Blue Dolphins*, $5.50; *Mr. Blue Jeans: The Story of Levi Strauss*, $5.95; *Coloring Books: California Missions* (Dover), $2.95; *California Missions* (Spizziri), $1.99; *California Indians*, $1.99.

The Story of Junipero Serra: Brave Adventurer, $3.99. Available from Excellence in Education, 2640 S. Myrtle Ave., Unit A-7, Monrovia, CA 91016; 626/821-0025; Fax: 626/357-4443; www.excellenceineducation.com. (See coupon.)

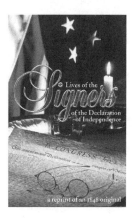

Lives of the Signers of the Declaration of Independence (Ages 15 to 18)

This 392-page reprint by B. J. Lossing of an 1848 original provides a brief biography of each of the 56 men who signed the Declaration of Independence. Learn the virtues of the venerated Americans who helped create the most stable and viable nation in the world. $9.95. Available from Excellence in Education, 2640 S. Myrtle Ave., Unit A-7, Monrovia, CA 91016; 626/821-0025; Fax: 626/357-4443; www.excellenceineducation.com. (See coupon.)

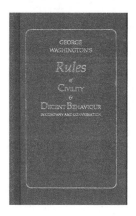

George Washington's Rules of Civility and Decent Behaviour (Ages 11 to adult)

The book the first president assembled as a guide for himself. $8.95 Available from Excellence in Education, 2640 S. Myrtle Ave., Unit A-7, Monrovia, CA 91016; 626/821-0025; Fax: 626/357-4443; www.excellenceineducation.com. (See coupon.)

The Bulletproof George Washington (Ages 15 to Adult) ✝

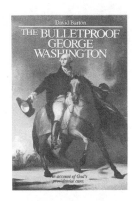

Read the thrilling account by David Barton of God's providential care of George Washington in the French and Indian War and of Washington's open gratitude for God's intervention. This encouraging story of God's sovereign preservation of our first President is a fast-reading book. $4.95. Available from Excellence in Education, 2640 S. Myrtle Ave., Unit A-7, Monrovia, CA 91016; 626/821-0025; Fax: 626/357-4443; www.excellenceineducation.com. (See coupon.)

Inventors and Scientists (Ages 9 to 12)

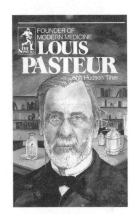

TROLL BIOGRAPHIES: *Louis Pasteur, Marie Curie, Wright Brothers, Young Einstein, Thomas Edison,* $3.50 each.

SOWER SERIES BIOGRAPHIES: *Samuel Morse, Johanes Kepler, Isaac Newton, Louis Pasteur, Wright Brothers,* $7.99 each.

CHILDHOOD OF FAMOUS AMERICANS: *Thomas Edison, Henry Ford, Benjamin Franklin, Thomas Jefferson, Wilbur and Orville Wright,* $4.95 each.

OTHER INVENTORS: *"Click:" The Story of George Eastman; Fine Print: The Story of Johann Gutenberg; Frontier Surgeons: The Story of the Mayo Brothers; Shoes for Everyone—Jan Matzelinger; We'll Race You Henry—Henry Ford; The Wizard of Sound—Thomas Edison,* $5.95 each.

HEALING WARRIORS: *Sister Elizabeth Kenny; Pioneer Plowmaker—John Deere; Rooftop Astronomer—Maria Mitchell; Forgotten Voyager—Amerigo Vespucci,* $15.95 each.

Native American Doctor, $6.95; *What Are You Figuring Now—Benjamin Banneker,* $5.95; *A Piece of the Mountain—Blaise Pascal,* $7.95. Available from Excellence in Education, 2640 S. Myrtle Ave., Unit A-7, Monrovia, CA 91016; 626/821-0025; Fax: 626/357-4443; www.excellenceineducation.com. (See coupon.)

The Mind of Plato (Ages 12 to adult)

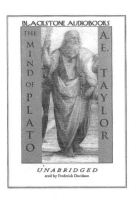

This series of three audiocassettes (4½-hours total) is a concise analysis by A. E. Taylor, examining the philosopher's theory of knowledge and doctrine of ideas; his ideal of the philosopher-king; and belief in the immortality of the soul. Item #S31075X, $24.95. Available from Audio-Forum, 96 Broad St., Ste. C70, Guilford, CT 06437; 203/453-9794; e-mail: info@audioforum.com; www.audioforum.com. (See coupon.)

History

Aristotle   (Ages 12 to adult)

A. E. Taylor developed this package on three audiocassettes (4½-hour total) to appeal to both the beginner and expert alike. He achieves a penetrating analysis of the philosopher's thought, covering formal logic, theory of knowledge, matter, and form. Taylor also deals with many of Aristotle's errors and weaknesses. Item #S31080X, $24.95. Available from Audio-Forum, 96 Broad St., Ste. C70, Guilford, CT 06437; 203/453-9794; e-mail: info@audioforum.com; www.audioforum.com. (See coupon.)

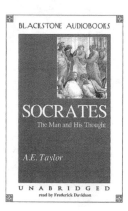

Socrates: The Man and His Thought   (Ages 12 to adult)

This program consists of three audiocassettes, a 4.5-hour total. Despite the fact that Socrates left no writings, A. E. Taylor has produced a body of knowledge about the philosopher through the writings of Plato, Aristotle, and Xenophon. Socrates believed that all wickedness was due to ignorance and that knowledge was virtue. Item #S31085X, $24.95. Available from Audio-Forum, 96 Broad St., Ste. C70, Guilford, CT 06437; 203/453-9794; e-mail: info@audioforum.com; www.audioforum.com. (See coupon.)

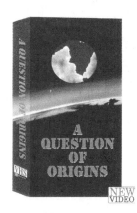

American Portrait Videos   (Ages 9 to adult) ✝

This company has a large line of excellent Christian video productions, which cover teen issues, secular humanism, pro-life issues, and many more. Each one is well produced and filled with information pertinent to the Christian living in this time. *Fossil Evidence of Creation*, BD049VN, 27 minutes; *The Grand Canyon Catastrophe*, BD048VN, 27 minutes; *In the Beginning*, BD050VN, 27 minutes; and *A Question of Origins*, BD079VN, 60 minutes. $19.95 each. *The Story of America's Liberty*, AH002VN, 65 minutes, $19.95. Available from American Portrait Films, P.O. Box 19266, Cleveland, OH 44119; 800/736-4567; e-mail: amport@amport.com; www.amport.com. (See coupon.)

Geography

The Complete *National Geographic* (Ages 9 to adult)
Experience 109 years of *National Geographic* magazine on these remarkable CD-ROMs. The search index on every disk points you easily to the correct one that contains every article, photograph, map, and magazine cover. Hybrid CD-ROM: MIN-DOO35-CDBS, $159.95. Available from Learning Services, P.O. Box 10636, Eugene, OR 97440-2636; Western Region: 800/877-9378; Eastern Region: 800/877-3278. (See coupon.)

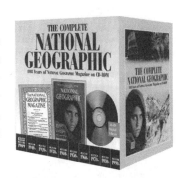

The Complete *National Geographic* Reference CD-ROM Bundle (Ages 9 to adult)
This program contains three *National Geographic* packages in one: (1) The Complete *National Geographic* (shown above). (2) *National Geographic Maps*. This comprehensive study resource includes every foldout map ever published in *National Geographic*, plus engaging multimedia map tours and an interactive timeline that traces the evolution of mapping. (3) *National Geographic: A World of Learning*. This is a comprehensive Teacher Resource Guide with 16 detailed lesson plans, student worksheets, transparencies, and a world map. LSPK1335-MPCS, $229.95. Available from Learning Services, P.O. Box 10636, Eugene, OR 97440-2636; Western Region: 800/877-9378; Eastern Region: 800/877-3278. (See coupon.)

DK Cartopedia (Ages 9 to adult)
This CD-ROM combines the map qualities of an atlas with the background information of an encyclopedia and the statistical and analytical depth of a gazetteer. Provides instant access to detailed maps and allows comparison of statistics. MAC CD-ROM: DOR-LOO4O-MCCD, $49.95. Available from Learning Services, P.O. Box 10636, Eugene, OR 97440-2636; Western Region: 800/877-9378; Eastern Region: 800/877-3278. (See coupon.)

Odyssey—the World's First Atlasphere   (Ages 5 to adult)
The atlasphere is a standard size globe on a mini-computer base, which contains numerous control buttons, a number keypad, and a digitally recorded narrator that guides you through various functions. You insert one of four cartridges into the base and can then access the various geography-based games or cultural information available, all of which are narrated for you. $399 plus tax. Explore Technologies, Inc., P.O. Box 2579, Santa Clara, CA 95055-2579; 888/456-2343.

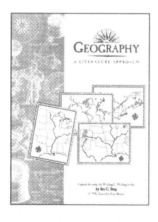

Learning Wrap-Ups' America Geography Sets   (Ages 10 and up)
In this exciting approach to memorizing states, capitals, and other facts, Learning Wrap-Ups makes the process much more interesting and attention-keeping. Each approximately 5" × 1½" plastic board contains geographic information about the United States. The precut length of yarn (supplied) is to be wrapped up on the plastic board in a certain pattern to match up the state with its capital. States and Capitals, LWU 105, $7.95; All About America (state abbreviations) LWU 150, $7.95. Available through Learning Wrap-Ups, 2122 East 6550 South, Ogden, UT 84405; 800/992-4966. (See coupon.)

Geography: A Literature Approach   (Ages 9 to 13) ✝
This teacher's guide by Rea C. Berg is designed to provide the teaching parent a framework for study, using four books by C. Holling. Suggested books covering U.S. geography and world geography are listed as well. $8.95. Beautiful Feet Books, 139 Main St., Sandwich, MA 02563; 800/889-1978; 508/833-8626; www.bfbooks.com. Call for catalog.

Geography Through Literature Pack
(Ages 9 to 13) †

This self-contained geography curriculum includes the *Geography Study Guide* by Rea C. Berg; four maps—three U.S. regions and one world—which are to be colored and labeled by your child; and four books by C. Holling: *Minn of the Mississippi, Paddle-to-the-Sea, Seabird,* and *Tree in the Trail.* $59.95. Beautiful Feet Books, 139 Main St., Sandwich, MA 02563; 800/889-1978; 508/833-8626; www.bfbooks.com. Call for catalog.

DK World Atlas CD-ROM (Ages 9 to adult)

Detailed maps, photos, and videos along with facts, statistics, charts, and graphs to satisfy any user. WIN CD-ROM: DORLO195-MPCS, $54.95. Available from Learning Services, P.O. Box 10636, Eugene, OR 97440-2636; Western Region: 800/877-9378; Eastern Region: 800/877-3278. (See coupon.)

The Canada Bundle (Ages 10 and up)

This excellent bundle of three different CD-ROMs will bring Canada to your homeschool geography program. (1) *Canadian Treasures:* discover rare photographs, maps, manuscripts, and paintings about Canada's history and culture. (2) *Adventure Canada:* over 70 movies, 300 slides, sound, graphics, narration, and music in this great CD-ROM. (3) *Totem Poles:* discover the major types of poles, plus stories related to the carved figures on the Pacific Northwest Coast. Explore the tribal nations. All three hybrid CD-ROMs: LSPK1175-CDBS, $119.95. Individually available: Canadian Treasures, DIDA0105-CDBS; Adventure Canada, DIDA0050-CDBS; Totem Poles, DIDA0085-CDBS, $49.95 each. Available from Learning Services, P.O. Box 10636, Eugene, OR 97440-2636; Western Region: 800/877-9378; Eastern Region: 800/877-3278. (See coupon.)

National Parks Live! (Ages 12 to 18)

This CD-ROM has over 20 activities that send your student to National Parks websites to work on geography, history, environmental studies, science, and language arts. Teacher instructions are included, as is a U.S. outline map. Hybrid CD-ROM: CUR-ROO05-CDB, $34.95. Available from Learning Services, P.O. Box 10636, Eugene, OR 97440-2636; Western Region: 800/877-9378; Eastern Region: 800/877-3278. (See coupon.)

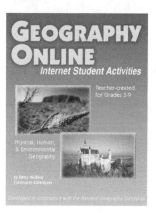

Geography Online (Ages 9 to 14)

Your student explores a variety of cultural and physical geography topics in the 20 Internet-based activities in this package. Hybrid CD-ROM: CURROO1O-CDB, $34.95. Available from Learning Services, P.O. Box 10636, Eugene, OR 97440-2636; Western Region: 800/877-9378; Eastern Region: 800/877-3278. (See coupon.)

DK Family Atlas (All ages)

This wonderfully illustrated DK book provides information on political, physical, and cultural geography in great detail. This 288-page hardcover includes a 16-page U.S. section. Item #375, $29.95. Available from DK Family Learning, 11124 N.E. Halsey, Suite 460, Portland, OR 97220; 888/225-3535. (See coupon.)

Geography

DK Eyewitness World Atlas   (Ages 12 and up)

This CD-ROM program presents graphics as only a CD-ROM can. Approximately 400 maps, thousands of charts, graphs, and 250 photos reproduced with dazzling vividness and clarity accompany 500,000 words of text in this great program of world geography. Includes flags of every country. WIN CD-ROM: $29.95. Available from DK Family Learning, 11124 N.E. Halsey, Suite 460, Portland, OR 97220; 888/225-3535. (See coupon.)

DK My First Amazing World Explorer 2.0   (Ages 3 to 9)

Treat your young student to this great introduction to geography on this excellent CD-ROM program. Five interactive games are included for fun learning along with more than one hour of audio narration, 44 full-color maps, and 16 "video" presentations of wildlife and people from across the globe. Hybrid CD-ROM: $29.95. Available from DK Family Learning, 11124 N.E. Halsey, Suite 460, Portland, OR 97220; 888/225-3535. (See coupon.)

DK World Atlas   (Ages 11 and up)

This 327-page atlas includes completely up-to-date entries of the world's countries. Eight large-scale, finely detailed, pullout maps depict important regions of the world. $60. Available from DK Family Learning, 11124 N.E. Halsey, Suite 460, Portland, OR 97220; 888/225-3535. (See coupon.)

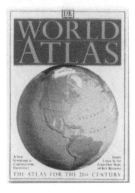

Geography

DK Essential World Atlas   (Ages 11 and up)

Here is a portable atlas (256 pages, flexibound) for your backpack, briefcase, car, or desk. It contains detailed maps of all countries of the world accompanied by a large amount of statistical information. This atlas is great for studying physical, political, or cultural geography. $14.95. Available from DK Family Learning, 11124 N.E. Halsey, Suite 460, Portland, OR 97220; 888/225-3535. (See coupon.)

DK Book of the World Atlas   (Ages 11 and up)

This little 432-page flex-bound pocket guide contains more than 10,000 key facts about every nation on the globe. Index of over 6,500 place names, too. $14.95. Available from DK Family Learning, 11124 N.E. Halsey, Suite 460, Portland, OR 97220; 888/225-3535. (See coupon.)

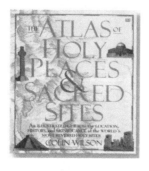

DK Atlas of Holy Places & Sacred Sites   (Ages 11 and up)

This unique 192-page hardcover volume by Colin Wilson contains more than 1,000 possible sites with beautiful illustrations and excellent text. $29.95. Available from DK Family Learning, 11124 N.E. Halsey, Suite 460, Portland, OR 97220; 888/225-3535. (See coupon.)

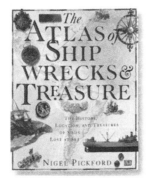

DK Atlas of Shipwrecks & Treasure   (Ages 11 and up)

This 200-page hardcover by Nigel Pickford is an unusual book to capture the imagination! From the days of the windjammers to modern commercial sinkings, if you are captivated by shipwrecks, this one's for you, mate! $29.95. Available from DK Family Learning, 11124 N.E. Halsey, Suite 460, Portland, OR 97220; 888/225-3535. (See coupon.)

DK Atlas of Archeology (Ages 11 and up)

This interesting 208-page hardcover by Tim Taylor and Mick Aston covers time periods from the Paleolithic Age through the Industrial Revolution. It offers a fresh perspective of the past and also provides details of archeological "digs" from the time they are discovered to their preservation. $29.95. Available from DK Family Learning, 11124 N.E. Halsey, Suite 460, Portland, OR 97220; 888/225-3535. (See coupon.)

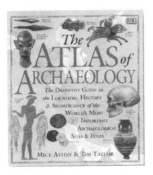

DK Ultimate Panoramic Atlas (Ages 10 and up)

With 42 pages plus 9 gatefolds, this hardcover from DK is composed of computer-generated foldout maps that have been exaggerated to produce a dazzling 3-D effect, illustrated in the unique DK style. $19.95. Available from DK Family Learning, 11124 N.E. Halsey, Suite 460, Portland, OR 97220; 888/225-3535. (See coupon.)

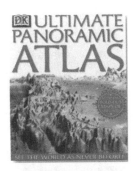

DK Oceans Atlas (Ages 10 and up)

This 64-page hardcover by Anita Ganeri is an excellent way to study the deep. Computer-generated maps of the ocean floor unlock and reveal its mysteries in the comfort of your home. $19.95. Available from DK Family Learning, 11124 N.E. Halsey, Suite 460, Portland, OR 97220; 888/225-3535. (See coupon.)

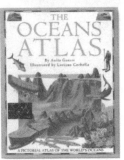

DK Earth Atlas (Ages 10 and up)

This 64-page hardcover is a wonderful addition to your atlas library. It was especially commissioned with an entertaining text style and full-color maps and is brimming with information. $19.95. Available from DK Family Learning, 11124 N.E. Halsey, Suite 460, Portland, OR 97220; 888/225-3535. (See coupon.)

Geography

DK Student World Atlas   (Ages 10 to adult)

This 160-page hardcover edited by DK is a well-written and richly illustrated text. It provides the perfect way for your child to learn about physical and cultural geography. $19.95. Available from DK Family Learning, 11124 N.E. Halsey, Suite 460, Portland, OR 97220; 888/225-3535. (See coupon.)

DK Atlas of the World   (Ages 10 to adult)

In the DK Books' tradition of their "eyewitness" series, this 160-page hardcover atlas by Deni Bown takes its place, ready to inform your child about physical and cultural geography through clear, intelligent text and dazzling photos and illustrations. $24.95. Available from DK Family Learning, 11124 N.E. Halsey, Suite 460, Portland, OR 97220; 888/225-3535. (See coupon.)

DK Geography of the World   (Ages 9 to adult)

This 304-page hardcover by David Green will aid your child as the ultimate geography reference book. Filled with descriptions of each country and its people, customs, resources, and more, it provides fun reading while informing. $39.95. Available from DK Family Learning, 11124 N.E. Halsey, Suite 460, Portland, OR 97220; 888/225-3535. (See coupon.)

DK Children Just Like Me   (Ages 7 to adult)

In this best-selling 80-page volume by Barnabas and Anabel Kindersley your child can read about other children around the world—their day, food, clothing, and customs. Dazzling illustrations and photos bring the world to life in this hardcover! $19.95. Available from DK Family Learning, 11124 N.E. Halsey, Suite 460, Portland, OR 97220; 888/225-3535. (See coupon.)

Runkle Geography   (Ages 12 to 18)

This seven-unit comprehensive geography course is new on the market. If studied in its entirety, it comprises three years of study—one year followed by five semesters. Each unit includes a teacher's guide and Testmasters. Unit 1: Physical World Geography, one-year course, #28-1, $70. Unit 2: Geography of N. America, one semester, #28-4, $60. Unit 3: Geography of Central & S. America, one semester, #28-7, $55. Unit 4: Geography of Europe, one semester, #38-4, $55. Unit 5: Geography of Asia, one semester, #38-1, $55. Unit 6: Geography of Africa, one semester, #48-1, $55. Unit 7: Map Packet (works with all units), #48-7, $52. Available from Runkle Publishers Inc., 3750 W. Main, 3 Park So., Norman, OK 73072; orders: 877/436-8398 toll free; Fax: 405/321-9644. (See coupon.)

Cobblestone Magazine   (Ages 8 to 15)

This is an inviting magazine for readers interested in cultural, physical, and political geography. Each issue is full of stories, diagrams, and factual sidebars, providing an in-depth view of the topic being written of, done in the most creative manner possible. Available from Cobblestone Publishing Company, 30 Grove St., Ste. C, Peterborough, NH 03458; 603/924-7209; 800/821-0115; e-mail: custsvc@cobbestone.mv.com; www.cobblestonepub.com.

Geography

DK Celebrations!   (Ages 8 to adult)

This 64-page hardcover by Anabel Kindersley chronicles the feasts, festivals, and carnivals that are celebrated around the world. A great way to study cultural geography. $19.95. Available from DK Family Learning, 11124 N.E. Halsey, Suite 460, Portland, OR 97220; 888/225-3535. (See coupon.)

World Citizen   (Ages 12 to 18)

Use the Worldwide Web to learn about current events in some other countries, such as Mexico, Central America, Hong Kong, Vietnam, India, and Ethiopia. Hybrid CD-ROM: BONUOOO5-CDBS, $32.95. Available from Learning Services, P.O. Box 10636, Eugene, OR 97440-2636; Western Region: 800/877-9378; Eastern Region: 800/877-3278. (See coupon.)

U.S. Atlas & Almanac   (Ages 9 to adult)

This CD-ROM program has been recently updated with full-color and 3-D relief maps. Indispensable for studies of geography or demographics, it also allows for customization of maps for printing. MAC CD-ROM: SWT09006-MCCDS or WIN CD-ROM: SWT09006-MPCS; $59.95 each. Available from Learning Services, P.O. Box 10636, Eugene, OR 97440-2636; Western Region: 800/877-9378; Eastern Region: 800/877-3278. (See coupon.)

World Atlas & Almanac   (Ages 9 to adult)

This CD-ROM program will improve your student's "world view" with its stunning graphics, satellite photos, and even audio reproductions of national anthems. The almanac includes information on world economy, agriculture, and more. MAC CD-ROM: SWT09010-MCCDS or WIN CD-ROM: SWT09010-MPCS, $59.95 each. Available from Learning Services, P.O. Box 10636, Eugene, OR 97440-2636; Western Region: 800/877-9378; Eastern Region: 800/877-3278. (See coupon.)

National Geographic: A World of Learning   (Parent use)

This CD-ROM program serves as a teacher resource guide companion to the complete *National Geographic* program. It includes lesson plans, worksheets, transparencies, a world map, and more. Hybrid CD-ROM: MIND1435-CDB, $59.95. Available from Learning Services, P.O. Box 10636, Eugene, OR 97440-2636; Western Region: 800/877-9378; Eastern Region: 800/877-3278. (See coupon.)

Compton's 3-D World Atlas Deluxe '98 Edition (Ages 11 to 18)

Besides geography, this CD-ROM program covers geology, climate, environmental issues, economies, and cultures. It includes narrated video documentaries, detailed articles, 1,500 photos, almost 200 national flags, 750 music clips, and common foreign phrases spoken in 43 languages. WIN CD-ROM: SKSW0180-MPC, $32.95. (Also see the Compton "Bundle" in the English section, page 184.) Available from Learning Services, P.O. Box 10636, Eugene, OR 97440-2636; Western Region: 800/877-9378; Eastern Region: 800/877-3278. (See coupon.)

Geography

GeoBee Challenge   (Ages 9 to adult)

This CD-ROM features a multimedia game based upon questions from the National Geography Bee, sponsored by the National Geographic Society. Children can compete against each other or the computer for a fun way to learn geography and some world history with the over 2,000 questions. Hybrid CD-ROM: NATG0035-CDB, $32.95. Available from Learning Services, P.O. Box 10636, Eugene, OR 97440-2636; Western Region: 800/877-9378; Eastern Region: 800/877-3278. (See coupon.)

Where in the World Is Carmen Sandiego?
(Ages 9 to adult)

In this fun and informative CD-ROM game, your student must track down the ex-secret agent Carmen Sandiego and her cronies across the globe, using clues in history, the arts, language, currency, and geography. Many different scenarios are offered. Includes access to the Carmen Sandiego website on the Internet. Hybrid CD-ROM: BROD1210-CDB, $27.95. Available from Learning Services, P.O. Box 10636, Eugene, OR 97440-2636; Western Region: 800/877-9378; Eastern Region: 800/877-3278. (See coupon.)

Where in the USA Is Carmen Sandiego?
(Ages 9 to adult)

In this CD-ROM program, your student will track down ex-secret agent Carmen Sandiego trying to recover stolen national treasures throughout the United States using clues relating to U.S. and state history, geography, economy, and culture. Many different scenarios are offered. Includes access to the Carmen Sandiego website on the Internet. Hybrid CD-ROM: BROD1215-CDB, $27.95. Available from Learning Services, P.O. Box 10636, Eugene, OR 97440-2636; Western Region: 800/877-9378; Eastern Region: 800/877-3278. (See coupon.)

Carmen Sandiego Jr. Detective Edition (Ages 5 to 9)

This CD-ROM program is designed to help pre-readers learn about countries and cultures around the world. Hybrid CD-ROM: BROD0900-CDB, $27.95. Available from Learning Services, P.O. Box 10636, Eugene, OR 97440-2636; Western Region: 800/877-9378; Eastern Region: 800/877-3278. (See coupon.)

U.S. Geography Series (Ages 10 to 14)

This series of eight CD-ROMs enables your student to learn about our country in the enjoyable format. The Overview disk covers all seven regions of the U.S., CLEA0881-CDB. The Northeast covers ME, VT, NH, MA, CT, RI, NY, NJ, PA, and DE, CLEA0082-CDB. The Southeast covers AL, AR, FL, GA, KY, LA, MD, MS, NC, SC, TN, VA, and WV, CLEA0083-CDB. The West covers WA, OR, CA, and NV, CLEA0084-CDB. The Rocky Mountain States covers MT, ID, WY, CO, and UT, CLEA0084-CDB. The North Central States covers OH, IA, IL, MI, WI, MN, IN, MO, ND, SD, NE, and KS, CLEA0087-CDB. The Southwest covers OK, TX, AZ, and NM, CLEA0088-CDB. AK & HI, CLEA0089-CDB. Each hybrid CD-ROM $59.95; or purchase all 8, CLEA0090-CDB, $429.95. Available from Learning Services, P.O. Box 10636, Eugene, OR 97440-2636; Western Region: 800/877-9378; Eastern Region: 800/877-3278. (See coupon.)

An Overview

Odyssey of Discovery: Mapping Concepts (Age 5 to 11)

This CD-ROM program contains five activities to instruct your child on how people and their products and ideas move across the earth. The units include Regions and Boundaries, Kinds of Maps, Reading Maps, Land and Water, and Movement and Communication. Hybrid CD-ROM: PIER1050-CDB, $29.95. Available from Learning Services, P.O. Box 10636, Eugene, OR 97440-2636; Western Region: 800/877-9378; Eastern Region: 800/877-3278. (See coupon.)

Geography

Odyssey of Discovery: Earth Systems   (Ages 10 and up)

Six activities in this CD-ROM program help develop an understanding of the relationship between people and earth. The units are Biosphere, Lithosphere, Hydrosphere, Climate and Atmosphere, People and the Environment, and People and Products. Hybrid CD-ROM: PIER1065-CDB, $29.95. Available from Learning Services, P.O. Box 10636, Eugene, OR 97440-2636; Western Region: 800/877-9378; Eastern Region: 800/877-3278. (See coupon.)

Map Skills   (Ages 8 to 13)

This series of high-quality workbooks in six volumes includes the basics of map reading and understanding and applying map-reading to a wide variety of geographic subjects—cultural, commercial, and physical geography, including weather maps. Level A (8), #2383-5, $3.10; Level B (9), #2384-3, $3.10; Level C (10), #2385-1, $3.20, Level D (11), #2386-X, $3.20; Level E (12), 2387-8, $3.35, Level F (12-13, remedial), #2417-3, $3.35. Teacher's Guide $2.50. Available from Continental Press, 520 E. Bainbridge St., Elizabethtown, PA 17022; 800/233-0759. (See coupon.)

Children's Atlas of World Wildlife   (Ages 9 to 14)

Explore animal habitats from every continent with this CD-ROM program. Contains over 60 full-motion videos, 200 photos, five exciting games, and detailed Rand McNally maps. Hybrid CD-ROM: RAND00005-CDB, $63.95. Available from Learning Services, P.O. Box 10636, Eugene, OR 97440-2636; Western Region: 800/877-9378; Eastern Region: 800/877-3278. (See coupon.)

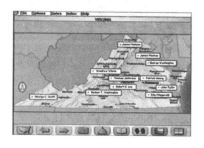

Children's Atlas of the United States   (Ages 8 to 14)

Your student can learn about the state capitals, largest cities, major rivers, and mountains via this CD-ROM program. Six exciting games are included, as well as Rand McNally maps. WIN CD-ROM: RAND00025-MPC or MAC CD-ROM: 0025-MCCD, $63.95 each. Available from Learning Services, P.O. Box 10636, Eugene, OR 97440-2636; Western Region: 800/877-9378; Eastern Region: 800/877-3278. (See coupon.)

Geography Audio Tapes   (Ages 8 to 12)

Sing Around The World Kit by Kathy Troxel contains a long-playing great musical cassette to teach you almost every country, region, and state in the world as well as the planets. A book of maps, words to the songs, and activities are included, as well as large maps of the world and USA to color. States and Capitals Kit is the easiest way known to learn the states and capitals and their locations. The package contains one audiocassette and a large map of the United States to color. States and Capitals Kit, $9.95; Sing Around the World Kit, $19.95; Songbook only, $6.95; map of the world, $3; Map of the United States, $3. Available from Excellence in Education, 2640 S. Myrtle Ave., Unit A-7, Monrovia, CA 91016; 626/821-0025; Fax: 626/357-4443; www.excellenceineducation.com. (See coupon.)

Read a Mat   (Ages 7 to adult)

More informative than a cereal box, more fun than the morning news! Read a Mats are entertaining tabletop teachers that stimulate family discussion. Each mat is made of thick, washable vinyl and measures 11½" × 17½". Choose Physical Terrain (U.S.), World (Political), World (Continental), and United States, $3.95 each. Available from Excellence in Education, 2640 S. Myrtle Ave., Unit A-7, Monrovia, CA 91016; 626/821-0025; Fax: 626/357-4443; www.excellenceineducation.com. (See coupon.)

U.S. and World Mark-It Laminated Maps   (Ages 7 to adult)

These write-on and wipe-off outline wall maps are laminated on both sides for years of use. Each laminated map measures 23" × 34" map. Use any water-based marking pen to label. The USA map includes insets of Alaska and Puerto Rico. World map places the Atlantic Ocean on center and does not divide Asia in two. U.S. Map, $6.95; World Map, $6.95; Double-sided (both maps back-to-back), $9.95. Available from Excellence in Education, 2640 S. Myrtle Ave., Unit A-7, Monrovia, CA 91016; 626/821-0025; Fax: 626/357-4443; www.excellenceineducation.com. (See coupon.)

Geography

Mapping the World by Heart   (Ages 11 to 12)

Can your student draw detailed maps without an atlas? They can now with this complete and proven approach to teaching geography. David Smith's curriculum promotes stunning results. Includes Comprehensive Teacher's Guide, detailed lesson plans, reproducibles, blank grid maps, blank outline maps, and a *Getting Started* video. Deluxe package contains 270 blank outline maps (30 each for nine world regions), $99.95; Lite package has master outline maps of only one for each of nine world regions (duplication required), $59.95. Available from Tom Snyder Productions, 80 Coolidge Hill Road, Watertown, MA 02472; 800/342-0236; e-mail: Ask@TeachTSP.com; www.mapping.com.

Music Programs and Materials

Melody Lane   (Ages 5 to 9)

This music course is nicely done on video tape. Children will cover the string, percussion, brass and woodwind families. It features many different composers and instrument making. Lessons and guidebooks are included along with hands-on activities, songs and games. $95. Available from Calvert School, 105 Tuscany Road, Baltimore, MD 21210; 888/487-4652; www.calvertschool.org.

Lives of the Musicians—Good Times, Bad Times (and What the Neighbors Thought)   (Ages 10 and up)

This unabridged book on two audiocassettes (two hours) is read by John C. Brown and Melissa Hughes. Author Kathleen Krull provides miniature biographies of the great musicians and how the people in their daily lives saw them. Cassette, Item #5-96, $15.95. Available from Audio Bookshelf, 174 Prescott Hill Road, Northport, ME 04849; 800/234-1713; audbkshf@agate.net. (See coupon.)

Madonna Woods' Piano Course for Christians   (Ages 5 to 11) ✝

This six-level book and two-cassette self-teaching course, developed by an experienced organist and piano teacher, uses church music and Bible-based pieces and text as the instructional material. A parent with a basic knowledge and ability in music can successfully teach his or her child with it. $27. Available from Davidsons Music Publications, 6727 Metcalf, Shawnee Mission, KS 66204; 913/262-4982; Fax 913/722-2980.

Julliard Music Adventure   (Ages 10 and up)

Using this CD-ROM, your student will be introduced to some basic elements of music: rhythm, melody, orchestration, and instrumentation in various musical styles, as he or she solves musical puzzles. Musical terms are defined and illustrated, musical notation is covered and a listening guide is provided for further exploration. Hybrid CD-ROM, THEA0020-CDB $29.95. Available from Learning Services, P.O. Box 10636, Eugene, OR 97440-2636; Western Region: 800/877-9378; Eastern Region: 800/877-3278. (See coupon.)

Making Music   (Ages 4 to 12)

This program presents the components of music aurally and visually to allow children to experience what composing music is like before they begin formal musical training. Allows children to let their imaginations run wild and have fun! Hybrid CD-ROM: VOYA350-CDB, $27.95. Available from Learning Services, P.O. Box 10636, Eugene, OR 97440-2636; Western Region: 800/877-9378; Eastern Region: 800/877-3278. (See coupon.)

Making More Music   (Ages 9 to 18)

This CD-ROM program offers a fun way to compose music. Develop a beat with nine different percussion instruments and create a musical composition while learning about the elements of music including tempo, scales, and dynamics. It offers classic examples to illustrate music fundamentals. Print compositions with an appropriate printer. Hybrid CD-ROM: VOYA8285-CDB, $27.95. Available from Learning Services, P.O. Box 10636, Eugene, OR 97440-2636; Western Region: 800/877-9378; Eastern Region: 800/877-3278. (See coupon.)

Music Programs and Materials

DK JAZZ   (Ages 12 to adult)

This is a DK Books' 216-page hardcover by John Fordham. If your student enjoys jazz, especially if he or she is a musician, this book will be a welcome addition to the home library. Filled with historical b&w as well as full-color photos, time charts, and drawings revealing America's true native musical form. $29.95. Available from DK Family Learning, 11124 N.E. Halsey, Suite 460, Portland, OR 97220; 888/225-3535. (See coupon.)

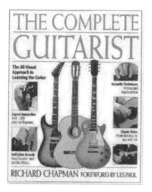

The Complete Guitarist   (Ages 12 to adul)

This 192-page paperback by Richard Chapman, foreword by Les Paul, is suitable for guitarists of any level. It is a complete instruction guide with a completely visual approach. $19.95. Available from DK Family Learning, 11124 N.E. Halsey, Suite 460, Portland, OR 97220; 888/225-3535. (See coupon.)

Music by Neil Ardley, with music by Paul Ruders (Ages 10 to adult)

This 80-page hardcover plus hybrid CD-ROM is an excellent way for your child to learn about music, primarily classical. A clearly written quality DK book filled with beautiful illustrations. $24.95. Available from DK Family Learning, 11124 N.E. Halsey, Suite 460, Portland, OR 97220; 888/225-3535. (See coupon.)

Classical Beginnings   (Ages 7 to adult)

This is a children's monthly newsletter devoted to classical music—its composers, players, pieces, etc. It includes cartoons, fun facts, and anecdotes kids will love. $12 for one year (12 issues). Available from Classical Beginnings, P.O. Box 940670, Simi Valley, CA 93094-0670; 805/522-9800; classical@earthlink.net.

DK The First Noel   (Ages 9 to adult) †

This is a beautiful 32-page hardcover Christmas song book by DK with 13 standard carols (words and music), including "Away in the Manger" and "Silent Night." $12.95. Available from DK Family Learning, 11124 N.E. Halsey, Suite 460, Portland, OR 97220; 888/225-3535. (See coupon.)

Apple Pie Music   (Ages 11 to 12)

This CD-ROM program brings you over 400 complete compositions, spanning nearly 350 years of American history in music. Approximately half of the total comes from archival recordings. A text section illuminates the social and political conditions of each era covered. Includes the music of Native Americans, settlers, revolutionaries, slaves, sailors, loggers, pioneers, the Civil War, and much more. Hybrid CD-ROM: QUEUOO14-CDB, $75. Available from Learning Services, P.O. Box 10636, Eugene, OR 97440-2636; Western Region: 800/877-9378; Eastern Region: 800/877-3278. (See coupon.)

Making Music with Children   (Ages 3 to 11)

Let's Sing! videos (two, 60 min. each) are for children under age 7. *Let's Keep Singing* videos (two, 45 min. each) are for older kids. John Langstaff is a noted music educator, children's author of 24 music books, and host of BBC's school's television series, *Making Music*. These videos capture Langstaff's dedication and enthusiasm for engaging children in music. $24.95 each. Available from The Langstaff Video Project, 685 Santa Barbara Road, Berkeley, CA 94707; 510/452-9335.

Latin Music Through the Ages   (Ages 12 to adult)

This unusual program consists of one 45-minute audiocassette and a 126-page book. Hear a selection of Latin choral music from the medieval, Renaissance, and modern periods performed by the Lafayette Chamber Singers. Accompanying text provides an English translation and background information on each lyric and a commentary on the arrangement. Item #SLT150, $29.50 Available from Audio-Forum, 96 Broad St., Ste. C70, Guilford, CT 06437; 203/453-9794; e-mail: info@audioforum.com; www.audioforum.com. (See coupon.)

Music Programs and Materials

Learning Wrap-Ups: Keyboard Theory (Ages 6 to 12)

The kit includes five different plastic boards with notches for the appropriate values and five bundles of thin yarn. Each board has two different columns of information. The yarn is wound around the plastic board in a particular pattern, right-to-left, and the information in the two columns matches up when done correctly. The correct pattern is embossed on the back of the board. $7.95. Available from Learning Wrap-Ups, 2122 East 6550 South, Ogden, UT 84405; 800/992-4966. (See coupon.)

Rhythm Band Instruments   (Ages 6 to 12)

This company offers a rhythm package of approximately nine instruments including triangles, recorder, castanets, maracas, and others. $24.95. Rhythm Band Instruments, P.O. Box 126 Fort Worth, Texas 76101-0126; 800/424-4724; e-mail: rhythmband@aol.com.

Biographies and Music History Books   (Ages 9 to 12)

Famous Children Series: *Beethoven, Brahms, Bach, Handel,* or *Tchaikovsky;* $5.95 each.

Introducing Beethoven, $7.95; *Introducing Bach* $7.95; *World of Music* $9.95.

TROLL BIOGRAPHIES: *Beethoven* $3.50; *Mozart* $3.50.

SOWER SERIES BIOGRAPHIES: *George F. Handel* $7.99; *Mahalia Jackson* $7.99; *Raggin—The Story of Scott Joplin* $5.95. Available from Excellence in Education, 2640 S. Myrtle Ave., Unit A-7, Monrovia, CA 91016; 626/821-0025; Fax: 626/357-4443; www.excellenceineducation.com. (See coupon.)

A History of Music of the Western World, 1100–1980   (Ages 12 to adult)

This 12-cassette or -CD-ROM collection is like a lecture course on medieval, renaissance, baroque, classical, romantic, modern, contemporary, popular, percussion instruments, reggae and calypso, and English folk music and instruments. Lively discussions by 15 authorities are illustrated with musical examples. 12 Cassesttes, #S11100, $59.95; 12 CD-ROMs, #SCD100, $99.95. Available from Audio-Forum, 96 Broad St., Ste. C70, Guilford, CT 06437; 203/453-9794; e-mail: info@audioforum.com; www.audioforum.com. (See coupon.)

The Joy of Bach (All ages)

This 60-minute video includes staged scenes from Bach's life (filmed on location in German cities) interspersed with performances of his music by violinist Yehudi Menuhin, Larry Adler on harmonica, the St. Thomas Boys Choir of Leipzig, and others. Item #V72338, $19.95 Available from Audio-Forum, 96 Broad St., Ste. C70, Guilford, CT 06437; 203/453-9794; e-mail: info@audioforum.com; www.audioforum.com. (See coupon.)

Kwanzaa Music: A Celebration of Black Cultures in Song (Ages 12 to adult)

This is a CD-ROM/booklet collection of songs of a holiday celebrating the best in people of African descent and their cultures. Includes spiritual, Bahamian junknoo, Zairean pop, and jazz. Languages you hear on the recording include French, Arabic, Spanish, Zulu, Cajun French, and Haitian Creole. Booklet contains in-depth notes on each song. Item #SCD114, $18.95 Available from Audio-Forum, 96 Broad St., Ste. C70, Guilford, CT 06437; 203/453-9794; e-mail: info@audioforum.com; www.audioforum.com. (See coupon.)

Voices of Forgotten Worlds (Ages 12 to adult)

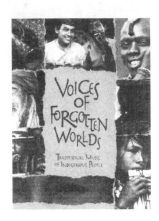

On these two audiocassettes you can experience these unique sounds of the human voice plus many more exotic sounds. Hear Mongolian Tuvan "throat" singing and the eerie, beautiful deep-throated overtone chanting of the Buddhist monks of Tibet. Aborigine didjeridoo music from Australia, Inuit drum songs, polyphonic singing from the Ba-Benjelle Pygmies, too. Includes an illustrated 96-page softcover book. Item #S11380, $29.95. Available from Audio-Forum, 96 Broad St., Ste. C70, Guilford, CT 06437; 203/453-9794; e-mail: info@audioforum.com; www.audioforum.com. (See coupon.)

Instruments Around the World (Ages 9 to adult)

Any serious student of music will welcome this audiocassette of instruments. Represented are the koto (Japanese zither), quena (Andean flute), atumpan (talking drum from Ghana), duda (Hungarian bagpipe), and many others. Item #C11112, $12.95 Available from Audio-Forum, 96 Broad St., Ste. C70, Guilford, CT 06437; 203/453-9794; e-mail: info@audioforum.com; www.audioforum.com. (See coupon.)

William Grant Still: Dean of Afro-American Composers (Ages 9 to adult)

Hear W. G. Still (1885–1978), one of the main American composers of his day, on this audiocassette. He played both oboe and cello in W. C. Handy's band and wrote the original band arrangements of two classics "Beale Street Blues" and "St. Louis Blues." He was the first African-American composer to write a symphony. Side two contains Henry Hadley, Salome. Includes booklet. Item #S11220, $12.95. Available from Audio-Forum, 96 Broad St., Ste. C70, Guilford, CT 06437; 203/453-9794; e-mail: info@audioforum.com; www.audioforum.com. (See coupon.)

Born To Sing   (Ages 12 to adult)

This program with four audiocassettes and a booklet is proven to help you develop quick results in your vocal control, power, and range. It teaches all of the basic and advanced voice techniques and all vocal styles—Broadway, classical, jazz, country, etc. Equivalent to hundreds of hours of private lessons. Item #S01985, $39.95 Available from Audio-Forum, 96 Broad St., Ste. C70, Guilford, CT 06437; 203/453-9794; e-mail: info@audioforum.com; www.audioforum.com. (See coupon.)

Real Music of Native Americans   (Ages 12 to adult)

These archival audiocassette recordings, culled from the Library of Congress, bring the true sounds of some of the American tribes to your ears. Songs of the Kiowa: narrow melodic range and no drums, 37-min. cassette and 21-page booklet, #S11154, $14.95; Songs of the Navajo: songs used in ceremonies, 36-min. cassette and 18-page booklet, #S11153, $14.95; Songs of the Sioux: songs from all three dialect groups, Lakota, Dakota, and Nakota, 2 cassettes, 75 min, and 2 booklets (30 pages total), #S11158, $29.50; Songs from the Iroquois Longhouse: 47-min cassette and 42-page booklet, #S11156, $16.95; Songs of the Apache: featuring the Apache violin, 35-min cassette and 14-page booklet, #S11157, $14.95. Available from Audio-Forum, 96 Broad St., Ste. C70, Guilford, CT 06437; 203/453-9794; e-mail: info@audioforum.com; www.audioforum.com. (See coupon.)

"Family Singing Is Fun" (Learn to Harmonize with the Lester Family) (All ages) ✝

Uplifting songs on four audiocassettes sung a capella (without accompaniment) by the six-member Lesters arranged in two to four parts for your family to memorize and sing together. Lyrics are included. Great ear training and a fun enriching family pastime. Tapes are 22 Traditional Rounds; Traditional Christmas Carols; Homestyle Harmony; Favorite Traditional Hymns. Available from the Lester Family, P.O. Box 203, Joshua Tree, CA 92252; 800/793-5309. (See coupon.)

HOMESTYLE HARMONY
with
The Lester Family

The Music Master Series   (Ages 9 to adult)

These three different CD-ROM or audiocassette collections present the lives and music of many great composers. A narrator discusses the composer's life as his music plays in the background. Following the narration, another 18 to 20 minutes of the composer's music is featured; total of 60 min. Series 1: Bach, Mozart, Chopin, Mendelssohn, Schubert, Schumann, and Grieg. Series 2: Handel, Beethoven, Haydn, Wagner, Vivaldi, Corelli, and Dvorak. Series 3: Tchaikovsky, Brahms, Strauss, Foster, Sousa, Berlioz, and Verdi. audiocassette $25 per series; CD-ROM: $36 per series. Available from Beautiful Feet Books, 139 Main St., Sandwich, MA 02563; 508/833-8626; 800/889-1978; www.bfbooks.com.

Beethoven Lives Upstairs   (Ages 8 to adult)

This audiocassette or CD-ROM tells how a young boy's life is disrupted by the idiosyncracies of his mother's new border—Beethoven, the famous composer. Cassette, $10.95; CD-ROM, $18.95. Available from Beautiful Feet Books, 139 Main St, Sandwich, MA 02563; 508/833-8626; 800/889-1978; www.bfbooks.com. Call for catalog.

Hallelujah, Handel!　(Ages 8 to adult)

This audiocassette or CD-ROM, set in 1750, tells the story of G. F. Handel who performs his tremendous oratorio "The Messiah" to an orphanage in London. A young boy there sings like an angel, but refuses to speak. The great composer helps to heal the boy with music. Cassette, $10.95; CD-ROM, $18.95. Available from Beautiful Feet Books, 139 Main St, Sandwich, MA 02563; 508/833-8626; 800/889-1978; www.bfbooks.com. Call for catalog.

Mr. Bach Comes to Call　(Ages 8 to adult)

On this audiocassette or CD-ROM, Mr. Bach visits a little girl in her living room as she practices his "Minuet in G" at her piano. Cassette, $10.95; CD-ROM, $18.95. Available from Beautiful Feet Books, 139 Main St, Sandwich, MA 02563; 508/833-8626; 800/889-1978; www.bfbooks.com. Call for catalog.

Vivaldi's Ring of Mystery　(Ages 8 to adult)

On this audiocassette or CD-ROM, a young violinist comes to the orphanage where Vivaldi is the music director, searching for clues to her unknown past. Cassette, $10.95; CD-ROM, $18.95. Available from Beautiful Feet Books, 139 Main St, Sandwich, MA 02563; 508/833-8626; 800/889-1978; www.bfbooks.com. Call for catalog.

Mozart's Magic Fantasy　(Ages 8 to adult)

This story on audiocassette or CD-ROM showcases Mozart's music. Cassette, $10.95; CD-ROM, $18.95. Available from Beautiful Feet Books, 139 Main St, Sandwich, MA 02563; 508/833-8626; 800/889-1978; www.bfbooks.com. Call for catalog.

Tchaikovsky Discovers America   (Ages 8 to adult)

This audiocassette or CD-ROM tells the story of the great Russian composer who has come to America to conduct the orchestra at the grand opening of Carnegie Hall in New York and takes an adventure to Niagara Falls. Cassette, $10.95; CD-ROM, $18.95. Available from Beautiful Feet Books, 139 Main St, Sandwich, MA 02563; 508/833-8626; 800/889-1978; www.bfbooks.com. Call for catalog.

Wee Sing America   (Ages 4 to 7)

This famous audiocassette/book program is a great way to teach your child songs of America such as "The Star Spangled Banner," "America the Beautiful," and folk songs of the U.S. Also features readings of the Preambles to the Declaration of Independence and the Constitution. Includes lead sheets with lyrics. $9.95. Available from Beautiful Feet Books, 139 Main St, Sandwich, MA 02563; 508/833-8626; 800/889-1978; www.bfbooks.com. Call for catalog.

Piano Discovery Software   (Ages 8 to adult)

This great CD-ROM-ROM program comes with an overlay miniature keyboard which fits over your computer keyboard and allows you to press "piano" keys which correspond to the appropriate notes in the program. If you have a MIDI keyboard you can plug it through the MIDI interface of your computer instead. Graphics and sound quality are both superb. WIN CD-ROM or MAC CD-ROM, $49.99. Available from Jump! Software, Mountain View, CA 94040; www.jumpmusic.com.

Thinking Skills

Critical Thinking

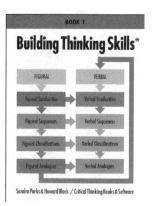

Building Thinking Skills Series   (Ages 9 to adult)

This series of books, designed to aid your child in building analytical thinking skills, has been successfully used by students for over 15 years. The activities are brief, sequenced, and easy to use; they enhance any curriculum. The teacher's manuals include discussion techniques to help you obtain the maximum benefit. Call for more information or to ask questions about using BTS with your current curriculum. Available from Critical Thinking Books & Software, 800/458-4849; Fax: 831/393-3277; www.criticalthinking.com. (See coupon.)

Building Thinking Skills, Primary (Prereading skill level, ages 5 to 8)

The hands-on, figural activities in this volume help prereaders develop reasoning skills in similarities and differences, sequences, classifications, and analogies. Primary book, #MP5213, $23.95; Teacher's Manual, #MP5214, $14.95; Plastic Manipulatives, #MP5215, $26.95; Interlocking Cubes, #MP5216, $14.95; Pattern Blocks, #MP5217, $20.95; Manipulative Bundle, #MP5218, $45. Available from Critical Thinking Books & Software, 800/458-4849; Fax: 831/393-3277; www.criticalthinking.com. (See coupon.)

Building Thinking Skills, Book 1   (Ages 8 to 10) and Book 2   (Ages 10 to 13)

These volumes are the next in the series of developing critical thinking abilities. Among the skills addressed are reading comprehension, following directions, antonyms and synonyms, several types of analogy, deductive reasoning, and mapping and directionality. Book 1, #MP5201, $23.95; Teacher's Manual, #MP5209, $18.95; Book 2, #MP5203, $23.95; Teacher's Manual, #MP5210, $18.95. Available from Critical Thinking Books & Software, 800/458-4849; Fax: 408/393-3277; www.criticalthinking.com. (See coupon.)

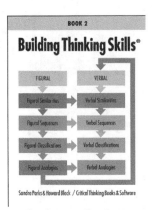

Building Thinking Skills, Book 3: Verbal and Book 3: Figural   (Ages 13 to adult)

These great, easy-to-use activity books help the student to develop a wide variety of reasoning skills, which produces better academic performance in most other subjects. With these volumes, students practice deductive reasoning, denotation/connotation, following/writing directions, map skills, logical connectives, and more. Verbal, #MP5207, $23.95; Teacher's Manual, #MP5212, $18.95; Figural, #MP5205, $23.95; Teacher's Manual, #MP5211, $18.95. Available from Critical Thinking Books & Software, 800/458-4849; Fax: 831/393-3277; www.criticalthinking.com. (See coupon.)

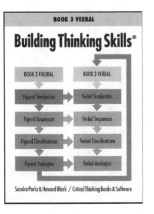

Critical Thinking, Book 1   (Ages 13 to 18); Book 2 (Ages 16 to adult)

Thinking critically is one of the most important—and least-taught—skills. Book 1 presents an introductory course in logic. Book 2 works on higher-level analytical and reasoning skills. The teacher's manuals provide support and include goals, comments, general suggestions, and thorough answers. Book 1, #MP1201, $16.95; Teacher's Manual #MP1202, $9.95; Book 2, #MP1203, $19.95; Teacher's Manual #MP1204, $10.95. Bundle of Books 1 and 2 and TMs #MP1200, $51.95. Available from Critical Thinking Books & Software, 800/458-4849; Fax: 408/393-3277; www.criticalthinking.com. (See coupon.)

Critical Thinking

Organizing My Learning (Ages 10 to 14)

This is a unique student planner, adaptable to any calendar year, with weekly assignments and a record of completed work. It teaches thinking skills, study skills, and thinking habits, which are practiced in three-week cycles. Student Planner, #MP6501, $14.95; Teacher's Manual, #MP6502, $2.95. Available from Critical Thinking Books & Software, 800/458-4849; Fax: 408/393-3277; www.criticalthinking.com. (See coupon.)

Organizing Thinking: Graphic Organizers (Ages 8 to 14)

These graphic book plus CD-ROM organizers will help your student to simplify complex tasks and improve organizational thinking. Book I (for grades 2 to 5) and Book II (for grades 4 to 8) have lessons to reinforce a number of skills, including classifying, sequencing, determining cause and effect, and evaluating. Twenty-three black-line master graphs are also available on disk for nearly any draw and desktop publishing programs but must be used in conjunction with the books. Book I, #MP6801, $34.95; MAC CD-ROM #MP6803, $19.95; WIN CD-ROM #MP6806, $19.95; Book II, #MP6802, $34.95; MAC CD-ROM #MP6804, $19.95; WIN CD-ROM #MP6807, $19.95. Available from Critical Thinking Books & Software, 800/458-4849; Fax: 408/393-3277; www.criticalthinking.com. (See coupon.)

Mind Benders Books (Ages 8 to adult)

These fun challenging books are perfect for sharpening the deductive reasoning skills. Clues are provided and you must deduce the answer. These books are effective for students with attention difficulties and great for adult practice in deductive reasoning, as well. All books are $7.95: *Warm-Up* (ages 5 to 8); A-level, four books (ages 8 to adult); B-level, four books (ages 12 to adult); C-level, three books (ages 13 to adult). Also available is *Instructions and Detailed Solutions* (ages 5 to adult), $10.95. Entire set, $89.95 Available from Critical Thinking Books & Software, 800/458-4849; Fax: 408/393-3277; www.criticalthinking.com. (See coupon.)

Mind Benders Software   (Ages 8 to Adult)

This is the software version of the Mind Benders series of books to sharpen deductive reasoning in all ages from. All disks are 3½ inches. $64.95 each. Available from Critical Thinking Books & Software, 800/458-4849; Fax: 408/393-3277; www.criticalthinking.com. (See coupon.)

Cornell Critical Thinking Tests   (Ages 11 to Adult)

If you want to test your student's critical thinking skills, these assessment test booklets will help you. Cornell tests are useful tools for general evaluation. Level X, for age 11 to college, has 72 items, multiple choice; Level Z is advanced secondary to adult, 52 items, multiple choice. Each level has a set of 10 test booklets. Level X, #MP5501, $16.95; Level Z, #MP5502, $16.95; Teacher's Manual for both levels, $6.95. Available from Critical Thinking Books & Software, 800/458-4849; Fax: 408/393-3277; www.criticalthinking.com. (See coupon.)

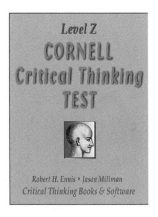

Cornell Critical Thinking Tests Software   (Ages 11 to Adult)

The same critical thinking evaluation tests available in booklet form are also available in this CD-ROM format. These tests for secondary students are self-timed, self-graded, and self-administered and yield printable reports. Level × (Age 11 to Adult), WIN CD-ROM: #MP5507; MAC CD-ROM: #MP5506; $64.95 each. Level Z (advanced secondary to adult), WIN CD-ROM: #MP5509; MAC CD-ROM: #MP5508, $64.95 each. Available from Critical Thinking Books & Software, 800/458-4849; Fax: 408/393-3277; www.criticalthinking.com. (See coupon.)

Creative Problem-Solving Activities   (Ages 9 to adult)

These activity book packages come in three levels: A1 for ages 9 to 11; B1 for ages 12 to 14; and C1 for ages 15 to adult. Each level contains 150 activities in seven different skill categories per book. Teaching suggestions and answers are included. With these fun and easy-to-use activities, your child will become a fluent and flexible problem solver. Improves creative and critical thinking. Level A1, #MP2201, $12.95; Level B1, #MP2202, $12.95; Level C1, #MP2203, $12.95. Available from Critical Thinking Books & Software, 800/458-4849; Fax: 408/393-3277; www.criticalthinking.com. (See coupon.)

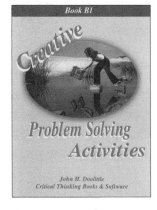

Critical Thinking

Fun Stuff

Arts and Crafts Supplies

Sax Aurora Watercolor Set   (Family use)

Designed with the student in mind! These attractively packaged sets have 11-inch diameter cakes of opaque, nontoxic watercolors set in sturdy plastic boxes, brush included. 12-Color Set, Item #146-0021, $3.85. Available from Sax Arts & Crafts, P.O. Box 510710, New Berlin, WI 53151-0710; 414/784-6880; 800/558-6696; e-mail: infor@saxarts.com; www.saxarts.com. (See coupon.)

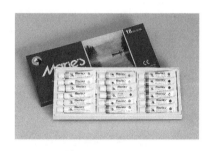

Tube Watercolors   (Family use)

This is an excellent value on high-quality student-grade watercolors that are certified nontoxic. Strong pigmentation delivers bright transparent colors with good lightfastness. Tubes are 0.4 oz. (12 ml) size and include white. Set of 18, Item #147-2042, $9.95. Available from Sax Arts & Crafts, P.O. Box 510710, New Berlin, WI 53151-0710; 414/784-6880; 800/558-6696; e-mail: infor@saxarts.com; www.saxarts.com. (See coupon.)

Glow-in-the-Dark Activity Paint Set   (Family use)

Fun, washable paint can be applied to almost any surface to safely light up in the dark. This water-based paint can be used with a brush or fingers to bring creative fun to classroom activities, craft projects, holidays, and parties. Contains six ¾-oz. (20 ml) jars of nontoxic paint in yellow, orange, red, violet, blue, and green. A 7¼-inch bristle brush is included. Item #160-6037, $10.50. Available from Sax Arts & Crafts, P.O. Box 510710, New Berlin, WI 53151-0710; 414/784-6880; 800/558-6696; e-mail: infor@saxarts.com; www.saxarts.com. (See coupon.)

Cave Painting Kit   (Ages 9 to adult)

Reconstruct the cave paintings of Lascaux with this fascinating interdisciplinary activity combining art, history, and sociology. Kit contains enough nontoxic materials to make 20 to 25 plaques measuring 6" × 8" × ⅜" thick. The kit includes a set of six half-pint Versatemp paints in "prehistoric paint colors" (red, yellow, peach, brown, black, and white), two 3-lb. bags of Sculptamold, and a project sheet. Item #64-0788, $24.95. Available from Sax Arts & Crafts, P.O. Box 510710, New Berlin, WI 53151-0710; 414/784-6880; 800/558-6696; e-mail: infor@saxarts.com; www.saxarts.com. (See coupon.)

Egg-Handled Brushes (Set of 5)   (Family use)

Quality brush set features egg-shaped natural hardwood handles with a flat side to prevent rolling. The easy-to-grasp, clear-coated handles are suitable for all ages and ideal for students with special needs. Unique ergonomic design allows for easy painting of vertical surfaces. This set of five synthetic golden taklon brushes with black enameled ferrules includes popular sizes and styles: rounds in 2, 6, and 10; and flats in 6 and 10. Item #201-5444, $25.95. Available from Sax Arts & Crafts, P.O. Box 510710, New Berlin, WI 53151-0710; 414/784-6880; 800/558-6696; e-mail: infor@saxarts.com; www.saxarts.com. (See coupon.)

Sax White Bristle Brush Assortment (Set of 24) (Family use)

This extremely versatile classroom set of 24 includes assorted sizes from 1 to 12 in flats and rounds. Clear-coated, short-handled brushes have seamless aluminum ferrules. Item #275-0297, $19.95. Available from Sax Arts & Crafts, P.O. Box 510710, New Berlin, WI 53151-0710; 414/784-6880; 800/558-6696; e-mail: infor@saxarts.com; www.saxarts.com. (See coupon.)

Arts and Crafts Supplies

Fiskars Paper Crimper   (Family use)

Take your paper crafting projects into the next dimension with this fun-to-use tool. Crimps a variety of papers, including card stock, foil, bond, and construction paper. Perfect for creating a unique rippled or corrugated effect on all kinds of paper up to 6½ inches wide. Comfortable and easy to operate—very little hand pressure is required. Item #315-2600, $16.95. Available from Sax Arts & Crafts, P.O. Box 510710, New Berlin, WI 53151-0710; 414/784-6880; 800/558-6696; e-mail: infor@saxarts.com; www.saxarts.com. (See coupon.)

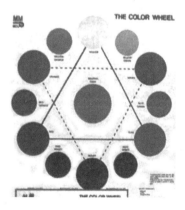

Sax 4-Ounce Mixing Cups   (Family use)

This package contains 100 durable white cups that are ideal for mixing paints, dyes, powdered tempera, inks, and glazes. Versatile small-size cups (3" × 1½") can hold watercolor or tempera cakes, beads, sequins, glitter, pins, or be used in dozens of other ways in your art room or craft center. Item #300-1351, $7.95. Available from Sax Arts & Crafts, P.O. Box 510710, New Berlin, WI 53151-0710; 414/784-6880; 800/558-6696; e-mail: infor@saxarts.com; www.saxarts.com. (See coupon.)

Color Wheel   (Family use)

Quality card-stock charts highlight the primary and secondary colors and teach color complements and color harmony. Mixing guides are printed on the back of these large (18¾" × 21") charts. Item #300-2508, $7.99. Available from Sax Arts & Crafts, P.O. Box 510710, New Berlin, WI 53151-0710; 414/784-6880; 800/558-6696; e-mail: infor@saxarts.com; www.saxarts.com. (See coupon.)

Color Mixing Recipe Cards   (Family use)

Thirteen double-sided coated cards show recipes for over 450 color combinations for oil and acrylic paint, and provide a color guide index covering more than 1,100 commonly used and generically labeled color names. Easy-to-understand instructions on tints, tones, and shades; complementary colors; mixing flesh tones; and five pages of color theory are featured. Laminated color-mixing grid for accurate paint measurement is also included. Item #300-2772, $7.95. Available from Sax Arts & Crafts, P.O. Box 510710, New Berlin, WI 53151-0710; 414/784-6880; 800/558-6696; e-mail: infor@saxarts.com; www.saxarts.com. (See coupon.)

Artist's Leaning Bridge   (Family use)

Lean on this 24-inch bridge instead of your work! Transparent bridge allows you to see your work at all times, while keeping hands clean and work smudge-free. Also serves as a 3-inch-wide straightedge when painting lines with brush or pen. Use with all wet or dry mediums. Item #300-2995, $22.95. Available from Sax Arts & Crafts, P.O. Box 510710, New Berlin, WI 53151-0710; 414/784-6880; 800/558-6696; e-mail: infor@saxarts.com; www.saxarts.com. (See coupon.)

Freshwater Rinse Well   (Family use)

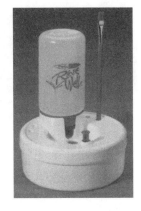

A plastic bottle holds 20 ounces of fresh water, while the base features a well for brush cleaning and a reservoir to hold used water. Press a button to drain used water and the well automatically refills with a clean supply. The well is ideal for watercoloring, acrylic painting, photo retouching, or crafts—a sensational idea for studios and small work areas. Item #300-381, $17.95. Available from Sax Arts & Crafts, P.O. Box 510710, New Berlin, WI 53151-0710; 414/784-6880; 800/558-6696; e-mail: infor@saxarts.com; www.saxarts.com. (See coupon.)

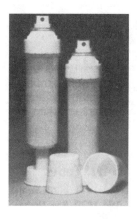

Safety Spray Aerosol Bottle   (Family use)

Fine, directed, push-button spray action without propellants! Transforms spray application of any media! Sprays paint, ink, dye, fixatives, or finishes without noxious, toxic fumes. A revolutionary push-button action dispenses the media of your choice. The bottle, which features one-piece construction, will spray approximately 3 fluid oz. of media. Item #310-9600 $3.95. Available from Sax Arts & Crafts, P.O. Box 510710, New Berlin, WI 53151-0710; 414/784-6880; 800/558-6696; e-mail: infor@saxarts.com; www.saxarts.com. (See coupon.)

Hot Air Balloon Activity Kit   (Ages 9 to adult)

It really flies! Making it takes only a couple of hours, and the result is a 5-foot-tall balloon. Decorate the balloon with authentic historical designs (included) or create your own aerial art. A couple of hair dryers or a popcorn popper will provide the heat needed for liftoff. Item #312-7461, $21.95. Available from Sax Arts & Crafts, P.O. Box 510710, New Berlin, WI 53151-0710; 414/784-6880; 800/558-6696; e-mail: infor@saxarts.com; www.saxarts.com. (See coupon.)

Fiskars Circle Cutter   (Family use)

The adjustable cutting arm—labeled with inch and metric markings—enables you to cut circles from 1 to 8 inches on paper, photos, cardstock, and other thin materials. The clear base allows you to see the exact position of the cut for perfect placement. You can choose either the needlepoint for precise realignment or the gripper foot for circles without pinholes. Item, #313-0101, $19.95; replacement Blades, two per package, Item #314-0100, $5. Sax Arts & Crafts, P.O. Box 510710, New Berlin, WI 53151-0710; 414/784-6880; 800/558-6696; e-mail: infor@saxarts.com; www.saxarts.com. (See coupon.)

Prang Poster Pastellos   (Family use)

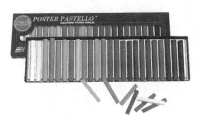

Slightly firmer than regular pastels, as well as grit-free and streak-resistant, nontoxic Prang Pastellos blend easily for full, rich coverage on any paper surface. Always a school favorite! 24-color set, round sticks ($3\frac{1}{4}$" × $\frac{3}{8}$"), Item #321-0382, $13.59; 12-color set, square sticks ($2\frac{1}{8}$" × $\frac{5}{16}$"), Item #321-0390, $6.29; 24-color set, square sticks, Item #321-0358, $9.39. Available from Sax Arts & Crafts, P.O. Box 510710, New Berlin, WI 53151-0710; 414/784-6880; 800/558-6696; e-mail: infor@saxarts.com; www.saxarts.com. (See coupon.)

Yarka Pastel Sets in Wooden Storage Boxes (Family use)

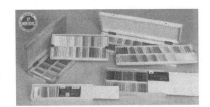

Medium-soft sticks lay down exceptionally lightfast color. Made from a nontoxic, time-tested recipe of durable, finely ground mineral and earth pigments combined with an exacting amount of Charsov Yar clay, the result is remarkable quality in professional-grade pastels. Full-sized sticks ($2\frac{1}{2}$" × $\frac{3}{8}$") come in a varnished wooden box for years of protected, elegant use. 30-color set, Item #321-3519, $29.95; 60-color set, Item #321-3527, $58.95; 130-color set, Item #321-3535, $124.95. Available from Sax Arts & Crafts, P.O. Box 510710, New Berlin, WI 53151-0710; 414/784-6880; 800/558-6696; e-mail: infor@saxarts.com; www.saxarts.com. (See coupon.)

True Draw System (Schoolpack of 6)   (Family use)

Using the nontoxic, odorless, water-based Aquawipe dry-erase marker, students learn to sketch what they see through the clear acrylic sheet. Students quickly learn about perspective, proportion, and relationships. This system is only a step away from drawing on paper. Pack kit includes six 18" × 24" × $\frac{1}{8}$" acrylic sheets, six Aquawipe black markers, and instructions and tips. Item #321-7460, $79.95. Available from Sax Arts & Crafts, P.O. Box 510710, New Berlin, WI 53151-0710; 414/784-6880; 800/558-6696; e-mail: infor@saxarts.com; www.saxarts.com. (See coupon.)

Gold and Silver Metallic Pencils   (Family use)

Draw or write in shimmering gold and sparkling silver. Elegant pencils yield dramatic effects—especially on black paper—and are ideal for scrapbooks, invitations, memory books, crafts, and fine art projects. A wonderful alternative to pens, these pencils are permanent, acid-free, and nontoxic. Package contains two pencils, one each in gold and silver, and a sharpener. Item #322-5851, $2.79. Available from Sax Arts & Crafts, P.O. Box 510710, New Berlin, WI 53151-0710; 414/784-6880; 800/558-6696; e-mail: infor@saxarts.com; www.saxarts.com. (See coupon.)

Watercolor Pencil Sets   (Family use)

Superior quality, water-soluble, colored pencils feature the finest pigments for rich color saturation and strong lightfastness. Clear, clean strokes of color are transformed into watercolor effects with the touch of a wet brush. This nontoxic set is packed in a sturdy metal storage box. Set of 12, Item #322-8608, $12.60. Available from Sax Arts & Crafts, P.O. Box 510710, New Berlin, WI 53151-0710; 414/784-6880; 800/558-6696; e-mail: infor@saxarts.com; www.saxarts.com. (See coupon.)

Prismacolor Colorless Blender Pencils (Family use)

This special formula is designed to soften hard edges, lighten, or blend colors. The effect is soft and subtle, moving just the right amount of color for a smooth, blended look. The clean laydown can be layered on top of any color without cloudy buildup—the colors below remain bright and brilliant. Colorless, nontoxic Blender works well with the other Prismacolor pencil products. Box of 12, Item #322-9622, $12. Available from Sax Arts & Crafts, P.O. Box 510710, New Berlin, WI 53151-0710; 414/784-6880; 800/558-6696; e-mail: infor@saxarts.com; www.saxarts.com. (See coupon.)

Faber-Castell 9000 Pencils—12-Piece Art Set (Family use)

This fine-quality set is specially assembled for drawing students, artists, and designers. Strong polymerized leads offer less breakage and exhibit even density throughout. Each set provides an ideal range of 12 different degrees of eraserless, sharpened, enameled pencils in a protective metal box. Set includes HB through 8B, plus F, H and 2H. Item #323-0547, $11.25. Available from Sax Arts & Crafts, P.O. Box 510710, New Berlin, WI 53151-0710; 414/784-6880; 800/558-6696; e-mail: infor@saxarts.com; www.saxarts.com. (See coupon.)

Dry Erase Boards   (Family use)

This package contains six 9" × 12" dry erase boards. Item #327-2812, $8.95. Available from Sax Arts & Crafts, P.O. Box 510710, New Berlin, WI 53151-0710; 414/784-6880; 800/558-6696; e-mail: infor@saxarts.com; www.saxarts.com. (See coupon.)

Pen with Metallic Ink   (Family use)

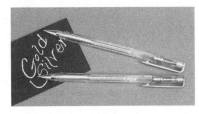

Add the glint of gold or the sparkle of silver to your drawings, announcements, special occasion cards, and other items. Gleaming metallic highlights create sensational effects when used on dark colors. Permanent, waterproof, and fade-resistant nontoxic ink glides on smoothly. Medium point pen has stainless steel tip for durability, while the hexagonal grip provides extra comfort and control. Gold, Item #327-4602, $1.49; Silver, Item #327-4610, $1.49. Available from Sax Arts & Crafts, P.O. Box 510710, New Berlin, WI 53151-0710; 414/784-6880; 800/558-6696; e-mail: infor@saxarts.com; www.saxarts.com. (See coupon.)

Sakura Gelly Roll Lightning Pen   (Family use)

Get this set of five brilliant nontoxic colors with the added attraction of a gleaming metallic silver outline. The precision tungsten ball glides smoothly across the paper, producing a fine, 0.3 mm line that's both waterproof and fade resistant. Set includes pink, purple, green, and two blue ink pens—all with silver outline. Item #327-6441, $4.95. Available from Sax Arts & Crafts, P.O. Box 510710, New Berlin, WI 53151-0710; 414/784-6880; 800/558-6696; e-mail: infor@saxarts.com; www.saxarts.com. (See coupon.)

Phantom Line Lettering & Drawing Instrument (Family use)

Trace or transfer any design with this unique, optical instrument! It reflects images onto any writing, painting, or drawing surface! Just attach a picture or guideline sheet to your Phantom Line and observe the reflected image through a plastic window. Includes one Phantom Line 500 (6 × 9-½-inch window) and three 8½" × 11" sheets, a blank transparency, a ruled sheet for writing, and a guideline sheet for calligraphy. Item #332-0033, $37.95. Available from Sax Arts & Crafts, P.O. Box 510710, New Berlin, WI 53151-0710; 414/784-6880; 800/558-6696; e-mail: infor@saxarts.com; www.saxarts.com. (See coupon.)

Unruly Rulers   (Family use)

This is a set of four templates for tracing and creating stencils and French curves for imaginative drawings, exciting designs, and abstract works of art. Simply pop out the interior shapes and start experimenting—assemble shapes to form pictures. Paints, pencils, markers, and crayons all work great with Unruly Rulers. Translucent tools are made of tough polyethylene and rinse clean with water. Item #334-2433, $6.49. Available from Sax Arts & Crafts, P.O. Box 510710, New Berlin, WI 53151-0710; 414/784-6880; 800/558-6696; e-mail: infor@saxarts.com; www.saxarts.com. (See coupon.)

Drawing Boards   (Family use)

This ¼-inch-thick laminated art board will perform the same functions that more costly drawing boards perform. This inexpensive board is great for sketching, easy-to-carry, durable, and lightweight. Item #334-4454 (18" × 24"), $9.95; #334-4462 (20" × 31"), $10.95. Available from Sax Arts & Crafts, P.O. Box 510710, New Berlin, WI 53151-0710; 414/784-6880; 800/558-6696; e-mail: infor@saxarts.com; www.saxarts.com. (See coupon.)

Sketch Box with Tabletop Easel   (Family use)

This lightweight, carry-along, natural wood box features a mixing palette and five interior bins for supplies. The back of the box converts to an easel, and with a simple adjustment, it holds canvases 5 to 27 inches tall. Luggage-type carrying handle provides comfortable portability. Box measures 13" × 17" × 3" with a 12" × 16" palette. Item #334-4470, $39.95. Available from Sax Arts & Crafts, P.O. Box 510710, New Berlin, WI 53151-0710; 414/784-6880; 800/558-6696; e-mail: infor@saxarts.com; www.saxarts.com. (See coupon.)

The Pen Pal (Light Box)   (Family use)

This 60" × 90" light box is complete with a 15-watt lightbulb, on/off switch, and six-foot cord. Item #334-5121, $16.95. Available from Sax Arts & Crafts, P.O. Box 510710, New Berlin, WI 53151-0710; 414/784-6880; 800/558-6696; e-mail: infor@saxarts.com; www.saxarts.com. (See coupon.)

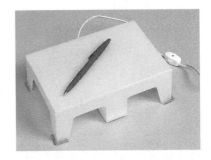

Safe-T 8-Piece Drawing Set   (Family use)

The perfect compact kit to carry into art, math, and science classes. Contains an mmArc compass, six-inch straightedge ruler, two triangles, four-inch protractor, pencil, sharpener, and eraser in a hinged-lid storage case with transparent cover. Instructional brochure gives tips on drawing circles and constructing artistic designs through geometry. Item #334-8091, $6.95. Available from Sax Arts & Crafts, P.O. Box 510710, New Berlin, WI 53151-0710; 414/784-6880; 800/558-6696; e-mail: infor@saxarts.com; www.saxarts.com. (See coupon.)

Nature Print Paper   (Family use)

Create beautiful prints without ink or presses! Nature Print Paper (5½" × 7½") creates prints by sunlight! Images appear in minutes—prints are white on blue. Use any flat natural or man-made object for exciting results. Place on paper, expose to sun, rinse in water, dry. Complete instructions detailing how to use this non-toxic paper are included. Package of 15 Sheets, Item #335-2143, $4.60; package of 30 sheets, Item 335-2150, $7.90. Available from Sax Arts & Crafts, P.O. Box 510710, New Berlin, WI 53151-0710; 414/784-6880; 800/558-6696; e-mail: infor@saxarts.com; www.saxarts.com. (See coupon.)

Fish Print Models   (Family use)

Originally, Japanese fishermen made fish prints to record the size and species of the fish they caught. Fish replicas may be rolled with paint or printing ink using a foam brayer. Realistic fish prints can then be done on Sax Print Paper, rice paper, fabric, T-shirts, and more. Stimulate learning about Japanese culture and fish anatomy while facilitating exciting art projects. 9-inch trout, Item #339-2222; 9-inch perch, Item #339-2255; 8-inch bass, Item #339-2230; 7½-inch blue gill, Item #339-2263; 8-inch starfish, Item #339-2248; 4½-inch sand dollar, Item # 339-2271, $9.95 each. Available from Sax Arts & Crafts, P.O. Box 510710, New Berlin, WI 53151-0710; 414/784-6880; 800/558-6696; e-mail: infor@saxarts.com; www.saxarts.com. (See coupon.)

Speedball Complete Silkscreen Unit   (Family use)

This complete 10" × 14" (inside measurement) heavy-duty frame with fabric attached is ready to use, conveniently mounted on a base with hinges and kick leg. Item #348-1009, $30.95. Available from Sax Arts & Crafts, P.O. Box 510710, New Berlin, WI 53151-0710; 414/784-6880; 800/558-6696; e-mail: infor@saxarts.com; www.saxarts.com. (See coupon.)

Paasche Hobby Kit   (Ages 13 to adult)

Model H includes single-action external mix airbrush, medium #3 color assembly and needle, two 12-oz. bottle assemblies, 6-foot × ⅛-inch airhose with coupling, airbrush hanger, wrench, Allen wrench, and airbrush lesson book. Item #390-1071, $46.55. Available from Sax Arts & Crafts, P.O. Box 510710, New Berlin, WI 53151-0710; 414/784-6880; 800/558-6696; e-mail: infor@saxarts.com; www.saxarts.com. (See coupon.)

Glow-in-the-Dark Paper   (Family use)

Exciting glow-in-the-dark paper cuts, folds, feels like regular paper, but it has an advanced coating that glows in the dark. After being exposed to direct light, it glows brightly for 30–60 minutes. The 8½" × 11" sheets are reusable and rechargeable. Use this fantastic paper for mask-making, costumes, party decorations, mobiles, or anything you can imagine. Package includes 30 nontoxic sheets. Item # 407-9018, $23.95. Available from Sax Arts & Crafts, P.O. Box 510710, New Berlin, WI 53151-0710; 414/784-6880; 800/558-6696; e-mail: infor@saxarts.com; www.saxarts.com. (See coupon.)

Pocket Sketchbook   (Family use)

This pocket sketchbook can go everywhere with you! The spiral-bound book has sturdy board backing and contains 80 sheets of 3½" × 4¾", 60-lb. medium-tooth drawing paper. It's made to comfortably fit a back pocket or handbag. 80-sheet pad, Item #411-1407, $2.99. Available from Sax Arts & Crafts, P.O. Box 510710, New Berlin, WI 53151-0710; 414/784-6880; 800/558-6696; e-mail: infor@saxarts.com; www.saxarts.com. (See coupon.)

Rice Paper   (Family use)

This white, acid-free rice paper in convenient 11-inch × 60-foot rolls is ideal for a variety of uses, including creating large Sumi paintings. Excellent as a dry media drawing/sketching paper, as well as woodblock printing. Retains its shape even when used in a wet-on-wet technique. Item #415-0033, $15. Available from Sax Arts & Crafts, P.O. Box 510710, New Berlin, WI 53151-0710; 414/784-6880; 800/558-6696; e-mail: infor@saxarts.com; www.saxarts.com. (See coupon.)

Imperial Sekishu   (Family use)

This heavy-weight rice paper (24" × 39") is handmade of a Kozo/sulphite mix and is acid-free for permanent, non-yellowing display of print techniques, drawings, and watercolors. White, Item #415-0108, $6.08. Available from Sax Arts & Crafts, P.O. Box 510710, New Berlin, WI 53151-0710; 414/784-6880; 800/558-6696; e-mail: infor@saxarts.com; www.saxarts.com. (See coupon.)

Wild Things Project Paper Rolls   (Family use)

Use nature's boldest graphics in collages or apply as faux finishes to vases, boxes, and frames; create paper clothing, accessories, and jewelry. Each pattern reverses to a solid color for more variety. This product comes in 30-inch × 20-foot rolls. Natural Zebra, Item #415-4019, $14.89; Birch Bark, Item #415-4027, $14.89; Natural Jaguar, Item #415-4035, $14.89. Available from Sax Arts & Crafts, P.O. Box 510710, New Berlin, WI 53151-0710; 414/784-6880; 800/558-6696; e-mail: infor@saxarts.com; www.saxarts.com. (See coupon.)

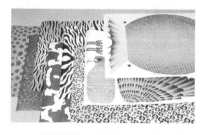

Really Big Animal Skins Paper   (Family use)

This 64-sheet package contains extra-big (23" × 35") realistic "animal skin" papers in eight different designs to create murals, costumes, large displays, mobiles, and more. Activity guide is included. Item #415-4050, $6.99. Available from Sax Arts & Crafts, P.O. Box 510710, New Berlin, WI 53151-0710; 414/784-6880; 800/558-6696; e-mail: infor@saxarts.com; www.saxarts.com. (See coupon.)

Hand-Embossed Paper Kit   (Ages to 13 to adult)

Create attractive embossed images without using costly presses, metal plates, or chemicals. Simply cut design in stencil board, lay paper over stencil, place on light table or window, then press design into paper with burnishers. Kit includes six 3-piece sets of burnishers; twenty-four 9" × 12" stencil boards; 20 sheets each of 12¼" × 15¼" lightweight, medium-weight, and heavy-weight embossing paper; small lettering guide, and instructions. Item #416-0644, $39.95. Available from Sax Arts & Crafts, P.O. Box 510710, New Berlin, WI 53151-0710; 414/784-6880; 800/558-6696; e-mail: infor@saxarts.com; www.saxarts.com. (See coupon.)

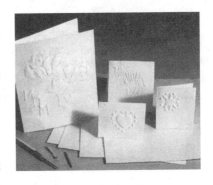

Bug Paper Assortment (Package of 40 Sheets) (Family use)

Use these colorful, 8½" × 11" papers to put together lots of creepy crawlies or flying bugs. Pair up "bugs" with a science project for a cross-curricular learning experience. Eight designs to make spiders, worms, ladybugs, dragonflies, bumblebees, and more. Cut the bug shapes and add faces, legs, antennae, and wings. Invent new insects by combining different shapes and papers. Item #417-0759, $4.59. Available from Sax Arts & Crafts, P.O. Box 510710, New Berlin, WI 53151-0710; 414/784-6880; 800/558-6696; e-mail: infor@saxarts.com; www.saxarts.com. (See coupon.)

Fossil Rubbing Plates   (Family use)

Watch as fascinating fossil shapes appear before your eyes! Simply place one of the 7" × 7" plastic templates under a sheet of paper and gently rub with crayons, pastels, or pencils to reveal striking fossil designs. Excellent for cross-curricular projects combining art, biology, history, and animal studies. Intriguing fossil shapes include amphibians, reptiles, birds, fish, dragonflies, sea creatures, and plant life. Item #417-2540, $6.49. Available from Sax Arts & Crafts, P.O. Box 510710, New Berlin, WI 53151-0710; 414/784-6880; 800/558-6696; e-mail: infor@saxarts.com; www.saxarts.com. (See coupon.)

Metallic Peel and Stick Paper   (Family use)

Gleaming vinyl paper exhibits a smooth, mirror-like finish that adds eye-catching excitement to jewelry, collages, masks, stage-craft, displays, holiday trims, and fillet work on matting. Special adhesive backing allows repositioning. The paper, which cuts cleanly with knife or scissors, comes in a package containing three 20" × 24" sheets. Silver, Item #426-0410, $6.95; Gold, Item #426-0428, $6.95. Available from Sax Arts & Crafts, P.O. Box 510710, New Berlin, WI 53151-0710; 414/784-6880; 800/558-6696; e-mail: infor@saxarts.com; www.saxarts.com. (See coupon.)

Computer-Generated Origami Paper   (Family use)

Modernize the ancient art of paperfolding! As you work with these hi-tech computer-generated papers, you will see new and interesting patterns emerge with each fold. Package contains 48 (6-inch) squares. Folder's Fantasy includes six designs in four colors, Item #427-5335, $5.30; Star Weave has two designs in four colors, Item #427-5343, $4.30. Available from Sax Arts & Crafts, P.O. Box 510710, New Berlin, WI 53151-0710; 414/784-6880; 800/558-6696; e-mail: infor@saxarts.com; www.saxarts.com. (See coupon.)

Building Design Patterned Paper   (Family use)

Create model homes of your own with this exciting assortment of paper! Choose the style and decor you want for every room from the eight interior and exterior designs—including great looks for wallpaper, carpeting, tile, wood, and brick. This paper is also ideal for paper sculpture or origami. Package includes 40 sheets in 8½" × 11" size as well as a resource guide. Item #427-5509, $4.59. Available from Sax Arts & Crafts, P.O. Box 510710, New Berlin, WI 53151-0710; 414/784-6880; 800/558-6696; e-mail: infor@saxarts.com; www.saxarts.com. (See coupon.)

Scratch-Brite Metallic Gold Scratchboard   (Family use)

This package of contains ten 8½" × 11" sheets of fine quality, heavy-duty, pre-inked scratchboard with added drama. The gleaming gold contrasts beautifully against the velvety black coating adding luster and scintillation to the art. Item #431-0777, $4.99. Available from Sax Arts & Crafts, P.O. Box 510710, New Berlin, WI 53151-0710; 414/784-6880; 800/558-6696; e-mail: infor@saxarts.com; www.saxarts.com. (See coupon.)

Drawing for Older Children & Teens   (Ages 10 to adult)

This 223-page softcover by Brookes includes 32 full-color and numerous b&w illustrations, plus proportion, perspective, special effects, and more. A special section for educators discusses drawing as a tool to develop self-expression and self-esteem. Lavishly illustrated with examples by students. Item #570-0422, $15.95. Available from Sax Arts & Crafts, P.O. Box 510710, New Berlin, WI 53151-0710; 414/784-6880; 800/558-6696; e-mail: infor@saxarts.com; www.saxarts.com. (See coupon.)

Compass Constructing Designs: Using a Compass and a Ruler   (Ages 10 to 12)

This 89-page softcover with b&w illustrations by Harst and Wiederhold helps students appreciate the beauty of geometric designs while strengthening their understanding of geometric concepts and vocabulary. Students gain satisfaction from creating works of art through the use of active mathematics. Item #570-0976, $10.95. Available from Sax Arts & Crafts, P.O. Box 510710, New Berlin, WI 53151-0710; 414/784-6880; 800/558-6696; e-mail: infor@saxarts.com. www.saxarts.com. (See coupon.)

Arts and Crafts Supplies

Create-A-Timeline Panels (Blank)   (Family use)

Timelines can be developed for many courses of study—ideal for art, history, literature, science, and social studies applications. Set includes six 27" × 13" panels; when joined they measure over 13 feet long. Pictures, articles, and artwork can be taped or glued to the timeline, then easily peeled off the special laminated surface. Teacher's guide and dry-erase marker are included. Item #581-0692, $19.95. Available from Sax Arts & Crafts, P.O. Box 510710, New Berlin, WI 53151-0710; 414/784-6880; 800/558-6696; e-mail: infor@saxarts.com; www.saxarts.com. (See coupon.)

Art History Poster Sets   (Family use)

Printed on heavy stock with pertinent background information and a short biography of the artist, these special poster sets feature 19" × 25" full-color reproductions of some of the world's most important masterpieces. Each set includes a teacher's guide with suggested activities and additional information. *Masterworks of Art*: Rembrandt, Toulouse-Lautrec, Picasso, Stuart, da Vinci, Cassatt, van Gogh, and Matisse, Item #581-1922, $19.95; *The Impressionists*: Renoir, Monet, Pissarro, and Manet, Item #581-1930, $44.95; *20th-Century Masterpieces*: Cezanne, Matisse, Hopper, Sloan, Picasso, Rothko, O'Keeffe, Kandinsky, Miro, and Dali, Item #581-1914, $36.95. Available from Sax Arts & Crafts, P.O. Box 510710, New Berlin, WI 53151-0710; 414/784-6880; 800/558-6696; e-mail: infor@saxarts.com; www.saxarts.com. (See coupon.)

Art Image Mini Kits   (Family use)

These sets of 30 small 5½" × 8½" full-color prints are laminated on both sides—the ideal size and durability for hands-on activities. It includes a teacher's guide. Kit 1 includes Cassatt, Gauguin, Klee, Picasso, and others, Item #581-6012; Kit 2 includes Calder, Hopper, Kandinsky, Stella, and others, Item #581-6020; Kit 3 includes Chagall, de Kooning, Pollock, Rembrandt, and others, Item #581-6038; Kit 4 includes Bingham, O'Keeffe, Rousseau, van Gogh, and others, Item #581-6046; Kit 5 includes Bruegel, Degas, Homer, Nevelson, and others, Item #581-6053; Kit 6 includes Botticelli, Feininger, Lichtenstein, Rothko, and others, Item #581-6061, $21.05 each kit. Master Set (all 6 kits), Item #581-5485, $119.95. Available from Sax Arts & Crafts, P.O. Box 510710, New Berlin, WI 53151-0710; 414/784-6880; 800/558-6696; e-mail: infor@saxarts.com; www.saxarts.com. (See coupon.)

Art Bulletin Board Pack Set of four Posters
(Ages 14 to adult)

Everything a teacher will need to create an artistic, eye-catching bulletin board. These four 17" × 22" posters feature realistic color portraits and brief biographies of 12 artists from Michelangelo and da Vinci to Georgia O'Keeffe and Andy Warhol. Includes eight activity cards containing challenging extension projects and corresponding headings for displaying student work. Item #581-8000, $6.95. Available from Sax Arts & Crafts, P.O. Box 510710, New Berlin, WI 53151-0710; 414/784-6880; 800/558-6696; e-mail: infor@saxarts.com; www.saxarts.com. (See coupon.)

Human-Shape Sponges   (Family use)

Paintings, collages, murals, and multicultural lessons come to life when you put humans in the picture. These inexpensive "sponge humans" can be easily used with paint to make prints or traced for cutouts. These 6-inch-tall and 1-inch-thick sponges are easy to grasp even for small hands, with no sharp edges. Pack of 6, Item #637-1918, $3.59. Available from Sax Arts & Crafts, P.O. Box 510710, New Berlin, WI 53151-0710; 414/784-6880; 800/558-6696; e-mail: infor@saxarts.com; www.saxarts.com. (See coupon.)

Large Polyclay Pattern Cutter Set   (Family use)

Unique tools are easy to use, yet give professional-quality results. Includes four shapes—round, teardrop, flower, and heart—in four sizes ready to provide concise detail in polymer clays and more. Each cutter is equipped with a spring-return plunger for ejecting clay cutouts with ease. Item #641-5400, $26.95. Available from Sax Arts & Crafts, P.O. Box 510710, New Berlin, WI 53151-0710; 414/784-6880; 800/558-6696; e-mail: infor@saxarts.com; www.saxarts.com. (See coupon.)

Sax Wax Carving Blocks   (Ages 10 to adult)

These 3" × 3" × 12" blocks are easy to carve and are reusable! Non-toxic brown-colored wax blocks are an excellent carving medium. They require no special or sharp tools. Cuttings, scraps, or mistakes can be remelted into new blocks or forms. Blocks can be formed into larger pieces by fusing with heat. Each block weighs approximately 3½ lbs. Item #651-4921, $9.60 each; 12 or more, $8.15 each. Available from Sax Arts & Crafts, P.O. Box 510710, New Berlin, WI 53151-0710; 414/784-6880; 800/558-6696; e-mail: infor@saxarts.com; www.saxarts.com. (See coupon.)

Make-a-Mask "Creative Craft" Kit   (Family Use)

Create dramatic, cultural, costume, and decorative masks with this fun-to-use kit. The possibilities are endless! All materials are nontoxic, nonflammable, and non-irritating to skin and eyes. Includes a reusable plastic facial form that provides the structure for your mask, plaster gauze for the mask itself, six colors with brush, and a 16-page illustrated instruction booklet. Item #651-6504, $12.95. Available from Sax Arts & Crafts, P.O. Box 510710, New Berlin, WI 53151-0710; 414/784-6880; 800/558-6696; e-mail: infor@saxarts.com; www.saxarts.com. (See coupon.)

A Beginner's Loom With Big Loom Features!

BRIO Student Table-Top Loom
(Ages to 10 to adult)

Even children can learn to weave on this 6-inch-wide, 5-pound loom of hardwood construction. The six dents per inch beater can be threaded with cotton or yarn warp. Top lever operates harness from low to high positions. When not in use, the loom folds flat for storage. With easy-to-follow detailed instructions, the loom comes fully assembled and warped, ready for weaving. Item #700-4310, $66.50. Available from Sax Arts & Crafts, P.O. Box 510710, New Berlin, WI 53151-0710; 414/784-6880; 800/558-6696; e-mail: infor@saxarts.com; www.saxarts.com. (See coupon.)

Student Inkle Looms   (Ages 10 to adult)

These classroom-tested inkle looms are made from selected hardwood, with birch dowels. Each inkle loom includes warping, weaving, and assembly instructions; shuttle; sample of string heddle; and strings for additional heddles. The loom requires glue and screwdriver for assembly. Both looms provide a weaving length of up to 85 inches. Item #700-5028 (6-inch weaving width), $17.95; Item #700-5036 (12½-inch weaving width), $21.95. Available from Sax Arts & Crafts, P.O. Box 510710, New Berlin, WI 53151-0710; 414/784-6880; 800/558-6696; e-mail: infor@saxarts.com; www.saxarts.com. (See coupon.)

Easy Weavers A and B   (Ages 9 and up)

These are two small, different-sized rigid heddle table looms for weaving cloth. The beautifully finished wood weaver fits on a small tabletop. Pre-threaded with yarn, both include two stick shuttles and an illustrated instruction book Weaver A comes with a warp of 100% pure virgin wool, 6½ inches wide by 2½ yards long. Size A: (17½-inch L. × 10-inch W. × 5½-inch H), Item #394, $89.95 plus shipping; Weaver B comes with a wool warp 15 inches wide × 13½ inches long. Size B: (18" L. × 18" W. × 6½" H.), Item #424, $134.95 plus shipping. Harrisville Designs, Inc., Center Village, Box 806, Harrisville, NH 03450; 603/827-3333; Fax: 603/827-3335.

Easy Weaver Refill Kits   (Family use)

These are refill kits made for use with the Easy Weavers A and B. Refill Kit for A contains a wool warp 6½ inches wide by 2½ yards long (enough yarn to weave the entire piece) and instructions. Refill Kit for B contains a wool warp 13½ inches wide by 3½ yards long (enough yarn to weave the entire piece) and illustrated instructions. Refill A, Item #433, $25.95; Refill B, Item #426, $39.95. Harrisville Designs, Inc., Center Village, P.O. Box 806, Harrisville, NH 03450; 603/827-3333; Fax: 603/827-3335.

Arts and Crafts Supplies

Lap Looms   (Ages 10 to adult)

These lap looms are portable, hardwood tapestry or frame looms that can be woven on while resting on a table, floor, or your lap! The loom comes with 1 ounce of cotton warp string, 100% pure virgin wool weft yarn (enough for one project), one tapestry needle, two wooden shed sticks, one 6-inch wooden stick shuttle, and illustrated instructions. Size A (12" × 16"), Item #376, $39.95 plus shipping. Size B (14½" × 18½"), Item #384, $49.95 plus shipping. Harrisville Designs, Inc., Center Village, Box 806, Harrisville, NH 03450; 603/827-3333; Fax: 603/827-3335. Write for catalog.

Schacht Open-Sided Inkle Loom (Family Use)

Simple, easy to master, and specially designed for rigorous use in schools, this loom is an excellent introduction to weaving. Made of unfinished, finely sanded, hard maple, the open-sided design of this inkle loom makes warping easy and uncomplicated. Loom is capable of handling warps of various lengths up to 8½ feet long and 4½ inches wide. Detailed instructions for warping are included. Dimensions: 6½" W × 9½" H × 31" L. Item #700-5051, $57.75. Available from Sax Arts & Crafts, P.O. Box 510710, New Berlin, WI 53151-0710; 414/784-6880; 800/558-6696; e-mail: infor@saxarts.com; www.saxarts.com. (See coupon.)

Adjustable Flat Looms (Family Use)

Create beautiful weaving projects up to 36" × 36". Easy to assemble and fully adjustable, these hardwood looms come in two popular sizes, with instructions included. Item #700-5358 (24" × 36"), $35.95; item #700-5366 (36" × 36"), $46.50. Available from Sax Arts & Crafts, P.O. Box 510710, New Berlin, WI 53151-0710; 414/784-6880; 800/558-6696; e-mail: infor@saxarts.com; www.saxarts.com. (See coupon.)

Chipboard Student Weaving Looms
(Ages 6 to adult)

This is an inexpensive loom that every student can afford! Cardboard looms are made of heavy ⅛-inch-thick chipboard with notches located at both ends, four notches per inch. The heavy board is practically indestructible. An economical starter loom for the very young or beginning student in textile weaving and design. Item #700-5614 (3¼" × 13"), $.45; #700-5622 (6½" × 13"), $.75; #700-5648 (9¾" × 13"), $1.05; #700-5630 (13" × 13"), $1.38. Available from Sax Arts & Crafts, P.O. Box 510710, New Berlin, WI 53151-0710; 414/784-6880; 800/558-6696; e-mail: infor@saxarts.com; www.saxarts.com. (See coupon.)

Peacock Finger Loom   (Ages 7 to 12)

Basic flat loom measures 10 × 12 inches and provides an inexpensive way to learn simple yet creative weaving. Easy to operate for all ages—even preschool—the loom holds 38 warp strands. Set includes 7-inch bobbin shuttle, 10½-inch lease stick, beater, and instruction sheet of special weaving knots. Assembly is required. Item #700-6653, $11.91. Available from Sax Arts & Crafts, P.O. Box 510710, New Berlin, WI 53151-0710; 414/784-6880; 800/558-6696; e-mail: infor@saxarts.com; www.saxarts.com. (See coupon.)

Schacht Tapestry Loom   (Ages 7 to 12)

This is a sturdy, well-constructed loom—simply designed for students and beginners learning traditional tapestry weaving. Continuous warp system is used and can be warped for 40- or 70-inch lengths and 18-inch widths. Four heddle bars are included so you can experiment with four-harness weaving. Instructions for assembling this maple loom are included. Item #700-7156, $72. Available from Sax Arts & Crafts, P.O. Box 510710, New Berlin, WI 53151-0710; 414/784-6880; 800/558-6696; e-mail: infor@saxarts.com; www.saxarts.com. (See coupon.)

Loom with Stand

Friendly Loom (Ages 7 to 12)

This superbly constructed and finished solid rock maple loom allows up to eight students to weave simultaneously. Equipped with unbreakable nylon pegs used to hold the warp in place, the loom adjusts in height from 44½ to 68½ inches. The loom stands 60 inches high and has a weaving area of 30-inch H × 48-inch W. Complete instructions and weaving techniques are included. Item #700-4450, $224.95. Available from Sax Arts & Crafts, P.O. Box 510710, New Berlin, WI 53151-0710; 414/784-6880; 800/558-6696; e-mail: infor@saxarts.com; www.saxarts.com. (See coupon.)

Friendly Loom Starter Kit (Family use)

This starter kit contains everything needed to begin projects: 2½ lbs. of assorted bulky yarns, ½ lb. of warp yarn, four shuttle sticks, four shed sticks, and a complete instruction book. Item #713-4455, $34.95. Available from Sax Arts & Crafts, P.O. Box 510710, New Berlin, WI 53151-0710; 414/784-6880; 800/558-6696; e-mail: infor@saxarts.com; www.saxarts.com. (See coupon.)

Iroquois Cornhusk Doll Classroom Kit (Ages 7 to 12)

Every student can create a winsome, handmade cornhusk doll, similar to the ones made centuries ago. Kits contain natural twist paper, 4-ply yarn, raffia in various colors, and instructions. Includes enough material for 28 dolls. Item #717-2166, $14.95. Available from Sax Arts & Crafts, P.O. Box 510710, New Berlin, WI 53151-0710; 414/784-6880; 800/558-6696; e-mail: infor@saxarts.com; www.saxarts.com. (See coupon.)

Design Your Own Mousepad (Family use)

This 8½" × 7½" mousepad can be decorated any way you wish. Do-it-yourself pad features a flip-up top with a vinyl window—simply slip in your favorite picture, original artwork, photo, fancy papers, etc. Change your design as often as you like! Artwork window measures 5" × 7". Item #717-9716, $5.95. Available from Sax Arts & Crafts, P.O. Box 510710, New Berlin, WI 53151-0710; 414/784-6880; 800/558-6696; e-mail: infor@saxarts.com; www.saxarts.com. (See coupon.)

Design Your Own Snowglobe   (Family use)

What a sensational, new way to add a little magic to small artwork or a favorite photo! Remove the bottom to reveal a plastic-encased slot for inserting your artwork or picture. Artwork can be two-sided or viewed "in-the-round" and will be magnified when placed into the globe. Dimensions: 4 inches high × 3 inches wide. Insert size: 2¾" × 1¾". Item #717-9724, $3.80. Available from Sax Arts & Crafts, P.O. Box 510710, New Berlin, WI 53151-0710; 414/784-6880; 800/558-6696; e-mail: infor@saxarts.com; www.saxarts.com. (See coupon.)

Design Your Own Clock   (Family use)

Display prized artwork or special photos on your own, uniquely personalized, snap-together craft clock. Use the preprinted die cut inserts or create original designs or mats to decorate the clock. The outer rim is black; one white die cut insert is provided. Requires one AA battery (not included). Item #718-0003 (8½-inch clock), $9.95. Available from Sax Arts & Crafts, P.O. Box 510710, New Berlin, WI 53151-0710; 414/784-6880; 800/558-6696; e-mail: infor@saxarts.com; www.saxarts.com. (See coupon.)

Jacquard Tie-Dye Kit   (Family use)

This all-inclusive, economical tie-dye kit produces professional results. Contains brilliant primary colors of premeasured Procion dye powders in convenient applicator bottles, soda ash, dye fixer, rubber bands, rubber gloves, easy directions, and an extra bottle for mixing secondary or pastel colors. Use it on natural fabric, it will dye up to 15 adult T-shirts. Item #721-0305, $19.95. Available from Sax Arts & Crafts, P.O. Box 510710, New Berlin, WI 53151-0710; 414/784-6880; 800/558-6696; e-mail: infor@saxarts.com; www.saxarts.com. (See coupon.)

Arts and Crafts Supplies

Beeswax Honeycomb Sheets   (Family use)

Fine-quality, multipurpose wax is ideal for making drip and smoke-free candles, and this pack includes a bonus of 10 wicks! Wax is soft and pliable enough to add beads and sequins or decorate with other shapes of wax cut-outs. Ten 8" × 16" pliable sheets per package, comes with directions. Natural, Item #723-0311; royal blue, #723-0345; white, #723-0329; navy, #723-0352; red, #723-0337; pine green, #723-0363, $15.99 each. Available from Sax Arts & Crafts, P.O. Box 510710, New Berlin, WI 53151-0710; 414/784-6880; 800/558-6696; e-mail: infor@saxarts.com; www.saxarts.com. (See coupon.)

Paint 'N Swirl Art Machine   (Family use)

Create beautiful circular designs assisted by a battery-powered rotation machine. Comes complete with non-toxic paints and decorative accents. It is particularly suited to the young or inexperienced artist. Make colorful designs for cards, patches, nature images, and free designs. Contents include art machine, four squeeze paints, paper, greeting cards, glitter, sand, and feathers. D-size battery is not included. Item #723-9981, $19.95. Available from Sax Arts & Crafts, P.O. Box 510710, New Berlin, WI 53151-0710; 414/784-6880; 800/558-6696; e-mail: infor@saxarts.com; www.saxarts.com. (See coupon.)

Renkly 3-Dimensional Paint   (Family use)

As a pigmented, glue-based product, Renkly 3-D paint can be used on virtually any surface to build 3-dimensional textured objects. Dries to a rubbery, vivid, flexible film with a high shine. Diluting it with water allows it to be used as a watercolor or as a papier-mâché paste. Mixable, nontoxic colors are lightfast, non-yellowing, and acid free. Item #724-7505, $24.95. Available from Sax Arts & Crafts, P.O. Box 510710, New Berlin, WI 53151-0710; 414/784-6880; 800/558-6696; e-mail: infor@saxarts.com; www.saxarts.com. (See coupon.)

Bucket-O-Beads   (Family use)

Over 3,000 plastic beads in assorted styles, sizes, and colors are a mix of traditional, top-quality USA beads and imported styles from Germany and China. Metallics, crystal-looks, brights, pastels, and multicolored styles are included in this eye-pleasing collection. Item #728-8400, $13.50. Available from Sax Arts & Crafts, P.O. Box 510710, New Berlin, WI 53151-0710; 414/784-6880;   800/558-6696;   e-mail: infor@saxarts.com; www.saxarts.com. (See coupon.)

Indian Seed Bead Loom   (Ages 7 to 12)

Simple to set up and operate, this bead loom has metal thread separators, correctly spaced, with no sharp edges to cut the threads. Includes beads, thread, needles, and instructions. Item #729-6155, $6.95. Available from Sax Arts & Crafts, P.O. Box 510710, New Berlin, WI 53151-0710; 414/784-6880; 800/558-6696; e-mail: infor@saxarts.com; www.saxarts.com. (See coupon.)

Solid Color Feathers   (Family use)

This 100-piece assortment includes all perfect feathers that are 12 to 14 inches in length. Tips may be sprayed for "eagle feather effect." Colors may vary. Item #729-8102, $13.95. Sax Arts & Crafts, P.O. Box 510710, New Berlin, WI 53151-0710; 414/784-6880; 800/558-6696; e-mail: infor@saxarts.com; www.saxarts.com. (See coupon.)

Classroom Pack of Natural Feathers   (Family use)

This pack of select quality natural feathers to enhance any jewelry or craft project contains approximately 200 assorted feathers in 10 styles. Feathers range from 2 to 3 inches in length. Item #729-8409, $12.95. Sax Arts & Crafts, P.O. Box 510710, New Berlin, WI 53151-0710; 414/784-6880; 800/558-6696; e-mail: infor@saxarts.com; www.saxarts.com. (See coupon.)

Arts and Crafts Supplies

Round Basket Kit   (Ages 7 to 12)

This kit contains everything you need for making a round basket, including a 5-inch wooden base with prepunched holes, heavy reed for stakes (uprights), lighter weight reed for the weaving, and complete, simple instructions. Item #730-2020, $4. Sax Arts & Crafts, P.O. Box 510710, New Berlin, WI 53151-0710; 414/784-6880; 800/558-6696; e-mail: infor@saxarts.com; www.saxarts.com. (See coupon.)

Colonial Footstool Kit   (Ages 7 to 12)

Enjoy making this authentic and attractive piece of furniture. Beautiful footstool (11" W × 9" H × 11" L comes with fiber rush, ready for completion. Item #730-5311, $12.50. Sax Arts & Crafts, P.O. Box 510710, New Berlin, WI 53151-0710; 414/784-6880; 800/558-6696; e-mail: infor@saxarts.com; www.saxarts.com. (See coupon.)

Styrofoam Sculpture Head   (Ages 7 to 12)

Use nonhardening modeling clay to form the facial features on the foam head, then cover with plaster or other molding material. Remove dry plaster and use the negative impression as a mold. The head is also suitable as an armature for additive sculpture. Sold by the dozen. Item #734-3254, $21.95. Sax Arts & Crafts, P.O. Box 510710, New Berlin, WI 53151-0710; 414/784-6880; 800/558-6696; e-mail: infor@saxarts.com; www.saxarts.com. (See coupon.)

Braid Craft Deluxe Tool Set   (Ages 7 to 12)

Three metal braidcrafters automatically turn in the edges of your fabric as you braid, thus allowing a more professional look. Include one braid lacer and 75 feet of lacing cord to assemble your braids into one solid piece; one braid clamp to secure your braid's starting point; and a 19-page illustrated instruction book with four projects. Item #734-9228, $16.50. Sax Arts & Crafts, P.O. Box 510710, New Berlin, WI 53151-0710; 414/784-6880; 800/558-6696; e-mail: infor@saxarts.com; com; www.saxarts.com.com. (See coupon.)

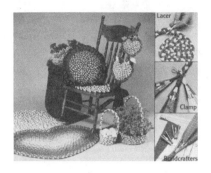

Authentic Glass Mosaic Tiles   (Family use)

Cast from colored glass in the centuries-old tradition of the master Italian glassmakers, these $\frac{3}{4}$" × $\frac{3}{4}$" square tiles are smooth on the front to reflect light and textured on the back to provide extra grip for the adhesive. Since these non-fading tiles are designed to be broken, they're easy to cut, nip, and apply in infinite combinations on nearly any smooth, hard surface. Ideal for mosaic art, over bottles or glass vases, for jewelry boxes,

pendants, and more. Bag contains 3 lbs. (approximately 450 tiles) of assorted colors—deep hues, pastels, earth tones, and brights. Item #742-3601, $49.95. Sax Arts & Crafts, P.O. Box 510710, New Berlin, WI 53151-0710; 414/784-6880; 800/558-6696; e-mail: infor@saxarts.com;.com; www.saxarts.com.com. (See coupon.)

Board Games

The Garden Game   (Ages 6 and up)

This is a beautifully hand-painted board game about gardening, plants, food, and fun. Players have a chance to nourish the soil, sow seeds, nurture their plants, and experience harvest. Whoever ends up with the largest garden and saves the most seeds is the "winner," although the spirit of the game is noncompetitive. $26.95 plus $6.95 shipping. Ampersand Press, 750 Lake St., Port Townsend, WA 98368; 800/624-4263. (See coupon.)

The Bug Game   (Ages 3 and up)

This is a favorite at our house! It is a matching, memory game that provides fun and learning at the same time. This is another of Ampersand Press' gorgeous illustrations. The game comes with a full-color poster, instructions for play, a bug sheet, glossary, and bibliography. $13.95 plus $4.95 shipping. Ampersand Press, 750 Lake St., Port Townsend, WA 98368; 800/624-4263.

Onto the Desert   (Ages 8 and up)

Ampersand Press does a great job on the breathtaking cards and illustrations in this game. The game consists of a deck of 41 cards, along with instructions, including seven ways to play. The set includes a full-color poster of desert habitat, "amazing" facts sheet, glossary, and a bibliography. $15.95 plus $4.95 shipping. Ampersand Press, 750 Lake St., Port Townsend, WA 98368; 800/624-4263.

Predator: The Forest Food Chain Game (Ages 8 and up)

In this board game the players learn about the food-chain relationships in a forest. There are 40 illustrated cards that represent a plant or animal commonly found in a temperate-zone forest. An animal takes what it eats and is taken by what eats it! There are several ways to play this great game. $9.95 plus $4.95 shipping. Ampersand Press, 750 Lake St., Port Townsend, WA 98368; 800/624-4263.

Into the Forest: Nature's Food Chain Game
(Ages 8 and up)

This is a nature game where players step into the forest and interact in the natural food chains of forest life. Each of the 41 playing cards has a picture of an animal, plant, or element. The players interact with each other based upon what cards they hold, whether they are "eaters" or "eaten" in conjunction with the other players' cards. $15.95 plus $4.95 shipping. Ampersand Press, 750 Lake St., Port Townsend, WA 98368; 800/624-4263.

Oh Wilderness: The Game of Backcountry Lore
(Ages 8 and up)

This is a card game for people who enjoy the outdoors. Easy to difficult questions about wildlife, wilderness skills, plants, animals, land, and sky. The rules assure that novices can enjoy playing as much as experienced people. $9.95 plus $4.95 shipping. Ampersand Press, 750 Lake St., Port Townsend, WA 98368; 800/624-4263.

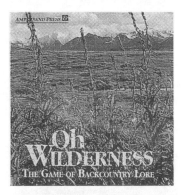

Good Heavens! (The Astronomy Game)
(Ages 10 and up)

There are 54 cards, each of which contains a question pertaining to astronomy, along with the answer. The object of the game is to answer questions using only the answers shown on the cards in your hand. $9.95 plus $4.95 shipping. Ampersand Press, 750 Lake St., Port Townsend, WA 98368; 800/624-4263.

KRILL: A Whale of a Game   (Ages 8 and up)

In playing this game, you will be submerged into the Antarctic Ocean community. There you will discover the food chain that exists amongst the ocean dwellers. Included are 77 cards, a glossary of terms, and instructions. On each card, the food chain member will be named and pictured, along with what it eats and what eats it. $9.95 plus $4.95 shipping. Ampersand Press, 750 Lake St., Port Townsend, WA 98368; 800/624-4263.

AC/DC Electricity Game   (Ages 8 and up)

Players use component cards to complete various electronic circuits. An understanding of electricity and its mysteries can be clarified through playing this game. $9.95 plus $4.95 shipping. Ampersand Press, 750 Lake St., Port Townsend, WA 98368; 800/624-4263.

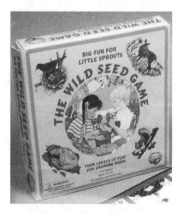

The Wild Seed Game   (Ages 4 to 10)

This board game is a simple way to help your child learn about wild seeds and the conditions that make them grow, or not. The 96 playing cards are pictures without writing, so reading does not enter into the game. Included are rules for playing four games with different levels of strategy and parent discussion topics. $20 plus $4.95 shipping. Ampersand Press, 750 Lake St., Port Townsend, WA 98368; 800/624-4263. (See coupon.)

Tangoes Puzzle Game   (Ages 5 to adult)

This game stretches your mind and aids abstract reasoning. Two players are shown a shape on a card and each one is provided with seven pieces with which to duplicate the picture on the card. Tangoes incorporates geometry, critical thinking, and analysis in a fun setting. $11.95. Additional puzzle set, $2.95 Available from Rex Games, 530 Howard St., Ste. 100, San Francisco, CA 94105-3007; 800/542-6375; www.rexgames.com.

Hexagonoes   (Ages 10 to adult)

Each edge of the hexagonal tiles has a number in either fraction, decimal, or percent form. Two to six players take turns matching the values on their tiles with those previously played. The more values a player matches on a turn, the more points earned. At the end of the game, the player with the most points wins. Item # EB-91-1934, $12.98. Available from Carolina Biological Supply Co., 2700 York Rd., Burlington, NC 27215; 800/334-5551; www.carolina.com.

Math Chase   (Ages 10 to 14)

The Intermediate Edition (ages 10 to 12) contains questions about geometry, fractions, decimals, percentages, integers, multiples, and computation using whole numbers and fractions. The Advanced Edition (ages 12 to 14) consists of questions about algebraic thinking, statistics/probability, measurement/geometry, and number theory. There are 192 cards containing questions in four categories. Each card has three questions at different levels of difficulty. Intermediate: EB-91-1931, $32.75; Advanced: EB-91-1932, $32.75. Available from Carolina Biological Supply Co., 2700 York Rd., Burlington, NC 27215; 800/334-5551; www.carolina.com.

Muggins!   (Ages 10 to adult)
and Opps!   (Ages 14 and up)

A double-sided playing board makes this two games in one. Muggins is a fun way to develop analytical and thinking skills. Using three ordinary dice, players add, subtract, multiply, and/or divide the results of the dice to produce a total and capture a corresponding spot on the board. Opps!, the game of positive and negative integers, is similar to Muggins, but uses four specially designed positive and negative six-face dice. Item #EB-91-1867, $38.95. Available from Carolina Biological Supply Co., 2700 York Rd., Burlington, NC 27215; 800/334-5551; www.carolina.com.

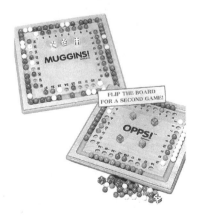

True Math Facts to Use and Amuse!
(Ages 10 and up)

Players race around a geometric board and answer entertaining and informative math questions. The 900 questions are in six categories: numbers, money, geometry, size and scale, logical thinking, and random access—in other words, "anything goes." Players have a choice of true/false or more difficult "genius" questions. Item #EB-91-1930, $25. Available from Carolina Biological Supply Co., 2700 York Rd., Burlington, NC 27215; 800/334-5551; www.carolina.com.

Mathematics Games for Fun and Practice   (Ages 10 to 13)

This 78-page softcover book (1992) by Alan Barson contains 38 games to motivate practice of math skills from measurement to geometry, computation to number properties. Playing boards and directions are on black-line masters for easy duplication. Item #EB-91-1928, $14.95. Available from Carolina Biological Supply Co., 2700 York Rd., Burlington, NC 27215; 800/334-5551; www.carolina.com.

Equations   (Ages 10 and up)

In this game for two or more, players seek to build statements of equality from sets of numerals and signs. The game can be played on increasingly challenging levels. The basic game uses the fundamental operations of arithmetic while more advanced rules incorporate further operations and various number bases. The game includes a teacher's manual. Item #EB-91-1901, $27. Available from Carolina Biological Supply Co., 2700 York Rd., Burlington, NC 27215; 800/334-5551; www.carolina.com.

Explorers Card Game   (Ages 10 to adult)

Here is a fun and interesting way to learn about 13 different explorers from Alexander the Great to Vasco De Gama and Francis Drake! 52-card deck, $6. Available from Beautiful Feet Books, 139 Main St., Sandwich, MA 02563; 800/889-1978; 508/833-8626; www.bfbooks.com. Call for catalog.

Algebra World   (Ages 13 and up)

This computer CD-ROM teaches and reinforces algebric concepts in a fun environment. Equations and their relationships to word problems are emphasized throughout the program. It combines detailed lessons with real-world examples. Students solve math challenges to earn map puzzle pieces. The challenges serve as an assessment of understanding. Hyrbrid CD-ROM: Item #EB-91-3150, $79.95. Available from Carolina Biological Supply Co., 2700 York Rd., Burlington, NC 27215; 800/334-5551; www.carolina.com.

Geometry World   (Ages 10 to 17)

This interactive computer CD-ROM game explores the world of geometry through beautiful 3-D graphics. Explore lines, angles, polygons, the Pythagorean Theorem, circles, perimeter, area, and solids. There are programming tools for exploration and building reasoning skills, as well as lessons and geometry challenges that promote geometric and logical reasoning. Hybrid CD-ROM: Item #EB-91-3250, $79.95. Available from Carolina Biological Supply Co., 2700 York Rd., Burlington, NC 27215; 800/334-5551; www.carolina.com.

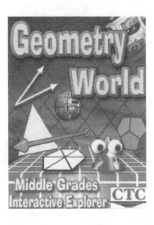

Visual Solid Geometry   (Ages 12 to 18)

This cross-platform CD-ROM demonstrates the principals of solid geometry all around us. Students easily understand difficult concepts as they watch the lesson virtually come to life before their eyes. Learning solid geometry has never been so easy and fun. Hybrid CD-ROM: Item #EB-91-3280, $39. Available from Carolina Biological Supply Co., 2700 York Rd., Burlington, NC 27215; 800/334-5551; www.carolina.com.

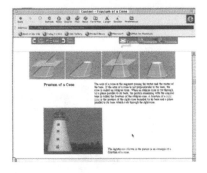

Board Games

Connections Game   (Ages 6 to 18)

A booklet and two decks of 55 card photos offer your child the opportunity to see buildings as ideas, visual images, and spatial forms. $18.95. Available from Architectural Education Resource Center (AERC), 131 Hillside Road, Franklin, MA 02038; 508/528-4517; e-mail: aerc@norfolk-county.com; www.norfolk-county.com./aerc. (See coupon.)

Art Memo Game   (Family use)

To play this simple yet challenging memory game similar to Concentration, players turn two cards up until they have a match. Players can match cards according to "works of art" or artist's styles (portraits, landscapes, abstracts, etc.) The set includes 72 cards that depict 36 paintings from the Renaissance to Pop Art. Also included is an instruction/information booklet listing the artist, title, and museum for each work. Item #573-1369, $22.95. Available from Sax Arts & Crafts, P.O. Box 510710, New Berlin, WI 53151-0710; 414/784-6880; 800/558-6696; e-mail: infor@saxarts.com; www.saxarts.com. (See coupon.)

Art Memo II Game   (Family use)

This memory matching game features 36 famous paintings from museums all over the world. The colorful variety of reproductions in this game range from Ancient Greek to Modern American works. A b&w descriptive booklet is included. Item #573-3092, $22.95. Available from Sax Arts & Crafts, P.O. Box 510710, New Berlin, WI 53151-0710; 414/784-6880; 800/558-6696; e-mail: infor@saxarts.com; www.saxarts.com. (See coupon.)

Impressionist Memo Game   (Family use)

This new version of Art Memo is an enjoyable memory game based on 36 inspiring Impressionist paintings. It is played like Concentration, with variations such as matching cards by genre or style. The game includes instructions and a b&w illustrated listing of the paintings, showing artist, title, and date. Item #573-0981, $22.95. Available from Sax Arts & Crafts, P.O. Box 510710, New Berlin, WI 53151-0710; 414/784-6880; 800/558-6696; e-mail: infor@saxarts.com; www.saxarts.com. (See coupon.)

Board Games

Art Bits—Apprentice Levels   (Ages 9 to 18)

Each deck of playing cards displays 17 full-color examples, including some of the most famous artworks in the world. A description sheet gives details about the specific work and artist. For three to five players or teams. "Painting" includes masterpieces by Michelangelo, Rembrandt, Degas, Gauguin, da Vinci, and others. "Sculpture" provides examples of relief, sculpture in the round, mobiles, and earth art. Painting, Item #573-1690, $13.95; Sculpture, #573-2698, $13.95 each. Available from Sax Arts & Crafts, P.O. Box 510710, New Berlin, WI 53151-0710; 414/784-6880; 800/558-6696; e-mail: infor@saxarts.com; www.saxarts.com. (See coupon.)

Where Art Thou? Details from 36
American Paintings   (Family use)

This challenging memory and chance art game revolves around details from 36 famous American paintings from 11 museums. The 72 cards can be played in four ways—Concentration, Bingo, Mix & Match, or Trivia. Item #573-1880, $19.95. Available from Sax Arts & Crafts, P.O. Box 510710, New Berlin, WI 53151-0710; 414/784-6880; 800/558-6696; e-mail: infor@saxarts.com; www.saxarts.com. (See coupon.)

ARTDECK Game   (Ages 13 to adult)

Winner of the Parents' Choice Award, this beautifully designed card game offers an enjoyable way to learn about modern art. The set features 52 paintings by 13 artists, reproduced in full color on a deck of playing cards. A second deck contains information on the artists whose work is highlighted. Players coordinate the Art and Artist cards, then earn extra points for stating facts listed on the latter. The game is for 2 to 4 players. Item #573-1518, $15. Available from Sax Arts & Crafts, P.O. Box 510710, New Berlin, WI 53151-0710; 414/784-6880; 800/558-6696; e-mail: infor@saxarts.com; www.saxarts.com. (See coupon.)

Board Games

ARTDECK Mexican Artist Playing Cards
(Ages 14 to adult)

Durable, coated, high-quality cards in full color feature 13 Mexican artists. Full deck of 52 celebrated paintings—four by each artist—from twentieth-century artists Rivera, Kahlo, Orozco, Dr. Atl, Siquieros, Murillo, Tamayo, and others. Includes brochure with historical notes and painting identification as to artist, title, medium, and year of creation. Item #573-1914, $9.95. Available from Sax Arts & Crafts, P.O. Box 510710, New Berlin, WI 53151-0710; 414/784-6880; 800/558-6696; e-mail: infor@saxarts.com; www.saxarts.com. (See coupon.)

ARTDECK African Artifacts Playing Cards
(Ages 14 to adult)

These high-quality playing cards feature beautiful 3-D and textile art objects from Africa. Artists from 13 countries are represented in the collection of headdresses, masks, figures, animals, and funeral cloths. The full-color, standard size deck includes 52 cards, and a brochure detailing information on each artifact. Item #573-2003, $9.95. Available from Sax Arts & Crafts, P.O. Box 510710, New Berlin, WI 53151-0710; 414/784-6880; 800/558-6696; e-mail: infor@saxarts.com; www.saxarts.com. (See coupon.)

Connections: A Visual Game   (Family use)

This challenging game encourages visual awareness and creative thinking. Adults and children will enjoy finding relationships between animals and humans, buildings and plants, art and industry. The deck includes 110 cards—96 inspiring and intriguing photos of nature, architecture, and the visual environment; 6 wild cards; and 8 museum works of art. Item #573-2433, $18.95. Available from Sax Arts & Crafts, P.O. Box 510710, New Berlin, WI 53151-0710; 414/784-6880; 800/558-6696; e-mail: infor@saxarts.com; www.saxarts.com. (See coupon.)

Board Games

The Fine Art Game   (Ages 9 to adult)

In this original art education game of strategy and luck, players try to learn more about the paintings from the guide while walking through the museum. The game, for three to five players, includes playing board, five tokens, five markers, 36 cards, and one museum guide. Duration of play is about 20 minutes. Item #573-3076, $22.95. Available from Sax Arts & Crafts, P.O. Box 510710, New Berlin, WI 53151-0710; 414/784-6880; 800/558-6696; e-mail: infor@saxarts.com; www.saxarts.com. (See coupon.)

Monet Memo Game   (Family use)

Monet's rich imagery is captured on 36 different squares to match in this entertaining game of memory and concentration. Item #573-3084, $22.95. Available from Sax Arts & Crafts, P.O. Box 510710, New Berlin, WI 53151-0710; 414/784-6880; 800/558-6696; e-mail: infor@saxarts.com; www.saxarts.com. (See coupon.)

Quizart, Two Games in One   (Ages 14 to adult)

Test your art knowledge in a fun, bingo-style game format! This game features 70 two-sided calling cards with questions on art materials and techniques on one side and questions on art history on the other side. The set also includes 36 two-sided game cards printed in a classic bingo format and includes 200 Quizmo markers/tokens for 2 to 36 players. Item #573-5170, $16.95. Available from Sax Arts & Crafts, P.O. Box 510710, New Berlin, WI 53151-0710; 414/784-6880; 800/558-6696; e-mail: infor@saxarts.com; www.saxarts.com. (See coupon.)

Blank Playing Cards   (Family use)

Design your own playing cards! Choose from jumbo ($3\frac{1}{2}$" × 5") or standard ($2\frac{3}{8}$" × $3\frac{3}{8}$") size. Each deck contains 60 cards with coated backs preprinted with cheery sun and stars motif. Create your own suits, draw designs, or paint pictures to play your favorite traditional or imaginative card games. Standard, Item #573-5253, $1.99; Jumbo, Item #573-5261, $2.99. Available from Sax Arts & Crafts, P.O. Box 510710, New Berlin, WI 53151-0710; 414/784-6880; 800/558-6696; e-mail: infor@saxarts.com; www.saxarts.com. (See coupon.)

Strategy Challenges Collection 1 (Ages 9 and up)

Let your student learn and use strategies for games (and possibly, for life) while playing the three games included on this CD-ROM: Mancala, Nine Men's Morris, or Go-Moku. Each game can be played against others or against characters depicted in the program. Hybrid CD-ROM: EDMKO25O-CDB, $19.95. Available from Learning Services, P.O. Box 10636, Eugene, OR 97440-2636; Western Region: 800/877-9378; Eastern Region: 800/877-3278. (See coupon.)

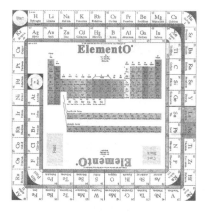

ElementO (Ages 11 and up)

This unique game combines the periodic table of elements with Monopoly-style layout. You utilize "electrons" or "neurons" to purchase element "properties" along the board path. There are also action cards that affect play. The person with the most elements at the end of the game wins, but the true object of the game is casually memorizing the table of elements and their atomic weights as you play. $31.95 each, plus $3.95 shipping and handling. Order from Lewis Educational Games, Box 727, Goddard, KS 67052; 800/557-8777. (See coupon.)

Number Quest (Ages 7 and up)

Play this fun family game and sharpen multiplication and other math skills. The set includes game board, play money, 200 plastic counters, four dice, cheat chart, and rule book. Item #308, $19.95, boxed. Available from DK Family Learning, 11124 N.E. Halsey, Suite 460, Portland, OR 97220; 888/225-3535. (See coupon.)

Board Games

Eyewitness Quiz Cards   (Ages 7 and up)

Use this great set of 90 color picture cards to teach science, nature, and history. Item #191, $8.95. Available from DK Family Learning, 11124 N.E. Halsey, Suite 460, Portland, OR 97220; 888/225-3535. (See coupon.)

Top 10 Quiz Book   (Ages 8 and up)

If your child is a budding trivia master, this 48-page hardcover book edited by the DK staff is just for him or her. The book has information about the biggest, tallest, longest, strangest things in the world. Item #187, $9.95. Available from DK Family Learning, 11124 N.E. Halsey, Suite 460, Portland, OR 97220; 888/225-3535. (See coupon.)

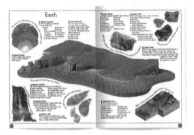

Rhymes & 'Nyms Card Game   (Ages 9 and up)

This unique easy-to-use card game challenges players' vocabulary knowledge, using old, new, amusing, and everyday words. Several games can be played with the deck. One focuses on homonyms, antonyms, and synonyms. $6.95 plus shipping. Available from Fireside Games, P.O. Box 82995, Portland, OR 97282-0995; 800/414-8990; www.firesidegames.com.

PART 3
Resources

The materials in this part are to aid you, the homeschooling parent, in expanding your knowledge of home education.

Books

Unless noted, books listed in part 3 are available through your local bookstore.

And What About College?
by Cafi Cohen
The author discusses how she helped her two homeschooled children apply to and get accepted by the colleges of their choice. This very readable and clear 176-page paperback helps you learn how to speak educationalese so you can compose your own transcripts and portfolios for college entrance use. Item #7116, $15.15. Available from FUN Books Catalog, 1688 Belhaven Woods Court, Pasadena, MD 21122-3727; voice/fax: 410/360-7330. (See coupon.)

The Art of Education: Reclaiming Your Family, Community and Self
by Linda Dobson
Home Education Magazine's Newswatch columnist shares refreshing insights she has gained through a decade of homeschooling her three children. In addition to thought-provoking commentary on the need for homeschooling, the book contains interesting quotations from a variety of sources. Contains a large index of books for further reading and a list of famous homeschoolers. Item #7140, $16.99. Available from FUN Books Catalog, 1688

Belhaven Woods Court, Pasadena, MD 21122-3727; voice/fax: 410/360-7330. (See coupon.)

The Big Book of Home Learning, Vol. 1, by Mary Pride
This 315-page book is a giant review book, one of three volumes. Products are listed and sometimes pictured, along with reviews by the author, a respected Christian homeschooling reviewer for many years. Mary Pride is also the publisher of *Practical Homeschooling Magazine.* $25. Available only from Home Life Publishing, 800/346-6322.

Christian Home Educator's Curriculum Manual by Cathy Duffy ✝
This is an all-encompassing, 360-page manual for the homeschooling Christian family. It has reviews, covers learning styles, tells what and how to teach, and includes a special planning and record-keeping section, as well as resources with addresses. Two manuals are available: K–6 and 7–12 (which includes goal setting, grades, transcripts and record keeping for college entrance; vocational and/or college preparation). $20. Available only from Grove Publishing, 16172 Huxley Circle, Westminster, CA 92683; 714/841-1220; fax: 714/841-5584.

The Complete Home Learning Source Book by Rebecca Rupp, Ph.D.
This 865-page volume is written by a homeschool mom of two boys and includes journal entries from Ms. Rupp's experiences with homeschooling. The rest of the book is a comprehensive listing of products and resources by category (math,

science, reading, etc.), which might be helpful to homeschooling families. $29.95. Three Rivers Press, New York; website: www.randomhouse.com.

Dumbing Us Down: The Invisible Curriculum of Compulsory Schooling by John Taylor Gatto

This superb 104-page paperback offers great insight into the public school mentality. John Taylor Gatto was a Manhattan junior high teacher for 30 years and knows the system from within. The book is not about homeschooling, but rather the primary cause of homeschooling—institutional schooling. But John's ability to communicate intellectual matters to Everyman makes his writings worth reading again and again. $9.95 plus $2.50 shipping. Available from Odysseus Group, 235 W. 76th St., New York, NY 10023.

The Exhausted School by John Taylor Gatto et al.

This very interesting book is a series of speeches about education reform and alternatives to public school given at a performance at Carnegie Hall. Some of the speakers are homeschool proponents, but most are not homeschoolers. $10.95 plus $2.50 shipping. Available from Odysseus Group, 235 W. 76th St., New York, NY 10023.

Homeschooling: The Early Years— Your Complete Guide to Successfully Homeschooling the 3- to 7- Year-Old Child by Linda Dobson

In this newly published 224-page paperback, Linda Dobson explores the early years of childhood, when lifelong learning foundations are established. She gives you keen advice on how to promote a love of learning in your child, how to not let a limited budget hamper your educational success, how to use online resources, and on many other topics. $14. Available from Prima Publishing, 916/632-4400.

Family Matters: Why Homeschooling Makes Sense by David Guterson

The most important lesson in this 254-page paperback is that no matter where education takes place, family matters; and homeschooling is just one way of embodying that neglected truth and reaffirming the bond between parents and children. Item #0001, $10.75. Available from FUN Books Catalog, 1688 Belhaven Woods Court, Pasadena, MD 21122-3727; voice/ fax: 410/360-7330. (See coupon.)

A Field Guide to Homeschooling by Christine M. Field ✝

This 269-page book is a practical guide for parents—from whether you should homeschool to how—written from the viewpoint of a homeschooling mom of four. Includes resources of varying types, including Internet resources. $12.99. Available from Revell Publishers, Baker House Books, P.O. Box 6287, Grand Rapids, MI 49516-6287.

Freedom Challenge: African American Homeschoolers, edited by Grace Llewellyn

Grace has put together 15 essays by and interviews with children, teenagers, and parents. There are lots of photos throughout this 316-page paperback. Item #9111, $14.99. Available from FUN Books Catalog, 1688 Belhaven Woods Court, Pasadena, MD 21122-3727; voice/fax: 410/360-7330. (See coupon.)

Government Nannies by Cathy Duffy

This 263-page paperback, with a foreword by John Taylor Gatto, is a tremendous book! Cathy Duffy wades through a swamp of government nonsense and doublespeak, to bring you understandable and enjoyable reading about a modern socialist agenda to turn the local public school into a depot of more government "services"—whether you want them or not! $14.95. Available only through Noble Publishing Associates, P.O. Box 2250, Gresham, OR 97030; 503/667-3942.

Hard Times in Paradise and Homeschooling for Excellence, both by David and Micki Colfax

These two books were written by the northern California couple who homesteaded a goat farm in the early 1980s. Their homeschooled sons attended Ivy League schools, proving that homeschooled children can make the grade in the wide world. This is a fascinating family story and very good reading. *Hard Times in Paradise,* $19.95 plus $2 shipping; *Homeschooling for Excellence,* $19.95 plus $2.50 shipping. Available from Mountain House Press, P.O. Box 353, Philo, CA 95466. (See coupon.)

The Homeschool Source Book by Donn Reed

This is the granddaddy of all resource books, originally compiled in 1982. It is a comprehensive catalog and directory of learning materials that the publisher deems challenging, constructive, or fun.

There are commentaries, essays, and notes about the family's liberal arts education at home from birth to adulthood. $20. Available only from Brook Farm Books, Bridgewater, ME; 506/375-4680.

Homeschooling: A Patchwork of Days by Nancy Lande

Wanting to offer beginning homeschoolers the opportunity to see how other parents homeschool on a day-to-day basis, homeschooling mom Nancy Lande decided to write a book that allows readers to "visit" a wide variety of families in their own homes. Find out how 30 different families go about their everyday tasks, from handling the cooking and cleaning to nurturing the husband/wife relationship. Different styles are represented to help you determine which one best suits your family. Experienced families will be interested in new resources, tips, and ideas for a change in style or scheduling. Item #0304, $10.35. Available from FUN Books Catalog, 1688 Belhaven Woods Court, Pasadena, MD 21122-3727; voice/fax: 410/360-7330. (See coupon.)

The Homeschooling Book of Answers by Linda Dobson

This 350-page book is structured to answer 88 of the most frequently asked questions by homeschooling's most respected voices. Some of them are the experienced homeschooling parents themselves. Others are teachers, such as John Taylor Gatto, or other people with experience in the homeschooling world, such as Susannah Sheffer of Holt Associates. The book, which has a loose interview-style format, is very easy reading and answers the questions homeschooling newcomers have. $22.95. Available from Prima Publishing, 916/632-4400.

The Homeschooling Handbook, 2nd ed., by Mary Griffith

A well-respected and experienced member of the homeschooling community, Mary has written a very thorough, enjoyable book that covers all the bases. She includes information on the primary, middle, and teen years; evaluation and record keeping; the legal "stuff"; handling special circumstances; the pluses and minuses of different homeschooling approaches; and much more. This 320-page paperback covers homeschooling resources, including helpful magazines, catalogs, websites, and local support groups. The opinions of a variety of homeschoolers who are quoted throughout are both useful and enjoyable. $14.95. Available from Prima Publishing, 916/632-4400.

Discover Your Child's Learning Style by Mariaemma Pelullo-Willis and Victoria Kindle Hodson

Two of the foremost learning styles experts in the homeschooling field put their 45 years of combined experience into this book, offering you a clear, easy-to-read guide into the concept of learning styles analysis. Everyone possesses seven different kinds of intelligence, some dominant, some not. Willis and Kindle Hodson take this concept further by defining peoples' learning styles on the basis of four other elements—such as environment—to develop a concise outline of an individual's "learning" personality. This is a fascinating, useful topic, and we have found the authors' results to be completely on-point

with us. $15. Available from Prima Publishing, 916/632-4400.

Learning All the Time: How Small Children Begin to Read, Write, Count, and Investigate the World, Without Being Taught by John Holt

John was working on this book before his death, and it was completed using his articles in *Growing Without Schooling* and other previously uncollected writing. This 169-page paperback demonstrates that children can and do pick up "the basics" from the world around them. I find many of his ideas very practical, not just theoretical, and every so often I pick up and skim this book to help remind me that my child is, indeed, learning all the time. Item #0911, $9.99. Available from FUN Books Catalog, 1688 Belhaven Woods Court, Pasadena, MD 21122-3727; voice/fax: 410/360-7330. (See coupon.)

The Moore Report, a periodical published monthly by The Moore Foundation

Dr. Raymond and Dorothy Moore were two of the earliest unschooling proponents, along with John Holt. Their viewpoint is very interesting and worth reading up on. $15 for a one-year subscription; $25 for a two-year subscription. Available only from The Moore Foundation, Box 1, Camas, WA 98607; 800/891-5255; 360/835-5500; fax: 360/835-5392; website: www.moorefoundation.com.

Real Lives: Eleven Teenagers Who Don't Go to School by Grace Llewellyn

Firsthand accounts written by teenagers about the things they can do when given the opportunity. It is reassuring for parents and kids to hear the voices of "real-life" teenagers. It is also fascinating to read all the different teenage stories and see the variety of interests they have and the different educational experiences they've gone through. Black-and-white photos accompany the text in this 318-page paperback. Item #9138, $15.99. Available from FUN Books Catalog, 1688 Belhaven Woods Court, Pasadena, MD 21122-3727; voice/fax: 410/360-7330. (See coupon.)

The Relaxed Home School
by Mary Hood

This 106-page paperback discusses how to help your children learn without an expensive curriculum and lesson plan. It also covers how to create units based on your child's interests, how to motivate reluctant teens, how to set goals and design your curriculum, and more. Item #4009, $9.85. Available from FUN Books Catalog, 1688 Belhaven Woods Court, Pasadena, MD 21122-3727; voice/fax: 410/360-7330. (See coupon.)

A Sense of Self: Listening to
Homeschooled Adolescent Girls
by Susannah Sheffer

If you've been discouraged by recent books and reports asserting that the self-esteem of adolescent girls plummets during their teenage years, this 191-page paperback will encourage you. The 55 in-depth interviews conducted with homeschooled girls ages 11 to 16 show that these homeschoolers are holding onto the strengths they had as children. Item #4052, $13.99. Available from FUN Books Catalog, 1688 Belhaven Woods Court, Pasadena, MD 21122-3727; voice/fax: 410/360-7330. (See coupon.)

The Well-Trained Mind: A Guide to
Classical Education at Home by Jessie
Wise and Susan Wise Bauer

This 764-page hardcover, authored by a mother-daughter team, provides excellent guidance into the trivium or classical approach to education, but also offers an insight into what sort of person a homeschooled child may grow up to be. Jessie, the mother and a former school teacher, taught Susan at home using the classical approach. Later, Susan began using the same method to homeschool her children. The result is a two-generation compilation of empirical information regarding the value of teaching the classical approach. $35. Published by W. W. Norton.

Teenage Liberation Handbook: How To
Quit School and Get a Real Life and
Education by Grace Llewellyn

This 443-page paperback is a terrific book! Written especially for teenagers and people with teenagers in their lives, it is also helpful for anyone who has ever gone to school. Grace discusses how to regain the natural ability to learn and be excited about it, ways of going to college, volunteering, apprenticeships, and more. The book leans toward an unschooling approach, which Grace is able to superbly articulate. The book is particularly popular for teenagers who plan on taking charge of their education, whether they are currently homeschooling, planning on homeschooling, or moving on to college. Highly recommended, this newly revised and expanded edition includes international information. Item #9103, $16.99. Available from FUN Books Catalog, 1688 Belhaven Woods Court, Pasadena, MD 21122-3727; voice/fax: 410/360-7330. (See coupon.)

The Unschooling Handbook: How to Use the Whole World as Your Child's Classroom by Mary Griffith

Just from the cover of Mary's new book, you can tell that this is not your typical homeschooling book—and not just because it has "unschooling" in the title! In this 230-page paperback, Mary has provided lots of good information, including resources for different subjects, real-life examples of what people do, and lots of great explanations. If you are already an ardent unschooler, it will still give you lots of good tips and insights into what other unschoolers may do, and lots of information to help you explain and defend your unschooling decision. Item #2764, $11.95. Available from FUN Books Catalog, 1688 Belhaven Woods Court, Pasadena, MD 21122-3727; voice/fax: 410/360-7330. (See coupon.)

Writing Because We Love To: Homeschoolers at Work by Susannah Sheffer

This book was written by the editor of *Growing Without Schooling*. Through her work with homeschoolers ages 10 to 15, the author explores how to help kids with their writing and looks at what children do when they are in charge of their own learning. This 122-page paperback provides many examples of young writers' work and their reflections on it. Item #3013, $11.95. Available from FUN Books Catalog, 1688 Belhaven Woods Court, Pasadena, MD 21122-3727; voice/fax: 410/360-7330. (See coupon.)

Prepackaged Curriculums and Consulting Services

A Beka ✝

Box 18000
Pensacola, FL 32523-9160
800/874-3592
fax: 800/874-3593
www.Abeka.org
A Beka provides textbooks that are popular for school-at-home use.

Alger Learning Center/ Independence High School

121 Alder Dr.
Sedro Woolley, WA 98284
800/595-2630
Alger offers homeschool assistance, individualized curriculum, long-distance learning programs, high school completion, and annual assessments for homeschoolers. They have been in business since 1980.

Alpha Omega ✝

300 N. McKemy Ave.
Chandler, AZ 85226-2618
800/622-3070
fax: 602/438-2702
This popular Christian publisher creates many of its own products for Christian homeschoolers, as well as offering manufacturers' products that have been made by other companies. It is an excellent resource for homeschoolers. See their online service as well in the Cybersources section.

The American School

2200 E. 170th
Lansing, IL 60438
708/418-2800

The American School offers high school correspondence courses and has been in business for over 100 years. It enables adults who did not receive the traditional diploma, as well as homeschoolers, to obtain a high school diploma. You may take one class at a time or entire grades. This is an accredited school, which means that a person who has left high school without enough credits to graduate may use it to obtain the needed credits.

At Home Publications

2826 Roselawn Ave.
Baltimore, MD 21214-1719
410/444-5465

This is a homeschool curriculum for grades K to 5, written by a homeschool family.

Bob Jones University Press ✝

Greenville, SC 29614
800/845-5731

Provides textbooks that are popular for school-at-home use.

Calvert School

105 Tuscany Rd.
Baltimore, MD 21210
410/243-6030
fax: 410/366-0674
website: www.calvertschool.org
e-mail: inquiry@calvertschool.org

This is a pre-K-through-8th-grade, free-standing day school in Baltimore, Maryland, founded over 100 years ago. The school itself has a stellar reputation for tra-

ditional, rigorous academics, and its complete curriculum-in-a-box is in an easy-to-use format. This homeschool favorite is rare in that it provides a classical education without any religious view. *Everything you need* comes in the box—including pencils and erasers! The price ranges from $300 to $450. An optional Teacher's Advisory Service is available for an additional charge. With this service, students turn in tests at their own pace and have them corrected and returned; they correspond with the same teacher throughout the entire grade.

Cambridge Academy

3855 S.E. Lake Weir Ave.
Ocala, FL 34474
352/401-3688
800/881-2717

A correspondence school for grades K to 6.

Curriculum Services

26801 Pine Ave.
Bonita Springs, FL 34135
941/992-6381
fax: 941/992-6473
website: www.curriculumservices.com

Curriculum Services offers customized homeschool programs across the United States.

Excellence in Education (EIE)

2640 S. Myrtle Ave., Unit A-7
Monrovia, CA 91016
626/821-0025
fax: 626/357-4443
website: www.excellenceineducation.com

EIE provides a bookstore and independent study program. This facility, based in Southern California, offers a complete line of services designed to meet the needs of any homeschooling family. EIE is owned and operated by a very broad-minded Christian couple who home-schooled their two daughters (who are now in college). The independent study program also has a game division through which they provide you with a curriculum guide and the opportunity to teach any subject through games.

Home Study International (HSI) †

12501 Old Columbia Pike
Silver Spring, MD 20904-6600
800/782-4769
website: www.hsi.edu
This company is a long-distance education provider offering individual, Christian-based courses from preschool through college, as well as degrees. Students can enroll in entire grades or individual courses, varying from business and secretarial to English, fine arts, religion, creation-based science courses, character-building Bible courses, theology, and much more—all taught by accomplished Christian instructors. HSI is a member of the Distance Education and Training Council, approved for accreditation in many states.

Indiana University

800/334-1011
website: www.extend.indiana.edu
In operation since 1912, IU Independent Study is one of the nation's leading independent study programs. It has won more national course awards than any other program of its kind. Choose from 105 high school courses, earn high school and university credits at the same time with 58 dual-credit courses, and enroll anytime. Call for a free catalog.

Jump Start Learning System

Learning Services
P.O. Box 10636
Eugene, OR 97440-2636
800/877-9378 (Western Region)
800/877-3278 (Eastern Region)
Complete grade-wise curriculums for preschool (ages 2 to 4) to 6th grade (ages 10 to 12). The program includes nine hybrid CD disks plus a CD-ROM typing program; each disk is $44.95. Preschool (ages 2 to 4): Comprehension, Phonics & Letter Sounds, Letters & Numbers (KADV0009-CDBS); pre-K (ages 3 to 5): Letter Order, Quantity, Vocabulary, Phonics & Letter Sounds (KADV0120-CDBS); kindergarten (ages 4 to 6): Letter Combinations, Reading & Sentences, Time Concepts (KADV0008-CDBS); grade 1 (ages 5 to 7): Spelling, Literature, Early Math, Science, Geography, Vocabulary (KADV0010-CDBS); grade 2 (ages 6 to 8) Basic Grammar, Higher Math, Social Studies, Science, Writing (KADV0018-CDBS); grade 3 (ages 7 to 9): Sentence Structure, Division, Multiplication, Addition, Subtraction, History, Earth Science (KADV0130-CDBLS); grade 4 (ages 8 to 10): History, Famous People, Earth Science, Parts of Speech, Story Creation, Equations, Division with Remainders, Geometry, Art History (KADV0135-CDBS); grade 5 (ages 9 to 11), U.S. History, Logic, Deductive Reasoning, Map Reading, Prepositions, Pronouns, Fractions, Long Division (KADV0020-CDBS); grade 6 (ages 10 to

12): Vocabulary, Analogies, Grammar, Spelling, Composition, Poetry, Comprehension, Percent, Biology, Geology (KADV0030-CDBS). (See coupon.)

Keystone National High School

Schoolhouse Station
420 W. 5th St.
Bloomsburg, PA 17815
717/784-5220
website: www.keystonehighschool.com
Keystone boasts that they are accessible (enroll at any time), affordable (no hidden costs), and accommodating. Study at your own pace and use quality materials supported by quality instructors. It is academically sound and achievement-oriented and has an outstanding student service department to help you achieve your goals. A student can enroll in one class at a time for $140; or in an entire grade and receive everything needed for $700. (Those wishing a creation-based science, please check first.) Keystone also offers driver's education courses and is a member of the Distance Education and Training Council, thereby being accepted in many states for accreditation.

Kolbe Academy Home School (Catholic) ✝

1600 F St.
Napa, CA 94559
707/255-7278
e-mail: kolbe@community.net
website: www.kolbe.org
This Catholic correspondence school features the Ignatian method, classical, content curriculum. Write for a free catalog.

Laurel Springs School

1002 E. Ojai Ave.
Ojai, CA 93024
805/646-2473
website: www.laurelsprings.com
This school offers customized, prepackaged curriculums for grades K to 12. They have an honors program, a special-needs curriculum, a book-based curriculum, and an online program. This is an excellent program for someone coming out of public or private school desiring the guidance and "feel" of a real school community and teachers in a real school. It is also a great program for those not wanting so much guidance. They will help you as much or as little as you like. (See coupon.)

Oak Meadow School

P.O. Box 740
Putney, VT 05346
802/387-2021
e-mail: oms@oakmeadow.com
website: www.oakmeadow.com
Oak Meadow has been in business for over 20 years. On their website, they state: "Children are sensitive, intelligent, creative spirits seeking to learn, to grow, and to express their unique excellence, and we believe the purpose of education is to provide a safe, supportive environment that will enable them to do this." Their philosophy is one that does not promote getting good grades for the sake of good grades.

The Robinson Self-Teaching Curriculum, Version 2.0

The Oregon Institute of Science & Medicine
2251 Dick George Rd.
Cave Junction, OR 97523

This is a complete grades 1 to 12 curriculum and source library on 22 CD-ROMs. It includes a complete course of study for all grades; a 120,000-page library resource; a 1911 *Encyclopaedia Britannica*; a 1913 *Noah Webster's Dictionary*; 2,000 historic illustrations; a 6,000-word vocabulary teacher; progress exams keyed to books; and an outstanding science program. The only additional materials required are Saxon math books, and if you purchase Dr. Robinson's curriculum, you will receive a 20% discount on these. This is not a program that children do on the computer; it is simply the way the program comes to you. The author cautions: "Do not use this curriculum unless you are willing for your children to be more academically learned than you." Entire program (22 CDs) $195.

The School of Tomorrow ✝

P.O. Box 299000
Lewisville, TX 75029-9000
800/925-7777
website: www.schooloftomorrow.com
This organization offers an individualized core curriculum, K through 12, with many extra electives to broaden your child's education. Biblical character building is an integral part of the curriculum in all subjects. This school has 25 years' experience, is a homeschool favorite among Christians, and offers a comprehensive homeschooling quick-start kit.

Schoolhouse Rock Collection

Learning Services
P.O. Box 10636
Eugene, OR 97440-2636
800/877-9378 (Western Region)
800/877-3278 (Eastern Region)

All four CD-ROMs and teachers' guides come in one complete package! Each CD explores a particular curriculum area with signature Schoolhouse Rock style. Original animated cartoons and songs combine with learning activities and games to reinforce every lesson. Each program includes multiple skill levels, providing an interactive experience that's appropriate for every learning style. Special teacher information and printable progress reports make this collection an ideal addition to your elementary school–level library. The package contains: America Rock (ages 7 to 15), Grammar Rock (ages 7 to 10), Math Rock (ages 7 to 10), Science Rock (ages 8 to 12). Item #CREW00D1-CDBS, $114.95. (See coupon.)

Seascape Educational Center

P.O. Box 1074
Thousand Oaks, CA 91358-0074
805/446-1917
website: pages.prodigy.com./SEAS
Seascape Educational Center is a nationwide program providing a complete curriculum for grades pre-K through 12. This service will provide diploma, report cards, record keeping, and transcripts, and will help you with step-by-step guidance for homeschooling your child.

The Sycamore Tree

The Sycamore Tree Center for Home
Education
2179 Meyer Pl.
Costa Mesa, CA 92627
800/779-6750
website: www.sycamoretree.com
This company offers a complete homeschool program, K to 8, for anyone interested worldwide. You can choose your own

curriculum from over 3,000 items in their catalog or join their school and let them choose for you. They include Bible-based, character-building courses. Sycamore also offers an online service. They have been in business since 1982.

TRISMS

1203 S. Delaware Pl.
Tulsa, OK 74104
918/585-2778
website: www.trisms.com
Time Related Integrated Studies for Mastering Skills (TRISMS) offers a partial curriculum covering world history, science, and language arts. It includes lesson plans that guide you to supplemental sources. The program does not include math.

University of Arizona

888 North Euclid Ave.
P.O. Box 210158
Tucson, AZ 85721-0158
800/772-7480
website: www.arizona.edu/~uaextend
e-mail: Idykstra@ccit.arizona.edu
The University of Arizona Correspondence Program was founded in 1912 and is a recognized leader in distance education. In the Elementary, Middle School, and High School Program, for grades 4 to 12, students and parents can choose from an extensive variety of quality courses. All classes are taught by certified practicing teachers experienced in their applicable age group. With the UA Correspondence Program, you will benefit from easy-to-follow curriculums, classes conveniently broken down by semester, the option to submit many assignments by e-mail, personal feedback

from helpful instructors, affordable prices, and a wide range of more than 145 courses.

Catalogs

The catalogs listed here are from mail-order companies specializing in the homeschool market.

Alpha Omega Publications ✝

300 N. McKemy Ave.
Chandler, AZ 85226-2618
800/622-3070
Alpha-Omega is "setting the standard for Christian homeschool education."

Bluestocking Press Catalog

P.O. Box 2030
Shingle Springs, CA 95682
916/621-1123
fax: 916/642-9222
This is an excellent resource for all homeschoolers.

Celestial Products

P.O. Box 801
Middleburg, VA 20118-0801
800/235-3783
Celestial offers fine astronomy products—galaxy posters, spectacular wall murals, comet posters, moon-phase posters, and much more.

The Eagle's Nest Educational Supplies Catalog

1411 Standiford Ave., Ste. A
Modesto, CA 95350
209/529-7720
fax: 209/529-1715

Catalogs

This company is so loaded with educational supplies for religious and secular home-schoolers that it's possibly the best home-school company around.

The Education Connection

P.O. Box 910367
St. George, UT 84791
800/863-3828
fax: 800/227-6609
website: www.educationconnection.com
This is an eclectic company featuring many arts and crafts products, owned by a homeschooling family with eight children. They have everything from curriculum to games, Saxon math to Italic writing. It has a very creative slant. Send for free catalog.

The Educators' Exchange

60 W. Ministorage
10755 Midlothian Turnpike
Richmond, VA 23235
804/794-6994
website: www.websvirginia.com./edex
Provides curriculums for the home-schooler up to the 12th grade.

The Elijah Company ✝

1053 Eldridge Loop
Crossville, TN 38558-9600
931/456-6284
888/2-ELIJAH
website: www.elijah.co
This is a Christian company; however, they also have products that appeal to all.

Emeth Educational Supplies

20618 Cypress Way
Lynnwood, WA 98036
425/672-8708
Emeth is primarily a Christian company that also carries products that appeal to all.

Family Christian Press Homeschool Warehouse ✝

483 Myatt Dr.
Madison, TN 37115
615/860-3000
800/788-0840 (orders)
Extensive product list suitable for home-schoolers and others.

Family Unschoolers Network (FUN)

1688 Belhaven Woods Court
Pasadena, MD 21122-3727
410/360-6265
website: www.iqcweb.com./fun
FUN Books carries a wide variety of products geared toward homeschooling and particularly, unschooling. They have software, craft kits, art supplies, history books, geography books, and much more. It is owned and operated by a home-schooling family. Send for free catalog. (See coupon.)

Family Works Unlimited

412 N. Fork Rd.
Metamora, IL 61548
801/565-9008
This company carries a general product line for all areas and grades K to 12. Call or write for catalog.

Farm Country General Store (FCGS)

Rt. 7, North Fork Rd.
Metamora, IL 61548
309/367-2844
800/551-FARM (orders only)
fax: 309/367-2844
website: www.homeschoolfcgs.com
e-mail: fcgs@mtco.com

Besides books and other products specifically for homeschoolers, FCGS carries interesting useful items like Indian Corn Soap, herbs, natural vitamins, and much more.

FUN Books Catalog

1688 Belhaven Woods Ct.
Pasadena, MD 21122-3727
410/360-7330 (voice/fax)

This is an excellent resource for everyone from unschoolers to school-at-home. They offer a diverse catalog of products.

Home Again

1825 N. 183rd St.
Seattle, WA 98133
888/666-0721
website: www.home-again.com

Hands-on learning in all curriculum areas including carpentry, handwork, and art is the focus in this catalog. Many Waldorf-inspired items are included. Call to request their free catalog.

Home Learner Catalog

1231 Manchester Dr.
El Dorado Hills, CA 95762
916/933-9838

This company specializes in history and literature.

The Home School

P.O. Box 308
N. Chelmsford, MA 01863-0308
800/788-1221

This catalog contains educational products geared toward the homeschooler.

Lehman's Catalog

One Lehman Cir.
P.O. Box 41
Kidron, OH 44636-0041
330/857-5757
fax: 330/857-5785
e-mail: GetLehmans@aol.com

This is a fascinating "Amish" products catalog from the heart of Ohio. It features woodburning stoves, hand-operated household machines, and other devices that are handy for independent families looking for more self-sufficiency.

Lynn's Homeschool Resources

P.O. Box 2305
1790 Betty St.
Wrightwood, CA 92397
760/249-6735

This Christian company provides products for the homeschooler.

Reprint Classroom Direct

P.O. Box 830677
Birmingham, AL 35283-0677
800/599-3040
website: www.classroomdirect.com

This company offers everything educational direct to you. Their catalog, which is almost 1½ inches thick, is not geared to homeschoolers. It does, however, have interesting arts and crafts, paper, paint, and markers—the types of things teachers would buy in bulk. It is worth calling for the free catalog and possibly making orders with other homeschool friends. In addition to bulk ordering, the company offers huge discounts on math software, social studies, reference software, and more. Save up to 76% on many mainstream products.

Rod & Staff Publishers, Inc. ✝

P.O. Box 3, Hwy 172
Crockett, KY 41413-0003
606/522-4348
Rod & Staff provides a Christian homeschool curriculum.

Roots & Wings Educational Catalog ✝

P.O. Box 19678
Boulder, CO 80308-2678
303/776-4796
800/833-1787
This company's target audience for educational supplies is K to 5. They specialize in multicultural, ecology-type products.

Timberdoodle Company

E. 1510 Spencer Lake Rd.
Shelton, WA 98584
360/426-0672
website: www.timberdoodle.com
Timberdoodle offers a very popular, diverse line of products in all subjects.

Tobin's Lab

P.O. Box 6503
Glendale, AZ 85312-6503
602/843-3520
800/522-4776
website: www.tobinlab.com
This is an excellent resource for science material for homeschoolers, run by a homeschool family.

Total Language Plus Catalog ✝

P.O. Box 12622
Olympia WA 98508
360/754-3660
Language arts products with a Christian perspective for middle and upper grades.

Whole Heart Catalogue ✝

P.O. Box 67
Walnut Springs, TX 76690
254/797-2142 (office)
800/311-2146 (orders)
e-mail: whm@wholeheart.org
website: www.wholeheart.org
This Christian catalog has many fine books and products that, in some cases, are suitable for the non-Christian as well. Write or call for their catalog.

Testing and Test Preparation

Pre-GED CD (Ages 15 to 18)

Use this tremendous CD to prepare your student who is not yet ready for high school equivalency. It contains the most extensive collection of material available anywhere—dozens of hours of material to be used over and over again—but at a much lower price than separately purchased software programs. MAC CD: QUEU0605-MCCD or WIN CD: QUEU0605-PCCD, $295.95. Available from Learning Services, P.O. Box 10636, Eugene, OR 97440-2636; Western Region: 800/877-9378; Eastern Region: 800/877-3278. (See coupon.)

GED CD (Ages 15 to 18)

This program prepares your student for the GED exam. Many hours of material can be used over and over for study. The program covers government, history, reading comprehension, chemistry, biology, writing skills, economics, physics, and health. All for much less than if the same material were purchased as separate titles. MAC CD: QUEU0610-MCCD or WIN CD: QUEU0610-PCCD, $295.95. Available from Learning Services, P.O. Box 10636, Eugene, OR 97440-2636; Western Region: 800/877-9378; Eastern Region: 800/877-3278. (See coupon.)

Kaplan CD-ROM Study Guides for the PSAT/SAT and ACT (Ages 15 to 18)

Give your student the advantage of this great study prep program! Over 2,700 test questions, scoring averages for hundreds of colleges, updated college admission information, Internet links to over 600 college websites, and 15 math review lessons. Hybrid CD: SAT: KADV0360-CDBS, $59.95; ACT: KADV0365-CDBS, $59.95. Available from Learning Services, P.O. Box 10636, Eugene, OR 97440-2636; Western Region: 800/877-9378; Eastern Region: 800/877-3278. (See coupon.)

Princeton Review: Inside the SAT & ACT '99 (Ages 14 to 19)

This study aid (two deluxe CD-ROMs) is packed with information to help your student increase his or her scores on the PSAT, SAT, and ACT tests. Instructors from the Princeton Review provide on-screen teaching and test-taking strategies. Hybrid CD: MIND9020-CDB,

$37.95. Available from Learning Services, P.O. Box 10636, Eugene, OR 97440-2636; Western Region: 800/877-9378; Eastern Region: 800/877-3278. (See coupon.)

Used Educational Supplies

The Back Pack
P.O. Box 125
Ernuel, NC 28527
252/244-0728
website: www.thebackpack.com
e-mail: thebackpack@coastalnet.com
This is your one-stop shopping place for grades K to 12. Whether you are home-schooling for religious reasons or have a secular point of view, you can happily shop here. This company, in business since 1990, is owned and operated by a homeschooling family with over 13 years' experience. They offer you personalized service, including free customized curriculum development for any grade. Please call or write for their catalog.

Home Text
283 Nevins St.
Brooklyn, NY 11217
888/466-3839
website: www.hometext.com
This company is a supplier of curriculums, both new and used, religious and secular, for all of your homeschooling needs. Home Text has developed their own K-to-12th-grade-level packages that are designed to provide homeschooling

families with the "essential" books they need for any given grade level at the absolutely best price possible.

Second Harvest
Rt. 1, Box 75
Humphrey, NE 68642
402/923-1682
website: www.secondharvest.com
website catalog:
megavision.com./~business/harvest
e-mail: rjnoona@megavision.com
This is a Christian company that carries new character-training material as well as a large pre-owned inventory at 25% to 75% off retail! Also sells Saxon math, Usborne, and other curriculums that any homeschooler would use. They also buy used books in good condition. Free catalog upon request.

The Home School
104 S. West Ave.
Arlington, WA 98223
800/788-1221 (orders only)
360/435-0376
fax: 360/435-1028
This is a Christian book and supplies company that offers material such as Usborne books at a 25% discount and is, therefore, attractive to any homeschooling family. They have been in business for over 10 years. Call or write for a free catalog.

Homeschool Discount.com
Bailey Advertising Co.
108 Windsong Dr.
Stockbridge, GA 30281
800/401-9931 or 770/474-5341
website: www.homeschooldiscount.com
Save up to 40% when you buy products through this website. They carry educational games, homeschool curriculums, math curriculums, science kits, and software games. They are a Christian company but carry something for everybody.

Excellence in Education (EIE) Bookstore
2640 S. Myrtle Ave., Unit A-7,
Monrovia, CA 91016
626/821-0025
fax: 626/357-4443
website: www.excellenceineducation.com
EIE's bookstore is designed to bring the joy of learning to your home. They offer books, activities, and games that can complement homeschool styles that range from formal to informal. Tap into their 15 years of homeschool experience and vast resources to make your homeschooling experience successful and joyful to all members of the family. Call for catalog. (See coupon.)

Laurelwood Publications
Rt. 1, Box 878
Bluemont, VA 20135
540/554-2670
Laurelwood offers used textbooks—Bob Jones University, A Beka, Saxon math, and more—with many new items at discount prices. The company also carries Pathway Readers, Writing Strands, Easy Grammar, Beautiful Feet, and other products.

Eagle's Nest Educational Supplies
1411 Standiford Ave, Ste. A
Modesto, CA 95350
209/529-7720
fax: 209/529-1715

This company carries an unbelievably large amount of homeschooling supplies for all homeschoolers. It is owned and operated by a Christian homeschool family. They carry everything from Saxon math to *Far Above Rubies*. Call for a free catalog.

Shekinah Curriculum Cellar

101 Meador Rd.
Kilgore, TX 75662
903/643-2760
fax: 903/643-2796
e-mail: customerservice@shekinahcc.com
website: www.shekinahcc.com
This company has a K-to-12 home-schooling catalog covering all subjects. Their products are highly discounted, and they match the lowest prices.

Atco School Supply

425 E. 6th St., Unit 105
Corona, CA 91719
909/272-2926
e-mail: atco@atco1.com
This is a K-to-12 catalog company with a Christian perspective; they do, however, carry many items that are useful to the non-Christian family as well, such as Saxon math and various phonics programs. The products are highly discounted. Send for catalog.

Barb's People Builders

3420 Highway 46 West
Templeton, CA 93465
805/237-9639
800/925-8587
e-mail: barb@barbsbooks.com
website: www.barbsbooks.com

This company sells products for the homeschooler, especially those focused on foreign language, English, or history. Please call for catalog.

Roots & Wings

P.O. Box 19678
Boulder, CO 80308-2678
303/776-4796
800/833-1787
website:
  www.books@rootsandwingscatalog.com
This company's specialty is multicultural products. They have an interesting line of educational supplies and books. Please call for catalog.

The Salt Seller

P.O. Box 56701
Phoenix, AZ 85079-6701
602/249-2699
e-mail: saltseller@aol.com
This company specializes in selling used curriculum. It is owned and operated by a homeschooling family. Please call for catalog.

Curriculum Services

26801 Pine Ave.
Bonita Springs, FL 34135
941/992-6473
website: www.curriculumservices.com
This company specializes in customizing homeschool programs. They have selected materials from over 150 suppliers of K to 12, public and non-religious private schools.

Alta Vista Curriculum
P.O. Box 1487
1936 N. Shiloh Dr.
Fayetteville, AR 72702-1487
501/443-9205
fax: 501/442-3064
This company provides a wide variety of resources.

Budgetext Home Education
P.O. Box 1487
1936 N. Shiloh Dr.
Fayetteville, AR 72702-1487
888/888-2272
email: sales@homeschoolmail.com
Budgetext is a company that has been offering quality textbooks at a savings since 1968.

Cybersources

Online Educational Programs

The Willoway School
610/678-0214
website: www.willoway.com
This school has a technology and science Web-based curriculum featuring authentic assessment, meaningful, personal relationships, and portfolio compilation. Peer inside the window to Willoway through the Web, where homeschoolers are inventing the future of education. Willoway students interactively use the Internet in all phases of their day and

meet via video-conferencing with their fellow students and teachers.

The Learning Odyssey (Grades 6 to 10)
800/457-4509
This online program boasts that it is the first complete curriculum available over the Internet, and it satisfies all state and national standards. Created by the Agency for Instructional Technology, the site offers interactive, contextualized lessons, multimedia support materials, real-life work situations, career exploration, and Web-based activities.

The Lyceum International Distance-Learning Program
2530 Perry Ave., Ste. 300
Bremerton, WA 98310
800/216-9708
webite: www.lyceumintl.com
Lyceum International is an online program offering university-level courses taught by outstanding intellectuals without the rampant relativism so prevalent on today's campuses. If you are looking for a rational, objective, non-politically correct educational alternative, join the many students from high school to university level, professionals, housewives, and people from all different walks of life who have gained from these programs.

Indiana University
800/334-1011
website: www.extend.indiana.edu
In operation since 1912, IU Independent Study is one of the nation's leading independent study programs. It has won more national course awards than any other

program of its kind. Choose from 105 high school courses, earn high school and university credits at the same time with 58 dual-credit courses, and enroll anytime! Call them and they will answer your questions about homeschooling with IU and send you a free catalog.

Laurel Springs School (Grades 5 to 12)
1002 East Ojai Ave.
Ojai, CA 93024
805/646-2473
website: www.laurelsprings.com
This is an accredited private school licensed by the state of California. Their online learning program provides fully approved curriculums to families statewide, nationwide, and worldwide. When your child graduates, she or he receives an academic diploma and transcript that is accepted by colleges and universities worldwide. Their unique online instruction provides students with the opportunity to work one-on-one with certified teachers who are just an e-mail away. The students access their lessons at the Laurel Springs School website. Some of these lessons are on CD-ROM. Students access specific websites to fulfill assignments. (See coupon.)

Bridgestone Online Academy ✝
300 N. McKemy Ave.
Chandler, AZ 85226-2618
800/682-7396
e-mail: bola@switched-onschoolhouse.com
website: www.switched-onschoolhouse
*   .com./bola*
This online site offers a Christ-centered, computer-based education for parents who want to homeschool yet are looking for the teaching and accreditation that a private school offers. Now you can have the best of homeschool, private school, and computer-based education all in one. Students use the Switched-On Schoolhouse multimedia curriculum and complete their studies daily at home on the computer by hooking up to Bridgestone's Internet site and then transfer their work to the academy's teachers. Comments and/or grading are e-mailed back to the student. Certified teachers, placement testing at the outset, progress reports, and report cards are featured.

Escondido Tutorial Service ✝
2634 Bernardo Ave.
Escondido, CA 92029
760/746-0980
website: www.gbt.org
ETS is dedicated to bringing classical Christian education to homeschoolers. Tutorials are available in your own home through the Internet. ETS is owned by Fritz Hinrichs, who believes that the study of great books is the backbone of a good education, just as it has been for centuries. He believes that the demise of great books was the demoralization of the Christian intellectual community.

University of Wisconsin Independent Learning Extension Course
432 N. Lake St., Room 104
Madison, WI 53706-1498
800/442-6460
UW offers extension courses in business, economics, mathematics, sciences, arts, and literature.

Websites

AIMS Education Foundation
www.aimsedu.org
AIMS stands for Activities Integrating Math, Science & Technologies; they offer an online catalog, teacher resources, *AIMS Magazine*, and workshop information.

Alpha Omega Publications ✝
www.home-schooling.com
This site shows the company's Christian materials.

Alta Vista Curriculum
www.valleyplaza.com
New and used homeschooling curriculums.

Amanda Bennett Unit Study ✝
www.unitstudy.com
This site has products and resources listed for all homeschoolers. It is Christian in nature.

America Student Travel
www.astravel.com
This is a company website that has a section profiling trips that homeschoolers have taken.

American Christian History Institute ✝
www.achipa.com
This site contains information about their homeschooling program and seminars and philosophy.

Atco School Supply ✝
www.atco1.com
This Christian company offers a wide variety of academic and study products for the Christian homeschooling family.

The Back Pack
www.thebackpack.com
This is an online used curriculum store.

Barb's People Builders
www.barbsbooks.com
This site shows reviews and educational resources for homeschoolers.

Beautiful Feet Books
www.bfbooks.com
This site shows the company's book catalog.

Best Picks
www.howtonews.com
A small website showing products and inspirational short articles.

Bethlehem Books
www.bethlehembooks.com
This is a company website that includes most of their books. They specialize in reprinting quality children's books.

Bob Jones University, Christian University ✝
www.bju.edu/press
This site shows company catalog, product support, advice on textbook purchasing.

Bold Christian Living ✝
www.BoldChristianLiving.com
The site is operated by the Lindvall family. Jonathan is a popular Christian speaker and writer; many of his articles can be found here.

Boston School Bookstore
www.bostonschool.org
Site shows homeschool bookstore as well as many educational links.

Calvert School

www.calvertschool.org

This site gives information about the day school and the homeschooling program, as well as individual products available.

Carolina Biological Supply Co.

www.carolinabiological.com

Large supplier of test tubes, many other scientific products, books, games, etc.

Catalog for Clasroomdirect.com Online

www.classroomdirect.com

A huge catalog carrying educational products.

Charlotte Mason Research & Supply Company

www.charlotte-mason.com

A resource place for homeschoolers interested in the Charlotte Mason approach to homeschooling.

A Child's Dream Catalogue

www.home.earthlink.net/~todream

An online catalog with baby items, dolls, toys, and gifts.

Christian Curriculum Cellar

ccc.simplenet.com

New and used curriculums and trades.

Christian Liberty Academy/Christian Liberty Press ✝

www.homeschools.org

This site has information about the online academy as well as the homeschool program.

Creative Teaching Associates ✝

www.mastercta.com

This site has many educational links for homeschoolers and product information.

Curriculum Services

www.curriculumservices.com

This site has listings of their products for homeschoolers.

Design-a-Study

www.designastudy.com

This is a company website telling all about the Design-a-Study products.

Discount Homeschool Supplies

www.dhss.com

This is an online catalog for discounted homeschool supplies.

The Elijah Company

www.elijahco.com

Articles, links, and a partial list of the Elijah catalog, which carries excellent products for homeschoolers.

Excellence in Education

www.excellenceineducation.com

This is a company website that has an online bookstore.

Explore Technologies

www.atlasphere.com

Information on the best geography tool ever!

Family Learning Organization

www.familylearning.org

This is a website that connects homeschoolers with testing and other resources.

Fireside Games

www.firesidegames.com

This website contains a demo of Rhymes & 'Nyms and ordering information; also homeschool links.

FUN Books

www.members.aol.com.FUNNews

Catalog of books about homeschooling as well as teaching books, etc.

The Gathering Place ✝

www.thegatheringplace.com

A Christian website with books, homeschool resources, and other links for Christians.

Gazelle Publications ✝

www.hoofprint.com

A homeschool resource website, Christian in nature with FAQs, Internet resources, and more.

Gordon School Of Art

www.newmasters.com

This site contains a student art gallery and information about the school and services.

Greek 'n' Stuff

home.earthlink.net/~timohs

Catalog of products for teaching Greek and Latin.

Green Leaf Press

www.greenleafpress.com

Family owned and operated, this site shows company catalog and reviews of new books.

Grove Publishing

www.grovepublishing.com

Sample reviews, articles, and resources

Growing Without Schooling

www.holtgws.com

Company site with information on homeschool consulting and John Holt's bookstore online.

History Alive

www.dianawaring.com

Waring history curriculum, online catalog, FAQs regarding Diana Waring's history products and more.

Home Education Magazine

www.home-ed-press.com

Many needed resources for the homeschooler, state-by-state resources, online newsletter, homeschooling library, and much more. One of the best websites around for homeschoolers.

Home Study International ✝

www.hsi.edu

This website contains information about the company's services for homeschoolers.

Homefires: The Journal Of Homeschooling

www.Homefires.com

This is one of the best homeschooling websites around. It has articles, resources, educational links.

Homeschool Curriculum Swap

www.theswap.com

Homeschoolers trade and sell products in a safe environment.

Homeschool Digest ✝
www.homeschooldigest.com
This quarterly journal for Christian homeschoolers is full of lengthy, intelligent articles relating to education, homeschooling, and the Christian faith.

Homeschool Discount
www.homeschooldiscount.com./home2/
Sedog.htm
Online store offering discounts on hundreds of products for homeschoolers.

Homeschool Fun
www.homeschoolfun.com
Provides an online magazine, educational supplies, classifieds, typical days section and more.

Homeschool Village
www.home-school-village.com
This site has many educational connections for homeschoolers.

The Homeschool Zone
www.homeschoolzone.com
Links, educational resources, bookstore, events, and more.

Indiana University School of Continuing Studies
www.extend.indiana.edu
This site has information about the Independent Study Program.

Insect Lore
www.insectlore.com
This is a company website with an awesome catalog online.

International Linguistics Corporation
www.learnables.com
Contains information regarding language programs.

Japanese Close Up
www.ccet.ua.edu
Information about University of Alabama's special projects.

Jon's Homeschool Resource Page
www.midnightbeach.com./hs
Probably the most popular homeschool spot on the Web; has something for every state and for every homeschooler.

KONOS, Inc.
www.konos.com
This is a company website that profiles their unit study materials.

Kaleidoscapes Homeschool
www.kaleidoscapes.com./wwboard
A basic information center for homeschoolers.

Keystone National High School
info@keystonehighschool.com
http://www.keystonehighschool.com
Information about the school's courses and services.

Laurel Springs School
www.laurelsprings.com
This site contains a detailed explanation and information regarding the school and its various services.

Lewis Educational Games
members.aol.com./dickwlewis
Company website showing their educational games.

Cybersources

The Link

www.homeschoolnewslink.com
The online version of *The Link, a Home-school Newspaper,* also includes links to many resources for homeschoolers.

Math Concepts

www.mathconcepts.com
Demos of company products and ordering information.

The Mining Company

www.homeschooling.miningco.com
An excellent information-gathering place for homeschoolers, articles, links, chats, and more.

On-Line Tutorial Services

www.supertutor.com
For a fee you can receive online help with homework

Patterns in Arithmetic

www.member.aol.com./patternpr
Company website showing arithmetic products along with links to educational articles and other websites.

Power-glide

www.power-glide.com
This is a company site profiling the many language courses that Power-glide carries.

Practical Homeschooling

www.home-school.com
Excellent resource for homeschoolers, state-by-state information, products, and more.

Progeny Press ✝

www.mgprogeny.com./progeny
Contains sample lessons, company catalog, and a discussion area.

Reflective Educational Perspectives

www.redp.com
This website has company information regarding "Self-Portrait" learning systems.

Rex Games

www.rexgames.com
This site has information regarding their product, Tangoes, and other company products.

School Is Dead, Learn in Freedom

www.learninfreedom.org
Many educational links and resources for homeschoolers. Many articles as well.

Seascape Educational Center

pages.prodigy.com./SEAS
This site includes information about the many services that the school offers to homeschoolers.

SmarterKids.com

www.SmarterKids.com
This is a company site with links to many other educational companies.

Space Camp

www.spacecamp.com
Find information regarding astronaut training and flight training programs for kids.

The Sycamore Tree Center for Home Education ✝

www.sycamoretree.com
This website shows the company's online catalog and has links for the Christian homeschooler.

Religious and Ethnic Resources

Catholic

Publishers

Bethlehem Books
15605 County Rd. 15
Minto, ND 58261
800/757-6831
website: www.bethlehembooks.com
Bethlehem Books is a publisher that reprints children's books set in a fictional Catholic/Christian background. They carry a wide variety of Catholic books, but their catalog is used by varied religions and homeschoolers.

Catholic Heritage Curricula
P.O. Box 125
Twain Harte, CA 95383-0125
website: www.sonnet.com./chc
This website is a catalog created by a homeschooling family. They publish a lot of their own materials but also carry materials from Neumann Press, Ignatius Press, and others. The catalog is available free of charge through the website.

Emmanuel Books
P.O. Box 321
Newcastle, DE 19720
800/871-5598
website: www.emmanuelbooks.com
Emmanuel is a distributor carrying a selection from the Kolbe Academy, Bethlehem Books, Neumann Press, Greenleaf, Our Father's House, and many more. Also carries Cuisinaire materials, Miqoun math, and much more.

Ignatius Press
P.O. Box 1339
Ft. Collins, CO 80522
800/651-1531
website: www.ignatius.com
This is a popular Catholic publisher who carries items enjoyed by homeschoolers, including *Homeward Bound, The Companion to the Catechism of the Catholic Church, Homeschooling Collection,* and *Designing Your Own Classical Curriculum.*

Leaflet Missal Company
976 W. Minnehaha Ave.
St. Paul, MN 55104-1556
800/328-9582
website: www.leafletmissal.org
This is a small gift company with rosaries, religious art, and cute, Catholic coloring books.

Neumann Press
Rt. 2, Box 30
Long Prairie, MN 56347
320/732-6358
website: www.rea-alp.com./~neumann
Neumann Press specializes in reprinting many of the old Catholic literature stories and textbooks. Among them are Catholic

National Readers, The American Cardinal Readers, and *The Outlaws of Ravenhurst.*

Priory Press
7200 W. Division St.
River Forest, IL 60305-1294
708/771-3030
773/478-3033 (shipping and ordering)
Priory Press specializes in the Dominicans' three-volume series of high school religion texts. Their homeschooler manuals are referenced to the new Catholic catechism.

Roman Catholic Books
P.O. Box 2286
Ft. Collins, CO 80522-2286
This company states their goal is "to preserve the best of Catholic literature for generations to come in the 21st Century." They have reprinted the *Catechism in Examples,* by Rev. D. Chisholm, and the *Mass Explained to Children,* by Dr. Maria Montessori. Please write for their catalog.

Saints & Scholars
c/o Palmer House Book Shop
34 N. Main St.
Waynesville, NC 28786
800/452-3936
This company carries a lot of materials for Catholic homeschoolers as well as DK Books, Saxon math, and others. It is well worth contacting.

St. Gabriel's Gift & Book Nook
website: www.stgabriel.com
This website is a fabulous way to obtain Catholic material online. Through it you can join a Catholic homeschool e-mail discussion group and view many of their

homeschool products from Ignatius Press, Bethlehem Books, and others.

Sursum Corda! The Catholic Revival
1331 Red Cedar Circle
Ft. Collins, CO 80524-20005
970/493-8781
This is a Catholic quarterly publication, published by *The Catholic Reform.* It has approximately 76 very attractive pages for about $6.75 per issue.

TAN Books
P.O. Box 424
Rockford, IL 61105
815/987-1800
website: www.tanbooks.com
This is a Catholic publisher carrying many Catholic homeschooling titles.

Catholic Homeschooling Programs

Kolbe Academy
1600 F St.
Napa, CA 94559
707/255-7278
website: www.com.munity.net/~kolbe
This is a Catholic correspondence school for homeschoolers. They offer an Ignatian method and classical content. Write for a free catalog.

Seton Homestudy
1350 Progress Dr.
Front Royal, VA 22630
540/636-9996
website: www.setonhome.org
Seton will sell you their own Catholic books and programs, even if you are not signed up with their homeschool program.

Catholic Websites of Interest

Traditions of Roman Catholic Homes (TORCH)

www.catholic-homeschool.com
This site has links for TORCH chapters, a catalog, activities, and general catholic information.

Jewish

Homeschooling Resources in the Jewish Community

Behrman House

235 Watchung Ave.
West Orange, NJ 07052
800/2212755 or 973/669-0447
website: www.behrmanhouse.com./catalog
Behrman House has many resources for Jewish/Hebrew education. They have a catalog with curriculum from preschool to high school that you can access by visiting their website.

Coalition for Advancement in Jewish Education (CAJE)

website: www.caje.org
This organization holds a convention each year and publishes some curriculum material.

Jewish Home Educators' Network (JHEN)

e-mail: Jhen@snj.com
website: http://snj.com./jhen
This is a quarterly networking newsletter with subscribers from all over the world who homeschool and observe Judaism at many different levels. They offer phone

and website support with much information available.

Jewish Homeschooling List

e-mail: jhlist@jewishmail.com
To connect with other Jewish families that are homeschooling, consider contacting the Jewish Homeschooling List of Jewish parents who are homeschooling their children. This is an attempt to build a community of Jewish homeschooling families to offer support, share ideas, and be together. It is not open to non-Jewish homeschoolers.

Jewish Homeschooling Support

www.geocities.com./Heartland/Hills/1259/
bmjwshed.htm
This website is a great resource for Jewish homeschooling. It has all kinds of links from curriculum to homeschooling, orthodox Jewish phone trees to websites, and much more.

The Jewish Publication Society (JPS)

800/237-1830
e-mail: JewishBook@aol.com
JPS is regarded as "The Jewish Publisher for the Jewish People." It is the oldest publisher of Jewish books in the English language. Their mission is to educate and enrich the Jewish community by publishing both classic and contemporary literature of outstanding quality. Membership is required. Please call or e-mail them for information.

The Learnables

800/237-1830
This is a language company that produces tapes for learning Hebrew.

Jewish

Lev Software

800/776-6538
Lev produces Hebrew software programs. No prior Hebrew knowledge is necessary to use their products.

Torah Aurah Productions

4423 Fruitland Ave.
Los Angeles, CA 90058
800/BE-TORAH
213/585-7312
This is another source for excellent materials from pre-school on up.

Latter-day Saint

LDS Websites

CTR Academy

www.geocities.com./Heartland/Pointe/1813
  /index.html
This is a good website for many links to a diverse group of homeschool sites, not all of which are LDS in nature. There is a suggested e-mail address: ldslearn-subscribe@egroups.com that one can subscribe to, but be forewarned that subscribers to this ring receive a lot of mail!

Charlotte's Page

www.geocities.com./Heartland/Plains/7038
  /BofM.html
This site is a broad website with many links. Charlotte has developed a study guide and lesson plan for the *Book of Mormon* consisting of 36 reading assignments based on a 36-week school year. She invites you to try it out and e-mail

her with any suggestions or comments you may have.

Latter-day Family Resources

www.ldfr.com./contact
On this website you'll find information about the LDS Education Convention, last held on August 14, 1999, in Provo, Utah. The convention coincides with the BYU Campus Education Week. A curriculum and LDS products fair is usually held as well.

Findlay Place

www.fly.hiwaay.net/~kfind/index.html
This website was created by the Findlay family. They are LDS, and their site has great links for LDS homeschooling families.

LDS Family Home Educators Exchange

www.members.xoom.com./ldfhe/index.html
This site has been called one of the best LDS homeschool links on the Web. They have everything from chat rooms to homeschool links.

ldscn (Latter-day Saints Church.net)

www.ldscn.com
A great website for LDS; many cooking, music, and fun links.

The Center for Educational Restoration

www.freewebmarket.com./lds/index.html
Site features LDS materials (curriculum and Web-ring links for LDS members).

Muslim

Alhumdillillah! For many years Muslim homeschoolers have had only three choices: unschooling, traditional schooling with parent-developed curriculum, or using prepared curriculum from non-Muslim sources, which required marking out what was not acceptable. Today, however, the situation is changing, and more resources and support are available than ever before.

Muslim Resources and Curriculum Material

Al-Hadi Curriculum
Al-Hadi is a full toolbox designed to help you build a Muslim intellect! According to Aziza Hutchinson, educator, Muslim children's author, and homeschool parent, "The MHSNR (Muslim Home School Network and Resource) curriculum has great language arts standards, including both Islamic and secular school material. This will make vital readers and writers who will be able to think, discriminate, and enhance English language materials from an Islamic perspective." A full Al-Hadi curriculum for grades K through 12 is currently available. Grades 1 to 8: $100 to $275, increasing with each grade. Grades 9 to 12 are $200 to $275, increasing with each grade. Available from Great Books Home School Store, 9895 W. Colfax Ave., Lakewood, CO 80215; 303/274-0680; fax: 303/274-0288; e-mail: PMcki63177@aol.com or MHSNR@aol.com.

Handbooks

Developing and Educating the Islamic Child by Umm Sulaimaan
This is a notebook by Zaynab Abdullah. Available only from Umm Sulaimaan, P.O. Box 77132, Seattle, WA 98133; 206/362-0204.

Muslim Books and Bookstores

Great Books Home School Store
9895 W. Colfax Ave.
Lakewood, CO 80215 303/274-0680
fax: 303/274-0288
e-mail: PMcki63177@aol.com
Great Books Home School Store is not affiliated with Great Christian Books (GCB).

Muslim Schools

ArabesQ Islamic Academy
Contact: Umm Sulaimaan
P.O. Box 77132
Seattle, WA 98133
206/362-0204
website: www.arabesq.com/hs/curricula.html
e-mail: Info@ArabesQ.com
ArabesQ offers a classic Islamic homeschool curriculum for grades K through 12. The curriculum, based on Quran and Sunnah, includes structured, eclectic, and unit studies in Quran, Islamic studies, and Arabic for all levels. Arabic as a second language is available from a program direct from the university in Medina and through elementary support in

Arabic. English as a second language is also available. The textbook-based program includes use of MHSNR's Al-Hadi Curriculum and the academy's on/offline courses. Request a tailor-made curriculum or use your own. Students can earn diplomas through ArabesQ's standard high school or college prep programs.

Helping Hands (Kindergarten Through 12th grade)

Contact: Latifah A. Sabur
215/747-2138
This state-certified two-year high school program is standard, tailored to the enrollment. Student work is delivered to your door. Testing includes entrance, quarterly, and final exams. Resource materials are available for remedial classes.

Laurel Springs School

P.O. Box 1440
Ojai, CA 93024-1440
805/646-2473
e-mail: lss@laurelsprings.com or
    LaurelSch@aol.com.
website: http://www.laurelsprings.com
To receive additional information, please inform Laurel Springs that you are a Muslim family and they will send you their brochure for Muslim families. Laurel Springs works with Muslim textbook author Susan Douglass in curriculum creation. This academy is accredited.

Muslim Girls Academy

websites: www.muslimgirlsacademy.net or
    info@muslimgirlsacademy.net
This school offers teacher-assisted home study leading to a high school diploma for Muslim girls ages 14 to 18. The curriculum follows New York State Education guidelines.

Muslim Websites

Muslim Homeschool and Arabic Resources

www.ArabesQ.com.
An excellent website and homeschooling connection. On it you will find a Muslim mall, Arabic resources, business center, foreign language, and more. One of the products available is the Medinah Arabic Language Program by Dr. V. Abdur-Raheem. In this program you will find help with grammar, reading, and writing, along with comprehension.

Muslim Homeschool Network & Resource

www.islam.org/MHSNR
This is another excellent website for Muslim homeschoolers. MHSNR can also be reached through P.O. Box 803, Attleborough, MA 02703; 508/226-1638.

IslamiCity

www.islamicity.org
A website of interest to Muslims, with a bookstore, a cyber mall, news and media, education, a science center, and more. The science links have incredible Web links to science websites in varying fields from agriculture to amateur radio to chemistry. Another online Islamic bookstore is located at www.sharaaz.com./home.html.

Native American

Homeschooling Resources

Native American Homeschool Association

Misty Dawn Thomas, Chairwoman
The Ani-Stohini/Unami Nation
P.O. Box 979
Fries, VA 24330
website: www.expage.com./page/
    nahomeschool2

Many Native Americans are choosing the advantages of homeschooling over the public or private forms of institutional schooling available. It allows them to maintain their religious and cultural autonomy within their own communities, while ensuring that their children receive a high-quality education that has the family's approval. There's a $25 fee to join this organization.

Native American Homeschooling Websites

Ani-Stohini/Unami Nation

www.ani-stohini-unami.com or
    www.myfreeoffice.com./tribe

This website gives Ani-Stohini/Unami nation information regarding crafts, herbs, news, and homeschool links.

Native American Homeschool Association Website

http://expage.com/page/nahomeschool

A Native American website that promotes homeschooling and awareness of cultural issues.

Seventh-day Adventist

Seventh-day Adventist Homestudy International

12501 Old Columbia Pike
Silver Spring, MD 20904-6600
800/782-4769
website: www.his.edu

Homestudy International offers Christian-based courses and degrees at all age levels from preschool through college. They have been offering a correspondence course for nearly 90 years. Call or write them for a free course catalog and more information.

The Moore Foundation

Box 1, Camas, WA 98607
360/835-5500
fax: 360/835-5392
website: www.moorefoundation.com

To receive a copy of The Moore Report, a periodical put out by The Moore Foundation (founded by Seventh-day Adventists Dr. Raymond and Dorothy Moore), please call 800/891-5255 or contact The Moore Foundation. The foundation provides help and instruction to all interested in homeschooling in the delayed academic approach. A family could customize the philosophy to fit any religion or do it in a non-religious fashion. The foundation also is a school that families can enroll in, having full guidance of a Moore Foundation teacher.

Seventh-day Adventist

Learning Styles

Consultants

Reflective Educational Perspectives

Contact: Victoria Kindle Hodson, M.A.,
and Mariaemma Pelullo-Willis, M.S.
1451 East Main Street, #200
Ventura, CA 93001;
805-648-1739
Victoria's e-mail: vkhodson@bigplanet.com
Mariaemma's e-mail: mepw1@aol.com
website: www.redp.com

Take the guesswork out of choosing a curriculum. Learn to use curriculums and strategies that work with all aspects of the student's learning style, including Talents, Interests, Modalities, Environment, and Dispositions. A consultation will help you to (1) discover and develop each student's unique intelligences and potentials; (2) eliminate destructive labels such as average, slow, dyslexic, ADD, hyperactive, learning disabled, unmotivated, and disruptive; and (3) educate for success in "real" life rather than success on tests. The consultation fee is $225 per child and includes a 1½-hour phone consultation, plus follow-up materials. Other services include educational assessments, family learning-team assessments, workshops and seminars, and expanded private consultations (in office or by phone or e-mail). Send for a free catalog. (See coupon for a discount on the Learning Styles Consultation.)

Books

Awakening Your Child's Natural Genius by Thomas Armstrong

Practical ideas for activities to do at home and advice on how to get the most out of your children's schools.

In Their Own Way by Thomas Armstrong

The author discusses children's distinct learning styles (linguistic, kinetic, interpersonal, etc.) and how to take full advantage of hidden aptitudes.

The Myth of ADD: 50 Ways to Improve Your Child's Behavior and Attention Span Without Drugs, Labels, Coercion by Thomas Armstrong

Expert Thomas Armstrong explores the many alternatives to traditional approaches to ADD.

No More Ritalin by Mary Ann Block and May A. Block

Authors discuss the dangers of Ritalin and give the reader alternatives.

Talking Back to Ritalin: What Doctors Aren't Telling You About Stimulants for Children by Peter R. Breggin

This 1998 book provides information about the dangers of Ritalin and other drugs.

Unschooling Method

Books

The Homeschooling Handbook by Mary Griffith

In this softcover, 320-page book, the author discusses everything pertinent to homeschoolers—structure, legal matters, obtaining information and resources, the teen years, and so on.

Teenage Liberation Handbook: How to Quit School and Get a Real Life and Education by Grace Llewellyn

This book profiles alternatives to traditional education, giving examples of situations and jobs that young people can find to carve out a meaningful and fulfilling life.

Real Lives: Eleven Teenagers Who Don't Go to School by Grace Llewellyn

In this book, the author profiles homeschooled teenagers, providing an inside view into their personalities and daily lives.

The following nine titles are available through John Holt's Bookstore, P.O. Box 8006, Walled Lake, MI 48391-8006; fax orders: 617/864-9235; phone orders: 617/846-3100; and Internet orders: www.holt.gws.com.

How Children Fail by John Holt

This revision of the 1964 version takes an inside look at the true experience children really have in schools and how they are affected by it.

How Children Learn by John Holt

This volume informs the reader on how early learning takes place and how parents and teachers can nurture and help its development.

Escape from Childhood by John Holt

In this book, Holt discusses his views on giving children "adult rights and responsibilities." He felt that children should be treated like "people," not "children."

Sharing Treasures: Book Reviews by John Holt, edited by Pat Farenga and J. P. Holcomb

This is a compilation of Holt's book review,s featured in *Harper's* and the *New York Review of Books*, and his introductions to various books. It also includes his personal list of homeschooling resource materials.

The Education of John Holt by Mel Allen

This is a 7-page biographical picture of John Holt.

What Do I Do Monday? by John Holt

This book has been updated with a new foreword and appendix. Holt provides practical advice on how to implement his teaching styles in the home and classroom.

Freedom and Beyond by John Holt

Possibly one of Holt's deepest books. He goes beyond the issues of "school" and "learning" and discusses differences between "structure" and "unstructure," discipline, helping kids make choices, and much more.

Unschooling Method

Teach Your Own by John Holt

A basic John Holt homeschooling "how-to" book. It deals with how to learn at home, answers common questions, and more.

Learning All the Time by John Holt

This book was in the works when John Holt passed away. It was finished by using articles he had written in *Growing Without Schooling*. Here he suggests that children will pick up the "basics" from the world around them if parents just guide them in small, subtle ways.

Child's Work: Taking Children's Choices Seriously by Nancy Wallace

The author shares with the reader her story of letting her children make their own decisions about what they learned and how this ultimately led to their growing up and finding work that they loved.

I Learn Better by Teaching Myself and Still Teaching Ourselves by Agnes Leistico

This volume contains two formerly separate books. They detail how the author, a homeschooling mom, dealt with the question of structure and making choices.

The following two titles are available only through Mountain House Press, P.O. Box 353, Philo, CA 95466.

Hard Times in Paradise by David and Micki Colfax

This 300-page hardcover tells the story of the Colfax parents homeschooling their four sons—ultimately to Ivy League colleges—on a goat farm in northern California. (See coupon.)

Homeschooling for Excellence by David and Micki Colfax

In this softcover book, the Colfax parents discuss specific aspects of homeschooling from the vantage point of raising their four sons. Included are the "Colfax 100 (more or less) Favorite Books" as well as other suggested resources and insights.

Audio

Learning Without a Curriculum

Two 60-minute cassettes from a Pat Farenga seminar that offer guidance into this way of teaching your children.

Magazines

Growing Without Schooling

2380 Mass Ave, Ste. 102
Cambridge, MA 02140
617/864-3100
This popular homeschooling magazine was started by John Holt, the well-known proponent of unschooling. (See coupon.)

Home Education Magazine

P.O. Box 1083
Tonasket, WA 98855
509/486-1351
This widely read magazine is full of resources and interesting columns for all homeschoolers.

Homefires: The Journal of Homeschooling

180 El Camino Real, Ste. 10
Millbrae, CA 94030
888/446-6333
website: www.Homefires.com
This eclectic journal is full of mindful articles about all aspects of homeschooling. (See coupon for one free issue.)

SKOLE: The Journal of Alternative Education

72 Phillip St.
Albany, NY 12202
518/432-1578
A quarterly publication, it discusses the issues pertinent to alternative education—for existing schools as well as homeschooling.

Newsletters

The Relaxed Homeschooler

P.O. Box 2524,
Cartersville, GA 30120
This newsletter is produced by Dr. Mary Hood, who is well known for her relaxed approach and has been referred to as a "Christian unschooler."

FUN News

1688 Belhaven Woods Court
Pasadena, MD 21122-3727
410/360-7330
website: http://members.aol.com/FUNNews
This newsletter and website focus on "unschooling"; however, materials are available for all homeschoolers.

The Moore Report

Box 1
Camas, WA 98607
360/835-2736
fax: 360/835-5392
This bi-monthly publication is useful to unschoolers because of its promotion of delayed academics.

Conferences

Unschoolers Network

Contact: Nancy Plent
732/938-2473
This is a large and diverse conference for unschoolers.

Growing Without Schooling

Annual Homeschool Conference
Contact: Holt Associates
617/864-3100
One of the largest unschooling conferences in the United States, it is sponsored by Growing Without Schooling magazine.

Mindfull: Rethinking Education

Dallas Texas
888/501-5244 (toll-free)
This annual conference centers on unschooling and beyond—dealing with issues of parenting styles, personal spiritual development, and more.

Unschooling Method

Websites

Fun Books Family Unschoolers Network

http://www.iqcweb.com/fun
This site sponsored by FUN Books has articles, reviews, resources, and websites.

Rethinking Education

www.rethinkingeducation.com
MINDFULL website gives information about their annual homeschooling conference; also contains resources.

Schools and Curriculums

Oak Meadow School

P.O. Box 740
Putney, VT 05346
802/387-2021
e-mail: oms@oakmeadow.com
website: www.oakmeadow.com
This non-religious correspondence school is well known for its academic and creative content.

Alger Learning Center and Independence High School

800/595-2630
website: www.independentlearning.com
Alger is an independent study program (ISP). They provide support and transcripts for both the unschooler and the more academically inclined.

Eclectic Method

Virtually everything in this book could be used by the eclectic homeschooling family. Even the right prepackaged curriculum would not be out of place. Feel free to use all materials and shape your own curriculum.

Websites

Eclectic Homeschool Website

http://www.eho.org/res.htm.
This website, with links to 600+ sites of educational value and interest, is filled with information about books, curricula, curriculum planners, chat rooms, articles, you name it. To obtain the printed version, which is not necessarily a 100 percent match with the online version, send $15 for six issues (one year) or $4 for a sample issue, to Eclectic Homeschool, P.O. Box 736, Dept. W, Bellevue, NH 68005-0736; e-mail: eclectic@eho.org.

Delayed Academic Method

Foundations

The Moore Foundation

Box 1
Camas, WA 98607
360/835-5500
fax: 360/835-5392
website: www.moorefoundation.com

Dr. Moore and Dorothy Moore are Seventh-day Adventists. Their foundation provides help and instruction to all interested in the delayed academic approach. A family could customize this homeschooling philosophy to fit any religion, or they could do it in a nonreligious fashion. The foundation also acts as a school in which families can enroll and have the full guidance of a Moore Foundation teacher. For information about delayed academic approach contact the Moores.

Books

The following six titles are by the Moores and can be ordered from The Moore Foundation (see above):

Better Late Than Early

Examines the research proving the dangers of early formal schooling for children under 8 or 10 years of age; resulted in the renaissance of homeschooling as a movement.

School Can Wait

This book can be considered the scholarly version of *Better Late Than Early*.

HomeSpun Schools

Tells about stories from homeschooling families who were among the first in the movement.

Homestyle Teaching

Time-tested insights on how to ensure your children the best education possible.

Home Grown Kids

Down-to-earth guidelines for emotional and intellectual development.

Home Built Discipline

The art of discipleship: balancing heart, hand, and health. Contains a study guide for parenting, church, and school groups.

What Educators Should Know About Home Schools

This booklet was written for the U.S. Department of Education and published by The Family Research Council to acquaint educators and others with the research results of home education and with its rationale.

Magazines

The Moore Report

800/891-5255
A periodical put out by The Moore Foundation.

Delayed Academic Method

Charlotte Mason Method

Books

A Charlotte Mason Education
by Catherine Levison

A concise "how to" manual, this book is a condensation of the practical aspects of the Charlotte Mason Method. Available by writing to: Charlotte Mason Communique-tions, PMB 500, 2522 N. Proctor, Tacoma, WA 98406 or calling 253/879-0433.

More Charlotte Mason Education
by Catherine Levison.

This one-of-a-kind "how-to" manual serves as a sequel to Catherine's first book. It is much larger, as it deals with such diverse subjects as high school, coping with homeschooling, the history of education, and how to keep a book of the centuries. Available by writing to Charlotte Mason Communique-tions, PMB 500, 2522 N. Proctor, Tacoma, WA 98406 or calling 253/879-0433.

The Charlotte Mason Companion, Personal Reflections on the Gentle Art of Daily Living by Karen Andreola

A Charlotte Mason expert, Karen writes the Charlotte Mason column for *Practical Homeschooling* magazine. Her catalog, featuring many Charlotte Mason products, can be ordered from Charlotte Mason Research and Supply Company, Box 1142, Rockland, ME 04841-1142; website: http://www.charlottemason.com.

Original Homeschooling Series (referred to as the "six-volume set") by Charlotte Mason

Reprints of Charlotte Mason's work, three volumes deal with education, three with parenting and children.

Magazines

Practical Homeschooling Magazine
P.O. Box 1250
Fenton, MO 63026-1850
314/343-6786
This bi-monthly publication features a regular Charlotte Mason column by Karen Andreola.

Study Guides

Charlotte Mason Study Guide

Penny Gardner brings you a simplified approach to a living education. A homeschooling mother of six and the coordinator of a Charlotte Mason study group, she is the author of the Nine-Note Recorder Method. Catalog available from Penny Gardner, P.O. Box 900983, Sandy, UT 84090. Pennygar@aol.com; website: cmsgpenny@aol.com.

Website

Good Life & Good Literature
http://members.aye.net/~mjf/index.html

Trivium Method

Teaching the Trivium

website: http://www.muscanet.com/~trivium
The Bluedorns' trivium catalog can be viewed online with pictures. They can be contacted at Bluedorn Family, c/o 139 Colorado Street, Ste. 168, Muscatine, IA 52761; 309/537-3641; e-mail: trivium@muscanet.com.

The American Communication Association

website: www.americancomm.org
This organization is dedicated to promoting academic and professional study using the basic principles of communication: argumentation; debate; classical; medieval, and renaissance rhetoric; freedom of speech; rhetorical theory and criticism; and more.

George Wythe College (GWC)

401 S. Main St.
Cedar City, UT 84720
435/586-6570
website: www.123inter.net/gwc/
    mainadmissions.html
Although not affiliated with the LDS church, approximately 90% of the students are LDS. This unusual college offers the only statesmanship "track" in the country to train future statesmen (rather than merely politicians) to serve the country's needs. GWC approaches education from the point of view of mentoring and reading of the classics. Their motto is "Creating Thomas Jeffersons one student at a time!" The college offers a very interesting newsletter about statesmanship, and their president, Dr. Oliver DeMille, is an interesting and intelligent thinker, writer, and lecturer.

Principle Approach

Foundation

The Foundation for American Christian Education

P.O. Box 9588
Chesapeake, VA 23321
800/352-3223
website: www.facel.net
Publisher of Noah Webster's 1828 dictionary, their mission is to publish and teach America's Christian history.

Distributor

Landmark Distributors

e-mail: lankmark@jps.net
website: http://www.jps.net/landmark/
    index.html
This company is owned and operated by Alan and Lori Harris. Lori is a popular speaker at homeschool conferences and is a regular columnist for *Practical Homeschooling* magazine.

Unit Study Method

Magazines

Homeschooling Today Magazine
954/962-1930.
This bi-monthly publication comes fully equipped with several unit studies in each issue. (See coupon for free issue.)

Unit Study Programs

KONOS, Inc. ✝
P.O. Box 250
Anna, TX 75409
972/924-2712
fax: 972/924-2701
e-mail: info@konos.com
website: www.konos.com
KONOS offers two types of unit study curriculum. One is designed so the parent need not plan anything. All planning is done for you. The other is designed so that the parent can assemble the materials using his/her own creativity and imagination.

Stewardship ✝
P.O. Box 164
Garden Valley, CA 95633
888/4R-UNITS (888/478-6487)
website: www.unitstudies.com
This is a Christian company, owned and operated by a homeschooling family with seven children. They provide a number of tools for the unit study approach, including their book, *Everything You Need to Know About Unit Studies*. They also provide unit study guides in a variety of topics.

Far Above Rubies ✝
Available through Eagle's Nest Educational Supplies
209/529-7720
fax: 209/529-1715
Designed to train girls to become Godly women. It is planned to cover all the subjects for a complete four-year high school education and includes many suggestions for expanding into specialized areas of interest. The main emphasis is on preparing daughters for the life calling of wife and mother. (See coupon.)

Design-a-Study
408 Victoria Ave.
Wilmington, DE 19804-2124
302/998-3889
This company helps you create your own unit study or other approach in science, math, history, critical conditioning, comprehensive composition, and spelling.

The Prairie Primer ✝
Available through Eagle's Nest Educational Supplies
209/529-7720
fax: 209/529-1715
This unit study, by Margie Gray, is designed around the Laura Ingalls Wilder books (*Little House on the Prairie*, etc.). The author has developed it so that parents can impress upon their children the way to walk faithfully with the Lord. (See coupon.)

How To Create Your Own Unit Study ✝

Available through Eagle's Nest Educational Supplies

209/529-7720

fax: 209/529-1715

By Valerie Bent, this book provides a framework for teaching life training using academics to assist in building a foundation of truth. Gives an explanation of the unit study approach and methods for implementing it for children of different ages. The materials allow you to develop unit studies based on your own family goals and interests. (See coupon.)

Books

Unit Study Idea Book
by Valerie Bent ✝

Available through Eagle's Nest Educational Supplies

209/529-7720

fax: 209/529-1715

Includes 20 complete unit studies in five subject areas and two to three years of plans. Study areas include aviation, birds, sign language, and much more. (See coupon.)

Training Our Daughters to Be Keepers At Home by Ann Ward ✝

Available through Eagle's Nest Educational Supplies

209/529-7720

fax: 209/529-1715

This 600-page hardbound home economics curriculum is for girls ages 11 to 18. Yearly curriculum includes studies of Godly womanhood, sewing, gardening, cooking, fiber arts, finances, serving others, and more. Projects increase in difficulty as the years go by. (See coupon.)

Treegate Publications (Literature Unit Studies for the Homeschooling Family)

833 Liberty Dr.

DeForest, WI 53532

608/846-8728

e-mail: treegt@aol.com

website: http://www.treegatepublications. com

These literature-based unit study guides are created by a homeschooling family and are perfect for home use. Study guides are available for *Alice's Adventures in Wonderland, Anne of Green Gables, The Prince and the Pauper, The Princess and the Goblin, The Secret Garden, The Wind in the Willows,* and *The Wonderful Wizard of Oz.*

Five In A Row

Available through Eagle's Nest Educational Supplies

209/529-7720

fax: 209/529-1715

This series was created by Jane Clair Lambert, a homeschooling mother with 12 years' experience. It is a unit study based on outstanding children's literature and provides lesson plans covering social studies, language arts, art, math, and science in a way that causes children to fall in love with learning. The lesson plans are simple in content but rich in results. Read the chosen book in its entirety over a period of at least a week (hence the name "Five in a Row"). Then, after each reading, choose an exercise to share with your child and watch his or her world expand as you begin to show facets of the story the child would not have recognized without your guidance. (See coupon.)

Unit Study Adventure Series by Amanda Bennett

Available through Eagle's Nest Educational Supplies
209/529-7720
fax: 209/529-1715

The author is an engineer and homeschooling mother of three. After using a standard textbook curriculum for a few months, she realized her children were bored and needed a greater challenge. When she was given a specific project as an engineer, she was expected to do research to thoroughly define and understand all facets of the problems, as well as come up with some solutions based on newly-gained knowledge. The unit study approach works on the same principle, exposing students to an area for in-depth study. Amanda decided to write science technology study guides. Topics available are oceans, baseball, home, gardens, computer, elections, pioneers, and more. (See coupon.)

Progeny Press Study Guides †

Progeny Press
200 Spring St.
Eau Claire, WI 54703-3225
715/833-5261; fax: 715/836-0105
e-mail: progeny@mgprogeny.com
website: http://www.mgprogeny.com/
progeny.

Progeny Press produces study guides for literature written with a Christian perspective. The company chooses high-quality books such as *The Red Badge of Courage*, *Hamlet*, *The Merchant of Venice*, *A Day No Pigs Would Die*, *Amos Fortune*, *Free Man*, and more. The guides, which average 50 pages, provide vocabulary lessons, biblical application, content questions, literary terms, and much more. The guide is designed to spend two months on a book or just do a cursory study of it.

PART 4

State-by-State Information: Organizations, Agencies, Groups, and Conferences

ALABAMA

Homeschooling is not an open "legal" option in Alabama per se, meaning if you contact the state Department of Education, they may say that you can't simply keep your children home and teach them without meeting certain requirements. (The applicable state law is *Code of Alabama*, Section 16-1-11.) For instance, you may be advised that a parent must either have a teaching certificate or be part of a private "church" school (also called a "cover" or "umbrella" school). Technically speaking, in order to form a church school, one must form a church. However, the state's definition of "church" is *very* broad, requiring only minor paperwork and timely fellowship meetings—not official state registration or the like. A church (or private) school need not have a certified teacher but must merely keep an attendance sheet. There are no requirements for curriculum choice and so forth, and many "Christian" schools are flexible in their denominational outlook as well. Support groups, which may also be private schools, provide social or extracurricular supplements through park days, field days, parent discussion groups, and so on. The designation "school" in the following list is used when the organization calls itself a school; the list does not denote different standings other than "support group." Contact the organizations listed below to find out their specifics.

STATEWIDE ORGANIZATIONS

Remember to contact your parent-run statewide organization before contacting any government agency. The parent-run organization will help you understand what to expect when you call the Department of Education.

Home Educators of Alabama Roundtable (HEART)

(256) 890-0515
website: www.heartofalabama.org
e-mail: bacons4@traveller.com

This statewide support group, operated by Susan Bacon, will help you with anything you need to know about homeschooling in Alabama. Membership is $1 per year.

GOVERNMENT AGENCY

Alabama State Department of Education

Prevention and Support Services
Charles Curley, Director
3316 Gordon Persons Building
P.O. Box 302101
Montgomery, AL 36130-2101
(334) 242-8165

SUPPORT GROUPS

Alabama Home Educators Network (AHEN)

Lisa Bugg
(256) 882-0208
605 Mountain Gap Dr.
Huntsville, AL 35803

This all-inclusive support group for home-schoolers meets once a month (in person and via e-mail) to discuss current homeschool issues and for mutual support. An AHEN member says: "We try to make everyone welcome, and we try desperately not to discuss religion."

North Alabama Friends School (NAFS)

Caroline Lampert, Director
(256) 650-0366
P.O. Box 2183
Huntsville, AL 35804
website: www.HSV.TIS.NET~NAFS
e-mail: nafs@traveller.com

This is a cover school that allows home-schooling. Although the school was founded by Quakers, there are no religious requirements; it has always been all-inclusive. All religions are respected, and those of any religious perspective can be accepted as members. The Friends School provides support and activities such as picnic/park days and spelling bees. The group tries to provide all activities a public school provides, to make homeschooling available and easy for all, and to support all homeschooling philosophies. NAFS follows a nondiscriminatory policy and discourages people from starting religious discussions during park days or meetings.

Faith Presbyterian Christian School

Dr. Steve Cloud, Administrator
P.O. Box 950
Robertsdale, AL 36567
(334) 947-5012
Laura Metz, Home School Coordinator
(334) 962-3582
e-mail: metzjjr@gulftel.com

This is a Christian day school that provides a homeschool service as well. No statement of faith or HSLDA* membership is required, and all denominations are welcome. Parents are free to choose their own curriculum (none is provided by the school), but one Bible course per year is required. The school is very flexible in its approach to homeschooling. Because group members strongly believe that the child's education is the parents' decision, they try to enhance that end. Cost is $300/year for grades 9–12; $200/year for elementary school. A 15 percent tuition discount is offered to families upon enrollment of subsequent children after the first child is enrolled.

Home Educators of Alabama Roundtable (HEART)

Susan Bacon
(256) 890-0515
website: www.heartofalabama.org
e-mail: bacons4@traveller.com

This statewide support group is operated by Susan Bacon, who is also the director of Franklin School (see next entry). Membership to HEART is $1 per year.

---

*Homeschool Legal Defense Association (www.hslda.org), a national organization that protects the legal rights of its member families wishing to homeschool.

Franklin School

Susan Bacon
P.O. Box 1433
Huntsville, AL 35807
(256) 830-2720
website:
www.hsv.tis.net/~bacons4/Franklin/
school.html
e-mail: bacons4@traveller.com

This is a church school in Huntsville, Alabama. Franklin requires beginning homeschool families to meet with a school advisor four or five times in the first school year via e-mail, phone, or in person—whichever suits the family's needs and conditions. Experienced families do not have to meet as often, but the number of meetings is based upon family needs. Cost: first-year family: 1–3 children, $215–$305/year (+$20 registration/administration fee); experienced family: 1–3 children, $170–260/year.

New Life Christian Academy

Kent or Terry McKee
(334) 541-3556 or (335) 541-4046
P.O. Box 211012
Montgomery, AL 36121
website: www.jubileeplus.com
e-mail: newlifechristianacademy@juno.com

This is a church school with no religious denominational affiliation. The group holds many thematic group meetings and sponsors some speakers throughout year. They also offer field trips, an extensive resource library, and the newsletter "Eclectic Home Schoolers of Alabama," which includes activities schedules, transcripts, counseling, and other information. No HSLDA membership is necessary to join, nor is the statement of faith mandatory (it's included for information only with the information packet). Their the statement of faith: "We believe that parents are responsible for the rearing and education of their children before God and that no one has the right to take away that responsibility or control from a parent."

Special Note: Terry McKee conducts a program called "The Masters' Touch," which is a co-op unit study program based upon her JUBILEE Curriculum. Once a week children in grades K–12 meet and do activities that are best suited for a group and which include supplies that are difficult for one family to provide (such as a full science lab, a car engine to rebuild, art materials, or musical instruments). The base fee is $40 per month per child. A family does not have to be resident in Alabama to participate. Contact the academy if you are interested in joining them or in setting up a program of your own. Cost is $25/year per family for new home educators; $10 per year for re-enrollment.

Our Lady of Good Counsel

Bob and Barbara Whitworth
6533 Bear Creek Rd.
Sterrett, AL 35147
(205) 672-7947
e-mail: BAH851@aol.com

This church school in the greater Birmingham area is intent upon providing a solid, conservative Catholic homeschool approach. They offer a curriculum guide, allowing families to customize their program and acquire the chosen books for themselves.

Southcrest Christian School

Tim and Donna McDow
4317 South Shades Crest Rd.
Bessemer, AL 35022
(205) 425-5705
e-mail: Tmacs6@aol.com

This Christian school requires mandatory signing of a statement of faith and HSLDA membership if the child is of school age. The school also requires letter grades and three meetings per year with an advisor.

CONFERENCES

The Alabama State Homeschooling Convention

Sponsored by Christian Home Education
Fellowship of Alabama
Birmingham, Alabama
(334) 645-5003

This Christian conference is in its ninth year and had attendance of about 2,500 at the April 30–May 1, 1999, event.

ALASKA

The citizens of Alaska enjoy a great deal of legal freedom in their practice of homeschooling. In 1997, Alaska created an exemption to the compulsory school attendance law "if a child is being educated in the child's home by a parent or guardian." No certification or qualification is required of parents; no government regulation of any kind is imposed; and there is no requirement that parents notify anyone of their intention to homeschool. There is also no testing, no required curriculum, and no evaluation of the results.

STATEWIDE ORGANIZATIONS

Remember to contact your parent-run statewide organization before contacting any government agency. The parent-run organization will help you understand what to expect when you call the Department of Education.

Alaska Private & Home Educators Association (APHEA)

Bob Parsons
P.O. Box 141764
Anchorage, AK 99514
(907) 566-3450
website: www.aphea.org

This statewide Christian organization holds an annual convention, publishes a monthly newsletter, and offers a homeschool starter packet with statewide information, including lists of support groups. There is an annual fee of $25.

GOVERNMENT AGENCY

Alaska Department of Education

801 W. 10th St.
Juneau, AK 99801-1878
(907) 465-2800

SUPPORT GROUPS

Alaska Homespun Educators

6731 E. 99th Ave.
Anchorage AK 99516
(907) 346-1776
e-mail: 102155.700@compuserve.com

This nondenominational organization includes Christians, Catholics, and pagans freely intermixing!

Sitka Home Education Association

Molly Jacobson
P.O. Box 1191
Sitka, AK 99835
(907) 747-1483

This all-inclusive local support group has approximately 15 families, publishes a bimonthly newsletter, and offers field trips.

Our Lady of Good Counsel Catholic Homeschool Support Group

Cynthia Cebuhar
9800 Buddy Werner
Anchorage, AK 99516-1051

This is a Catholic support group that meets for mass once a week and also for field trips.

CONFERENCES

Alaska Private & Home Educators Association (APHEA)

Anchorage, Alaska
Contact: Bob Parsons
(907) 566-3450
e-mail: www.aphea.org

The Annual Christian Homeschool Conference (last held March 19–20 of 1999) features vendors and speakers.

ARIZONA

The superintendent of each county school district in Arizona is mandated to maintain the homeschool program. However, in sparsely populated counties, the Maricopa County (Phoenix) Director of Homeschool Services oversees the forms and information services. Current law requires the filing of an affidavit of intent to homeschool (form) and a certified copy of the student's birth certificate for each student with the local school superintendent. The affidavit form can be obtained from the local district or the Maricopa County address listed below. The parent must be the primary teacher and must teach reading, grammar, math, science, and social studies. Curriculum approval is not necessary. Students are not evaluated or tested during homeschooling; however, placement testing is required if the homeschooler wants to enter a school after having homeschooled. The compulsory education law applies only to students between the ages of 6 and 16.

Parents should contact the Department of Education or local superintendent to ask for homeschooling information and the homeschooling and affidavit packet. Ms. Beadleston was very helpful and encouraging to homeschoolers when we spoke with her. This is another great state to homeschool in!

STATEWIDE ORGANIZATIONS

Remember to contact your parent-run statewide organization before contacting any government agency. The parent-run organization will help you understand what to expect when you call the Department of Education.

Arizona Families for Home Education (AFHE)

P.O. Box 4661
Scottsdale, AZ 85261
(602) 443-0612 (Maricopa County only)
(800) 929-3927 (all other Arizona counties)
website: www.primenet.com/~afhe
e-mail: AFHE@primenet.com

This nonprofit educational corporation offers a wide variety of services and information. Among these are pre-startup information, start-up information, legislative monitoring and alerting, bimonthly newsletter, annual curriculum fair, state convention, and membership in HSLDA for AFHE members. Annual membership fees are $25 for the first year, $20 each year thereafter. You do not have to be a member to obtain start-up information. Simply send $3 payable to the AFHE at the above address, requesting your information.

The Salt Seller

Tammy Lopez
P.O. Box 56701
Phoenix, AZ 85079-6701
(602) 249-SALT (7258) (24-hour hotline)
(602) 249-2699
(602) 249-6151 (fax)
e-mail: SaltSeller@aol.com

AFHE and The Salt Seller are affiliated organizations. The Salt Seller publishes a statewide, quarterly publication, *The Salt Seller*, which promotes all activities throughout Arizona. It features announcements of activities and speakers, discounts, and so forth at a cost of only $5 per year. It also offers free classifieds for selling used curricular materials. The Salt Seller is staffed by families who volunteer their time to aid homeschooling families and prospective homeschoolers. (See Conference section also.)

GOVERNMENT AGENCY

Maricopa County School Superintendent

Ann Beadleston
Director of Homeschooling Services
301 W. Jefferson, Ste. 660 HSD
Phoenix, AZ 85003
(602) 506-3144

SUPPORT GROUPS

SPICE

Sue Taniguchi
10414 W. Mulberry Dr.
Avondale, AZ 85323
(602) 877-3642
e-mail: pompey@juno.com

The group is not very active right now; but if you call, they will provide you with some resource information, especially for an un-schooling point of view.

East Valley Educators (EVE)

Sylvia Acuna or Sue Lullo
(602) 987-1404 or (602) 983-5660

This all-inclusive group of 35–40 families holds park days the second and fourth Tuesday of each month from October to May, publishes a newsletter, and sponsors field trips and social activities.

Families Forever

Linda Zollinger
(602) 241-7864

This nondenominational group of nine families in the Central Phoenix area meets the first week of each month. The group has a picnic in the evening so the dads and extended family members can participate; childrens' activities are also connected with the picnic. Families Forever sponsors field trips, guest speakers, and projects of various types. The last week of each month, the group meets again and the children tell what they learned during the preceding month.

Christian Home Educators of Tucson, South East

Wendy Weekly
8850 E. Rose Tree St.
Tucson, AZ 85730
(520) 751-8901

A Statement of Faith is required for membership in this Christian, nondenominational support group that serves like-minded people. They feature physical education every Friday, a small sister-to-sister (mothers) support group, a girls' club called "Keepers at Home," and a boys' club called "Contenders of the Faith." The group also publishes a monthly newsletter. Membership is $20 per year.

Flagstaff Home Educators

P.O. Box 31236
Flagstaff, AZ 86003-1236
(520) 773-8068

This group has a number of activities listed on their phone message. Past activities have included a field trip to Lowell Observatory, a spelling bee, a Young Homemakers meeting, and a curriculum swap meet. Call for information and calendar of events.

Christian Home Educators (CHE)

P.O. Box 20685
Mesa, AZ 85277-0685
(602) 530-8733 (recorded message)
e-mail: Jwiebe8553@aol.com

If you call the recorded message number, you'll get the schedule and contact numbers for more information on monthly activities (such as bowling day or business meetings). Features workshops, newsletter, field trips, Moms' Night Out, and more.

CONFERENCES

Arizona Families for Home Education (AFHE)

Phoenix Civic Convention Center
(800) 929-3927
(602) 443-0612 (Maricopa County)

Over 4,000 attended the organization's 1998 Annual Statewide Homeschool Convention.

The Salt Seller

Contact: Tammy Lopez
North Phoenix Baptist Church
5757 N. Central Ave.
Phoenix, AZ
(602) 249-2699

In June 1999, the Salt Seller sponsored its 5th Annual State-Wide Used Curriculum and Book Fair.

ARKANSAS

Homeschooling has been legal in Arkansas since 1985. Parents must determine their teaching approach and curriculum, locate and obtain textbooks, and fill out and file a Notice of Intent at the local school district, along with a waiver releasing the state from liability for the education of their child(ren). Children will be tested by a standardized test. The ages for testing and locations of sites may change, so this information should be checked regularly. Then parents need to locate support groups and websites to get more information to help them homeschool.

STATEWIDE ORGANIZATIONS

Remember to contact your parent-run statewide organization before contacting any government agency. The parent-run organization will help you understand what to expect when you call the Department of Education.

Home Educators of Arkansas (branch of CAP)

Home Ed
1 Patriot Ct.
Little Rock, AR, 72212
(501) 847-4942

If you call the phone number listed, you'll be given a menu of phone messages to listen to for information. This organization has many services for homeschoolers, so it is worth the call.

You can become a member by subscribing to Home Ed's school-year monthly (10 issues) newsletter and annual directory. The newsletter provides news and information related to the Little Rock area. The newsletter subscription is $15 and includes the directory and a membership card, which also serves as a homeschooling ID for discounts from selected bookstores. Send your check for $15, payable to "Home Ed." Please provide both parents' names, mailing address, home phone number, and the names, gender, and full date of birth of all children.

Arkansas Homeschooling Resource Directory (AHRD)

2703 Grist Mill Rd.
Little Rock, AR 72227

This is a 20-page statewide, newspaper-format directory, featuring information about the law, how to fill out the forms, testing, and curriculum guidance. Lists support groups, resources, and other areas of interest. Send your name, address, and $1 to AHRD at the address listed above.

Education Alliance (branch of Family Council)

Peri
414 S. Palaski, Ste 2
Little Rock, AR 72212
(501) 375-7000
(501) 664-4566
website: www.familycouncil.org

GOVERNMENT AGENCY

Arkansas Department of Education

4 State Capitol Mall
Little Rock, AR 72201
(501) 682-4475 (main number)
(501) 682-4251 (Homeschool Department)

SUPPORT GROUPS

Family Association for Instruction and Teaching at Home (FAITH)

P.O. Box 1041
Ft. Smith, AR 72902
website: www.ilovejesus.com/school/
*   faithhomeschool/index.html*

This is a large (169-family) Christian support group serving the greater Ft. Smith/ Eastern Oklahoma area. Membership is $25 per year. Benefits include a subscription to the monthly newsletter; access to all activities, such as the spelling bee, skate days, and speech fair; monthly Parents Encouraging Parents meetings; annual family picnic; field trips; and more.

This is a statewide, nonprofit organization that supports homeschooling in Arkansas. The group sponsors an annual book fair and convention and provides information on all facets of homeschooling. Call for support groups in your area.

CONFERENCES

Northwest Arkansas Christian Curriculum Fair, Inc.

Springdale, Arkansas
Contact: Kathy Parker
(501) 524-4094

This Annual Christian Curriculum Fair was on April 17, 1999.

CALIFORNIA

California is a private school state, which means that it is legal to educate your children at home by establishing a private school. There are two other ways to homeschool. First, you can register your kids with a private or public school independent study program (ISP). Second, if you're a parent with a current teaching credential, you may teach under the private tutorial exemption. The greatest scope of independence and freedom comes from establishing your home as a private school.

STATEWIDE ORGANIZATIONS

Remember to contact your parent-run statewide organization before contacting any government agency. The parent-run organization will help you understand what to expect when you call the Department of Education.

California Homeschool Network (CHN)

(800) 327-5339
website: www.comenius.orgchnpage.htm
e-mail: CHNmail@aol.com

CHN is an inclusive, statewide homeschooling organization serving families across a diverse spectrum of homeschooling styles and philosophies. The organization empowers families and educates the public through seminars, publications, a bimonthly newsletter, network of local contacts, and legal and legislative monitoring. The organization also educates the public by placing information notebooks in public libraries and maintaining an active media presence.

Homeschool Association of California (HSC)

P.O. Box 2442
Atascadero, CA 93423
(888) HSC-4440
website: www.hsc.org
e-mail: info@hsc.org

HSC is a statewide organization that honors the diversity of homeschoolers and supports and promotes the entire spectrum of homeschooling by providing information, monitoring and influencing legislation, and providing an opportunity for families to get together.

GOVERNMENT AGENCY

California Department of Education

Carolyn Pirillo
721 Capitol Mall, Room 552
Sacramento, CA 95814
(916) 657-2453

SUPPORT GROUPS

Southern California

Excellence in Education (EIE)

Martin and Carolyn Forte
2650 S. Myrtle Ave.
Monrovia, CA 91016
(626) 821-0025
website: www.excellenceineducation.com

This large, all-inclusive support group is run by Martin and Carolyn Forte. They are experienced homeschooling parents with two grown daughters. EIE is also a large, popular, private ISP and an excellent bookstore. The organization offers a wide variety of classes, curriculum, field trips, SAT preparation, high school graduation ceremonies, a yearbook, an excellent monthly newsletter, and a great deal more.

L. A. (Los Angeles) Homeschoolers

Lauren Brenner-Katz or Maryanne Clair
(310) 458-2633 or (310) 559-5476
e-mail: copykatz@aol.com

This all-inclusive support group of approximately 50 families welcomes all families. L. A. Homeschoolers sponsors monthly park days, meets for socializing and fun, and provides a monthly calendar of events. A member states: "This is a very fun group!"

Family-Centered Education of Los Angeles (FaCE-LA)

Marsha Lennox or Terry Polcene-King
11100-8 Sepulveda Blvd, Ste. 567
Mission Hills, CA 91345
(818) 766-8914 or (818) 503-6205
e-mail: writer42@aol.com or
*   rolterking@msn.com*

This nonreligious, nonpolitical support group welcomes all homeschoolers and all philosophies. Anyone interested in home education is welcome to join the exchange of ideas, skills, knowledge, and enthusiasm offered on a voluntary participation level. The subscription price for their newsletter is $20.00.

Inland Empire Area Home Learners (Rancho Cucamonga)

Roberta Jackson
(909) 980-7262
e-mail: DWILLi8906@aol.com

Here's another all-inclusive, friendly support group open to families of different religious backgrounds and teaching styles in the Inland Empire and San Bernardino areas. The group meets the second and fourth Wednesdays of each month at 11:00 A.M. For ages 5–12, field trips and special events are planned. For teenagers, more social events are scheduled, and field trips are aimed at their interest levels. A monthly newsletter, "Teen Times," is composed by the teens involved in the program. There is also a special Mom & Tots group. They invite you to "Please visit any time!"

Rainbow Kids Support Group

Jocelyn Vilter
4604 Glen Arden Ave.
Covina, CA 91724
(626) 939-0318
website: http://members.aol.com/
*   RainboKids/Times.html*
(Note: Web address is case sensitive.)
e-mail: jvilter@aol.com

This all-inclusive homeschooling group consists of approximately 35 families living in Orange, San Bernardino, Los Angeles, Riverside, and Ventura Counties. Formed more than 10 years ago by a few families interested in homeschooling their children, the group has grown to include many families with a wide variety of approaches to homeschooling and life. Rainbow Kids publishes a monthly newsletter for $11/year or online for free (see website).

Thalassa!

Isabelle Nidever
(626) 287-8595
e-mail: AMEUSROGO@LOOP.COM

This is an independent study and support group that would love to have anyone interested in joining contact them.

Riverside Area Home Learners (RAHL)

Charlie Miles
(909) 279-4026
e-mail: moonsong@ix.netcom.com

An all-inclusive, secular group, Riverside Home Learners values diversity, respecting everyone and all kinds of educational philosophies. The group offers twice-monthly park days, field trips, and more. They're also open to adding new classes or activities should you want to lead one.

Cumorah Association of Inland Empire

Deena Ortiz
11965 Palo Alto St.
Rancho Cucamonga, CA 91739-9777

This is an LDS group, but not exclusively so. The group's activities include park day (first Wednesday of each month) and field trips.

Heritage Academy (Ontario, CA)

Rachel
(909) 988-3456

This smaller group is a full-service, private ISP that places its main emphasis on families. They do many things together, including field trips, park days, parties, and barbecues. The group is Christian-oriented but sponsors mixed park days.

Whittier Area Homeschoolers

Marian
P.O. Box 90638
Industry, CA 91715
(562) 693-4232
e-mail: fun2study@aol.com

This inclusive group emphasizes children 8 and under. Activities include a park-day group meeting once a month, as well as field trips throughout the month.

High Desert Homeschoolers (Victorville area)

Karen Taylor
(760) 956-1588
e-mail: taylors@mscomm.com

Approximately 50 families comprise this inclusive group, which sponsors weekly park days and field trips. There is no charge for participation in these activities; please drop in to visit.

Homeschoolers United

Linda Davis
(805) 532-2276

This all-inclusive homeschool group serves the Thousand Oaks, Simi Valley, and Moorpark areas. The organization offers support, socialization, field trips, activities, weekly park days, monthly family night, a private ISP for those who wish it, and more.

Westside Academy (private ISP)

Pam Owens
12593 Westmont Dr.
Moorpark, CA 93021
(805) 378-5153

This inclusive group has weekly park days, field trips, classes, and "many, many activities."

Conejo Valley Homeschoolers

Sandra Katz
(805) 373-6586

This secular homeschool support group, which serves the Thousand Oaks–Westlake Village area, is open to all. They schedule weekly park days, classes, drama, sports, tennis, skate days, field trips, and much more! If you're considering homeschooling, stop by for a park day (call for details).

The Innovative Homeschoolers Support

Carin
(805) 649-5063

This group, located in the Ventura/Santa Barbara area, welcomes all who support homeschooling, regardless of religious affiliation. Homeschoolers meet for field trips, art classes, special interest classes, and so forth.

Orange County (Irvine)

Jean Bellinger
(949) 559-0973
e-mail: jbellinger@yahoo.com

Jean Bellinger knows many people and has much experience in the homeschooling arena.

North (San Diego) County Homeschoolers

Janeen Dell'Acqua and Anita Peterson
(619) 484-8318 and (619) 578-5350
Janeen's e-mail: dellrogers@aol.com
Anita's e-mail: momofaj@aol.com

Approximately 30 families comprise this nonsectarian homeschooling group, which places its main emphasis on children 7 years old and younger. They publish a large Northern County San Diego newsletter, schedule monthly parent meetings, and sponsor park days every Wednesday at two different locations.

Northern California

East Bay Family Educators

Barbara Donovan and Jane Ahrens
(510) 527-9428 or (510) 524-1224
e-mail: donovanb@uclink4.berkeley.edu

This all-inclusive, secular, informal group encompasses an area from approximately Richmond through Oakland. They sponsor park days on the second and fourth Tuesdays of each month and publish a monthly newsletter.

Homeschool Cooperative of Sacramento

Claudia Camuso
2850 Acevido Dr.
Sacramento, CA 95833
(916) 927-6181

This support group's purpose is to "create a cooperative community of homeschool families without regard for educational, political, or religious philosophies." They offer park days, skate days, field trips, classes, and many other activities.

Yolo County Homeschoolers

Katje Sabin-Newmiller
2816 Loyola Dr.
Davis, CA 95616
(530) 758-6459
e-mail: klsabin@dcn.davis.ca.us

A member of this Yolo County group states: "We are an informal homeschool support group that does not discriminate based on age, sex, philosophy, or shoe size. Call us and come and join the fun!" They sponsor a monthly park day, publish a newsletter, and maintain a phone tree and directory in the area.

CONFERENCES

Southern California

The Link "kid comfortable" Homeschool Conference

Warner Center Marriott Hotel
Woodland Hills, California
   (NW Los Angeles metro area)
(805) 492-1373
website: www.homeschoolnewslink.com
e-mail: hompaper@gte.net

Sponsored by *The Link* Homeschool Newspaper, this all-inclusive conference offers 55 workshops over three days (May 21–23 of 1999) for children and adults, and includes 50-plus exhibitors. The conference has something for everyone—unschooling, academic, Christian, and non-Christian.

Bayshore Homeschooling Conference

Long Beach, CA
(562) 434-3940

This is one-day conference (April 24, 1999) put on by the Bayshore Homeschool Group. It is all-inclusive, mostly focusing on unschooling. There are vendors and approximately six workshops.

Annual Christian Home Educators' Association (CHEA) Conference

Disneyland Hotel
Anaheim, California
(562) 864-2432 or (800) 564-2432
website: www.cheaofca.org

This is the largest Christian Conference in Southern California (July 9–11, 1999), with approximately 6,000 in attendance and hundreds of vendors. The workshops are mostly Christian.

Christian Family Schools (San Diego)

Todd Cooper
(619) 484-2544

The 15th Annual Curriculum Fair/Homeschool Conference (May 14–15, 1999) drew attendance of about 1,000.

Northern California

Homeschool Association of California (HSC)

Sacramento, CA
(707) 765-5375 or (888) HSC-4440
website: www.hsc.org

This group will sponsor "Home = Education," an annual homeschooling conference with an eclectic, secular focus. The three-day conference (August 1999) offers many workshops, vendors, and much more. It focuses on making friends and networking with other homeschoolers, as well as providing "how-to" information to the new homeschooler. Many families return to this conference year after year.

CHEA Home Educators of Santa Clara (San Francisco Bay Area)

Santa Clara Convention Center
Contact: Julie Horn
(562) 864-2432

The 16th Annual Christian Home Educators' Convention (April 30–May 1, 1999) is a Christian conference with an attendance of about 2,200. It's geared toward both those new to homeschooling and experienced Christian families.

HOPE School International

Redding, California
Contact: Dee Haselhuhn
(530) 222-2095

The 1999 conference was held in April. Please call them for details of their Conference 2000.

Central California

Valley Home Educators (Modesto area)

Big Bear Water Park
Waterford, California
(209) 548-0436

The two-day annual homeschool conference (July 30–31, 1999) features 35 workshops and many exhibits.

COLORADO

To homeschool children between the ages of 7 and 16 in Colorado, a parent must do two things: (1)test during the odd grades (beginning with 3rd grade), using a nationally recognized standardized test, such as the Iowa or Stanford and (2)file a letter of intent to homeschool annually with the school district. A homeschooling family does not have to report its curriculum or the subjects are being taught. This is a very easy state in which to homeschool.

STATEWIDE ORGANIZATIONS

Remember to contact your parent-run statewide organization before contacting any government agency. The parent-run organization will help you understand what to expect when you call the Department of Education.

Christian Home Educators of Colorado (CHEC)

3739 E. 4th Ave.
Denver, CO 80206
(303) 338-1888 (information message)
(303) 393-6587 (office)
website: www.chec.org

Call the information line for news about various services provided—such as park days, local support groups, and legal updates.

Colorado Home Educators Association

1616 17th St.
Denver, CO 80209
(303) 441-9938

You can get a newcomer's packet by calling their voice mail and leaving your name and address along with your request.

GOVERNMENT AGENCY

Colorado State Board of Education

Department of Education
201 E. Colfax Ave.
Denver, CO 80203
(303) 866-6817

SUPPORT GROUPS

West River Unschoolers

Peggy Nishikawa
2420 N. 1st St.
Grand Junction, CO 81501
(970) 241-4137
e-mail: wru2420@aol.com

Approximately 80 families are members of this organization, which is open to all.

Boulder County Home Educators

Valerie Berg
(303) 449-5916

Call this group for information about Boulder County–area homeschooling.

Secular Homeschool Support Group

Kerry Kantor
(719) 634-4098
website: http://members.iex.net/
~mkantor/SHSSH_Frame_Set.htm
e-mail: mkantor@usa.net

This is an all-inclusive group to which approximately 50 families of many different religious beliefs belong. Members keep their beliefs private.

Support Parents in Christian Education (SPICE)

Jan Voltmer
(970) 255-8324

This is a Christian group of 50 families that meet to support each other in the realm of Christian home education. They sponsor park days, field trips, and more.

Colorado Springs Homeschool Support Group

P.O. Box 26117
Colorado Springs, CO 80936
(719) 598-2636 (volunteer parents)
website: www.hschool.com

This all-inclusive group meets monthly, publishes a bimonthly newsletter, and hosts a website. The group offers support, friendship, field trips, and much more.

Rocky Mountain Education Connection

Cindy
(303) 341-2242
e-mail: connect@pcisys.net

"We are an all-inclusive support group with a newsletter, park days, field trips, and fun."

CONFERENCES

Northwest Colorado Homeschool Association

Craig, Colorado
Contacts: Steve and Ren Berkoff
(970) 842-3198

This association sponsored its 7th Annual Christian Homeschool Convention in April 1999.

Christian Home Educators of Colorado

Denver, Colorado
Sherri Wilson
(303) 393-6587

The 9th Annual Christian Homeschool Conference took place June 24–26, 1999.

Colorado Home Educator's Book Fair

Colorado Christian
Lakewood, Colorado
(303) 670-0673

The 12th Annual Book Fair was held May 22, 1999.

CONNECTICUT

Parent Luz Schosie says this about homeschooling in Connecticut: "Connecticut is one of best states for homeschooling. The state law, which was written in the 1600s, is still the same. The law gives parents responsibility for educating their children. They can teach them at home or send them to school. There is no testing required."

In Connecticut, 99 percent of the homeschool groups fall under the interest of the two statewide organizations listed below. For a fee of under $20, you can join whichever one suits your family best. They will put you in touch with the numerous groups in the state. We found in our research that every group referred us back to those two primary organizations.

STATEWIDE ORGANIZATIONS

Remember to contact your parent-run statewide organization before contacting any government agency. The parent-run organization will help you understand what to expect when you call the Department of Education.

Connecticut Home Educators' Association (CHEA)

Dale Schneider
10 Ellen Ln.
Deep River, CT 06417
(203) 781-8569
website: www.connix.com/
 ~dschroth/chea/RCT.html

The purpose of CHEA is to provide support and disseminate information to people interested in homeschooling in Connecticut. The group welcomes all styles and religions.

The Education Association of Christian Homeschoolers (TEACH)

(800) 205-7844 (within Connecticut)
(860) 231-2930 (outside Connecticut)

This is a statewide organization for people seeking information about Christian homeschooling. You can obtain information about conventions, support groups, and much more by contacting TEACH.

GOVERNMENT AGENCY

Connecticut Department of Education

Room 246-A
165 Capitol Ave.
Hartford, CT 06106
(860) 566-8263 or (860) 566-5982

SUPPORT GROUPS

CT's CURE (Citizens to Uphold the Right to Educate)

Debi Stevenson-Michener
(203) 354-3590
website: www.connix.com/
  ~dschroth/chea/RCT.html

CURE is a legislative watchdog organization. See the CHEA website for more information.

Unschoolers Support

Luz Schosie
22 Wildrose Ave.
Guilford, CT 06437
(203) 458-7402

Anyone interested is welcome to join this group of about 100 families that meets every other month. Although originally founded for unschoolers, the group excludes no one.

CONFERENCES

The Education Association of Christian Homeschoolers (TEACH)

(Location to be announced)
(800) 205-7844 (in Connecticut)
(860) 677-4538 (outside Connecticut)

TEACH sponsors an Annual Conference & Curriculum Fair featuring 100 vendors and many, many workshops held over a two-day period (last held June 1999). It has a Christian feel but could be of interest to all. Contact TEACH for conference location and dates.

DELAWARE

There are three ways to homeschool in the state of Delaware:

1. A family may enroll in an existing and registered private home education school (called a private academy in Delaware). If a family chooses this method, they will not need to fill out any forms with the Department of Education.

2. Have the superintendent of your local school district sign a "Homeschool Under Local Superintendent Registration Form."

3. Start your own nonpublic school. To do this, please call Vicki Fjelsted Fields at the Department of Education at (302) 475-0574.

STATEWIDE ORGANIZATIONS

Remember to contact your parent-run statewide organization before contacting any government agency. The parent-run organization will help you understand what to expect when you call the Department of Education.

Delaware Home Education Association (DHEA)

John Poe, President
Suite 172, 1712 Marsh Rd.
Wilmington, DE 19810-4611
(302) 475-0574

DHEA is a statewide network for private academies in Delaware. The organization functions as a clearinghouse for information to homeschooling families and also performs legislative watchdog duties toward maintaining the best legal environment in Delaware. They provide information concerning the ten private academies they represent (most of those in the state). Their membership includes approximately 800 families and over 1,300 students.

GOVERNMENT AGENCY

Delaware State Department of Education

Townsend Building
P.O. Box 1402
Dover, DE 19903
(302) 739-4583

SUPPORT GROUPS

Tri-State Homeschool Network

Mike and Kate
P.O. Box 7193
Newark, DE 19714
(302) 322-2018

Because of the great differences in homeschooling laws of Pennsylvania, New Jersey, and Delaware, this group may not be useful to some families in these states for strictly educational support, but for field trips and other similar activities, it is a good group. This homeschool support group provides field trips, skating, academic activities, choir, and band to the 350–400 families that are members. They will also help you get in contact with groups in all areas of Delaware. Please call for information specific to your needs.

CONFERENCES

Delaware Home Education Association (DHEA)

Wilmington, Delaware
Contact: John Poe
Suite 172, 1712 Marsh Rd.
Wilmington, DE 19810-4611

The 6th Semi-Annual Inclusive Homeschooling Conference, planned for April 7–8, 2000, will feature keynote speaker Ken Hammond, vendors, and more.

FLORIDA

To homeschool legally in Florida, parents must file with the superintendent of schools in the district in which they live and intend to homeschool. You do not have to be under an umbrella school. The state requires that you have some form of year-end status evaluation by any currently certified teacher. Testing can be done around the state and with home support or with the public school. Florida is a homeschool-friendly state.

STATEWIDE ORGANIZATIONS

Remember to contact your parent-run statewide organization before contacting any government agency. The parent-run organization will help you understand what to expect when you call the Department of Education.

Florida Parent Educator's Association

P.O. Box 50685
Jacksonville Beach, FL 32240
(877) 275-3732

This is the statewide group to join if you want information about homeschooling in Florida. They will put you in touch with any group in the area in which you live. They have a yearly conference, put out a guide to homeschooling booklet, and will guide you to legally homeschool in the state.

GOVERNMENT AGENCY

Florida Department of Education

325 West Gaines St., Suite 532
Tallahassee, FL 32399
(850) 487-8428

To get further information on homeschooling in Florida, ask for Mary Lou Carothers.

SUPPORT GROUPS

Home Education Resource & Information (HERI)

Kristen Mock
711 St. Johns Bluff Rd.
Jacksonville, FL 32225
(904) 565-9121
e-mail: herijax@juno.com

This networking support group holds a curriculum convention, publishes a monthly newsletter, sponsors field trips, and maintains a lending library.

Parkland Home Educators

Sandra D. Coburn
(407) 677-1891
e-mail: abercrom@netwide.net

Approximately 28 families comprise this all-inclusive support group that focuses on Christian leadership. The group publishes a monthly newsletter-calendar and offers civic theater, 4-H group, park days, and field trips, as well as testing.

West Florida Home Education Support League

Mark Chivers
P.O. Box 11720
Pensacola, FL 32524
(850) 995-9444
websites: (FPEA) www.fpa.org
www.wfhesl.org

This group of approximately 300 families includes several cell groups that offer field trips and park days.

Indian River Homeschoolers

(561) 388-2066

This all-inclusive support group of 140 families in Indian River County has Christian leadership. Families get together for bowling, skating, physical education, talent night (once a year), and graduation.

Home Educators Resource and Information (HERI)

Lori Fox
711 St. John's Bluff Rd.
Jacksonville, FL 32225
(904) 565-9121
e-mail: herijax@yahoo.com

This group of 500–600 families includes 30–40 subgroups. They maintain a library and sponsor a curriculum convention in July with 60 to 70 workshops.

CONFERENCES

Home Educators Resource and Information (HERI)

Jacksonville, Florida
(904) 565-9121

HERI sponsors an Annual Curriculum Fair and Conference with 60 to 70 workshops and hundreds of vendors in mid-July.

Circle Christian School

Orlando, Florida
Contact: Sarah Grandstaff
(407) 740-8877

The 14th Homeschool Conference (Christian) was held July 9–10 of 1999.

Emerald Coast Homeschool Organization (ECHO)

Pensacola, Florida
Contact: Tim Grant
(850) 994-1470

The group held its 3rd Homeschool Conference (Christian) June 4–5, 1999.

Florida Parent-Educators Association (FPEA)

Orlando, Florida
Contact: David Exley
(877) 275-3732 or (904) 241-5538

The 13th Homeschool Conference, which is an all-inclusive annual event, was held May 27–29 of 1999.

West Florida Home Education Support League

Pensacola, Florida
Contact: Mark Chivers
(850) 995-9444

The 11th Homeschool Conference, an inclusive event, was held May 14–15, 1999.

Florida Parent Educator's Association (FPEA)

World Marriott Resort
Orlando, Florida
(877) 275-3732 (FPEA)

The 12th Annual Homeschool Conference was held May 29–31, 1999. Over 6,000 attend this conference, which is all-inclusive, serving all religions. It features hundreds of vendors, a homeschool band, graduating ceremony, and over 70 great workshops.

GEORGIA

To homeschool legally in Georgia, parents must file a letter of intent with the local school superintendent 30 days after the establishment of their homeschool program the first year and by September 1 each year thereafter. The family is required to homeschool for 4.5 hours each day, covering a daily curriculum that includes English, math, social studies (geography and history), and science. The parents must prepare an annual progress report on their child and retain it for 3 years. They must also test the child every 3 years after 3rd grade and are required to keep the test scores on hand for 3 years thereafter, but don't have to report them. Parents must also fill out a monthly attendance form (including the name and address of the home-school site) 180 days per year and send it in to the local Board at the end of each month.

STATEWIDE ORGANIZATIONS

Remember to contact your parent-run statewide organization before contacting any government agency. The parent-run organization will help you understand what to expect when you call the Department of Education.

Georgia Home Education Association (GHEA)

(770) 461-3657
website: www.ghea.org

This is a statewide Christian homeschooling organization with a huge network of local member support groups all over Georgia. They offer a wealth of information for Christian homeschooling families. They also offer the Christian "Connector," which provides free information on numerous Christian functions, including Christian colleges, concerts, short-term missions, and more. Call (800) 667-0600 for information or visit their large and informative website.

Home Educators Information Resource (HEIR)

P.O. Box 2111
Roswell, GA 30077-2111
(404) 861-HEIR (4347) (voice mail)
website: www.heir.org

This is a statewide, nonpartisan and nonsectarian volunteer organization. They work to ensure the freedom to homeschool in Georgia and provide legal information as well. Since HEIR is not a nonprofit organization, members can lobby all they please. They advise that the best way to contact them is via their (excellent) website. (Their "snail mail" address is also available, but takes longer.)

GOVERNMENT AGENCY

Georgia Department of Education

205 Butler St.
Atlanta, GA 30334
(404) 656-2446

SUPPORT GROUPS

Family Education for Christ

Becky Gianino
P.O. Box 16619
Savannah, GA 31416
(912) 354-5204
e-mail: fefc.savh@juno.com

This expressly Christian support group of 140 families requires a Statement of Faith. They publish a monthly newsletter, plan monthly field trips, and sponsor a chess club and Boy Scout troop.

Coweta Home Educators Association

Judy Floyd
9 Ashley Oaks Ln.
Newnan, GA 30263
(770) 502-9375

This 46-family support group is all-inclusive and requires no membership fee. They sponsor a monthly newsletter and field trips.

Gwinnett Home Educators

Sandra Rush
1981 Clinton Pl.
Lawrenceville, GA 30043
(770) 963-0713

This group of 300 Christian families requires a Statement of Faith. Field trips, park days, and a bimonthly newsletter are among their planned activities.

North Fulton Home Educators Encouragers

Kelly Ling
24 Windsor Ln.
Alpharetta, GA 30004
(770) 664-0960
e-mail: ladyscham@bellsouth.net

This local support group, which includes 100 families, is all-inclusive with Christian leadership. The group publishes a newsletter (11 issues per year).

CONFERENCES

Catholic Home Educators of Georgia

Contact: Karen Donaldson
(706) 367-2437
e-mail: kadonald@juno.com

The group's Annual Catholic Homeschool Conference was last held in Atlanta, Georgia June 18–19, 1999.

Georgia Home Education Association

Contacts: Ken or Mary Jo Patterson
(770) 461-3657
e-mail: ghea@mindspring.com

The Annual Homeschool Conference, last held April 23–24, 1999 in Atlanta, Georgia, is Christian but inclusive.

Gwinnett Christian Home Educators Association (GCHA)

Atlanta, Georgia
Contact: Sandra Rush
(770) 963-0713
e-mail: mathusee@juno.com

GCHA's Annual Christian Conference was held March 26–27, 1999, in Atlanta, Georgia.

Harvest Home Educators

Atlanta, Georgia
Contact: Veronica F. Bowen
(770) 271-2360
e-mail: harvesthomeeducators@juno.com

Call to learn the dates of this Annual Inclusive Homeschool Conference.

HAWAII

To homeschool legally in Hawaii, parents must notify their local district. Parents do not need to be certified, but they are expected to participate in statewide testing of students in grades 3, 6, 8, and 10. Homeschools are, however, permitted to turn in alternative assessments.

STATEWIDE ORGANIZATIONS

Remember to contact your parent-run statewide organization before contacting any government agency. The parent-run organization will help you understand what to expect when you call the Department of Education.

The Hawaii Homeschool Association

(808) 944-3339
e-mail: Tgthrngplc@aol.com

This is an all-inclusive, statewide organization staffed by volunteers. For information (a packet is available) on fun, activities, legalities, park days, and more, please contact them via phone or e-mail.

GOVERNMENT AGENCY

Hawaii Department of Education

641 18th Ave., Room 210
Honolulu, HI 96816
(808) 733-9895

SUPPORT GROUPS

Homeschool Adventure Programs for Parents & Youngsters (HAPPY)

Gail Nagasako
777 Kolani St.
Wailuku, HI 96793
(808) 242-8225

"HAPPY" is a loose co-op group ("a wonderful mix of people!") in which different ideas from everyone are welcome. The group has a newsletter.

Christian Homeschoolers of Hawaii

John or Arlene
(808) 689-6398

This is the base for a network of Christian support groups throughout the Hawaiian Islands. They provide information about the laws, conferences, and so forth to anyone interested in homeschooling. They have Christian leadership, but will make contact with anyone.

Hawaiian Island Christian Home Educators

Ruth
(808) 965-6373

"We are a Christian homeschooling group that offers support and information for Christian families." Call for the address or information about this group, which is located on the big island.

Hawaiian Homeschool Association

Linda
(808) 944-3339
e-mail: tgthrngplc@aol.com

This is an all-inclusive group with people from many different backgrounds. They welcome people of all religions and all styles of homeschooling. Members plan activities, as well as meet for park day twice a month. Call to request an information packet, which will include a resource packet for homeschoolers in the Hawaii area that will answer frequently asked questions and more.

CONFERENCES

Christian Homeschoolers of Hawaii

Ewa Beach, Hawaii
Contact: Arlene
(808) 689-6398

The 10th annual Homeschool Conference was held March 19–20 of 1999 at the Kalihi Union Church on the Big Island. The conference (the only one we know of in Hawaii) is mostly a Christian focus, but all are welcome. Approximately 600 attend this event, which features vendors and workshops.

IDAHO

Larry Nelson, a founding member of Idaho Coalition of Home Educators, says that Idaho has no requirements whatsoever for homeschoolers. "Idaho is the easiest and most friendly state to homeschool in," says Nelson.

STATEWIDE ORGANIZATIONS

Remember to contact your parent-run statewide organization before contacting any government agency. The parent-run organization will help you understand what to expect when you call the Department of Education.

Idaho Coalition of Home Educators

Larry Nelson
P.O. Box 7
Hope, ID 83836
(208) 264-5212

This statewide group watches legislation and sponsors a yearly legislation day, where they set up tables at the state capitol building and show legislators the types of work homeschoolers are doing.

GOVERNMENT AGENCY

Idaho Department of Education

P.O. Box 83720
Boise, ID 83720-0027
(208) 332-6800

SUPPORT GROUPS

Boise Home Educators

Deena Kolb
(208) 322-3937

This all-inclusive group meets monthly for park days and field trips.

83709 & Friends

Janine Sonoda
(208) 362-0235

Please call Janine, who puts together a list of homeschool families in the 83709 zip code area and beyond (thus the name "83709 & Friends"). She'll give you their address to which you can send your self-addressed stamped envelope requesting information.

Treasure Valley Homeschool Newsletter

Diane Schrader
(208) 463-2331
e-mail: BSCHRADE@micron.net

Call or e-mail Diane to request this 12-page monthly newsletter, which explains all you need to know about homeschooling in Idaho.

Southwestern Idaho Christian Home Educators (SWICHE)

Carol Dunn
(208) 323-2741

SWICHE is a newly formed Christian homeschooling group that meets for support and friendship and sponsors park days, a newsletter, and more.

The Regional Christian Home Educators (Pocatello, Idaho)

Teresa Tapia
(208) 238-0850

This Christian homeschooling group requires no statement of faith, only a statement of conduct.

Magic Valley Home Educators (MVHE)

David and Shirley Blakeslee
2392 Grandview Dr. N
Twin Falls, ID 83301
(208) 733-8378
e-mail: dsblake@magiclink.com

MVHE, located in south central Idaho, is an all-inclusive support group for all homeschoolers. The organization publishes a newsletter and sponsors regularly scheduled events such as roller-skating, skiing, and a teen support group.

The Family Unschooling Network of Boise

Neysa Jensen
(208) 345-2703
e-mail: neysajensen@compuserve.com

This is an "unschooling group" that welcomes all styles of homeschoolers for park days, theme days, friendship, and fun.

CONFERENCES

Southwest Idaho Christian Home Educators (SWICHE)

Capital Christian Center
Boise, Idaho
Contact: Carol Dunn
(208) 323-2741

SWICHE plans an annual two-day Conference (last held July 16 and 17, 1999) focusing on Christian homeschooling, new to homeschooling, teen homeschooling, and home health.

Pocatello Regional Christian Home Educators Conference

Gate City Christian Church
Pocatello, Idaho
Contact: Teresa Tapia
(208) 238-0850

A one-day conference for Christian homeschoolers featuring workshops and vendors was held May 22, 1999.

Magic Valley Home Educators

Twin Falls, Idaho
Contact: Shirley Blakeslee
(208) 733-8378
e-mail: dsblake@magiclink.com

This Christian Homeschooling Conference with workshops and exhibitors was held March 19–20, 1999.

ILLINOIS

The only thing a parent must do to homeschool in Illinois is teach their child at home. No regulations or registering or testing of any kind is in place, nor are parents required to register with the Board of Education at all. If you wish help in any area, please call Chuck Stoeckel. He was very helpful when we called and extremely positive toward homeschooling. This would be a great state in which to homeschool!

As for the state's political climate, according to Teresa Sneade, "It is very easy to homeschool in Illinois, where a homeschool is considered a private school. Some people have a problem with a particular district but just teach the educational subjects that are taught in public school."

STATEWIDE ORGANIZATIONS

Remember to contact your parent-run statewide organization before contacting any government agency. The parent-run organization will help you understand what to expect when you call the Department of Education.

Home Oriented Unique Schooling Experience (HOUSE)

Teresa Sneade
2508 East 222 Pl.
Sauk Village, IL 60411
(708) 758-7374
website: www.geocities.com/Athens/
   Acropolis/7804
e-mail: ASERET70@aol.com

Call this statewide organization to request support information on homeschooling anywhere in the state and to learn about the annual conference in the Chicago area. HOUSE has 25 chapters in Illinois, with the greater proportion in the Chicagoland area, but they have chapters downstate as well. Call Teresa Sneade for the chapter contact in your area.

Illinois Christian Home Educators (ICHE)

Roger Erber
P.O. Box 775
Harvard, IL 60033
(847) 662-1909
e-mail: iche83@juno.com

ICHE is a nondenominational organization that has been in existence since 1983. It is not a membership group, but rather works with support groups around Illinois in maintaining a network. They sponsor two state conventions each year—the Northern version is held in Naperville in the middle of May, and the downstate event is held in Mount Vernon in April. ICHE offers a beginner packet, which includes much useful information on Illinois education law, how to withdraw your child from school, and curriculum publisher information. The organization also connects the beginning family to support groups.

Network of Illinois Catholic Home Educators

Karen Dempsey
690 Red Bridge Rd.
Lake Zurich, IL 60047
e-mail: dempsey@uss.net

This is the Catholic Network of support groups in Illinois. They offer virtually the same services to Catholic homeschoolers as the above organizations do to their respective user groups.

GOVERNMENT AGENCY

Illinois State Board of Education

Chuck Stoeckel
100 North First St.
Springfield, IL 62777
(217) 782-3950

SUPPORT GROUPS

Evanston Home Educators

Nancy Guenther
P.O. Box 1914
Evanston, IL 60204-1914
(847) 604-3541
e-mail: 102723,2764@compuserve.com

The all-inclusive HOUSE group, which was started 15 years ago, encompasses 70 families. Group offerings include foreign language classes, nature classes, sports classes, gymnastics, swimming, drama, field trips, monthly meeting for parents, a separate group for newcomers, discussion topics, and living history.

Homeschooling Families of Illinois

(630) 548-4349

Call for information about this inclusive group of 50 families. They conduct two daytime meetings per summer months and one per month during the winter, as well as publish a monthly newsletter. HFI serves the Southwestern Chicago suburbs.

CONFERENCES

The Association of Christian Home Educators

Peoria, Illinois
Contact: Janice Price
(309) 589-1307

The Heart of Illinois Convention of Home Educators held its 10th annual conference on April 16–17, 1999, with approximately 1,000 people in attendance.

INDIANA

Parents of homeschoolers in Indiana must report enrollment data to the Department of Education and provide instruction that is equivalent to the public school system. Parents must keep attendance and teach 180 days per year.

STATEWIDE ORGANIZATIONS

Remember to contact your parent-run statewide organization before contacting any government agency. The parent-run organization will help you understand what to expect when you call the Department of Education.

Indiana Association of Home Educators (Christian)

(317) 859-1202

This is a statewide Christian organization that provides information for those interested in homeschooling. If you contact this group, staff members can put you in touch with the group in your area, no matter where you live in the state of Indiana. The organization also publishes a bimonthly magazine and offers an annual conference and a moms' retreat. Call the office for further information.

GOVERNMENT AGENCY

Indiana Department of Education

Room 229, State House
Indianapolis, IN 46204-2798
(317) 232-9135

SUPPORT GROUPS

Families Learning Together

Jill
(317) 255-9298
e-mail: whelan.mullen@juno.com

This all-inclusive group offers park days, field trips, socializing, and fun.

Life Education and Resource Network (L.E.A.R.N.)

Barbara Benson
9577 E State Rd. 45
Unionville, IN 47468
(812) 336-8028

This all-inclusive group publishes a newsletter, holds a park day each month, and meets for socializing and field trips.

Northern Indiana Christian Home Educators (NICHE)

Joanne Stas
(219) 923-1270
e-mail: NICHESUPRT@aol.com

This is a Christian organization whose purpose is to help Christian families in their efforts to homeschool. They meet for park days, field trips, academic activities, and more.

CONFERENCES

Ft. Wayne Area Homeschools

Ft. Wayne, Indiana
Contact: Kathy Prentice
(219) 483-2807

May 8, 1999, was the date of this organization's 15th Annual Home Educator's Curriculum Fair, which featured over 45 vendors.

Indiana Association of Home Educators (IAHE)

Indianapolis, Indiana
Contact: Joyce Johnson
(317) 859-1202
e-mail: iahe@inhomeeducators.org

IAHE held its 14th Annual (Christian) Home Educators Convention June 18–19 of 1999, featuring vendors, workshops, and various activities.

IOWA

To homeschool in the state of Iowa, parents have three alternatives:

1. Submit a portfolio to an approved portfolio evaluator.

2. Administer an annual Iowa Test of Basic Skills. (You can buy them from an independent source or get them from the school district.)

3. Dual enroll and join a homeschool assistance program that involves many visits.

Most people are in the various state programs. This tends to undermine the local grassroots groups. It was very difficult to find grassroots groups in this state.

STATEWIDE ORGANIZATIONS

Remember to contact your parent-run statewide organization before contacting any government agency. The parent-run organization will help you understand what to expect when you call the Department of Education.

Network of Iowa Christian Home Educators (NICHE)

P.O. Box 158
Dexter, IA 50070

Contact this statewide group before you do anything, to ensure that you protect your rights as best you can.

GOVERNMENT AGENCY

Iowa Department of Education

Jim Tyson
Grimes State Office Bldg.
Des Moines, IA 50319-0416
(515) 281-5001 (homeschooling)
(515) 281-5811 (main number)

SUPPORT GROUPS

XYZ (temporary name)

Rebecca Leach
(712) 274-0472
e-mail: homNhearth@aol.com

XYZ is the temporary name for this new, inclusive nonsectarian group that advocates unschooling. Everyone is welcome.

CONFERENCES

Network of Iowa Christian Home Educators (NICHE)

Des Moines, Iowa
Contact: Julie Naberhaus
(800) 723-0438 (inside Iowa)
(515) 830-1614 (outside Iowa)
website: www.the-niche.org
e-mail: NICHE@netins.net

NICHE sponsors an Annual Christian Homeschool Conference during the summer (June 11–12 in 1999).

KANSAS

The only requirement parents must meet to legally homeschool in Kansas is to request, fill out, and return a homeschooling registration form that will be kept on file in Topeka. The form is obtained through the state's Department of Education. The state does not perform follow-ups, testing, or any other monitoring. However, if a neighbor complains to Social Services because children seem to be outside too much, for instance, a family would do well to have attendance records or other documents to verify that they are actually instructing their children. The reason for this is that Kansas has a law that all children must be educated until they are 18.

STATEWIDE ORGANIZATIONS

Remember to contact your parent-run statewide organization before contacting any government agency. The parent-run organization will help you understand what to expect when you call the Department of Education.

Christian Home Educators Conference of Kansas (CHECK)

David Barfield, Chairman
P.O. Box 3564
Shawnee Mission, KS 66203
(785) 843-9207
website: www.kansashomeschool.org
e-mail: barfield@cjnetworks.com
info@kansashomeschool.org (for general inquiries)

CHECK encompasses 52 local member chapters and 2 large regional chapters: Teaching Parents Association (TPA) of Wichita with 1,500 members (see below) and Johnson County Parent Educators of Kansas City with nearly 1,000 members (see below). The organization's mission statement reads: "CHECK is an association of support groups from across the State which serves as an information clearinghouse and an advocate for homeschooling in Kansas. CHECK is committed to the preservation of the rights of parents to direct the education of their children, in accordance with Biblical mandates, and to the provision of encouragement and assistance to all parents in the exercise of that responsibility."

Teaching Parents Association (TPA)

Cathy Middleton
P.O. Box 3968
Wichita, KS 67201
(316) 945-0810
e-mail: bdmiddle@aol.com

This Christian group of 1,500 families requires no statement of faith. The organization sponsors an annual convention, newsletter, resource center, testing, field trips, classes, and sports activities.

Johnson County Parent Educators (JCPE)

P.O. Box 14391
Lenexa, KS 66285-4391
(913) 397-9506 (during business hours CST, Monday–Friday)
(913) 791-8089 (recorded information)

GOVERNMENT AGENCY

Kansas State Department of Education

Maria Collins
120 Southeast 10th Ave.
Topeka, KS 66612-1182
(785) 296-3201

SUPPORT GROUPS

Lawrence Area Unaffiliated Group of Homeschoolers (LAUGH)

Pete and Elizabeth Laufer
407 East 10th St.
Lawrence KS 66044
(785) 841-6020
e-mail: sandheron@earthlink.net

This all-inclusive secular group describes itself as follows: "We do not support any sort of curriculum or religion. Our main goals are to share strength, encourage and give information."

Heartland Area Homeschoolers' Association

Gary and Ranae Wyatt
(316) 343-7376
e-mail: orion@carrollsweb.com

The group itself is dormant but the Wyatts are a local referral for those contemplating homeschooling. Ranae gives a balanced view of what it is all about. Gary is a professor at the university in Emporia, Kansas.

Flinthill Educators Group (Christian)

Cheryl Repp
2365 Angus
Neosho Rapids, KS 66864
(316) 342-9137
e-mail: curtrepp@cadvantage.com

This Christian group requires a Statement of Faith for leadership roles, but doesn't exclude anyone from participating. They schedule park days the second Tuesday of each month and offer science projects, moms' days, and testing for those who wish it.

CONFERENCES

Johnson County Parent Educators

College of The Nazarene
Olathe, Kansas
(913) 791-8089

The Johnson Parent Educators Curriculum Fair and Homeschool Conference was held April 23–24 of 1999.

Teaching Parents Association (TPA)

Century 2 Convention Center
Wichita, Kansas
Contact: Cathy Middleton
(316) 755-2159

TPA held its 14th Annual Teaching Parents Association Homeschool Conference June 4–5 of 1999. This large conference draws about 3,000 attendees for approximately 50 workshops (all geared toward Christian homeschooling) and over 160 vendors.

 # KENTUCKY

Kentucky has compulsory attendance laws for children between 6 and 16. Home schools are considered private schools. Instruction must be in English and must be in the branches of study offered in public schools. This includes at least reading, writing, spelling, grammar, history, mathematics, and civics. Minimum annual school term is 185 days, equivalent of 175 days × 6 hours = 1,050 instructional hours. Attendance and grades must be kept just as is required in public schools. Inspections of private school is required by law; however, since the school is within a home and the 4th Amendment of the U.S. Constitution protects against unwarranted searches and seizures, government officials should not be allowed to come into the home without a warrant or court order. Parents must notify the local school board of the enrollment of their child in a private school within the first two weeks of each school year. There are a number of other points of which parents in Kentucky should make themselves aware.

STATEWIDE ORGANIZATIONS

Remember to contact your parent-run statewide organization before contacting any government agency. The parent-run organization will help you understand what to expect when you call the Department of Education.

Christian Home Educators of Kentucky (CHEK)

691 Howardstown Rd.
Hodgensville, KY 42748
(502) 358-9270
website: www.check.org

This is a statewide, Christian group with local support group information, legal oversight, guidance, and information for all Kentucky homeschoolers. The organization also sponsors an annual convention.

Kentucky Home Education Association (KHEA)

P.O. Box 81
Winchester, KY 40392
(606) 737-3338
website: http://ky-on-line.com/bhe

This is a secular statewide group that offers much information for homeschoolers who live in Kentucky. From what we read on the association's great website, the Christian and secular homeschooling leaders in Kentucky seem to engage in a spirit of united cooperation. The group benefits all homeschoolers in the state by working to protect their basic rights and freedoms to teach their own children. Hear, hear.

GOVERNMENT AGENCY

Kentucky Department of Education

Joe Clark
500 Mero St., 8th Floor, Capitol Plaza Tower
Frankfort, KY 40601-1957
(502) 564-3791 (Joe Clark)
(502) 564-4770 (main number)

SUPPORT GROUPS

Central Kentucky Christian Home School Association (CKCHSA)

e-mail: ckchsa@hotmail.com

Bluegrass Home Educators

Cherie Carroll
600 Shake Rag Rd.
Waynesburg, KY
website: http:ky-on-line.com/bhe
e-mail: bhe@ky-on-line.com

This website contains an excellent aid for Kentucky homeschoolers: the "Best Practice Document," which was developed by Kentucky Home Education Association (KHEA), Christian Home Educators of Kentucky (CHEK), and the Kentucky Directors of Pupil Personnel (DDPs). (The DDPs are county peace officers who oversee compliance with the state's homeschooling laws but do not have the authority to issue warrants.) The document describes the best practice for Kentucky homeschooling parents to follow in their homeschooling and dealing with the state department of education and the laws.

CONFERENCES

Christian Home Educators of Kentucky (CHEK)

Louisville, Kentucky
Contact: Don Woolett
(502) 358-9270
website: www.chek.org
e-mail: chek@kynet.org

The organization's Annual Christian Conference, held July 16–17, 1999, featured vendors, speakers, and other activities.

Our Lady of the Rosary School

Louisville, Kentucky
Contact: Robert Brindle
(502) 348-1338
website: www.olrs.com
e-mail: information@olrs.com

The group's Annual Catholic Homeschool Conference was held July 23–24, 1999.

LOUISIANA

A homeschool can operate as a private school and must teach 180 days per year. The subjects taught have to be the equivalent of that offered in the public schools, including the Declaration of Independence and the Federalist Papers. Parents are not required to have any qualifications. Notification of the intention to homeschool must be provided to the state department of education within the first 30 days of each school year. No recordkeeping or testing is required. The other way to homeschool is to establish and operate a homeschool as approved by the board of education. This approach has filing, recordkeeping, and testing requirements.

STATEWIDE ORGANIZATIONS

Remember to contact your parent-run statewide organization before contacting any government agency. The parent-run organization will help you understand what to expect when you call the Department of Education.

Christian Home Educators Fellowship of Louisiana

P.O. Box 74292
Baton Rouge, LA 70874-4292
(888) 876-2433
e-mail: burger6@juno.com

This is a statewide Christian organization with local support group and other information.

Louisiana Home Education Network (LAHEN)

*website: http://members.aol.com/La-
    HomeED/Lahen.html*
e-mail: lahmednet@usa.net

This statewide, inclusive association has a very good website from which this information is extracted. LAHEN respects the diversity of philosophies and styles that compose homeschooling and therefore has no official political, philosophical, or religious orientation. Their purpose is to help homeschoolers protect the fundamental right of the family to educate its children in the manner it deems appropriate without regulation or interference by federal, state, or local agencies. LAHEN also monitors and responds to relevant legislation. It is not a membership organization; therefore, your choosing to sign up seems to imply your willingness to become part of the LAHEN network by placing your e-mail address (kept confidential) with them.

GOVERNMENT AGENCY

Louisiana Department of Education

Home Study Program
P.O. Box 94064
Baton Rouge, LA 70804-9064
(504) 342-3473

SUPPORT GROUPS

Wild Azalea Unschoolers

Tracey Sherry
6055 General Meyer Ave.
New Orleans, LA 70131
(504) 392-5647

This is an all-inclusive local support group with over 30 families. They have weekly meetings, plan occasional outings, and provide support for parents.

CONFERENCES

Christian Home Educators Fellowship of Louisiana (CHEF)

Baker, Louisiana
Contact: Eric R. Burges, President
(888) 876-2433

CHEF's Annual Christian Homeschool Conference, which was held April 23–24 of 1999, highlighted vendors and various activities.

MAINE

To homeschool in Maine, you must apply to the state Department of Education, in writing, notifying them of how many children you will be homeschooling. You can either keep track of what you do academically or you can use a form provided, which allows you to check a box stating: "I don't use a regular instructional plan." This translates into what most home-schoolers know as "unschooling." Your child has to be assessed quarterly. Please note that you can do this in one of several ways. Two methods are through a homeschool group that has a portfolio night or by a public school teacher who is licensed in Maine. Therefore, it is necessary to belong to a homeschool group. You could also be a non-approved private school.

Regarding the state's political climate, Eileen Yoder, homeschooling mother and co-founder of Southern Maine Home Education Support Network, states: "Our state does not make it difficult to homeschool. We are a notification state, and there are several methods of notification available."

STATEWIDE ORGANIZATIONS

Remember to contact your parent-run statewide organization before contacting any government agency. The parent-run organization will help you understand what to expect when you call the Department of Education.

Maine Home Education Associates (MHEA)

Vicki Limberger
P.O. Box 421
Topsham, ME 04086
(800) 520-0577

This is a legal contact information service run by homeschoolers. It publishes a newsletter and distributes the legal guidelines and support group lists geographically. The Maine Department of Education provides this association's number to prospective homeschool families. (The state homeschool application requires that a family be affiliated with a support group.) Call for information and to get free answers to your questions.

GOVERNMENT AGENCY

Maine Department of Education

Edwin Kastuck
23 State House Station
Augusta, ME 04333-0023
(207) 287-5922

SUPPORT GROUPS

Southern Maine Home Education Support Network

Eileen Yoder
76 Beech Ridge Rd.
Scarborough, ME 04074
(207) 883-9621
e-mail: smhesn@hotmail.com

Eclectic, nonsectarian group of about 200 families that welcomes all religions and "gathers around activities people are interested in." Because members range from strict curriculum users to the far end of the spectrum, everybody fits in.

Homeschool Associates of New England

Steve Moitozo
(800) 882-2828
e-mail: homeschool@
*   homeschoolassociates.com*

This association provides all sorts of services in Maine, from conference information to high school diplomas and group referrals.

Sebago Lake Homeschoolers Support Group

Mary
5 School St.
Standish, ME 04084
(207) 642-4368

From born-again Christians to unschoolers, these 10 to 15 families provide a great resource for area people. Not at all rigid, they provide what their people need. Right now, for example, they are offering Chinese, cello, and a science class.

Home Education and Family Services

Jane Boswell and Shirley Minster
P.O. Box 1056
Gray, ME 04039
(207) 657-2800

Jane and Shirley are professional teachers who provide consulting services for homeschoolers for a fee. They help in setting up a curriculum and also provide educational testing.

Central Maine Self-Learners

Suzanne Cook
36 Country Acres
Monmouth, ME 04259-6530
(207) 933-5055
website:
http://members.aol.com/scookie5/cmfl.html

This homeschool group of families in central Maine is all-inclusive, open to anyone. Families take turns hosting field trips and different activities. Parents meet monthly and are committed to satisfying families' needs as they go.

Maine Catholic Home Education Network

Tamara and Bob Konczal
210 Beech Ridge Rd.
Scarborough, ME 04074-9151
(207) 839-6351
website: http://members.aol.com/
    moosenews

The website offers insights and thoughtful information from a Catholic perspective on a variety of topics, including community service.

CONFERENCES

Homeschoolers of Maine (Christian)

Bethel, ME
Contact: Ed Green
(207) 763-4251
e-mail: homeschl@midcoast.com;
website: www.homeschool-maine.org

The 9th Annual Homeschools of Maine Convention was held April 16–17, 1999.

MARYLAND

A family who wishes to homeschool in Maryland must give the board of education 15 days notice of intent and sign an assurance of consent. Then the family has two options for review:

1. Be reviewed by the board of education.

2. Go with an oversight group.

Most families choose evaluation by an oversight group that is not part of the board of education. We have been told it is much more flexible and comfortable for families not to have a member of the board of education come to their home to evaluate.

STATEWIDE ORGANIZATIONS

Remember to contact your parent-run statewide organization before contacting any government agency. The parent-run organization will help you understand what to expect when you call the Department of Education.

Maryland Home Education Association

Manfred W. Smith
9085 Flamepool Way
Columbia, MD 21045
(410) 730-0073

This organization provides information on the legalities of homeschooling in the state of Maryland. A family can also find contacts in the state and request group information.

GOVERNMENT AGENCY

Maryland State Department of Education

Richard Scott, Director
People's Services Branch
200 West Baltimore St.
Baltimore, MD 21201
(410) 767-0288

SUPPORT GROUPS

Educating Our Own

686 Geneva Dr.
Westminster, MD 21157
(410) 857-0168 or (410) 848-3390

This support group for the north-central Maryland area offers information for home-schoolers in their state.

Prince George's Home Learning Network

Jacqui Walpole or Sydney Jacobs
3730 Marlbrough Way
College Park, MD 20740
(301) 935-5456 or (301) 431-1838

This is the local homeschooling support group for central Maryland, near Bethesda.

Montgomery Home Learning Network

(301) 320-5125

This local support group offers a monthly newsletter from September to June ($15 subscription price) that provides activity information. They sponsor field trips and other events.

Kaleidscope

(301) 320-5125

This support group in the Baltimore area publishes a newsletter (available for $12 per year) that offers information about activities and events such as field trips.

Christian Home Educators Network

P.O. Box 2010
Ellicott City, MD 21043
(301) 474-9055
website: www.Chenmd.org

This is a statewide Christian networking system for homeschoolers.

CONFERENCES

Maryland Association of Christian Home Educators

Frederick, Maryland
Contact: John Shilts
(301) 607-4284

The organization held its 17th Annual Curriculum Fair & Homeschool Conference on April 16–17, 1999.

Maryland Home Education Association

Manfred Smith
(410) 730-0073

This group's all-inclusive 20th Annual Homeschool Conference was held March 27, 1999. Vendors and workshops were featured at the event.

Christian Home Educators Network

Baltimore County, Maryland
Contact: Cindy Krohe
(410) 467-6785
website: www.Chenmd.org

June 25–26, 1999, was the date of the 11th Annual Conference, featuring Christian vendors and workshops.

MASSACHUSETTS

Massachusetts is an "approval" state, which means that parents or guardian must obtain approval from the government before they begin homeschooling their children. It is also considered a "patchwork quilt" state, meaning that it is a loose framework of many different districts, each of which can choose to make parents adhere to testing, evaluations, examination of subject material, and other authoritarian practices. However, there is no central law governing these areas.

STATEWIDE ORGANIZATIONS

Remember to contact your parent-run statewide organization before contacting any government agency. The parent-run organization will help you understand what to expect when you call the Department of Education.

The Massachusetts Home Learning Association

Loretta Heuer
P.O. Box 1558
Marstons Mills, MA 02648
(508) 429-1436

This is the secular statewide group, offering information and other services.

Mass H.O.P.E.

5 Atwood Rd.
Cherry Valley, MA 01611
(508) 755-4467

This is a statewide Christian homeschool group, offering information to anyone interested in homeschooling.

GOVERNMENT AGENCY

State Department of Education

350 Main St.
Malden, MA 02148-5023
(781) 388-3300

SUPPORT GROUPS

The Home Club (Greater Boston)

Phoebe Wells
19 Florence St.
Cambridge, MA 02139
(617) 876-7273

This is an all-inclusive group that meets to support each other and share field trips, activities, and friendship.

Merrmack Valley Home Learners

Alysa Dudley
13 Ashdale Rd.
North Billerica, MA 01862
(978) 663-2755
e-mail: garyd@chelmsford.com

This secular homeschool group provides fun and support, activities, field trips, and more to home learners.

The Franklin County Home Learning Families

Jean Johnson
72 Prospect St.
Greenfield, MA 01301
(413) 773-9280

This eclectic support group welcomes all people from all backgrounds. They meet for field trips, academic activities, socialization, and fun.

Holt Associates

2380 Massachusetts Ave., Ste. 104,
Cambridge, MA 02140-1226
(617) 864-3100
website: www.holtgws.com
e-mail: holtgws@erols.com

This is John Holt's Bookstore, where *Growing Without Schooling* is produced and lots of homeschooling information is to be had. There are books and tapes about homeschooling and an annual conference.

Franklin City H.O.P.E. Group

Tamara Little
(413) 863-2701

This Christian subsidiary of the statewide Mass HOPE group in the Franklin City area follows a Statement of Faith that is handed down by the statewide group. The homeschool families that form the group gather together to do field trips, gymnastics, activities, science days, co-op days (which are days where certain topics are picked and a theme is built around them).

CONFERENCES

Growing Without Schooling

Great Barrington, Massachusetts (The Berkshires)
John Holt's Bookstore
2380 Mass Ave., Suite 104
Cambridge, MA 02140
(617) 864-3100
website: www.holtgws.com
e-mail: holtgws@erols.com

This Annual Conference is an unschooling conference sponsored by Holt Associates, Inc. The 1999 conference, which took place September 24–26 in Great Barrington, Massachusetts (The Berkshires), offered workshops and vendors.

Mass HOPE

Worchester, Massachusetts
(508) 755-4467

The Annual Christian Homeschool Conference sponsored by Mass HOPE was held April 23–24 of 1999.

MICHIGAN

Parents must register in order to homeschool their children. You can do this in any of three ways:

1. Call (517) 373-0796 to receive a homeschool packet with a one-page registration form.

2. Register through your local school district.

3. Apply for exemption "A," which is a religious exemption.

In this state, it is highly recommended that you call the parent-run group first.

STATEWIDE ORGANIZATIONS

Remember to contact your parent-run statewide organization before contacting any government agency. The parent-run organization will help you understand what to expect when you call the Department of Education.

The Homeschool Support Network (HNS)

Jackie Beattie
P.O. Box 2457
Riverview, MI 48192
(734) 284-1249
e-mail: HSNMom@aol.com

If you need any information about home-schooling in Michigan, call this group before you do anything else. They will send you their information packet, which includes resources and support group listings, a copy of the pertinent Michigan law, and a copy of *Family Times* magazine. HSN helps parents homeschool their children, without regard for religion, educational philosophy, or other differences. HSN also holds a conference in the south of Detroit area each year. Call for dates.

GOVERNMENT AGENCY

Michigan Department of Education

P.O. Box 30008
Lansing, MI 48909
(517) 335-4074

SUPPORT GROUPS

Home Educator's Circle

Karin Corliss
1280 John Hix St.
Westland, MI 48186
(734) 326-5406
e-mail: krcorliss@aol.com

This all-inclusive group of about 20 families serves the Detroit metro area. They get together for many family field trips and activities, and for weekly park days in summer.

Families Learning and Schooling at Home (FLASH)

Jose and Natalie Valle
21671 B. Drive North
Marshall, MI 49068
(616) 781-1069

This all-inclusive group of 40 families in South Central Michigan offers classes; play days; field trips; and recreational, service, and support group activities.

Celebrating Home Under Rome— Catholic Homeschoolers (CHURCH) aka Greater Lansing Catholic Homeschoolers

Rachel Mackson
P.O. Box 198
Okemos, MI 48805-0198
(517) 349-6389
e-mail: Rwittlans@aol.com

Approximately 70 families from the Greater Lansing area of central Michigan comprise this loosely organized Catholic homeschooling group. A very democratic organization, CHURCH has many activities going on—park days, chess club, show and tell, field trips, and a monthly newsletter, as well as First Friday mass and rosary.

Older Homeschooler's Group

Diane Lynn
(313) 331-8406

This organization serves "older" (12- to 18-year-old) homeschool students in the southeastern Michigan and Windsor, Ontario, area. Each member (they currently have 65) is asked to plan one activity per year; most activities cost $10 or less. The group also operates classes in higher academics taught by inspired teachers who give neither grades nor tests. The current 20 programs cover topics such as foreign languages, advanced science, history, great books, and (most popular) opera!

CONFERENCES

The Homeschool Support Network (HSN)

Contact: Jackie Beattie
(734) 284-1249

HSN, an organization that provides state-wide support and information, sponsors an annual all-inclusive conference in a southern suburb of Detroit to which everyone is welcome. Call for dates and exact location.

Information Network for Christian Homes (INCH)

Lansing, Michigan
Contacts: Dennis and Roxanne Smith
(616) 874-5656

INCH held their 1999 Annual Christian homeschooling conference on May 21–22. Activities included workshops and over 100 vendors.

MINNESOTA

Basically, parents who wish to homeschool their children in Minnesota must contact their local superintendent's office. (To find out more about this, please call Traci at the Department of Children, Families and Learning, listed below.) Many have told us that Minnesota is not a friendly homeschool state. Apparently some of the political thinking of Goals 2000 (see glossary) is in place here, so that when you register with the State Department of Education, you are put on a list and "kept track of." The reason so few groups are listed in Minnesota is because parents simply told us to go through the parent-run statewide groups listed on p. 561. As in many states, a large number of homeschooling families are underground; the number in Minnesota seems particularly high.

STATEWIDE ORGANIZATIONS

Remember to contact your parent-run statewide organization before contacting any government agency. The parent-run *organization will help you understand what to expect when you call the Department of Education.*

Homebased Educators' Accrediting Association

P.O. Box 32122
Fridley, MN 55432
(651) 223-0333

This is basically an accrediting agency that will also provide information about support groups, state laws, and any other home-schooling information a family might need.

Minnesota Homeschoolers Alliance

P.O. Box 23072
Richfield, MN 55423
(612) 288-9662

For $18, members receive numerous materials, including a guidance handbook for homeschooling in Minnesota, subscription to the newsletter, directory of support groups, and much more. Call the number for recorded message information.

GOVERNMENT AGENCY

Department of Children, Families and Learning

Traci LaFerriere
1500 Highway 36 West
Roseville, MN 55113-4266
(651) 582-8593

Please contact Traci to learn Minnesota's homeschooling requirements.

SUPPORT GROUPS

Minnesota Association of Christian Home Educators (MACHE)

P.O. Box 32308
Fridley, MN 55432-0308
(651) 717-9070
website: www.mache.org/who/who.htm
   (legal information)
e-mail: www.mache.org

MACHE is the primary Christian group in Minnesota. Call for information about their spring conference and other services.

CONFERENCES

Minnesota Association of Christian Home Educators

Saint Paul, Minnesota
(612) 717-9070

MACHE held its 16th Annual Homeschool Conference in April 1999.

MISSISSIPPI

In Mississippi, a child must attend school from the ages of 6 through 17. There is no specific requirement for attendance, curriculum choice, testing, or recordkeeping. There is an annual filing requirement, and written notice must be given to the district attendance officer.

STATEWIDE ORGANIZATIONS

Remember to contact your parent-run statewide organization before contacting any government agency. The parent-run organization will help you understand what to expect when you call the Department of Education.

Mississippi Home Educators Association (MHEA)

Jack Rutland
P.O. Box 945
Brookhaven, MS 39602
(601) 833-9110

Send $8.00 for general information about homeschooling in Mississippi, including legal and curriculum information.

GOVERNMENT AGENCY

Mississippi Department of Education

P.O. Box 771
Jackson, MS 39205-0771
(601) 359-2098

SUPPORT GROUPS

Home Educators of Central Mississippi

Jo Ann Tullos
419 Thomasville Rd.
Florence, MS 39073
(601) 978-2204

This large group of 350–400 families has Christian leadership and requires that members sign a Statement of Faith. Highlights of their activities include a bi-monthly newsletter and field trips.

Byhalia, Mississippi (from Memphis HEA info)

Steve and Theresa Montgomery
(601) 895-5545

Hernando/Nesbit, Mississippi (from Memphis HEA info)

Steve and Charlotte Joyce or Billy and
*   Cindy Brant*
(601) 429-2092 or (601) 429-1771
website: www.geocities.com/
*   Heartland/Meadows/7342*

Horn Lake, Mississippi (from Memphis HEA info)

Elizabeth Willoughby
(601) 280-4042

Olive Branch, Mississippi

Michelle Taylor or Carol O'Kelly
(601) 895-8516 or (601) 895-3068

Southhaven, Mississippi

Bobbie Cooksey
(601) 342-2221

CONFERENCES

Mississippi Home Educators Association

Clinton, Mississippi
(601) 833-9110
e-mail: MHEA@juno.com

The 1999 Spring Conference & Curriculum Fair was held May 21–22 in Clinton, Mississippi.

MISSOURI

Currently, Missouri law does not require parents to register or notify anyone that they are homeschooling, though parents may choose to notify the local school district. While not required to have a teaching certificate or meet any education requirements, parents are required to provide 1,000 hours of instruction per year, with at least 600 hours in the basic academics, such as reading, math, science, and social studies. Parents must also maintain records that show the subjects taught and activities engaged in, a portfolio of samples of each student's academic work, and a record of evaluation of the student's academic progress.

STATEWIDE ORGANIZATIONS

Remember to contact your parent-run statewide organization before contacting any government agency. The parent-run organization will help you understand what to expect when you call the Department of Education.

Families for Home Education (FHE)

6209 NW Tower Dr.
Platte Woods, MO 64151

Region V
St. Louis, Missouri
Contact: Patricia
(417) 782-8833

Region VI
2450 N. Campbell
Springfield, MO 65638
Contact: Henry Long
(417) 865-5170

The networking in Missouri is very well organized, set up as follows: FHE has six different chapters around the state. Call the St. Louis number above, and ask for the referral closest to you. They have much information.

GOVERNMENT AGENCY

Department of Education

P.O. Box 480
Jefferson City, MO 65102
(573) 751-3527

SUPPORT GROUPS

Christian Home Educators of Carthage

1415 S. Maple St.
Carthage, MO 64836
(417) 394-3056

Field trips, potlucks, mothers' meetings, and American History night are among this group's featured events.

Springfield Home Education (SHELL)

Donna Culbertson
P.O. Box 1412
Springfield, MO 65801
(314) 534-1171
e-mail: all6cf@aol.com

This small support group of about 25–30 families is nonsectarian and all-inclusive. Among their activities are weekly park days, bowling, skating, camping, and field trips.

Ozark Lore Society

Deborah Eisenmann
H.C. 73, Box 160
Drury, MO 65638
(417) 679-3391

All are welcome to this nonreligious group that offers various clubs (such as History, Skating, and Girls' Club) that meet for activities.

LEARN

P.O. Box 10105
(913) 383-7888

This homeschool organization support line provides information for those who are interested.

CONFERENCES

Families for Home Education (FHE)

Kansas City, Missouri
Contact: Deana Haines
(816) 763-4820
e-mail: fhe@microlink.com

LEARN's Annual Inclusive State Convention in Kansas City, Missouri, included over 50 vendors.

Mid-Missouri Home Education Conference

Columbia, Missouri
Contact: David Swartz
(573) 682-3635
e-mail: davidswartz@juno.com

The group's Annual Christian Conference, held May 1, 1999, included over 40 vendors.

Missouri Association of Teaching Christian Homes (MATCH)

West Plains, Missouri
Contact: Michael and Orilla Crider
(417) 255-2824
e-mail: mathc@christiannmail.net

MATCH's Annual Christian Homeschool Conference was held June 12, 1999.

Southwest Home Education Ministry

Springfield, Missouri
Contact: Mary Douglas
(417) 376-3647

SHEM's 10th Annual Curriculum Conference, held April 30–May 1, 1999, in Springfield, drew over 45 vendors.

MONTANA

Montana has a Parents' Rights Law in place. That means parents must submit a request to their local school board, which has no choice but to approve the request. Parents must report attendance (the standard is 180 days per year attendance).

STATEWIDE ORGANIZATIONS

Remember to contact your parent-run statewide organization before contacting any government agency. The parent-run organization will help you understand what to expect when you call the Department of Education.

Montana Coalition of Home Educators

P.O. Box 43
Gallatin Gateway, MT 59730
(406) 587-6163
website:
  www.3.gomontana.com/white/mche.htm

This is a statewide organization providing information to all who are interested in homeschooling in Montana.

News Resource

The Grapevine Montana News

Pascal Redfern, Publisher
P.O. Box 3228
Missoula, MT 59806
(406) 542-8721

Published bimonthly during the school year, The Grapevine gives information about homeschooling statewide—activities, laws, get-togethers, and more.

Pascal Redfern is also the Athletic Director for the Missoula Homeschool Athletic Association and the Executive Director of the Rocky Mountain Homeschool Basketball Tourney in Denver.

GOVERNMENT AGENCY

Montana Department of Education

Office of Public Instruction
1227 11th Street
Helena, MT 59602
(406) 444-3095

SUPPORT GROUPS

Bozeman Homeschool Network

Heleen Bloethe
8799 Huffman Ln.
Bozeman, MT 59715
(406) 586-1025

Monthly newsletter (event calendar) and park days are among the activities of this nondenominational group of 15–20 families.

Mid-Mountain Home Education Network

Karen Semple
P.O. Box 2182, Montana City Station
Clancy, MT 59634
(406) 443-3376
e-mail: mhen2@juno.com

This activity-based, nonsectarian support group of 100 families does not require membership to participate, but invites anyone to "just come." They publish a broad informational monthly newsletter ($15/year) and sponsor Lunch at the Library in Helena with a speaker and/or activity for children the first Friday of the month.

Central Mountain Homeschoolers of Montana

Karen Seyfert
(406) 538-3949

This local support group for homeschoolers meets for fun and park days.

NEBRASKA

Rose Yonekura, a homeschooling parent in Nebraska, says: "Since 1984, the law has required homeschooling families to fill out a state-provided form, which is then filed with the state department of education. The wording of the law states that one is homeschooling 'Due to sincerely held religious beliefs.' Such a condition has not, however, been imposed. The law provides for yearly testing and visitation by the superintendent or his representative, but in the larger counties, that has not occurred. In the smaller counties, it has from time to time."

STATEWIDE ORGANIZATIONS

Remember to contact your parent-run statewide organization before contacting any government agency. The parent-run organization will help you understand what to expect when you call the Department of Education.

Nebraska Christian Home Education Association (NCHEA)

P.O. Box 57041
Lincoln, NE 68505
(402) 423-4297

This statewide homeschooling group offers local support group information and guidance.

GOVERNMENT AGENCY

Nebraska Department of Education

301 Centennial Mall
Lincoln, NE 68509
(402) 471-2784

SUPPORT GROUPS

Lincoln Educators-At-Residence Network (LEARN)

Rose Yonekura
7741 E. Avon Ln.
Lincoln, NE 68505
(402) 488-7741

Although all-inclusive, the six families in this group are primarily unschoolers who do much information-disseminating for Nebraska homeschooling. They also get together for park days twice a month.

CONFERENCES

Home Educators Network (HEN)

Bellevue, Nebraska
Contact: Lori Darby
(402) 451-3459
e-mail: mdarby@creighton.edu

HEN's Annual Christian Conference features vendors and various activities.

Nebraska Christian Home Educators (NCHEA)

Lincoln, Nebraska
Contact: Nick and Kathleen Lenzen
(402) 432-4297
e-mail: nchea@navix.net

NCHEA's Annual Christian Homeschool Conference, featuring vendors and workshops, is held each spring.

NEVADA

Nevada parents must apply to the local school board for an application to homeschool their children. The testing requirement has been dropped within the last two years. If a parent has been homeschooling for less than one year, they must stay in touch with a "consultant," either a credentialed teacher or a homeschooling parent who has been homeschooling for three years or more.

STATEWIDE ORGANIZATIONS

Remember to contact your parent-run statewide organization before contacting any government agency. The parent-run organization will help you understand what to expect when you call the Department of Education.

Home Schools United—Vegas Valley

P.O. Box 93564
Las Vegas, NV 89193-3564
(702) 870-9566 (recorded message)
e-mail: HSU.VegasValley@juno.com

This is a nonprofit, volunteer group. Call their recorded message at the above number to obtain a great deal of information about the group and its services, and about homeschooling in Nevada. They offer park days, field trips, a newsletter for $20/year, two teen groups, and much more. To obtain a list of qualified consultants (which are required by Nevada law), send a self-addressed stamped envelope along with your request to the above address.

GOVERNMENT AGENCY

Department of Education

Holly Walton-Buchanan
700 East 5th St.
Carson City, NV 89701-5096
(775) 687-9134

SUPPORT GROUPS

Northern Nevada Homeschools, Inc.

P.O. Box 21323
Reno, NV 89515
(702) 852-6647
e-mail: NNHS@aol.com

This homeschool organization will put you in touch with other homeschoolers. Please call for information.

Homeschool Melting Pot

Nancy Barcus
1778 Antelope Valley Ave.
Henderson, NV 89012
(702) 269-9101
website: www.angelfire.com/nv/
homeschoolmeltingpot/
e-mail: barcus@lvcm.com

This all-inclusive group for all religions and homeschooling styles offers park days, field trips, newsletter, e-mail, and a website.

Home Education and Righteous Training (HEART)

P.O. Box 422
Las Vegas, NV 89116
(702) 391-7219

HEART is a homeschool group that meets once a month for support and information about homeschooling in the Christian household. Please call for more information (they return calls twice a week).

CONFERENCES

Northern Nevada Homeschooling Association

Reno, Nevada
Contact: Debbie Owens
(702) 852-0366

The group hosts a small Christian conference with vendors and workshops for those interested in homeschooling. Approximately 300 people attend in May.

Schooling at Home in Northeastern Nevada

Elko, Nevada
Contact: Nancy Corn
(775) 738-4447

Hometeaching and Exposition and Curriculum Sale is a conference with vendors and workshops. About 150 people attended May 7, 1999.

Northern Nevada Homeschools (NNHS)

Carson City, Nevada
Contact: Nancy Ziese
(775) 849-3835

NNHS's Curriculum Fair (held June 12, 1999) is a small, cozy conference that offers various workshops.

NEW HAMPSHIRE

New Hampshire has no school attendance requirement. The required curriculum is the "standard" that most states follow for homeschooling and is basically the same as the public schools': reading, writing, other English skills, basic math, American history, and so on. An Intent to Homeschool must be filed with either a private school principal, state commissioner of education, or a local school superintendent annually. There is also extensive recordkeeping required, including a detailed portfolio with a log of reading materials used, student's writing samples, and workbooks or worksheets. The state requires testing to be completed by July 1 of each year, and the parents must file their choice of (1) standardized test results, (2) local school district assessment test results, (3) written evaluation by a certified teacher, or (4) any other method agreeable to the local school board.

STATEWIDE ORGANIZATIONS

Remember to contact your parent-run statewide organization before contacting any government agency. The parent-run organization will help you understand what to expect when you call the Department of Education.

New Hampshire Homeschool Coalition

Abbey Lawrence
P.O. Box 2224
Concord, NH 03304
(603) 539-7233

This statewide group consists of homeschooling families that support each other in their endeavors. The inclusive group meets for friendships and activities.

GOVERNMENT AGENCY

The New Hampshire Department of Education

State Office Park South
101 Pleasant St.
Concord, NH 03301
(603) 271-3144

SUPPORT GROUPS

The Christian Home Educators of New Hampshire

Lee and Connie Button
P.O. Box 961
Manchester, NH 03105
(603) 569-2343

A Statement of Faith is required of those wishing to join this Christian homeschooling group. They meet for field trips, activities, and fellowship.

Catholics United for Home Education

George D'Orazio
(603) 623-3377

This is a Catholic homeschool group dedicated to helping Catholic families with their homeschool needs.

New Hampshire Alliance for Home Education

Betsy Westgate
(603) 880-8629

This support group of families in the greater Nashua area and surrounding towns meets for field trips, social events, and fun! The all-inclusive group welcomes all homeschoolers.

CONFERENCES

New Hampshire Homeschooling Coalition

Concord, New Hampshire
Contact: Abbey Lawrence
(603) 539-7233

The coalition held its Annual Homeschooling Panel Workshop May 15, 1999.

Christian Home Educators of New Hampshire

Concord, New Hampshire
Contact: Rick Amador
(603) 623-0914

The Annual Christian Conference, offering vendors, workshops, and more, was held April 9–10, 1999.

NEW JERSEY

The prospective homeschooling family in New Jersey must submit documentation outlining their proposed curriculum to the superintendent of the school district in which they live. Then they proceed to teach their children. No approval must be granted by the school district. No testing or any other requirement is necessary either.

STATEWIDE ORGANIZATIONS

Remember to contact your parent-run statewide organization before contacting any government agency. The parent-run organization will help you understand what to expect when you call the Department of Education.

North Jersey Home Schoolers Association (NJHSA)

P.O. Box 34
Hillsdale, NJ 07642
(201) 666-6025 (information only; no messages)

This is a network of support groups comprising approximately 200 families around North New Jersey. If you send $3 (payable to Christa Grajcar), she will send you the NJHSA information packet. This includes newsletter information, support group locations and contact people, and other items to aid you with homeschooling in New Jersey. If you call the above number, you will hear the same information printed here.

Educational Network of Christian Homeschoolers (ENOCH)

Box 308
Atlantic Highlands, NJ 07716-0308
(732) 291-7800
e-mail: enochnji@uscom.com

This large statewide organization offers many services and activities. Call to obtain their information packet.

GOVERNMENT AGENCY

Department of Education

John Lalley
100 Riverview Plaza, P.O. Box 500
Trenton, NJ 08625-0500
(609) 984-7814

SUPPORT GROUPS

Homeschoolers of South Jersey

Rose
1239 Whitaker Ave.
Millville, NJ 08332
(609) 327-1224
website: www/cyberenet/net/home/tutor
e-mail: tutor@cyberenet.net

This all-inclusive group of approximately 35 families meets once a month to go over itinerary for the month's activities. The group's various activities include bowling, nature classes, workshops, rollerskating days, field trips, a lending library with books about homeschooling, and park days in appropriate weather.

Cape May County Home Educators

Karen Lange
49 Springer's Mill Rd.
Cape May Ct.house, NJ 08210
(609) 465-9796
e-mail: klange5@juno.com

Anyone is welcome in this mostly Christian but all-inclusive group. "Homeschooling is what we have in common," according to their spokesperson. Activities include park days (weather permitting), rollerskating, bowling, monthly field trips, monthly meetings, and a teaching co-op where families come together to teach each other's children specific subjects.

Homeschoolers Network of Ocean City

Gail "Peaches" Luken
300 Central Ave.
Ocean City, NJ 08226
(609) 398-8781

Peaches acts as a homeschool liaison, aiding families leaving the Ocean City public schools. She conducts informal mini-workshops on homeschooling for them, shows them curriculum resource catalogs, provides an overview of different schedules to use in starting out, and maintains a lending library that's especially useful to new people. This support group of approximately fifteen families (majority of children are 8 and under) is Christian (they do have a statement of faith), but welcomes all. They organize monthly library days, field trips, and other activities.

Light Fellowship

Mike and Karen Elwell
419 Fairton-Millville Rd.
Bridgeton, NJ 08302
(609) 451-7518

This nondenominational mixed group of approximately 50 homeschooling families was founded by Baptists. Membership has since changed and gradually broadened to include Catholics, Presbyterians, Pentecostals, Mennonites, and others. The group's activities include park days, field trips, monthly skate days, bowling, swimming days, used curriculum sales, and parent breakfasts. They also feature a legislative hotline and a drama coordinator who arranges trips to college drama performances.

Unschoolers Network

Nancy Plent
(732) 938-2473

Nancy maintains a network of unschoolers and homeschoolers in general and can put you in touch with support groups throughout the state.

CONFERENCES

Education Network of Christian Homeschoolers of New Jersey, Inc. (ENOCH)

Florence, New Jersey
(609) 222-4283

The 10th Annual Christian Homeschooling Conference was held during April of 1999.

Unschoolers Network

Brookdale, New Jersey
Contact: Nancy Plent
(732) 938-2473

The network held its 22nd Annual Inclusive Homeschool Conference in June 1999.

NEW MEXICO

To homeschool legally in New Mexico, the family must notify either the superintendent of the local school district or the New Mexico Department of Education in Santa Fe for the Homeschool Procedure Manual and the Notification form. These must then be filled out and filed with the local school district superintendent. Currently, the student must be tested in Grades 4, 6, and 8, using the C.T.B.S.5/Terra Nova assessment test. The student can test in all areas or opt for just the reading/language portion. (The state legislature can change these requirements as it sees fit, so check with the Department of Education for up-to-date information.) The teaching must be done by only the parent/guardian of the student. The teaching parent must have a high school diploma or GED.

STATEWIDE ORGANIZATIONS

Remember to contact your parent-run statewide organization before contacting any government agency. The parent-run organization will help you understand what to expect when you call the Department of Education.

New Mexico Family Educators

P.O. Box 92276
Albuquerque, NM 87199-2276
(505) 275-7053

This group offers a beginner's packet with all the pertinent legal and procedural information for those beginning homeschooling in New Mexico. It also offers monthly meetings, a newsletter, and support information. To obtain the beginner's packet, send $7 (payable to NMFE) at the above address. Call the above phone number for a calendar of events.

GOVERNMENT AGENCY

New Mexico Department of Education

Management Support and Intervention
Sally Rynott, Director
300 Don Gaspar
Santa Fe, NM 87501-2786
(505) 827-6582

SUPPORT GROUPS

Homeschooling PACT

Barbara Klepperich-Senn
P.O. Box 961
Portales, NM 88130
(505) 359-1618
e-mail: homeschoolingpact@yahoo.com

PACT is an informal, inclusive group in Eastern New Mexico. Activities include weekly play days and annual special events, such as an award ceremony, science fair, and student art exhibit. The group's membership charge of $15/year includes the newsletter ($10/year subscription price for non-members).

Unschoolers of Albuquerque

Sandra Dodd
2905 Tahiti Ct., NE
Albuquerque, NM 87112
(505) 299-2476
e-mail: SandraDodd@aol.com

This relaxed group of unschoolers schedules play days (weather permitting) during which kids play and parents talk. They have no business meetings or field trips.

East Mountain Family Educators

Elise Kraf
P.O. Box 369
Tijeras, NM 87059
(505) 281-3865

Park days, field trips, and intermittent specialized classes taught by parents are highlights of this group.

Home Educators of Dona Ana (Las Cruces area)

Sarah Jones
(505) 526-7174
website: www.mission-control/heda

This all-inclusive group of approximately 6–12 families plans regular social days and publishes a newsletter. The membership fee is $15/year.

CONFERENCES

Glorietta Conference Center

Glorietta, New Mexico
(505) 757-6161

Homeschool '99 (September 19–23, 1999) is a Christian conference featuring many vendors and workshops. Its main focus is on Christian homeschooling, although all are welcome.

The Christian Association of Parents

Albuquerque, New Mexico
(505) 898-8548

The second annual Christian Homeschool Convention of New Mexico on April 22–24, 1999 drew about 2,200 interested in Christian homeschooling.

NEW YORK

Parent Ann Hog says this about homeschooling in New York: "Although there are a lot of hoops to jump through and a lot of paperwork to be filed, homeschooling is not difficult to do in New York. No degree is required to teach, but there are student-testing requirements. The local school districts have the power (rather than the state) so no one knows what everyone else is doing."

STATEWIDE ORGANIZATIONS

Remember to contact your parent-run statewide organization before contacting any government agency. The parent-run organization will help you understand what to expect when you call the Department of Education.

Loving Education at Home (LEAH)

P.O. Box 88
Cat, NY 13088
(716) 346-0939
website: www.leah.org

This Christian group has many chapters statewide.

New York Home Education Network (NYHEN)

Ann Hog
39 North St.
Saratoga Springs, NY 12866
(518) 584-9110
e-mail: nyhen@juno.com

This secular organization welcomes everyone. The purpose is to spread homeschooling information, put families in touch with each other, and also serve as a legislative watchdog organization.

Alliance for Parental Involvement in Education (ALLPIE)

P.O. Box 59
East Chatham, NY 12060-0059
(518) 392-6900
website: www.croton.com/allpie

GOVERNMENT AGENCY

Office for Nonpublic School Services

New York State Education Department
P.O. Box 12846
Albany, NY 12234
(518) 474-3879

Prospective homeschool families should contact this office.

SUPPORT GROUPS

Fingerlakes Unschoolers Network

Linda Holzbaur
249 Coddington Rd.
Ithaca, NY 14850
(607) 277-6300
e-mail: rittholz@lightlink.com

No philosophy or belief is necessary to belong to this social support group. The group charges no membership fee, and has a sliding-scale subscription rate for its newsletter (published every other month). Group activities include conference, classes, and workshops.

Homeschoolers Network of the Mid-Hudson Valley

Cathy Belcher
Rd. 2, P.O. Box 211P
Bloomingburg, NY 12721-0211
(914) 733-1002

Cathy Belcher, the contact person for the entire Hudson Valley region, will direct you to various groups in that area.

Ulster County Home Educators

Kim Kimble
(914) 256-0464
e-mail: kimsquared@aol.com

This inclusive group focuses on supporting homeschooling families.

Long Islanders Growing at Home Together (LIGHT)

Devorah Weimann
186 East Ave.
Freeport, NY 11520
(516) 868 5766
e-mail: devww2@aol.com

LIGHT, which provides support for families that educate at home, welcomes all religions and all styles. They publish a newsletter (essential for activities) for $15/year.

Tri-County Homeschoolers

Chris or Andy Hofer
P.O. Box 190
Ossining, NY 10562
(914) 941-5607

Tri-County Homeschoolers serves approximately 100 families in suburban New York City, Connecticut, Westchester County, and New Jersey. All families are welcome.

Rochester Area Homeschoolers Association

(716) 234-0298 (voice mail)

This all-inclusive community of families supports and welcomes all styles of homeschooling.

New York City Home Educators Alliance

Elizabeth Isaksen
464 A 16th St.
Brooklyn, NY 11215
(212) 505/9884

This support group serves the New York City area.

Long Island Family Teachers United in Prayer (LIFTUP)

Ralph and Pam Cipriano
753 Greenlawn Ave.
Islip Terrace, NY 11752-1701
(516) 277-6646

LIFTUP is an overtly Christian group with an open-door attitude, providing mutual support for families and activities for children. They watch legislation as it relates to family issues, as well as to homeschooling. The group holds a monthly meeting and communicates via an Internet chain.

Dutchess County Homeschoolers

Tracey Covell
(914) 473-1044

This loosely organized support group of approximately 30 homeschool families welcomes all homeschoolers.

The Alter Learning Center

Wendy Barnett-Mulligan
c/o 143 Hudson Ave.
Chatham, NY 12037
(518) 392-2943

This group of families dedicated to home-learning comes together for field, fun, and classes. They meet 10 hours a week at a specific site. Everyone is welcome. Call for more details about the group and its membership fee.

Families for Home Education

Peg Moore
3219 Coulter Rd.
Cazenovia, NY 13035
(315) 655-2574

This group of 30 families gets together to support each other and do activities related to homeschooling. Any religion is welcome (some members are Christian, some are not). Their newsletter is available for $10 per year.

CONFERENCES

LEAH

Syracuse, New York
(315) 363-3877
website: www.leah.org

The 15th Annual New York State Loving Education at Home Convention was held from May 20–22, 1999. This Christian conference (the only one in New York state of which we're aware) draws approximately 4,100 attendees.

NORTH CAROLINA

To homeschool in North Carolina, parents must possess at least a high school diploma and register their household as a homeschool with the state. Once you register your homeschool status with the state, you must comply with the state's laws and test your child(ren) annually.

STATEWIDE ORGANIZATIONS

Remember to contact your parent-run statewide organization before contacting any government agency. The parent-run organization will help you understand what to expect when you call the Department of Education.

North Carolinians for Home Education

Susan Van Dyke
419 N. Boylan Ave.
Raleigh, NC 27603
(919) 834-6243
e-mail: NCHE@mindspring.com

This nonprofit organization provides information on all aspects of homeschooling in North Carolina, including local resources, legal regulations, and curriculum guidance.

They host the second largest national homeschooling conference and book fair. Contact them for membership information (there is a fee).

GOVERNMENT AGENCY

Division of Non-Public Education

530 N. Wilmington St.
Raleigh, NC 27604
(919) 733-4276

SUPPORT GROUPS

Cabarrus County Home School Association

Linda Paskiewicz
(704) 933-8764

All are welcome to participate in this Christian organization that approaches home education from a Biblical perspective. Field trips, gym classes, teen group, moms' night out, a quarterly mom and dads' night out, and a group band are a few of the activities they sponsor.

Grace Homeschool Group

Tammy Munden
(704) 583-1015
Charlotte, NC

This all-inclusive group with Christian leadership meets for support, field trips, presentation platform, plays, and more.

Homeschoolers Offering Practical Encouragement (HOPE)

(704) 753-1612
e-mail: ncfried6@aol.com

HOPE is a Christian homeschool group that gathers together for fun and centers on including the entire family for activities.

CONFERENCES

North Carolinians for Home Education

Winston-Salem, North Carolina
Contact: Susan Van Dyke
(919) 834-6243

The Annual Christian Homeschool Conference, held May 13–15, 1999, featured approximately 100 vendors.

Heritage Education, Inc.

Asheville, North Carolina
Contact: Sue Lamm
(828) 885-2311
e-mail: blamm@sitcom.net

The group sponsors an Annual Inclusive Homeschool Conference highlighting vendors and workshops (held May 28–29 in 1999).

NORTH DAKOTA

If you live in North Dakota, do not do anything until you contact the parent-run statewide homeschooling group. We are told the climate is very inhospitable and restrictive. Please see the legal requirements below.

Mandatory school attendance is required between the ages of 7 through 16, 175 days per year, four hours per day. The standard curriculum is required with a few "health" class additions. The parent-teacher must be qualified in one of the following ways: (1) hold a valid teaching certificate, (2) possess a bachelor's degree, (3) possess a high school diploma or GED equivalent (in which case, the parent must be monitored until the child completes third grade or for the first two years of homeschooling, whichever is longer), or (4) provide proof of having met or exceeded the cutoff score of the national teaching exam. There is a filing notice requirement and mandatory testing in Grades 3, 4, 6, 8 and 11 by a certified teacher; the test results must be filed with the local school superintendent. If a parent possesses a teaching certificate, he or she can establish a private home school approved by county and state. This option allows the parent to waive the recordkeeping and testing requirements.

STATEWIDE ORGANIZATIONS

Remember to contact your parent-run statewide organization before contacting any government agency. The parent-run organization will help you understand what to expect when you call the Department of Education.

North Dakota Homeschool Association

Box 74000
Bismarck, ND 58507
(701) 223-4080
e-mail: ndsa@wdata.com

The association provides beginner's packets, legal information, and support group information. Every other year they sponsor a Home Education Day at the state capitol.

GOVERNMENT AGENCY

North Dakota Department of Public Instruction

600 East Blvd.
Bismarck, ND 58505
(701) 328-4572

CONFERENCES

North Dakota Homeschool Association

Bismarck, North Dakota
Contact: Gail Bilby
(701) 223-4080
e-mail: ndhsa@wdata.com

The Annual Christian Homeschool Conference (featuring vendors and activities) will be held March 17–18, 2000.

OHIO

In Ohio, a parent or legal guardian must notify the local school district of their intent to homeschool. Homeschooling parents must also sign a letter stating that they will cover the following subjects: language, reading, spelling and writing, geography, history, math, science, health, physical education, fine arts/music, and first aid. They must also submit an outline of curriculum (for informational purposes only).

STATEWIDE ORGANIZATIONS

Remember to contact your parent-run statewide organization before contacting any government agency. The parent-run organization will help you understand what to expect when you call the Department of Education.

Ohio Home Educators Network (OHEN)

Barb Sommer
P.O. Box 23054
Chagrin Falls, OH 44023
(330) 274-0542

This organization, which serves Greater Cleveland, Akron, and Canton, was started to help families learn how to homeschool legally. They say, "We welcome all families. We are more of an 'unschooling' group, interest-based, project-oriented." The group publishes a monthly calendar that ties the area together, as well as a directory of homeschool families.

GOVERNMENT AGENCY

The Ohio Department of Education

65 S. Front St.
Columbus, OH 43266-0308
(614) 466-2937

SUPPORT GROUPS

Families Unschooling in the Neighborhood

Laurie Clark
5668 Township Rd. 105
Mount Gilead, OH 43338
(419) 947-6351
e-mail: clark@redbird.net

This is a small group of families that unschool and get together for socializing. They say: "We are an all-inclusive group welcoming diversity."

Learning in Family Environments (LIFE)

Chris O'Connor
P.O. Box 2512
Columbus, OH 43216
(614) 241-6957
e-mail: www.Karenemaillistandwebsite

LIFE is an inclusive, eclectic group that welcomes families of all backgrounds. Park days and field trips are published through the statewide e-mail list. Monthly parent support meetings are held at Hilliard Branch Library.

Youngstown Home Learners

Marla Herrmann
846 E. Boston
Youngstown, OH 44502
(330) 788-5027

This eclectic mix of about 25 homeschooling families schedules park days, field trips, and academic activities.

Newark Area Home Learners

Cassie Holderman or Nancy Dobbelaer
9005 Hidden Springs Rd.
Hopewell, OH 43746
(740) 787-1073 or (740) 366-0118
e-mail: homeEdfam@aol.com

This loosely organized collection of approximately 20 families gets together for park days, field trips, play days, and parents' night out.

Pathways Homeschool Group

Pam Parsons
(740) 927-9186

At least one parent must sign a Statement of Faith to join this Christian group of about 50 families. Park days, field trips, rollerskating, bowling, science fair, international festival, arts festival, and a monthly "classroom" type activity are among their scheduled events.

CONFERENCES

Christian Home Educators of Ohio

Columbus, Ohio
Contact: Bruce Purdy
(740) 687-5474

"Training a Godly Generation" is the name of the conference scheduled June 24–26, 1999. The organization's annual Christian conference attracts approximately 4,000 to 5,000 attendees.

The Christian Parents' Educational Fellowship

Findlay, Ohio
Contact: Shari Wiseman
(419) 422-9371

Approximately 130 families attend the Annual Small Christian Homeschooling Conference (held April 16–17, 1999).

The Mansfield Christian School

Mansfield, Ohio
Contact: Linda Hoefilch
(419) 756-5651

April 24 was the date of the school's 1999 Annual Homeschool Curriculum Fair.

OKLAHOMA

Linda Duntley of T.H.E. Coalition of Oklahoma says this of the state's political climate: "Homeschooling in Oklahoma is recognized as a constitutional right of parents to guide the education of their children. We are one of the few—if not the only—state which has such a constitutional guarantee." At the present time there are no laws in effect with regard to home-schooling. Dorris Sims, secretary to the superintendent, explains how you homeschool in Oklahoma: "There are no rules in the state of Oklahoma. The parent simply has to notify the local school district with a letter of intent to homeschool."

STATEWIDE ORGANIZATIONS

Home Educator's Resource Organization (HERO) of Oklahoma

Leslie Moyer
302 N. Coolidge
Enid, OK 73703
(918) 396-0108 (Leslie Moyer, Contact Person)
(580) 446-5679 (Julie Miller, Coordinator)
website: www.geocities.com/Athens/Forum/3236
e-mail: moyerles@wiltel.net

HERO, the only statewide homeschooling organization in Oklahoma, has many affiliated organizations throughout the state. Services of this all-inclusive group include statewide e-mail, legislative and chat, conference directory, Oklahoma Homeschool Handbook (which describes how to homeschool in Oklahoma).

SUPPORT GROUPS

Bartlesville Christian Home Educators Fellowship (BCHEF)

Carolyn Morgan
P.O. Box 3591
Bartlesville, OK 76006
(918) 335-2291

This Christian-oriented group of 80 families from the Bartlesville area (30-mile radius) requires a Statement of Faith.

CORNERSTONE

Kathy Witt
P.O. Box 459
Sperry, OK 74073-0459
(918) 425-4162
e-mail: okwitt@aol.com

This inclusive basic support group for family educators serves the Tulsa area. Monthly meetings, e-mail loop, newsletter, and other activities are part of their program.

Green Country (HERO) Home Educators Resource Organization

Cathy Sweany
183 Fox Run Cir.
Jenks, OK 74037
(918) 461-8560 (information)
(918) 245-8460

Membership to this HERO group is open, but leaders are required to sign a Christian Statement of Faith. Services include field trips and support meetings.

Eastern Oklahoma Catholic Home School Association (EOCHSA)

Rebecca Gaskill
1708 N. 30th
Broken Arrow, OK 74014
(918) 355-4149
e-mail: gaskill-tulsa@msn.com

This Catholic-based organization primarily celebrates religious holidays.

Tulsa Home Educator's Leadership Coalition (T.H.E. Coalition)

Linda Duntley
(918) 322-3984

This group for leadership of homeschool support groups only meets twice a year. Current membership includes leaders of 31 groups representing 1,500 families. The organization publishes *T.H.E. News*, a bi-monthly newsletter of 20 to 30 pages (individual subscriptions available) and serves as a clearinghouse for information for support groups. Information supplied to group leaders includes sports information, how to homeschool teens, book fair information, and special class offerings. Leaders of any support group (3–5 families meeting regularly constitutes a support group), co-oping schools, alternative education schools (meet 3 times a week), or those offering tutorship services can belong.

Oklahoma City Association of Home Educators

P.O. Box 270601
Oklahoma City, OK 73137
(405) 521-8439

This is the largest group in Oklahoma; it encompasses 40 affiliate groups.

Christian Home Educators Fellowship of Oklahoma (CHEF)

(918) 583-READ

This group of Christian families gathers together to lend support to those interested in homeschooling. Parent volunteers answer phone calls.

CONFERENCES

CHEF of Oklahoma

Great Mont Baptist Church
Tulsa, Oklahoma
Contact: Debbie Smith
(918) 455-8315

The Annual Curriculum Fair (held June 11–12, 1999) is a Christian homeschool conference with vendors and workshops, many of which would be of interest to non-Christians as well. All who are interested in homeschooling are welcome. Approximately 800 attendees were expected at the 14th annual conference (held in 1999).

Central Home Educators Association

Marriott Convention Center
Oklahoma City, Oklahoma
Contact: Lisa Parks
(405) 521-8439

Approximately 3,000 attended the 1999 Homeschooling Convention held April 30–May 1. Exhibits and workshops were aimed toward those interested in home-schooling.

OREGON

To learn about homeschooling in Oregon, visit the Department of Education website (www.ode.state.or.us/stusvc/homesch/index.htm) to review the Administrative Rules and Laws and to get information on county contacts, test publishers, and support group people. Don Perkins is Student Services Specialist at the Department of Education.

The law applies to students who are at least 7 but not older than 18 on September 1 of the school year in question. Parents must contact the Educational Service District of the county in which they live and register their intent to homeschool with that agency or institution. The child is then required to take one of the five approved tests within 8 weeks of that registration. If the student scores a certain level, she or he does not take it again. The state also has a requirement for annual verification of satisfactory progress.

It's possible that you can avoid all of this by filing to become your own private school, but look into this carefully.

Oregon allows three kinds of private schools:

1. Schools accredited by the Association of Northwest Schools and Colleges.

2. Schools registered by the state Department of Education. (Presumably, the reason for registering is to enable the Department of Education to refer callers looking for private schools in a certain geographic location to an on-file registered school.)

3. Non-registered private schools (the majority in the state fall into this category).

We were advised that the wisest way to go with the non-registered fashion is to ask the Department of Education for its packet on private schools. We recommend that you contact OHEN for more parent-friendly information before contacting the Department of Education.

STATEWIDE ORGANIZATIONS

Remember to contact your parent-run statewide organization before contacting any government agency. The parent-run organization will help you understand what to expect when you call the Department of Education.

Oregon Home Education Network (OHEN)

4470 SW Hall Blvd., # 286
Beaverton, OR 97005
503/321-5166

This all-inclusive statewide nonprofit organization is committed to supporting homeschooling families throughout the state. For a complete information packet, please send $5.00 to the above address. For an annual subscription to *The Oregon Connection*, a homeschooling newsletter, send $12.

Oregon Christian Home Education Network (OCEAN)

(503) 288-1285 (automated number)

This is a private, statewide Christian-to-Christian group.

Parents Political Action Committee (PPAC)

(503) 693-0724

This for-profit group provides political oversight and a call to action, when necessary. Since non-profit organizations are prohibited from engaging in political influencing, a group like this one can work freely to ensure protection of homeschoolers' rights.

GOVERNMENT AGENCY

Oregon Department of Education

255 Capitol St. NE
Salem, OR 93710-0203
(503) 378-5585, ext. 677 (Home Education Department)
(503) 378-8004, ext. 222 (Private School Department)

SUPPORT GROUPS

Greater Portland Homeschoolers

Jeanne Biggerstaff
P.O. Box 82415
Portland, OR 97282
(503) 241-5350
e-mail: sassenak@msn.com

This all-inclusive group offers support to all homeschooling families.

The Homeschool Information and Service Network (HISNET) of Oregon

1044 Bismark
Klamath Falls, OR 97601-1212
(541) 782-2466
website: www.efn.org/~hisnet
e-mail: hisnet@efn.org

This statewide organization offers information on a variety of services, including a newcomer booklet. The board is Christian, but the group serves anyone who calls.

Westside Counties Associated Christian Homeschoolers

10235 SW Clydesdale Ter.
Beaverton, OR 97008
(503) 699-9241
e-mail: www.wscoach@juno.com

This group of 350 families welcomes Christians exclusively. They hold monthly meetings, stage student presentation nights, and publish a newsletter.

Holy Rosary Homeschool Group

Holly Denman
14656 SE Charjan St.
Clackamas, OR 97015-9344
(503) 658-3099
e-mail: www.denman@teleport.com

All 75 families that constitute this group are Catholic, and activities are from a Catholic point of view. They do, however, welcome all to their monthly support activities.

The Ln. County Inter-Christian Guild of Home Teachers (LIGHT)

P.O. Box 70498
Eugene, OR 97401
(541) 782-2466
website: www.efn.org/~light
e-mail: light@efn.org

Over 200 families under Christian leadership welcome all to participate in their monthly meetings, annual fair, field trips, children's classes, and newsletter publication.

Willamette Valley Homeschoolers

Karen Wildish
110 Deer Valley Dr.
Eugene, OR 97405
(541) 344-0170
e-mail: wildbkw@aol.com

All are welcome to join the 100 families that form this group. They have a newsletter and social activities, including a weekly park day.

Alternative Bethel Homesource

Richard
P.O. Box 40884
Eugene, OR 97404
(541) 689-9959
e-mail: DickH@betheltech.com

Everyone is welcome to join this state-funded private alternative resource center governed by a parent board. Over 500 children are involved in classes taught in all subject areas for all grades.

Jackson County Home Educators

Bev Huard
4733 Hillcrest Rd.
Medford, OR 97504
(541) 734-3243
website: http://home.cdsnet.net/
    ~normrowe/jche
e-mail: rwarrick@cdsnet.net

This group of approximately 200 families has Christian leadership, but welcomes all. Activities include monthly meetings, newsletter, yearbook, grad lending library, and biannual curriculum fair. The group also sponsors a trip to Washington D.C. and Europe.

Grande Ronde Association of Christian Educators

Peg Wallace
141 E. Bryson St.
Union, OR 97883
(541) 562-5014

Christian leaders head this group of 50 families that welcomes everyone. Their schedule includes annual achievement testing and regular meetings.

E-mail Loop Groups

The Oregon Special Interest Group

e-mail: Orsig@listserv.aol.com

The Oregon Christian Homeschoolers

e-mail: ORChristianHS@onelist.com

Homeschooling in Oregon: The 1998 Handbook

Nettlepatch Press
P.O. Box 80214
Portland, OR 97280-1214
e-mail: www.nettlepatch.net

This book, written by Ann Lahrson-Fisher and published by Nettlepatch Press, is a must-have for anyone homeschooling in the state of Oregon.

CONFERENCES

Northwest Curriculum Exhibition

Portland, Oregon
(503) 784-4398
website: www.teleport/~chesso/nwce

This Christian Conference celebrated its tenth year with approximately 2,200 in attendance June 18–19, 1999. Vendors, workshops, and vendor workshops were part of the fare.

Oregon Christian Home Education Network (OCEAN)

Portland, Oregon
(503) 288-1285

This conference (August 27–28, 1999) attracts approximately 450 people.

Oregon Home Education Network (OHEN)

Portland State Community College
Rock Creek Campus
Hillsboro, Oregon
Contact: (503) 321-5166
e-mail: ohen@teleport.com

OHEN held its Annual All-inclusive Conference March 27, 1999.

PENNSYLVANIA

Homeschooling parents in Pennsylvania must possess a high school diploma or GED equivalent certification. They must file an affidavit each year with the superintendent of the local school district, which includes a general educational objective. A parent cannot homeschool if he or she has been convicted of various crimes, mostly child-abuse-related. Testing is required in grades 3, 5, and 8 and cannot be done by the parent, but can be administered by a friend. For the yearly work, the family must have a certified teacher or psychologist as an evaluator. The evaluator must be approved and on file with the school district. Call a statewide group before you do anything in Pennsylvania.

STATEWIDE ORGANIZATIONS

Remember to contact your parent-run statewide organization before contacting any government agency. The parent-run organization will help you understand what to expect when you call the Department of Education.

Pennsylvania Home Education Network

Kathy Terleski
285 Allegheny St.
Meadville, PA 16335
(412) 561-5288
e-mail: normommY@aol.com

This large statewide, nonprofit corporation offers inclusive membership and a networking function for anyone interested in homeschooling. They direct people to local groups and to area contact people around the state.

Catholic Homeschoolers of Pennsylvania

Ellen Kramer
101 S. College St.
Myerstown, PA 17067
(717) 866-5425
(717) 866-9383 (fax)
e-mail: cathmschpa@ihs2000.com

This statewide, exclusively Catholic network provides legislative alerts, a bimonthly newsletter, and a yearly conference and curriculum fair.

GOVERNMENT AGENCY

School Services Unit of the Pennsylvania Department of Education

Sarah Pearce
333 Market St., 5th Floor
Harrisburg, PA 17126-0333
(717) 787-4860

SUPPORT GROUPS

Bucks County Homeschoolers

Pat Porter
125 Mountain Oaks Rd.
Yardley, PA 19067
(215) 428-3865
e-mail: renee321@juno.com

Approximately 30 families belong to this all-inclusive group that plans field trips and publishes a newsletter.

The McKeesport Area Homeschoolers

Jan Conrad
404 Owens Ave.
Liberty Borough, PA
(412) 672-7056
e-mail: pageclan@msn.com

Unabashedly Christian yet all-inclusive, this group of approximately 40 families uses Mom teachers as well as outside teachers, puts out a weekly newsletter giving Friday school news, and offers weekly enrichment classes and some field trips.

Christian Home Educators Fellowship of Lycoming County

Greg and Lisa Schaeffer
RR#1, Box 348B
Cogan Station, PA 17728
(717) 435-0717
e-mail: lisasch@csrlink.net

Explicitly Christian, this group of about 100 families requires a Statement of Faith. In addition to regular homeschooling activities, they have monthly business meetings and publish a monthly newsletter.

Fayette County Christian Homeschoolers

Melissa Lough
Box 219
Mt. Braddock, PA 15465
(724) 438-5003
e-mail: andi@hhs.net

Approximately 40 families comprise this Christian organization that requires a Statement of Faith. Monthly parent meetings, a monthly newsletter, a YMCA program, and co-op classes are highlighted activities.

Johnstown Christian Homeschoolers

Dawn Defibaugh
202 Weible Dr.
Hooversville, PA 15936
(814) 479-7202

This group of approximately 60 families has Christian leadership but is inclusive. They feature a monthly newsletter (calendar of events), field trips, and park days.

Catholic Homeschoolers of Scranton

Michele Fitzgerald
1317 St. Ann St.
Scranton, PA 18504
(717) 344-8866
e-mail: anchoracad@aol.com

This Catholic group of about 25 families with Catholic leadership is inclusive ($10 per year membership fee). In addition to a monthly newsletter, the group sponsors two or more activities per month, including adult night, youth gatherings, and 4-H projects.

Hosanna Homeschoolers

Linda Dovey
1615 Termon Ave.
Pittsburgh, PA 15212
(412) 734-1086
e-mail: ldovey@aol.com

"Seeking excellence, not perfection" is the motto of this growing Christian-led group of seven families that welcomes everyone. They meet bimonthly (10:00 A.M. to 2:00 P.M.) for a writers club, brown-bag lunch, and afternoon craft activity. Other activities include field trips, guest speakers, and an e-mail newsletter.

TITUS II (Quakertown area)

Judy Scheetz
(215) 536-0186

This small nondenominational Christian group of 10 families in the Quakertown area is very active. Members must try to attend as many of the monthly Bible studies as possible. A project fair each winter features science, history, music, or whatever the children like. Standardized testing is done each spring. Activities are offered whenever a parent or family wants to sponsor one. The group also has a monthly newsletter.

Lehigh County Home Educators

Cathy Mills
6385 Manzanita Dr.
Macungie, PA 18062
(610) 965-5932

This group consists of 132 families located in the Lehigh County area (about 50 miles north of Philadelphia). These home educators publish a newsletter and a "How to Get Started" brochure, hold various classes, and take field trips together.

LIGHT (Learning Is Great Homeschooling Together)

Peg Donnelly or Debbie Genua
(215) 721-9656

This 40-family organization encourages small groups within the larger group. The group publishes a monthly newsletter for members ($40/year). Activities include Moms' meetings and monthly get-togethers, newspaper, and academic club for children. The Hi-Lighters group for Junior and Senior High School ages meets semimonthly.

CONFERENCES

Ferg N Us

Berean Bible Church
Pottstown, Pennsylvania
Contact: Bonnie Ferguson
(610) 282-0780

Jim and Bonnie Ferguson run the company that puts on this Christian conference with workshops and vendors (held April 16–17, 1999). All are welcome.

Christian Homeschool Association of Pennsylvania (CHAP)

Pennsylvania Complex in Harrisburg
Contact: Kim Huber
(717) 661-2428
website: www.chapboard.org

The 16th Annual CHAP homeschool convention (May 7–8, 1999) featured vendors and workshops of a Christian nature. All are welcome.

RHODE ISLAND

To homeschool legally in the state of Rhode Island, a family must submit its plan to the Committee at the State Department of Education. The family must agree to teach reading, writing, arithmetic, U.S. history, Rhode Island history, and physical education, as well as keep attendance.

STATEWIDE ORGANIZATIONS

Remember to contact your parent-run statewide organization before contacting any government agency. The parent-run organization will help you understand what to expect when you call the Department of Education.

Rhode Island Guild of Home Teachers (RIGHT)

P.O. Box 11
Hope, RI 02831
(401) 821-7700 (message phone)
(401) 351-5991 (call for Brenda after 2:00
  P.M. EST)

This state parent-run organization is the only organization in the state. It is a Christian organization with eight geographic chapters (listed below).

Newport County	Washington County
Northwest	Northeast
Greater Providence	East Bay
West Bay	South Central

It's mission statement: "RIGHT is an organization of about 300 families committed to educational excellence and freedom. Our goals are to promote home education for those wishing to do so and to support efforts that protect parental authority and educational freedom. We believe that all families have the right to homeschool their children. We operate on the basis of Biblical principles by upholding Judeo-Christian ethics." All religions are welcome to call for information and to find out about their park days and other activities.

GOVERNMENT AGENCY

Department of Education

225 Westminster St., 4th Fl.
Providence, RI 02903
(401) 222-4600 ext. 2503

SOUTH CAROLINA

To homeschool in South Carolina, a parent can use any of three methods (the first and the third being the easiest):

1. Register with the local school district.

2. Register through SCAIHS, not under control of state department.

3. Form a local accountability group.

STATEWIDE ORGANIZATIONS

Remember to contact your parent-run statewide organization before contacting any government agency. The parent-run organization will help you understand what to expect when you call the Department of Education.

South Carolina Association of Independent Homeschools (SCAIHS)

P.O. Box 2104
Irmo, SC 29063
(803) 551-1003
website: www.scaihs.org
e-mail: scaihs@aol.com

This is a large homeschooling group in South Carolina. They sponsor an annual conference (see below) as well make as local support group referrals.

South Carolina Home Educators Association (SCHEA)

P.O. Box 3231
Columbia, SC 29230
(803) 754-6425
website: http://members.aol.com/
schea1/index.html

This statewide group offers a resource center open to all homeschoolers. They provide information for local support groups throughout the state of South Carolina. They also have a newsletter and offer testing services, diplomas, and transcripts for a small charge.

South Carolina Homeschool Support Group

Sherry Huston
242 Weathers Ferry Rd.
Bowman, SC 29018
(843) 563-9322
e-mail: sherryh@bellsouth.net

This is a statewide network resource, directing people to local groups and area contact people and serving as an information hub statewide.

Teachers Ink Homeschooling Association

Deborah Tobus-White
P.O. Box 13386
Charleston, SC 29422-3386
(803) 795-9982
(803) 795-2683 (fax)

This association offers legal information regarding homeschooling to families in South Carolina.

Piedmont Home Educators Association (PHEA)

Mark and Martha
115 Buist Ave.
Greenville, SC 29609
(864) 255-9520

This organization screens applications, publishes a newsletter, and offers information on support groups. There is a fee.

Website

SCHS (South Carolina Home Schoolers)

website: www.icpn.com/homeschool

GOVERNMENT AGENCY

South Carolina Department of Education

Mary Kay Jones
1429 Senate St.
Columbia, SC 29201
(803) 734-8493

SUPPORT GROUPS

Tri-County Educational Association of Community Homeschoolers

Maria Schich
107 Prairie Ln.
Sommerville, SC 29483
(843) 871-6683

This family support group of approximately 25 families publishes a newsletter, takes field trips, and provides a teaching handout.

Greenville Homeschool Resource Center

Mark and Martha
(864) 255-9520

This organization provides courses from 5th grade to high school for homeschool students. There is a fee.

Crusaders

Patricia Sweatt
(803) 547-4323
e-mail: frogs18@juno.com
Columbia, SC area

This Christian organization was established to serve members in fellowship, educational opportunities, and activities. Although all families are welcome, the group is run with a Biblical perspective.

Sumter Area Family Educators

Diane Setzer
90 Hope Ct.
Sumter, SC 29154
(803) 481-5987

This support group has a newsletter, field trips, and other activities.

Home Education Links for Parent Support

Pamela Berthume
53 Cobblestone Rd.
Greenville, SC 29615
(864) 233-2450 (voice mail)

This support group conducts field trips, offers other activities, and publishes a newsletter.

CONFERENCES

South Carolina Association of Independent Home Schools (SCAIHS)

Irmo, South Carolina
Contact: Kathy Carper, Vice President
(803) 407-2155
e-mail: scaihs@aol.com

SCAIHS 3rd Annual Curriculum Exposition & Convention was held April 9–10, 1999.

SOUTH DAKOTA

To homeschool in South Dakota, the parent must fill out an Exemption form, file it with the local school board, and comply with a mandatory testing requirement for children in grades 4, 8, and 11. Testing can be done by a local testing agency or in your own home.

STATEWIDE ORGANIZATIONS

Remember to contact your parent-run statewide organization before contacting any government agency. The parent-run organization will help you understand what to expect when you call the Department of Education.

GOVERNMENT AGENCY

South Dakota Department of Education

700 Governor's Dr.
Pierre, SD 57501-2291
(605) 773-6934

SUPPORT GROUPS

Western Dakota Christian Home Schools

Judi Sigafoos
P.O. Box 528
Blackhawk, SD 57718
(605) 745-4203

This is a Christian group that meets to support each other in their efforts to homeschool. They will help you get in touch with other groups around South Dakota.

South Dakota Homeschool Association

Mr. Carroway
P.O. Box 882
Sioux Falls, SD 57101
(605) 335-1125

This nonreligious group meets for fun and support.

CONFERENCES

Western Dakota Christian Home Schools (WDCHS)

Spearfish, South Dakota
Contact: Joel Fink
(605) 341-3257

WDCHS sponsors an Annual Christian Homeschool Conference each spring.

TENNESSEE

In Tennessee, a homeschooling parent must have a high school diploma (or GED equivalent) to teach his or her own children from grades K–8 and a bachelor's degree to teach grades 9–12. There are two kinds of home schools: church-related and independent. Church-related means that it must be affiliated with a recognized, bona fide church organization. These must meet standards of accreditation of various accrediting agencies set by law [T.C.A. 49-50-801]. Independent home schools are those in which parents or guardians teach their own children. These home schools must register with the local school district by August 1 each year. Mandatory testing is required in grades 5, 7, and 9. If a previously homeschooled child then enters a public school, they must meet various testing requirements to receive credit for work done in the homeschool setting.

Tennessee has the usual attendance requirements—4 hours per day, 180 days per year, with attendance records sent to the local superintendent at the end of the school year. Procure the "Homeschooling in Tennessee Basic Information Packet" before you do anything else. The procedures are extensive (but not confusing if you read them carefully).

STATEWIDE ORGANIZATIONS

Remember to contact your parent-run statewide organization before contacting any government agency. The parent-run organization will help you understand what to expect when you call the Department of Education.

Tennessee Home Education Association

3677 Richbriar Ct.
Nashville, TN 37211
(615) 834-3529 or (615) 794-3259

This organization has eight chapters statewide (listed below).

Tennessee Home Education Association — Memphis

P.O. Box 240402
Memphis, TN 38124-0402
(901) 362-2620
website: MemphisHomeEd.org
e-mail: MHEA@MemphisHomeEd.org

The Memphis Chapter has a large number of activities. Its excellent newsletter, "News & Views," is 20 pages long and filled with science fair, conference, support group, and basketball schedule information.

The other Chapters are:

Jackson: (901) 664-6740

Middle Tennessee: (931) 487-9888

South Middle Tennessee: (931) 723-4312

Smokey Mountains: (423) 675-3073

Middle East Tennessee: (423) 263-3308

South East Tennessee: (423) 266-4663

North East Tennessee: (423) 288-7658

Please call the chapter in your geographic area to request specific information regarding its newsletter and activities. Many have an annual curriculum fair, book fair, and other activities.

GOVERNMENT AGENCY

Tennessee State Department of Education

Donna Cross
Accountability Department
Andrew Johnson Tower, Sixth Floor
710 James Robertson Parkway
Nashville, TN 37243-0375
(615) 741-2731 (will transfer your call)

SUPPORT GROUPS

Mid-South LDS Home Educators

Tina Rowden
(901) 365-4676
e-mail: rowdencmtn@aol.com

This is a Latter-day Saints support group.

CONFERENCES

Bill Rice Ranch Home School Conference (Christian)

Murfreesboro, Tennessee
Contact: Registrar
(615) 893-2767 or (800) 253-RICE
e-mail: BillRiceRanch@
*   WORLDNET.ATT.NET*

The school's Annual Homeschool Conference (held April 15–17 in 1999) offers fine arts competition, speech competition, and more.

Chattanooga Southeast Tennessee Home Education Association (CSTHEA)

East Ridge, Tennessee
Contact: Gary or Carole Hargraves
(423) 266-4663
e-mail: carole@voy.net

CSTHEA's Annual Christian/Inclusive Educational Expo & Curriculum Fair (July 23–24, 1999) features vendors, literature bags, and more.

Memphis-Area Home Education Association

Memphis, Tennessee
Contact: Judy Pierce
(901) 362-2620
e-mail: MHEA@MemphisHomeEd.org

The Memphis area held its Annual Christian Homeschool Conference May 21–22, 1999.

Tennessee Home Education Association (Mid-East THEA)

Athens, Tennessee
Contact: Lisa Bell
(423) 263-3308
e-mail: Mideastthea@juno.com

The Annual Christian/Inclusive Conference & Curriculum Fair with vendors and various activities is held each spring.

Middle Tennessee Home Education Association (MTHEA)

Nashville, Tennessee
Contact: (615) 794-3259

Call to get dates and other information about MTHEA's Annual Christian Conference.

West Tennessee Home Education Association (WTHEA)

Milan, Tennessee
Contact: Elizabeth Hall
(901) 664-9936
e-mail: nodullmoments@juno.com

Call to get dates and other information about WTHEA's Annual Christian Homeschool Conference featuring 30 vendors and more.

TEXAS

Refer to *Texas Education Code Section 25-085*, and you'll learn that to homeschool in Texas, you have to teach reading, writing, arithmetic, grammar, and good citizenship in a bona fide manner. There is no testing or any other requirements.

In a landmark case in Texas, the Class Action *Leeper v. Arlington Ind. School District*, the State Supreme Ct. ruled unanimously that homeschools are private schools and that the state has no jurisdiction over them.

STATEWIDE ORGANIZATIONS

Remember to contact your parent-run statewide organization before contacting any government agency. The parent-run organization will help you understand what to expect when you call the Department of Education.

Texas Homeschool Coalition (THC)

Tim Lambert, President
P.O. Box 6982
Lubbock, TX 79493
(806) 797-4927
(806) 797-4629 (fax)
website www.thsc.org
email: staff@thsc.org

This statewide homeschool group in Texas performs legislative watchdog activities and offers a Capitol Day during which homeschool parents meet and speak with their state senators. The organization helps new homeschoolers by pointing them in the right direction for curriculum resources and support groups in their area. If a family is harassed by a school district, this group will aid them by reminding the district with a form letter from the Texas Education Commissioner about the Texas law pertinent to homeschooling. The THC also publishes a 77-page *Handbook for Texas Homeschoolers* ($15 + $3 shipping & handling), which tells a family all it needs to know to homeschool in Texas—laws, resources, groups, how to, and more. Information is listed by county and area code.

GOVERNMENT AGENCY

Texas Education Agency

1701 Congress Ave.
Austin, TX 78701
(512) 463-9734

SUPPORT GROUPS

Apostolate of Roman Catholic Home Schoolers

Tyna Leonard
608 Sun Ct.
Friendswood, TX 77546 (Houston area)
(281) 482-4271

This exclusively Catholic homeschoolers support group offers park days, field trips, and a newsletter.

El Paso Christian Home Educators

P.O. Box 3549
El Paso, TX 79923
(915) 755-1803

This Christian support group of 70 families requires a Statement of Faith. Park days, swimming, and a 50-child choir are featured activities.

The Carthage Area Homeschool Association

Vonnez Kincheloe
10181 County Rd.
Carthage, TX 75633 (East Texas)
(903) 693-5306

This Christian homeschool group welcomes those of all religions ("Please call!"). They meet for semi-organized sports, Keeper of the Faith sessions, and friendly meetings in members' homes.

Texas Education Achieved in Christian Homes (TEACH)

Colleen Reid
611 Ave. "A"
El Campo, TX 77437 (near Houston)
(409) 543-1999

This exclusively Christian homeschooling support group (members must sign a Statement of Faith) meets for park days, field trips, and monthly business meetings.

Christian Home Educators of The Colony (CHEC)

Terri Goebel
P.O. Box 561027
The Colony, TX 75056
(972) 625-6829

Located in a Dallas suburb, this exclusively Christian group requires a Statement of Faith. Field trips and a newsletter are featured.

The Houston Unschoolers Group

Holly Furgason
(713) 695-4888
e-mail: NHFurgason@hotmail.com

This unschoolers' group just gets together to have fun. They also have a yearly conference with just under 100 people (which is great fun, too!).

Family Educators Alliance of South Texas (FEAST)

Ruth Perez
4719 Blanco Rd.
San Antonio, TX 78212
(210) 342-4674
e-mail: office@homeschoolfeast.com

This Christian organization has a curriculum bookstore and Resource Center located in South Central Texas. A monthly newsletter, workshops, seminars, science fair, used book sale, annual basketball tournament, and a yearly conference are featured activities.

West Texas Regional Homeschoolers

t'Charles and Sharon Carr
P.O. Box 717
Brookesmith, TX 76827-0717
(915) 646-3414
e-mail: texsota@web-access.net

This Central Texas–based group serves as a liaison between the homeschooling family and local support groups and information.

North Texas Self-Educators

Sarah Jordan
150 Forest Ln.
Double Oak, TX 75067
(817) 430-4835
e-mail: jordan@wininternet.com

This is an inclusive group of 70 families in the Forth Worth area who follow mostly unschooling philosophies. They publish a newsletter and sponsor regular gatherings.

CONFERENCES

Family Educators Alliance of South Texas (FEAST)

Contact: Ruth Perez
(210) 342-4674

Please call to get dates and information about the group's Annual National Basketball Tournament and Conference.

Christian Home Education Association (CHEA) of Central Texas

Austin, Texas
Contact: Chris Parrish
(512) 450-0070
e-mail: hiswayhome@juno.com

CHEA of Central Texas put on its 12th Annual Bookfair & Family Conference July 9–10, 1999.

Big Country Home Educators (BCHE)

Abilene, Texas
Contact: B. J. Pollan
(915) 673-2040

On April 17, 1999, BCHE held its Annual Christian Homeschool Conference.

Southeast Texas Home School Association (SETHSA)

Houston, Texas
Contact: Jonathan Weidner
(281) 370-8787
website: www.sethsa.org
e-mail: sethsa@sethsa.org

SETHSA's Gulf Coast Home Education Conference was held June 4–5 of 1999.

MINDFULL

Dallas, Texas
Contact: Barb Lundgren
(817) 540-6423 or (817) 430-4835
website: www.flashnet/~lisadahl
e-mail: source@flash.net

"Rethinking Education" was the theme of MINDFULL's 5th Annual Conference, held May 28–31, 1999.

UTAH

To homeschool legally in Utah, all that is required is that parents notify the local school district, teach all the subjects required by law, and conduct learning activity for a specified number of hours. No testing is required by the state and no home visits are performed. Dual enrollment, in which homeschool children are entitled to take classes in public schools, is also an option.

STATEWIDE ORGANIZATIONS

Remember to contact your parent-run statewide organization before contacting any government agency. The parent-run organization will help you understand what to expect when you call the Department of Education.

Utah Home Education Association (UHEA)

P.O. Box 167
Roy, UT 84067
(888) 887-UHEA (hotline)
website: www.itsnet.com/~uhea

UHEA is a statewide support group.

GOVERNMENT AGENCY

Utah State Office of Education

250 E. 500th S.
So. Salt Lake City, UT 84111
(801) 538-7801

SUPPORT GROUPS

Latter-day Saints Home Education Association

Joyce Kinmont
2770 S. 1000 W.
Perry, UT 84302
(435) 723-5355
website: ldshea.org

This worldwide LDS homeschooling support group helps Mormon families connect with other homeschoolers. Members stay well informed through the group's quarterly newsletter, website, e-mail newsletter, and annual conference.

Salt Lake Home Educators

Holly Godard
(801) 501-0345
e-mail: shark@xmission.com

This all-inclusive homeschool group serves Christian, Mormon, Jewish, and nonreligious families—all together. Their spokesperson states: "Join us for park days, monthly meetings, newsletter, field trips. Each month our group has a theme."

Charlotte Mason Homeschool Study Group

Penny Gardner
P.O. Box 900983
Sandy, UT 84090
(801) 943-3146
website: http://members.aol.com/PennyGar

This informal association provides a "comfortable forum for people from various backgrounds and denominations." They wish to establish positive relations with each other as they explore this gentle approach to learning and homeschooling. No membership fees are charged.

The Utah Christian Home School Association (UTCH)

P.O. Box 3942
Salt Lake City, UT 84110-3942
(801) 296-7198 (voice mail)
website: utch@utch.org

This Christian support group requires a Statement of Faith and membership fee. Field trips, workshops, regular meetings, a high school graduation ceremony, monthly newsletter, and an annual conference are highlighted activities.

CONFERENCES

Utah Home Education Association

Brigham Young University
Provo, Utah
Contact: Brian Smith
(801) 774-0495
website: www.itsnet.com/~uhea

UHEA's 18th Annual Convention & Curriculum Fair was held June 12, 1999.

Ben Franklin Academy

Contact: Steve Adams
(801) 886-0188

Call to get the location of the LDS Forum–Homeschool Curriculum Fair & Workshops (held August 18, 1999).

Charlotte Mason Convention

Salt Lake City Christian Fellowship
Sandy, Utah
Contact: Penny Gardner
(801) 943-3146

The Fellowship's 4th Annual Convention was held April 10, 1999.

Utah Christian Home School Association (UTCH)

The E-center
3200 S. Decker Lake Dr. (I-125 & 3500 S)
Salt Lake City, UT 84110-3924
Contact: (801) 296-7198 (voice mail)
e-mail: utch@utch.org

The 7th Annual Convention was held March 20, 1999. Visit the UTCH website for complete schedule and details of next conference.

VERMONT

To homeschool in Vermont, each family must perform a yearly enrollment process through the Department of Education. The family is required to supply the state with this basic information about each child: name, age, parents' names, addresses, which parent will do the teaching, and what public school the child would have attended. The family must include the curriculum they intend to follow—not materials, but content of the course or skills they will cover to teach the eight subjects required by law. For the first year, parents must complete a beginning-year and ending-year assessment. Each year after that, only an end-of-year assessment is required.

STATEWIDE ORGANIZATIONS

Remember to contact your parent-run statewide organization before contacting any government agency. The parent-run organization will help you understand what to expect when you call the Department of Education.

Vermont Homeschoolers Directory

Published by Gnarly Branch Press
Contact: Cindy Wade
RR 2, Box 145
E. Wallingford, VT 05742
(802) 259-3493
e-mail: cwade@vertmontel.com

This 32-page booklet covers homeschooling in Vermont; it tells readers where to begin, lists 100 homeschoolers who are willing to help others get started, and provides resources (both state and national) and helpful publications.

GOVERNMENT AGENCY

Vermont Department of Education

Natalie Casco, Home Study Consultant
120 State St.
Montpelier, VT 05602
(802) 828-5406

Natalie is also a homeschooling mom. She has 17 years' experience!

SUPPORT GROUPS

Kingdom Country Homeschoolers

Cheryl Pelkey
9 Pelkey Rd.
Newport, VT 05855
(802) 754-2946
e-mail: ncuser4@nccc.k12.vt.us

This is an inclusive group of about 15 families with Christian leadership. They offer park days, field trips, and a bimonthly newsletter.

Chittenden County Homeschool Cooperative

Michael Healy
66 Scarff Ave.
Burlington, VT 05401
(802) 864-9724

This all-inclusive group is located in the heart of Vermont's largest city. They have approximately 45 member families, publish a newsletter, and offer ongoing play days, field trips, many study activities, and more.

Franklin County Homeschoolers Cooperative

Kathleen Engstrom
(802) 524-5453

This all-inclusive group of approximately 30 families meets for a monthly potluck. Field trips are organized by parents who wish to lead them. The group also publishes a statewide newsletter, "Resource Center for Homeschooling." Please contact the editor/publisher, Marieken Volz at liberty@together.net for further resource information.

Harvest Home School Group

Beth
P.O. Box 8408
Essex, VT 05451
(802) 434-2934

Harvest Home is under Christian leadership and requires a Statement of Faith, but is open to others as well. This group has a novel approach: As an enrichment supplement, they hire teachers to create and teach a class for an entire school year (students meet once a week for five hours). They currently employ four teachers and one aide to teach 1st through 6th grades.

CONFERENCES

The nearest conferences are in Massachusetts (please see Massachusetts conference listing).

VIRGINIA

To homeschool in Virginia, parents must have a bachelor's or master's degree, or they must submit their curriculum choice to the state. All children must be tested yearly. To avoid testing, parents can request religious exemption. Please call your state organization to find out details of the exemption.

STATEWIDE ORGANIZATIONS

Remember to contact your parent-run statewide organization before contacting any government agency. The parent-run organization will help you understand what to expect when you call the Department of Education.

Virginia Home Education Association (VHEA)

William Shaw
P.O. Box 5131
Charlottesville, VA 22905
(540) 832-3578
e-mail: vhea@juno.com

This statewide organization describes itself as politically nonpartisan and religiously neutral, representing a diverse homeschooling community. VHEA also publishes a bimonthly newsletter.

GOVERNMENT AGENCY

Virginia Department of Education

Charles Findlay
P.O. Box 2120
Richmond, VA 23218
(804) 786-9421

SUPPORT GROUPS

Family-Oriented Learning Co-operative

Shay Seborne
(703) 494-6021
website: http://expage.com/page/folcfolks
e-mail: s/seaborne@juno.com

Approximately 40 families comprise this relaxed, all-inclusive group. Their monthly calendar of events features activities such as German language courses, teen group, toddler group, field trips, park days, and an annual open house.

Richmond Educational Alternatives for Children at Home (REACH)

Melinda Sellers
P.O. Box 36174
Richmond, VA 23235
(804) 795-7624

This nonreligious, all-inclusive group for families interested in homeschooling meets for park days, field trips, and fun.

Home Educators Are Restoring the Heritage (HEARTH)

Kathy or Chris Davis
P.O. Box 69
Linden, VA 22642
(540) 636-3713

This Christian group requires a Statement of Faith, but they are open to anyone who is comfortable with HEARTH's mission. The group offers field trips, park days, and other fun activities.

Beach Educators Association for Creative Homeschooling (BEACH)

Howard Douthit
P.O. Box 64516
Virginia Beach, VA 23467-4516
(757) 579-3139 (hotline)
(757) 482-7369
e-mail: handr@integrityonline18.com

This is a network of Christian home educators whose purpose is to serve Christian families in their efforts to homeschool. They have sports teams, science fairs, classes, field trips, and much, much more.

CONFERENCES

Home Educators Association of Virginia

Richmond Center Marriott Hotel
Richmond, Virginia
Contact: 804/288-1608

The group held its 16th Annual Home-school Conference & Curriculum Fair June 17–19, 1999. This is a Christian conference, but all are welcome.

Beach Educators Association for Creative Homeschooling

Virginia Beach Pavilion
Virginia Beach, Virginia
Contact: Howard Douthit
(757) 482-7369
website: www.homeschools.to/va/beach

The 13th Annual Christian Homeschooling Curriculum Fair & Conference was held May 22–23, 1999.

WASHINGTON

In the state of Washington, any child over the age of 8 and under 18 must attend school in the district in which the child resides unless: (1) the child is attending an approved private school or is enrolled in an extension program of an approved private school, (2) is receiving home-based instruction, (3) is attending an education center, (4) is excused from attendance by the school district superintendent for various reasons, (5) is 16 or older and is regularly or lawfully employed and either parent agrees that the child must not attend school, or (6) is emancipated.

STATEWIDE ORGANIZATIONS

Remember to contact your parent-run statewide organization before contacting any government agency. The parent-run organization will help you understand what to expect when you call the Department of Education.

The Washington Homeschool Organization

6632 S. 191st Pl., Ste. E-100
Kent, WA 98032
(425) 251-0439

Family Learning Organization

P.O. Box 7247
Spokane, WA 99207-0247
(509) 467-2552

GOVERNMENT AGENCY

Department of Education

Old Capitol Building
Olympia, Washington 98504

SUPPORT GROUPS

St. Thomas More Home Educators

Katherine Eames
7248 SE 27th St.
Mercer Island, WA 98040
(206) 230-0455
e-mail: jreames@aol.com OR
Jfogassy@aol.com

This 10-year-old Catholic home educators' support group of 150 families provides academic, social, and spiritual support for children and parents. They schedule year-round park days and sponsor a conference each May.

Valley Home Educators

Emilie Fogle
1413 Easthills Terrace
East Wenatchee, WA 98802
e-mail: gardnfev@nwi.net

This inclusive group of over 100 families holds informal meetings once a month (usually evenings). They cover subject-matter academics, math, foreign language, and offer a program called Running Start.

Also at the e-mail address is Washington Home Educators' E-mail Network (WHEN), which focuses on legislation affecting homeschoolers and provides a newsline service for statewide homeschooling events.

Teaching Parents Association

Laurie McDonald or Diana Franklin
P.O. Box 1934
Woodinville, WA 98072
(425) 739-8562 or (425) 844-3047
website: www.bess.net~mosk/page3.htm
e-mail: mosk@bess.net

This nonsectarian support group sponsors monthly park days, field trips, and other special events. They also offer information on legalities and beginning guidance. Call (425) 739-8562 for a recorded message.

Peninsula Homeschool Exchange

Deborah Carroll
419 Benton St.
Port Townsend, WA 98368
(360) 385-3830
e-mail: dcarroll@olympus.net

Everyone is welcome to participate with this inclusive, diverse group of 40 families. This is actually more a network than a group, since they disseminate information via their quarterly newsletter ($5 per year). They do have beach days in summer.

Granite Falls Homeschoolers

Barbara Maitland
3526 Robe Menzel Rd.
Granite Falls, WA 98252
(360) 691-7429

Everyone is welcome to participate in this inclusive group that meets monthly and provides classes for kids and field trip/play days. Those interested can get the group's newsletter for the cost of postage only.

Network of Vancouver Area Homeschoolers (NOVAH)

Lori Loranger
162 Krogstad Rd.
Washougal, WA 98671
(360) 837-3760
e-mail: lori@data-serve.com

This group of 50 families from Clark, Skamania, and Cowlitz Counties is not religiously oriented, therefore is open to everyone. All volunteer in this loosely organized network, which features twice monthly park days during the summer and meets at a community center during the winter.

CONFERENCES

Washington Homeschool Organization (WHO)

Bellevue, Washington
Contact: (425) 251-0439

The Annual WHO Conference, a large, all-inclusive event, held its 15th conference May 21–22, 1999. Approximately 3,900 attended what could be considered Washington State's Conference.

St. Thomas More Educators

Seattle Police Academy Pavilion
Seattle, Washington
Contact: (206) 230-0455
e-mail: jfogassy@aol.com

The 5th Annual Catholic Family Educational Conference was held May 28–29, 1999. This strictly Catholic homeschooling conference features many good speakers, vendors, and presentations.

Washington Christian Home Educators Conference (WATCH)

Redmond, Washington
Contact: (509) 678-5440
website: www.WATCHhome.org

The 5th annual conference sponsored by WATCH occurred April 23–24, 1999. This Christian conference draws approximately 800 attendees.

Kitsap County Mini Convention

Bremerton, Washington
Contact: (360) 373-0477

The Kitsap Homeschool Mini Convention (held June 26, 1999) is a small Christian conference with approximately 200 in attendance.

WEST VIRGINIA

The state of West Virginia currently has a law in effect, the 4-year law, which requires a parent teaching at home to have at least 4 years of education more than the highest level he or she is teaching to his or her offspring. In other words, to teach 8th grade to your child, you must have a high school diploma; to teach high school, a bachelor's degree, and so on. This law may be changed by the legislature this year.

In addition, parents must submit to yearly standardized testing of their children by a certified teacher or they can opt to have a certified teacher visit their home and review the child's portfolio of work each year.

STATEWIDE ORGANIZATIONS

Remember to contact your parent-run statewide organization before contacting any government agency. The parent-run organization will help you understand what to expect when you call the Department of Education.

West Virginia Home Educators Association (WVHEA)

Mary Beth Stenger
P.O. Box 3707
Charleston, WV 25337
(800) 736-9843
website: http://members.tripod.com/
  ~WVHEA
e-mail: Whvea@bigfoot.com

This statewide group provides testing, which is required by the state; sponsors an annual conference and an annual family day; publishes a bimonthly newsletter; and sponsors a Legislative Day where the group goes en mass to the West Virginia legislature. Call them first to get information about homeschooling. They also have an excellent website with abundant information about West Virginia homeschooling.

GOVERNMENT AGENCY

West Virginia Department of Education

1900 Kanawha Blvd., East
Bldg. 6, Room 262
Charleston, WV 25305
(304) 558-2118

SUPPORT GROUPS

Jackson County Homeschoolers

Karen Weaver
P.O. Box 333
Cottageville, WV 25239
(304) 372-4333

This all-inclusive group offers support to families through park days, field trips, and other fun activities. Karen advises that homeschooling is on the rise in West Virginia.

Christian Home Educators of West Virginia

P.O. Box 8770
S. Charleston, WV 25303-0770
(304) 776-4664

This is a state-wide group with Christian leadership. They can provide local support group information. Please call them to learn more.

Tri-State Home Schoolers

Martha Mishoe
29 Rosemont Ct.
Huntington, WV 25705
e-mail: wvmishmom@juno.com

This is a network of families interested in homeschooling offers swimming, skating, bowling, gymnastics, field trips, picnics, and other activities; it also publishes a newsletter.

CONFERENCES

Christian Home Educators of West Virginia

Charleston, West Virginia
Contact: Mike Hutchison
(304) 776-4664
e-mail: chewvadm@aol.com

May 28–29 were the dates of this group's 1999 Annual Christian Conference featuring vendors and various activities.

West Virginia Home Educators Association, Inc.

Weston, West Virginia
Contact: Mary Beth Stenger
(800) 736-9843;
e-mail: MBS26385@aol.com

The group's Annual Inclusive Homeschool Conference, which includes vendors, workshops, and more was September 25, 1999.

WISCONSIN

To homeschool in Wisconsin, parents must register with their local department of instruction and provide an accepted curriculum of instruction in the following areas: social studies, science, health, math, language arts, and reading.

STATEWIDE ORGANIZATIONS

Remember to contact your parent-run statewide organization before contacting any government agency. The parent-run organization will help you understand what to expect when you call the Department of Education.

Wisconsin Parents Association (WPA)

P.O. Box 2502
Madison, WI 53701
(608) 283-3131 (voice mail)

This grassroots, statewide organization performs legislative watchdog activities, publishes a quarterly newsletter, and provides an information packet that includes local support group listings. Contact them before you do anything about homeschooling in Wisconsin.

GOVERNMENT AGENCY

Wisconsin Department of Public Instruction

125 S. Webster St., Box 7841
Madison, WI 53707-7841
(608) 266-3390

SUPPORT GROUPS

Milwaukee Area Home Learners

Erich Moraine
(414) 246-3604

This local support group conducts weekly meetings, publishes a newsletter, and sponsors field trips and other activities. They charge a fee for membership.

Unschooling Families

Sarah Gilbert
1908 N. Clark St.
Appleton, WI 54911
(920) 735-9832

This all-inclusive local support group of about 20 families publishes a monthly newsletter and schedules park days and field trips.

Ozaukee Explorers

Tommy Lee Forbes
W 59 N, 450 Hilgen Ave.
Cedarburg, WI 53012

This local support group has no regular meetings but publishes a newsletter and organizes field trips (nominal fee charged).

The HOME Group

Alison McKee
5745 Bittersweet Pl.
Madison, WI 53705
(608) 238-3302
e-mail: amckee@hotmail.com

This local support group of 90 families publishes a newsletter and holds monthly parents' meetings, potlucks, and field trips, as well as other activities. Annual fees are $15.

Washington County Homeschool Information

Sharon Keselick
(414) 338-2650

This group holds meetings every Friday. Call for further information.

CONFERENCES

Wisconsin Christian Home Educators Association

Brookfield, Wisconsin
Contact: Al and Jan Gnacinski
(414) 637-5127

The Annual Christian Homeschool Conference, featuring vendors and more, took place May 20–22, 1999.

Wisconsin Parents Association (WPA)

Stevens Point, Wisconsin
Contact: Jim Schultze
(920) 435-9101 or (920) 826-7632
website: www.homeschooling.wpa.org

WPA's Annual Inclusive Homeschool Conference (held April 30–May 1, 1999) featured over 50 vendors and various activities.

WYOMING

In Wyoming, the compulsory school attendance is from ages 7 through 15, or completion of 10th grade. For homeschoolers, there are two options a family can utilize. The first is to establish and operate a homeschool. The parents have to instruct their children for 175 days per year and follow "the standard curriculum" of reading, writing, math, history, literature, civics, and science. There are no teacher qualifications required. There is no testing nor recordkeeping required. The second option is to operate a homeschool under the auspices of a church or congregation. In this case there are no requirements at all.

STATEWIDE ORGANIZATIONS

Remember to contact your parent-run statewide organization before contacting any government agency. The parent-run organization will help you understand what to expect when you call the Department of Education.

Homeschoolers of Wyoming

Cindy Munger
P.O. Box 3151
Jackson, WY 83001
(307) 733-2834
e-mail: mungermtrr@compuserve.com

This statewide homeschooling networking organization has Christian leadership, but is inclusive. HSLDA summary information is available for the various counties, as is local support group information. The group holds a homeschool convention once a year and maintains a calling chain for legislative alert.

GOVERNMENT AGENCY

Wyoming Department of Education

Jim Lindino
Hathaway Bldg 2nd Floor
2300 Capitol Ave.
Cheyenne 82002-0050
(307) 777-7670

SUPPORT GROUPS

Big Horn Basin Schoolers

Donna Hiltz
(307) 754-3271

This support group of over 120 families plans outings and provides support to homeschooling families. They also publish a newsletter and charge a membership fee of $7.50 per year.

TEACH

Cindy Munger
(307) 733-2834

Please call this local support group for the Jackson area to learn about the various services they provide.

Gillette Christian Homeschoolers

Mary Becker
(307) 686-2567

This support group for the Gillette, Wyoming, area has monthly meetings, publishes a newsletter, sponsors field trips, and charges a membership fee.

Grable Basin Homeschoolers

Teresa Olsen
(307) 568-2987

This support group holds monthly meetings, publishes a newsletter, and conducts free field trips.

Christian Homeschoolers At Task (CHAT) — Big Horn Basin area

Jeannie Ferris
(307) 366-2685

This very active group of about 19 families has weekly meetings, publishes a newsletter, plans field trips, and charges a fee to join.

CONFERENCES

Homeschoolers of Wyoming

Gillette, Wyoming
Contact: Mary Becker
(307) 686-2567

The group's Annual Christian Homeschool Conference with vendors, speakers, and more, was held May 14–15, 1999.

Who's Who and What's What in Homeschooling

For further information on the magazines and books below, please see part 3, "Resources."

Accreditation   Certification of a school by an accrediting board that inspects a school and, on approval, provides it with a certificate of approval or a certificate of accreditation.

Beechick, Ruth   Author of the books *An Easy Start in Arithmetic, A Home Start in Reading, Language and Thinking for Young Children, You Can Teach Your Child Successfully,* and *A Strong Start in Language.* She is also a popular speaker and writer.

Blumenfeld, Sam   Author of eight books on the topic of education, including *Is Public Education Necessary,* which contains a history of public education in America. He is also the creator of the reading program Alpha Phonics and a popular teacher, speaker, and writer.

Boomerang   A monthly kids' audio magazine created, written, and produced by David Strohm. It is popular and unique, featuring an all-child cast of characters who interview historic people, discuss current events, tell jokes, and explore vocabulary, geography, and many other topics relevant to kids.

Charlotte Mason Approach   Method of homeschooling founded by Charlotte Mason, a teacher in England who advocated educating by living a gentle, full life with much observation of nature, music, the use of living books, and other high quality activities.

Charter School   A school that is recognized and funded by the government to operate as an at-home public school. The charter school is owned by an individual or independent company. The difference between a charter school and an independent study program (ISP) is the freedom the charter school's owner has in running the facility.

Child-led   An approach to child rearing in which the child's needs and interests are considered first and foremost, as opposed to expecting the child to simply conform to parental authority.

Cohen, Cafi   Homeschooling mother of two grown children and author of *And What About College,* a popular book detailing how to think of and translate what you do into "transcript language" for college applications. She is also a popular speaker at homeschool conferences nationwide and specializes in simplifying the forbidding process of college admission.

Colfax, David and Micki   Couple who homeschooled their four boys on a goat farm in Northern California in the early 1980s and attained national attention as their first son (and subsequently two more) was accepted at Harvard and Yale. They are the authors of two books on homeschooling: *Home Schooling for Excellence* and *Hard Times in Paradise.*

Correspondence School   Provides long-distance educational services, giving students the option of mailing in assignments that are graded by a staff teacher and returned.

Curriculum   Course of study, homeschooling or otherwise. It may be composed of textbooks, workbooks, and other prepackaged materials or may be completely made up from scratch to fit parents' objectives.

Decompression   In the homeschooling sense, the act of releasing the negative pressure built up from a school setting once a child begins homeschooling.

Delayed Academics   Philosophy that young children should not be pressured with instruction in the "academic subjects" (such as reading, writing, and math), but rather be allowed to mature into their skills at their own rate. This philosophy was brought to light by Dr. Raymond Moore and his wife, Dorothy.

DeMille, Dr. Oliver   Founder and president of George Wythe College in Cedar City, Utah. Dr. DeMille has developed an approach to homeschooling using the classics and mentorship as its core, which was the method used to teach many of the founding fathers.

Dewey, John (1859–1952)   American philosopher and educator. While a professor at the University of Chicago, he did much work in experimental mass schooling and was an influential educator in the early twentieth century. Dewey was responsible for much of the socialist nature of mass education.

Dobson, Linda   Homeschooling mother and popular speaker, she is also the news editor for *Home Education Magazine*. Linda is the author of *The Art of Education*, *The Homeschooling Book of Answers*, and *Homeschooling: The Early Years*.

Dodd, Sandra   Homeschooling mother of three and a columnist on unschooling for *Home Education Magazine*. She is also a popular speaker at conferences.

Duffy, Cathy   Veteran Christian homeschooling mother and author of the *Christian Home Educators' Curriculum Manuals* and the widely acclaimed book *Government Nannies*, which details the government's effort to extend its influence over the home and family through its *Goals 2000* public school program. She is also a sought-after conference speaker.

Eclectic Approach   Method of homeschooling that uses materials from any and all sources.

Farenga, Pat and Day   President and conference coordinator, respectively, of Holt Associates. The Farengas homeschool their three daughters and sponsor the annual Growing Without Schooling conference. Pat is a frequent speaker at conferences nationwide and is one of the most esteemed unschoolers in the field.

Farris, Mike   President and founder of the Home School Legal Defense Association as well as a homeschooling father and popular author.

Gardner, Howard   Harvard psychologist who discovered, researched, and wrote about the seven intelligences all humans possess.

Gatto, John Taylor   A 30-year veteran teacher of Manhattan public junior high schools and three-time winner of the New York City and New York State Teacher of the Year; education reformer, thinker, and author of many books about public education and life.

Goals 2000   Federal government program that seeks to make each public school into a sort of village center for dispensing and monitoring a wide variety of medical, social, and family programs. The wording of its provisions is mandatory, not voluntary, and it is viewed by its critics as a further encroachment upon personal and family freedom for those families within the public school system. For more information about Goals 2000, please see the book *Government Nannies* by Cathy Duffy.

Growing Without Schooling   Bimonthly publication started by John Holt over 20 years ago. Along with the *Moore Report*, *GWS* was one of the first publications devoted to unschooling.

Guterson, David   Public school teacher, father of four homeschooled children, and author of *Family Matters* and other books.

Harris, Greg   Homeschooling father, author, and popular conference speaker. Author of *The Christian Homeschool* and other books.

Harris, Lori   Homeschooling mother of six and columnist for *Practical Homeschooling* magazine. She is a popular speaker and an expert in the principle approach and, along with her husband, owner of Landmark Book Distributors.

Hegener, Mark and Helen   Parents of five exclusively homeschooled children (oldest is 21) and publishers of *Home Education Magazine*. They also are frequent conference speakers.

Holt, John   The late pioneer researcher, teacher and founder of *Growing Without Schooling* magazine. Coined the term "unschooling" and authored many books about children and learning.

Holt Associates   Company that publishes *Growing Without Schooling* magazine; operates John Holt's Bookstore in Cambridge, Massachusetts; sponsors a yearly conference in Massachusetts; and publishes many homeschooling books.

Home Education Magazine   Published by Mark and Helen Hegener, this bimonthly magazine has been in existence since 1983. Full of informative articles and resources for homeschoolers.

Homeschool Dad   A bimonthly Christian magazine geared toward encouraging fathers' homeschooling involvement, with articles and tips for dads.

The Homeschool Digest   A Christian-based quarterly educational journal.

Homeschool Legal Defense Association   A nationwide, membership organization which, for a flat annual fee, will provide legal defense and advice to homeschool families regarding legal difficulties in the realm of home education.

Homeschooling Today   A bimonthly Christian magazine that is extremely popular for its inclusion of curriculum within the publication.

Hood, Dr. Mary   A veteran Christian homeschooling mother with a Ph.D. in Education. She and her husband have homeschooled their five children for 15 years. She is the author of several books, including *The Relaxed Homeschool* and *The Joyful Homeschooler* and has written a series of guidebooks for homeschoolers[EM]*Relaxed Recordkeeping* and *Helping Children Learn to Write*. She is a popular conference speaker and editor of *The Relaxed HomeSchooler* newsletter.

Independent Study Program (ISP)   A program offered by your local public school in which you can homeschool your children using the same curriculum and schedule offered in the day school. Every state has a different designation for this facility. Please check yours.

Kaseman, Larry and Susan   Homeschooling parents of four and authors of *Taking Charge Through Homeschooling: Personal and Political Empowerment*. They write a column called "Taking Charge" for *Home Education Magazine*.

Keith, Diane   Homeschooling mother of two, editor and publisher of *Homefires: A Journal of Homeschooling*, and popular speaker and writer.

Kindle Hodson, Victoria, M.A.   Author of many books including co-author of *Discover Your Child's Learning Styles*. Consultant and co-owner of Reflective Educational Perspectives, a learning styles consultation firm in Ventura, California.

Kinesthetic Learner   One who learns best by feeling or touching.

Klicka, Chris   Homeschool father and author *of The Right Choice: The Incredible Failure of Public Education, The Rising Hope of Homeschooling, The Right to Homeschool: A Guide to the Law on Parents' Rights in Education*, and *Homeschooling in the United States: A Statutory Analysis*.

KONOS   A popular unit-study company.

Language Arts   The study of the English language, reading, spelling, grammar, and literature.

Layne, Marty   A homeschooling mother of four and author of the book *Learning at Home: A Mother's Guide to Homeschooling*.

Llewellyn, Grace   This homeschooled young adult is the author of *The Teenage Liberation Handbook*.

The Link   A free, nationwide, nonreligious, nonsecular homeschooling newspaper .

Mann, Horace (1776–1859)   Instrumental in establishing the public school elementary system in Massachusetts, which later served as a model for the United States system. Helped put together the first state board of education and was its secretary for more than ten years. He served on the Massachusetts state legislature and was later elected to the House of Representatives, where he was an aggressive advocate for public education. Was the president of Antioch College in Ohio from 1853 until he died in 1859.

McKee, Allison   Homeschooling mother and author of *From Homeschool to College and Work*.

Moore, Dr. Raymond and Dorothy   Parents of two partially homeschooled children and the developers of the Moore method of homeschooling. They are pioneers in the homeschooling movement and responsible for many of the homeschooling laws in California. They are also authors of *Better Late Than Early, School Can Wait, Home Grown Kids, Home Spun Schools, Home Built Discipline, Home Made Help, Minding Your Own Business*, and *The Successful Family Handbook*.

Moore Formula   Philosophy developed by the Moores, which says that work and service along with study from books provides a balanced education. The formula also advocates not forcing academics until the child is mature and ready.

Moore Foundation   Serves homeschool families with educational material that supports the Moore Formula. Can also be used as a correspondence school.

Neill, A. S.   Founder and headmaster of Summerhill School in England

Parental Approach   Method of homeschooling based on simply being the child's parent and making choices according to the family philosophy.

Pelullo-Willis, Mariaemma   Popular homeschool consultant and co-owner of Reflective Educational Perspectives. Author of *What to Do When They Don't Get It,*, *Homeschooling the Child with Learning Problems*, and co-author of *Discover Your Child's Learning Style.*

Phonics   A method of teaching the act of reading, spelling, and pronunciation by using the phonetic sounds of letters.

Pride, Mary   Publisher of the popular Christian homeschool magazine *Practical Homeschooling.* Author of *The Big Book of Home Learning, The Way Home, All the Way Home, Schoolproof, The Child Abuse Industry*, and co-author of both the *Unholy Sacrifices of the New Age* and *Ancient Empires of the New Age.*

Principle Approach   Method of homeschooling based on Biblical principles.

Priesnitz, Wendy   Canadian homeschooling mother, advocate, speaker, and author of the book *School Free: The Homeschooling Handbook.* She is also recognized as a home-business expert. Wendy has authored eight other books, including *Bringing It Home: A Startup Guide for You and Your Family.*

Prystowsky, Richard   Popular conference speaker, college professor, and homeschooling father of three.

Reflective Educational Perspectives   Company in Ventura, California that provides Learning Style Evaluations and consultation for homeschool families and families in general. They specialize in children who have been negatively labeled.

Robinson Self-Teaching Curriculum   A 22-set CD-ROM program with which Dr. Robinson taught his six children how to teach themselves.

Rosseau, Jean-Jacques   Eighteenth-century French philosopher and writer who inadvertently influenced educators with his book *Emile* (1762), which ultimately led to both public school and unschooling.

Rupp, Rebecca   Homeschooling mother of three and author of several books, including *Everything You Never Learned about Birds, Good Stuff, Committed to Memory, The Dragon of Lonely Island, The Home Learning Source Book*, and *Getting Started in Homeschooling.* She is also a columnist for *Home Education Magazine.*

Sheffer, Susannah   Editor of *Growing Without Schooling* Magazine. Popular writer and conference speaker.

Socialization   Process of shaping and molding behavior within a certain realm.

Summerhill   Experimental boarding school in England founded by A. S. Neill that took "problem" students and offered them a completely non-compulsory atmosphere in which to learn. Classes were held, but no student was required to attend.

Tactile Learner   Same as kinesthetic; one who learns best by touching.

The Teaching Home   Popular conservative Christian homeschooling magazine, published bimonthly.

Trivium Approach   Method of teaching that focuses on grammar, logic, and rhetoric.

Umbrella School   School or church that functions as a legal cover.

Unit Study   Method of study by which an entire theme is created to study one topic.

Unschooling Method   Method of schooling in which learning is child-led.

Visual Learner   One who learns best by seeing things laid out for them.

Voucher   In the schooling sense, a credit given by the government for taxpayers to use for their choice of private, public, or correspondence school.

Weiss, Jim   Highly gifted storyteller whose tapes and CD-ROMs for Greathall Productions include many of the Sherlock Holmes adventures, Greek myths, and stories from the Old Testament. He also performs at conferences, libraries, and bookstores around the nation.

White, Donna-Nichols   Homeschooling mother of three, popular conference speaker and editor and publisher of *The Drinking Gourd*. She also owns a catalog company that sells products for homeschoolers.

Whole Language   Method of teaching reading or other subjects which advocates having experiences and memorizing words to develop a total experience that is then blended together to learn the material in a more "whole" approach.

Index

Homeschooling Today

- Expires 1/1/2001
- Use original coupon; no photocopies permitted.
- Valid for one use only.
- See page 361.
- Check with company for any shipping and handling costs.
- May not be combined with any other offer.

The Link

- Expires 1/1/2001
- Use original coupon; no photocopies permitted.
- Valid for one use only.
- See page xv.
- Check with company for any shipping and handling costs.

Homefires

- Expires 1/1/2001
- Use original coupon; no photocopies permitted.
- Valid for one use only.
- See page 507.
- Check with company for any shipping and handling costs.

The Teaching Home

- Expires 1/1/2001
- Use original coupon; no photocopies permitted.
- Valid for one use only.
- Check with company for any shipping and handling costs.

The Homeschool Digest

- Expires 1/1/2001
- Use original coupon; no photocopies permitted.
- Valid for one use only.
- See page 495.
- Check with company for any shipping and handling costs.
- May not be combined with other offer.
- Offer good only for nonsubscribers.

Growing Without Schooling

- Expires 1/1/2001
- Use original coupon; no photocopies permitted.
- Valid for one use only.
- See page 506.
- Check with company for any shipping and handling costs.

The Journal of Family Life

- Expires 1/1/2001
- Use original coupon; no photocopies permitted.
- Valid for one use only.
- Check with company for any shipping and handling costs.

The Homeschool Digest

- Expires 1/1/2001
- Use original coupon; no photocopies permitted.
- Valid for one use only.
- See page 495.
- Check with company for any shipping and handling costs.
- May not be combined with other offer.

Hard Times in Paradise

- Expires 1/1/2001
- Use original coupon; no photocopies permitted.
- Valid for one use only.
- See page475.
- Check with company for any shipping and handling costs.

Homeschool Dad Magazine

- Expires 1/1/2001
- Use original coupon; no photocopies permitted.
- Valid for one use only.
- Check with company for any shipping and handling costs.

Boomerang Audio Magazine

- Expires 1/1/2001
- Use original coupon; no photocopies permitted.
- Valid for one use only.
- Check with company for any shipping and handling costs.

Newsweek Magazine

- Expires 1/1/2001
- Use original coupon; no photocopies permitted.
- Valid for one use only.
- Check with company for any shipping and handling costs.

Power-glide

- Expires 1/1/2001
- Use original coupon; no photocopies permitted.
- Valid for one use only.
- See page 240 for this company's product featured in *Homeschooling Almanac*.
- Check with company for any shipping and handling costs.
- Please request a catalog.

Power-glide

- Expires 1/1/2001
- Use original coupon; no photocopies permitted.
- Valid for one use only.
- See page 240 for this company's product featured in *Homeschooling Almanac*.
- Check with company for any shipping and handling costs.
- Please request a catalog.

Draw Today!

- Expires 1/1/2001
- Use original coupon; no photocopies permitted.
- Valid for one use only.
- See page 341 for this company's product featured in *Homeschooling Almanac*.
- Check with company for any shipping and handling costs.
- Please request a catalog.

Art Extension Press

- Expires 1/1/2001
- Use original coupon; no photocopies permitted.
- Valid for one use only.
- See page 341 for this company's product featured in *Homeschooling Almanac*.
- Check with company for any shipping and handling costs.
- There is no obligation.

Globe Pequot Press

- Expires 1/1/2001
- Use original coupon; no photocopies permitted.
- Valid for one use only.
- See page 395 for this company's product featured in *Homeschooling Almanac*.
- Check with company for any shipping and handling costs.
- Please request a catalog.

Gordon School of Art

- Expires 1/1/2001
- Use original coupon; no photocopies permitted.
- Valid for one use only.
- See page 360 for this company's product featured in *Homeschooling Almanac*.
- Check with company for any shipping and handling costs.

COUPONS COUPONS COUPONS COUPONS COUPONS

Home Science Adventures

- Expires 1/1/2001
- Use original coupon; no photocopies permitted.
- Valid for one use only.
- See page 457 for this company's product featured in *Homeschooling Almanac.*
- Check with company for any shipping and handling costs.

Ampersand Press

- Expires 1/1/2001
- Use original coupon; no photocopies permitted.
- Valid for one use only.
- See page 457 for this company's product featured in *Homeschooling Almanac.*
- Check with company for any shipping and handling costs.

CTI

- Expires 1/1/2001
- Use original coupon; no photocopies permitted.
- Valid for one use only.
- See pages 185 and 228 for this company's product featured in *Homeschooling Almanac.*
- Check with company for any shipping and handling costs.

CTI

- Expires 1/1/2001
- Use original coupon; no photocopies permitted.
- Valid for one use only.
- See pages 185 and 228 for this company's product featured in *Homeschooling Almanac.*
- Check with company for any shipping and handling costs.

Audio Bookshelf

- Expires 1/1/2001
- Use original coupon; no photocopies permitted.
- Valid for one use only.
- See index entry for this company's products featured in *Homeschooling Almanac..*
- Check with company for any shipping and handling costs.

Lost Classics Books

- Expires 1/1/2001
- Use original coupon; no photocopies permitted.
- Valid for one use only.
- See index entry for this company's products featured in *Homeschooling Almanac.*
- Check with company for any shipping and handling costs.

Effective Educational Systems

- Expires 1/1/2001
- Use original coupon; no photocopies permitted.
- Valid for one use only.
- See page 208 for this company's products featured in *Homeschooling Almanac*.
- Check with company for any shipping and handling costs.

Sax Arts & Crafts

- Expires 1/1/2001
- Use original coupon; no photocopies permitted.
- Valid for one use only.
- See index entry for this company's products featured in *Homeschooling Almanac*.
- Check with company for any shipping and handling costs.
- Discount does not apply to taxes or shipping and handling and cannot be combined with any other discount or coupons.

American Portrait Films

- Expires 1/1/2001
- Use original coupon; no photocopies permitted.
- Valid for one use only.
- See page 400 for this company's product featured in *Homeschooling Almanac*.
- Check with company for any shipping and handling costs.

AMG Publishers

- Expires 1/1/2001
- Use original coupon; no photocopies permitted.
- Valid for one use only.
- See page 197 for this company's product featured in *Homeschooling Almanac*.
- Check with company for any shipping and handling costs.

Reflective Educational Perspectives

- Expires 1/1/2001
- Use original coupon; no photocopies permitted.
- Valid for one use only.
- See pages 66, 67, and 68 for this company's product featured in *Homeschooling Almanac*.
- Check with company for any shipping and handling costs.

A.D.D. Warehouse

- Expires 1/1/2001
- Use original coupon; no photocopies permitted.
- Valid for one use only.
- Check with company for any shipping and handling costs.
- For family use only, please; no institutions. Only one coupon per family.

Lewis Educational Games

- Expires 1/1/2001
- Use original coupon; no photocopies permitted.
- Valid for one use only.
- See pages 468 and 495 for this company's products featured in *Homeschooling Almanac*.
- Check with company for any shipping and handling costs.

Ring-of-Fire

- Expires 1/1/2001
- Use original coupon; no photocopies permitted.
- Valid for one use only.
- See page 329 for this company's product featured in *Homeschooling Almanac*.
- Check with company for any shipping and handling costs.

Greek 'n' Stuff

- Expires 1/1/2001
- Use original coupon; no photocopies permitted.
- Valid for one use only.
- See page 245 for this company's product featured in *Homeschooling Almanac*.
- Check with company for any shipping and handling costs.

Mastery Publications

- Expires 1/1/2001
- Use original coupon; no photocopies permitted.
- Valid for one use only.
- Check with company for any shipping and handling costs.

Progeny Press

- Expires 1/1/2001
- Use original coupon; no photocopies permitted.
- Valid for one use only.
- See page 197 for this company's product featured in *Homeschooling Almanac*.
- Check with company for any shipping and handling costs.

Lester Family Tapes

- Expires 1/1/2001
- Use original coupon; no photocopies permitted.
- Valid for one use only.
- See page 423.
- Check with company for any shipping and handling costs.

$7 OFF

Send in this coupon for $7 off
the deluxe set.

Visual Manna

Send to: Visual Manna
P.O. Box 553, Salem, MO 65560;
orders: (888) 275-7309

10% OFF

Send in this coupon
for 10% off any order.

Visual Manna

Send to: Visual Manna
P.O. Box 553, Salem, MO 65560;
orders: (888) 275-7309

$20 OFF

Send in this coupon for $20 off the pur-
chase price of the software program.

Stars & Stories

(normally $89.95)

Send to: Wildridge Software
Wildridge Farm Road, Newark, VT 05871;
(888) 244-4379

$5 OFF

Send in this coupon for
$5 off the curriculum set.

Trisms

Send to: Trisms
1203 S. Delaware Pl., Tulsa, OK 74104;
(918) 585-2778

$5 OFF!

Send in this coupon
for $5 off any order.

StartWrite

Send to: IdeaMaker, Inc.
80 S. Redwood Road, Ste. 212, North Salt Lake, UT
84054; (888) WRITE-ABC or (801) 936-7779

SAVE 10%

Send in this coupon
for 10% off any order.

Activities for Learning

Send to: Activities for Learning
21161 York Rd., Hutchinson, MN 55350-6705;
(320) 587-9146

Visual Manna

- Expires 1/1/2001
- Use original coupon; no photocopies permitted.
- Valid for one use only.
- See page 361 for this company's product featured in *Homeschooling Almanac.*
- Check with company for any shipping and handling costs.
- May not be combined with any other offer or coupon

Visual Manna

- Expires 1/1/2001
- Use original coupon; no photocopies permitted.
- Valid for one use only.
- See page 361 for this company's product featured in *Homeschooling Almanac.*
- Check with company for any shipping and handling costs.
- May not be combined with any other offer or coupon

Trisms

- Expires 1/1/2001
- Use original coupon; no photocopies permitted.
- Valid for one use only.
- See page 483 for this company's product featured in *Homeschooling Almanac.*
- Check with company for any shipping and handling costs.

Stars & Stories

- Expires 1/1/2001
- Use original coupon; no photocopies permitted.
- Valid for one use only.
- See page 325 for this company's product featured in *Homeschooling Almanac.*
- Check with company for any shipping and handling costs.

Activities for Learning

- Expires 1/1/2001
- Use original coupon; no photocopies permitted.
- Valid for one use only.
- See page 287 for this company's product featured in *Homeschooling Almanac.*
- Check with company for any shipping and handling costs.

SmartWrite

- Expires 1/1/2001
- Use original coupon; no photocopies permitted.
- Valid for one use only.
- See page 238 for this company's products featured in *Homeschooling Almanac.*
- Check with company for any shipping and handling costs.

Meridian Creative Group

- Expires 1/1/2001
- Use original coupon; no photocopies permitted.
- Valid for one use only.
- See pages 295 and 294 for this company's products featured in *Homeschooling Almanac*.
- Check with company for any shipping and handling costs.

The Happy Homeschool

- Expires 1/1/2001
- Use original coupon; no photocopies permitted.
- Valid for one use only.
- See page 270 for this company's products featured in *Homeschooling Almanac*.
- Check with company for any shipping and handling costs.

Audio-Forum Cassettes

- Expires 1/1/2001
- Use original coupon; no photocopies permitted.
- Valid for one use only.
- See index entry for this company's products featured in *Homeschooling Almanac*.
- Check with company for any shipping and handling costs.

Architectural Education Resource

- Expires 1/1/2001
- Use original coupon; no photocopies permitted.
- Valid for one use only.
- See index entry for this company's products featured in *Homeschooling Almanac*.
- Check with company for any shipping and handling costs.

Trail Mix CD Bundle

- Expires 1/1/2001
- Use original coupon; no photocopies permitted.
- Valid for one use only.
- See page 253 for this product featured in *Homeschooling Almanac*.
- Check with company for any shipping and handling costs.

Critical Thinking Books & Software

- Expires 1/1/2001
- Use original coupon; no photocopies permitted.
- Valid for one use only.
- See pages 426–429 for this company's products featured in *Homeschooling Almanac*.
- Check with company for any shipping and handling costs.
- Coupon good only when products are ordered directly from Critical Thinking.

$5 OFF

Send in this coupon for $5 off:

Teacher's Roadmap to the InterNET

(reference item #FORE005-CDB).
School version only

Send to: Learning Services, P.O. Box 10636, Eugene, OR 97440-2636; Western Region: (800) 877-9378; Eastern Region: (800) 877-3278

$5 OFF

Send in this coupon for $5 off:

Field Trap

(reference item #APTE0040-CDB).
School version only

Send to: Learning Services, P.O. Box 10636, Eugene, OR 97440-2636; Western Region: (800) 877-9378; Eastern Region: (800) 877-3278

$5 OFF

Send in this coupon for $5 off:

Science Investigator

(normally $106.50)
Reference item #BONU0030-CDBS
School version only

Send to: Learning Services, P.O. Box 10636, Eugene, OR 97440-2636; Western Region: (800) 877-9378; Eastern Region: (800) 877-3278

$15 OFF

Send in this coupon for $15 off:

The Complete National Geographic CD Bundle

(reference item #LSPK1335-MPCS).
School version only

Send to: Learning Services, P.O. Box 10636, Eugene, OR 97440-2636; Western Region: (800) 877-9378; Eastern Region: (800) 877-3278

$5 OFF!

Send in this coupon for $5 off:

Geography Online

(reference item #CURR0010CDB)
School version only

Send to: Learning Services, P.O. Box 10636, Eugene, OR 97440-2636; Western Region: (800) 877-9378; Eastern Region: (800) 877-3278

$8 OFF

Send in this coupon for $8 off:

U.S. Atlas & Almanac

(reference item #SWTO9006)
School version only

Send to: Learning Services, P.O. Box 10636, Eugene, OR 97440-2636; Western Region: (800) 877-9378; Eastern Region: (800) 877-3278

Field Trap

- Expires 1/1/2001
- Use original coupon; no photocopies permitted.
- Valid for one use only.
- See page 263 for this product featured in *Homeschooling Almanac*.
- Check with company for any shipping and handling costs.

Roadmap to the Internet

- Expires 1/1/2001
- Use original coupon; no photocopies permitted.
- Valid for one use only.
- See page 262 for this product featured in *Homeschooling Almanac*.
- Check with company for any shipping and handling costs.

National Geographic CD Bundle

- Expires 1/1/2001
- Use original coupon; no photocopies permitted.
- Valid for one use only.
- See page 411 for this product featured in *Homeschooling Almanac*.
- Check with company for any shipping and handling costs.

Science Investigator

- Expires 1/1/2001
- Use original coupon; no photocopies permitted.
- Valid for one use only.
- See page 295 for this product featured in *Homeschooling Almanac*.
- Check with company for any shipping and handling costs.

U.S. Atlas & Almanac

- Expires 1/1/2001
- Use original coupon; no photocopies permitted.
- Valid for one use only.
- See page 410 for this product featured in *Homeschooling Almanac*.
- Check with company for any shipping and handling costs.

Geography Online

- Expires 1/1/2001
- Use original coupon; no photocopies permitted.
- Valid for one use only.
- See page 404 for this product featured in *Homeschooling Almanac*.
- Check with company for any shipping and handling costs.

Student Writing Center

- Expires 1/1/2001
- Use original coupon; no photocopies permitted.
- Valid for one use only.
- See page 236 for this product featured in *Homeschooling Almanac*.
- Check with company for any shipping and handling costs.

Storybook Weaver Deluxe

- Expires 1/1/2001
- Use original coupon; no photocopies permitted.
- Valid for one use only.
- See page 236 for this product featured in *Homeschooling Almanac*.
- Check with company for any shipping and handling costs.

The American Pioneer Experience

- Expires 1/1/2001
- Use original coupon; no photocopies permitted.
- Valid for one use only.
- See page 387 for this product featured in *Homeschooling Almanac*.
- Check with company for any shipping and handling costs.

U.S. Government Bundle

- Expires 1/1/2001
- Use original coupon; no photocopies permitted.
- Valid for one use only.
- See page 387 for this product featured in *Homeschooling Almanac*.
- Check with company for any shipping and handling costs.

Greathall Productions

- Expires 1/1/2001
- Use original coupon; no photocopies permitted.
- Valid for one use only.
- See page 230 for this product featured in *Homeschooling Almanac*.
- Check with company for any shipping and handling costs.

Learning Services

- Expires 1/1/2001
- Use original coupon; no photocopies permitted.
- Valid for one use only.
- See index entry for this company's products featured in *Homeschooling Almanac*.
- Check with company for any shipping and handling costs.

FUN Books

- Expires 1/1/2001
- Use original coupon;
  no photocopies permitted.
- Valid for one use only.
- See index entry for this company's
  products featured in *Homeschooling
  Almanac.*
- Check with company for any shipping
  and handling costs.

Runkle Geography

- Expires 1/1/2001
- Use original coupon;
  no photocopies permitted.
- Valid for one use only.
- See page 409 for this product featured
  in *Homeschooling Almanac.*
- Check with company for any shipping
  and handling costs.

DK Books

- Expires 1/1/2001
- Use original coupon;
  no photocopies permitted.
- Valid for one use only.
- See index entries for this company's
  products featured in *Homeschooling
  Almanac.*
- Check with company for any shipping
  and handling costs.

Excellence in Education

- Expires 1/1/2001
- Use original coupon;
  no photocopies permitted.
- Valid for one use only.
- See index entry for this company's
  products featured in *Homeschooling
  Almanac.*
- Check with company for any shipping
  and handling costs.

Ball-Stick-Bird

- Expires 1/1/2001
- Use original coupon;
  no photocopies permitted.
- Valid for one use only.
- See page 212 for this product featured
  in *Homeschooling Almanac.*
- Check with company for any shipping
  and handling costs.

Learning Wrap-Ups

- Expires 1/1/2001
- Use original coupon;
  no photocopies permitted.
- Valid for one use only.
- See index entry for this company's
  products featured in *Homeschooling
  Almanac.*
- Check with company for any shipping
  and handling costs.

Alpha Phonics

- Expires 1/1/2001
- Use original coupon; no photocopies permitted.
- Valid for one use only.
- See page 213 for this product featured in *Homeschooling Almanac.*
- Ground shipping only.

TV program on homeschooling

- Expires 1/1/2001
- Use original coupon; no photocopies permitted.
- Valid for one use only.
- Twenty families offer their stories. Commercially broadcast infomercial was broadcast by PAX TV network.

The Wild Seed Game

- Expires 1/1/2001
- Use original coupon; no photocopies permitted.
- Valid for one use only.
- See index entry for this company's products featured in *Homeschooling Almanac.*
- Check with company for any shipping and handling costs.

Continental Press

- Expires 12/31/1999
- Use original coupon; no photocopies permitted.
- Valid for one use only.
- See page 460 for this company's products featured in *Homeschooling Almanac.*
- Check with company for any shipping and handling costs.

Laurel Springs School

- Expires 1/1/2001
- Use original coupon; no photocopies permitted.
- Valid for one use only.
- See page 502.
- Check with company for any shipping and handling costs.

Laurel Springs School

- Expires 1/1/2001
- Use original coupon; no photocopies permitted.
- Valid for one use only.
- See page 502.
- Check with company for any shipping and handling costs.